HIGH PERFORMANCE

Don Burleson ... or

ORACLE8 SQL PROGRAMMING and Tuning

GW01005951

Publisher
Keith Weiskamp

Acquisitions
Jeff Duntemann
Stephanie Wall

Project Editor
Ann Waggoner Aken

Production Coordinator
Wendy Littley

Cover Design
Anthony Stock

Layout Design
April Nielsen

CD-ROM Development
Robert Clarfield

High Performance Oracle8 SQL Programming & Tuning

Copyright © 1998 by The Coriolis Group, Inc.

All rights reserved. This book may not be duplicated in any way without the express written consent of the publisher, except in the form of brief excerpts or quotations for the purposes of review. The information contained herein is for the personal use of the reader and may not be incorporated in any commercial programs, other books, databases, or any kind of software without written consent of the publisher. Making copies of this book or any portion for any purpose other than your own is a violation of United States copyright laws.

Limits of Liability and Disclaimer of Warranty

The author and publisher of this book have used their best efforts in preparing the book and the programs contained in it. These efforts include the development, research, and testing of the theories and programs to determine their effectiveness. The author and publisher make no warranty of any kind, expressed or implied, with regard to these programs or the documentation contained in this book.

The author and publisher shall not be liable in the event of incidental or consequential damages in connection with, or arising out of, the furnishing, performance, or use of the programs, associated instructions, and/or claims of productivity gains.

Trademarks

Trademarked names appear throughout this book. Rather than list the names and entities that own the trademarks or insert a trademark symbol with each mention of the trademarked name, the publisher states that it is using the names for editorial purposes only and to the benefit of the trademark owner, with no intention of infringing upon that trademark.

The Coriolis Group, Inc.
An International Thomson Publishing Company
14455 N. Hayden Road, Suite 220
Scottsdale, Arizona 85260

602.483.0192
FAX 602.483.0193
http://www.coriolis.com

Library of Congress Cataloging-In-Publication Data

Cassidy, Pete.
High performance Oracle8 SQL programming and tuning / by Pete Cassidy.
p. cm.
Includes index.
ISBN 1-57610-213-0
1. Relational databases. 2. Oracle (Computer file) 3. SQL (Computer program language) I. Title.
QA76.9.D3C38235 1998
005.75'85—dc21 97-47339
CIP

Printed in the United States of America
10 9 8 7 6 5 4 3 2 1

CORIOLIS GROUP BOOKS
an International Thomson Publishing company I(T)P®

Albany, NY • Belmont, CA • Bonn • Boston • Cincinnati • Detroit
Johannesburg • London • Madrid • Melbourne • Mexico City
New York • Paris • Singapore • Tokyo • Toronto • Washington

For my children, Debra and Paige, and for my wife of twenty-five years, Carole. I want to thank my mother, Maryellen Warren, for teaching me the value of laughter and for being able to bring "light" and a smile to my students.

People are just about as happy
as they make up their minds to be.
— Abraham Lincoln

Acknowledgments

I want to thank Donald Burleson for his inspiration, encouragement, and friendship while I wrote this book, and Mike Ault for his Oracle8 object help. I also want to thank Keith Weiskamp for his vision in making this book a reality. Thanks to Bart Reed, whose editing saved me; to Ann Waggoner Aken, my project editor, for believing in me and encouraging me during some very trying times; to Rob Clarfield who managed the CD; to Wendy Littley, production coordinator of the book; to Tony Stock, who designed the cover; to Josh Mills, marketing specialist; and to the many employees here at Database Consultants Inc. Thanks also to Kerry and Kevin Osborne for their support and use of their equipment; to Stan and Theresa Feighny for helping and encouraging me on many occasions; to Ruby Sauvignet, Patti Steele, and Angie Whiteside for encouraging me throughout the entire project; to Mike Stewart and Dave Renner for their sense of humor, wit, and for promoting my book; to Brad Johnson and Greg Grimes for their support on hardware issues; and to Joe Cairns, of Database Consultants Inc., for technical assistance and advice.

A Note From Don Burleson

Today's Oracle professionals are standing at the turning point. As Oracle technology moves into the twenty-first century we are seeing the complexity of database systems becoming almost unfathomable. Today's Oracle professional must be an expert in database performance and tuning, database administration, data warehousing, using Oracle with the Web, using OLAP and spatial data, and many other areas. These robust new features of Oracle present unique challenges to anyone who must use Oracle technology to deliver solutions to complex data-oriented challenges.

Oracle, the world's leading database management system, provides a mind-boggling wealth of features and options—far more than one Oracle professional can easily digest. The Oracle market is filled with new possibilities as Oracle introduces the management of objects, data warehouses, and Web-enabled applications; Oracle professionals everywhere are struggling to understand how to exploit these new features.

It is no longer acceptable for Oracle professionals to be generalists—they must become intimately familiar with all facets of Oracle technology and understand how these technologies interoperate. Rather than simply breadth of knowledge, the Oracle professional must have enough depth to effectively apply the technology. To get this knowledge we must rely on experts to guide us through the labyrinth of complicated tools and techniques, and we do not have the luxury of wading through mundane technical manuals.

What we need is clear, concise advice from seasoned Oracle professionals. That is the purpose of The Coriolis Group's High Performance Oracle series. As you are challenged to keep pace with this exciting new technology, we are challenged to provide on-point books to help guide you through the myriad of Oracle features and ensure your success.

— Don Burleson

Introduction

This book is aimed at Oracle developers and database administrators who work with either Oracle8 (or Oracle7). The format of this book is one of a kind. Many queries are written showing the actual elapsed times and Explain Plans of a one million-row table named **STATS**. Of particular note is the last chapter of the book, Chapter 16, which shows Explain Plans and elapsed times using Oracle8 objects. *This is the only book in the world that attempts such a feat.* Throughout the entire book, I share as many real-life situations as possible from my ten years of experience working with Oracle at 150 customer sites. All code listings were actually executed, and for Chapters 1 through 14, the database was shut down and started up between commands, as was necessary to do.

The book is broken down into the following chapters:

Chapter 1 provides meaningful information about Oracle's cost-based and rule-based optimizer to help you write more efficient SQL statements.

Chapter 2 covers rowids, btree indexes, concatenated btree indexes, how and when to use histograms, and how to identify and repair index fragmentation. There are plenty of Explain Plans and execution times to help you learn the proper use of btree indexes.

Chapter 3 illustrates the proper and improper use of btree index clusters using Explain Plans and execution times.

Chapter 4 shows the correct and incorrect use of hash clusters using Explain Plans and execution times.

Chapter 5 provides many examples of bitmap and concatenated bitmap indexes using Explain Plans, SQL Trace/TKPROF, and execution times.

Chapter 6 covers analyzing tables, clusters, indexes, and creating histograms.

Chapter 7 shows how to use and interpret Explain Plans on many types of SQL statements.

Chapter 8 covers how to use and interpret SQL Trace/TKPROF on many SQL statements.

Chapter 9 provides many examples of SQL statements using hints.

Chapter 10 shows the importance of understanding the join chain, the driving table, the four types of table joins, and hints used to join tables. Many examples are shown using Explain Plans and execution times.

Chapter 11 provides examples of SQL statements using the parallel option.

Chapter 12 illustrates true-life "adventure" application sagas and the proper solutions for them.

Chapter 13 illustrates storage problems and their solutions, from row chaining to tables with too many extents.

Chapter 14 provides many practical SQL statements used by people who work with Oracle.

Chapter 15 covers the new features in Oracle8, such as partitions.

Chapter 16 provides information about Oracle8 application tuning and shows Explain Plans and execution time comparisons between traditional SQL joins and the Oracle8 objects using OIDs.

Appendix A contains most of the SQL scripts that created the tables and objects used throughout this book.

Appendix B contains the tuning SQL scripts you will use frequently.

CD-ROM contains demo copies of BMC's Patrol SQL Explorer, Patrol Pathfinder, Patrol DB Voyager, and most of the SQL statements used in this book.

Contents

HIGH PERFORMANCE

The Optimizers

HIGH PERFORMANCE

CHAPTER 1

The purpose of an optimizer is to execute statements via the fastest, most efficient method possible by making the best decision for each step of the execution plan. The more you know about the Oracle optimizers, the more likely you are to write faster running SQL statements. In this chapter, we'll take a closer look at the two optimizers—Rule and Cost. Then, we'll observe how Oracle optimizes SQL statements. We'll also identify various methods of controlling which optimizer is used.

The Optimizers

What Is An Optimizer?

Most dictionaries define "optimize" as "improving to the greatest extent possible" or "to use most effectively." This is exactly what the Oracle optimizers attempt to do for SQL statements. For each SQL statement, at parse time, Oracle decides how to execute the statement. This is called the "execution plan," and most of the time the plan contains multiple steps. (See Figure 1.1.) These steps can be observed by using Explain Plan, one of Oracle's tuning tools. The plan is based on the syntax of the statement, the conditions in the **WHERE** clause, definitions of objects stored in the data dictionary, and any indexes that exist on the table(s) in the SQL statement. The execution plan also selects an optimizer (Rule or Cost), an access path, a "join chain" if the statement joins two or more tables, and a method for joining tables. The join chain is the order in which the tables are joined. It also evaluates constants and expressions and, perhaps, rewrites the statement. The cost-based optimizer was new in Oracle7, but the rule-based optimizer has always existed within Oracle.

The Rule-Based Optimizer

Rumors of the untimely demise of the rule-based optimizer have existed since the inception of Oracle7. However, as of Oracle8, it is still functioning quite well. If it ever does die, it will be in Oracle9 or Oracle10. The rule-based optimizer is still very widely used, particularly in On-Line Transaction Processing (OLTP) applications. This optimizer is based on a ranking scheme. The ranking starts with 1 and ends with 14. A ranking of 1 is the fastest—it uses the **ROWID** to retrieve the row(s). A ranking of 14 is the slowest—it uses a full table scan to retrieve the row(s) in the active set.

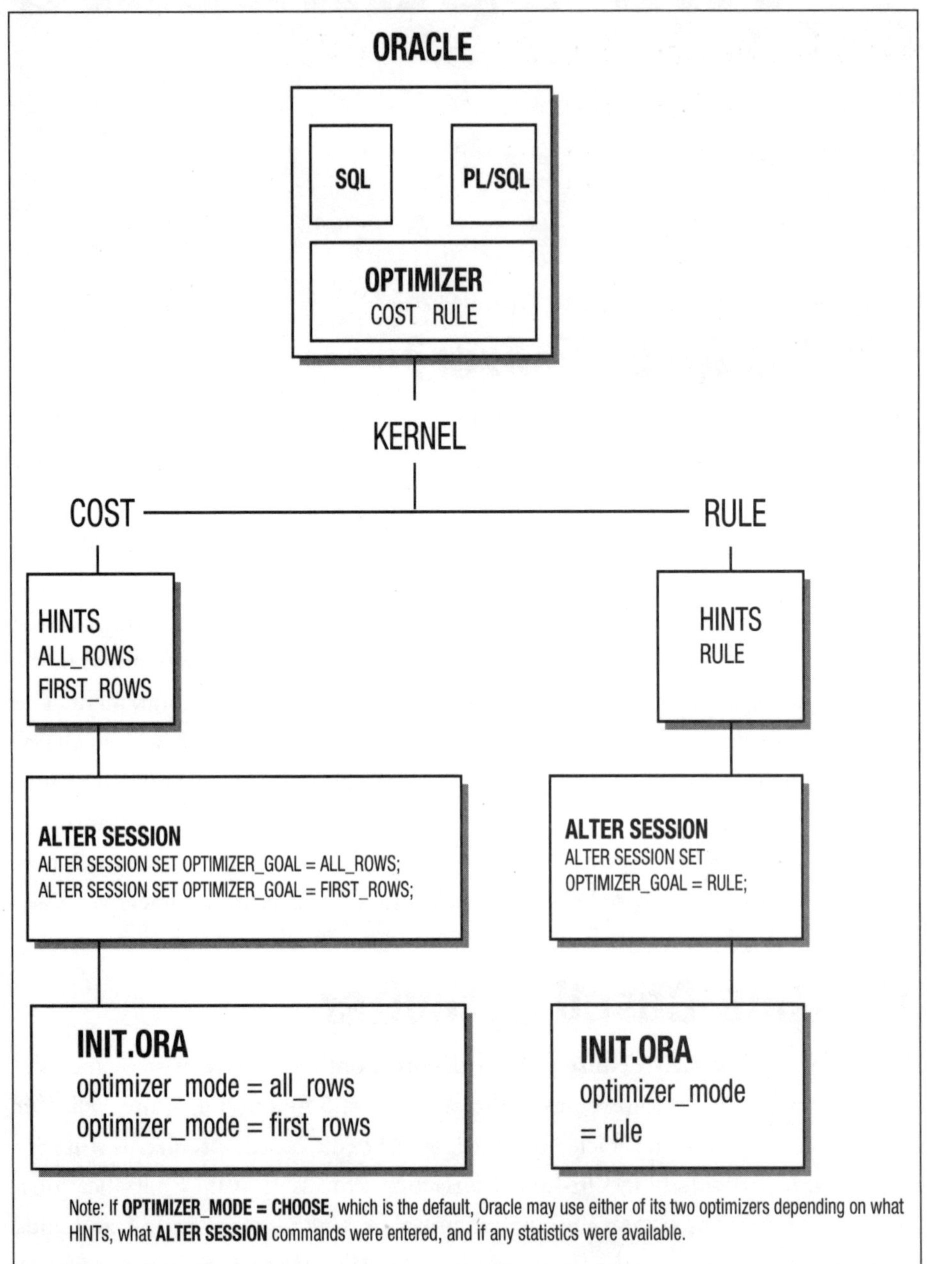

Figure 1.1
The Oracle kernel and optimizer.

The Cost-Based Optimizer

The cost-based optimizer was introduced in Oracle7. It uses a numerical value assigned to a SQL statement based on estimated amounts of memory, input/output, and CPU time. There may be four or five different methods of executing a SQL statement. The cost-based optimizer executes the method with the lowest cost estimate.

The Original Statement May Be Transformed

The following SQL statement demonstrates how Oracle transforms a SQL statement so that it can be executed more quickly than originally written. In versions 5 and 6 of Oracle, this statement would have caused a full table scan. But now, Oracle knows more about the data in the index, because it has been analyzed. Oracle knows that out of this one-million=row table, **STATS**, only two rows are in the active set. **SNO** is 1 or **SNO** is 1,000,000. Obviously, it would be much faster to use the unique index on the **SNO** column to retrieve the two rows. Therefore, Oracle transforms the SQL statement in the following Explain Plan (see Listing 1.1).

```
SELECT *
FROM   STATS
WHERE  SNO = 1  OR
SNO   = 1000000;
```

The word **CONCATENATION** in the output of Explain Plan suggests that this is the case. Also, the appearance of **INDEX RANGE SCAN** indicates that the unique btree index on the SNO column would be used both times—once for **SNO=1** and once for **SNO=1000000**.

Listing 1.1 Statement transformation.

```
SQL> EXPLAIN PLAN FOR
  2  SELECT *
  3  FROM   STATS
  4* WHERE  SNO NOT BETWEEN 2 AND 999999;
Explained.

SQL> @explain
Query Plan                                                     COST
-------------------------------------------------------------  ----
SELECT STATEMENT   RULE
  CONCATENATION
```

```
  TABLE ACCESS BY ROWID STATS ANALYZED
    INDEX RANGE SCAN BTREE_UNIQUE_SNO ANALYZED
  TABLE ACCESS BY ROWID STATS ANALYZED
    INDEX RANGE SCAN BTREE_UNIQUE_SNO ANALYZED
```

Oracle Selects An Optimizer

Oracle must select either the cost-based or the rule-base optimizer to execute the SQL statement. The optimizer can be selected at the instance, session, or statement levels. However, **HINT**s at the statement level supersede the session and instance settings. At the instance level, a parameter named **OPTIMIZER_MODE** is set to **FIRST_ROWS, RULE, ALL_ROWS**, or **CHOOSE**. At the session level, the **ALTER SESSION** command is used to set **OPTIMIZER_GOAL** to any one of the four settings. Session settings for **OPTIMIZER_GOAL** override the instance settings of **OPTIMIZER_MODE**. Also, using **HINT**s you can use all four settings as well. The settings of **ALL_ROWS** and **FIRST_ROWS** invoke the cost-based optimizer. **RULE** invokes the rule-based optimizer. And, finally, **CHOOSE** uses either one of the two optimizers. Listing 1.2 indicates that Oracle selected the cost-based optimizer because the number 3 appears in the **COST** column of the table **PLAN_TABLE**. If the **COST** column were null, then Oracle would have selected the rule-based optimizer.

Listing 1.2 Cost- or rule-based optimizer selected.

```
SQL> EXPLAIN PLAN FOR
  2  SELECT  *
  3  FROM    STATS
  4  WHERE   SNO = 99999;
Explained.

SQL> @explain
Query Plan                                                    COST
------------------------------------------------------------  ----
SELECT STATEMENT   CHOOSE                                        3
  TABLE ACCESS BY ROWID STATS ANALYZED                           3
    INDEX UNIQUE SCAN BTREE_UNIQUE_SNO ANALYZED
```

Oracle Selects An Access Path

Oracle must retrieve the rows in the active set by any one of the following methods: rowid, bitmap index, btree index, hash cluster index, btree index cluster, or full table scan. If the table has been analyzed, Oracle should make a pretty good decision unless the data in the index is heavily skewed. In that case, you would want to have histograms for the skewed columns. I will discuss this later in Chapters 2 and 6. Before Oracle can use any of its four index types to access rows, several conditions must exist. First, the index must have been created. Also, the indexed column must be referenced in the predicate of the SQL statement. The predicate clause is usually the **WHERE** clause. Also, the referenced index column cannot have any functions applied to it, any numbers added to it, or anything concatenated to it. Finally, Oracle must decide it would be faster to use the index or indexes. By using hints, you can help Oracle select a better access path for a SQL statement than what it would select itself. However, be sure you know what you are asking for. The following hint is terrible (see Listing 1.3). Sure, Oracle took the hint and used the bitmap index on the **SEX** column. But, is this any faster than a full table scan? The estimated cost here is 14,074, compared to 3,958 for a full table scan. Once again, Oracle makes a much better decision without the help.

Listing 1.3 Access path selected.

```
SQL> EXPLAIN PLAN FOR
  2  SELECT /*+ INDEX_COMBINE(STATS BITMAP_SEX) */    *
  3  FROM    STATS
  4* WHERE   SEX = 'F';
Explained.

SQL> @explain
Query Plan                                                          COST
----------------------------------------------------------- ------
SELECT STATEMENT   CHOOSE                                     14,074
  TABLE ACCESS BY ROWID STATS ANALYZED                        14,074
    BITMAP CONVERSION TO ROWIDS
      BITMAP INDEX SINGLE VALUE BITMAP_SEX

SQL> TRUNCATE TABLE PLAN_TABLE;
Table truncated.

SQL> EXPLAIN PLAN FOR
  2  SELECT  *
  3  FROM    STATS
  4* WHERE   SEX = 'F';
Explained.
```

```
SQL> @explain
Query Plan                                                      COST
--------------------------------------------------------------  ----
SELECT STATEMENT    CHOOSE                                      3,958
  TABLE ACCESS FULL STATS ANALYZED                              3,958
```

Oracle Selects A Join Chain

Oracle must decide the order in which it will join tables. The most important decision in this process is deciding which table to start with first. This table should return the fewest rows. Some will say the table with the fewest rows should always be the "driving table." However, this is not always the case. If a table with many rows can use a unique index in the query, then the table with many rows would probably be the "driving table." The first table in the join chain is referred to as the "driving table." You can tell Oracle in what order to join the tables by using the **ORDERED** hint in the SQL statement. By reading the output of an Explain Plan from the top down, you can observe the driving table. The first table name you see is the driving table. In the following example (Listing 1.4), **STATS2** is the driving table.

Listing 1.4 Join chain selected.

```
SQL> EXPLAIN PLAN FOR
  2  SELECT STATS2.SNO, STATS.SEX
  3  FROM   STATS,      STATS2
  4  WHERE  STATS.SNO = STATS2.SNO;
Explained.

SQL> @explain
Query Plan                                                      COST
--------------------------------------------------------------  ----
SELECT STATEMENT    CHOOSE                                      20,010
  NESTED LOOPS                                                  20,010
    TABLE ACCESS FULL STATS2 ANALYZED                               10
    TABLE ACCESS BY ROWID STATS ANALYZED
      INDEX UNIQUE SCAN BTREE_UNIQUE_SNO ANALYZED
```

Oracle Selects A Join Method

Oracle must also select a method of joining tables. The methods are sort merge, nested loops, cluster, and hash join. From the previous listing, the **NESTED LOOPS** method would be used.

Oracle Selects The Degree Of Parallelism

Oracle selects the degree of parallelism from the instance, the data dictionary information on a table, or from a hint. Chapter 11, "The Oracle Parallel Query Option," discusses this more thoroughly.

Controlling Which Optimizer Oracle Uses

You can control which optimizer Oracle will use on SQL statements at the instance, session, and statement levels. At the instance level, the init.ora parameter **OPTIMIZER_MODE** is used. At the session level, the **ALTER SESSION** command is used to select the optimizer. At the statement level, the optimizer is selected using HINTs, which always overrides the instance- and session-level settings. The ALTER SESSION command overrides the settings of the parameter **OPTIMIZER_MODE** for the particular session.

Instance Level

OPTIMIZER_MODE may be set to either **FIRST_ROWS**, **RULE**, **ALL_ROWS**, or **CHOOSE** (the default). If the table has been analyzed and **OPTIMIZER_MODE** is set to **CHOOSE**, the cost-based optimizer is used. Listing 1.5 suggests that this is the case, because there is a cost of 39. When the **COST** column is null, the rule-based optimizer is invoked. Note: If you don't have DBA privileges, you will not be able to query **V$ PARAMETER**.

Listing 1.5 Optimizer mode **CHOOSE**, table analyzed.

```
SQL> SELECT SUBSTR(VALUE,1,45) "Current Setting"
  2  FROM   V$PARAMETER
  3  WHERE  NAME = LOWER('&Parameter');
Enter value for parameter: OPTIMIZER_MODE
Current Setting
---------------------------------------------
CHOOSE

SQL> EXPLAIN PLAN FOR
  2  SELECT *
  3  FROM   STATS
  4  WHERE  SNO > 999000;
Explained.
```

```
SQL> @explain
Query Plan                                                        COST
---------------------------------------------------------------   ----
SELECT STATEMENT   CHOOSE                                           39
  TABLE ACCESS BY ROWID STATS ANALYZED                              39
    INDEX RANGE SCAN BTREE_UNIQUE_SNO ANALYZED
```

If the table has been analyzed and **OPTIMIZER_MODE** is set to **ALL_ROWS**, the cost-based optimizer is used. Listing 1.6 suggests that this is the case, because there is a cost of 39 and the **OPTIONS** column of the table **PLAN_TABLE** contains **ALL_ROWS**.

Listing 1.6 Optimizer mode **ALL_ROWS**, table analyzed.

```
SQL> SELECT SUBSTR(VALUE,1,45) "Current Setting"
  2  FROM   V$PARAMETER
  3* WHERE  NAME = LOWER('&Parameter');
Enter value for parameter: OPTIMIZER_MODE
Current Setting
----------------------
ALL_ROWS

SQL> EXPLAIN PLAN FOR
  2  SELECT  *
  3  FROM    STATS
  4  WHERE   SNO > 999000;
Explained.

SQL> @explain
Query Plan                                                        COST
---------------------------------------------------------------   ----
SELECT STATEMENT   ALL_ROWS                                         39
  TABLE ACCESS BY ROWID STATS ANALYZED                              39
    INDEX RANGE SCAN BTREE_UNIQUE_SNO ANALYZED
```

If the table has been analyzed and **OPTIMIZER_MODE** is set to **FIRST_ROWS**, the cost-based optimizer is used. Listing 1.7 suggests that this is the case, because there is a cost of 39 and the **OPTIONS** column of the table **PLAN_TABLE** contains **FIRST_ROWS**. **FIRST_ROWS** uses the cost-based optimizer, but it is different than **ALL_ROWS**. **FIRST_ROWS** causes Oracle to execute the SQL statement that will return the first row the fastest way possible, whereas **ALL_ROWS** executes the SQL statement that returns all the rows in the active set the quickest.

For this example, the estimated cost is identical for ALL_ROWS and FIRST_ROWS. However, when the SQL statement joins tables, the cost is different for ALL_ROWS and FIRST_ROWS.

Listing 1.7 Optimizer mode **FIRST_ROWS**, table analyzed.

```
SQL> SELECT SUBSTR(VALUE,1,45) "Current Setting"
  2  FROM   V$PARAMETER
  3* WHERE  NAME = LOWER('&Parameter');
Enter value for parameter: OPTIMIZER_MODE
Current Setting
-----------------------
FIRST_ROWS

SQL> EXPLAIN PLAN FOR
  2  SELECT  *
  3  FROM    STATS
  4  WHERE   SNO > 999000;
Explained.

SQL> @explain
Query Plan                                                        COST
--------------------------------------------------------------   ----
SELECT STATEMENT   FIRST_ROWS                                       39
  TABLE ACCESS BY ROWID STATS ANALYZED                              39
    INDEX RANGE SCAN BTREE_UNIQUE_SNO ANALYZED
```

If the table has been analyzed and **OPTIMIZER_MODE** is set to RULE, the rule-based optimizer is used. Listing 1.8 suggests that this is the case, because there is no cost and the **OPTIONS** column of the table **PLAN_TABLE** contains RULE.

Listing 1.8 Optimizer mode **RULE**, table analyzed.

```
SQL> SELECT SUBSTR(VALUE,1,45) "Current Setting"
  2  FROM   V$PARAMETER
  3* WHERE  NAME = LOWER('&Parameter');
Enter value for parameter: OPTIMIZER_MODE
Current Setting
----------------------
RULE

SQL> EXPLAIN PLAN FOR
  2  SELECT  *
  3  FROM    STATS
  4* WHERE   SNO > 999000;
Explained.
```

```
SQL> @explain
Query Plan                                                          COST
------------------------------------------------------------------  ----
SELECT STATEMENT   RULE
  TABLE ACCESS BY ROWID STATS ANALYZED
    INDEX RANGE SCAN BTREE_UNIQUE_SNO ANALYZED
```

If the table has not been analyzed and **OPTIMIZER_MODE** is set to **CHOOSE**, the rule-based optimizer is used. Listing 1.9 suggests that this is the case, since there is no cost.

Listing 1.9 Optimizer mode **CHOOSE**, table not analyzed.

```
SQL> SELECT SUBSTR(VALUE,1,45) "Current Setting"
  2  FROM   V$PARAMETER
  3  WHERE  NAME = LOWER('&Parameter');
Enter value for parameter: OPTIMIZER_MODE
Current Setting
-----------------------
CHOOSE

SQL> EXPLAIN PLAN FOR
  2  SELECT *
  3  FROM   STATS
  4  WHERE  SNO > 999000;
Explained.

SQL> @explain
Query Plan                                                          COST
------------------------------------------------------------------  ----
SELECT STATEMENT   CHOOSE
  TABLE ACCESS BY ROWID STATS
    INDEX RANGE SCAN BTREE_UNIQUE_SNO
```

If the table has not been analyzed and **OPTIMIZER_MODE** is set to **ALL_ROWS**, the cost-based optimizer is used. Listing 1.10 suggests that this is the case, because the cost is 237 and the **OPTIONS** column of the table **PLAN_TABLE** contains **ALL_ROWS**. Notice that the cost-based optimizer would have been used even though there are no statistics available for the **STATS** table. Oracle had to estimate the cost with no statistics in the data dictionary. Obviously, with no real data to base its cost on, Oracle quickly—on the fly—derived an estimated cost of 237. In previous listings, Oracle estimated the cost to be 39 when there was statistical data in the data dictionary. The data dictionary is populated with statistical information when a table or index is analyzed.

Listing 1.10 Optimizer **ALL_ROWS**, table not analyzed.

```
SQL> SELECT SUBSTR(VALUE,1,45) "Current Setting"
  2  FROM   V$PARAMETER
  3  WHERE  NAME = LOWER('&Parameter');
Enter value for parameter: OPTIMIZER_MODE
Current Setting
----------------------
ALL_ROWS

SQL> EXPLAIN PLAN FOR
  2  SELECT *
  3  FROM   STATS
  4  WHERE  SNO > 999000;
Explained.

SQL> @explain
Query Plan                                                    COST
------------------------------------------------------------  ----
SELECT STATEMENT   ALL_ROWS                                   237
  TABLE ACCESS BY ROWID STATS                                 237
    INDEX RANGE SCAN BTREE_UNIQUE_SNO
```

If the table has not been analyzed and **OPTIMIZER_MODE** is set to FIRST_ROWS, the cost-based optimizer is used. Listing 1.11 illustrates this. The cost is 237 and the **OPTIONS** column of the table **PLAN_TABLE** contains FIRST_ROWS.

Listing 1.11 Optimizer mode **FIRST_ROWS**, no statistics.

```
SQL> SELECT SUBSTR(VALUE,1,45) "Current Setting"
  2  FROM   V$PARAMETER
  3  WHERE  NAME = LOWER('&Parameter');
Enter value for parameter: OPTIMIZER_MODE
Current Setting
----------------------
FIRST_ROWS

SQL> EXPLAIN PLAN FOR
  2  SELECT *
  3  FROM   STATS
  4  WHERE  SNO > 999000;
Explained.
```

```
SQL> @explain
Query Plan                                                     COST
-------------------------------------------------------------  ----
SELECT STATEMENT   FIRST_ROWS                                   237
  TABLE ACCESS BY ROWID STATS                                   237
    INDEX RANGE SCAN BTREE_UNIQUE_SNO
```

If the table has not been analyzed and **OPTIMIZER_MODE** is set to **RULE**, the rule-based optimizer is used. Listing 1.12 suggests that this is the case, because there is no cost and the **OPTIONS** column of the table **PLAN_TABLE** contains **RULE**.

Listing 1.12 Optimizer mode **RULE**, no statistics.

```
SQL> SELECT SUBSTR(VALUE,1,45) "Current Setting"
  2  FROM   V$PARAMETER
  3  WHERE  NAME = LOWER('&Parameter');
Enter value for parameter: OPTIMIZER_MODE

Current Setting
----------------------
RULE

SQL> EXPLAIN PLAN FOR
  2  SELECT *
  3  FROM   STATS
  4  WHERE  SNO > 999000;
Explained.

SQL> @explain
Query Plan                                                     COST
-------------------------------------------------------------  ----
SELECT STATEMENT   RULE
  TABLE ACCESS BY ROWID STATS
    INDEX RANGE SCAN BTREE_UNIQUE_SNO
```

Session Level

At the session level, the optimizer can be chosen using the **ALTER SESSION** command. This command overrides the current setting of the parameter **OPTIMIZER_MODE** at the instance level. Notice that **OPTIMIZER_GOAL** is used in the **ALTER SESSION** command as opposed to **OPTIMIZER_MODE**. One way to remember is to remind yourself that you are a GOAL setter. Listing 1.13 contains the **ALTER SESSION** commands that invoke the use of either the cost-based or rule-based optimizer.

Listing 1.13 ALTER SESSION SET OPTIMIZER_GOAL.

```
ALTER SESSION SET OPTIMIZER_GOAL = CHOOSE;          (Either)
ALTER SESSION SET OPTIMIZER_GOAL = ALL_ROWS;        (Cost)
ALTER SESSION SET OPTIMIZER_GOAL = FIRST_ROWS;      (Cost)
ALTER SESSION SET OPTIMIZER_GOAL = RULE;            (Rule)
```

If the table has been analyzed and **OPTIMIZER_GOAL** is **CHOOSE**, the cost-based optimizer is used. Listing 1.14 suggests that this is the case, because there is a cost of 39. The parameter **OPTIMIZER_MODE** is set to **RULE**. Notice that the **ALTER SESSION** command using **OPTIMIZER_GOAL (CHOOSE)** overrides the init.ora setting for **OPTIMIZER_MODE (RULE)**.

Listing 1.14 OPTIMIZER_GOAL CHOOSE, with statistics.

```
SQL> SELECT SUBSTR(VALUE,1,45) "Current Setting"
  2  FROM   V$PARAMETER
  3  WHERE  NAME = LOWER('&Parameter');
Enter value for parameter: OPTIMIZER_MODE
Current Setting
------------------
RULE

SQL> ALTER SESSION SET OPTIMIZER_GOAL = CHOOSE;
Session altered.

SQL> EXPLAIN PLAN FOR
  2  SELECT *
  3  FROM   STATS
  4  WHERE  SNO > 999000;
Explained.

SQL> @explain
Query Plan                                                      COST
--------------------------------------------------------------  ----
 SELECT STATEMENT   CHOOSE                                        39
  TABLE ACCESS BY ROWID STATS ANALYZED                            39
    INDEX RANGE SCAN BTREE_UNIQUE_SNO ANALYZED
```

If the table has been analyzed and **OPTIMIZER_GOAL** is set to **ALL_ROWS**, the cost-based optimizer is used. Listing 1.15 suggests that this is the case, because there is a cost of 39. The parameter **OPTIMIZER_MODE** is **RULE**. Notice that the

ALTER SESSION command using **OPTIMIZER_GOAL** (**ALL_ROWS**) overrides the init.ora setting for **OPTIMIZER_MODE** (**RULE**).

Listing 1.15 OPTIMIZER_GOAL ALL_ROWS, with statistics.

```
SQL> SELECT SUBSTR(VALUE,1,45) "Current Setting"
  2  FROM   V$PARAMETER
  3  WHERE  NAME = LOWER('&Parameter');
Enter value for parameter: OPTIMIZER_MODE
Current Setting
-----------------------
RULE

SQL> ALTER SESSION SET OPTIMIZER_GOAL = ALL_ROWS;
Session altered.

SQL> EXPLAIN PLAN FOR
  2  SELECT *
  3  FROM   STATS
  4  WHERE  SNO > 999000;
Explained.

SQL> @explain
Query Plan                                                      COST
-------------------------------------------------------------  ----
SELECT STATEMENT   ALL_ROWS                                      39
  TABLE ACCESS BY ROWID STATS ANALYZED                           39
    INDEX RANGE SCAN BTREE_UNIQUE_SNO ANALYZED
```

If the table has been analyzed and **OPTIMIZER_GOAL** is set to **FIRST_ROWS**, the cost-based optimizer is used. Listing 1.16 suggests that this is the case, because there is a cost of 39. The parameter **OPTIMIZER_MODE** is **RULE**. Notice that the **ALTER SESSION** command using **OPTIMIZER_GOAL** (**FIRST_ROWS**) overrides the init.ora setting for **OPTIMIZER_MODE** (**RULE**).

Listing 1.16 OPTIMIZER_GOAL FIRST_ROWS, with statistics.

```
SQL> SELECT SUBSTR(VALUE,1,45) "Current Setting"
  2  FROM   V$PARAMETER
  3  WHERE  NAME = LOWER('&Parameter');
Enter value for parameter: OPTIMIZER_MODE
Current Setting
----------------------
RULE
```

```
SQL> ALTER SESSION SET OPTIMIZER_GOAL = FIRST_ROWS;
Session altered.

SQL> EXPLAIN PLAN FOR
  2  SELECT *
  3  FROM   STATS
  4  WHERE  SNO > 999000;
Explained.

SQL> @explain
Query Plan                                                          COST
--------------------------------------------------------------    ----
SELECT STATEMENT   FIRST_ROWS                                         39
  TABLE ACCESS BY ROWID STATS ANALYZED                                39
    INDEX RANGE SCAN BTREE_UNIQUE_SNO ANALYZED
```

If the table has been analyzed and **OPTIMIZER_GOAL** is **RULE**, the rule-based optimizer is used. Listing 1.17 suggests that this is the case, because there is no cost and the **OPTIONS** column of the table **PLAN_TABLE** contains **RULE**. The parameter **OPTIMIZER_MODE** is also **RULE**.

Listing 1.17 **OPTIMIZER_GOAL RULE**, with statistics.

```
SQL> SELECT SUBSTR(VALUE,1,45) "Current Setting"
  2  FROM   V$PARAMETER
  3  WHERE  NAME = LOWER('&Parameter');
Enter value for parameter: OPTIMIZER_MODE
Current Setting
-------------------------
RULE

SQL> ALTER SESSION SET OPTIMIZER_GOAL = RULE;
Session altered.

SQL> EXPLAIN PLAN FOR
  2  SELECT *
  3  FROM   STATS
  4  WHERE  SNO > 999000;
Explained.

SQL> @explain
Query Plan                                                          COST
--------------------------------------------------------------    ----
```

```
SELECT STATEMENT   RULE
  TABLE ACCESS BY ROWID STATS ANALYZED
    INDEX RANGE SCAN BTREE_UNIQUE_SNO ANALYZED
```

Statement Level

At the statement level, the optimizer can be chosen using **HINTs**. Chapter 9, "Hints," discusses hints in much greater detail. Hints override both the instance-level parameter setting of **OPTIMIZER_MODE** and the session-level setting of **OPTIMIZER_GOAL**. Listing 1.18 is a result of **OPTIMIZER_MODE** being set to **CHOOSE** and a hint to use the rule-based optimizer even though the table has been analyzed. Oracle uses the hint **RULE**, and the **COST** column of the table **PLAN_TABLE** is null.

Listing 1.18 The hint **RULE**.

```
SQL> SELECT SUBSTR(VALUE,1,45) "Current Setting"
  2  FROM   V$PARAMETER
  3  WHERE  NAME = LOWER('&Parameter');
Enter value for parameter: OPTIMIZER_MODE
Current Setting
------------------------
CHOOSE

SQL> EXPLAIN PLAN FOR
  2  SELECT /*+ RULE */   *
  3  FROM   STATS
  4  WHERE  SNO > 999000;
Explained.

SQL> @explain
Query Plan                                                        COST
--------------------------------------------------------------    ----
SELECT STATEMENT   HINT: RULE
  TABLE ACCESS BY ROWID STATS ANALYZED
    INDEX RANGE SCAN BTREE_UNIQUE_SNO ANALYZED
```

Listing 1.19 is a result of **OPTIMIZER_MODE** being set to **CHOOSE**, an **OPTIMIZER_GOAL** of **RULE**, and a hint of **ALL_ROWS**. Oracle uses the hint **ALL_ROWS**, and the cost of 39 indicates that the cost-based optimizer is used. This listing also illustrates that hints do override both the instance- and session-level settings for **OPTIMIZER_MODE** and **OPTIMIZER_GOAL**, respectively.

Listing 1.19 The hint **ALL_ROWS**.

```
SQL> SELECT SUBSTR(VALUE,1,45) "Current Setting"
  2  FROM   V$PARAMETER
  3  WHERE  NAME = LOWER('&Parameter');
Enter value for parameter: OPTIMIZER_MODE
Current Setting
-------------------------
CHOOSE

SQL> ALTER SESSION SET OPTIMIZER_GOAL = RULE;
Session altered.

SQL> EXPLAIN PLAN FOR
  2  SELECT --+ ALL_ROWS
  3  *
  4  FROM   STATS
  5  WHERE  SNO > 999000;
Explained.

SQL> @explain
Query Plan                                                     COST
-------------------------------------------------------------  ----
SELECT STATEMENT   HINT: ALL_ROWS                                39
  TABLE ACCESS BY ROWID STATS ANALYZED                           39
    INDEX RANGE SCAN BTREE_UNIQUE_SNO ANALYZED
```

Listing 1.20 is a result of **OPTIMIZER_MODE** being set to **CHOOSE**, an **OPTIMIZER_GOAL** of **RULE**, and a hint of **FIRST_ROWS**. Oracle uses the hint **FIRST_ROWS**, and the cost of 39 indicates that the cost-based optimizer is used. This listing also illustrates that hints do override both the instance- and session-level settings for **OPTIMIZER_MODE** and **OPTIMIZER_GOAL**, respectively.

Listing 1.20 The hint **FIRST_ROWS**.

```
SQL> SELECT SUBSTR(VALUE,1,45) "Current Setting"
  2  FROM   V$PARAMETER
  3  WHERE  NAME = LOWER('&Parameter');
Enter value for parameter: OPTIMIZER_MODE
Current Setting
-------------------------
CHOOSE

SQL> ALTER SESSION SET OPTIMIZER_GOAL = RULE;
Session altered.
```

```
SQL> EXPLAIN PLAN FOR
  2  SELECT --+ FIRST_ROWS
  3  *
  4  FROM   STATS
  5  WHERE  SNO > 999000;
Explained.

SQL> @explain
Query Plan                                                        COST
----------------------------------------------------------------  ----
SELECT STATEMENT   HINT: FIRST_ROWS                                 39
  TABLE ACCESS BY ROWID STATS ANALYZED                              39
    INDEX RANGE SCAN BTREE_UNIQUE_SNO ANALYZED
```

Listing 1.21 is a result of **OPTIMIZER_MODE** being set to **RULE**, an **OPTIMIZER_GOAL** of **ALL_ROWS**, and a hint of **CHOOSE**. Oracle uses the hint **CHOOSE**, and the cost of 39 indicates that the cost-based optimizer is used. This listing also illustrates that hints do override both the instance- and session-level settings for **OPTIMIZER_MODE** and **OPTIMIZER_GOAL**, respectively.

Listing 1.21 The hint **CHOOSE**.

```
SQL> SELECT SUBSTR(VALUE,1,45) "Current Setting"
  2  FROM   V$PARAMETER
  3  WHERE  NAME = LOWER('&Parameter');
Enter value for parameter: OPTIMIZER_MODE

Current Setting
---------------------------
RULE

SQL> ALTER SESSION SET OPTIMIZER_GOAL = ALL_ROWS;
Session altered.

SQL> EXPLAIN PLAN FOR
  2  SELECT --+ CHOOSE
  3  *
  4  FROM   STATS
  5  WHERE  SNO > 999000;
Explained.

SQL> @explain
Query Plan                                                        COST
```

```
----------------------------------------------------------  ----
SELECT STATEMENT   HINT: CHOOSE                               39
  TABLE ACCESS BY ROWID STATS ANALYZED                        39
    INDEX RANGE SCAN BTREE_UNIQUE_SNO ANALYZED
```

Summary

Which optimizer is used—cost or rule—can be controlled in the init.ora file by the setting of **OPTIMIZER_MODE**. The optimizer can also be selected at the session level using the **ALTER SESSION** command. Finally, at the statement level, hints can be used. Hints override the settings of both **OPTIMIZER_MODE** and **OPTIMIZER_GOAL**. For all three levels, there are four parameters. A method I use to recall these settings is to remember an old comedy ice-skating team on television many years ago. They went by the stage names of Fric and Frac. Taking the name of Frac from Fric and Frac, you can derive the names of the settings.

The "F" in Frac denotes **FIRST_ROWS**, which uses the cost-based optimizer. The "R" denotes **RULE**, which uses the rule-based optimizer. The "A" denotes **ALL_ROWS**, which uses the cost-based optimizer. And, finally, the "C" denotes **CHOOSE**, which uses either of the two optimizers.

Btree Indexes

CHAPTER 2

*The purpose of a btree index is either to implement a primary key on a table or to provide faster access to table data. This chapter illustrates the use of **ROWIDS**, how **ROWIDS** are used in a btree index, and how to create btree indexes on single and multiple columns. You'll also learn how to use histograms, how to detect and repair index fragmentation, and how to suppress the use of indexes. You'll also observe the output from Explain Plan on queries that reference indexed columns in the predicate or WHERE clause.*

Btree Indexes

What Is A Btree Index?

A btree index is used to implement part of the primary key definition of a table. You can cause Oracle to create a unique btree index on the primary key column(s) using the **CONSTRAINT** syntax either in the **CREATE TABLE** or **ALTER TABLE** commands. Or, you can create a btree index explicitly using either the **CREATE INDEX** or the **CREATE UNIQUE INDEX** commands. Btree indexes are also used to reduce retrieval access times of rows in a table. Btree indexes may include up to 16 columns from the same table.

A btree index consists of root, branch, and leaf blocks (see Figure 2.1). A leaf block contains two pieces of information. The first piece is the **KEY**, which is the indexed column sorted in ascending order. The second piece is the **ADDRESS**, which is the **ROWID** (also sorted in ascending order). Listing 2.1 shows the creation of a nonunique index on the **JOB** column of Oracle's **EMP** table. Included is a query that indicates the data found in a leaf block of the index.

Listing 2.1 Leaf blocks.

```
SQL> CREATE INDEX EMP_JOB_INDX
            ON EMP(JOB)
            TABLESPACE USER_DATA;
Index created.

SQL> SELECT JOB KEY,
            ROWID ADDRESS
     FROM   EMP
     ORDER  BY KEY, ADDRESS;

KEY       ADDRESS
--------  ------------------
ANALYST   00000003.0007.0007
```

```
ANALYST   00000003.000C.0007
CLERK     00000003.0000.0007
CLERK     00000003.000A.0007
CLERK     00000003.000B.0007
CLERK     00000003.000D.0007
MANAGER   00000003.0003.0007
MANAGER   00000003.0005.0007
MANAGER   00000003.0006.0007
PRESIDENT 00000003.0008.0007
SALESMAN  00000003.0001.0007
SALESMAN  00000003.0002.0007
SALESMAN  00000003.0004.0007
SALESMAN  00000003.0009.0007

14 rows selected.
```

Oracle7 ROWID

ROWID is one of Oracle's pseudocolumns and is comprised of three pieces of information about a row in a table. The rowid contains 18 hex characters. Positions 1 through 8 indicate the block number. Position 9 contains a period. Positions 10 through 13 indicate the row number within the block. Four zeros in positions 10 through 13 represent the first row for that block. Position 14 contains a period. Positions 15 through 18 represent the file number. Listing 2.2 indicates **FORD** is in row 13 of block 3 in file 7. See Chapters 15 and 16 for Oracle8 **ROWIDs**

Listing 2.2 ROWID.

```
SQL> SELECT ENAME,
  2         JOB,
  3         ROWID
  4  FROM   EMP
  5* WHERE  ENAME = 'FORD';

ENAME      JOB       ROWID
---------- --------- ------------------
FORD       ANALYST   00000003.000C.0007
```

Number Of Table Blocks Containing Data

The **ROWID** can also be used to calculate the number of table blocks containing rows. Remember that each file will contain identical block numbers. To obtain an

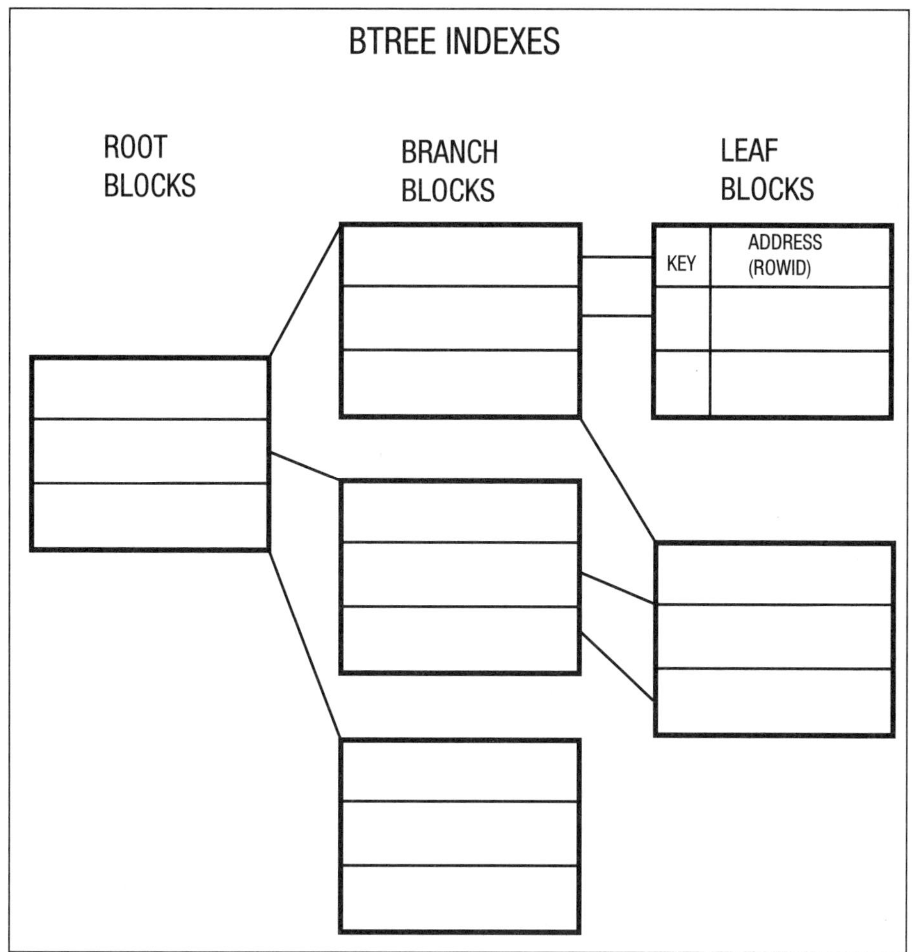

Figure 2.1
A conceptual diagram of a btree index.

accurate count, you must count the concatenation of the block number with the file number. Listing 2.3 indicates the number of blocks in the **STATS** table.

Listing 2.3 Number of data blocks containing rows.

```
SQL> SELECT COUNT(DISTINCT SUBSTR(ROWID,1,8) ||
                           SUBSTR(ROWID,15,4)) BLKS
   FROM   STATS;
   BLKS
-------
  26071

Elapsed: 00:02:38.23
```

Notice from Listing 2.3 that 26,071 blocks actually contain data, or rows; also, the query required 2 minutes and 38 seconds to execute. The **STATS** table contains one million rows.

Number Of Rows Per Block

The **ROWID** can also be used to calculate the number of rows per block. Listing 2.4 indicates the number of rows in each block in the **STATS** table.

Listing 2.4 Number of rows per block.

```
SQL> SELECT SUBSTR(ROWID,1,8) "Block",
            COUNT(*) "Rows In Block"
     FROM   STATS
     GROUP  BY SUBSTR(ROWID,1,8);

BLOCK    Rows In Block
-------- -------------
........            ..
00001892            38
00001893            39
00001894            39
........            ..
000065D4            44
000065D5            44
000065D6            44
000065D7            44
000065D8            44
000065D9            24

26071 rows selected.

Elapsed: 00:08:51.57
```

Average Number Of Rows Per Block

The **ROWID** can also be used to calculate the average number of rows per block. Listing 2.5 indicates the average number of rows in each block in the **STATS** table.

Listing 2.5 Average number of rows per block.

```
SQL> get cor5
  1  SET     PAUSE    OFF
  2  BREAK   ON  REPORT
```

```
  3  COMPUTE AVG OF "Rows In Block" ON REPORT
  4  SELECT  SUBSTR(ROWID,1,8) Block,
  5          COUNT(*) "Rows In Block"
  6          FROM   STATS
  7  GROUP   BY SUBSTR(ROWID,1,8);
  8  CLEAR   BREAKS
  9* CLEAR   COMPUTES

SQL> start cor5

BLOCK    Rows In Block
-------- -------------
........ .............  (Just the last few rows displayed)
000065D7            44
000065D8            44
000065D9            24
         -------------
avg            38.3568

26071 rows selected.

Elapsed: 00:10:43.43
```

Deleting Duplicate Rows

The **ROWID** can also be used to delete duplicate rows. Listing 2.6 indicates one method of deleting duplicate rows based on the primary key column value. This example deletes the larger values of **ROWID** and keeps the smallest values for all rows that have duplicate employee numbers. Two sets of duplicate employee numbers exist. Martin, Blake, and Clark all have employee number 7698. Adams, James, Ford, and Miller all have employee number 7902. The smallest **ROWID** values for the two sets of duplicate employee numbers belong to Martin (00000003.0004.0007) and Adams (00000003.000A.0007). Reader beware! The statement is a correlated update that can run forever on a large table.

Listing 2.6 Deleting duplicate rows.

```
SQL> SELECT EMPNO,
  2         ROWID,
  3         ENAME
  4  FROM   EMP
  5* ORDER  BY EMPNO, ROWID;
```

```
  EMPNO ROWID              ENAME
------- ------------------ -----
   7369 00000003.0000.0007 SMITH
   7499 00000003.0001.0007 ALLEN
   7521 00000003.0002.0007 WARD
   7566 00000003.0003.0007 JONES
   7698 00000003.0004.0007 MARTIN
   7698 00000003.0005.0007 BLAKE
   7698 00000003.0006.0007 CLARK
   7788 00000003.0007.0007 SCOTT
   7839 00000003.0008.0007 KING
   7844 00000003.0009.0007 TURNER
   7902 00000003.000A.0007 ADAMS
   7902 00000003.000B.0007 JAMES
   7902 00000003.000C.0007 FORD
   7902 00000003.000D.0007 MILLER

14 rows selected.

SQL> DELETE FROM EMP X
  2       WHERE X.ROWID > (SELECT MIN(EMP.ROWID) -- Keep Smallest
  3                        FROM   EMP  -- Save ADAMS and MARTIN
  4*                       WHERE  X.EMPNO = EMP.EMPNO);

5 rows deleted.

SQL> SELECT EMPNO,
  2         ROWID,
  3         ENAME
  4  FROM   EMP
  5* ORDER  BY EMPNO, ROWID;

  EMPNO ROWID              ENAME
------- ------------------ -----
   7369 00000003.0000.0007 SMITH
   7499 00000003.0001.0007 ALLEN
   7521 00000003.0002.0007 WARD
   7566 00000003.0003.0007 JONES
   7698 00000003.0004.0007 MARTIN
   7788 00000003.0007.0007 SCOTT
   7839 00000003.0008.0007 KING
   7844 00000003.0009.0007 TURNER
   7902 00000003.000A.0007 ADAMS

9 rows selected.
```

Fastest Retrieval Of A Row

The **ROWID** can also be used to fetch a row from an Oracle table. This is absolutely, positively the fastest method in all versions of Oracle for retrieving a row. No index is required. However, rowids can and will change if the table is exported, dropped, and imported because of fragmentation. While teaching tuning classes I usually ask my students, "Does anyone still live in the same house you lived in when you were born?" People change addresses and so does Oracle. By the way, only one of my students during the past nine years answered yes. Listing 2.7 illustrates the quickest method for retrieving **FORD** from the **EMP** table. Moreover, the cost of using **ROWID** to retrieve rows is one.

Listing 2.7 Fastest retrieval of a row.

```
SQL>  SELECT ENAME
      FROM   EMP
      WHERE  ROWID = '00000003.000C.0007';

ENAME
-----
FORD
```

Determining Which Rows Are Chained

The **ROWID** can also be used to determine which rows of a table are chained. If you do not already have a table named **CHAINED_ROWS** in your Oracle account, execute the following script, named utlchain.sql, shown in Listing 2.8. On most Unix platforms, the script can be located in $ORACLE_HOME/rdbms/admin. Next, analyze the table, **EMP** in our case, listing any chained row information into the table **CHAINED_ROWS**. Finally, join the table just analyzed, **EMP**, to the **CHAINED_ROWS** table using the **ROWID** in the analyzed table, **EMP**, to the **HEAD_ROWID** column of **CHAINED_ROWS**.

Listing 2.8 Determining which rows are chained.

```
SQL> @$ORACLE_HOME/rdbms/admin/utlchain
Table created.

SQL> ANALYZE TABLE EMP
             LIST CHAINED ROWS
             INTO CHAINED_ROWS;
Table analyzed.
```

```
SQL> SELECT ENAME
     FROM   EMP E, CHAINED_ROWS C
     WHERE  E.ROWID = C.HEAD_ROWID;

ENAME
-----
SMITH
WARD
MARTIN
SMITH
SCOTT
TURNER

6 rows selected.
```

If a table contains chained rows, you should eliminate the chaining. One method of resolving chained rows is to export the table, drop the table, and then import the table. Chained rows degrade the performance of queries against the chained table.

When To Use Btree Indexes

You want to use btree indexes for primary key columns, foreign key columns, and columns that are frequently referenced in **WHERE** clauses. However, btree indexes are normally not much of an advantage for a table with less than six Oracle blocks. When I worked for Oracle Corporation, I heard people from the Kernel group indicate that six to eight Oracle blocks are required for an index to be useful.

Selectivity Or Cardinality

Selectivity or cardinality is simply the ratio of the number of distinct values in a column to the total number of rows in a table. A higher selectivity or cardinality of data in the indexed column and fewer rows returned in an SQL statement are ideal for btree indexes. As an example, a table named **STATS** has a column named **SNO** that contains numbers from 1 to 1,000,000. The selectivity or cardinality of the **SNO** column is 1. A cardinality of 1 is as good as it gets for a btree index. The formula for deriving the selectivity or cardinality is the number of distinct column values divided by the total number of rows in the table. Therefore, in the **STATS** table, the cardinality is

```
1,000,000 values/1,000,000 rows = 1
```

Obviously, if you needed to see rows with a **SNO** number between 1 and 100, you would expect Oracle to use the unique btree index on the **SNO** column. Because much less than one percent of the rows from the one-million-row table are in the active set, an index scan is much faster than a full table scan. This leads to an old industry unofficial standard: the 80/20 rule.

The 80/20 Rule

"The 80/20 rule" states that if 20 percent or less of the rows of a table are returned, an index would probably return the rows faster than a full table scan. However, this standard has changed over time. With the advent of data warehouse tables of 150 million to 200 million rows, it just isn't practical for Oracle to use a btree index to retrieve 20 percent of the rows from a 200-million-row table. If Oracle did use the btree index to retrieve 40 million rows from a 200-million-row table, the disk heads would be very busy reading the index blocks and the data blocks. To make a better decision, Oracle has changed the optimizer with each release. Oracle7.0 appeared to be close to a 90/10 rule, Oracle7.1 a 95/5 rule, Oracle7.2 a 96/4 rule, and Oracle7.3 varies. Keep in mind that these are not exact percentages. In addition, Oracle uses many other factors to decide whether or not to use an index. Something else to consider are the conditions under which Oracle uses a btree index. Oracle uses a btree index under the following conditions:

- An index has been created.
- An indexed column is referenced in the predicate or **WHERE** clause.
- An indexed column is not changed in the **WHERE** clause.
- Oracle decides to use the btree index.

Distribution Of Data In An Indexed Column

The distribution of data on a btree indexed column is very important. If the data is badly skewed on the indexed column, Oracle might not use an index when it should. For example, consider a one-million-row table named **OIL_WELLS** with a column named **STATE** consisting of either **TX** or **OK**. Only one oil well is in Oklahoma, whereas 999,999 oil wells are in Texas. Listing 2.9 is the easiest method for quickly determining the distribution of data on the indexed column. Please realize you would never place a btree index on a column with just two distinct values. The selectivity is

2/1,000,000. Btree indexes work best with high selectivity (cardinality). However, if the CEO's administrative assistant complained loudly enough concerning the length of time required for the oil well in Oklahoma to be returned, you would probably try placing a btree index on the **STATE** column to preserve your corporate position.

Listing 2.9 Distribution of data on an indexed column.

```
SQL> SELECT STATE,
            COUNT(*)
     FROM   OIL_WELLS
     GROUP  BY STATE;

STATE COUNT(*)
----- --------
TX      999999
OK           1
```

If the table has been analyzed without using histograms, Oracle makes an incorrect assumption. Oracle assumes there are 500,000 oil wells in Texas and 500,000 oil wells in Oklahoma. This is a fairly logical assumption because there are 1,000,000 rows containing two values. Nevertheless, Oracle performs a full table scan when retrieving oil wells from either Texas or Oklahoma. Later, you'll see the importance of histograms to alleviate this problem.

Another method for determining the distribution of data on an indexed column is to use the **VALIDATE INDEX** command. This command was used in version 6 of Oracle and can be used in Oracle7. Listing 2.10 is an example. The output from **INDEX_HISTOGRAM** suggests there are eight values. The column **KEYS_WITH_REPEAT_COUNT** contains a 3, 4, 1, and a number of zeroes, which indicate there are eight distinct values in the index. The column **REPEAT_COUNT** contains the number of occurrences of each value in the **KEYS_WITH_REPEAT_COUNT** column. For example, four index values occur 98,304 times, and one index value occurs 491,520 times One entry suggests three index values occur zero times, and that is incorrect. Since 1 row is in the Southeast, 1,000 rows are in the Northwest, and 4,000 rows are from the West, Oracle considers them as a zero in the **REPEAT_COUNT** column because the **STATS** table contains one-million rows. Notice it requires nearly 53 seconds to validate a btree index on a one-million-row table. If the **VALIDATE INDEX** command indicates that the index is corrupt, you should drop and re-create the index. Otherwise, write one query against **INDEX_STATS** and another against **INDEX_HISTOGRAMS** to determine the distribution of data on the index (as well as to determine a wealth of other information).

Listing 2.10 Validate index.

```
SQL> SET TIMING ON
SQL> VALIDATE INDEX BTREE_REGION;
Index analyzed.

Elapsed: 00:00:52.56

SQL> SELECT SUBSTR(NAME,1,15) "Name",
  2         LF_ROWS,
  3         DISTINCT_KEYS,
  4         MOST_REPEATED_KEY,
  5         PCT_USED
  6* FROM   INDEX_STATS;

Name             LF_ROWS  DISTINCT_KEYS MOST_REPEATED_KEY PCT_USED
--------------- -------- ------------- ----------------- --------
BTREE_REGION     1000000             8             49500       89

SQL> SELECT *
  2* FROM   INDEX_HISTOGRAM;

REPEAT_COUNT KEYS_WITH_REPEAT_COUNT
----------- ----------------------
          0                      3
      32768                      0
      65536                      0
      98304                      4
     131072                      0
     163840                      0
     196608                      0
     229376                      0
     262144                      0
     294912                      0
     327680                      0
     360448                      0
     393216                      0
     425984                      0
     458752                      0
     491520                      1

16 rows selected.
```

```
SQL> SELECT REGION_BTREE,
            COUNT(*)
     FROM   STATS
     GROUP  BY REGION_BTREE;

REG COUNT(*)
--- --------
E     125000
N     124999
NE    125000
NW      1000
S     125000
SE         1
SW    495000
W       4000

8 rows selected.

Elapsed: 00:03:00.99
```

From Listing 2.10, you can conclude that one row has a value of **SE** in the **REGION_BTREE** column of the **STATS** table (and you certainly want Oracle to use the btree index on the **REGION_BTREE** column to retrieve one row from this one-million-row table). You can also deduce that 495,000 rows contain **SW** in the **REGION_BTREE** column of the **STATS** table; the use of an index to retrieve all rows containing **SW** in the **REGION_BTREE** column would be very, very slow compared to a full table scan.

Another method for determining the distribution of data on an indexed column is to use the **ANALYZE INDEX** command. This is the Oracle7 equivalent to the Version 6 **VALIDATE INDEX** command. However, the **ANALYZE INDEX** command also populates data dictionary views as well. Listing 2.11 illustrates one use of this command. Notice that it requires nearly 1 minute to validate an index on a one-million-row table; also, as with the Version 6 **VALIDATE INDEX** command, the views **INDEX_STATS** and **INDEX_HISTOGRAM** are populated with data concerning the index. From the output, you can see that there are eight distinct values in the **BTREE_REGION** column. Also, one of the values occurs 495,000 times.

Listing 2.11 ANALYZE INDEX using VALIDATE STRUCTURE.

```
SQL> ANALYZE INDEX BTREE_REGION
              VALIDATE STRUCTURE;
```

```
Index analyzed.

Elapsed: 00:00:55.16

SQL> SELECT SUBSTR(NAME,1,15) "Name",
  2         LF_ROWS,
  3         DISTINCT_KEYS,
  4         MOST_REPEATED_KEY,
  5         PCT_USED
  6* FROM   INDEX_STATS;

Name             LF_ROWS  DISTINCT_KEYS MOST_REPEATED_KEY PCT_USED
--------------- -------- ------------- ----------------- --------
BTREE_REGION     1000000             8            495000       89


SQL> SELECT *
  2* FROM   INDEX_HISTOGRAM;

REPEAT_COUNT KEYS_WITH_REPEAT_COUNT
------------ ----------------------
           0                      3
       32768                      0
       65536                      0
       98304                      4
      131072                      0
      163840                      0
      196608                      0
      229376                      0
      262144                      0
      294912                      0
      327680                      0
      360448                      0
      393216                      0
      425984                      0
      458752                      0
      491520                      1

16 rows selected.
```

Creating Btree Indexes

Unique btree indexes are used on primary key column(s) whenever a primary key constraint is associated with a table. This is accomplished using the CREATE TABLE or

ALTER TABLE command. You can also explicitly create a unique index using the **CREATE UNIQUE INDEX** command. You can create btree indexes that permit duplicates by using the **CREATE INDEX** command. The unique btree index should *not* be in the same tablespace as the data for the table. Hopefully, the tablespace for the data and the tablespace for the index will be on different physical drives. Spreading the input/output across several disk drives maximizes throughput and produces much faster queries.

NOSORT Option

To speed up the process of creating an index on a large table, consider loading data into the table sorted in ascending order on the column(s) to be indexed. The largest piece of overhead in creating indexes is the sorting of the key column(s). Therefore, if the data is already sorted in ascending order, you should use the **NOSORT** option. If the data in the indexed column(s) is not sorted and you attempt to use the **NOSORT** option, you'll receive an Oracle error. Another option to speed up the creation of an index is to use the **UNRECOVERABLE** option.

UNRECOVERABLE Option

UNRECOVERABLE speeds up the index creation process. When you specify **UNRECOVERABLE**, no information is written to the redo logs.

PARALLEL Option

You can have Oracle create the index using several processes if the proper entries have been made in the init.ora file. The number of concurrent processes is the degree of parallelism, which is specified using either the **CREATE TABLE** or **ALTER TABLE** command. The **CREATE UNIQUE INDEX** statement in Listing 2.12 illustrates this option. Four processes are used to create the unique btree index.

You can verify that Oracle automatically created the unique index because of the existence of the primary key constraint by writing a query against **USER_INDEXES**.

Listing 2.12 Primary keys.

```
SQL> CREATE TABLE STATS                 /*  One Million Rows      */
    (SNO            NUMBER(7,0),        /*  Values 1 to 1,000,000 */
     SNAME          VARCHAR2(30),
     REGION_BTREE   VARCHAR2(3), /*  Values N, NE, E, SE, S, SW, W, NW  */
     REGION_BIT_MAP VARCHAR2(3), /*  Values N, NE, E, SE, S, SW, W, NW */
```

```
    REGION_HASH NUMBER(1,0), /* Values
      1=NE,2=E,3=SE,4=S,5=SW,6=W,7=NW,8=N */
    GENDER             VARCHAR2(1), --  500,000 Fs And 500,000 Ms
    FIVE_HUNDRED_FIFTY NUMBER(4,0)
    CONSTRAINT PK_STATS_SNO
                    PRIMARY KEY(SNO)
                    USING INDEX  -- Unique Btree Index In Different TS
                         TABLESPACE USER_INDEXES);
Table created.

SQL> SELECT INDEX_NAME,    --  PK Constraint Creates Unique Index.
  2         UNIQUENESS,    --  Index Has Same Name As Constraint
  3         DISTINCT_KEYS
  4  FROM   USER_INDEXES
  5  WHERE  TABLE_NAME = UPPER('&TABLE');
Enter value for table: STATS

INDEX_NAME                       UNIQUENESS DISTINCT_KEYS
------------------------------ ------------------------
PK_STATS_SNO                     UNIQUE

SQL> ALTER TABLE    STATS
             ADD      CONSTRAINT PK_STATS_SNO
             PRIMARY KEY(SNO)
             USING INDEX
             TABLESPACE USER_INDEXES
    UNRECOVERABLE     --No Redo Written Which Is Faster
    NOSORT;

Elapsed: 00:09:04.76

SQL> CREATE UNIQUE INDEX PK_STATS_SNO
              ON STATS(SNO)
    TABLESPACE USER_INDEXES
    UNRECOVERABLE
    NOSORT
    PARALLEL(DEGREE 4);
Index created.
```

Disabling And Enabling Primary Key Constraints

You can disable primary key constraints before performing a large table load. After the table has been loaded, you can enable the primary key constraint. However, several problems might occur. One possible problem is duplicate rows existing after the table is loaded; therefore, the enabling of the primary key constraint will fail. You'll have to repair the duplicate problem before the primary key constraint can be successfully enabled. To resolve this problem, you need the table named **EXCEPTIONS.** You can create it manually, or you can run the script utlexcpt.sql. On most Unix platforms, this script is located in $ORACLE_HOME/rdbms/admin. By including this table in the **ALTER TABLE** statement, you can determine which rows are violating the primary key constraint. Listing 2.13 illustrates this problem and one method of repairing it.

Listing 2.13 Duplicate rows.

```
SQL> ALTER TABLE EMP -- Next Load EMP using SQL* Loader
  2        DISABLE CONSTRAINT PK_EMP_EMPNO;
Table altered.

SQL> ALTER TABLE EMP
  2        ENABLE CONSTRAINT PK_EMP_EMPNO;
ALTER TABLE EMP
*
ERROR at line 1:
ORA-02437: cannot enable (OPS$PCASSIDY.PK_EMP_EMPNO)
                  - primary key violated

SQL> @$ORACLE_HOME/rdbms/admin/utlexcpt
Table created.

SQL> LIST
  1  CREATE TABLE EXCEPTIONS(ROW_ID ROWID,
  2                      OWNER VARCHAR2(30),
  3                      TABLE_NAME VARCHAR2(30),
  4*                     CONSTRAINT VARCHAR2(30))

SQL> ALTER TABLE EMP
  2        ENABLE CONSTRAINT PK_EMP_EMPNO
  3*       EXCEPTIONS INTO EXCEPTIONS;
ALTER TABLE EMP
*
ERROR at line 1:
ORA-02437: cannot enable (OPS$PCASSIDY.PK_EMP_EMPNO)
                  - primary key violated
```

```
SQL> DESC EXCEPTIONS
 Name                            Null?    Type
 ------------------------------- -------- -----
 ROW_ID                                   ROWID
 OWNER                                    VARCHAR2(30)
 TABLE_NAME                               VARCHAR2(30)
 CONSTRAINT                               VARCHAR2(30)

SQL> SELECT ENAME, EMPNO
  2  FROM   EMP E, EXCEPTIONS X
  3  WHERE  E.ROWID = X.ROW_ID;

ENAME        EMPNO
------------ -----
FORD          7902
MILLER        7902

SQL> UPDATE EMP
  2  SET    EMPNO = 7934
  3  WHERE  ENAME = 'MILLER';

1 row updated.

SQL> ALTER TABLE EMP
  2         ENABLE PRIMARY KEY;

Table altered.
```

Another problem you might encounter when enabling a primary key constraint is that the unique index is created in the default tablespace of the user. This problem is easy to eliminate—just add the **USING INDEX** clause to the **ALTER TABLE** statement. Listing 2.14 shows you how to prevent the index and the table data from being stored in the same tablespace after enabling a primary key constraint.

Listing 2.14 Enabling the primary key constraint caveat.

```
SQL> COL INDEX_NAME      FORMAT A15
SQL> COL TABLESPACE_NAME FORMAT A15
SQL> SELECT INDEX_NAME, TABLESPACE_NAME,
  2         UNIQUENESS,
  3         DISTINCT_KEYS
  4  FROM   USER_INDEXES
  5* WHERE  TABLE_NAME = UPPER('&TABLE');
```

```
Enter value for table: EMP

INDEX_NAME      TABLESPACE_NAME UNIQUENES DISTINCT_KEYS
--------------- --------------- --------- -------------
PK_EMP_EMPNO    USER_INDEXES    UNIQUE

SQL> ALTER TABLE EMP
  2         DISABLE PRIMARY KEY;

Table altered.

SQL> ALTER TABLE EMP
  2         ENABLE PRIMARY KEY;

Table altered.

SQL> SELECT INDEX_NAME, TABLESPACE_NAME,
  2          UNIQUENESS,
  3          DISTINCT_KEYS
  4   FROM   USER_INDEXES
  5* WHERE   TABLE_NAME = UPPER('&TABLE');

Enter value for table: EMP

INDEX_NAME      TABLESPACE_NAME UNIQUENES DISTINCT_KEYS
--------------- --------------- --------- -------------
PK_EMP_EMPNO    USER_DATA       UNIQUE

SQL> ALTER TABLE EMP
  2         DISABLE PRIMARY KEY;

Table altered.

SQL> ALTER TABLE EMP
  2         ENABLE PRIMARY KEY
  3         USING INDEX
  4         TABLESPACE USER_INDEXES;

Table altered.

SQL> SELECT INDEX_NAME, TABLESPACE_NAME,
  2          UNIQUENESS,
  3          DISTINCT_KEYS
  4   FROM   USER_INDEXES
  5* WHERE   TABLE_NAME = UPPER('&TABLE');
```

```
Enter value for table: EMP

INDEX_NAME      TABLESPACE_NAME UNIQUENES DISTINCT_KEYS
--------------- --------------- --------- -------------
PK_EMP_EMPNO    USER_INDEXES    UNIQUE
```

Estimating The Size Of A Btree Index

First of all, many formulas exist for estimating the size of an index. In a btree index block are three major areas. The first is the header, and it contains a fixed area as well as a variable. The second is the free space reserved for entries that could not fit in the third area. The third area is used for index entries.

Assume that the fixed header is 110 bytes. The variable header is the product of 24 bytes and the value of **INITRANS**. The default value of **INITRANS** is 2. You can conclude that **HEADER SIZE** is 158 bytes (110 + (24 * 2)). The default value of **PCTFREE** (percent free) is 10. If the Oracle block size is 2,048 bytes (db_block_size init.ora) and **HEADER SIZE** is 158, then that leaves 1,890 bytes not in the header. If **PCTFREE** is 10, then ten percent of 1,890 bytes (that is, 189 bytes) is allocated for the free space. Subtracting 189 from 1,890 results in 1,701 bytes reserved for index entries per block.

Next, you must calculate or estimate the average value of an index. You can fudge a little here, because the index has already been created. Listing 2.15 uses the **AVG** function and the **VSIZE** functions to calculate the actual average value of the indexed column **REGION_BTREE**, which has a data type of **VARCHAR2**(3). Note that it requires nearly 7 minutes to execute the query.

Listing 2.15 Estimating the average value of an index.

```
SQL> SELECT AVG(VSIZE(REGION_BTREE)) AVG_INDEX_COL
  2* FROM   STATS;

AVG_INDEX_COL
-------------
        1.621

Elapsed: 00:06:51.98
```

Next, you must calculate the number of bytes for each index entry. Each entry of the index has 2 bytes of overhead and 6 bytes for the ROWID. Each entry also has a 1-byte column length indicator if the data is less than or equal to 127 bytes. If the indexed column contains data longer than 127 bytes, the length indicator is 2 bytes. Finally, the last part of each index entry is the average value length of each indexed column in the index. In this example, each index entry has an estimated size of 10.621 bytes (2 + 6 + 1 + 1.621).

The number of index entries per block is approximately 160 (1,701 bytes/10.621 bytes). Therefore, the estimated number of blocks required for the index on the **REGION_BTREE** column of the **STATS** table is 6,250 (1,000,000 rows/160 per block). Oracle says to allow five percent additional blocks for the branch blocks of the index. Therefore, the total estimated blocks required for the index on the **BTREE_REGION** column is 6,563 blocks. This equates to 13.4MB.

When Not To Use Btree Indexes In SQL Statements

Believe it or not, there are times when a full table scan outperforms an index. If the table has been analyzed, the cost-based optimizer makes the decision on how to access the data. For the most part, Oracle selects the fastest path. If you want to rigidly control full table scans for a particular query, you can deliberately suppress the use of indexes by the way you write your query. Suppressing indexes is used most frequently in the OLTP, On-Line Transaction Processing, world. You can use one of Oracle's many hints, or you can use one of the following sophisticated techniques on numeric, character, or date columns.

Suppressing Indexes On Numeric Columns

To cause Oracle to always perform a full table scan on the query shown in Listing 2.16, just add a zero to the numeric indexed column in the **WHERE** clause. This is true for both the cost-based and rule-based optimizers.

Listing 2.16 Adding a zero to a numeric indexed column.

```
SQL> EXPLAIN PLAN FOR
  2  SELECT  *    -- SNO HAS A BTREE INDEX ON IT
  3  FROM    STATS
  4* WHERE   SNO + 0 > 700000;
Explained.
```

```
SQL> @explain
Query Plan                                                      COST
------------------------------------------------------------    ----
SELECT STATEMENT   CHOOSE
  TABLE ACCESS FULL STATS
```

Suppressing Indexes On Character Columns

To cause a full table scan on a table containing a VARCHAR2 indexed column in the WHERE clause, concatenate a null to the indexed column. You can also use functions on the indexed column to produce a full table scan. Any one of the following WHERE clauses will cause a full table scan:

- WHERE UPPER(REGION_BTREE) = 'SW'
- WHERE LOWER(REGION_BTREE) = 'sw'
- WHERE INITCAP(REGION_BTREE) = 'Sw'

Listing 2.17 is an example of suppressing an index on a VARCHAR2 column using the concatenation technique.

Listing 2.17 Concatenating a null to a **VARCHAR2** column.

```
SQL> EXPLAIN PLAN FOR
  2  SELECT  *              -- 495,000 Rows
  3  FROM    STATS
  4  WHERE   REGION_BTREE || '' = 'SW';
Explained.
SQL> @explain
Query Plan                                                      COST
------------------------------------------------------------    ----
SELECT STATEMENT   CHOOSE
  TABLE ACCESS FULL STATS ANALYZED
```

Suppressing Indexes On DATE Columns

To cause a full table scan on a table containing a DATE indexed column in the WHERE clause, concatenate a null to the indexed column. You can also use functions on the indexed column to produce a full table scan. Listing 2.18 illustrates suppressing an index on a DATE column.

Listing 2.18 Concatenating a null to a **DATE** column.

```
SQL> EXPLAIN PLAN FOR
  2  SELECT  *
```

```
  3  FROM    EMP
  4  WHERE   HIREDATE || '' = '03-MAY-88';
Explained.

SQL> @explain
Query Plan                                                      COST
--------------------------------------------------------------- ----
SELECT STATEMENT   CHOOSE
  TABLE ACCESS FULL EMP

SQL> TRUNCATE TABLE PLAN_TABLE;
Table truncated.
SQL> EXPLAIN PLAN FOR
  2  SELECT  *
  3  FROM    EMP
  4* WHERE   TRUNC(HIREDATE) = '29-JAN-97';
Explained.

SQL> @explain
Query Plan                                                      COST
--------------------------------------------------------------- ----
SELECT STATEMENT   CHOOSE
  TABLE ACCESS FULL EMP

SQL> EXPLAIN PLAN FOR
  2  SELECT  *
  3  FROM    EMP
  4* WHERE   TO_DATE(HIREDATE, 'MM/DD/YY') = '02-MAR-78';
Explained.

SQL> @explain
Query Plan                                                      COST
--------------------------------------------------------------- ----
SELECT STATEMENT   CHOOSE
  TABLE ACCESS FULL EMP
```

Explain Plan And Elapsed Times

In Chapter 7, "Explain Plan," you'll take a closer look at Explain Plan and how to interpret its output. Referencing Explain Plan in this chapter is used to show whether or not Oracle performs a full table scan or uses an index. You'll run SQL statements through Explain Plan using both types of optimizers and then review the results. It is very important to realize that Explain Plan does *not* actually execute the SQL statement. Instead, it writes recursive call SQL statements to the data dictionary and derives a plan tree to execute the statement. Most plans contain more than one step. Each step of the plan becomes an inserted row into the table named **PLAN_TABLE**. The SQL script explain.sql that I use is included in Listing 2.19. This script is a query written against the table **PLAN_TABLE**. The output from this query is used to view how Oracle executes the SQL statement at this time. It also indicates which of the two optimizers gets utilized. Let's take a look what happens when **IN** is used on an indexed column in the **WHERE** clause.

Listing 2.19 SQL script file explain.sql.

```
SQL> get explain
COL      COST             FORMAT 99,999
COL      CARDINALITY      FORMAT 99,999,999
COL      'Query Plan'     FORMAT A60
SELECT   LPAD(' ', 2*(LEVEL-1)) ||
         OPERATION || ' ' ||
         OPTIONS || ' ' ||
         OBJECT_NAME || ' ' || OPTIMIZER "Query Plan",
         COST
FROM     PLAN_TABLE
START    WITH ID = 0
CONNECT BY PRIOR ID = PARENT_ID
```

IN

When **IN** is used on an indexed column in a **WHERE** clause, Oracle sometimes translates the SQL statement so that the index can be used multiple times, as you will observe in Chapter 4. Listing 2.20 indicates what action would take place if the rule-based optimizer were used. The value of **SW** appears 495,000 times in the **STATS** table out of a possible 1,000,000 rows. This represents nearly one-half of the rows in this table. You absolutely, positively do *not* want Oracle to use the btree index on the **REGION_BTREE** column to retrieve all those rows. The poor disk heads would be flying all over the place to retrieve every row. Remember, a rule is a rule. There is an index—it is referenced in the **WHERE** clause—and no function or modification such as concatenating a null to the column has taken place. And, because the rule-based optimizer is used, Oracle uses the index to retrieve 495,000 rows! This is the time to force Oracle to perform a full table scan by using one of the techniques discussed previously in the "Suppressing Indexes On **DATE** Columns" section. If the table was analyzed, the cost-based optimizer is used, and a full table scan is performed, as illustrated in Listing 2.21. Remember, when a number is displayed in the **COST** column of the table **PLAN_TABLE**, the cost-based optimizer is used.

Listing 2.20 IN with the rule-based optimizer.

```
SQL> ALTER SESSION SET OPTIMIZER_GOAL = RULE;
Session altered.

SQL> EXPLAIN PLAN FOR
  2  SELECT  *
  3  FROM    STATS
  4* WHERE   REGION_BTREE IN ('SW');
Explained.

SQL> @explain
Query Plan                                                    COST
------------------------------------------------------------  ----
SELECT STATEMENT   RULE
  TABLE ACCESS BY ROWID STATS
    INDEX RANGE SCAN BTREE_REGION
```

Listing 2.21 IN with the cost-based optimizer.

```
SQL> EXPLAIN PLAN FOR                  -- Statistics Estimated
  2  SELECT  *                         -- Choose
  3  FROM    STATS                     -- 495,000 Rows
  4  WHERE   REGION_BTREE IN ('SW');
Explained.

SQL> @explain
Query Plan                                                    COST
------------------------------------------------------------  ----
SELECT STATEMENT   CHOOSE                                    3,958
  TABLE ACCESS FULL STATS ANALYZED                           3,958
```

NOT IN

Now let's see if you can determine if Oracle might make an assumption when using the rule-based optimizer, which is not always correct. The following query in Listing 2.22 returns all rows whose **BTREE_REGION** column does not contain **SW**, **W**, **NW**, **N**, **NE**, **E**, and **S**. The only region remaining is the southeastern region (**SE**). There is only one row in this region. Obviously, to return this row, you want Oracle to use the btree index. However, with the rule-based optimizer,

Oracle performs a full table scan. When the query is executed, a full table scan requires 2 minutes and 43 seconds to return one row from the **STATS** table. However, in Listing 2.23, the cost-based optimizer makes the same decision as the rule-based optimizer.

Listing 2.22 **NOT IN** with the rule-based optimizer.

```
SQL> EXPLAIN PLAN FOR
  2 SELECT  *            /* Only One Row In REGION_BTREE 'SE'  */
  3 FROM    STATS
  4 WHERE   REGION_BTREE NOT IN('N','NE','E','S','SW','W','NW');
Explained.

SQL> @explain
Query Plan                                                      COST
--------------------------------------------------------------  ----
SELECT STATEMENT   RULE
  TABLE ACCESS FULL STATS

SQL> SET TIMING ON
SQL> SELECT  SNO, SNAME, REGION_BTREE
  2 FROM    STATS
  3* WHERE   REGION_BTREE NOT IN('N','NE','E','S','SW','W','NW');

    SNO SNAME                        REGION_BTREE
------- ------------------------- ------------
 375000 BETWEEN 300001 AND 600000 SE

Elapsed: 00:02:43.38
```

Oracle assumes, because it sees **NOT IN** at parse time, that most of the rows will be returned. Because the table does not contain any statistics, this assumption is usually correct. However, this is one time when the assumption is definitely incorrect. Performing a full table scan to return one row is very slow and costly.

Listing 2.23 **NOT IN** with the cost-based optimizer.

```
SQL> EXPLAIN PLAN FOR
  2 SELECT  *
  3 FROM    STATS
  4 WHERE   REGION_BTREE NOT IN('N','NE','E','S','SW','W','NW');
Explained.

SQL> @explain
```

```
Query Plan                                                      COST
-------------------------------------------------------------   ----
SELECT STATEMENT   CHOOSE                                      3,958
  TABLE ACCESS FULL STATS ANALYZED                             3,958
```

Looks like a great opportunity for histograms. Let's try creating histograms; you can observe the effect in Listing 2.24. Histograms are discussed later in this chapter in the section entitled "Histograms."

Listing 2.24 NOT IN with cost and histogram.

```
SQL> ANALYZE TABLE STATS
             COMPUTE STATISTICS
             FOR COLUMNS REGION_BTREE
             SIZE 8;
Table analyzed.

Elapsed: 00:04:47.89

SQL>  EXPLAIN PLAN FOR
  2   SELECT  *
  3   FROM    STATS
  4*  WHERE   REGION_BTREE NOT IN('N','NE','E','S','SW','W','NW');
Explained.

SQL> @explain
Query Plan                                                      COST
-------------------------------------------------------------   ----
SELECT STATEMENT   CHOOSE                                      3,958
  TABLE ACCESS FULL STATS ANALYZED                             3,958
```

Not even a histogram would cause Oracle to use the btree index on the **REGION_BTREE** column using **NOT IN**. This is a perfect example of a query that should be rewritten. Listing 2.25 uses the index.

Listing 2.25 Rewriting the query.

```
SQL> EXPLAIN PLAN FOR
  2  SELECT  *
  3  FROM    STATS
  4* WHERE   REGION_BTREE = 'SE';
Explained.
```

```
SQL> @explain
Query Plan                                                    COST
------------------------------------------------------------  ----
SELECT STATEMENT   CHOOSE                                    2,621
  TABLE ACCESS BY ROWID STATS ANALYZED                       2,621
    INDEX RANGE SCAN BTREE_REGION ANALYZED
```

BETWEEN

BETWEEN is an inclusive range with Oracle. For example, let's return all rows with an **SNO** number between 1 and 1,000,000. Such a query would return every row in the table because **SNO** numbers range from 1 to 1,000,000. Obviously, a full table scan would perform much faster than using an index. This column is indexed with a btree index. Listing 2.26 indicates what Oracle would do using the rule-based optimizer. Listing 2.27 uses the cost-based optimizer, and it would perform much faster if a full table scan was used to retrieve every row from the **STATS** table.

Listing 2.26 **BETWEEN** with the rule-based optimizer.

```
SQL> EXPLAIN PLAN FOR
  2  SELECT  *
  3  FROM    STATS
  4  WHERE   SNO BETWEEN 1 AND 1000000;
Explained.

SQL> @explain
Query Plan                                                    COST
------------------------------------------------------------  ----
SELECT STATEMENT   RULE
  TABLE ACCESS BY ROWID STATS
    INDEX RANGE SCAN BTREE_UNIQUE_SNO
```

Listing 2.27 **BETWEEN** with the cost-based optimizer.

```
SQL> EXPLAIN PLAN FOR
  2  SELECT  *
  3  FROM    STATS
  4  WHERE   SNO BETWEEN 1 AND 1000000;
Explained.

SQL> @explain
Query Plan                                                    COST
------------------------------------------------------------  ----
```

```
SELECT STATEMENT   CHOOSE                                          3,958
  TABLE ACCESS FULL STATS ANALYZED                                 3,958
```

Even though hints will be discussed in Chapter 9, "Hints," let's use one now to cause Oracle to use the unique btree index on the SNO column. Notice the cost of 43,468 in Listing 2.28 compared to 3,958 for a full table scan. The cost to use the index for a full table scan is nearly 11 times greater than a full table scan.

Listing 2.28 Cost of **BETWEEN** using index full table scan.

```
SQL> EXPLAIN PLAN FOR
  2  SELECT --+ INDEX(STATS BTREE_UNIQUE_SNO)
  3  *
  4  FROM       STATS
  5  WHERE      SNO BETWEEN 1 AND 1000000;
Explained.

SQL> @explain
Query Plan                                                          COST
------------------------------------------------------------------ ----
SELECT STATEMENT   CHOOSE                                         43,468
  TABLE ACCESS BY ROWID STATS ANALYZED                            43,468
    INDEX RANGE SCAN BTREE_UNIQUE_SNO ANALYZED
```

NOT BETWEEN

Let's return all SNO numbers not in the inclusive range of 2 and 999,999. You are really wanting Oracle to return just two rows from the one-million-row table. In other words, you want to see the rows where **SNO** is 1 or **SNO** is 1,000,000. This certainly warrants the use of an index. In Chapter 1, "The Optimizers," you observed Oracle translating this statement and using the index to retrieve both rows. However, that was using the cost-based optimizer. Now look at Listing 2.29 to see how Oracle executes this query using the rule-based optimizer.

Listing 2.29 **NOT BETWEEN** with the rule-based optimizer.

```
SQL> EXPLAIN PLAN FOR
  2  SELECT  *
  3  FROM    STATS
  4* WHERE   SNO NOT BETWEEN 2 AND 999999;
Explained.
```

```
SQL> @explain
Query Plan                                                      COST
--------------------------------------------------------------  ----
SELECT STATEMENT   RULE
  CONCATENATION
    TABLE ACCESS BY ROWID STATS
      INDEX RANGE SCAN BTREE_UNIQUE_SNO
    TABLE ACCESS BY ROWID STATS
      INDEX RANGE SCAN BTREE_UNIQUE_SNO

6 rows selected.
```

Oracle has continuously improved both optimizers with each new release. There was a time when Oracle would have performed a full table scan for this query. Internally, Oracle has transformed this query into the following query shown in Listing 2.30, which uses the btree index twice—once for each row.

Listing 2.30 **NOT BETWEEN** transformed.

```
SELECT *
FROM   STATS
WHERE  SNO = 1        -- Uses Index
UNION
SELECT *
FROM   STATS
WHERE  SNO = 1000000  -- Uses Index
```

LIKE

For Oracle to have any chance of using a btree index on a character column, either **VARCHAR2** or **CHAR**, the first position must be included in the **LIKE** portion of the **WHERE** clause. Listing 2.31 uses **LIKE** in the **WHERE** clause. Notice that the first position contains "S". However, a closer look at the data in the **REGION_BTREE** column reveals the following: First of all, regions **S**, **SE**, and **SW** would all be returned using the btree index on the **REGION_BTREE** column. Second, **S** is in 125,000 rows, **SE** is in 1 row, and **SW** is in 495,000 rows. The result set is 620,001 rows. It is very slow to use a btree index to retrieve 62 percent of the rows from a table with 1,000,000 rows.

Listing 2.31 **LIKE 'S%'** with the rule-based optimizer.

```
SQL> EXPLAIN PLAN FOR
  2  SELECT  *
  3  FROM    STATS
  4  WHERE   REGION_BTREE LIKE 'S%';
Explained.

SQL> @explain
Query Plan                                                    COST
------------------------------------------------------------  ----
SELECT STATEMENT   RULE
  TABLE ACCESS BY ROWID STATS
    INDEX RANGE SCAN BTREE_REGION
```

Listing 2.32 indicates the course of action using the cost-based optimizer. Notice that a full table scan is used to retrieve over 60 percent of the rows from the one-million-row table—and that is a very good decision.

Listing 2.32 **LIKE** using the cost-based optimizer.

```
SQL> EXPLAIN PLAN FOR
  2  SELECT  *
  3  FROM    STATS
  4* WHERE   REGION_BTREE LIKE 'S%';
Explained.

SQL> @explain
Query Plan                                                    COST
------------------------------------------------------------  ----
SELECT STATEMENT   CHOOSE                                     3,958
  TABLE ACCESS FULL STATS ANALYZED                            3,958
```

By switching the **LIKE** from 'S%' to '%S%', you cause Oracle to perform a full table scan. Here, Oracle is making a great decision using the rule-based optimizer. The cost-based optimizer also performs a full table scan. Listing 2.33 indicates the action taken under the rule-based optimizer.

Listing 2.33 **LIKE '%S%'** with the rule-based optimizer.

```
SQL> EXPLAIN PLAN FOR
  2  SELECT  *
  3  FROM    STATS
  4* WHERE   REGION_BTREE LIKE '%S%';
Explained.
```

```
SQL> @explain
Query Plan                                                    COST
------------------------------------------------------------- ----
SELECT STATEMENT   RULE
  TABLE ACCESS FULL STATS
```

IS NULL

In Oracle, a "null" is simply an unknown value. In addition, one unknown value does not equal another unknown value. For every column in every row of a table, there is a length byte. If the column is null, the length byte is zero. Null values are not stored in single-column btree indexes. If the index is concatenated or composite, only the first column of the composite index must not be null. If it is, the index entry is skipped. Listing 2.34 shows a column being added to the **STATS** table. Five rows in the **STATS** table are updated in the new column. Then, a btree index is created on the new column. An Explain Plan reveals that Oracle performs a full table scan. That is the only access method possible here, because nulls are not stored in the index. This is a great decision because 999,995 rows are retrieved. Listing 2.35 indicates that the cost-based optimizer is also forced to perform a full table scan.

Listing 2.34 **IS NULL** with the rule-based optimizer.

```
SQL> ALTER TABLE STATS
  2        ADD TEMPERATURE NUMBER(4,1);
Table altered.

SQL> UPDATE STATS
  2  SET     TEMPERATURE = 103.9
  3  WHERE   SNO IN(200000,400000,600000,800000,1000000);
5 rows updated.

SQL> CREATE INDEX TEMP_INDX
  2          ON STATS(TEMPERATURE)
  3* TABLESPACE USER_INDEXES;
Index created.

Elapsed: 00:05:41.21

SQL> EXPLAIN PLAN FOR
  2  SELECT  *
  3  FROM    STATS
  4  WHERE   TEMPERATURE IS NULL;
Explained.
```

```
SQL> @explain
Query Plan                                                      COST
--------------------------------------------------------------  ----
SELECT STATEMENT   RULE
  TABLE ACCESS FULL STATS
```

Listing 2.35 **IS NULL** with the cost-based optimizer.

```
SQL> EXPLAIN PLAN FOR
  2  SELECT  *
  3  FROM    STATS
  4* WHERE   TEMPERATURE IS NULL;
Explained.

SQL> @explain
Query Plan                                                      COST
--------------------------------------------------------------  ----
SELECT STATEMENT   CHOOSE                                      3,958
  TABLE ACCESS FULL STATS ANALYZED                             3,958
```

IS NOT NULL

Oracle sometimes makes a bad decision because of an untrue assumption with the rule-based optimizer. When the **WHERE** clause contains an **IS NOT NULL** on an indexed column, the assumption is that most rows have data. In the case of the **STATS** table, this assumption is false. Only five rows contain a value in the **TEMPERATURE** column. Because Oracle assumes that most rows contain data in the indexed column, it performs a full table scan. The fastest method for retrieving those five rows is by index. Listing 2.36 serves as an illustration of this point.

Listing 2.36 **IS NOT NULL** with the rule-based optimizer.

```
SQL> EXPLAIN PLAN FOR
  2  SELECT  *
  3  FROM    STATS
  4  WHERE   TEMPERATURE IS NOT NULL;
Explained.

SQL> @explain
Query Plan                                                      COST
--------------------------------------------------------------  ----
SELECT STATEMENT   RULE
  TABLE ACCESS FULL STATS
```

Even using the cost-based optimizer, without histograms a full table scan is used to retrieve the five rows from the one-million-row table. Listing 2.37 indicates that this is the case. So, try using a histogram. You can observe the results in Listing 2.38.

Listing 2.37 **IS NOT NULL** with the cost-based optimizer.

```
SQL> EXPLAIN PLAN FOR
  2  SELECT  *
  3  FROM    STATS
  4* WHERE   TEMPERATURE IS NOT NULL;
Explained.

SQL> @explain
Query Plan                                                    COST
------------------------------------------------------------  ----
SELECT STATEMENT   CHOOSE                                     3,958
  TABLE ACCESS FULL STATS ANALYZED                            3,958
```

Listing 2.38 **IS NOT NULL** cost-based and histograms.

```
SQL>  ANALYZE TABLE STATS
  2           ESTIMATE STATISTICS
  3           FOR TABLE
  4*          FOR COLUMNS TEMPERATURE SIZE 8;
Table analyzed.

Elapsed: 00:00:18.87

SQL> EXPLAIN PLAN FOR
  2  SELECT  *
  3  FROM    STATS
  4  WHERE   TEMPERATURE IS NOT NULL;
Explained.

SQL> @explain
Query Plan                                                    COST
------------------------------------------------------------  ----
SELECT STATEMENT   CHOOSE                                     3,958
  TABLE ACCESS FULL STATS ANALYZED                            3,958
```

Not even a histogram will cause Oracle to use an index when using **IS NOT NULL**. The assumption is that most rows have data in the **TEMPERATURE** column, which is not correct.

AND

When the **WHERE** clause contains an **AND** and more than one indexed column is referenced, Oracle will use the most selective index, or it might use both indexes by merging the rowids in the btree indexes. Merging btree indexes can be very expensive. The **AND-EQUAL** indicates that both btree indexes are used to retrieve the rows, and the indexes are merged. Listing 2.39 describes what happens. Notice that it only required .85 seconds to retrieve one row even though the rule-based optimizer merged the two btree indexes.

Listing 2.39 **AND** with the rule-based optimizer.

```
SQL> EXPLAIN PLAN FOR
  2  SELECT *
  3  FROM   STATS
  4  WHERE  REGION_BTREE = 'SE'    -- One Row
  5         AND
  6         TEMPERATURE = 103.9    -- Five Rows
  7*
SQL> /
Explained.

SQL> @explain
Query Plan                                                      COST
--------------------------------------------------------------  ----
SELECT STATEMENT   RULE
  TABLE ACCESS BY ROWID STATS
    AND-EQUAL
      INDEX RANGE SCAN BTREE_REGION
      INDEX RANGE SCAN TEMP_INDX

SQL> ALTER SESSION SET OPTIMIZER_GOAL = RULE;
Session altered.

SQL> get cortemp
  1  SELECT     SNO, SNAME
  2  FROM   STATS
  3  WHERE  REGION_BTREE = 'SE'
  4         AND
  5*        TEMPERATURE = 103.9
SQL> SET TIMING ON
SQL> /
```

```
    SNO SNAME
------- ------------------------
 375000 BETWEEN 300001 AND 600000

Elapsed: 00:00:00.85
```

After the queries in Listing 2.39 are run, a shutdown is performed. Then, in Listing 2.40 the cost-based optimizer is used to execute the query. The query actually runs somewhat slower than the rule-based query in Listing 2.39. The rule-based query requires .85 seconds, whereas the cost-based query requires 1.29 seconds. The rule-based query uses and merges both indexes, and the cost-based query uses only the index on the **TEMPERATURE** column. You might be thinking, because Oracle parses bottom-up, maybe that's why the **TEMPERATURE** index is chosen. By merely switching the order of the columns in the **WHERE** clause, you can test this theory. (See Listing 2.41 for further details.)

Listing 2.40 **AND** with the cost-based optimizer.

```
SQL> EXPLAIN PLAN FOR
  2  SELECT *
  3  FROM   STATS
  4  WHERE  REGION_BTREE = 'SE'
  5         AND
  6*        TEMPERATURE = 103.9;
Explained.

SQL> @explain
Query Plan                                                      COST
--------------------------------------------------------------  ----
SELECT STATEMENT   CHOOSE                                          2
  TABLE ACCESS BY ROWID STATS ANALYZED                             2
    INDEX RANGE SCAN TEMP_INDX ANALYZED

SQL> SET        TIMING ON
SQL> SELECT     SNO, SNAME
  2  FROM   STATS
  3  WHERE  REGION_BTREE = 'SE'
  4         AND
  5*        TEMPERATURE = 103.9;

    SNO SNAME
------- ------------------------
 375000 BETWEEN 300001 AND 600000

Elapsed: 00:00:01.29
```

Listing 2.41 proves that the parse direction does not determine which of the indexes gets used in a SQL statement. Oracle goes to the database buffer pool first. If one index already has index blocks in the pool, Oracle will use that index—that is, if they are both nonunique indexes. If one of the indexes is unique, then the unique index is used.

Listing 2.41 Parse direction myth.

```
SQL> EXPLAIN PLAN FOR
  2  SELECT *
  3  FROM   STATS
  4  WHERE  TEMPERATURE = 103.9
  5         AND
  6*        REGION_BTREE = 'SE';
Explained.

SQL> @explain
Query Plan                                                   COST
------------------------------------------------------------ ----
SELECT STATEMENT   CHOOSE                                       2
  TABLE ACCESS BY ROWID STATS ANALYZED                          2
    INDEX RANGE SCAN TEMP_INDX ANALYZED
```

OR

When the **WHERE** clause contains an **OR** and more than one indexed column is referenced, Oracle will use both indexes. The **CONCATENATION** indicates that both btree indexes are used to retrieve the rows. If one side of the "**OR**" has a column with no index, Oracle must perform a full table scan. Picture a row boat with two oars. For a straight ride, you place both oars in the water. Imagine each oar as being one side of the **OR**. Listing 2.42 describes this situation.

Listing 2.42 **OR** with the rule-based optimizer.

```
SQL> EXPLAIN PLAN FOR
  2  SELECT  *
  3  FROM    STATS
  4  WHERE   TEMPERATURE = 103.8 OR  --        5 Rows
  5*         REGION_BTREE = 'SW'     -- 495,000 Rows
SQL> /
Explained.

SQL> @explain
Query Plan                                                   COST
------------------------------------------------------------ ----
```

```
SELECT STATEMENT   RULE
  CONCATENATION
    TABLE ACCESS BY ROWID STATS
      INDEX RANGE SCAN BTREE_REGION
    TABLE ACCESS BY ROWID STATS
      INDEX RANGE SCAN TEMP_INDX

6 rows selected.
```

Listing 2.43 indicates, for this particular query anyway, that Oracle executes it exactly the same way, regardless of the optimizer selected.

Listing 2.43 **OR** with the cost-based optimizer.

```
SQL> EXPLAIN PLAN FOR
  2  SELECT  *
  3  FROM    STATS
  4  WHERE   TEMPERATURE = 103.8 OR  --        5 Rows
  5*         REGION_BTREE = 'SW'     -- 495,000 Rows
SQL> /
Explained.

SQL> @explain
Query Plan                                                        COST
--------------------------------------------------------------   ----
SELECT STATEMENT   CHOOSE                                        2,623
  CONCATENATION
    TABLE ACCESS BY ROWID STATS ANALYZED                             2
      INDEX RANGE SCAN BTREE_REGION ANALYZED
    TABLE ACCESS BY ROWID STATS ANALYZED                             2
      INDEX RANGE SCAN TEMP_INDX ANALYZED

6 rows selected.
```

Listing 2.44 shows what occurs if one side of the **WHERE** clause is not indexed. You can simulate this by concatenating a null to the **REGION_BTREE** column, which causes Oracle not to use the index on that column with either one of the optimizers.

Listing 2.44 **OR** with one side indexed.

```
SQL> EXPLAIN PLAN FOR
  2  SELECT  *
  3  FROM    STATS
  4  WHERE   TEMPERATURE = 103.8 OR  --        5 Rows
```

```
  5*        REGION_BTREE || '' = 'SW' --    495,000 Rows
SQL> /
Explained.

SQL> @explain
Query Plan                                                      COST
--------------------------------------------------------------- ----
SELECT STATEMENT   CHOOSE                                       3,958
  TABLE ACCESS FULL STATS ANALYZED                              3,958
```

The Equal Sign (=)

When the **WHERE** clause contains an equal sign (=), the rule-based optimizer will more than likely use the btree index. If your query returns 495,000 rows out of a 1,000,000 rows, you might want Oracle to perform a full table scan. However, Oracle knows what is best. Listing 2.45 examines this situation.

Listing 2.45 The equal sign (=) with the rule-based optimizer.

```
SQL> EXPLAIN PLAN FOR
  2  SELECT  *
  3  FROM    STATS          -- 495,000 Rows
  4  WHERE   REGION_BTREE = 'SW';
Explained.

SQL> @explain
Query Plan                                                      COST
--------------------------------------------------------------- ----
SELECT STATEMENT   RULE
  TABLE ACCESS BY ROWID STATS
    INDEX RANGE SCAN BTREE_REGION
```

Now let's use the cost-based optimizer to determine whether Oracle still uses the index that returns 495,000 rows or performs a full table scan. Oracle knows by the statistics in the data dictionary that the estimated cost for a full table scan on the **STATS** table is 3,958. For this query, the estimated cost of using the index is 2,621. Therefore, because 2,621 is lower than 3,958, Oracle uses the btree index to fetch the 495,000 rows. For further details, see Listing 2.46.

Listing 2.46 The equal sign (=) with the cost-based optimizer.

```
SQL> EXPLAIN PLAN FOR
  2  SELECT  *
```

```
  3  FROM    STATS          -- 495,000 Rows
  4* WHERE   REGION_BTREE =  'SW'
SQL> /
Explained.

SQL> @explain
Query Plan                                                     COST
-------------------------------------------------------------  ----
SELECT STATEMENT   CHOOSE                                      2,621
  TABLE ACCESS BY ROWID STATS ANALYZED                         2,621
    INDEX RANGE SCAN BTREE_REGION ANALYZED
```

Less Than (<)

When the **WHERE** clause contains a less than sign (<), the rule-based optimizer will more than likely use the btree index. If your query returns most of the rows out of a table with 1,000,000 rows, you'll want Oracle to perform a full table scan. Amazing, isn't it? Oracle will access the index and then the data for 999,999 rows. Here is where one of Oracle's many hints can be used. Refer to Chapter 9, "Hints," for more details. Listing 2.47 indicates the results.

Listing 2.47 Less than (<) with the rule-based optimizer.

```
SQL> EXPLAIN PLAN FOR
  2  SELECT  *
  3  FROM    STATS
  4* WHERE   SNO < 1000000;
Explained.

SQL> @explain
Query Plan                                                     COST
-------------------------------------------------------------  ----
SELECT STATEMENT   RULE
  TABLE ACCESS BY ROWID STATS
    INDEX RANGE SCAN BTREE_UNIQUE_SNO
```

Listing 2.48 illustrates the beauty of the cost-based optimizer. It is intelligent enough to know that a full table scan would be much more efficient in returning all the rows than using the btree index.

Listing 2.48 Less than (<) with the cost-based optimizer.

```
SQL> EXPLAIN PLAN FOR
  2  SELECT  *
```

```
  3  FROM     STATS
  4* WHERE    SNO < 1000000;
Explained.

SQL> @explain
Query Plan                                                    COST
------------------------------------------------------------  ----

SELECT STATEMENT   CHOOSE                                     3,958
  TABLE ACCESS FULL STATS ANALYZED                            3,958
```

Greater Than (>)

When the **WHERE** clause contains a greater than sign (>), the rule-based optimizer will more than likely use the btree index. If your query returns most of the rows out of a table with 1,000,000 rows, you want Oracle to perform a full table scan. Here is where one of Oracle's many hints could be used. Refer to Chapter 9, "Hints," for more details. Listing 2.49 indicates the results.

Listing 2.49 Greater than (>) with the rule-based optimizer.

```
SQL> EXPLAIN PLAN FOR
  2  SELECT  *
  3  FROM     STATS
  4* WHERE    SNO > 1;
Explained.

SQL> @explain
Query Plan                                                    COST
------------------------------------------------------------  ----

SELECT STATEMENT   RULE
  TABLE ACCESS BY ROWID STATS
    INDEX RANGE SCAN BTREE_UNIQUE_SNO
```

Listing 2.50 determines the cutoff point for full table scans as well as the starting point for Oracle to use the unique btree index on the **SNO** column. Oracle will perform a full table scan on the **STATS** table when 908,775 rows or fewer are returned. If 91,224 rows or fewer are returned, Oracle uses the index. As mentioned earlier, this is the 80/20 rule (with some major modifications). To be precise, it appears to be more like the 91/9 rule (TRUNC(100*(91224/1000000))).

Listing 2.50 Greater than (>) with the cost-based optimizer.

```
SQL> EXPLAIN PLAN FOR
  2  SELECT  *
  3  FROM    STATS
  4* WHERE   SNO > &no;
Enter value for no: 908775
Explained.

SQL> @explain
Query Plan                                                     COST
-------------------------------------------------------------  ----
SELECT STATEMENT   CHOOSE                                     3,958
  TABLE ACCESS FULL STATS ANALYZED                            3,958


SQL> EXPLAIN PLAN FOR
  2  SELECT  *
  3  FROM    STATS
  4* WHERE   SNO > &no;
Enter value for no: 908776
Explained.

SQL> @explain
Query Plan                                                     COST
-------------------------------------------------------------  ----
SELECT STATEMENT   CHOOSE                                     3,958
  TABLE ACCESS BY ROWID STATS ANALYZED                        3,958
    INDEX RANGE SCAN BTREE_UNIQUE_SNO ANALYZED
```

Histograms

Oracle uses height-balanced histograms as opposed to width-balanced histograms. Each bucket of the height-balanced histogram contains the same number of elements. The purpose of the histogram is to produce a clearer picture of the distribution of data on the indexed column and to reduce or eliminate full table scans when an index would be more efficient. The following command creates histograms for the STATS table:

```
SQL> ANALYZE TABLE STATS COMPUTE STATISTICS FOR COLUMNS
  REGION_BTREE SIZE 8;
Elapsed: 00:04:49.56
```

In this command, "8" represents the number of **BUCKETS** for the histogram. The default number of buckets is 75, and the maximum is 256. The number of buckets may change the performance of certain SQL statements, so you might try experimenting. You cannot have too many buckets.

In Oracle 8, the data dictionary views pertaining to histograms are **USER_HISTOGRAMS, ALL_HISTOGRAMS,** and **DBA_HISTOGRAMS.** Listing 2.51 shows information concerning the histograms just created.

Listing 2.51 USER_HISTOGRAMS.

```
SQL> get p9
  1  BREAK   ON "Column" SKIP 1
  2  SELECT  SUBSTR(COLUMN_NAME,1,15) "Column",
             ENDPOINT_NUMBER,
             ENDPOINT_VALUE
  5  FROM    USER_HISTOGRAMS
  6  WHERE   TABLE_NAME = 'STATS'
  7  ORDER   BY "Column", ENDPOINT_NUMBER;
  8* CLEAR   BREAKS
SQL> @p9

Column          ENDPOINT_NUMBER ENDPOINT_VALUE
--------------- --------------- --------------
REGION_BIT_MAP                0     3.5827E+35
                              1     4.5173E+35

REGION_BTREE                  1     3.5827E+35
                              2     4.0640E+35
                              3     4.0676E+35
                              4     4.3096E+35
                              7     4.3273E+35
                              8     4.5173E+35
REGION_HASH                   0              1
                              1              8
GENDER                        0     3.6346E+35
                              1     3.9981E+35
SNAME                         0     3.4410E+35
                              1     3.7032E+35
SNO                           0              1
                              1        1000000

16 rows selected.
```

Notice that there are only two "buckets" for all of the columns except the **REGION_BTREE** column, which was just analyzed. For character and date columns, the endpoint values include E+35 or some other combination of numbers other than 35. However, with the **SNO** column, which is numeric, the endpoint value of bucket 0 is 1, and the endpoint value of bucket 1 is 1,000,000. Even though you requested eight intervals, or buckets, on the **REGION_BTREE** column, Oracle used only six. Nevertheless, Oracle will now make a wiser choice on whether to use an index because it has a much better view of how the data is distributed on the column. This prevents full table scans where there are few values on the indexed column(s) and the percentage for each value is totally skewed. The **REGION_BTREE** column contains eight values, but one of those values occurs once.

At one of my customer's sites, this query resembled the following (not showing all buckets):

```
Column          ENDPOINT_NUMBER  ENDPOINT_VALUE
--------------- ---------------- ---------------
VALUE                        70             .18
                             71           .2052
                             72           .2232
                             73            .252
                             74           .2736
                             75           .3096
                             76           .3384
                             77
```

From this output, all numbers greater than .2736 and less than or equal to .3096 fall into bucket 75, whereas all numbers greater than .3096 and less than or equal to .3384 land in bucket 76. This continues all the way up to bucket 100. To cause Oracle to construct a histogram on the **REGION_HASH** column with eight buckets and to compute statistics for the table, refer to Listing 2.52.

Listing 2.52 FOR COLUMNS.

```
SQL> ANALYZE TABLE STATS
  2          COMPUTE STATISTICS
  3          FOR TABLE        -- Calculate Statistics For The Table
  4*         FOR COLUMNS REGION_HASH SIZE 8;
Elapsed: 00:04:52.85

SQL> COL TABLE_NAME FORMAT  A10
SQL> COL COLUMN_NAME FORMAT A20
SQL> SELECT *
```

```
     FROM  USER_HISTOGRAMS
     WHERE COLUMN_NAME = 'REGION_HASH'
     ORDER BY ENDPOINT_VALUE;

TABLE_NAME COLUMN_NAME         ENDPOINT_NUMBER ENDPOINT_VALUE
---------- ------------------- --------------- --------------
STATS      REGION_HASH                       1              1
STATS      REGION_HASH                       2              2
STATS      REGION_HASH                       3              4
STATS      REGION_HASH                       6              5
STATS      REGION_HASH                       7              7
STATS      REGION_HASH                       8              8
```

Oracle places the same number of elements in each of the eight buckets of the histogram for the **REGION_HASH** column. Because the **STATS** table contains 1,000,000 rows, each bucket contains 125,000 values. Notice that Oracle derives only six endpoints, but eight were requested. The data is skewed on the value 5 because it occurs 495,000 times.

Listing 2.53 reveals the distribution of data in the **REGION_HASH** column.

Listing 2.53 Distribution of data using GROUP BY.

```
SQL> SELECT REGION_HASH, COUNT(*)
  2  FROM   STATS
  3  GROUP  BY REGION_HASH;
REGION_HASH COUNT(*)
----------- --------
          1   125000
          2   125000
          3        1
          4   125000
          5   495000
          6     4000
          7     1000
          8   124999

Elapsed: 00:03:17.93
```

By using this distribution of data, you can conclude the following:

- Bucket 1 starts with 1; contains 125,000 ones; and has an endpoint of 1.
- Bucket 2 starts with 2; contains 125,000 twos; and has an endpoint of 2.
- Bucket 3 starts with 3; contains 1 three and 124,999 fours; and has an endpoint of 4.

- Bucket 4 starts with 4; contains 1 four and 124,999 fives; and has an endpoint of 5.
- Bucket 5 starts with 5; contains 125,000 fives; and has an endpoint of 5.
- Bucket 6 starts with 5; contains 125,000 fives; and has an endpoint of 5.
- Bucket 7 starts with 5; contains 120,001 fives, 4,000 sixes, and 999 sevens; and has an endpoint of 7.
- Bucket 8 starts with 7; contains 1 seven and 124,999 eights; and has an endpoint of 8.
- Buckets 4, 5, and 6 have endpoints of 5. Because bucket 7 consists mainly of fives (120,001), Oracle combines buckets 4, 5, 6, and 7 into one bucket. It appears that Oracle only needs five buckets. (Buckets 1, 2, 3, 4 [4, 5, 6, 7 combined], 5 (8)). Listing 2.54 suggests that this is the case.

Listing 2.54 Determining the actual number of buckets.

```
SQL> SELECT COLUMN_NAME, NUM_BUCKETS
  2  FROM   USER_TAB_COLUMNS
  3* WHERE  TABLE_NAME = 'STATS' AND COLUMN_NAME = 'REGION_HASH';
COLUMN_NAME          NUM_BUCKETS
-------------------- -----------
REGION_HASH                    5
```

Listing 2.55 used against **USER_HISTOGRAMS** indicates the number of endpoints and their endpoint values.

Listing 2.55 Number of endpoints and their values.

```
SQL> SELECT COLUMN_NAME, ENDPOINT_NUMBER, ENDPOINT_VALUE
  2  FROM   USER_HISTOGRAMS
  3  WHERE  TABLE_NAME = 'STATS' AND COLUMN_NAME = 'REGION_HASH'
  4  ORDER  BY ENDPOINT_VALUE;

COLUMN_NAME          ENDPOINT_NUMBER ENDPOINT_VALUE
-------------------- --------------- --------------
REGION_HASH                        1              1
REGION_HASH                        2              2
REGION_HASH                        3              4
REGION_HASH                        6              5
REGION_HASH                        7              7
REGION_HASH                        8              8
6 rows selected.
```

If all of the endpoints are unique, try reanalyzing with more columns. Eight buckets seems like a good choice for the **REGION_HASH** column. (See Listing 2.56.)

Listing 2.56 Oracle uses a histogram for better decision making.

```
SQL> EXPLAIN PLAN FOR
  2  SELECT  *
  3  FROM    STATS
  4* WHERE   REGION_BTREE = 'SE';

SQL> @explain

Query Plan                                         COST
-------------------------------------------------- ----
SELECT STATEMENT   CHOOSE                          2,144
  TABLE ACCESS BY ROWID STATS ANALYZED             2,144
    INDEX RANGE SCAN BTREE_REGION ANALYZED

SQL> SELECT REGION_BTREE
  2  FROM   STATS
  3  WHERE  REGION_BTREE = 'SE';

REGION_BTREE
------------
SE

Elapsed: 00:00:01.02
```

As you can see from Listing 2.56 and the Explain Plan, Oracle makes the correct decision this time, and it uses the btree index to retrieve one row. What a difference a histogram makes—1 second compared to 2 minutes and 54 seconds (as illustrated in the following listing). Listing 2.57 indicates that Oracle will perform a full table scan. Note that it requires nearly 3 minutes to return one row.

Listing 2.57 No histogram, but the table is analyzed.

```
SQL> EXPLAIN PLAN FOR
  2  SELECT  *
  3  FROM    STATS          -- One Row
  4  WHERE   REGION_BTREE = 'SE';
Explained.

SQL> @explain
```

```
Query Plan                                                    COST
------------------------------------------------------------  ----
SELECT STATEMENT   CHOOSE                                     3,958
  TABLE ACCESS FULL STATS ANALYZED                            3,958

SQL> SELECT REGION_BTREE
  2  FROM   STATS
  3  WHERE  REGION_BTREE = 'SE';

REGION_BTREE
------------
SE

Elapsed: 00:02:54.13
```

Concatenated Btree Indexes

Composite, or concatenated, btree indexes can contain up to 16 columns from the same table. Typically, they are used whenever a primary key is composed of multiple columns. They are also useful for queries that consistently use the same columns in the **WHERE** clause. The underlying assumption is that an index with more columns is more selective than a single-column index. The order in which the columns are defined in the **CREATE INDEX**, **CREATE UNIQUE INDEX**, **CREATE TABLE**, and **ALTER TABLE** commands is very important. The column with the highest selectivity should be first, and so on. You can create unique, concatenated indexes as well as nonunique, concatenated indexes. Listing 2.58 is an example of how to create a concatenated btree index as well as how to view the results from the data dictionary view **USER_IND_COLUMNS**.

Listing 2.58 Creating concatenated btree indexes.

```
SQL> DESC STATS2
 Name                            Null?    Type
 ------------------------------- -------- -----------
 SNO                                      NUMBER(7)
 REGION                                   VARCHAR2(3)

SQL> CREATE INDEX STATS2_SNO_REGION
  2*        ON STATS2(SNO, REGION);
Index created.

Elapsed: 00:00:11.62
```

```
SQL> BREAK ON NAME SKIP 1
SQL> SELECT SUBSTR(INDEX_NAME,1,17) NAME,
  2         COLUMN_POSITION POS,
  3         SUBSTR(COLUMN_NAME,1,17) "Column"
  4  FROM   USER_IND_COLUMNS
  5  WHERE  TABLE_NAME = 'STATS2'
  6* ORDER  BY NAME, COLUMN_POSITION;

NAME                                     POS Column
---------------------------------------- --- ------
STATS2_SNO                                 1 SNO
STATS2_SNO_REGION                          1 SNO
                                           2 REGION
```

Listing 2.59 analyzes the **STATS2** table so that Oracle can use the cost-based optimizer by relying on statistics in the data dictionary. One way to verify that a table has been analyzed is to view the contents of the **NUM_ROWS** column in **USER_TABLES**. As you can see, the **STATS2** table contains 10,000 rows. If a number exists, the table is analyzed. If no number exists, the table is not analyzed.

Listing 2.59 The **NUM_ROWS** column in **USER_TABLES**.

```
SQL> ANALYZE TABLE STATS2 COMPUTE STATISTICS;
Table analyzed.

Elapsed: 00:00:02.04

SQL> SELECT NUM_ROWS
  2  FROM   USER_TABLES
  3* WHERE  TABLE_NAME = 'STATS2';

NUM_ROWS
--------
   10000
```

The Leading Edge

The first column in a concatenated btree index must be referenced in the **WHERE** clause before Oracle will use the index. The **COLUMN_POSITION** column in the data dictionary view **USER_IND_COLUMNS** contains a 1 if the column of the index is the first column. Some Oracle users refer to the first column of a concatenated btree index as "the leading edge." Regardless of the optimizer (cost or rule), the first column of a composite btree index must be referenced in the **WHERE** clause before Oracle will even consider using it. Listing 2.60 illustrates the use of the leading column.

Listing 2.60 Referencing the first column.

```
SQL> EXPLAIN PLAN FOR
  2  SELECT  REGION
  3  FROM    STATS2
  4  WHERE   SNO > 9000;
Explained.

SQL> @explain
Query Plan                                                    COST
------------------------------------------------------------  ----
SELECT STATEMENT   CHOOSE                                       11
  TABLE ACCESS FULL STATS2 ANALYZED                             11

SQL> --  Not selective enough.  1,000 Rows = 10% Of 10,000

SQL> TRUNCATE TABLE PLAN_TABLE;
Table truncated.

SQL> EXPLAIN PLAN FOR
  2  SELECT  REGION     -- Now We Will Retrieve Only 10 Rows
  3  FROM    STATS2
  4  WHERE   SNO > 9990;
Explained.

SQL> @explain
Query Plan                                                    COST
------------------------------------------------------------  ----
SELECT STATEMENT   CHOOSE                                        2
  INDEX RANGE SCAN STATS2_SNO_REGION ANALYZED                    2
```

Not only must the first column of the composite index be referenced, but the value used in the **WHERE** clause must be very selective. Listing 2.61 illustrates that the first column must be referenced or else the index does not get used (even though there is only one index entry with a **REGION** of SE).

Listing 2.61 Referencing all columns but the first.

```
SQL> EXPLAIN PLAN FOR
  2  SELECT  REGION
  3  FROM    STATS2
  4* WHERE   REGION = 'SE';
Explained.
```

```
SQL> @explain
Query Plan                                                      COST
--------------------------------------------------------------- ----
SELECT STATEMENT   CHOOSE                                         11
  TABLE ACCESS FULL STATS2 ANALYZED                               11
```

Rule-Based Optimizer

With the rule-based optimizer, Oracle automatically uses the concatenated btree index if the first column is referenced in the **WHERE** clause. Listing 2.62 substantiates this claim.

Listing 2.62 The rule-based optimizer uses the concatenated index.

```
SQL> EXPLAIN PLAN FOR
  2  SELECT  REGION
  3  FROM    STATS2
  4* WHERE   SNO > 9000;
Explained.

SQL> @explain
Query Plan                                                      COST
--------------------------------------------------------------- ----
SELECT STATEMENT   RULE
  INDEX RANGE SCAN STATS2_SNO_REGION
```

Detecting Index Fragmentation

Indexes become fragmented over time if many index entries have been deleted. Index entries are deleted when rows from a table are deleted. Listing 2.63 analyzes the concatenated index on the **STATS2** table. The **VALIDATE STRUCTURE** populates **INDEX_STATS** with some very meaningful information concerning the analyzed index. The **DEL_LF_ROWS** column indicates the number of deleted index entries. The **LF_ROWS** column indicates the total number of index entries. Index **STATS2_SNO_REGION** is in great shape. No index entries have been deleted so far. The **PCT_USED** column indicates what percentage of the index block contains index information. If this number drops below 70 to 75 percent, consider rebuilding the index. The sample index uses 89 percent of the index block—and that's great. Ten percent of the block is allocated (**PCTFREE**) as free space for updates.

Listing 2.63 Determining if indexes are fragmented.

```
SQL> ANALYZE INDEX STATS2_SNO_REGION
  2           VALIDATE STRUCTURE;
Index analyzed.

SQL> SELECT TRUNC(100*(DEL_LF_ROWS/LF_ROWS)) PCT_DELETED,  PCT_USED
  2  FROM   INDEX_STATS;

PCT_DELETED PCT_USED
----------- --------
          0       89
```

Now let's simulate index fragmentation. Listing 2.64 uses a PL/SQL block to delete every third row from the **STATS2** table, committing every one-hundredth row. Then, the index is reanalyzed. Notice that 22 percent of the index entries have been deleted and that the **PCT_USED** column has dropped from 89 percent in Listing 2.63 to 76 percent.

Listing 2.64 Producing index fragmentation.

```
SQL> SET TIMING ON
SQL> BEGIN
  2      FOR i IN 1..10000 LOOP
  3        IF MOD(i,3) = 0 THEN
  4           DELETE FROM STATS2 WHERE SNO = i;
  5        END  IF;
  6        IF MOD(i,100) = 0 THEN
  7           COMMIT;
  8        END  IF;
  9      END  LOOP;
 10  END;
 11  .
SQL> /
PL/SQL procedure successfully completed.

Elapsed: 00:01:26.15

SQL> ANALYZE INDEX STATS2_SNO_REGION
  2*          VALIDATE STRUCTURE;
Index analyzed.

Elapsed: 00:00:00.74
```

```
SQL> SELECT TRUNC(100*(DEL_LF_ROWS/LF_ROWS)) PCT_DELETED,
  2         PCT_USED
  3* FROM   INDEX_STATS;

PCT_DELETED PCT_USED
----------- --------
         22       76
```

Eliminating Index Fragmentation

If an index is fragmented, you should rebuild the index. You can either drop and re-create the index, or you can rebuild the index. Sorting has a lot of overhead associated with it, whereas rebuilding bypasses the sorting, because the index entries are already sorted.

Listing 2.65 rebuilds the fragmented index. Then, the index is reanalyzed and compared to the results in Listing 2.63, where **PCT_DELETED** was 0 and **PCT_USED** was 89. Now **PCT_DELETED** is 0 and **PCT_USED** is 88.

Listing 2.65 Rebuilding an index.

```
SQL> ALTER INDEX STATS2_SNO_REGION
  2        REBUILD;
Index created.
Elapsed: 00:00:08.12

SQL> ANALYZE INDEX STATS2_SNO_REGION
  2          VALIDATE STRUCTURE;
Index analyzed.
Elapsed: 00:00:00.44

SQL> SELECT TRUNC(100*(DEL_LF_ROWS/LF_ROWS)) PCT_DELETED, PCT_USED
  2* FROM   INDEX_STATS;

PCT_DELETED PCT_USED
----------- --------
          0       88
```

Summary

Btree indexes are the most widely used of Oracle's four types of indexes. Btree indexes can be unique, or they can permit duplicates (nonunique indexes). They can be created implicitly using primary key constraints, or explicitly using the **CREATE INDEX** and **CREATE UNIQUE INDEX** commands. For a nonunique index, Oracle scans the key and uses the **ROWID** to retrieve the row(s). The major use of a btree index is to enforce the primary key constraint. A second major use is to speed up queries by indexing frequently referenced columns in the **WHERE** clause where the selectivity of the column to be indexed is high.

Indexes can be altered, analyzed, created, dropped, or validated. When creating large indexes, try to take advantage of the **NOSORT**, **PARALLEL**, and **UNRECOVERABLE** options.

You can control which index is used by the way the SQL statement is written. You can either suppress indexes or use hints. You can suppress an index in the **WHERE** clause. To suppress an index on a **CHAR**, **VARCHAR2**, or **DATE** column, place a function on the column or concatenate a null to the column. The following two examples are partial SQL statements showing only the **WHERE** clause:

```
WHERE UPPER(ENAME) = 'DEBRA'
```

or

```
WHERE ENAME || ''  = 'PAIGE'
```

You can also control which index you want Oracle to use by using the **INDEX** hint. If you want Oracle not to use any indexes, you can use the **FULL** hint. Hints are discussed in Chapter 9, "Hints."

The optimizer used can have a dramatic impact on performance. The rule-based optimizer is easier to predict, but it will someday vanish. Rule-based queries are more suited for OLTP applications. Decision Support Systems, or DSS applications, are better suited for the cost-based optimizer.

If data is badly skewed on an indexed column, use histograms to help the cost-based optimizer make a better choice for accessing the rows.

Concatenated btree indexes can contain up to a maximum of 16 columns from the same table. The most crucial column position is the first position. If the first column is not referenced in the **WHERE** clause, regardless of the optimizer, Oracle will perform a full table scan.

By validating the structure of your btree indexes and observing the data in the **INDEX_STATS** view, you can determine whether or not your indexes are fragmented. If they are fragmented, drop and re-create; otherwise, rebuild the index.

Btree Index Clusters

CHAPTER 3

In this chapter you'll learn how and when to create a btree index cluster. You'll also observe the explain plans and elapsed times of queries against clustered and unclustered tables.

Btree Index Clusters

What Is A Btree Index Cluster?

A btree index cluster, if used, typically prejoins tables on-disk. Sometimes a table can be clustered to itself. Either way, poor performance is the reason this type of index is even attempted, which is normally when joining tables. If tables are joined, the primary key and foreign key columns should be indexed. This still does not return rows as quickly as desired or expected. You can then experiment with the **ORDERED** hint, perhaps, to change Oracle's join chain and observe the elapsed times.

To create a btree index cluster, you must pick the cluster key column and the average block size for each cluster block. In the case of employees and departments, the cluster key column would be the department number column. The problem is the distribution of data around the cluster key column. In this case, it is the number of employees in each department. If you have 100 departments, and each department contains one percent of all employees, then a btree index cluster *might* help improve performance. However, the real challenge is determining the average cluster block size. If the size is too small, you'll experience chained cluster blocks, which translates into queries that run anywhere from 50 to 100 times slower than before the tables were clustered. On the other hand, if the cluster block size is too large, you'll have wasted space and have slower-running queries.

If you are frequently joining tables or master detail tables and normal joins execute too slowly, you *might* want to consider creating btree index clusters. But, if the cluster key column is updated frequently, rows might have to be migrated from one block to another. In addition, full table scans on individual clustered tables are slower than full table scans of unclustered tables. Because the clustered tables are prejoined on-disk in cluster blocks, the full table scan on the clustered table will read more blocks than on the unclustered table.

Unclustered Tables

Let's examine the unclustered tables **PARTS** and **TESTS** in Listing 3.1. The **PARTS** table contains 10,000 rows with part numbers, **PNO**s, ranging from 1 to 10,000. The **TESTS** table contains 470,692 rows with part numbers ranging from 1 to 10,000. In addition, each part has a number of tests associated with it. For part numbers 1 through 93, the part number is squared and 1 is added to the result to determine the number of tests. For example, part number 90 has 8,101 tests (90 squared is 8,100; add 1 to 8,100 and you get 8,101). Part number 93 has 8,650 tests (93 squared is 8,649). Part numbers 94 through 10,000 all have 20 tests each. Indexes are created on the **PNO** columns of both tables. Both tables are also analyzed.

Listing 3.1 **PARTS** and **TESTS** tables.

```
SQL> DESC PARTS
 Name                            Null?    Type
 ------------------------------- -------- ------------
 PNO                                      NUMBER(7)
 PNAME                                    VARCHAR2(15)
 TIME_OF_INSERT                           DATE

SQL> SELECT MIN(PNO),
  2         MAX(PNO),
  3         COUNT(*)
  4  FROM   PARTS;

MIN(PNO) MAX(PNO) COUNT(*)
-------- -------- --------
       1    10000    10000

SQL> DESC TESTS
 Name                            Null?    Type
 ------------------------------- -------- ---------
 PNO                                      NUMBER(7)
 TNO                                      NUMBER(4)
 RESULTS                                  CHAR(1)

SQL> SELECT MAX(PNO),      --Largest Part Number
  2         MAX(TNO),      --Largest Number Of Tests On A Part
  3         COUNT(*)       --# Of Rows In The TESTS Table
  4* FROM   TESTS;
```

```
MAX(PNO) MAX(TNO)                           COUNT(*)
-------- -------- ------------------------------
   10000     8650                             470692

SQL> SELECT PNO, MAX(TNO)
  2  FROM   TESTS
  3  WHERE  PNO IN
  4         (1,50,80,90,100,1000,2000,6000,7000,8000,9000,10000)
  5  GROUP  BY PNO;

    PNO MAX(TNO)
------- --------
      1        2
     50     2501
     80     6401
     90     8101
    100       20
   1000       20
   2000       20
   6000       20
   7000       20
   8000       20
   9000       20
  10000       20

12 rows selected.

SQL> SELECT *
  2  FROM   TESTS
  3* WHERE  TNO IN(SELECT MAX(TNO) FROM TESTS);

    PNO     TNO R
------- ------- -
     93    8650 P

SQL> CREATE INDEX PARTS_PNO_UNIQUE_INDX ON PARTS(PNO);
Index created.
Elapsed: 00:00:10.53

SQL> ANALYZE TABLE PARTS COMPUTE STATISTICS;
Table analyzed.
Elapsed: 00:00:09.75

SQL> CREATE INDEX TESTS_PNO_INDEX ON TESTS(PNO);
Index created.
Elapsed: 00:04:31.41
```

```
SQL> ANALYZE TABLE TESTS COMPUTE STATISTICS;
Table analyzed.
Elapsed: 00:02:58.13
```

Clustered Tables

Let's create a btree index cluster and compare the execution times of queries against clustered tables and unclustered tables. Listing 3.2 shows the creation of the btree index cluster. The cluster key is the **PNO** column. The **SIZE** parameter is not nearly large enough. This is done on purpose to produce poorer performance on the btree index cluster. Because part numbers from 1 through 93 are squared plus 1, the distribution is clearly not consistent with respect to the cluster key column **PNO**. Analyzing the cluster also produces statistics for both of the clustered tables as well as the index on the cluster. The cluster contains two tables. One of the two tables in the cluster is **PARTS_IN_CLUSTER**. It contains 10,000 rows or part numbers. The other table in the cluster is **TESTS_IN_CLUSTER**.It contains nearly 500,000 rows. Each part has a varying range of tests and results stored in **TESTS_IN_CLUSTER**. For example, part number 40 has 1,601 tests and part number 50 has 2,501 tests.

Listing 3.2 PARTS_IN_CLUSTER and TESTS_IN_CLUSTER.

```
SQL> CREATE CLUSTER PARTS_AND_TESTS
  2         (PNO      NUMBER(7,0))
  3* SIZE 650;
Cluster created.

SQL> CREATE TABLE PARTS_IN_CLUSTER
  2         (PNO            NUMBER(7,0),
  3          PNAME          VARCHAR2(15),
  4          TIME_OF_INSERT DATE)
  5* CLUSTER PARTS_AND_TESTS(PNO);
Table created.

SQL> CREATE TABLE TESTS_IN_CLUSTER
  2         (PNO     NUMBER(7,0),
  3          TNO     NUMBER(4,0),
  4          RESULTS CHAR(1))
  5* CLUSTER PARTS_AND_TESTS(PNO);
Table created.
```

```
SQL> CREATE INDEX INDX_PARTS_AND_TESTS
  2*        ON CLUSTER PARTS_AND_TESTS;
Index created.

(Load Both Tables With PL/SQL Scripts)

SQL> ANALYZE CLUSTER PARTS_AND_TESTS COMPUTE STATISTICS;
Cluster analyzed.
Elapsed: 00:03:29.90
```

Storage

Now let's examine and compare the storage of the btree index cluster to that of the unclustered tables. Listing 3.3 shows that there are 9,935 blocks for both unclustered tables and the two indexes on the **PNO** columns.

Listing 3.3 Unclustered tables and their indexes.

```
SQL> BREAK ON REPORT
SQL> COMPUTE SUM OF BLOCKS_USED ON REPORT
SQL> COL BLOCKS_USED FORMAT 99,999
SQL> SELECT SUBSTR(SEGMENT_NAME,1,25) "Name",
  2         SUM(BLOCKS) BLOCKS_USED
  3  FROM   DBA_EXTENTS
  4  WHERE  SEGMENT_NAME IN('PARTS','TESTS','PARTS_PNO_UNIQUE_INDX',
  5         'TESTS_PNO_INDEX')
  6* GROUP  BY SUBSTR(SEGMENT_NAME,1,25);

Name                                        BLOCKS_USED
------------------------------------------- -----------
PARTS                                               195
PARTS_PNO_UNIQUE_INDX                               130
TESTS                                             4,805
TESTS_PNO_INDEX                                   4,805
                                            -----------
sum                                               9,935
```

Now, let's examine the number of blocks required for the btree index cluster and the cluster index in Listing 3.4. The cluster uses 7,205 Oracle blocks to store the prejoined clustered tables on-disk. The cluster index requires 89 blocks. Therefore, the cluster and its index utilize 7,294 blocks. By comparing this figure to the 9,935 blocks for the two unclustered tables, you can see that btree index clusters can save you disk storage space. In this case, a savings of 2,641 blocks at 2,048 bytes per block. This is equivalent to saving 5.4MB of disk space.

Listing 3.4 Clustered tables and the cluster index.

```
SQL> BREAK ON REPORT
SQL> COMPUTE SUM OF BLOCKS_USED ON REPORT
SQL> COL BLOCKS_USED FORMAT 99,999
SQL> SELECT SUBSTR(SEGMENT_NAME,1,25) "Name",
  2         SUM(BLOCKS) BLOCKS_USED
  3   FROM   DBA_EXTENTS
  4  WHERE  SEGMENT_NAME
  5         IN('PARTS_AND_TESTS','INDX_PARTS_AND_TESTS')
  6* GROUP  BY SUBSTR(SEGMENT_NAME,1,25);

Name                                             BLOCKS_USED
---------------------------------------------  -----------
INDX_PARTS_AND_TESTS                                     89
PARTS_AND_TESTS                                       7,205
                                                -----------
sum                                                   7,294
```

USER_CLUSTERS

Listing 3.5 shows the results of a query against the data dictionary view **USER_CLUSTERS**. The btree index cluster, **PARTS_AND_TESTS**, has a key size of 650, which is much too small. This cluster is not a hash cluster, but a btree index cluster.

Listing 3.5 USER_CLUSTERS.

```
SQL> COL CLUSTER_TYPE FORMAT A12
SQL> SELECT CLUSTER_NAME,
  2         KEY_SIZE,
  3         AVG_BLOCKS_PER_KEY ABPERKEY,
  4         CLUSTER_TYPE
  5* FROM   USER_CLUSTERS;

CLUSTER_NAME                    KEY_SIZE ABPERKEY CLUSTER_TYPE
------------------------------ -------- -------- ------------
DEPT_AND_EMP                       30720       10 HASH
HUEY_DEWEY_LEWIE                    2816        1 HASH
PARTS_AND_TESTS                      650        1 INDEX
```

USER_CLU_COLUMNS

The data dictionary view **USER_CLU_COLUMNS** contains the names of the tables in the cluster as well as the cluster key column in each of the clustered tables. This view contains information about hash clusters and btree index clusters. Listing 3.6 indicates the name of the btree index cluster (**PARTS_AND_TESTS**), the two clustered tables (**PARTS_IN_CLUSTER** and **TESTS_IN_CLUSTER**), and the cluster key column in both clustered tables (**PNO**).

Listing 3.6 USER_CLU_COLUMNS.

```
SQL> BREAK ON CLUSTER_NAME SKIP 1
SQL> SELECT *
  2* FROM   USER_CLU_COLUMNS;

CLUSTER_NAME          CLU_COL_NAME TABLE_NAME         TAB_COLUMN_NAME
-------------------- ------------ ----------------- ---------------

DEPT_AND_EMP          DEPTNO       EMP_IN_HASH        DEPTNO
HUEY_DEWEY_LEWIE      EMPNO        DON_AND_DAFFY      EMPNO

PARTS_AND_TESTS       PNO          PARTS_IN_CLUSTER   PNO


PARTS_AND_TESTS       PNO          TESTS_IN_CLUSTER   PNO
```

Joins

First of all, the joins in this chapter are not necessary. All of the data resides in the **TESTS_IN_CLUSTER** clustered table and in the **TESTS** table, which is unclustered. But I deliberately joined the two tables for the sake of timings and comparisons. Listing 3.7 could have been written as: **SELECT COUNT(TNO) FROM TESTS WHERE TNO BETWEEN 50 AND 90**. When you join tables, Oracle has several methods to choose from to retrieve the rows. If the init.ora parameter **HASH_JOIN_ENABLED** is set to **TRUE**, Oracle might use the hash join method to retrieve the rows, as in Listing 3.7. To count the number of tests for part numbers 50 through 90, the estimated cost is only 39. However, the elapsed time was 5 minutes and 4 seconds. The driving table is **PARTS**, and both indexes on the **PNO** columns are used.

Listing 3.7 An unclustered hash join.

```
SQL> SELECT SUBSTR(NAME,1,25) PARAM,
  2         SUBSTR(VALUE,1,25) CURRENT_SETTING
  3  FROM   V$PARAMETER
  4* WHERE  NAME LIKE '%' || LOWER('&Parameter') || '%';
Enter value for parameter: hash_join

PARAM                     CURRENT_SETTING
------------------------- ---------------
hash_join_enabled         TRUE

SQL> EXPLAIN PLAN FOR
  2  SELECT COUNT(TNO)
  3  FROM   PARTS P,
  4         TESTS T
  5  WHERE  P.PNO = T.PNO AND
  6*        P.PNO BETWEEN 50 AND 90;

SQL> @explain
Query Plan                                                    COST
------------------------------------------------------------- ----
SELECT STATEMENT   CHOOSE                                       39
  SORT AGGREGATE
    HASH JOIN                                                   39
      INDEX RANGE SCAN PARTS_PNO_UNIQUE_INDX ANALYZED            2
      TABLE ACCESS BY ROWID TESTS ANALYZED                      36
        INDEX RANGE SCAN TESTS_PNO_INDEX ANALYZED

SQL> SELECT COUNT(TNO)
  2  FROM   PARTS P,
  3         TESTS T
  4  WHERE  P.PNO = T.PNO AND
  5*        P.PNO BETWEEN 50 AND 90;

COUNT(TNO)
----------
    206681

Elapsed: 00:05:04.18
```

Another method of retrieving rows from joined tables is "sort merge join." This method, illustrated in Listing 3.8, is normally the worst and slowest method for joining tables. However, sometimes Oracle has no choice. For instance, if none of the tables being joined has an index, then a sort merge join will be performed. Furthermore, the driving table is completely irrelevant. If the init.ora parameter **HASH_JOIN_ENABLED** is set to **FALSE**, Oracle will not use the hash join method to retrieve the rows as it did in Listing 3.7. To count the number of tests for part numbers 50 through 90, the estimated cost is only 43. However, the elapsed time is 5 minutes and 57 seconds. The driving table is **TESTS**, and both indexes on the **PNO** columns are used.

Listing 3.8 An unclustered merge join.

```
SQL> ALTER SYSTEM SET HASH_JOIN_ENABLED = FALSE;
ALTER SYSTEM SET HASH_JOIN_ENABLED = FALSE
                 *
ERROR at line 1:
ORA-02095: Specified initialization parameter cannot be modified

SQL>host vi initPETE.ora
hash_join_enabled = false

SVRMGR> show parameter hash_join
NAME                                TYPE    VALUE
----------------------------------- ------- ------------------
hash_join_enabled                   boolean FALSE

SQL> EXPLAIN PLAN FOR
  2  SELECT COUNT(TNO)
  3  FROM   PARTS P,
  4         TESTS T
  5  WHERE  P.PNO = T.PNO AND
  6*        P.PNO BETWEEN 50 AND 90;

SQL> @explain
Query Plan                                                    COST
------------------------------------------------------------  ----
SELECT STATEMENT   CHOOSE                                       43
  SORT AGGREGATE
    MERGE JOIN                                                  43
      TABLE ACCESS BY ROWID TESTS ANALYZED                      36
        INDEX RANGE SCAN TESTS_PNO_INDEX ANALYZED
      SORT JOIN
        INDEX RANGE SCAN PARTS_PNO_UNIQUE_INDX ANALYZED          2

SQL> SELECT COUNT(TNO)
  2  FROM   PARTS P,
```

```
  3         TESTS T
  4  WHERE  P.PNO = T.PNO AND
  5*        P.PNO BETWEEN 50 AND 90;

COUNT(TNO)
----------
    206681

Elapsed: 00:05:57.14
```

Another method for retrieving rows from joined tables is to use a btree index cluster—that is, if the cluster exists and the tables are part of the cluster. Also, Oracle may choose to use the "nested loops" approach within the index cluster to retrieve the rows. Listing 3.9 illustrates this. To count the number of tests for part numbers 50 through 90, the estimated cost is 67. However, the elapsed time is extremely quick—only 27 seconds! This is another example indicating that cost is truly an estimation. Even though this query had the highest cost of the three join queries, 67 (compared to the lowest cost of 43), it ran 5 minutes and 30 seconds faster than the query with the estimated cost of 43. The driving table is **PARTS_IN_CLUSTER**, and the cluster index is used.

Listing 3.9 Clustered nested loops join.

```
SQL> EXPLAIN PLAN FOR
  2  SELECT COUNT(TNO)
  3  FROM   PARTS_IN_CLUSTER P,
  4         TESTS_IN_CLUSTER T
  5  WHERE  P.PNO = T.PNO AND
  6*        P.PNO BETWEEN 50 AND 90;

SQL> @explain
Query Plan                                                     COST
-------------------------------------------------------------  ----
SELECT STATEMENT   CHOOSE                                        67
  SORT AGGREGATE
    NESTED LOOPS                                                 67
      TABLE ACCESS CLUSTER PARTS_IN_CLUSTER ANALYZED             24
        INDEX RANGE SCAN INDX_PARTS_AND_TESTS ANALYZED
      TABLE ACCESS CLUSTER TESTS_IN_CLUSTER ANALYZED

SQL> SELECT COUNT(TNO)
  2  FROM   PARTS_IN_CLUSTER P,
```

```
  3         TESTS_IN_CLUSTER T
  4  WHERE  P.PNO = T.PNO AND
  5*        P.PNO BETWEEN 50 AND 90;

COUNT(TNO)
----------
    206681

Elapsed: 00:00:27.12
```

Table 3.1 shows the results of these three queries that join two tables.

Full Table Scans

Full table scans of individual clustered tables run slower than full table scans of unclustered tables. Listing 3.10 indicates a cost of 1,045 to perform a full table scan of the clustered tables **TESTS_IN_CLUSTER** and **PARTS_IN_CLUSTER**. The elapsed time to perform the full table scan is 26.5 seconds for **TESTS_IN_CLUSTER**, which scans nearly a half million rows. **PARTS_IN_CLUSTER** only requires a little more than 16 seconds to scan 10,000 rows. The **FULL** hint is not necessary—it is used merely as an example. (See Chapter 9, "Hints," for more information on this topic.)

Listing 3.10 Full table scans of clustered tables.

```
SQL> EXPLAIN PLAN FOR
  2  SELECT --+ FULL(TESTS_IN_CLUSTER)
  3  COUNT(*)
  4* FROM  TESTS_IN_CLUSTER;

SQL> @explain
Query Plan                                                    COST
-------------------------------------------------------------- ----
SELECT STATEMENT   CHOOSE                                     1,045
  SORT AGGREGATE
    TABLE ACCESS FULL TESTS_IN_CLUSTER ANALYZED               1,045

SQL> SELECT --+ FULL(TESTS_IN_CLUSTER)
  2  COUNT(*)
  3  FROM  TESTS_IN_CLUSTER;
```

```
COUNT(*)
--------
  470692

Elapsed: 00:00:26.54


SQL> EXPLAIN PLAN FOR
  2  SELECT --+ FULL(PARTS_IN_CLUSTER)
  3  COUNT(*)
  4* FROM  PARTS_IN_CLUSTER;

SQL> @explain
Query Plan                                                      COST
--------------------------------------------------------------  ----
SELECT STATEMENT   CHOOSE                                      1,045
  SORT AGGREGATE
    TABLE ACCESS FULL PARTS_IN_CLUSTER ANALYZED                1,045

SQL> SELECT --+ FULL(PARTS_IN_CLUSTER)
  2  COUNT(*)
  3* FROM  PARTS_IN_CLUSTER;

COUNT(*)
--------
   10000

Elapsed: 00:00:16.13
```

Now, let's try executing full table scans on the two unclustered tables, **PARTS** and **TESTS** (see Listing 3.11). Notice how much lower the cost is for full table scans against the **TESTS** table (571) and the **PARTS** table (26) than for the clustered tables. The elapsed times are also quicker—**TESTS** requires nearly 20 seconds and **PARTS** requires a little more than 1 second.

Table 3.1 Join summary.

Clustered/Unclustered	Type Of Join	Cost	Elapsed Time
Unclustered	Merge	43	5 min 57 sec
Unclustered	Hash	39	5 min 4 sec
Clustered	Nested Loops	**67**	**27 sec**

Listing 3.11 Full table scans of unclustered tables.

```
SQL> EXPLAIN PLAN FOR
  2  SELECT --+ FULL(TESTS)
  3  COUNT(*)
  4* FROM  TESTS;

SQL> @explain
Query Plan                                                    COST
------------------------------------------------------------  ----
SELECT STATEMENT   CHOOSE                                      571
  SORT AGGREGATE
    TABLE ACCESS FULL TESTS ANALYZED                           571

SQL> SELECT --+ FULL(TESTS)
  2  COUNT(*)
  3  FROM  TESTS;

COUNT(*)
--------
  470692

Elapsed: 00:00:19.96


SQL> EXPLAIN PLAN FOR
  2  SELECT COUNT(*)
  3* FROM   PARTS;

SQL> @explain
Query Plan                                                    COST
------------------------------------------------------------  ----
SELECT STATEMENT   CHOOSE                                       26
  SORT AGGREGATE
    TABLE ACCESS FULL PARTS ANALYZED                            26

SQL> SELECT COUNT(*)
  2  FROM   PARTS;

COUNT(*)
--------
   10000

Elapsed: 00:00:01.11
```

Table 3.2 Full table scan summary.

Clustered	Table Name	Cost	Elapsed Time
Yes	TESTS_IN_CLUSTER	1,045	26.54 sec
Yes	PARTS_IN_CLUSTER	1,045	16.13 sec
No	TESTS	**571**	**19.96 sec**
No	PARTS	**26**	**1.11 sec**

Table 3.2 indicates that full table scans against unclustered tables perform much faster than full table scans against clustered tables.

BETWEEN

Listing 3.12 illustrates the use of **BETWEEN** in the **WHERE** clause of a query that joins two tables. The first example joins the two clustered tables, and the second example joins the two unclustered tables. In both cases, the query counts the number of tests that passed for part numbers between 50 and 93. Once again, this is an example of a higher estimated cost query actually outperforming a lower cost query—by 5 minutes. The clustered table join has a cost of 71 and an elapsed time of 28.35 seconds, whereas the unclustered join has a lower cost of 45, but has an elapsed time of 5 minutes 49 seconds—5 minutes slower than the query with a lower estimated cost.

Listing 3.12 BETWEEN.

```
SQL> EXPLAIN PLAN FOR
  2  SELECT COUNT(*)
  3  FROM   PARTS_IN_CLUSTER P,
  4         TESTS_IN_CLUSTER T
  5  WHERE  P.PNO = T.PNO     AND
  6         T.RESULTS = 'P'   AND
  7*        T.PNO BETWEEN 50 AND 93;

SQL> @explain
Query Plan                                                   COST
------------------------------------------------------------ ----
SELECT STATEMENT   CHOOSE                                      71
  SORT AGGREGATE
    NESTED LOOPS                                               71
      TABLE ACCESS CLUSTER PARTS_IN_CLUSTER ANALYZED           25
```

```
        INDEX RANGE SCAN INDX_PARTS_AND_TESTS ANALYZED
      TABLE ACCESS CLUSTER TESTS_IN_CLUSTER ANALYZED

SQL> SELECT COUNT(*)
  2  FROM   PARTS_IN_CLUSTER P,
  3         TESTS_IN_CLUSTER T
  4  WHERE  P.PNO = T.PNO     AND
  5         T.RESULTS = 'P'   AND
  6*        T.PNO BETWEEN 50  AND 93;

COUNT(*)
--------
  116028

Elapsed: 00:00:28.35

SQL> EXPLAIN PLAN FOR
  2  SELECT  COUNT(*)
  3  FROM    PARTS P,
  4          TESTS T
  5  WHERE   P.PNO = T.PNO    AND
  6          T.RESULTS = 'P'  AND
  7*         T.PNO BETWEEN 50 AND 93;

SQL> @explain
Query Plan                                                     COST
-------------------------------------------------------------  ----
SELECT STATEMENT   CHOOSE                                        45
  SORT AGGREGATE
    MERGE JOIN                                                   45
      TABLE ACCESS BY ROWID TESTS ANALYZED                       38
        INDEX RANGE SCAN TESTS_PNO_INDEX ANALYZED
      SORT JOIN
        INDEX RANGE SCAN PARTS_PNO_UNIQUE_INDX ANALYZED           2

SQL> SELECT COUNT(*)
  2  FROM   PARTS P,
  3         TESTS T
  4  WHERE  P.PNO = T.PNO    AND
  5         T.RESULTS = 'P'  AND
  6*        T.PNO BETWEEN 50 AND 93;
COUNT(*)
--------
  116028

Elapsed: 00:05:49.31
```

NOT BETWEEN

Listing 3.13 illustrates the use of **NOT BETWEEN** in the **WHERE** clause of a query that joins two tables. The first example joins the two clustered tables, and the second example joins the two unclustered tables. In both cases, the query counts the number of tests that passed for part numbers not between 94 and 10,000. Once again, this is an example of a higher estimated cost query actually outperforming a lower cost query by a tremendous amount of elapsed time. The clustered table join has a cost of 142 (and I cancelled the query with a Ctrl+C after 55 minutes), whereas the unclustered join has a cost of 169, but has an elapsed time of 7 minutes and 6 seconds.

Listing 3.13 NOT BETWEEN.

```
SQL> EXPLAIN PLAN FOR
  2  SELECT  COUNT(*)
  3  FROM    PARTS_IN_CLUSTER P,
  4          TESTS_IN_CLUSTER T
  5  WHERE   P.PNO       = T.PNO     AND
  6          T.RESULTS = 'P'         AND
  7*         T.PNO NOT BETWEEN 94 AND 10000;

SQL> @explain
Query Plan                                                       COST
--------------------------------------------------------------   ----
SELECT STATEMENT   CHOOSE                                         142
  SORT AGGREGATE
    CONCATENATION
      NESTED LOOPS                                                115
        TABLE ACCESS CLUSTER TESTS_IN_CLUSTER ANALYZED              5
          INDEX RANGE SCAN INDX_PARTS_AND_TESTS ANALYZED
        TABLE ACCESS CLUSTER PARTS_IN_CLUSTER ANALYZED
      NESTED LOOPS                                                115
        TABLE ACCESS CLUSTER TESTS_IN_CLUSTER ANALYZED              5
          INDEX RANGE SCAN INDX_PARTS_AND_TESTS ANALYZED
        TABLE ACCESS CLUSTER PARTS_IN_CLUSTER ANALYZED

SQL> SELECT COUNT(*)
  2  FROM    PARTS_IN_CLUSTER P,
  3          TESTS_IN_CLUSTER T
  4  WHERE   P.PNO       = T.PNO     AND
  5          T.RESULTS = 'P'         AND
  6*         T.PNO NOT BETWEEN 94 AND 10000;
```

```
^CERROR:
ORA-01013: user requested cancel of current operation
no rows selected

Elapsed: 00:55:06.59


SQL> EXPLAIN PLAN FOR
  2  SELECT   COUNT(*)
  3  FROM     PARTS P,
  4           TESTS T
  5  WHERE    P.PNO     = T.PNO     AND
  6           T.RESULTS = 'P'       AND
  7*          T.PNO NOT BETWEEN 94 AND 10000;

SQL> @explain
Query Plan                                                          COST
-------------------------------------------------------------    ----
SELECT STATEMENT   CHOOSE                                            169
  SORT AGGREGATE
    CONCATENATION
      NESTED LOOPS                                                    92
        TABLE ACCESS BY ROWID TESTS ANALYZED                          42
          INDEX RANGE SCAN TESTS_PNO_INDEX ANALYZED
        INDEX RANGE SCAN PARTS_PNO_UNIQUE_INDX ANALYZED               92
      MERGE JOIN                                                     141
        INDEX FULL SCAN PARTS_PNO_UNIQUE_INDX ANALYZED                92
        SORT JOIN
          TABLE ACCESS BY ROWID TESTS ANALYZED                        42
            INDEX RANGE SCAN TESTS_PNO_INDEX ANALYZED

SQL> SELECT COUNT(*)
  2  FROM   PARTS P,
  3         TESTS T
  4  WHERE  P.PNO     = T.PNO     AND
  5         T.RESULTS = 'P'       AND
  6*        T.PNO NOT BETWEEN 94 AND 10000;

COUNT(*)
--------
  136253

Elapsed: 00:07:06.38
```

IN

Listing 3.14 illustrates the use of **IN** in the **WHERE** clause of a query that joins two tables. The first example joins the two clustered tables, and the second example joins the two unclustered tables. In both cases, the query counts the number of tests that passed for part numbers 88, 90, or 91. Part number 89 is skipped on purpose. If 89 were included, we could use **BETWEEN** instead of **IN**. Once again, this is an example of a higher estimated cost query actually outperforming a lower cost query. The clustered table join has a cost of 78 and an elapsed time of 6 minutes and 20 seconds, whereas the unclustered join has a higher cost of 84, but has an elapsed time of only 46 seconds—nearly 6 minutes faster. Most of the time, a query with a higher cost executes slower than a query with a lower cost.

Listing 3.14 IN.

```
SQL> EXPLAIN PLAN FOR
  2  SELECT COUNT(*)
  3  FROM   PARTS_IN_CLUSTER P,
  4         TESTS_IN_CLUSTER T
  5  WHERE  P.PNO     = T.PNO AND
  6         T.RESULTS = 'P'   AND
  7*        T.PNO IN(88,90,91);

SQL> @explain
Query Plan                                                     COST
-------------------------------------------------------------  ----

SELECT STATEMENT   CHOOSE                                        78
  SORT AGGREGATE
    CONCATENATION
      NESTED LOOPS                                               26
        TABLE ACCESS CLUSTER TESTS_IN_CLUSTER ANALYZED            2
          INDEX UNIQUE SCAN INDX_PARTS_AND_TESTS ANALYZED
        TABLE ACCESS CLUSTER PARTS_IN_CLUSTER ANALYZED
      NESTED LOOPS                                               26
        TABLE ACCESS CLUSTER TESTS_IN_CLUSTER ANALYZED            2
          INDEX UNIQUE SCAN INDX_PARTS_AND_TESTS ANALYZED
        TABLE ACCESS CLUSTER PARTS_IN_CLUSTER ANALYZED
      NESTED LOOPS                                               26
        TABLE ACCESS CLUSTER TESTS_IN_CLUSTER ANALYZED            2
          INDEX UNIQUE SCAN INDX_PARTS_AND_TESTS ANALYZED
        TABLE ACCESS CLUSTER PARTS_IN_CLUSTER ANALYZED
```

```
SQL> SELECT COUNT(*)
  2  FROM   PARTS_IN_CLUSTER P,
  3         TESTS_IN_CLUSTER T
  4  WHERE  P.PNO     = T.PNO AND
  5         T.RESULTS = 'P'   AND
  6*        T.PNO IN(88,90,91);

COUNT(*)
--------
   12063

Elapsed: 00:06:20.46


SQL> EXPLAIN PLAN FOR
  2  SELECT  COUNT(*)
  3  FROM    PARTS P,
  4          TESTS T
  5  WHERE   P.PNO     = T.PNO AND
  6          T.RESULTS = 'P'   AND
  7*         T.PNO IN(88,90,91);

SQL> @explain
Query Plan                                                        COST
------------------------------------------------------------      ----
SELECT STATEMENT   CHOOSE                                           84
  SORT AGGREGATE
    CONCATENATION
      NESTED LOOPS                                                  28
        TABLE ACCESS BY ROWID TESTS ANALYZED                         4
          INDEX RANGE SCAN TESTS_PNO_INDEX ANALYZED
        INDEX RANGE SCAN PARTS_PNO_UNIQUE_INDX ANALYZED
      NESTED LOOPS                                                  28
        TABLE ACCESS BY ROWID TESTS ANALYZED                         4
          INDEX RANGE SCAN TESTS_PNO_INDEX ANALYZED
        INDEX RANGE SCAN PARTS_PNO_UNIQUE_INDX ANALYZED
      NESTED LOOPS                                                  28
        TABLE ACCESS BY ROWID TESTS ANALYZED                         4
          INDEX RANGE SCAN TESTS_PNO_INDEX ANALYZED
        INDEX RANGE SCAN PARTS_PNO_UNIQUE_INDX ANALYZED

SQL> SELECT COUNT(*)
  2  FROM   PARTS P,
  3         TESTS T
```

```
     WHERE  P.PNO     = T.PNO AND
            T.RESULTS = 'P'   AND
            T.PNO IN(88,90,91);

COUNT(*)
--------
   12063

Elapsed: 00:00:46.22
```

NOT IN

Listing 3.15 illustrates the use of **NOT IN** in the **WHERE** clause of a query that joins two tables. The first example joins the two clustered tables, and the second example joins the two unclustered tables. In both cases, the query counts the number of tests that passed for odd-numbered part numbers from 1 through 93. Once again, this is an example of a higher estimated cost query actually outperforming a lower cost query. The clustered table join has a cost of 10,999 and an elapsed time of 3 minutes and 46 seconds, whereas the unclustered join has a lower cost of 7,713, but has a much slower elapsed time (5 minutes and 22 seconds).

Listing 3.15 NOT IN.

```
SQL> EXPLAIN PLAN FOR
     SELECT COUNT(*)
     FROM   PARTS_IN_CLUSTER P,
            TESTS_IN_CLUSTER T
     WHERE  P.PNO     = T.PNO AND
            T.RESULTS = 'P'   AND
            T.PNO NOT IN(2,4,6,8,10,12,14,16,18,20,22,24,26,28,30,
                         32,34,36,38,40,42,44,46,48,50,52,54,56,58,60,62,
                         64,66,68,70,72,74,76,78,80,82,84,86,88,90,92,94);

SQL> @explain
Query Plan                                                     COST
------------------------------------------------------------   ----
SELECT STATEMENT   CHOOSE                                    10,999
  SORT AGGREGATE
    NESTED LOOPS                                             10,999
      TABLE ACCESS FULL PARTS_IN_CLUSTER ANALYZED             1,045
      TABLE ACCESS CLUSTER TESTS_IN_CLUSTER ANALYZED
```

```
SQL> SELECT COUNT(*)
  2  FROM   PARTS_IN_CLUSTER P,
  3         TESTS_IN_CLUSTER T
  4  WHERE  P.PNO      = T.PNO AND
  5         T.RESULTS = 'P'   AND
  6         T.PNO NOT IN(2,4,6,8,10,12,14,16,18,20,22,24,26,28,30,
  7         32,34,36,38,40,42,44,46,48,50,52,54,56,58,60,62,
  8*        64,66,68,70,72,74,76,78,80,82,84,86,88,90,92,94);

COUNT(*)
--------
  168291

Elapsed: 00:03:45.57

SQL> EXPLAIN PLAN FOR
  2  SELECT COUNT(*)
  3  FROM   PARTS P,
  4         TESTS T
  5  WHERE  P.PNO      = T.PNO AND
  6         T.RESULTS = 'P'   AND
  7         T.PNO NOT IN(2,4,6,8,10,12,14,16,18,20,22,24,26,28,30,
  8                      32,34,36,38,40,42,44,46,48,50,52,54,56,58,60,62,
  9*                     64,66,68,70,72,74,76,78,80,82,84,86,88,90,92,94);

SQL> @explain
Query Plan                                                    COST
--------------------------------------------------------------  ----
SELECT STATEMENT   CHOOSE                                      7,713
  SORT AGGREGATE
    MERGE JOIN                                                 7,713
      SORT JOIN
        TABLE ACCESS FULL TESTS ANALYZED                         571
      SORT JOIN
        TABLE ACCESS FULL PARTS ANALYZED                          26

SQL> SELECT COUNT(*)
  2  FROM   PARTS P,
  3         TESTS T
  4  WHERE  P.PNO      = T.PNO AND
  5         T.RESULTS = 'P'   AND
  6         T.PNO NOT IN(2,4,6,8,10,12,14,16,18,20,22,24,26,28,30,
  7         32,34,36,38,40,42,44,46,48,50,52,54,56,58,60,62,
  8*        64,66,68,70,72,74,76,78,80,82,84,86,88,90,92,94);
```

```
COUNT(*)
--------
  168291

Elapsed: 00:05:22.01
```

Summary

A btree cluster index can be used (although very rarely) when tables joined in queries execute too slowly. If few full table scans are performed on the clustered tables, the data is fairly evenly distributed around the cluster key column, and the cluster key column is not updated very often on any of the clustered tables, then maybe as a last-ditch effort you should try creating a btree index cluster. If you do try creating an index cluster and response time is worse, dropping the index cluster is difficult and time consuming.

Hash Cluster Indexes

CHAPTER 4

The purpose of a hash cluster index is to execute queries faster than using btree indexes. This chapter examines when and when not to use hash cluster indexes. You'll also learn how to create and analyze hash clusters and write queries against the appropriate data dictionary views pertaining to hash clusters.

Hash Cluster Indexes

What Is A Hash Cluster Index?

The result of applying a hash function to a column (or columns) of a table is the disk location. This can be slightly more efficient than a btree index. With a btree index, the root, branch, and leaf blocks must be retrieved to return rows using the index, whereas a table that is clustered using a hash function requires only one I/O to locate the data. The only exception would be when many rows are stored with the same hash function result. You can define your own hash function or use Oracle's default hash function. This usually requires one or two I/Os less than a btree index. However, the **WHERE** clause must use an equality operator, "="; otherwise, Oracle performs a full table scan to retrieve the data. For this reason alone, hash cluster indexes are very rarely used.

Creating A Hash Cluster

You might consider using hash clusters when the following conditions exist:

- The table is static.
- The hash cluster key column will not be updated.
- The size of the table is known at creation time.
- All or most of the queries use equality.

On the other hand, a hash cluster requires a large amount of disk space. Dropping a hash cluster is no easy task and is time consuming on large hash clusters. The following command in Listing 4.1 creates a hash cluster named **HASH_CLUSTER**, and the cluster key column is **SNO**. The **SIZE** parameter of 23 indicates that the size of all the rows for a particular cluster key is 23 bytes. The **HASH IS** parameter indicates a column containing the hash value or a user-defined hash function. In this case, because the **SNO** column is numeric (with a scale of zero) and contains only positive values, the hash value is the contents of the **SNO** column.

Listing 4.1 Creating a hash cluster.

```
SQL> CREATE CLUSTER
              HASH_CLUSTER (SNO  NUMBER(7,0)) -- Multiple columns OK
              TABLESPACE HASH_CLUSTER
     STORAGE(INITIAL      2M
              NEXT         2M
              MINEXTENTS  2
              PCTINCREASE 0)
     SIZE     23
     HASH IS SNO --  Column in cluster key, pos numbers,no internal hash
     HASHKEYS 500000;  -- Deliberately set to 1/2 of what it should be
```

HASH IS is used in the **CREATE CLUSTER** command because the cluster column **SNO** is numeric with a zero scale. **HASH IS** does not use Oracle's internal hash function. The data is populated into the **SNO** column and is sorted by **SNO**. However, the data does not have to be sorted. Also, note that you can use Oracle's internal hash function, or you can create your own. To use Oracle's internal hash function, omit the **HASH IS SNO** line from the previous command. To use your own hash function, enter something like **HASH IS (MOD(SNO,17))**. The command in Listing 4.2 creates a table in the hash cluster. The table contains two columns: **SNO** and **SEX**. The cluster key is on **SNO**, ranging from 1 to 1,000,000. The table in the cluster is loaded using a PL/SQL script.

Listing 4.2 Creating and analyzing a hash cluster.

```
SQL> CREATE TABLE HASH_TABLE
            (SNO  NUMBER(7),
             SEX  VARCHAR2(1))
     CLUSTER HASH_CLUSTER(SNO);

SQL> ANALYZE CLUSTER HASH_CLUSTER COMPUTE STATISTICS;
Elapsed: 00:09:34.40
```

USER_CLUSTERS

Information on the hash cluster is stored in several data dictionary views. One of those views is **USER_CLUSTERS**. Listing 4.3 is a query using the view **USER_**

CLUSTERS. From this listing, you can see that the average blocks per key is 2, **HASH_CLUSTER** has a type of **HASH**, the hash function is on the **SNO** column, and there are 500,009 hash keys.

Listing 4.3 Creating and analyzing a hash cluster.

```
SQL> SELECT SUBSTR(CLUSTER_NAME,1,15) NAME,
            KEY_SIZE,
            AVG_BLOCKS_PER_KEY "BLKS/KEY",
            CLUSTER_TYPE TYPE,
            FUNCTION, HASHKEYS
     FROM   USER_CLUSTERS;

NAME           KEY_SIZE BLKS/KEY TYPE  FUNCTION        HASHKEYS
-------------- -------- -------- ----- -------------- --------
HASH_CLUSTER         23        2 HASH  COLUMN           500009
```

If the hash cluster is not analyzed, then **AVG_BLOCKS_PER_KEY** will be null. Because the query in Listing 4.3 shows 2 in the **AVG_BLOCKS_PER_KEY** column, the cluster is analyzed.

CLU

Another data dictionary view that contains information about index and hash clusters is **CLU**. Listing 4.4 illustrates the creation of another hash cluster and information stored in **CLU**. The first query indicates the data distribution on the **DEPTNO** column. The **DEPTNO** column will have an Oracle hash function applied to its contents. The result of the hash function being applied to the data in the **DEPTNO** column is the location of the row. The second statement analyzes the **EMP** table. The query against **USER_TABLES** indicates the average row length. Notice that the average row length for rows in the **EMP** table is 40 and that there are at most 768 employees in one department—department 30. Therefore, the **SIZE** setting in the **CREATE CLUSTER** command is 30,720 bytes (40 * 768). Notice how Oracle rounds up to the nearest prime number for the number of hash keys. For 4 hash keys, Oracle rounds up to the next prime number, which is 5. Oracle performs this operation to reduce the number of collisions. Next, the table **EMP_IN_HASH** is created to be included in the hash cluster **HASH_ON_EMP**. Then, the table in the hash cluster is loaded with 1,792 rows, and it requires nearly 13 seconds. Also, the cluster is analyzed in 1.72 seconds. Finally, another query against **CLU** indicates that the average blocks per key is 10.

Listing 4.4 Viewing the contents of **CLU**.

```
SQL> SELECT DEPTNO, COUNT(*)
  2  FROM   EMP
  3  GROUP  BY DEPTNO;

 DEPTNO COUNT(*)
 ------ --------
     10      384
     20      640
     30      768

SQL> ANALYZE TABLE EMP COMPUTE STATISTICS;
Table analyzed.

SQL> SELECT NUM_ROWS,AVG_ROW_LEN
  2  FROM   USER_TABLES
  3* WHERE  TABLE_NAME = 'EMP';

NUM_ROWS AVG_ROW_LEN
-------- -----------
    1792          40

SQL> CREATE CLUSTER HASH_ON_EMP (DEPTNO NUMBER(2,0))
  2         SIZE 30720     -- AVG_ROW_LEN(40) * 768 Emps
  3         HASHKEYS 4;
Cluster created.

SQL> SELECT CLUSTER_NAME,
  2         KEY_SIZE,
  3         AVG_BLOCKS_PER_KEY ABPK,
  4         CLUSTER_TYPE,
  5         FUNCTION,
  6         HASHKEYS
  7  FROM   CLU
  8* ORDER  BY CLUSTER_NAME;

CLUSTER_NAME KEY_SIZE    ABPK CLUSTER_TYPE FUNCTION HASHKEYS
------------ -------- ------ ------------ -------- --------
HASH_ON_EMP     30720         HASH         DEFAULT2        5

SQL> CREATE TABLE EMP_IN_HASH
  2  (EMPNO     NUMBER(4),
  3   ENAME     VARCHAR2(10),
```

```
       JOB           VARCHAR2(9),
       MGR           NUMBER(4),
       HIREDATE      DATE,
       SAL           NUMBER(7,2),
       COMM          NUMBER(7,2),
       DEPTNO        NUMBER(2))
       CLUSTER HASH_ON_EMP(DEPTNO);

SQL> INSERT INTO EMP_IN_HASH
            SELECT * FROM EMP;
1792 rows created.
Elapsed: 00:00:12.91

SQL> ANALYZE CLUSTER HASH_ON_EMP
             COMPUTE STATISTICS;
Cluster analyzed.
Elapsed: 00:00:01.72

SQL> SELECT CLUSTER_NAME,
            KEY_SIZE,
            AVG_BLOCKS_PER_KEY ABPK,
            CLUSTER_TYPE
            FUNCTION,
            HASHKEYS
     FROM   CLU
     ORDER  BY CLUSTER_NAME;

CLUSTER_NAME KEY_SIZE    ABPK FUNCTION HASHKEYS
------------ --------  ------ -------- --------
HASH_ON_EMP     30720      10     HASH        5
```

USER_CLU_COLUMNS

The data dictionary view **USER_CLU_COLUMNS** indicates basic information about the cluster—the name of the cluster, the column on which the cluster is based, the table(s) in the cluster, and the column name in the table to which the hash function is applied. A column name in one of the clustered table(s) could be different from the column name in the other clustered table. Listing 4.5 shows information about the hash cluster **HASH_ON_EMP**. The cluster column of the cluster is **DEPTNO**; the table named **EMP_IN_HASH** is in the cluster; and the column **DEPTNO** of the table **EMP_IN_HASH** has the Oracle hash function applied to it.

Listing 4.5 Viewing **USER_CLU_COLUMNS**.

```
SQL> COL CLUSTER_NAME     FORMAT A12
SQL> COL CLU_COLUMN_NAME FORMAT A15
SQL> COL TABLE_NAME       FORMAT A11
SQL> COL TAB_COLUMN_NAME FORMAT A15
SQL> SELECT *
  2  FROM    USER_CLU_COLUMNS;

CLUSTER_NAME CLU_COLUMN_NAME TABLE_NAME   TAB_COLUMN_NAME
------------ --------------- -----------  ---------------
HASH_ON_EMP  DEPTNO          EMP_IN_HASH  DEPTNO
```

USER_CLUSTER_HASH_EXPRESSIONS

Listing 4.6 contains information concerning user-defined hashing algorithms or functions. A very common error is to make the **SIZE** parameter too small. As you can see, Oracle error number 2454 occurs. Just by increasing the **SIZE** parameter from 20 bytes to 25 bytes, you eliminate the problem.

Listing 4.6 User-defined hash functions.

```
SQL> CREATE CLUSTER HUEY_DEWEY_LEWIE (EMPNO NUMBER(6,0))
  2  SIZE 20
  3  HASH IS TRUNC(MOD(EMPNO,3))
  4* HASHKEYS 14;
CREATE CLUSTER HUEY_DEWEY_LEWIE (EMPNO NUMBER(6,0))
*
ERROR at line 1:
ORA-02454: Number of hash keys per block (96) exceeds maximum of 87

SQL> CREATE CLUSTER HUEY_DEWEY_LEWIE (EMPNO NUMBER(6,0))
  2  SIZE 25
  3  HASH IS TRUNC(MOD(EMPNO,3))
  4* HASHKEYS 14;
Cluster created.

SQL> COL OWNER            FORMAT A12
SQL> COL CLUSTER_NAME     FORMAT A17
SQL> COL HASH_EXPRESSION FORMAT A19
SQL> SELECT *
  2* FROM    USER_CLUSTER_HASH_EXPRESSIONS;

OWNER        CLUSTER_NAME      HASH_EXPRESSION
------------ ----------------  ------------------
OPS$PCASSIDY HUEY_DEWEY_LEWIE  TRUNC(MOD(EMPNO,3))
```

Storage

See Listing 4.7 to determine the amount of disk space for hash clusters. The cluster on the one-million-row table requires 20,500 blocks, which is approximately 42MB.

Listing 4.7 Disk space for hash clusters.

```
SQL> get corhc13
COL     SEGMENT_NAME   FORMAT A25
SELECT SEGMENT_NAME, SEGMENT_TYPE,
       SUM(BLOCKS) BLOCKS_USED
FROM   DBA_EXTENTS
WHERE  SEGMENT_NAME =  'HASH_CLUSTER'
GROUP  BY SEGMENT_TYPE, SEGMENT_NAME
SQL> @corhc13

SEGMENT_NAME              SEGMENT_TYPE     BLOCKS_USED
------------------------- ---------------- -----------
HASH_CLUSTER              CLUSTER                20500
HUEY_DEWEY_LEWIE          CLUSTER                   25
```

Explain Plan

Now let's take a closer look at the plan trees for several different SQL statements using the hash cluster. The major point to remember is only the equality operator, "=", uses the hash cluster access method to retrieve the rows in the active set. This is an incredible disadvantage.

IN

Listing 4.8 shows how Oracle retrieves five rows from the hash cluster named **HASH_CLUSTER** using **IN** in the **WHERE** clause. Notice that Oracle uses the hash cluster five times to retrieve all five rows. The word **CONCATENATION** means that Oracle rewrites the **WHERE** clause to use the hash cluster method of access for each of the five rows. The estimated cost using the hash cluster retrieval method is only 2. The translated **WHERE** clause looks like this:

```
WHERE SNO = 222     OR
      SNO = 5500    OR
      SNO = 175000  OR
      SNO = 800000  OR
      SNO = 999000
```

This is a much faster query than a full table scan.

Listing 4.8 Using **IN** for a hash cluster.

```
SQL> EXPLAIN PLAN FOR
  2  SELECT  *       /* GOOD_HASH  */
  3  FROM    HASH_TABLE
  4  WHERE   SNO IN(222,5500,175000,800000,999000);
Explained.

SQL> @explain
Query Plan                                              COST
------------------------------------------------------  ----
SELECT STATEMENT   CHOOSE                                 10
  CONCATENATION
    TABLE ACCESS HASH HASH_TABLE ANALYZED      2           1
    TABLE ACCESS HASH HASH_TABLE ANALYZED      2           1
    TABLE ACCESS HASH HASH_TABLE ANALYZED      2           1
    TABLE ACCESS HASH HASH_TABLE ANALYZED      2           1
    TABLE ACCESS HASH HASH_TABLE ANALYZED      2           1
```

Elapsed Time Using IN

Listing 4.9 illustrates the elapsed time for executing a query against a one-million-row table that returns five rows. Each of the five returned rows is retrieved using the hash cluster retrieval method. In other words, the hash cluster method of access is used five times for this query. This only requires a little more than 1 second.

Listing 4.9 Time for retrieving 5 rows using a hash cluster.

```
SQL> SELECT  *       /* GOOD_HASH  */
  2  FROM    HASH_TABLE
  3* WHERE   SNO IN(222,5500,175000,800000,999000);

    SNO S
 ------ -
 999000 M
 800000 M
 175000 M
   5500 M
    222 M
Elapsed: 00:00:01.17
```

Greater Than (>)

Hash clusters work well when the **WHERE** clause contains an equal sign. However, if >, <, <>, >=, <=, **BETWEEN**, **NOT BETWEEN**, **LIKE**, **NOT LIKE**, or **NOT IN** are used, Oracle performs a full table scan. Let's examine a query against the table

HASH_TABLE that returns 1,000 rows for verification (see Listing 4.10). Oracle performs a full table scan at a cost of 3,069. In the previous example, the hash cluster was used at a cost of 2 using **IN**.

Listing 4.10 Using greater than (>) in a hash cluster.

```
SQL> EXPLAIN PLAN FOR
  2  SELECT  *
  3  FROM    HASH_TABLE
  4* WHERE   SNO > 999000;
Explained.

SQL> @explain
Query Plan                                             COST
-----------------------------------------------------  -----
SELECT STATEMENT   CHOOSE                              3,069
  TABLE ACCESS FULL HASH_TABLE ANALYZED                3,069
```

Elapsed Time Using Greater Than (>)

One of the drawbacks of using a hash cluster, shown in Listing 4.11, is that Oracle will perform a full table scan to retrieve 1,000 rows from a one-million-row table in a hash cluster. The actual time required is 1 minute and 55 seconds. Note that a btree index on the **SNO** column would have been used here instead of a full table scan—yet another example of the many drawbacks of using hash clusters.

Listing 4.11 Time for retrieving 1,000 rows in a full table scan.

```
SQL> SELECT  *
  2  FROM    HASH_TABLE
  3* WHERE   SNO > 999000;
.
999975 F
999976 M
1000 rows selected.
Elapsed: 00:01:54.68
```

NOT BETWEEN

What if you want to retrieve rows not in a particular range? In this case, you need only two rows—where **SNO** is 1 or **SNO** is 1,000,000. Listing 4.12 shows the outcome. Oracle executes a full table scan to retrieve two rows. A btree index would certainly use the index. If there is no equal sign in the **WHERE** clause (for example **WHERE SNO =** ***any number***) then Oracle will perform a full table scan instead of using the hash cluster.

Listing 4.12 Using **NOT BETWEEN** in a hash cluster.

```
SQL> EXPLAIN PLAN FOR
  2  SELECT   *
  3  FROM     HASH_TABLE
  4* WHERE    SNO NOT BETWEEN 2 AND 999999;
Explained.

SQL> @explain
Query Plan                                                        COST
------------------------------------------------------------ ------
SELECT STATEMENT    CHOOSE                                    3,069
  TABLE ACCESS FULL HASH_TABLE ANALYZED                       3,069
```

Elapsed Time Using NOT BETWEEN

Listing 4.13 indicates **NOT BETWEEN** requires 2 minutes and 21 seconds to return two rows! Compare this elapsed time to the query that returned five rows in 1.17 seconds.

Listing 4.13 Time for retrieving 2 rows using NOT BETWEEN.

```
SQL> SELECT   *
  2  FROM     HASH_TABLE      -- UGLY_HASH
  3* WHERE    SNO NOT BETWEEN 2 AND 999999;

    SNO SEX
 ------ ---
      1 F
1000000 M
Elapsed: 00:02:20.97
```

The query in Listings 4.12 and 4.13 can be rewritten so that Oracle will access the table using the hash cluster. The following Explain Plan (shown in Listing 4.14) indicates that rewriting this query would certainly be beneficial. A cost of 4, using the hash cluster, compared to a cost of 3,069, using a full table scan, would make a great deal of difference with the execution times.

Listing 4.14 The rewritten query using the equal sign (=).

```
SQL> EXPLAIN PLAN FOR
  2  SELECT   *
  3  FROM     HASH_TABLE
  4  WHERE    SNO = 1 OR SNO = 1000000;
Explained.
```

```
SQL> @explain
Query Plan                                                COST
-------------------------------------------------------- ----
SELECT STATEMENT   CHOOSE                                   4
  CONCATENATION
    TABLE ACCESS HASH HASH_TABLE ANALYZED                   2
    TABLE ACCESS HASH HASH_TABLE ANALYZED                   2
```

Elapsed Time Using The Equal Sign (=)

It's time to execute the statement and observe the actual time for this rewritten query. Listing 4.15 illustrates the dramatic increase in performance. One second is superb! It is usually a good idea to rewrite long-running queries. Many times the rewritten query will run faster. Sometimes, however, the rewritten query will run slower. See Chapter 8, for more details. The bottom line is: Some queries can be resolved using different accessing methods. However, the response times can be significantly different. In Chapter 8, the same problem is solved using **NOT IN**, **NOT EXISTS**, and MINUS—all with very different elapsed times. Oracle gives you the flexibility to try many things before you throw in the towel. Listing 4.15 indicates the actual execution time.

Listing 4.15 Time for retrieving 2 rows using the equal sign (=).

```
SQL> SELECT *
  2  FROM   HASH_TABLE   /* SUPER_HASH  */
  3  WHERE  SNO = 1 OR SNO = 1000000;
     SNO S
  ------ -
 1000000 M
       1 F
Elapsed: 00:00:01.02
```

NOT IN

Once again, if the equality symbol is not used in the WHERE clause for a hash cluster column, Oracle performs a full table scan. Listing 4.16 supports this fact.

Listing 4.16 Using **NOT IN** for the hash cluster.

```
SQL> EXPLAIN PLAN FOR
  2  SELECT   *
  3  FROM     DON_AND_DAFFY
  4* WHERE    EMPNO NOT IN(8000,8001,8002);
```

```
Explained.

SQL> @explain
Query Plan                                                         COST
-----------------------------------------------------------     ------
SELECT STATEMENT   CHOOSE                                        1,880
  TABLE ACCESS FULL DON_AND_DAFFY ANALYZED                       1,880
```

BETWEEN

Listing 4.17 shows that equality predicates are necessary for using a hash cluster to retrieve rows from the hash-clustered table.

Listing 4.17 Using **BETWEEN** for the hash cluster.

```
SQL> EXPLAIN PLAN FOR
  2  SELECT  *
  3  FROM    DON_AND_DAFFY      -- 8 Rows In Active Set
  4* WHERE   EMPNO BETWEEN 8000 AND 8001;
Explained.

SQL> @explain
Query Plan                                                         COST
-----------------------------------------------------------     ------
SELECT STATEMENT   CHOOSE                                        1,880
  TABLE ACCESS FULL DON_AND_DAFFY ANALYZED                       1,880
```

LIKE

Using LIKE on a numeric column is not normally performed. However, Listing 4.18 shows the results. Once again, nothing surprising.

Listing 4.18 Using **LIKE** for the hash cluster.

```
SQL> EXPLAIN PLAN FOR
  2  SELECT  *
  3  FROM    DON_AND_DAFFY
  4* WHERE   EMPNO LIKE '800%';
Explained.

SQL> @explain
Query Plan                                                         COST
-----------------------------------------------------------     ------
SELECT STATEMENT   CHOOSE                                        1,880
  TABLE ACCESS FULL DON_AND_DAFFY ANALYZED                       1,880
```

IS NULL

Listing 4.19 shows that using **IS NULL** also produces a full table scan, because an equal sign isn't used in the **WHERE** clause on the **EMPNO** column. However, first a few nulls had to be placed in the **EMPNO** column. In the real world, that could never happen on a primary key column.

Listing 4.19 Using **IS NULL** for the hash cluster.

```
SQL> UPDATE DON_AND_DAFFY
  2  SET     EMPNO = NULL
  3  WHERE   EMPNO = 8000;

4 rows updated.

SQL> EXPLAIN PLAN FOR
  2  SELECT  *
  3  FROM     DON_AND_DAFFY
  4* WHERE    EMPNO IS NULL;
Explained.

SQL> @explain
Query Plan                                                        COST
------------------------------------------------------------  ------
SELECT STATEMENT   CHOOSE                                        1,880
  TABLE ACCESS FULL DON_AND_DAFFY ANALYZED                       1,880
```

IS NOT NULL

Listing 4.20 indicates that using **IS NOT NULL** produces another full table scan. This is no surprise, however. For Oracle to use the hash cluster to access most of the rows from the clustered table takes longer than a full table scan.

Listing 4.20 Using **IS NOT NULL** in a hash cluster.

```
SQL> EXPLAIN PLAN FOR
  2  SELECT  *
  3  FROM     DON_AND_DAFFY
  4* WHERE    EMPNO IS NOT NULL;
Explained.

SQL> @explain
Query Plan                                                        COST
------------------------------------------------------------  ------
SELECT STATEMENT   CHOOSE                                        1,880
  TABLE ACCESS FULL DON_AND_DAFFY ANALYZED                       1,880
```

In Listing 4.21, a hint tries to force Oracle to use the hash cluster. However, the cost-based optimizer has a much better plan, and it completely ignores the hint.

Listing 4.21 Using a hint in a hash cluster.

```
SQL> EXPLAIN PLAN FOR
  2  SELECT --+ HASH(DON_AND_DAFFY)
  3  *
  4  FROM    DON_AND_DAFFY
  5* WHERE   EMPNO IS NOT NULL;
Explained.

SQL> @explain
Query Plan                                                      COST
------------------------------------------------------------  ------
SELECT STATEMENT   CHOOSE                                       1,880
  TABLE ACCESS FULL DON_AND_DAFFY ANALYZED                      1,880
```

AND

In Listing 4.22, the hash cluster is used to return four rows from a table with 19,106 rows, even though there is no index on the **SALARY** column.

Listing 4.22 Using **AND** in a hash cluster.

```
SQL> EXPLAIN PLAN FOR
  2  SELECT *
  3  FROM   DON_AND_DAFFY    -- 4 Rows In Active Set Out Of 19,106 Rows
  4* WHERE  EMPNO = 8001 AND SALARY = 1300;
Explained.

SQL> @explain
Query Plan                                                      COST
------------------------------------------------------------  ------
SELECT STATEMENT   CHOOSE                                           1
  TABLE ACCESS HASH DON_AND_DAFFY ANALYZED                          1
```

OR

In Listing 4.23, the hash cluster access method is, once again, ignored. Each side of the **WHERE** clause must be clustered before the hash cluster can be used to access the rows.

Listing 4.23 Using **OR** in a hash cluster.

```
SQL> EXPLAIN PLAN FOR
  2  SELECT  *
  3  FROM    DON_AND_DAFFY    -- 512 Rows Out Of 19,106 Rows
```

```
  4* WHERE  EMPNO = 7839 OR SALARY = 5000;
Explained.

SQL> @explain
Query Plan                                                      COST
-------------------------------------------------------------  ------
SELECT STATEMENT   CHOOSE                                       1,880
  TABLE ACCESS FULL DON_AND_DAFFY ANALYZED                      1,880
```

MAX

In Listing 4.24, the single group function **MAX** is used on the hash-clustered column **EMPNO**, but to no avail. This makes sense because the rows are stored in a location on-disk as a result of the hash function being applied to the **EMPNO** column. There really is no other choice—Oracle must perform a full table scan.

Listing 4.24 Using MAX in a hash cluster.

```
SQL> EXPLAIN PLAN FOR
  2  SELECT MAX(EMPNO)
  3  FROM   DON_AND_DAFFY;
Explained.

SQL> @explain
Query Plan                                                      COST
-------------------------------------------------------------  ------
SELECT STATEMENT   CHOOSE                                       1,880
  SORT AGGREGATE
    TABLE ACCESS FULL DON_AND_DAFFY ANALYZED                    1,880
```

Joins

In Listing 4.25, Oracle uses the hash cluster to access the one row in the hash-clustered table **DON_AND_DAFFY**. That row is then used to retrieve rows from the **EMP** table. Note that **DON_AND_DAFFY** is the "driving" table—that is, the table Oracle starts with or the first table in the "join chain."

Listing 4.25 Using joins in a hash cluster.

```
SQL> EXPLAIN PLAN FOR
  2  SELECT EMP.ENAME, D.SALARY
  3  FROM   EMP,
  4         DON_AND_DAFFY D
  5  WHERE  EMP.EMPNO = D.EMPNO AND
  6         D.EMPNO   = 8588;
Explained.
```

```
SQL> @explain
Query Plan                                                        COST
---------------------------------------------------------------  ------
SELECT STATEMENT   CHOOSE                                             3
  NESTED LOOPS                                                        3
    TABLE ACCESS HASH DON_AND_DAFFY ANALYZED                          1
    TABLE ACCESS FULL EMP
```

Deleting Hash Clusters

If hash clusters contain a table with many rows, you may experience many errors in the process of trying to drop the hash cluster. You might run out of rollback segment space or temporary space. One of the quickest methods for deleting a hash cluster is shown in Listing 4.26. However, the **INCLUDING TABLES** clause drops the tables in the cluster.

Listing 4.26 Deleting a hash cluster.

```
SQL> DROP CLUSTER HUEY_DEWEY_LEWIE
          INCLUDING TABLES;
Cluster dropped.
```

Summary

Be careful of the limitations and the amount of disk space required for hash clusters. The best situation for hash clusters is when the cardinality is high, the percentage of rows returned is low, and most queries use equality in the **WHERE** clause. Also, the table should be very static; very few updates should be performed on the hash column; and the table size should be known at table creation time. Dropping a hash cluster may require a lot of time. Table 4.1 summarizes the estimated costs and elapsed times for the hash cluster and full table scan access methods.

Table 4.1 Hash cluster versus full table scans.

Access Method	Estimated Cost	Elapsed Time
Hash cluster	4	1.02 sec
Full table scan	3,069	2 min 20 sec

HIGH PERFORMANCE

Bitmap Indexes

CHAPTER 5

This chapter examines the creation and use of bitmap indexes. You'll learn how to create and use bitmap indexes correctly as well as how to create and use concatenated bitmap indexes.

Bitmap Indexes

What Are Bitmap Indexes?

Bitmap indexes are not new. They have been around since the old Model 204 days. However, they are new to Oracle. The best use of a bitmapped index is on a column with very low cardinality (that is, few distinct values) such as the **SEX** column of the **STATS** table (it contains only "F" or "M"). The **REGION_BIT_MAP** column has eight distinct values, so a bitmap index on that column might be justifiable. However, a bitmap index on the **SNO** column would be utterly ridiculous. The **SNO** column is the primary key column of the **STATS** table. The values for **SNO** range from 1 to 1,000,000. That would produce one million index entries with one bit for each row stored in each entry. The bitmap index on the **SEX** column resembles this:

```
                        Row 1  Row 2  Row 3   Row4 .........Row 1,000,000
Bitmap Index Entry: F      1      0      1      0                      0
Bitmap Index Entry: M      0      1      0      1                      1
```

From here you can observe that odd rows contain F and even rows contain M. Oracle uses bitmap indexes when users or applications refer to columns with very few distinct values in the **WHERE** clause. For example, the query

```
SELECT * FROM STATS WHERE SEX = 'F'
```

could use a bitmap index on the **SEX** column, if one existed.

Oracle7.3.2 Bitmap Caveat

You can use bitmap indexes in Oracle7.3.2, but beware. Unless you have set some very special init.ora parameters, you'll experience internal errors (ORA-0600). I had to rebuild two databases before I learned of these init.ora parameters (refer to page 381 of the Oracle Press book titled *Advanced Oracle Tuning and Administration.* These special parameters prevent the internal errors from occurring.). The errors I received, as well as the special init.ora parameters that prevent corruption, are shown in Listing 5.1.

Listing 5.1 Special init.ora parameters.

```
SQL> @$ORACLE_HOME/rdbms/admin/utlxplan
create table PLAN_TABLE (
*
ERROR at line 1:
ORA-00600: internal error code,
           arguments: [4097], [], [], [], [], [], [], []
```

I could not create any objects in the database, and I had to rebuild it.

```
SQL> SELECT REGION_BIT_MAP,
  2         COUNT(*)
  3  FROM   STATS
  4* GROUP  BY REGION_BIT_MAP;

ERROR:
ORA-00600: internal error code,
           arguments: [711], [10691072], [], [], [], [].[}, []
no rows selected
Elapsed: 00:02:24.27

SVRMGR> !more initpete.ora
event = "10111 trace name context forever"
event = "10112 trace name context forever"
event = "10114 trace name context forever"
```

Here are other Oracle7.3.2 init.ora parameters that pertain to bitmap indexes:

```
create_bitmap_area_size =8000000    # Default 8Mb Memory For Creation
bitmap_merge_area_size  =1000000    # Memory To Merge Scans
v733_plans_enabled      = true      # Bitmap Access For btree Indexes
b_tree_bitmap_plans     = true      # No Explain Plan Without It
```

When To Use Bitmap Indexes

Bitmap indexes are very useful for queries that use equality and AND or ORs on columns where the cardinality is very low. In other words, columns that have few distinct values like the **SEX** column, which has two distinct values, and the **REGION_BIT_MAP** column, which has eight distinct values are likely candidates for a bitmap index. By dividing the number of distinct values in a column by the number of rows in a table, you have the selectivity of a column. The **SEX** column has a very low selectivity, 2/1,000,000, and the **SNO** column has a very high selectivity, 1,000,000/1,000,000 = 1. Oracle's bitmap indexes exist for low selectivity columns. Otherwise, Oracle performs a full table scan. The following two commands create two bitmap indexes — one on the **SEX** column, and the other on the **REGION_BIT_MAP** column. It required approximately five minutes to create each one. Listing 5.2 shows the creation of two bitmap indexes.

Listing 5.2 Creating bitmap indexes.

```
SQL>  CREATE BITMAP INDEX BITMAP_SEX ON STATS(SEX)
  2   TABLESPACE     BITMAP_INDEXES    -- 5 Min 5 Seconds To Create
  3                  STORAGE(INITIAL 300K
  4   NEXT 300K MINEXTENTS 3  MAXEXTENTS 121  PCTINCREASE  0);

SQL> CREATE BITMAP INDEX BITMAP_REGION_BIT_MAP
  2        ON STATS(REGION_BIT_MAP)      -- 4 Min 38 Seconds To Create
  3   TABLESPACE   BITMAP_INDEXES
  4   STORAGE(INITIAL 300K  NEXT 300K  MINEXTENTS 3  MAXEXTENTS 121
          PCTINCREASE  0);
```

Data Dictionary View USER_INDEXES

Now let's write a simple query against the data dictionary view **USER_TABLES** to indicate whether or not the table **STATS** has been analyzed. Oracle will not use the bitmap index unless the table has been analyzed, or unless you use the **INDEX_COMBINE**, **FIRST_ROWS**, or **ALL_ROWS** hints. Listing 5.3 illustrates this. Because the **NUM_ROWS** column is null, no statistics exist on the **STATS** table.

Listing 5.3 Determining if a table has been analyzed.

```
SQL> SELECT  NUM_ROWS
  2  FROM    USER_TABLES
  3* WHERE   TABLE_NAME = 'STATS';
NUM_ROWS
--------
```

Explain Plan

Notice in Listing 5.4 that the index is not used. This is because there are no statistics for the table. Before you can execute Explain Plan, you must first create the table named **PLAN_TABLE**. The utlxplan.sql script ($ORACLE_HOME/rdbms/admin/utlxplan.sql on most Unix platforms) creates the table named **PLAN_TABLE**. Next, you need to write a query against **PLAN_TABLE**. After I wrote a query against **PLAN_TABLE**, I saved it into a Unix file called explain.sql. Remember that when you run an Explain Plan, Oracle does not execute the statement. Instead, Oracle inserts one row for each step of its plan into **PLAN_TABLE**. The plan depends on the current data found in the data dictionary. You can drastically change a plan by adding or dropping indexes on one of the tables in the SQL statement, or by rewriting the query.

Listing 5.4 No statistics.

```
SQL> EXPLAIN PLAN FOR
  2  SELECT  SNO, REGION_HASH
  3  FROM    STATS               /* 2,000 ROWS   */
  4* WHERE   REGION_BIT_MAP = 'W' AND SEX = 'F';

SQL> @explain
Query Plan                                     COST
-------------------------------------------    ----
SELECT STATEMENT    CHOOSE
  TABLE ACCESS FULL STATS
```

Causing Oracle To Use Bitmap Indexes

Oracle will use the bitmap index when it recognizes the hints **INDEX_COMBINE**, **FIRST_ROWS**, or **ALL_ROWS**, even if the table has not been analyzed. Listing 5.5 shows the power of a hint.

Listing 5.5 **INDEX_COMBINE** hint.

```
SQL> EXPLAIN PLAN FOR
  2  SELECT /*+ INDEX_COMBINE(STATS BITMAP_SEX) */  SNO, REGION_HASH
  3  FROM   STATS            /* 2,000 ROWS    */
  4* WHERE  REGION_BIT_MAP = 'W' AND SEX = 'F';
```

```
SQL> @explain
Query Plan                                                      COST
-----------------------------------------------------------     -----
SELECT STATEMENT   CHOOSE                                           5
  TABLE ACCESS BY ROWID STATS                                       5
    BITMAP CONVERSION TO ROWIDS
      BITMAP AND
        BITMAP INDEX SINGLE VALUE BITMAP_SEX
        BITMAP INDEX SINGLE VALUE BITMAP_REGION_BIT_MAP
```

Notice in Listing 5.5 that both bitmap indexes are used because of the new hint **INDEX_COMBINE**. This hint is designed for bitmap indexes. Also, Oracle computes the "cost" by combining the estimated amount of memory, I/O, and CPU. I tell my students and customers that they should think "MIC" when it comes to how Oracle estimates the cost. The lowest possible cost is 1, which you can observe by writing a query that returns a single row from a table using the rowid in the **WHERE** clause. For example, **SELECT * FROM STATS WHERE ROWID = '00000C06.0000.000B'** retrieves one row. However, you must first determine the **ROWID** by writing a query such as **SELECT ROWID, SNO FROM STATS WHERE SNO = 222**. Just be aware that rowids change when the table is exported/imported. **BITMAP CONVERSION TO ROWIDS** indicates that the bits are converted to actual rowids. **BITMAP AND** indicates that the two bitmap indexes are merged into one, whereas **BITMAP INDEX SINGLE VALUE** merely indicates that Oracle will use the bitmap index. In Oracle7.3.3, **BITMAP AND** can be replaced by **BITMAP MERGE**. The query in Listing 5.6 indicates information from the columns **OPERATION** and **OPTIONS** that pertains to bitmap indexes. **TABLE ACCESS BY ROWID STATS** indicates the access method—in this case, by rowid, which has always been the fastest method for retrieving a row from a table.

Listing 5.6 PLAN_TABLE columns OPERATION and OPTIONS.

```
SQL> SELECT OPERATION, OPTIONS
  2  FROM   PLAN_TABLE          -- New Bitmap Data In Plan Table
  3* WHERE  OPERATION LIKE 'BIT%';
```

```
OPERATION                        OPTIONS
------------------------------   ------------------------------
BITMAP CONVERSION                TO ROWIDS
BITMAP AND
BITMAP INDEX                     SINGLE VALUE
BITMAP INDEX                     SINGLE VALUE
```

Here are the remaining bitmap operations not shown in Listing 5.6:

- **BITMAP OR**
- **BITMAP MINUS**
- **BITMAP MERGE (BITMAP AND)**

The next query, shown in Listing 5.7, will not use an index argument in the **INDEX_COMBINE (STATS)** hint. This permits Oracle to use the boolean combination of bitmap indexes with the lowest cost estimate. In this case, Oracle uses the union of both bitmap indexes, converts the bitmaps to rowids, and then uses the rowids to retrieve the rows in the active set. Please note that this command is entered *after* the **STATS** table had been analyzed.

Listing 5.7 **INDEX_COMBINE** hint.

```
SQL> EXPLAIN PLAN FOR  --   STATS  Analyzed
  2  SELECT --+ INDEX_COMBINE(STATS)
  3  *
  4  FROM     STATS
  5  WHERE    SEX = 'F'  OR
  6           REGION_BIT_MAP = 'SE';

SQL> @explain
Query Plan                                                    COST
------------------------------------------------------------  ------
SELECT STATEMENT   CHOOSE                                     17,172
  TABLE ACCESS BY ROWID STATS ANALYZED                        17,172
    BITMAP CONVERSION TO ROWIDS
      BITMAP OR
        BITMAP INDEX SINGLE VALUE BITMAP_SEX
        BITMAP INDEX SINGLE VALUE BITMAP_REGION_BIT_MAP
```

FIRST_ROWS

Now, let's continue to cause Oracle to use the cost-based optimizer even though the STATS table has not been analyzed. Listing 5.8 illustrates, once again, how powerful hints are. Note that the cost is computed without the statistics. Later you'll see the actual estimated cost.

Listing 5.8 Using the **FIRST_ROWS** hint.

```
SQL> EXPLAIN PLAN FOR
  2  SELECT --+ FIRST_ROWS
  3         SNO, REGION_HASH
  4  FROM   STATS              /* 2,000 ROWS   */
  5* WHERE  REGION_BIT_MAP = 'W' AND SEX = 'F';

SQL> @explain
Query Plan                                                     COST
-------------------------------------------------------        ----
SELECT STATEMENT   HINT: FIRST_ROWS                               5
  TABLE ACCESS BY ROWID STATS                                     5
    BITMAP CONVERSION TO ROWIDS
      BITMAP AND
        BITMAP INDEX SINGLE VALUE BITMAP_REGION_BIT_MAP
        BITMAP INDEX SINGLE VALUE BITMAP_SEX
```

Notice in Listing 5.8 that Oracle uses both bitmap indexes again—this is because the hint **FIRST_ROWS** is used. The plan for both **ALL_ROWS** and **FIRST_ROWS** is identical. Hints override the init.ora parameter **OPTIMIZER_MODE** and the **ALTER SESSION SET OPTIMIZER_GOAL** commands.

ALL_ROWS

The cost-based optimizer will use bitmap indexes, but the rule-based optimizer will not. The hint **ALL_ROWS** invokes the cost-based optimizer, as illustrated in Listing 5.9, and it uses both bitmap indexes. The cost-based optimizer is invoked in several ways:

- Using the hint **ALL_ROWS** or **FIRST_ROWS**
- Entering **ALTER SESSION SET OPTIMIZER_GOAL = ALL_ROWS**
- Entering **ALTER SESSION SET OPTIMIZER_GOAL = FIRST_ROWS**
- Analyzing the table

The hint **INDEX_COMBINE**, new in Oracle7.3.3, is used with bitmap indexes. This hint causes Oracle to use the bitmap index with the lowest cost, if more than one is specified. However, in this case, Oracle knows it's best to use both bitmapped indexes.

Listing 5.9 Using the **ALL_ROWS** hint.

```
SQL> EXPLAIN PLAN FOR
  2  SELECT --+ ALL_ROWS
  3         SNO, REGION_HASH
  4  FROM   STATS                /* 2,000 ROWS    */
  5* WHERE  REGION_BIT_MAP = 'W' AND SEX = 'F';

SQL> @explain
 Query Plan                                                  COST
----------------------------------------------------------   -----
SELECT STATEMENT   HINT: ALL_ROWS                                5
  TABLE ACCESS BY ROWID STATS                                    5
    BITMAP CONVERSION TO ROWIDS
      BITMAP AND
        BITMAP INDEX SINGLE VALUE BITMAP_REGION_BIT_MAP
        BITMAP INDEX SINGLE VALUE BITMAP_SEX
```

Analyze Indexes

Now let's see what Oracle does if you analyze the bitmap indexes on the table **STATS**. Listing 5.10 shows the impact of analyzing these bitmap indexes. By the way, analyzing an index will not cause Oracle to use the cost-based optimizer. However, analyzing the table will cause Oracle to use the cost-based optimizer as well as analyze all indexes on the table.

Listing 5.10 Analyzing the bitmap indexes.

```
SQL> ANALYZE INDEX BITMAP_SEX
             COMPUTE STATISTICS;
     Required 1.12 Secs

SQL> ANALYZE INDEX BITMAP_REGION_BIT_MAP
             COMPUTE STATISTICS;
     Required 0.57 Sec

SQL> EXPLAIN PLAN FOR
  2  SELECT  SNO, REGION_HASH
  3  FROM    STATS                /* 2,000 ROWS    */
  4* WHERE   REGION_BIT_MAP = 'W' AND SEX = 'F';

SQL> @explain
Query Plan                                          COST
-------------------------------------------------   ----
SELECT STATEMENT   CHOOSE
  TABLE ACCESS FULL STATS
```

Analyze The STATS Table

The table, not the index, must be analyzed in order for the bitmap index to be used. Listing 5.11 indicates that Oracle needs nearly 11 minutes to perform a full-blown compute of one million rows in the STATS table.

Listing 5.11 Analyzing the **STATS** table.

```
SQL> SET TIMING ON
SQL> ANALYZE TABLE STATS
               COMPUTE STATISTICS;
Elapsed: 00:10:50.32
```

The query in Listing 5.12 suggests that **NOT EQUAL** will suppress the use of a bitmapped index and that Oracle estimates a full table scan on the **STATS** table to cost 3,958. The bitmap index is very beneficial when used with **ORs** or **ANDs**. Also, a bitmap index exists on the columns referenced in **WHERE** clauses containing **ORs** or **ANDs**, as in Listing 5.13.

Listing 5.12 Not equal.

```
SQL> EXPLAIN PLAN FOR
  2  SELECT *         -- Return 999,999 Rows
  3  FROM   STATS
  4* WHERE  REGION_BIT_MAP <> 'SE';

SQL> @explain
Query Plan                                                       COST
-------------------------------------------------------------   -----
SELECT STATEMENT   CHOOSE                                       3,958
  TABLE ACCESS FULL STATS ANALYZED                              3,958
```

Listing 5.13 Explain Plan using **AND**.

```
SQL> EXPLAIN PLAN FOR
  2  SELECT  SNO, REGION_HASH
  3  FROM    STATS   -- 2,000 ROWS IN ACTIVE SET
  4  WHERE   REGION_BIT_MAP = 'W' AND SEX = 'F';

SQL> @explain
Query Plan                                                            COST
--------------------------------------------------------------       ------
SELECT STATEMENT   CHOOSE                                             2,032
  TABLE ACCESS BY ROWID STATS ANALYZED                                2,032
```

```
BITMAP CONVERSION TO ROWIDS
  BITMAP AND
    BITMAP INDEX SINGLE VALUE BITMAP_REGION_BIT_MAP
    BITMAP INDEX SINGLE VALUE BITMAP_SEX
```

The "cost" of 5 in Listing 5.8 is based on estimates made "on the fly" because of the hints **INDEX_COMBINE, ALL_ROWS,** and **FIRST_ROWS.** These three hints force Oracle to estimate statistics at runtime (because no statistics were available) and to use the bitmap index. Following a full-blown "analyze" of the table, which requires 10 minutes and 50 seconds, Oracle has more accurate information in the data dictionary as well as a more reliable cost number of 2,032.

SQL Trace/TKPROF

Now, let's execute a query that returns 2,000 rows and then observe the elapsed time and the output produced by SQL Trace/TKPROF (see Listing 5.14). If the output contains zeroes, you forgot to set the init.ora parameter **TIMED_STATISTICS = TRUE.** You can either update your init.ora file and then "bounce" the database, or you can enter the following command:

```
SQL> ALTER SYSTEM SET TIMED_STATISTICS = TRUE;
```

Or, you can enter

```
ALTER SESSION SET TIMED_STATISTICS = TRUE;
```

without bouncing the database.

Listing 5.14 Elapsed time using AND.

```
SQL> SET      TIMING    ON
SQL> ALTER    SESSION   SET   SQL_TRACE    =    TRUE;
SQL> SELECT SNO, REGION_HASH GOOD_BITMAP
     FROM   STATS          /* 2,000 ROWS RETURNED  */
     WHERE  REGION_BIT_MAP = 'W' AND SEX = 'F';
 ......               .
 998999               6
2000 rows selected.

Elapsed: 00:00:09.76
```

Locating The Trace File

SQL Trace and TKPROF (Trace Kernel Profile) are fully explained in Chapter 8. The Unix commands in Listing 5.15 are used to locate the correct trace dump file. The column alias **GOOD_BITMAP** is easily located using the **grep** command.

Listing 5.15 Unix commands for locating the trace file.

```
> cd $ORACLE_HOME/rdbms/log
> grep GOOD_BITMAP *.trc
pete_ora_23837.trc:SELECT SNO, REGION_HASH GOOD_BITMAP
```

TKPROF

Because the trace file is so cryptic, you should submit it to the Trace Kernel Profile program TKPROF. This utility reformats the trace dump file into a more readable format file, as illustrated in Listing 5.16. The reformatted file has a .prf extension.

Listing 5.16 TKPROF output file.

```
> tkprof pete_ora_23837.trc $HOME/good_bitmap.prf
> more good_bitmap.prf
call     count       cpu    elapsed       disk      query    current
-------- -----   ------- ----------   --------  ---------- ----------

Parse        1      0.43       0.46         13         80          0
Execute      1      0.00       0.07          0          0          0
Fetch      134      1.98       2.43         97       2007          0
-------- ------  -------- ----------  --------  ---------- ----------

total      136      2.41       2.96        110       2087          0
```

Bad Example

Now, let's force Oracle to perform a full table scan and then compare both Explain Plans, the elapsed times, and the output from SQL Trace/TKPROF of the good bitmap index query and the full table scan query (see Listings 5.17 and 5.18). You can accomplish this dastardly deed using the hint **FULL(STATS)**. Hints are discussed in Chapter 9.

Listing 5.17 Full table scan.

```
SQL> EXPLAIN PLAN FOR
 2   SELECT /*+ FULL(STATS) */  SNO,
 3              REGION_HASH SUPPRESS_BITMAP
 4   FROM        STATS            -- 2,000 ROWS IN ACTIVE SET
```

```
 5* WHERE      REGION_BIT_MAP = 'W' AND SEX = 'F';

SQL> @explain
Query Plan                                                        COST
------------------------------------------------------------ -----
SELECT STATEMENT   CHOOSE                                         3,958
  TABLE ACCESS FULL STATS ANALYZED                                3,958
```

Listing 5.18 Actual times.

```
SQL> ALTER SESSION SET SQL_TRACE = TRUE;

SQL> SELECT /*+ FULL(STATS) */  SNO,
  2  REGION_HASH SUPPRESS_BITMAP
  3  FROM       STATS           -- 2,000 ROWS
  4* WHERE  REGION_BIT_MAP = 'W' AND SEX = 'F';

Elapsed: 00:02:12.15

> tkprof pete_ora_23876.trc $HOME/bad_bitmap.sql explain=/
> more bad_bitmap.sql
call     count       cpu    elapsed       disk      query    current
------  ------  --------  ----------  ------  --------  --------
Parse        1      0.43        0.49        13         80          0
Execute      1      0.00        0.00         0          0          0
Fetch      134    120.24      124.50     26075      26207          2
------  ------  --------  ----------  -------  -------  -------
total      136    120.67      124.99     26088      26287          2
```

The use of bitmap indexes clearly surpasses the performance of a full table scan for this query that returns 2,000 rows from a table containing 1,000,000 rows. CPU and I/O are much lower when Oracle's cost-based optimizer uses the two bitmap indexes. The "disk" column in the TKPROF output indicates the number of physical buffer reads from disk. Table 5.1 compares the results of the two queries. The number of disk reads is high for a full table scan.

Terrible Bitmap Example

The absolute worst use of a bitmap index is on a column with a large number of distinct values or a very high cardinality (for example, the **SNO** column, which has exactly 1,000,000 distinct values ranging from 1 to 1,000,000). Because disk space and time are at a premium, we'll do the next best thing. We'll place

Table 5.1 Good and bad bitmap summary.

	SQL>SET TIMING ON	TKPROF Total CPU	TKPROF Total Elapsed	TKPROF Total Disk	EXPLAIN Cost
Bitmap Indexes Used:	9.76 Secs	2.41 Secs	2.96 Secs	110	2,032
Full Table Scan:	2 Min 12 Secs	**2 Min. 7 Secs**	2 Min 4.99 Secs	**26,088**	**3,958**

550 distinct values in the column **FIVE_HUNDRED_FIFTY** with the following data distribution:

```
FIVE_HUNDRED_FIFTY                    NUMBER OF OCCURRENCES
         1                                       10,000
         2                                       10,000
         3                                       20,000
         4                                       40,000
         5                                       80,000
         6 -  15                                 20,000
        16                                       10,000
        17 -  20                                 20,000
        21 - 549                                  1,000
       550                                       21,000
```

Now, let's create the bitmap index on a column that has 550 distinct values and then analyze the **STATS** table again (see Listing 5.19). Hmm, I wonder if it will require more time now that another index is on the **STATS** table.

Listing 5.19 Actual times.

```
SQL> CREATE BITMAP INDEX
  2         BITMAP_FIVE_HUNDRED_FIFTY   -- 5 Min 23.7 Secs
  3         ON STATS(FIVE_HUNDRED_FIFTY)
  4  TABLESPACE BITMAP_INDEXES
  5  STORAGE(INITIAL 800K  NEXT 800K
  6                      MINEXTENTS 2  MAXEXTENTS
  7                      121  PCTINCREASE 0)
  8* UNRECOVERABLE;

Elapsed: 00:05:23.70

SQL> ANALYZE TABLE STATS COMPUTE STATISTICS;    -- 12 Min 51 Seconds
Elapsed: 00:12:51.18
```

This query requires 12 minutes and 51 seconds to analyze **STATS** with the new bitmap index. Before this index was added, it required 10 minutes and 50 seconds to analyze **STATS**.

Now, let's execute an Explain Plan on a query that will retrieve one row (see Listing 5.20).

Listing 5.20 Returns one row.

```
SQL> EXPLAIN PLAN FOR
  2  SELECT  *
  3  FROM    STATS    -- ACTIVE SET  10,000 ROWS
  4  WHERE   FIVE_HUNDRED_FIFTY    = 17  AND      --   20,000 Rows
  5          SEX                   = 'M' AND      --  500,000 Rows
  6*         REGION_BIT_MAP        = 'SE'         --        1 Row
SQL> /

SQL> @explain
Query Plan                                                         COST
----------------------------------------------------------   -----

SELECT STATEMENT   CHOOSE                                             7
  TABLE ACCESS BY ROWID STATS ANALYZED                                7
    BITMAP CONVERSION TO ROWIDS
      BITMAP AND
        BITMAP INDEX SINGLE VALUE BITMAP_FIVE_HUNDRED_FIFTY
        BITMAP INDEX SINGLE VALUE BITMAP_REGION_BIT_MAP
        BITMAP INDEX SINGLE VALUE BITMAP_SEX
```

Full Table Scan Or Bitmap Index

BITMAP AND in Listing 5.20 indicates that the three bitmap indexes are merged, where the cost of 7 is exceptionally low. Now let's compare the previous Explain Plan to the Explain Plan in Listing 5.21, which suppresses both the bitmap indexes on the **FIVE_HUNDRED_FIFTY** and **REGION_BIT_MAP** columns. The percent sign (a wildcard) in front of "SE" will always prevent Oracle from using indexes—and so does a function, such as **MOD**, on an indexed column. Oracle has to choose between performing a full table scan and using the bitmap index on the **SEX** column. Let's see which choice Oracle makes.

Listing 5.21 Bitmap index or full table scan.

```
SQL> EXPLAIN PLAN FOR
  2  SELECT  *
  3  FROM    STATS
```

```
  4  WHERE    MOD(FIVE_HUNDRED_FIFTY, 17) = 0   AND
  5           SEX                         = 'M' AND
  6*          REGION_BIT_MAP              LIKE '%SE%';

SQL> @explain
Query Plan                                                  COST
--------------------------------------------------------- -----
SELECT STATEMENT   CHOOSE                                  3,958
TABLE ACCESS FULL STATS ANALYZED                           3,958
```

Sure enough, Listing 5.21 indicates that Oracle resolves this query by performing a full table scan. However, a well-intentioned individual might try to help a little with a hint of "--+ **INDEX_COMBINE(STATS BITMAP_SEX)**" or "/*+ **INDEX_COMBINE(STATS BITMAP_SEX)** */". This is where the plot thickens and gets really, really ugly.

Terrible Hint

Be careful what you ask. The cost of forcing Oracle to use a bitmapped index can be really high. Listing 5.22 shows a cost of 14,074, compared to a full table scan cost of 3,958. Wow!

Listing 5.22 Explain Plan.

```
SQL> EXPLAIN PLAN FOR
  2  SELECT --+ INDEX_COMBINE(STATS BITMAP_SEX)
  3  *
  4  FROM     STATS
  5  WHERE    MOD(FIVE_HUNDRED_FIFTY, 17) = 0   AND
  6           SEX                         = 'M' AND
  7*          REGION_BIT_MAP              LIKE '%SE%';

SQL> @explain
Query Plan                                                  COST
------------------------------------------------------ -----------
SELECT STATEMENT   CHOOSE                                  14,074
    TABLE ACCESS BY ROWID STATS ANALYZED                   14,074
    BITMAP CONVERSION TO ROWIDS
    BITMAP INDEX SINGLE VALUE BITMAP_SEX
```

Now, let's look at the real times for the two queries and observe the output from SQL Trace/TKPROF (see Listing 5.23). It requires 2 minutes and 21 seconds to retrieve one row from a one-million-row table. This is not very good, but it could always get worse.

Listing 5.23 Actual times.

```
SQL>  ALTER SESSION SET SQL_TRACE = TRUE;

SQL> SELECT   *
  2  FROM     STATS
  3  WHERE    MOD(FIVE_HUNDRED_FIFTY, 17) = 0   AND
  4           SEX                           = 'M' AND
  5*          REGION_BIT_MAP                LIKE '%SE%';
   SNO  SNAME                    REG  REG  REGION_HASH  SEX
------  ------------------------ ---  ---  -----------  ---
375000  BETWEEN 300001 AND 600000 SE   SE            3    M
Elapsed: 00:02:21.77

> tkprof pete_ora_4613.trc $HOME/bmuglya.prf explain=/
> more bmuglya.prf
call       count     cpu     elapsed       disk       query   current
---------- --  ---------  ---------  ---------  ----------  --------
Parse          1      0.53      0.57         14        105         0
Execute        1      0.00      0.00          0          0         0
Fetch          1    131.63    140.49      26075      26074         2
---------- --  ---------  ---------  --------  ----------  ---------

total          3    132.16    141.06      26089      26179         2
```

Now, let's try to help Oracle with the **INDEX_COMBINE** hint and let the chips fall as they may. Listing 5.24 shows that things really can get worse by using a bad hint.

Listing 5.24 Bad hint.

```
SQL> ALTER SESSION SET SQL_TRACE = TRUE;
SQL> SELECT --+ INDEX_COMBINE(STATS BITMAP_SEX)
  2  *
  3  FROM     STATS
  4  WHERE    MOD(FIVE_HUNDRED_FIFTY, 17) = 0   AND  --  REALLY_UGLY
  5           SEX                           = 'M' AND
  6*          REGION_BIT_MAP                LIKE  '%SE%';
SNO     SNAME                    REG   REG   REGION_HASH  SEX
------  ------------------------ ----  ----  -----------  ---
375000  BETWEEN 300001 AND 600000 SE    SE             3    M
Elapsed: 00:07:15.25
```

```
> cd $ORACLE_HOME/rdbms/log
> grep REALLY_UGLY *.trc

> tkprof pete_ora_4690.trc $HOME/bmugly.prf explain=/
> more bmugly.prf
call     count       cpu    elapsed       disk        query     current
------ ------    -------   --------    -------   ----------  ----------
Parse        1      0.59       0.64         14          124           0
Execute      1      0.01       0.01          0            0           0
Fetch        1    404.71     432.08      26326       500255           0
------  -----   --------   --------    -------   ----------   ---------
total        3    405.31     432.73      26340       500379           0
Misses in library cache during parse: 1
Optimizer goal: CHOOSE
Parsing user id: 8  (OPS$PCASSIDY)

   Rows  Execution Plan
-------  --------------------------------------------------
      0  SELECT STATEMENT   GOAL: CHOOSE
 500000   TABLE ACCESS   GOAL: ANALYZED (BY ROWID) OF 'STATS'
 500000    BITMAP CONVERSION (TO ROWIDS)
    254     BITMAP INDEX (SINGLE VALUE) OF 'BITMAP_SEX'
```

The major difference in the TKPROF reports in Listings 5.23 and 5.24 is the **query** column, which denotes the number of buffers retrieved by a consistent read. For a full table scan, there were 26,179 buffers, compared to 500,379 for the bitmap index on the SEX column—this is nearly 20 times the number of consistent buffer reads for the bitmap index compared to the full table scan as shown in Table 5.2.

Concatenated Bitmap Indexes

A concatenated bitmap index can contain as many as 14 columns from the same table, whereas concatenated btree indexes have a maximum of 16 columns. If you

Table 5.2 Terrible bitmap summary.

TKPROF SET TIMING ON	TKPROF Total CPU	TKPROF Total Elapsed	TKPROF Total Disk	EXPLAIN Query	Cost
Bitmap: **7 Min 15 Sec**	6 Min 45 Sec	7 Min 12 Sec	26,340	**500,379**	**14,074**
Full Scan: 2 Min 21 Sec	2 Min 12 Sec	2 Min 21 Sec	26,089	26,179	3,958

try to create a concatenated bitmap index with more than 14 columns, you'll receive the error message shown in Listing 5.25 that is not correct. In other words, Oracle error ORA-25112 is in error. The second example in Listing 5.25 shows how to create a concatenated bitmap index on 14 columns. The error message displays if your concatenated bitmap index is on more than 14 columns. The error message should say, "ORA-25112: a bitmap index may index up to 14 columns".

Listing 5.25 Bogus error message.

```
SQL> CREATE BITMAP INDEX BM_MANY
 2   ON BM_CONCATENATED(C1,C2,C3,C4,
 3          C5,C6,C7,C8,C9,C10,C11,C12,C13,C14,C15);
                                                   *
ERROR at line 2:
ORA-25112: a bitmap index may index only one column


SQL> CREATE BITMAP INDEX BM_MANY
 2   ON BM_CONCATENATED(C1,C2,C3,C4,
 3     C5,C6,C7,C8,C9,C10,C11,C12,C13,C14);
Index created.
```

The reason you should consider using concatenated bitmap indexes is the same as for concatenated btree indexes: because several columns are consistently used together in the **WHERE** clause. Usually, an index on more than one column is more efficient than an index on each of the individual columns. The command in Listing 5.26 creates a concatenated bitmap index on the three columns **SEX**, **FIVE_HUNDRED_FIFTY**, and **REGION_BIT_MAP** of the **STATS** table. The ordering of the columns is extremely important when using btree indexes. With a btree index, the most selective column should go first. Also, if the first column of the concatenated btree index is referenced in the **WHERE** clause, the index can be used. In this concatenated bitmap index, the least selective column, **SEX**, which has two values, has been deliberately placed first.

Listing 5.26 Concatenated bitmap index.

```
SQL> CREATE BITMAP INDEX
  2        BITMAP_SEX_550_REGION       -- 11 Minutes 59 Secs
  3        ON STATS(SEX,FIVE_HUNDRED_FIFTY,REGION_BIT_MAP)
  4        TABLESPACE BITMAP_INDEXES
  5        STORAGE(INITIAL  200K
```

```
  6             NEXT         200K
  7             MINEXTENTS      1
  8             MAXEXTENTS    121
  9             PCTINCREASE     0)
 10   UNRECOVERABLE;
Index created.

Elapsed: 00:11:59.46
```

Listing 5.27 shows all the indexes currently on the STATS table.

Listing 5.27 Current indexes on the **STATS** table.

```
SQL>  SELECT INDEX_NAME,
   2         UNIQUENESS, PCT_FREE,
   3         DISTINCT_KEYS

   4  FROM   USER_INDEXES
   5* WHERE  TABLE_NAME = 'STATS';

INDEX_NAME                      UNIQUENESS   PCT_FREE  DISTINCT_KEYS
------------------------------- -----------  --------  -------------
BITMAP_FIVE_HUNDRED_FIFTY       BITMAP             10            550
BITMAP_REGION_BIT_MAP           BITMAP             10              8
BITMAP_SEX                      BITMAP             10              2
BITMAP_SEX_550_REGION           BITMAP             10           1111
BTREE_REGION                    NONUNIQUE          10              8
BTREE_UNIQUE_SNO                UNIQUE             10        1000000
```

Listing 5.28 examines how Oracle executes the SQL statement Explain Plan. First, you should reanalyze the STATS table; otherwise, you'll have to use hints in order for Oracle to use the concatenated bitmap index.

Listing 5.28 Reanalyzing the **STATS** table.

```
SQL> ANALYZE TABLE STATS COMPUTE STATISTICS;
Elapsed: 00:27:21.61
```

Referencing All Columns But The First

The query in Listing 5.29 to be explained will reference the second and third columns of the concatenated bitmap index created in Listing 5.26 (FIVE_ HUNDRED_FIFTY and REGION_BIT_MAP), but it will not reference the first column, SEX. Notice that Oracle merges the two individual bitmap indexes as opposed to using the concatenated bitmap index. Also notice the very low cost of 9.

Listing 5.29 Not referencing the first column.

```
SQL> EXPLAIN PLAN FOR
  2  SELECT  *
  3  FROM    STATS
  4  WHERE   FIVE_HUNDRED_FIFTY  =  17  AND
             REGION_BIT_MAP      =  'SE';

SQL> @explain
Query Plan                                                          COST
-----------------------------------------------------------       ------
SELECT STATEMENT   CHOOSE                                              9
  TABLE ACCESS BY ROWID STATS ANALYZED BITMAP CONVERSION TO ROWIDS     9
      BITMAP AND
        BITMAP INDEX SINGLE VALUE BITMAP_FIVE_HUNDRED_FIFTY
        BITMAP INDEX SINGLE VALUE BITMAP_REGION_BIT_MAP
```

Trying To Force Use Of The Concatenated Index

Often, the Big "O" (Oracle) is very smart. For example, it ignores really dumb hints. The output in Listing 5.30 illustrates this. Even though Oracle is instructed to use the bitmap index **BITMAP_SEX_550_REGION**, the bitmap indexes **BITMAP_FIVE_HUNDRED_FIFTY** *and* **BITMAP_REGION_BIT_MAP** are merged and used.

Listing 5.30 Oracle ignores really dumb hints.

```
SQL> EXPLAIN PLAN FOR
SELECT  /*+ INDEX_COMBINE(STATS BITMAP_SEX_550_REGION) */  *
  3  FROM   STATS
  4  WHERE  FIVE_HUNDRED_FIFTY          = 17 AND
                       REGION_BIT_MAP = 'SE';

SQL> @explain
Query Plan                                                      COST
-----------------------------------------------------------    -----
 SELECT STATEMENT   CHOOSE                                         9
        TABLE ACCESS BY ROWID STATS ANALYZED                       9
           BITMAP CONVERSION TO ROWIDS
      BITMAP AND
        BITMAP INDEX SINGLE VALUE BITMAP_FIVE_HUNDRED_FIFTY
        BITMAP INDEX SINGLE VALUE BITMAP_REGION_BIT_MAP
```

Concatenated Bitmap Index Only

Because Oracle did not accept the hint, we'll drop the other two bitmap indexes. Maybe Oracle will now use the concatenated bitmap index. Listing 5.31 examines this situation. As you can see, Oracle does not use the bitmap index. Instead, a full table scan is performed.

Listing 5.31 Reanalyzing the **STATS** table.

```
SQL> DROP INDEX BITMAP_FIVE_HUNDRED_FIFTY;
SQL> DROP INDEX BITMAP_REGION_BIT_MAP;
SQL> ANALYZE TABLE STATS COMPUTE STATISTICS;
SQL> EXPLAIN PLAN FOR
  2  SELECT  *
  3  FROM    STATS
  4  WHERE   FIVE_HUNDRED_FIFTY = 17  AND
  5*         REGION_BIT_MAP     = 'SE';

SQL> @explain
Query Plan                                                          COST
------------------------------------------------------------       -----
SELECT STATEMENT   CHOOSE                                          3,958
  TABLE ACCESS FULL STATS ANALYZED                                 3,958
```

A Really Bad Hint (Be Careful What You Ask For!)

I once heard a rumor that it's not necessary to reference the leading edge of a concatenated bitmap index in order for the index to be used, but judging by the results in Listing 5.31, it appears that this *is* necessary. Let's try one more time to give Oracle a hint (see Listing 5.32). Yes, it can be done, but does anyone want a cost of 28,170? The cost for a full table scan is 3,958, as illustrated in Listing 5.31. Using the hint, the cost is 28,170. This is a tremendously large gap between the two costs. It is safe to assume the query using the hint would be at least eight times slower than without the hint. This is the main purpose of using Explain Plan on statements. The query with the lowest cost normally executes faster than a query with a higher cost.

Listing 5.32 Oracle takes the hint.

```
SQL> EXPLAIN PLAN FOR
  2  SELECT --+ INDEX_COMBINE(STATS BITMAP_SEX_550_REGION)
  3  *
```

```
  4  FROM     STATS
  5  WHERE    FIFTY_FIVE_HUNDRED = 17 AND
              REGION_BIT_MAP     = 'SE';

SQL> @explain
Query Plan                                                          COST
------------------------------------------------------------------- ------
SELECT STATEMENT   CHOOSE                                            28,170
          TABLE ACCESS BY ROWID STATS ANALYZED                       28,170
             BITMAP CONVERSION TO ROWIDS
                BITMAP INDEX FULL SCAN BITMAP_SEX_550_REGION
```

Concatenated Or Merged? That's The Question

Now, let's re-create the indexes dropped a few minutes ago, analyze the table, and then reference all three columns in the concatenated bitmap index. Note whether Oracle uses the concatenated bitmap index or merges the other three bitmap indexes (see Listing 5.33).

Listing 5.33 All columns referenced.

```
SQL> EXPLAIN PLAN FOR
  2  SELECT   *
  3  FROM     STATS
  4  WHERE    FIVE_HUNDRED_FIFTY = 17    AND
              REGION_BIT_MAP = 'SE' AND
              SEX = 'M';

SQL> @explain
Query Plan                                                     COST
-------------------------------------------------------------- -----
 SELECT STATEMENT   CHOOSE                                         7
          TABLE ACCESS BY ROWID STATS ANALYZED                     7
            BITMAP CONVERSION TO ROWIDS
                BITMAP INDEX SINGLE VALUE BITMAP_SEX_550_REGION
```

Sure enough, the concatenated bitmap index is used.

Which Column Is The Leading Edge?

Listing 5.34 contains one of my favorite queries for determining the column position in concatenated indexes. The output indicates the order of the columns in the concatenated bitmap index **BITMAP_SEX_550_REGION**. The first column is SEX, the second column is **FIVE_HUNDRED_FIFTY**, and the third column is **REGION_BIT_MAP**.

Listing 5.34 The first column of the concatenated index.

```
SQL> get col
SELECT INDEX_NAME, COLUMN_POSITION CP,
       COLUMN_NAME CN
FROM   USER_IND_COLUMNS
WHERE  TABLE_NAME = 'STATS' AND
       INDEX_NAME LIKE 'BITMAP%'
ORDER  BY INDEX_NAME, COLUMN_POSITION;
SQL> @col

INDEX_NAME                                 CP  CN
------------------------------------------ --- ---------------------
BITMAP_FIVE_HUNDRED_FIFTY                    1 FIVE_HUNDRED_FIFTY
BITMAP_REGION_BIT_MAP                        1 REGION_BIT_MAP
BITMAP_SEX                                   1 SEX
BITMAP_SEX_550_REGION                        1 SEX
                                             2 FIVE_HUNDRED_FIFTY
                                             3 REGION_BIT_MAP
```

Bitmap Storage

Listing 5.35 determines the disk space actually used by each bitmap index. The concatenated bitmap index requires 300 2KB blocks. The btree index on the **REGION_BTREE** column requires 9,220 2KB blocks. The hash cluster requires 20,500 2KB blocks. (The btree index and the hash cluster are created later.) The unique btree index on the **SNO** column has been dropped, and a bitmap index has been created on the **SNO** column, but this is absurd because there are 1,000,000 distinct values in the **SNO** column. This bitmap index on the **SNO** column requires 15,300 blocks, or 31.3MB.

Listing 5.35 Disk storage for indexes.

```
SQL> get bmstorage
COL     SEGMENT_NAME    FORMAT A25
SELECT SEGMENT_NAME,
       SUM(BLOCKS) BLOCKS_USED
FROM   DBA_EXTENTS
```

```
  5  WHERE  SEGMENT_NAME LIKE '%BIT%' AND
  6         SEGMENT_TYPE = 'INDEX'
  7* GROUP  BY SEGMENT_NAME

SQL> @bmstorage
SEGMENT_NAME                                  BLOCKS_USED
------------------------------------------    -----------
BITMAP_FIVE_HUNDRED_FIFTY                             800
BITMAP_REGION_BIT_MAP                                 450
BITMAP_SEX                                            450
BITMAP_SEX_550_REGION                                 300
```

V733_plans_enabled init.ora Parameter

When **v733_plans_enabled** is set to "true" in the init.ora parameter file, the optimizer permits access paths using bitmap indexes for btree indexes on tables that have at least one bitmap index. In Listing 5.36, a unique btree index is created on the **SNO** column of the **STATS** table. Oracle converts the rowids from the unique btree index to bitmaps (**BITMAP CONVERSION FROM ROWIDS**); then the two bitmaps are sorted (**SORT ORDER BY**), merged (**BITMAP OR**), and converted from bitmaps back to rowids (**BITMAP CONVERSION TO ROWIDS**). Finally, Oracle retrieves the two rows by their respective rowids! Oracle converts the SQL statement into two statements using the set operator union. Then the btree index **BTREE_UNIQUE_SNO** has its rowids converted into two bitmaps. The union of the two bitmaps is converted back to rowids, and the rowids are used to retrieve the two rows. Note the elapsed time of 1.7 seconds—which is outstanding.

Listing 5.36 The impact of parameter **V733_plans_enabled.**

```
SQL> CREATE UNIQUE INDEX
            BTREE_UNIQUE_SNO   -- Took 9 Minutes 4.76 Secs
  2         ON STATS(SNO)
  3  TABLESPACE BTREE_INDEXES
  4  STORAGE(INITIAL 12M   NEXT 3M
              MINEXTENTS 1   MAXEXTENTS 121
              PCTINCREASE 0)
  5  UNRECOVERABLE
  6  NOSORT;
```

```
SQL> EXPLAIN PLAN FOR
  2  SELECT   *
  3  FROM     STATS
  4* WHERE    SNO NOT BETWEEN 2 AND 999999;

SQL> @explain
Query Plan                                                          COST
-------------------------------------------------------------      ----
 SELECT STATEMENT   CHOOSE                                             6
          TABLE ACCESS BY ROWID STATS ANALYZED                         6
              BITMAP CONVERSION TO ROWIDS
      BITMAP OR
        BITMAP CONVERSION FROM ROWIDS
          SORT ORDER BY
            INDEX RANGE SCAN BTREE_UNIQUE_SNO ANALYZED
        BITMAP CONVERSION FROM ROWIDS
          SORT ORDER BY
            INDEX RANGE SCAN BTREE_UNIQUE_SNO ANALYZED

SQL> ALTER SESSION SET SQL_TRACE = TRUE;
SQL> SELECT *     -- BTREE_AND_BITMAP
  2  FROM   STATS
  3  WHERE  SNO NOT BETWEEN 2 AND 999999;

    SNO  SNAME                    REG      REG      REGION_HASH   SEX
-------  --------------------     ------   -----   ------------   ---
      1  BETWEEN 1 AND 100000     N        N                  8   F
1000000  GREATER THAN 950,000     NW       N                  7   M
 Elapsed: 00:00:01.70

> cd $ORACLE_HOME/rdbms/log
> grep BTREE_AND_BITMAP *.trc
pete_ora_923.trc:SELECT *     -- BTREE_AND_BITMAP

> tkprof pete_ora_923.trc $HOME/btandbm.prf explain=/
> cd/home2/dci2/pcassidy/v7322

> more btandbm.prf
call     count       cpu    elapsed       disk      query    current
------ ------  -------  ---------  ---------  --------  --------
Parse        1      0.70       0.73         16        119          0
Execute      1      0.00       0.06          0          0          0
Fetch        1      0.03       0.22          7          8          0
------ ------  -------  ---------- ---------- ---------- ----------
total        3      0.73       1.01         23        127          0
```

```
Misses in library cache during parse: 1
Optimizer goal: CHOOSE
Parsing user id: 8  (OPS$PCASSIDY)

   Rows  Execution Plan
-------  ---------------------------------------------------
      0  SELECT STATEMENT   GOAL: CHOOSE
      2   TABLE ACCESS   GOAL: ANALYZED (BY ROWID) OF 'STATS'
      2    BITMAP CONVERSION (TO ROWIDS)
      0     BITMAP OR
      0      BITMAP CONVERSION (FROM ROWIDS)
      1       SORT (ORDER BY)
      2        INDEX   GOAL: ANALYZED (RANGE SCAN) OF
                   'BTREE_UNIQUE_SNO' (UNIQUE)
      0      BITMAP CONVERSION (FROM ROWIDS)
      1       SORT (ORDER BY)
      2        INDEX   GOAL: ANALYZED (RANGE SCAN) OF
                   'BTREE_UNIQUE_SNO' (UNIQUE)
```

Which Is Faster, Btree Or Bitmap?

Is the query in Listing 5.36 really faster than just using the old unique btree index? In Listing 5.37, Oracle is given a hint (**RULE**) to use the unique btree index without any bitmaps. The cost-based optimizer uses bitmap indexes, but the rule-based optimizer does not. Oracle transforms this query into two "unionized" queries so that the index is used for both (**CONCATENATION**). You'll also see **CONCATENATION** when the **WHERE** clause has several **OR**s and each column associated with each **OR** has an index. The two queries look like this:

```
SELECT * FROM STATS WHERE SNO < 2
UNION
SELECT * FROM STATS WHERE SNO > 999999
```

The query that uses the cost-based optimizer and bitmaps is slower than the rule-based optimizer in this case. The rule-based query requires an elapsed time of 0.96 seconds, compared to the cost-based query's elapsed time of 1.7 seconds. The rule-based query is 0.74 seconds faster.

Listing 5.37 Speed of unique btree index.

```
SQL> EXPLAIN PLAN FOR
  2  SELECT --+ RULE
```

```
  3  *
  4  FROM       STATS
  5  WHERE      SNO NOT BETWEEN 2 AND 999999;

SQL> @explain
Query Plan                                                      COST
------------------------------------------------------------ -----
SELECT STATEMENT   HINT: RULE
 CONCATENATION
   TABLE ACCESS BY ROWID STATS ANALYZED
     INDEX RANGE SCAN
                  BTREE_UNIQUE_SNO ANALYZED
   TABLE ACCESS BY ROWID STATS ANALYZED
     INDEX RANGE SCAN
                  BTREE_UNIQUE_SNO ANALYZED

SQL> SELECT --+ RULE
  2  *
  3  FROM      STATS
  4* WHERE     SNO NOT BETWEEN 2 AND 999999;

     SNO  SNAME                    REG  REG   REGION_HASH  SEX
--------  ------------------------ ---- ----  -----------  ----
       1  BETWEEN 1 AND 100000     N    N               8  F
 1000000  GREATER THAN 950,000     NW   N               7  M
Elapsed: 00:00:00.96

> tkprof pete_ora_984.trc $HOME/btrule.prf explain=/
> cd
> more btrule.prf
call     count       cpu    elapsed       disk      query    current
------  ------  -------  ---------  -------  --------  --------
Parse        1      0.63       0.64          0          0          0
Execute      1      0.00       0.00          0          0          0
Fetch        1      0.03       0.03          7          9          0
------  ------  -------  ---------  -------  --------  --------
total        3      0.66       0.67          7          9          0
```

If you compare the totals from TKPROF, you can see a *slight* difference:

```
                                 Total CPU     ELAPSED     DISK
Cost Based - Uses Bitmaps          0.73         1.01        23
Rule Based - Btree Only            0.66         0.67         7
```

Cost Of Using A Btree Index

To determine the actual cost of using the unique btree index on **SNO** without the help of bitmaps, the init.ora parameter **v733_plans_enabled** is set to **FALSE** to disallow access paths for btree indexes on tables that have at least one bitmap index. To verify the current setting of this parameter, refer to Listing 5.38. Here is a perfect example of a query with a lower cost (6) executing slightly slower than a query with a higher cost (8). I have seen this situation, occasionally, in all versions of Oracle7. Remember that the cost from an Explain Plan is an *estimate.*

Listing 5.38 Verify current **v733_plans_enabled** setting.

```
SQL> SELECT SUBSTR(NAME,1,25) PARAM,
  2         SUBSTR(VALUE,1,25) CURRENT_SETTING
  3  FROM   V$PARAMETER
  4  WHERE  NAME LIKE '%' || LOWER('&Parameter') || '%';
Enter value for parameter: V73

PARAM                     CURRENT_SETTING
------------------------- -------------------------

v733_plans_enabled        FALSE

SQL> EXPLAIN PLAN FOR
  2  SELECT *    /* v733_plans_enabled set to false  */
  3  FROM   STATS
  4  WHERE  SNO NOT BETWEEN 2 AND 999999;

SQL> @explain
Query Plan                                                 COST
---------------------------------------------------------- -----

 SELECT STATEMENT   CHOOSE                                     8
          CONCATENATION
    TABLE ACCESS BY ROWID STATS ANALYZED                        4
                 INDEX RANGE SCAN
                 BTREE_UNIQUE_SNO ANALYZED
    TABLE ACCESS BY ROWID STATS ANALYZED                        4
                 INDEX RANGE SCAN
                 BTREE_UNIQUE_SNO ANALYZED
```

Summary

First of all, Oracle uses bitmap indexes if you are using the cost-based optimizer for the SQL statement through the use of one of these three hints:

- ALL_ROWS
- FIRST_ROWS
- INDEX_COMBINE

You can also enter either one of the following **ALTER SESSION** commands:

- ALTER SESSION SET OPTIMIZER_GOAL = ALL_ROWS
- ALTER SESSION SET OPTIMIZER_GOAL = FIRST_ROWS

In other words, you can force Oracle to use a bitmap index even if there are no statistics on the table. Without hints or an altered session, Oracle uses a bitmap index if the table is analyzed. Second, using **AND**s or **OR**s in the **WHERE** clause on bitmap indexed columns is a very fast and efficient method, because the bitmaps are actually merged in memory before the table is accessed. The same holds true when the **WHERE** clause contains **OR**s on bitmap indexed columns. Third, the storage requirements are very low compared to btree and hash clusters. Fourth, using **NOT IN** (or "<>") suppresses the use of a bitmap index. Finally, the hint **INDEX_FFS** apparently has no effect on bitmap indexes.

HIGH PERFORMANCE

Analyzing Tables, Clusters, And Indexes; And Creating Histograms

CHAPTER 6

The purpose of the **ANALYZE** *command is to produce statistics in the data dictionary so that the cost-based optimizer can be used. In this chapter, you'll learn how to use this command to analyze indexes, tables, and btree index clusters. You'll also learn how to create and use histograms when btree indexes contain badly skewed data.*

Analyzing Tables, Clusters, And Indexes; And Creating Histograms

What Is The ANALYZE Command?

The ANALYZE command (see Figure 6.1) is used to compute, estimate, or delete statistics on indexes, tables, or clusters. This command can also be used to validate the structure of an index, to pinpoint row chaining, and to create histograms. Results from this command are stored in 9 to 12 data dictionary views, depending on the type of object being analyzed. The following data dictionary views are updated:

- USER_TABLES
- ALL_TABLES
- DBA_TABLES
- USER_INDEXES
- ALL_INDEXES
- DBA_INDEXES
- USER_TAB_COLUMNS
- ALL_TAB_COLUMNS
- DBA_TAB_COLUMNS

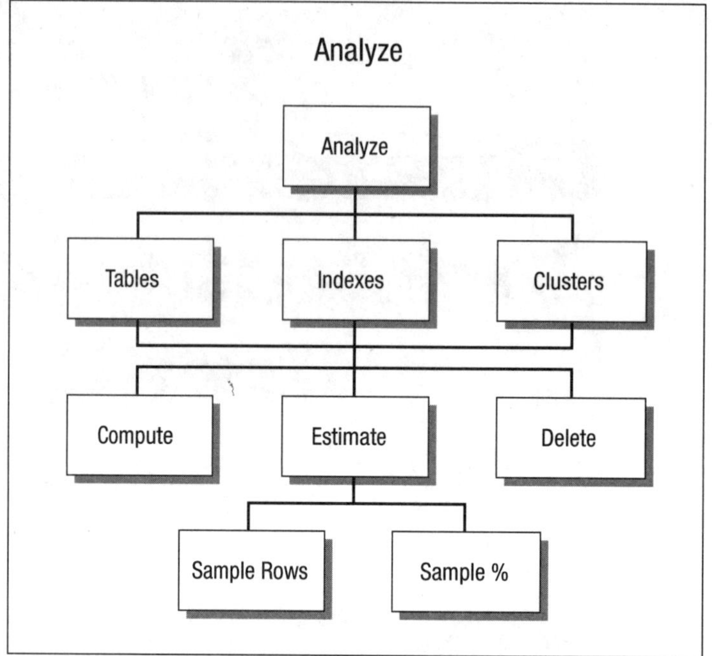

Figure 6.1
Analyze.

- USER_CLUSTERS
- ALL_CLUSTERS
- DBA_CLUSTERS

The three views that contain information about clusters are updated only if a cluster is analyzed. If statistics are available for a table at parse time, the cost-based optimizer is invoked (unless a hint to do otherwise is entered in the SQL statement). If statistics are not available at parse time, the rule-based optimizer is invoked (unless a hint to use the cost-based optimizer is included in the SQL statement).

Analyzing Tables

Let's see what Oracle does when you analyze the one-million-row table **STATS**. By the way, analyzing an index will not cause Oracle to use the cost-based optimizer.

However, analyzing a table will cause Oracle to use the cost-based optimizer as well as analyze all indexes on the table. Listing 6.1 illustrates that tables must be analyzed in order for Oracle to best use the cost-based optimizer. Also, notice that it takes 12 minutes and 51 seconds to perform a *compute* on a one-million-row table. However, the really huge difference is between the elapsed times. When the table is not analyzed, Oracle performs a full table scan and requires 2 minutes and 12 seconds to execute. If the **STATS** table is analyzed, Oracle uses the bitmap indexes and requires only 9 seconds to execute. That's a difference of 2 minutes and 3 seconds for a query against a one-million-row table.

Listing 6.1 Analyzing tables versus analyzing indexes.

```
SQL> ANALYZE INDEX BITMAP_SEX COMPUTE STATISTICS;
Elapsed: 00:00:01.12   (1.12 Seconds)

SQL> ANALYZE INDEX BITMAP_REGION_BIT_MAP COMPUTE STATISTICS;
Elapsed: 00:00:00.57

SQL> EXPLAIN PLAN FOR
  2  SELECT SNO, REGION_HASH
  3  FROM   STATS    /* 2,000 ROWS RETURNED   */
  4* WHERE  REGION_BIT_MAP = 'W' AND SEX = 'F';

SQL> @explain
Query Plan                                                COST
-------------------------------------------------------- -----
 SELECT STATEMENT   CHOOSE
  TABLE ACCESS FULL STATS

SQL> SELECT SNO, REGION_HASH
  2  FROM   STATS   /* 2,000 ROWS RETURNED   */
  3* WHERE  REGION_BIT_MAP = 'W' AND SEX = 'F';

Elapsed: 00:02:12.15

SQL> ANALYZE TABLE STATS COMPUTE STATISTICS;
Elapsed: 00:12:51.18

SQL> EXPLAIN PLAN FOR
  2  SELECT  SNO, REGION_HASH
  3  FROM    STATS  -- 2,000 ROWS IN ACTIVE SET
  4  WHERE   REGION_BIT_MAP = 'W' AND SEX = 'F';
```

```
SQL> @explain
Query Plan                                                           COST
-------------------------------------------------------------------- -----
SELECT STATEMENT   CHOOSE                                            2,032
   TABLE ACCESS BY ROWID STATS ANALYZED                              2,032
       BITMAP CONVERSION TO ROWIDS
          BITMAP AND
              BITMAP INDEX SINGLE VALUE
                              BITMAP_REGION_BIT_MAP
              BITMAP INDEX SINGLE VALUE
                              BITMAP_SEX

SQL> SELECT  SNO, REGION_HASH
  2  FROM    STATS  /* 2,000 ROWS RETURNED   */
  3* WHERE   REGION_BIT_MAP = 'W' AND SEX = 'F';

Elapsed: 00:00:09.76
```

Analyzing tables has some other uses as well. You can analyze a table to determine the number of blocks containing data. However, as Listing 6.2 indicates, analyzing is slower than writing a **SELECT** statement. How much faster is counting the blocks using the **COUNT** function as opposed to using the **ANALYZE** command? Notice two things in Listing 6.2: First of all, the **ANALYZE** command is slower than using **COUNT DISTINCT** by nearly 1 minute for a table with 470,692 rows. Imagine what the difference would be for a data warehouse fact table containing 175 million rows. Second, there's a difference in the number of blocks. **COUNT DISTINCT** counts blocks that actually contain data—in this case 3,755 blocks, whereas the **ANALYZE** command populates the **BLOCKS** column of the data dictionary views **USER_TABLES**, **ALL_TABLES**, and **DBA_TABLES** with 3,759 blocks—four more blocks than **COUNT DISTINCT**. The **ANALYZE** command includes the two blocks of overhead plus any empty blocks preallocated beneath the high-water mark.

Listing 6.2 Counting the number of blocks in a table.

```
SQL> SET TIMING ON
SQL> ANALYZE TABLE TESTS COMPUTE STATISTICS;
Table analyzed.

Elapsed: 00:02:50.52
```

```
SQL> SELECT BLOCKS
  2  FROM   USER_TABLES
  3  WHERE  TABLE_NAME = 'TESTS';

 BLOCKS
-------
   3759

SQL> SELECT COUNT(DISTINCT
  2  SUBSTR(ROWID,1,8) || SUBSTR(ROWID,15,4)) BLKS
  3* FROM   TESTS;

   BLKS
-------
   3755

Elapsed: 00:01:52.20
```

In Listing 6.3, you can see that using a sample of one row is 2 minutes and 49 seconds faster than a full **COMPUTE STATISTICS** of the table. Also, the sample of one row is 1 minute and 50 seconds faster than the **SELECT** statement. Therefore, the **ANALYZE TABLE** command that estimates statistics using a sample of one row is extremely fast compared to a **SELECT** or a **COMPUTE STATISTICS** command. However, you do not receive all of the statistics, just the number of blocks, when you use the **SAMPLE 1 ROWS** clause.

Listing 6.3 The fastest way to determine the number of blocks.

```
SQL> ANALYZE TABLE TESTS
  2            ESTIMATE STATISTICS
  3*           SAMPLE 1 ROWS;
Table analyzed.

Elapsed: 00:00:01.28

SQL> SELECT BLOCKS
  2  FROM   USER_TABLES
  3  WHERE  TABLE_NAME = 'TESTS';

 BLOCKS
-------
   3759
```

```
SQL> ANALYZE TABLE TESTS COMPUTE STATISTICS;
Table analyzed.

Elapsed: 00:02:50.52
```

COMPUTE STATISTICS

You can analyze tables, indexes, and clusters. Furthermore, the **ANALYZE** command has three options. The three options are **COMPUTE, ESTIMATE,** and **DELETE**. The **COMPUTE** option requires more time, but analyzes the entire object, whether it is a table, index, or cluster. Some will tell you to always use the **COMPUTE** option. But, the **ESTIMATE** option is much faster than the **COMPUTE** option and does an excellent job with a very small degree of error. Finally, the **DELETE** option removes entries from the data dictionary views. This section uses the **COMPUTE** option of the **ANALYZE** command.

FOR TABLE

In Listing 6.4, data dictionary views **USER_TABLES, USER_INDEXES,** and **USER_TAB_COLUMNS** are queried before the **PARTS** table is analyzed. Null values in the statistical columns indicate that the table or index has not been analyzed. Then, the **PARTS** table is analyzed using the **FOR TABLE** clause. This clause prevents Oracle from analyzing the indexes. Without the **FOR TABLE** clause, Oracle analyzes all of the indexes on the table being analyzed.

Listing 6.4 FOR TABLE.

```
SQL> SELECT SUBSTR(TABLE_NAME,1,16) "Table Name",
  2         NUM_ROWS,
  3         BLOCKS,
  4         AVG_ROW_LEN
  5  FROM   USER_TABLES
  6* WHERE  TABLE_NAME = 'PARTS';

Table Name               NUM_ROWS        BLOCKS
---------------- ---------------- ------------
PARTS

SQL> SELECT SUBSTR(INDEX_NAME,1,20) NAME,
  2         UNIQUENESS,
  3         DISTINCT_KEYS,
```

```
  4         STATUS
  5  FROM   USER_INDEXES
  6* WHERE  TABLE_NAME = 'PARTS';

NAME                             UNIQUENESS  DISTINCT_KEYS STATUS
-------------------------------  ----------  --------------------
PARTS_PNO_UNIQUE_IND             NONUNIQUE   VALID

SQL> SELECT SUBSTR(COLUMN_NAME,1,15) "Column",
  2         NUM_DISTINCT DIS,
  3         DENSITY DEN,
  4         NUM_NULLS NULLS,
  5         NUM_BUCKETS BUCKETS
  6  FROM   USER_TAB_COLUMNS
  7* WHERE  TABLE_NAME = UPPER('&TN');

Enter value for tn: parts

Column                   DIS  DEN  NULLS   BUCKETS
------------------------ ---  ---  ------  -------
PNO
PNAME
TIME_OF_INSERT

SQL> ANALYZE TABLE PARTS
  2          COMPUTE STATISTICS FOR TABLE;
Table analyzed.
Elapsed: 00:00:01.34

SQL> SELECT SUBSTR(TABLE_NAME,1,16) "Table Name",
  2         NUM_ROWS,
  3         BLOCKS,
  4         AVG_ROW_LEN
  5  FROM   USER_TABLES
  6* WHERE  TABLE_NAME = 'PARTS';

Table Name        NUM_ROWS  BLOCKS  AVG_ROW_LEN
----------------  --------  ------  -----------
PARTS                10000     169           25
```

FOR ALL INDEXED COLUMNS SIZE

The **FOR ALL INDEXED COLUMNS** clause causes histograms to be created on each of the indexed columns of the analyzed table. In Listing 6.5, **SIZE 10** indicates the number of desired buckets for each indexed column. Information about the histograms is stored in the data dictionary views **USER_HISTOGRAMS, ALL_HISTOGRAMS,** and **DBA_HISTOGRAMS.** Listing 6.5 shows a description of all of the columns in the **STATS** table. Then, the names of all the indexes on the **STATS** table are listed as well as the column names on which the btree indexes are created.

Listing 6.5 FOR ALL INDEXED COLUMNS SIZE.

```
SQL> DESC STATS
 Name                                      Null? Type
 ----------------------------------------- ------ -------------------------
 SNO                                              NUMBER(7)
 SNAME                                            VARCHAR2(30)
 REGION_BTREE                                     VARCHAR2(3)
 REGION_BIT_MAP                                   VARCHAR2(3)
 REGION_HASH                                      NUMBER(1)
 SEX                                              VARCHAR2(1)
 ONE_THOUSAND_NUMBERS                             NUMBER(4)
 TEMPERATURE                                      NUMBER(4,1)

SQL> SELECT INDEX_NAME,
  2         COLUMN_POSITION CPOS,
  3         COLUMN_NAME CNAME
  4  FROM   USER_IND_COLUMNS
  5  WHERE  TABLE_NAME = 'STATS'
  6* ORDER  BY INDEX_NAME, CPOS;

INDEX_NAME                      CPOS  CNAME
------------------------------ -----  ----------------------
BTREE_REGION                       1  REGION_BTREE
BTREE_REGION_HASH                  1  REGION_HASH
BTREE_UNIQUE_SNO                   1  NO
TEMP_INDX                          1  TEMPERATURE

SQL> ANALYZE TABLE STATS
  2          COMPUTE STATISTICS
  3          FOR ALL INDEXED COLUMNS SIZE 10;
Table analyzed.

Elapsed: 00:17:35.33

SQL> BREAK  ON COLUMN_NAME SKIP 1
SQL> SELECT COLUMN_NAME,
  2         ENDPOINT_NUMBER EPN,
  3         ENDPOINT_VALUE EPV
  4  FROM   USER_HISTOGRAMS
```

```
  5  WHERE  TABLE_NAME = 'STATS'
  6* ORDER  BY COLUMN_NAME, EPN;

COLUMN_NAME                      EPN          EPV
------------------------------ ---  ------------
REGION_BTREE                       1       3.6E+35
                                   2       4.0E+35
                                   3       4.1E+35
                                   5       4.3E+35
                                   9       4.3E+35
                                  10       4.5E+35

REGION_HASH                        1             1
                                   2             2
                                   3             4
                                   8             5
                                  10             8

SNO                                0             1
                                   1        100000
                                   2        200000
                                   3        300000
                                   4        400000
                                   5        500000
                                   6        600000
                                   7        700000
                                   8        800000
                                   9        900000
                                  10       1000000

TEMPERATURE                       48          22.2
                                 196          30.7
                                 296          55.5
                                 302         103.9
```

FOR COLUMNS

If the data is badly skewed on an indexed column, the index will not be used in certain situations. These situations result in full table scans, which can be devastatingly slow on large tables. A method for preventing full table scans when an index would be much faster is to create histograms. The **FOR COLUMNS** clause in Listing 6.6 creates histograms for the **TEMPERATURE** and **SNO** columns. Histograms are examined more closely later in this chapter in the section "FOR ALL INDEXED COLUMNS."

Listing 6.6 FOR COLUMNS.

```
SQL> ANALYZE TABLE STATS
  2          COMPUTE STATISTICS
  3*         FOR COLUMNS TEMPERATURE, SNO SIZE 4;
Table analyzed.

Elapsed: 00:05:54.16

SQL> BREAK  ON COLUMN_NAME SKIP 1
SQL> SELECT COLUMN_NAME,
  2         ENDPOINT_NUMBER EPN,
  3         ENDPOINT_VALUE EPV
  4  FROM   USER_HISTOGRAMS
  5  WHERE  TABLE_NAME = 'STATS'
  6* RDER   BY COLUMN_NAME, EPN;

COLUMN_NAME                          EPN          EPV
------------------------------ ---- ------------
SNO                                    0            1
                                       1       250000
                                       2       500000
                                       3       750000
                                       4      1000000

TEMPERATURE                           48         22.2
                                     196         30.7
                                     296         55.5
                                     302        103.9
9 rows selected.
```

FOR ALL INDEXES

If you want statistics on all the indexed columns of a table and do not want to use histograms, then use the **FOR ALL INDEXES** clause in the **ANALYZE** command. Listing 6.7 shows that no rows were selected from **USER_HISTOGRAMS**, which indicates that no histograms were created.

Listing 6.7 FOR ALL INDEXES.

```
SQL> ANALYZE TABLE STATS
  2          COMPUTE STATISTICS
  3          FOR ALL INDEXES;
Table analyzed.
```

```
Elapsed: 00:03:54.73

SQL> BREAK  ON COLUMN_NAME SKIP 1
SQL> SELECT COLUMN_NAME,
  2         ENDPOINT_NUMBER EPN,
  3         ENDPOINT_VALUE EPV
  4  FROM   USER_HISTOGRAMS
  5  WHERE  TABLE_NAME = 'STATS'
  6* ORDER  BY COLUMN_NAME, EPN;

no rows selected

SQL> SELECT SUBSTR(INDEX_NAME,1,20) NAME,
  2         UNIQUENESS,
  3         DISTINCT_KEYS DIS,
  4         STATUS
  5  FROM   USER_INDEXES
  6* WHERE  TABLE_NAME = 'STATS';

NAME                                UNIQUENESS              DIS    STATUS
-------------------------------- ------------------ ------    ------
BTREE_REGION                        NONUNIQUE                 8    VALID
BTREE_REGION_HASH                   NONUNIQUE                 8    VALID
BTREE_UNIQUE_SNO                    UNIQUE              1000000    VALID
TEMP_INDX                           NONUNIQUE                 4    VALID
```

FOR ALL INDEXED COLUMNS

The **FOR ALL INDEXED COLUMNS** clause creates histograms for the indexed columns. Notice in Listing 6.8 that the default number of buckets is 75. Also note that no index statistics are gathered in **USER_INDEXES**, but statistics are gathered and placed into **USER_TAB_COLUMNS**. In addition, no table statistics exist in **USER_TABLES**.

Listing 6.8 FOR ALL INDEXED COLUMNS.

```
SQL> ANALYZE TABLE STATS
  2          COMPUTE STATISTICS
  3          FOR ALL INDEXED COLUMNS;
Table analyzed.

Elapsed: 00:17:59.54

SQL> BREAK  ON COLUMN_NAME SKIP 1
SQL> SELECT COLUMN_NAME,
```

```
       ENDPOINT_NUMBER EPN,
       ENDPOINT_VALUE EPV
FROM   USER_HISTOGRAMS
WHERE  TABLE_NAME = 'STATS'
ORDER  BY COLUMN_NAME, EPN;

COLUMN_NAME                                EPN          EPV
---------------------------------------- -----  -----------
REGION_BTREE                                 9      3.6E+35
                                            18      4.0E+35
                                            28      4.1E+35
                                            37      4.3E+35
                                            74      4.3E+35
                                            75      4.5E+35

REGION_HASH                                  9            1
                                            18            2
                                            28            4
                                            65            5
                                            75            8

SNO                                          0            1
                                             1        13334
                                             2        26668
                                             3        40002
                                             4        53336
                                             5        66670
                                             6        80004
                                             7        93338
                                             8       106672
                                             9       120006
                                            10       133340
                     <<< Rows Of Output Skipped Here >>>
                                            71       946714
                                            72       960048
                                            73       973382
                                            74       986716
                                            75      1000000

TEMPERATURE                                 48         22.2
                                           196         30.7
                                           296         55.5
                                           302        103.9

91 rows selected.
```

```
SQL> SELECT SUBSTR(INDEX_NAME,1,20) NAME,
  2         UNIQUENESS,
  3         DISTINCT_KEYS DIS,
  4         STATUS
  6  FROM   USER_INDEXES
  7* WHERE  TABLE_NAME = 'STATS';

NAME                           UNIQUENESS         DIS STATUS
------------------------------ ----------------- ----- ------
BTREE_REGION                   NONUNIQUE              VALID
BTREE_REGION_HASH              NONUNIQUE              VALID
BTREE_UNIQUE_SNO               UNIQUE                 VALID
TEMP_INDX                      NONUNIQUE              VALID

SQL> SELECT SUBSTR(COLUMN_NAME,1,20) "Column",
  2         NUM_DISTINCT DIS,
  3         DENSITY DEN,
  4         NUM_BUCKETS BUCKETS,
  5         SAMPLE_SIZE SAMPLE
  6  FROM   USER_TAB_COLUMNS
  7* WHERE  TABLE_NAME = UPPER('&TN');

Enter value for tn: stats

Column                       DIS      DEN     BUCKETS  SAMPLE
---------------------- --------- -------- ----------- ----------
SNO                      1000000  1.0E-06          75  1000000
SNAME
REGION_BTREE                   8  .000999           5  1000000
REGION_BIT_MAP
REGION_HASH                    8  .003399           4  1000000
SEX
ONE_THOUSAND_NUMBERS
TEMPERATURE                    4  .008197           3  1000000

SQL> SELECT NUM_ROWS,
  2         AVG_ROW_LEN
  2  FROM   USER_TABLES
  4* WHERE  TABLE_NAME = 'STATS';

NUM_ROWS           AVG_ROW_LEN
---------------    ----------------------
```

FOR TABLE FOR ALL INDEXED COLUMNS

The **FOR TABLE FOR ALL INDEXED COLUMNS** clause creates histograms for all the indexed columns in the **STATS** table. The command in Listing 6.9 requests six buckets, but the **REGION_HASH** and **TEMPERATURE** columns do not require six buckets, Statistical information pertaining to the indexes is also populated in **USER_TAB_COLUMNS**. Because the **FOR TABLE** syntax is used, statistics are also gathered for the table and are populated in **USER_TABLES**.

Listing 6.9 FOR TABLE FOR ALL INDEXED COLUMNS.

```
SQL> ANALYZE TABLE STATS
  2          COMPUTE STATISTICS
  3          FOR TABLE FOR ALL INDEXED COLUMNS SIZE 6;
Table analyzed.

Elapsed: 00:17:39.24

SQL> SELECT COLUMN_NAME,
  2         ENDPOINT_NUMBER EPN,
  3         ENDPOINT_VALUE EPV
  4  FROM   USER_HISTOGRAMS
  5  WHERE  TABLE_NAME = 'STATS'
  6* ORDER  BY COLUMN_NAME, EPN;

COLUMN_NAME                                EPN  EPV
---------------------------------------- ----- -------------
REGION_BTREE                                 0       3.6E+35
                                             1       4.0E+35
                                             2       4.1E+35
                                             3       4.3E+35
                                             5       4.3E+35
                                             6       4.5E+35

REGION_HASH                                  0             1
                                             1             2
                                             2             4
                                             5             5
                                             6             8

SNO                                          0             1
                                             1        166667
                                             2        333334
                                             3        500001
                                             4        666668
```

```
                                                    5          833335
                                                    6         1000000

TEMPERATURE                                        48            22.2
                                                  196            30.7
                                                  296            55.5
                                                  302           103.9
22 rows selected.

SQL> SELECT SUBSTR(COLUMN_NAME,1,20) "Column",
  2         NUM_DISTINCT DIS,
  3         DENSITY DEN,
  4         NUM_BUCKETS BUCKETS,
  5         SAMPLE_SIZE SAMPLE
  6    FROM USER_TAB_COLUMNS
  7*   WHERE TABLE_NAME = UPPER('&TN');

Enter value for tn: stats

Column                       DIS       DEN    BUCKETS     SAMPLE
------------------------- -------- -------- ----------- ----------
SNO                        1000000  1.0E-06           6    1000000
SNAME
REGION_BTREE                     8  .083333           5    1000000
REGION_BIT_MAP
REGION_HASH                      8  .083333           4    1000000
SEX
TEMPERATURE                      4  .083333           3    1000000

8 rows selected.

SQL> SELECT NUM_ROWS,
  2         EMPTY_BLOCKS,
  3         AVG_ROW_LEN
  4   FROM   USER_TABLES
  5   WHERE  TABLE_NAME = 'STATS';

NUM_ROWS         EMPTY_BLOCKS  AVG_ROW_LEN
---------------  ------------  -----------
        1000000             0           47
```

ESTIMATE STATISTICS

Estimating statistics has some very outstanding advantages over the full-blown COMPUTE STATISTICS command. First of all, ESTIMATE is much, much faster than

COMPUTE—particularly on large tables. Second, the statistics are very close to the statistics of a **COMPUTE** command. In every case I have ever tested, **ESTIMATE** has been within one percent of predicting the number of rows in the table. More information is available for comparing these two methods of gathering statistics a little later in this chapter in the section "**COMPUTE** Versus **ESTIMATE** Elapsed Times And Accuracy." Listing 6.10 shows that the amount of time required for the **ESTIMATE STATISTICS** command on a one-million-row table is 31 seconds. With respect to accuracy, **ESTIMATE** guessed that the **STATS** table contains 997,928 rows, which means that Oracle is less than one percent off in estimating the number of rows in the table. Also, remember that maintaining this degree of accuracy requires only 31 seconds, as compared to 17 minutes using the **COMPUTE** option. However, the **USER_INDEXES** column **DISTINCT_KEYS** is a little inaccurate. For example, we know there are one-million **SNO**s and eight values in the columns **BTREE_REGION** and **BTREE_REGION_HASH**. In addition, the **ENDPOINT_NUMBER** column of **USER_HISTOGRAMS** contains either 0 or 1. This indicates that no histograms exist. The **BUCKETS** column of **USER_TAB_COLUMNS** contains a 1 for every column in the **STATS** table. This indicates that no histograms exist for any of the columns in the **STATS** table. Finally, **ESTIMATE STATISTICS** samples 1,064 rows. Listing 6.10 illustrates all this.

Listing 6.10 ESTIMATE STATISTICS.

```
SQL> ANALYZE TABLE STATS ESTIMATE STATISTICS;
Table analyzed.

Elapsed: 00:00:31.39

SQL> SELECT NUM_ROWS,
  2         EMPTY_BLOCKS,
  3         AVG_ROW_LEN
  4  FROM   USER_TABLES
  5* WHERE  TABLE_NAME = 'STATS';

NUM_ROWS  EMPTY_BLOCKS  AVG_ROW_LEN
--------  ------------  -----------
  997928             0           47

SQL> SELECT (1000000-997928)/1000000
  2  FROM   DUAL;
```

```
(1000000-997928)/1000000
------------------------
                 .002072

SQL> SELECT SUBSTR(INDEX_NAME,1,20) NAME,
  2         UNIQUENESS,
  3         DISTINCT_KEYS DIS,
  4         STATUS
  5   FROM  USER_INDEXES
  6*  WHERE TABLE_NAME = 'STATS';

NAME                                UNIQUENESS       DIS  STATUS
--------------------------------  ----------  --------  ------
BTREE_REGION                        NONUNIQUE          5  VALID
BTREE_REGION_HASH                   NONUNIQUE          6  VALID
BTREE_UNIQUE_SNO                    UNIQUE        999728  VALID
TEMP_INDX                           NONUNIQUE          4  VALID

SQL> SELECT COLUMN_NAME,
  2         ENDPOINT_NUMBER EPN,
  3         ENDPOINT_VALUE EPV
  4  FROM   USER_HISTOGRAMS
  5  WHERE  TABLE_NAME = 'STATS'
  6* ORDER  BY COLUMN_NAME, EPN;

COLUMN_NAME                 EPN        EPV
-------------------------- --- ---------
REGION_BIT_MAP                0    3.6E+35
                              1    4.5E+35

REGION_BTREE                  0    3.6E+35
                              1    4.5E+35

REGION_HASH                   0          1
                              1          8

SEX                           0    3.6E+35
                              1    4.0E+35

SNAME                         0    3.4E+35
                              1    3.7E+35

SNO                           0       3898
                              1     999364
```

```
SQL> SELECT SUBSTR(COLUMN_NAME,1,20) "Column",
  2         NUM_DISTINCT DIS,
  3         DENSITY DEN,
  4         NUM_BUCKETS BUCKETS,
  5         SAMPLE_SIZE SAMPLE
  6  FROM   USER_TAB_COLUMNS
  7* WHERE  TABLE_NAME = UPPER('&TN');

Enter value for tn: stats

Column                   DIS        DEN    BUCKETS     SAMPLE
-------------------- ------- ---------- ---------- ----------
SNO                   997928    1.0E-06          1       1064
SNAME                      5     .2              1       1064
REGION_BTREE               7     .142857         1       1064
REGION_BIT_MAP             6     .166667         1       1064
REGION_HASH                7     .142857         1       1064
SEX                        2     .5              1       1064
TEMPERATURE                0    1.0E-06          1       1064
```

Now let's estimate the statistics using a number of rows for Oracle to sample. Listing 6.11 samples nearly one-half of the **STATS** table. For the nearly 14 minutes that this requires, just computing the statistics would have worked better. Notice that the **DISTINCT_KEYS** column in **USER_INDEXES** shows 1,000,222 keys for the unique index on the **SNO** column, but there are actually 1,000,000. No histograms are created. That's the reason no query is shown against **USER_HISTOGRAMS**.

Listing 6.11 Estimating statistics using a sample number of rows.

```
SQL> ANALYZE TABLE STATS
             ESTIMATE STATISTICS
             SAMPLE 499999 ROWS;
Table analyzed.

Elapsed: 00:13:42.79

SQL> SELECT  NUM_ROWS,
  2          EMPTY_BLOCKS,
  3          AVG_ROW_LEN
  4  FROM    USER_TABLES
  5* WHERE   TABLE_NAME = 'STATS';

NUM_ROWS EMPTY_BLOCKS AVG_ROW_LEN
-------- ------------ -----------
 1000000            0          47
```

```
SQL> SELECT SUBSTR(INDEX_NAME,1,20) NAME,
  2         UNIQUENESS,
  3         DISTINCT_KEYS DIS,
  4         STATUS
  5  FROM   USER_INDEXES
  6* WHERE  TABLE_NAME = 'STATS';

NAME                             UNIQUENESS                 DIS  STATUS
------------------------------ ------------------ ---------- ---------
BTREE_REGION                     NONUNIQUE                    8  VALID
BTREE_REGION_HASH                NONUNIQUE                    8  VALID
BTREE_UNIQUE_SNO                 UNIQUE                 1000222  VALID
TEMP_INDX                        NONUNIQUE                    4  VALID

SQL> SELECT SUBSTR(COLUMN_NAME,1,20) "Column",
  2         NUM_DISTINCT DIS,
  3         DENSITY DEN,
  4         NUM_BUCKETS BUCKETS,
  5         SAMPLE_SIZE SAMPLE
  6  FROM   USER_TAB_COLUMNS
  7* WHERE  TABLE_NAME = UPPER('&TN');

Enter value for tn: stats

Column                         DIS        DEN        BUCKETS     SAMPLE
----------------------- --------- ---------- ------------ ---------
SNO                         1000000  1.0E-06              1     499948
SNAME                             5    .2                 1     499948
REGION_BTREE                      7    .142857            1     499948
REGION_BIT_MAP                    6    .166667            1     499948
REGION_HASH                       7    .142857            1     499948
SEX                               2    .5                 1     499948
TEMPERATURE                       4    .25                1     499948
```

In Listing 6.12, the **ESTIMATE** clause uses a sampling percentage as opposed to a sampling of rows. A little more than 5 minutes are required to analyze 10 percent of the table's rows via estimating. The estimated sampling calculated that 1,000,018 rows exist in the **STATS** table. That's a very accurate number considering that 10 percent (or 100,000 rows) of a one-million-row table is sampled. Moreover, only a little more than 5 minutes are required to execute the command, compared to 15 plus minutes to perform a **COMPUTE STATISTICS** on the entire table. The **DISTINCT_KEYS** column in **USER_INDEXES** shows 1,000,222 values, but only

1,000,000 actually exist. The **SAMPLE_SIZE** column in **USER_TAB_COLUMNS** indicates that Oracle actually sampled 96,460 rows instead of 100,000. Finally, the **DENSITY** column of **USER_TAB_COLUMNS** represents the mathematical probability of selecting any particular value from the column. For example, the **SEX** column contains two values: "M" for male and "F" for female. There are 500,000 males and 500,000 females. Therefore, the probability of picking an "F" is 500,000/1,000,000. This ratio is the same as .5. Density is not to be confused with selectivity. *Selectivity* is defined as the number of distinct values divided by the total number of rows in a table. Therefore, the selectivity of the **SEX** column is very, very low (2/1,000,000 = .000002). On the other hand, the selectivity of the **SNO** column is 1,000,000/1,000,000, which equals 1. The highest selectivity a column can have is 1. Also, the density of the **SNO** column is 1/1,000,000, which is .000001, or 1.0E-06.

Listing 6.12 An estimate using a sample percentage of rows.

```
SQL> ANALYZE TABLE STATS
             ESTIMATE STATISTICS
             SAMPLE 10 PERCENT;
Table analyzed.

Elapsed: 00:05:08.24

SQL> SELECT NUM_ROWS,
  2         EMPTY_BLOCKS,
  3         AVG_ROW_LEN
  4  FROM   USER_TABLES
  5* WHERE  TABLE_NAME = 'STATS';

NUM_ROWS EMPTY_BLOCKS  AVG_ROW_LEN
-------- ------------  -----------
 1000018            0           47

SQL> SELECT SUBSTR(INDEX_NAME,1,20) NAME,
  2         UNIQUENESS,
  3         DISTINCT_KEYS DIS,
  4         STATUS
  5  FROM   USER_INDEXES
  6* WHERE  TABLE_NAME = 'STATS';

NAME                           UNIQUENESS DIS       STATUS
------------------------------ ---------- -------   -------
BTREE_REGION                   NONUNIQUE        8   VALID
```

```
BTREE_REGION_HASH             NONUNIQUE        8  VALID
BTREE_UNIQUE_SNO              UNIQUE     1000222  VALID
TEMP_INDX                     NONUNIQUE        4  VALID

SQL> SELECT SUBSTR(COLUMN_NAME,1,20) "Column",
  2         NUM_DISTINCT DIS,
  3         DENSITY DEN,
  4         NUM_BUCKETS BUCKETS,
  5         SAMPLE_SIZE SAMPLE
  6  FROM   USER_TAB_COLUMNS
  7* WHERE  TABLE_NAME = UPPER('&TN');

Enter value for tn: stats

Column                     DIS      DEN       BUCKETS     SAMPLE
-------------------- --------- -------- ------------ ----------
SNO                    1000018  1.0E-06            1      96460
SNAME                        5   .2                1      96460
REGION_BTREE                 7   .142857           1      96460
REGION_BIT_MAP               6   .166667           1      96460
REGION_HASH                  7   .142857           1      96460
SEX                          2   .5                1      96460
TEMPERATURE                  4   .25               1      96460
```

DELETE STATISTICS

Deleting statistics from a table causes all entries in the data dictionary views—mentioned at the beginning of the chapter—to be removed. Consequently, unless you override your queries at the instance, session, or statement level, the rule-based optimizer is used after the statistics are deleted. Listing 6.13 is an example of removing statistics from the data dictionary for the STATS table.

Listing 6.13 Deleting statistics.

```
SQL> ANALYZE TABLE STATS DELETE STATISTICS;
Table analyzed.
```

LIST CHAINED ROWS

Under certain circumstances, rows can become chained from one Oracle block to another. If a row is chained, Oracle recommends that you correct this situation as quickly as possible. However, row spanning cannot usually be corrected. Row spanning occurs when a single row will not fit into an Oracle block. If a table has a column with a data type **LONG**, obviously 2 GB of data is never going to fit into one Oracle block. Typically, Oracle block sizes are 2K, 4K, 8K, 16K, or even 32K in size for data warehousing applications. Other terms linked with chained rows are row splitting, row spanning, and row migration. The major cause of chained rows is improper settings for the percent free space of an Oracle data block. The default value is 10 percent. This space is reserved for column updates when the data is actually longer than what is currently in the column. For example, if Paige Smith marries Nathan Perrygamos, then Oracle will place "Perrygamos" in the percent free space of the data block. Oracle does not expand the column containing Smith so that it is large enough to hold Perrygamos. Every column has a length indicator, followed by the data. If a column contains a null value, the length byte contains a zero, unless it is the last column of a table. Obviously, then, any column that contains a null, uses the percent free space of the data block when updated. If columns are regularly updated from null values to non-null values or if the data to be placed in a column is wider or longer than the data currently in the column, then the setting for the percent free space should be higher than the default value of 10 percent. If it is not set higher, you'll experience "chaining." This means that queries against the table containing chained rows will execute slower. Several methods exist for correcting this problem.

One method is to change the setting of percent free, export, drop, and import the table. Frequently, the area reserved for column expansion from updates, the percent free area, is not large enough. The default value for percent free is 10 percent. For a table that updates frequently by placing data values into null columns, the percent free area of the block fills up quickly. Future updates needing space in the percent free area of the current block, get chained to another block. This causes poor response time and performance when queries are written against the chained blocks. Another method is to create a temporary table, copy the chained rows to the temporary table, delete the chained rows from the original table, and then insert the rows back into the original table from the temporary table.

The method used to detect chained rows is shown in Listing 6.14. First, to determine the current setting of percent free, you write a query against **USER_TABLES**. Notice, the setting for percent free is the default value of 10. Then, the percent free value is deliberately set to 1 percent to cause row chaining after the next several commands. Then a new column, named **COMMENTS**, is added to the **EMP** table. This is a variable-length character column that allows up to 50 characters. The next step is absolutely absurd in the real world. I did it here to populate the table very easily and quickly. You would never insert rows into a table using this command. First of all, if you have a primary key constraint on the table, inserts from the table to itself would fail. However, for this demonstration, it is a quick, appropriate technique to illustrate row chaining. This **INSERT** statement is executed several times until there are 224 rows in the **EMP** table. Note that the table is not chained as of yet, because all 224 rows contain null values for the **COMMENTS** column.

The **UPDATE** statement of all 224 rows causes row chaining. Forty-nine characters are placed in each row of the **EMP** table in the **COMMENTS** column, which currently contains nulls. Therefore, the percent free space of the Oracle data block is used to store this new data. Obviously, there simply isn't enough room for 224 rows of 49 characters plus pointers to be placed in the percent free area. The Oracle block size for this database is 2K (or 2,048 bytes), so 1 percent of 2,048 is around 20 bytes. This means that every row of newly acquired blocks will be chained. Next, the table **CHAINED_ROWS** is created using the Oracle-supplied SQL script file utlchain.sql. Then, the **EMP** table is analyzed, inserting information into the table **CHAINED_ROWS** for every chained row in the **EMP** table. The next query indicates the number of chained rows. The last query joins the **EMP** table to the **CHAINED_ROWS** table to view the rows that are chained. **ROWNUM** is used to limit the output from 138 chained rows to 4.

Listing 6.14 Chained rows.

```
SQL> SELECT PCT_FREE
  2  FROM   USER_TABLES
  3* WHERE  TABLE_NAME = 'EMP';

PCT_FREE
--------
      10

SQL> ALTER TABLE EMP  --  Set Too Low Deliberately
           PCTFREE 1;
Table altered.

SQL> ALTER TABLE EMP
  2        ADD COMMENTS VARCHAR2(50);
Table altered.
```

```
SQL> INSERT INTO EMP SELECT * FROM EMP;
14 rows created.

SQL> /
28 rows created.

SQL> /
56 rows created.

SQL> /
112 rows created.

SQL> SELECT COUNT(*) FROM EMP;

COUNT(*)
--------
     224

SQL> UPDATE EMP
 2   SET COMMENTS =
 3   'THIS SHOULD CAUSE CHAINING SINCE THERE WERE NULLS';
224 rows updated.

SQL> @$ORACLE_HOME/rdbms/admin/utlchain
SQL> CREATE TABLE CHAINED_ROWS (
  2    owner_name        VARCHAR2(30),
  3    table_name        VARCHAR2(30),
  4    cluster_name      VARCHAR2(30),
  5    head_rowid        ROWID,
  6    timestamp         DATE
  7  );
Table created.

SQL> ANALYZE TABLE EMP
  2          LIST CHAINED ROWS
             INTO CHAINED_ROWS;
Table analyzed.

SQL> SELECT COUNT(*)
  2  FROM   CHAINED_ROWS;

COUNT(*)
--------
     138
```

```
SQL> SELECT EMPNO, ENAME
  2  FROM   EMP E,
  3         CHAINED_ROWS C      -- Only Want To See 4
  4  WHERE  E.ROWID = C.HEAD_ROWID AND
  5         ROWNUM < 5;

EMPNO   ENAME
------- ---------
   7369 SMITH
   7521 WARD
   7654 MARTIN
   7698 BLAKE
```

COMPUTE Versus ESTIMATE Elapsed Times And Accuracy

One of my customers had a 27-million-row table that required just 33 seconds to estimate the histograms using the parallel query option. After this, we wanted to see just how accurate **ESTIMATE** really was. Just minutes before, we fully analyzed (using **COMPUTE STATISTICS**) the 27-million-row table and found exactly 27,329,308 rows. When we executed the query again after estimating the statistics, Oracle returned 27,266,335 rows in the **NUM_ROWS** column. We were all very impressed and excited that Oracle's ability to estimate statistics on large tables was so accurate. The reason for this excitement was that **ESTIMATE STATISTICS** was much, much faster than **COMPUTE STATISTICS**. Also, the margin of error was less than a quarter of a percentage point. Listing 6.15 shows all this.

Listing 6.15 **COMPUTE** versus **ESTIMATE** accuracy.

```
SQL> SET TIMING ON
SQL> ANALYZE TABLE  T27MILLION
                    ESTIMATE STATISTICS
                    FOR COLUMNS
                    VALUE SIZE 100;
Elapsed:  00:00:33.71

SQL> SELECT DEGREE,
            NUM_ROWS,
            CACHE
     FROM   DBA_TABLES
     WHERE  OWNER = 'CLINT' AND
                          TABLE_NAME = 'T27MILLION';
```

```
DEGREE  NUM_ROWS    CACHE
------  ----------  -----
     3  27,329,308  N

SQL> SELECT 100 * ((27329308 - 27266335)/27329308) PCT_OFF
  2  FROM   DUAL;

PCT_OFF
-------
.230423
```

Listing 6.16 illustrates the quickness of **ESTIMATE** compared to **COMPUTE**. To analyze the one-million-row table with four or five indexes requires nearly 13 minutes, whereas **ESTIMATE STATISTICS** requires just under 39 seconds. **ESTIMATE STATISTICS** is 12 minutes and 47 seconds faster for a one-million-row table. Also, notice the degree of accuracy. **ESTIMATE** indicates that 997,928 rows exist in the **STATS** table—and we know that there are actually 1,000,000 rows. This results in an error of less than one-fifth of one percent! Therefore, don't believe it when people say you should use **COMPUTE** because it's more accurate.

Listing 6.16 COMPUTE and ESTIMATE times.

```
SQL> ANALYZE TABLE STATS COMPUTE STATISTICS;
Elapsed: 00:12:51.18

SQL> SELECT NUM_ROWS
  2  FROM   USER_TABLES
  3  WHERE  TABLE_NAME = 'STATS';

NUM_ROWS
--------
 1000000

SQL> ANALYZE TABLE STATS ESTIMATE STATISTICS;
Elapsed: 00:00:38.77

SQL> SELECT NUM_ROWS
  2  FROM   USER_TABLES
  3  WHERE  TABLE_NAME = 'STATS';

NUM_ROWS
--------
  997928
```

```
SQL> SELECT (1000000 - 997928)/1000000 PCT_OFF
     FROM   DUAL;

PCT_OFF
-------
.002072
```

Analyzing Clusters

Notice in Listing 6.17 that analyzing a cluster has several positive side effects. First of all, the index on the cluster is analyzed. Second, the tables in the cluster are also analyzed.

Listing 6.17 Analyzing clusters.

```
SQL> SELECT SUBSTR(TABLE_NAME,1,16) "Table Name",
            NUM_ROWS,  -- Clustered Tables Not Analyzed
            BLOCKS,
            AVG_ROW_LEN
       FROM USER_TABLES
      WHERE TABLE_NAME
            IN('PARTS_IN_CLUSTER','TESTS_IN_CLUSTER');

Table Name                           NUM_ROWS        BLOCKS  AVG_ROW_LEN
--------------------------    ----------------   ------------  -----------
PARTS_IN_CLUSTER
TESTS_IN_CLUSTER

SQL> SELECT INDEX_NAME,   -- Cluster Not Analyzed
            UNIQUENESS,
            PCT_FREE PFREE,
            DISTINCT_KEYS DIS,
            CLUSTERING_FACTOR CLUSFAC
     FROM   USER_INDEXES
     WHERE  INDEX_NAME = 'INDX_PARTS_AND_TESTS';

INDEX_NAME                    UNIQUENESS  PFREE   DIS  CLUSFAC
----------------------------- ---------- ------ ---- -------
INDX_PARTS_AND_TESTS          NONUNIQUE       10

SQL> ANALYZE CLUSTER PARTS_AND_TESTS
             COMPUTE STATISTICS;
```

```
Cluster analyzed.
Elapsed: 00:03:29.90

(Analyzing a cluster automatically analyzes the cluster index)
SQL> SELECT TABLE_NAME,
  2         LEAF_BLOCKS,
  3         DISTINCT_KEYS DKEYS,
  4         AVG_LEAF_BLOCKS_PER_KEY ALBPK,
  5         AVG_DATA_BLOCKS_PER_KEY ADBPK,
  6         CLUSTERING_FACTOR CLUSFAC
  7  FROM   USER_INDEXES
  8  WHERE  INDEX_NAME = 'INDX_PARTS_AND_TESTS';

TABLE_NAME       LEAF_BLOCKS DKEYS ALBPK ADBPK CLUSFAC
---------------- ----------- ----- ----- ----- -------
PARTS_AND_TESTS           86 10000     1     0    5042

SQL> SELECT SUBSTR(TABLE_NAME,1,16) "Table Name",
  2         NUM_ROWS,
  3         BLOCKS,
  4         AVG_ROW_LEN,
  5  FROM   USER_TABLES
  6* WHERE  TABLE_NAME
                IN('PARTS_IN_CLUSTER','TESTS_IN_CLUSTER');

Table Name                      NUM_ROWS    BLOCKS  AVG_ROW_LEN
------------------------------ ---------    ------  -----------
PARTS_IN_CLUSTER                   10000      6879           47
TESTS_IN_CLUSTER                  470692      6879           32
```

Analyzing Indexes

First of all, analyzing indexes does *not* cause the cost-based optimizer to be invoked. You must analyze a table, which automatically analyzes the indexes, to cause Oracle to use the cost-based optimizer. Or, set the parameter **OPTIMIZER_MODE** to either **ALL_ROWS** or **FIRST_ROWS** to cause Oracle to use the cost-based optimizer. Or, use the **ALTER SESSION** command or the hints **ALL_ROWS** or **FIRST_ROWS** to invoke the cost-based optimizer.

VALIDATE STRUCTURE

Although many methods are available, here are two ways to determine the amount of disk space consumed by the index. Two very special tables are populated as a result of the **VALIDATE INDEX** and **ANALYZE** commands using the **VALIDATE STRUCTURE** syntax. The tables populated by **VALIDATE** are **INDEX_STATS** and **INDEX_HISTOGRAMS**. If you receive an error message after validating an index on a table, you can drop and re-create the index. You can also use **INDEX_HISTOGRAMS** to determine if your indexes are fragmented. Listing 6.18 shows both methods of validating indexes on a table as well as a query written against the **INDEX_STATS** table.

Listing 6.18 Validating index structure.

```
SQL> VALIDATE INDEX BTREE_REGION;   Version 6 Method
Elapsed: 00:01:17.11

SQL> ANALYZE INDEX BTREE_REGION
             VALIDATE STRUCTURE;   Version 7 Method
Elapsed: 00:00:49.84

SQL> SELECT NAME,
  2         PCT_USED,
  3         BLOCKS BLKS,
  4         MOST_REPEATED_KEY MOST,
  5         DISTINCT_KEYS DIS
  6* FROM  INDEX_STATS;

NAME                         PCT_USED      BLKS       MOST   DIS
---------------------- -------------- -------- ---------- ----
BTREE_REGION                       89      9220     495000     8
```

Histograms

The distribution of data on a btree indexed column is very important. If the data is badly skewed on the indexed column, Oracle might not use an index when it should. Consider the example of a one-million-row table named **OIL_WELLS** with a column named **STATE** that contains either TX or OK. Only one oil well is in Oklahoma, whereas 999,999 oil wells are in Texas. Listing 6.19 shows the easiest method for quickly determining the distribution of data on the indexed column. Please understand that you would never place a btree index on a column with just two distinct values. The selectivity is 2/1,000,000. Btree indexes work best with high selectivity (cardinality). However, if the CEO's administrative assistant complains loudly enough concerning the length of time required to return the oil well in Oklahoma, you would probably try placing a btree index on the **STATE** column to preserve your position.

Listing 6.19 Distribution of data on an indexed column.

```
SQL> SELECT STATE,
             COUNT(*)
     FROM   OIL_WELLS
     GROUP  BY STATE;

STATE       COUNT(*)
--------    --------
TX            999999
OK                 1
```

If the table has been analyzed without using histograms, Oracle makes an incorrect assumption. Oracle assumes that there are 500,000 oil wells in Texas and 500,000 oil wells in Oklahoma. This is a fairly logical assumption because there are 1,000,000 rows and only two values. Nevertheless, Oracle performs a full table scan when retrieving oil wells from either Texas or Oklahoma. To correct this problem, use histograms.

Oracle uses height-balanced histograms as opposed to width-balanced histograms. Each bucket of the height-balanced histogram contains the same number of elements. The purpose of a histogram is to produce a clearer picture of the distribution of data on the indexed column and to reduce or eliminate full table scans when an index would be more efficient. Listing 6.20 creates histograms for the **STATS** table. Here, "8" represents the number of buckets for the histogram. The default number of buckets is 75, and the maximum is 256. The number of buckets might change the performance of certain SQL statements, so you'll want to experiment. You can't have too many buckets.

Listing 6.20 Creating histograms.

```
SQL> ANALYZE TABLE STATS
             COMPUTE STATISTICS
             FOR COLUMNS
             REGION_BTREE SIZE 8;
Elapsed: 00:04:49.56
```

In Oracle8, the data dictionary views pertaining to histograms are **USER_HISTOGRAMS**, **ALL_HISTOGRAMS**, and **DBA_HISTOGRAMS**. In Listing

6.21, information about the histograms is shown. Notice that there are only two buckets for all the columns except the **REGION_BTREE** column, which we just analyzed. For character and date columns, the endpoint values include E+35, or some other combination of numbers other than 35. However, with the **SNO** column, which is numeric, the endpoint value of bucket zero is 1, and the endpoint value of bucket one is 1,000,000. Even though eight intervals (or buckets) are requested on the **REGION_BTREE** column, Oracle uses only six. Nevertheless, Oracle will now make a better choice whether to use an index, because it has a clearer view of how the data is distributed on the column. This prevents full table scans where there are few values on the indexed column(s) and the percentage for each value is totally skewed. The **REGION_BTREE** column contains eight values, but one of those values occurs only once.

Listing 6.21 USER_HISTOGRAMS.

```
SQL> get p9
  1  BREAK  ON "Column" SKIP 1
  2  SELECT SUBSTR(COLUMN_NAME,1,15) "Column",
  3         ENDPOINT_NUMBER EPN,
  4         ENDPOINT_VALUE EPV
  5  FROM   USER_HISTOGRAMS
  6  WHERE  TABLE_NAME = 'STATS'
  7  ORDER  BY "Column", EPN;
  8* CLEAR  BREAKS
SQL> @p9

Column                                   EPN         EPV
-------------------------- ------------- -----------
REGION_BIT_MAP                             0  3.5827E+35
                                           1  4.5173E+35
REGION_BTREE                               1  3.5827E+35
                                           2  4.0640E+35
                                           3  4.0676E+35
                                           4  4.3096E+35
                                           7  4.3273E+35
                                           8  4.5173E+35
REGION_HASH                                0           1
                                           1           8
GENDER                                     0  3.6346E+35
                                           1  3.9981E+35
SNAME                                      0  3.4410E+35
                                           1  3.7032E+35
```

```
SNO                                        0          1
                                           1    1000000
16 rows selected.
```

At a site of one of my customers, the output resembled this (not showing all buckets):

```
Column       ENDPOINT_NUMBER  ENDPOINT_VALUE
----------   ---------------  --------------
VALUE                     70             .18
                          71           .2052
                          72           .2232
                          73           .2520
                          74           .2736
                          75           .3096
                          76           .3384
```

From this output, you can see that all numbers greater than .2736 and less than or equal to .3096 fall into bucket 75, whereas all numbers greater than .3096 and less than or equal to .3384 land in bucket 76. This continues up to bucket 100.

Listing 6.22 shows how to cause Oracle to construct a histogram on the **REGION_HASH** column with eight buckets and to compute the statistics for the table. Oracle places the same number of elements in each of the eight buckets of the histogram for the **REGION_HASH** column. Because the **STATS** table contains 1,000,000 rows, each bucket contains 125,000 values. Notice that Oracle derives only six endpoints, but eight were requested. The data is "skewed" on the value 5, because 5 occurs 495,000 times. The **FOR COLUMNS** clause causes Oracle to construct histograms as in listing 6.22.

Listing 6.22 FOR COLUMNS.

```
SQL> ANALYZE TABLE STATS
  2          COMPUTE STATISTICS
  3          OR TABLE  -- Calculate Statistics For The Table
  4          FOR COLUMNS
  5          REGION_HASH SIZE 8;
Elapsed: 00:04:52.85

SQL> COL TABLE_NAME   FORMAT  A10
SQL> COL COLUMN_NAME  FORMAT  A20
SQL> SELECT TABLE_NAME,
            COLUMN_NAME,
```

```
          ENDPOINT_NUMBER EPN,
          ENDPOINT_VALUE EPV
    FROM  USER_HISTOGRAMS
    WHERE COLUMN_NAME = 'REGION_HASH'
    ORDER BY ENDPOINT_VALUE;

TABLE_NAME             COLUMN_NAME                 EPN       EPV
--------------------   ------------------------    --------  ------
STATS                  REGION_HASH                 1         1
STATS                  REGION_HASH                 2         2
STATS                  REGION_HASH                 3         4
STATS                  REGION_HASH                 6         5
STATS                  REGION_HASH                 7         7
STATS                  REGION_HASH                 8         8
```

Listing 6.23 shows another method to determine the distribution of data on the **REGION_HASH** column. This is much easier than analyzing and writing a query. But, the more methods you have to choose from, the more productive you become.

Listing 6.23 Distribution of data using **GROUP BY**.

```
SQL> SELECT REGION_HASH, COUNT(*)
  2         FROM   STATS
  3  GROUP  BY REGION_HASH;

REGION_HASH      COUNT(*)
-----------   -----------
          1        125000
          2        125000
          3             1
          4        125000
          5        495000
          6          4000
          7          1000
          8        124999

Elapsed: 00:03:17.93
```

By using the distribution of data, we can conclude the following:

- Bucket 1 starts with 1, contains 125,000 ones, and has an endpoint of 1.
- Bucket 2 starts with 2, contains 125,000 twos, and has an endpoint of 2.

- Bucket 3 starts with 3, contains 1 three and 124,999 fours, and has an endpoint of 4.
- Bucket 4 starts with 4, contains 1 four and 124,999 fives, and has an endpoint of 5.
- Bucket 5 starts with 5, contains 125,000 fives, and has an endpoint of 5.
- Bucket 6 starts with 5, contains 125,000 fives, and has an endpoint of 5.
- Bucket 7 starts with 5, contains 120,001 fives, 4,000 sixes, and 999 sevens, and has an endpoint of 7.
- Bucket 8 starts with 7, contains 1 seven and 124,999 eights, and an endpoint of 8.
- Buckets 4, 5, and 6 have endpoints of 5. Because bucket 7 consists mainly of fives (120,001), Oracle combines buckets 4, 5, 6, and 7 into one bucket. It appears that Oracle only needs five buckets (buckets 1, 2, 3, 4 [4, 5, 6, 7 combined], 5 [8]). Listing 6.24 suggests that this is the case.

Listing 6.24 Determining the actual number of buckets.

```
SQL> SELECT COLUMN_NAME, NUM_BUCKETS
  2  FROM   USER_TAB_COLUMNS
  3  WHERE  TABLE_NAME  = 'STATS' AND
  4*        COLUMN_NAME = 'REGION_HASH';

COLUMN_NAME                  NUM_BUCKETS
------------------------     -----------
REGION_HASH                            5
```

Listing 6.25 uses a query on **USER_HISTOGRAMS** that indicates the number of endpoints and their endpoint values.

Listing 6.25 The number of endpoints and their values.

```
SQL> SELECT COLUMN_NAME,
  2         ENDPOINT_NUMBER EPN,
  3         ENDPOINT_VALUE EPV
  4  FROM   USER_HISTOGRAMS
  5  WHERE  TABLE_NAME  = 'STATS' AND
  6         COLUMN_NAME = 'REGION_HASH'
  7  ORDER  BY EPV;
```

```
COLUMN_NAME                     EPN         EPV
------------------------  ---------- ------------
REGION_HASH                       1            1
REGION_HASH                       2            2
REGION_HASH                       3            4
REGION_HASH                       6            5
REGION_HASH                       7            7
REGION_HASH                       8            8
6 rows selected.
```

If all of the endpoints are unique, try reanalyzing with more columns. Eight buckets seems like a good choice for the **REGION_HASH** column.

As you can see from Listing 6.26 and the Explain Plan, Oracle makes the correct decision using histograms—it uses the btree index to retrieve one row. What a difference a histogram makes!

Listing 6.26 Oracle uses histograms to make better decisions.

```
SQL> EXPLAIN PLAN FOR
  2  SELECT  *              -- One Row In Active Set
  3  FROM    STATS
  4* WHERE   REGION_BTREE = 'SE';

SQL> @explain
Query Plan                                                    COST
--------------------------------------------------------------  -----
SELECT STATEMENT   CHOOSE                                     2,144
  TABLE ACCESS BY ROWID STATS ANALYZED                        2,144
    INDEX RANGE SCAN BTREE_REGION ANALYZED

SQL> SELECT REGION_BTREE  -- One Row In Active Set
  2  FROM   STATS
  3  WHERE  REGION_BTREE = 'SE';

REGION_BTREE
------------
SE

Elapsed: 00:00:01.02
```

Because there are eight distinct values in the **REGION_BTREE** column, Oracle incorrectly assumes that each value occurs 12.5 percent in 1,000,000 rows (that is,

125,000 occurrences for each value of the **REGION_BTREE** column). Because this assumption is obviously not true, Oracle performs a full table scan, as indicated in Listing 6.27. That's why Oracle7.3 uses histograms to eliminate this problem. Let's actually execute the query. Remember that only one row from a one-million-row table is being retrieved. One second compared to 2 minutes and 54 seconds is quite a difference. Nearly 3 minutes are required to return one row.

Listing 6.27 Oracle makes a bad assumption.

```
SQL> EXPLAIN PLAN FOR
  2  SELECT  *              -- One Row In Active Set
  3  FROM    STATS
  4* WHERE   REGION_BTREE = 'SE';

SQL> @explain
Query Plan                                                  COST
----------------------------------------------------------- -----
SELECT STATEMENT   CHOOSE                                   3,958
  TABLE ACCESS FULL STATS ANALYZED                          3,958

SQL> SELECT   *
  2  FROM     STATS
  3* WHERE    REGION_BTREE = 'SE';

       SNO SNAME                    REG    REG    REGION_HASH S
---------- ------------------------ ------ ------ ----------- --
    375000 BETWEEN 300001 AND 600000 SE    SE               3 M
Elapsed: 00:02:54.55
```

Analyzing All Tables In A Schema

Using SQL to generate SQL, you can produce a SQL script file that analyzes all tables in a particular schema. Listing 6.28 estimates statistics on all tables in the schema OPS$PCASSIDY.

Listing 6.28 Analyzing all tables in a schema.

```
SET ECHO     OFF
SET HEADING  OFF
SET FEEDBACK OFF
SET PAUSE    OFF
SET TIMING   OFF
```

```
SPOOL        estimate.sql
Select 'ANALYZE TABLE ' || table_name || ' ESTIMATE STATISTICS;'
From    user_tables
Order   By table_name;
SPOOL        OFF
SET HEADING  ON
SET FEEDBACK ON
SET ECHO     ON
START estimate

SQL> start cor6s2s

SQL> set timing off
SQL> set pause off
SQL> set echo off
ANALYZE TABLE DEPT ESTIMATE STATISTICS;
ANALYZE TABLE DON_AND_DAFFY ESTIMATE STATISTICS;
ANALYZE TABLE EMP ESTIMATE STATISTICS;
ANALYZE TABLE PARTS ESTIMATE STATISTICS;
ANALYZE TABLE PARTS_IN_CLUSTER ESTIMATE STATISTICS;
ANALYZE TABLE STATS ESTIMATE STATISTICS;
ANALYZE TABLE STATS2 ESTIMATE STATISTICS;
ANALYZE TABLE TESTS ESTIMATE STATISTICS;
ANALYZE TABLE TESTS_IN_CLUSTER ESTIMATE STATISTICS;

SQL> start estimate

SQL> ANALYZE TABLE DEPT ESTIMATE STATISTICS;
Table analyzed.

SQL> ANALYZE TABLE DON_AND_DAFFY ESTIMATE STATISTICS;
Table analyzed.

SQL> ANALYZE TABLE EMP ESTIMATE STATISTICS;
Table analyzed.

SQL> ANALYZE TABLE PARTS ESTIMATE STATISTICS;
Table analyzed.

SQL> ANALYZE TABLE PARTS_IN_CLUSTER ESTIMATE STATISTICS;
Table analyzed.

SQL> ANALYZE TABLE STATS ESTIMATE STATISTICS;
Table analyzed.
```

```
SQL> ANALYZE TABLE STATS2 ESTIMATE STATISTICS;
Table analyzed.

SQL> ANALYZE TABLE TESTS ESTIMATE STATISTICS;
Table analyzed.

SQL> ANALYZE TABLE TESTS_IN_CLUSTER ESTIMATE STATISTICS;
Table analyzed.
```

Analyzing Objects In A Schema

Using Oracle's package **DBMS_UTILITY**, you can analyze objects in a particular account using the procedure **ANALYZE_SCHEMA**. In Listing 6.29, the first query shows the names of the procedures, assuming that the procedure names are lowercase. If you need more detailed information on the number and data types of arguments that a procedure or function in a package is expecting, use the **DESCRIBE** command. The output from the **DESCRIBE** command indicates that two **VARCHAR2** input arguments are expected. You can specify up to five input arguments to the procedure **ANALYZE_SCHEMA** in the package **DBMS_UTILITY**. Next, to analyze all tables, indexes, and clusters in the schema **OPS$PCASSIDY**, the **ANALYZE_SCHEMA** procedure in the package **DBMS_UTILITY** is executed. This example uses **ESTIMATE**. You can also use either **COMPUTE** or **DELETE**. The last query in Listing 6.29 strips out all comments from the package **DBMS_UTILITY**. This is a very useful query in determining what the package and its components are actually performing. Not all of the output from the last query has been included in Listing 6.29 because there could be several hundred lines of output.

Listing 6.29 DBMS_UTILITY procedures.

```
SQL> SELECT  SUBSTR(TEXT,1,75) CODE
  2  FROM    DBA_SOURCE
  3  WHERE   NAME = UPPER('&DBMS') AND
  4          TEXT NOT LIKE '%--%' AND
  5*         TEXT LIKE '%procedure%';

Enter value for dbms: dbms_utility
```

```
CODE
------------------------------------------------------------------
procedure compile_schema(schema varchar2);
procedure analyze_schema(schema varchar2, method
procedure analyze_database(method varchar2,
procedure name_resolve(name in varchar2, context in
procedure name_tokenize(name in varchar2,

SQL> DESCRIBE DBMS_UTILITY.ANALYZE_SCHEMA
PROCEDURE DBMS_UTILITY.ANALYZE_SCHEMA
Argument Name                  Type              In/Out  Default?
------------------------------ ----------------- ------  --------
SCHEMA                         VARCHAR2          IN
METHOD                         VARCHAR2          IN
ESTIMATE_ROWS                  NUMBER            IN      DEFAULT
ESTIMATE_PERCENT               NUMBER            IN      DEFAULT
METHOD_OPT                     VARCHAR2          IN      DEFAULT

SQL> EXECUTE DBMS_UTILITY.ANALYZE_SCHEMA
             ('OPS$PCASSIDY','ESTIMATE')
PL/SQL procedure successfully completed.
Elapsed: 00:01:43.85

SQL> SELECT  SUBSTR(TEXT,1,75) CODE
  2  FROM    DBA_SOURCE
  3  WHERE   NAME = UPPER('&DBMS') AND
  4          TEXT  LIKE '%--%'
  5* ORDER   BY LINE;

Enter value for dbms: dbms_utility

CODE
------------------------------------------------------------------
  --  OVERVIEW
  --
  --  This package provides various utility routines.
  ----------------------------
  --  PL/SQL TABLES
  --
  --  Lists of "USER"."NAME"."COLUMN"@LINK should be stored here
  --  Lists of NAME should be stored here
  --  Lists of database links should be stored here
  ----------------------------
 PROCEDURES AND FUNCTIONS
```

Summary

If you're using Oracle's cost-based optimizer, volatile or dynamic tables should be analyzed frequently, maybe even daily. However, large tables can require a large amount of time if the **COMPUTE** clause is used. **ESTIMATE STATISTICS** used on large tables is very accurate, and it is certainly much, much faster than a full-blown **COMPUTE**. Remember that when a table is analyzed, all the indexes on the table are also analyzed. Use histograms on indexed columns that contain skewed data to minimize full table scans. To analyze all tables in a particular schema, you can use SQL to generate SQL. Or, if you need to analyze all objects in an Oracle account, you can use the package **DBMS_UTILITY**.

Explain Plan

HIGH PERFORMANCE

CHAPTER 7

*The purpose of Explain Plan is to help you write faster-executing SQL statements by clearly showing you how the Oracle optimizer executes SQL statements. You'll learn how to create the table **PLAN_TABLE**, how to execute Explain Plan, how to write queries against **PLAN_TABLE**, and how to interpret the output of queries against **PLAN_TABLE**.*

Explain Plan

What Is Explain Plan?

Explain Plan is an application performance-tuning tool used by developers, database administrators, and some end users. The purpose of this tool is to indicate the steps in the plan tree for a particular SQL statement. The statement is not executed, but Oracle does formulate a plan tree for the statement based on the contents of the data dictionary. For each step, a row is inserted into the table **PLAN_TABLE**. After the SQL statement has been explained, you write a query against **PLAN_TABLE**, interpret the results, and then take corrective action.

Information stored in the **PLAN_TABLE** includes the optimizer, the mode, the table access method, the driving table, and the estimated cost to execute the statement being explained. The estimated cost is based on three areas. The first area is the estimated amount of CPU. The second is the estimated I/O (input/output) required. The third is the estimated amount of memory. If you combine the first letters of Memory, I/O, and CPU, you end up with "MIC," which reminds me of a very popular mouse.

To use Explain Plan, you must have a table in which to place the steps of the plan. You can manually create your own table using the **CREATE TABLE** command, or you can execute the SQL script file utlxplan.sql, provided by Oracle Corporation. On most Unix platforms, this file can be found in $ORACLE_HOME/rdbms/admin, and on NT platforms, the file is in C:\ORANT\RDBMS\73\ADMIN. Once you have a table to contain the steps of the plan tree, you are ready to use this tuning tool.

To use Explain Plan, simply place the string **EXPLAIN PLAN FOR** in front of the SQL statement, then execute. Several extensions to this command exist and are illustrated later in this chapter in the "Explain Plan Syntax" section. After you execute the plan, you are ready to write a query against the table containing the steps of the plan.

You can write a simple query, or you can write a recursive query using **CONNECT BY** and **START WITH** against the table containing the steps of the plan tree. Most of the time, this is the table **PLAN_TABLE**. Both queries are illustrated in this chapter.

The last step is to interpret the results of the query against the table **PLAN_TABLE**. Maybe a full table scan is performed because an index was dropped and never re-created. Maybe the indexed column needs a histogram for the cost-based optimizer to make a better decision. Or, maybe Oracle doesn't choose the best table as the driving table. If the number of steps is somewhat overwhelming, or the problem is not easily recognizable, then consider using SQL Trace and TKPROF, which are discussed in Chapter 8. Figure 7.1 shows the steps to use Explain Plan. You only need to execute utLxplan.sql once.

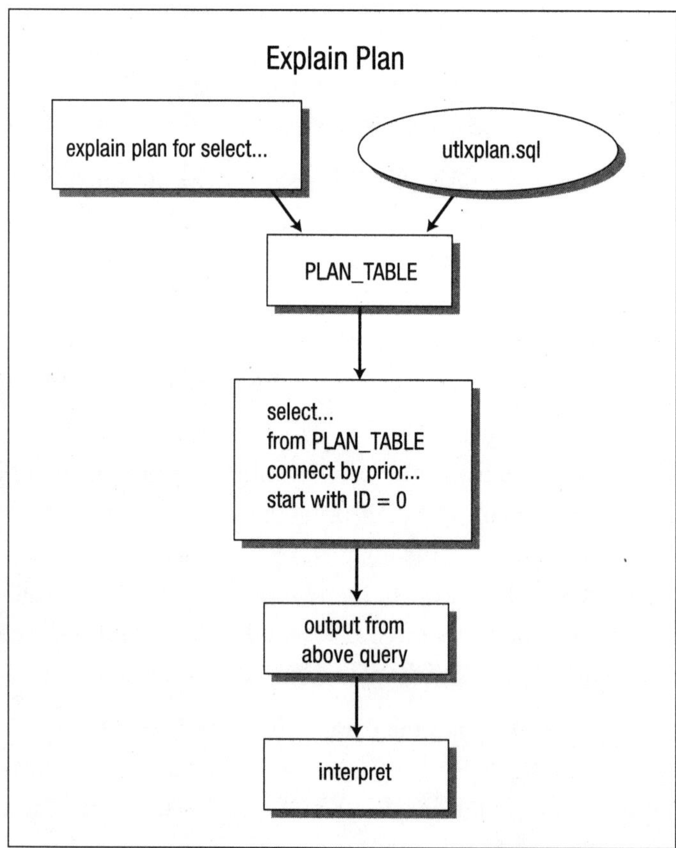

Figure 7.1
Using Explain Plan.

Checking On Indexes

Before using Explain Plan on a slow-running query, consider writing a query against **USER_INDEXES** or **USER_IND_COLUMNS**. Both of these data dictionary views store information about indexes. Perhaps an index does not exist on a column referenced in the **WHERE** clause of the slow-executing query. You can easily identify this using either one of these views in a query. Listing 7.1 shows a query you can use to identify what indexes exist for a particular table. If the name of the index contains the column name the index is on, this query works just fine. Notice that all indexes have been analyzed. If they were not analyzed, the **DISTINCT_KEYS** column would contain nulls. Also, notice that the names of the indexes include the column names. If the length of the column name is 30 characters, this is impossible. For example, if a column name **LARRY_CURLY_AND_MORBID** on the **COMEDIANS** table needs an index, you cannot create the index name with the name of the table and the column name combined. The table name, **COMEDIANS**, contains 9 characters. And, the column name, **LARRY_CURLY_AND_MORBID**, contains 22 characters. The maximum length of any type of object in Oracle is 30 characters. Because the sum of 22 and 9 is 31, the **CREATE INDEX** command fails. Listing 7.1 also includes another query against **USER_IND_COLUMNS**. This is an even better query, particularly if the btree indexes are concatenated. Of particular importance is the first column of the concatenated index. If the first column is not referenced in the **WHERE** clause, the index cannot be used. Two concatenated indexes were created on the **EMP** table. Notice that the **JOB** or **SAL** columns must be referenced in the **WHERE** clause in order for Oracle to consider using either one of the two concatenated btree indexes on the **EMP** table.

Listing 7.1 USER_INDEXES and USER_IND_COLUMNS.

```
SQL> SELECT  SUBSTR(INDEX_NAME,1,20) "Name",
  2          UNIQUENESS,
  3          DISTINCT_KEYS DIS
  4   FROM    USER_INDEXES
  5   WHERE   TABLE_NAME = UPPER('&Table_Name');
Enter value for table_name: STATS

Name                       UNIQUENES            DIS
------------------------   -------------   --------
BTREE_REGION               NONUNIQUE              8
BTREE_REGION_HASH          NONUNIQUE              8
```

```
BTREE_UNIQUE_SNO                UNIQUE            1000222
TEMP_INDX                       NONUNIQUE               4

SQL> CREATE INDEX JOB_SAL_COMM
  2*        ON EMP(JOB, SAL, COMM);
Index created.

SQL> CREATE INDEX SAL_COMM_HIREDATE
  2         ON EMP(SAL, COMM, HIREDATE);
Index created.

SQL> get con_emp
  1  BREAK  ON NAME SKIP 1
  2  SELECT SUBSTR(INDEX_NAME,1,25) NAME,
  3  COLUMN_POSITION "POSITION",
  4         SUBSTR(COLUMN_NAME,1,25) COL_NAME
  5  FROM   USER_IND_COLUMNS
  6  WHERE  TABLE_NAME = 'EMP'
  7  ORDER  BY NAME, "POSITION";
  8* CLEAR  BREAKS

SQL> @con_emp

NAME                  POSITION   COL_NAME
-------------------   --------   ---------
JOB_SAL_COMM                 1   JOB
                             2   SAL
                             3   COMM

SAL_COMM_HIREDATE            1   SAL
                             2   COMM
                             3   HIREDATE
```

Creating The Table PLAN_TABLE

To use Explain Plan, you must have a table in which to store the steps of the plan tree for explained SQL statements. You can create your own using the **CREATE TABLE** command, or you can execute the SQL script file utlxplan.sql (provided by Oracle). Normally, you'll execute utlxplan. Listing 7.2 shows this process.

Listing 7.2 Creating **PLAN_TABLE**.

```
SQL> @$ORACLE_HOME/rdbms/admin/utlxplan
Table created.
```

```
SQL> list
  1  create table       PLAN_TABLE (
  2     statement_id       varchar2(30),
  3     timestamp          date,
  4     remarks            varchar2(80),
  5     operation          varchar2(30),
  6     options            varchar2(30),
  7     object_node        varchar2(128),
  8     object_owner       varchar2(30),
  9     object_name        varchar2(30),
 10     object_instance    numeric,
 11     object_type        varchar2(30),
 12     optimizer          varchar2(255),
 13     search_columns     numeric,
 14     id                 numeric,
 15     parent_id          numeric,
 16     position           numeric,
 17     cost               numeric,
 18     cardinality        numeric,
 19     bytes              numeric,
 20     other_tag          varchar2(255),
 21*    other              long)
```

Explain Plan Syntax

The basic syntax of the Explain Plan command is very simple. However, you might want to use the **SET STATEMENT_ID** clause if you're storing the plans of several SQL statements. The **INTO schema.TABLE@dblink** clause is also optional. If you're not using the table **PLAN_TABLE**, then you want to use this clause. Oracle assumes that the schema is the same as the connected session. If this is not the case, you want to include the schema where the table to hold the plan is located. For instance, if the table name is **MY_PLAN_TABLE** and it exists in the **SCOTT** schema, the **INTO** clause would be **INTO SCOTT.MY_PLAN_TABLE**. Furthermore, if **MY_PLAN_TABLE** is located on another node of the network, a database link exists, and you're running Oracle using the distributed option, then the **INTO** clause would be **INTO SCOTT.MY_PLAN_TABLE@maui**. Listing 7.3 contains examples using all the clauses.

Listing 7.3 Executing the Explain Plan.

```
SQL> EXPLAIN PLAN FOR   -- The Most Used And Practical
             SELECT  *
```

```
            FROM    ISLANDS
            WHERE   INAME = 'MAUI';

SQL> EXPLAIN PLAN  -- To Save Plans Use STATEMENT_ID
            SET STATEMENT_ID = 'HERE TODAY'
            FOR
            SELECT  *
            FROM    ISLANDS
            WHERE   INAME = 'OAHU';

SQL> EXPLAIN PLAN
            SET STATEMENT_ID = 'GONE TO MAUI'
            INTO MY_PLAN_TABLE    --  Not PLAN_TABLE
            FOR
            SELECT  *
            FROM    ISLANDS
            WHERE   INAME = 'KAUAI';

SQL> EXPLAIN PLAN
            SET STATEMENT_ID = 'ALOHA'
            INTO SCOTT.MY_PLAN_TABLE
            FOR    --  Not My Schema, But In Scott's
            SELECT *
            FROM   ISLANDS
            WHERE  INAME = 'KAUAI';

SQL> EXPLAIN PLAN
            SET STATEMENT_ID = 'MAHALO'
            INTO SCOTT.MY_PLAN_TABLE@HKAUAI
            FOR       -- And It Is Not My Schema, But In Scott's
            SELECT  *  -- And It Is On Another Machine With
            FROM    ISLANDS  -- A Database Link Name Of HAWAII
            WHERE   INAME = 'KAUAI';
```

Simple Query Against PLAN_TABLE

After you have explained a SQL statement, you must write a query against the table containing the steps in the plan tree for the statement. From now on, we'll assume the table is named **PLAN_TABLE**. You have your choice as to the type of statement you'll write. You can either write a simple query, as shown in Listing 7.4, or you can write a much more sophisticated recursive query. Let's use the simple, nonrecursive query first. This query, if actually executed, returns two rows from the **PARTS** table, which contains 10,000 rows. Obviously, it would be faster and more efficient for

Oracle to retrieve the two rows using the unique btree index on the **PNO** column of the **PARTS** table. The **OPERATION** column contains **INDEX**, indicating that the index will be used twice in this query—once for each of the two rows. The **OPTIONS** column contains **BY ROWID**, indicating that the address of the index (rowid) will be used to retrieve each of the two rows. As mentioned earlier, retrieving a row by its rowid is the fastest possible retrieval method. **CONCATENATION** in the **OPERATION** column suggests that Oracle will transform the original statement into two separate statements using the **UNION** set operator to retrieve the two rows. The transformation is made so that the index on the **PNO** column can be used twice. Here's the transformed statement:

```
SELECT * FROM PARTS WHERE PNO = 1
UNION
SELECT * FROM PARTS WHERE PNO = 10000;
```

Because both **WHERE** clauses contain references to the **PNO** column and no functions are applied to the **PNO** column in the **WHERE** clauses, Oracle might decide to use the index. Because the **OPTIMIZER** column contains **ANALYZED** for the **PARTS** table, the cost-based optimizer will be used. Another indication that the cost-based optimizer will be used for this query is the presence of non-null values in the **COST** column. The total estimated cost of this statement is 6. Because the data dictionary has been populated with statistics and Oracle knows the **PNO** column in the **PARTS** table contains 10,000 distinct values, the unique index on the **PNO** column will be used. Also note that the **OPTIMIZER** column contains **CHOOSE**. As previously explained, four possible values for the optimizer mode or optimizer goal exist. Remember Fric and Frac? The four values are **FIRST_ROWS**, **RULE**, **ALL_ROWS**, and **CHOOSE**.

Figure 7.2 shows another method of viewing the steps of the plan. Label each step of the plan with the ID number, and note the number in the **PARENT_ID** column. The **PARENT_ID** column contains the ID number that the step feeds into. For example, ID 3 contains a **PARENT_ID** of 2. In other words, ID 3 feeds into ID 2. Finally, notice that the primary key column of the **PLAN_TABLE** table is **ID** and the foreign key column is **PARENT_ID**. What's so unusual about the **PARENT_ID** column is that it references the values in the **ID** column in the same table. When a foreign key column like **PARENT_ID** references the values in the primary key column like ID and both volumns are in the same table, the table (**PLAN_TABLE**) is referred to as a *recursive table*. Oracle's **EMP** table is also recursive. The **EMPNO**

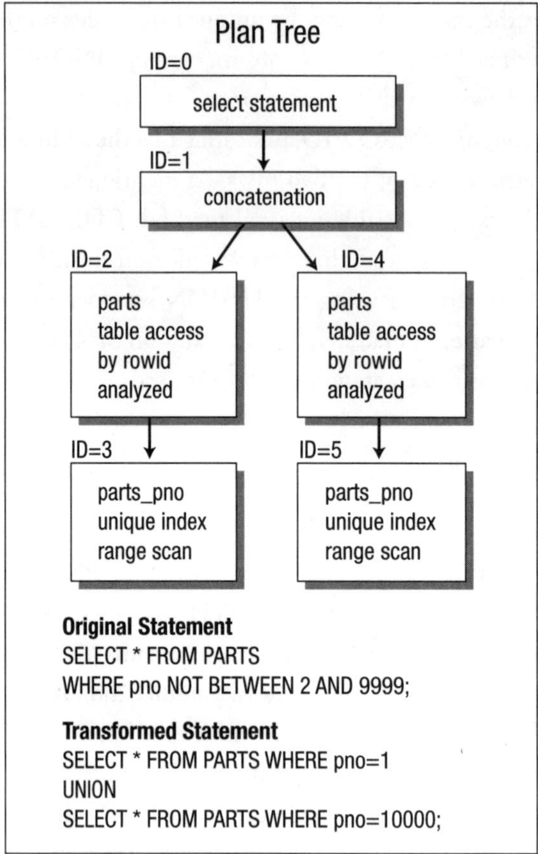

Figure 7.2
The plan tree.

column is the primary key column, and the MGR column is a foreign key column referencing the EMPNO column.

Listing 7.4 Nonrecursive SELECT statement.

```
SQL> EXPLAIN PLAN
  2  SET STATEMENT_ID = 'PARTS1' FOR
  3  SELECT *
  4  FROM   PARTS  -- PNO=1 And PNO=10,000
  5* WHERE  PNO NOT BETWEEN 2 AND 9999;
Explained.
```

```
SQL> SET NUMWIDTH 5
SQL> SELECT ID,
     SUBSTR(OBJECT_NAME,1,12) "Name",
     SUBSTR(OBJECT_TYPE,1,6) "Type",
     SUBSTR(OPERATION,1,16) "Operation",
     SUBSTR(OPTIONS,1,10) "Options"
     FROM   PLAN_TABLE
     ORDER  BY ID, PARENT_ID;

ID  Name              Type        Operation                 Options
--  ----------------  ----------  ------------------------- -----------
 0                                SELECT STATEMENT          CHOOSE
 1                                CONCATENATION
 2  PARTS                         TABLE ACCESS              BY ROWID
 3  PARTS_PNO         UNIQUE      INDEX                     RANGE SCAN
 4  PARTS                         TABLE ACCESS              BY ROWID
 5  PARTS_PNO         UNIQUE      INDEX                     RANGE SCAN
```

Recursive Tables

When a foreign key column references the primary key column, and both columns are in the same table, the table is referred to as a "recursive table." Oracle's **EMP** table is a recursive table. The **EMPNO** column is the primary key, and the **MGR** column is a foreign key referencing the **EMPNO** column. Because each manager might manage one or more employees, the **EMP** table is a one-to-many recursive table. When you have a recursive table in Oracle, you write two types of queries. You can write a **SELF JOIN** or you can use two special clauses: **CONNECT BY** and **START WITH**. You use the **CONNECT BY** and **START WITH** clauses to interpret the information stored in the table **PLAN_TABLE**—it is also a recursive table. However, let's examine the **EMP** table first in Listing 7.5 and then **PLAN_TABLE** in Listing 7.6.

Notice that King is the president and reports to nobody. This is the case because the **MGR** column for King contains a null. Three managers report to King: Blake, Clark, and Jones. This is true because the **MGR** columns for all three managers contain the employee number of King—7839. To make the output much more readable, you can use a function named **LPAD** to indent each employee's name to the right, placing spaces to the left of the name. The technique is to use one of Oracle's pseudocolumns, **LEVEL**, to do the indenting. King is in LEVEL 1, and the three managers are in LEVEL 2. The other technique is to walk down the recursive tree for the **EMP** table, which is accomplished using the **CONNECT BY PRIOR** clause. To tell Oracle where to start walking, use the **START WITH** clause.

Listing 7.5 Recursive **SELECT** statement on **EMP**.

```
SQL> SELECT  EMPNO, ENAME, JOB, MGR
  2  FROM    EMP
  3  ORDER   BY ENAME;

  EMPNO    ENAME        JOB             MGR
-------- ------------ ---------------- ------
   7876    ADAMS        CLERK            7788
   7499    ALLEN        SALESMAN         7698
   7698    BLAKE        MANAGER          7839
   7782    CLARK        MANAGER          7839
   7902    FORD         ANALYST          7566
   7900    JAMES        CLERK            7698
   7566    JONES        MANAGER          7839
   7839    KING         PRESIDENT
   7654    MARTIN       SALESMAN         7698
   7934    MILLER       CLERK            7782
   7788    SCOTT        ANALYST          7566
   7369    SMITH        CLERK            7902
   7844    TURNER       SALESMAN         7698
   7521    WARD         SALESMAN         7698

14 rows selected.

SQL> SELECT  LPAD(' ',2*LEVEL) || ENAME "Corp Structure"
  2  FROM    EMP
  3  CONNECT BY PRIOR EMPNO = MGR
  4  START   WITH JOB = 'PRESIDENT';

Corporate Structure
--------------------------------------------------
  KING
    JONES
      SCOTT
        ADAMS
      FORD
        SMITH
    BLAKE
      ALLEN
      WARD
      MARTIN
      TURNER
      JAMES
    CLARK
      MILLER

14 rows selected.
```

Figure 7.3 shows a diagram of the EMP table, followed by a description of the physical table.

The Table PLAN_TABLE

PLAN_TABLE is also a recursive table. The primary key column is **ID**. The PARENT_ID column is a foreign key column that references the **ID** column.

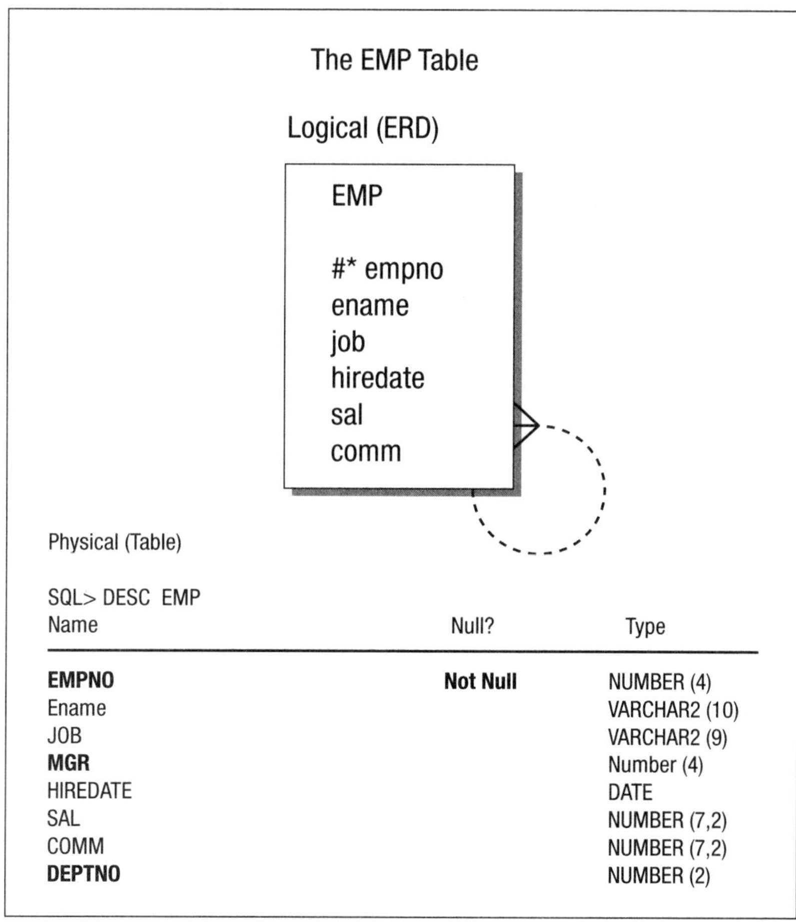

Figure 7.3
The **EMP** table.

Instead of employees in the **EMP** table, there are steps of a plan tree that feed into each other, with **PRESIDENT** being the statement type. You can run Explain Plan on selects, updates, deletes, and so on. All of these are examples of statement types. Listing 7.6 shows the recursive query against the table **PLAN_TABLE**. This query is very similar to the one shown in Listing 7.5, which goes against the **EMP** table. You must write this query yourself—it is not shipped with Oracle. I saved the script to an operating system file named explain.sql so that I won't forget the name of the file. The output has already been explained in Listing 7.4.

Listing 7.6 Recursive SELECT statement on PLAN_TABLE.

```
SQL> get explain
  1  COL      COST            FORMAT 99,999
  2  COL      CARDINALITY     FORMAT 99,999,999
  3  COL      "Query Plan"    FORMAT A60
  4  SELECT   LPAD(' ', 2*(LEVEL-1)) ||
  5           OPERATION || ' ' ||
  6           OPTIONS || ' ' ||
  7           OBJECT_NAME || ' ' || OPTIMIZER "Query Plan",
  8           COST
  9  FROM     PLAN_TABLE
 10  WHERE    STATEMENT_ID = UPPER('&STMT_ID')
 11  START    WITH ID = 0
 12* CONNECT BY PRIOR ID = PARENT_ID

SQL> @explain
Enter value for stmt_id: parts1
Query Plan                                                         COST
------------------------------------------------------------------ ----
SELECT STATEMENT   CHOOSE                                             6
  CONCATENATION
    TABLE ACCESS BY ROWID PARTS ANALYZED                              3
          INDEX RANGE SCAN PARTS_PNO
    TABLE ACCESS BY ROWID PARTS ANALYZED                              3
          INDEX RANGE SCAN PARTS_PNO

6 rows selected.
```

Figure 7.4 illustrates the logical and physical design of the **PLAN_TABLE** table. This table is a recursive table just like the table **EMP**. The primary key of the table **PLAN_TABLE** is **ID**, and the foreign key column is **PARENT_ID**. The **PARENT_ID** column is based upon the data found in the **ID** column.

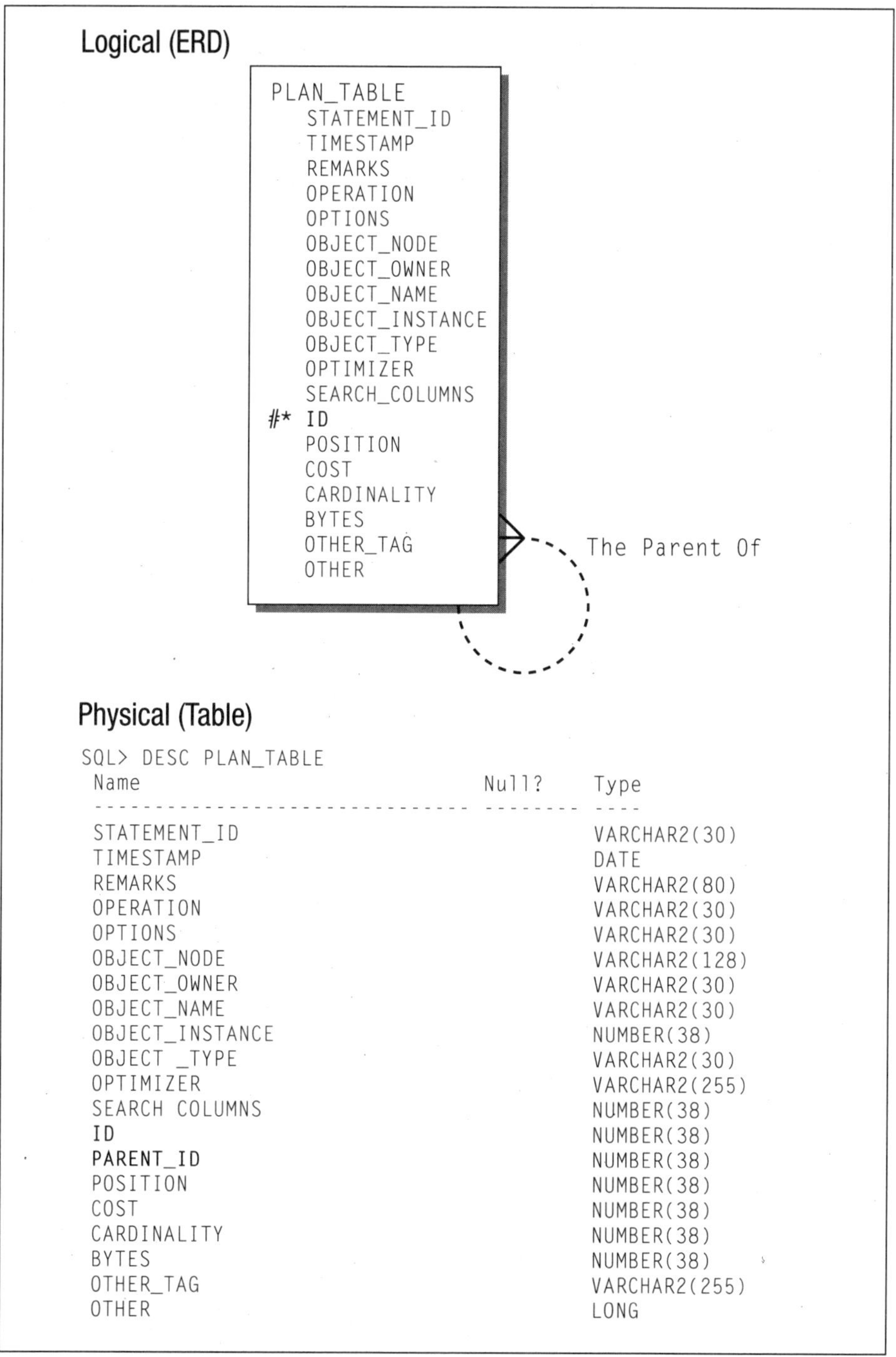

Figure 7.4
The Table **PLAN_TABLE**.

Examples

Let's use Explain Plan on several statements and then interpret the results. The first example, shown in Listing 7.7, indicates that Oracle will return the rows using a full table scan. This makes good sense, because there are 10,000 part numbers, and the query will return all but 99 of them. It would be ridiculous for Oracle to read an index block, then data, and so on. The I/O for reading index and data blocks for 9,901 rows is at least twice as much I/O as just performing one full table scan and returning the rows that match the criteria. The **PARTS** table has been analyzed, and the estimated cost to perform a full table scan on the **PARTS** table is 26. A full table scan on one table does not have the same cost as a full table scan on the other.

Listing 7.7 Full table scan.

```
SQL> EXPLAIN PLAN
  2         SET     STATEMENT_ID = 'PARTS2'
  3         FOR
  4         SELECT  *
  5         FROM    PARTS
  6         WHERE   PNO > 99;
Explained.

SQL> get explain
  1  SELECT  LPAD(' ', 2*(LEVEL-1)) ||
  2          OPERATION || ' ' ||
  3          OPTIONS || ' ' ||
  4          OBJECT_NAME || ' ' || OPTIMIZER "Query Plan",
  5          COST
  6  FROM    PLAN_TABLE
  7  START   WITH ID = 0
  8* CONNECT BY PRIOR ID = PARENT_ID
SQL> /

Query Plan                                                     COST
-------------------------------------------------------------- -----
SELECT STATEMENT   CHOOSE                                         26
  TABLE ACCESS FULL PARTS ANALYZED                                26
```

Many queries join tables. The selection of a driving table is absolutely crucial in order for a query of this type to execute fast. Most of the time, Oracle makes the best selection of a driving table. You must be able to detect which table is the join table by observing the output from the table **PLAN_TABLE**. This is very simple. Reading from the top down, the first table name encountered is the driving table. This is the table Oracle starts with in the join chain. The driving table should be the most selective table; however, this does not mean it's always the table with the fewest rows. Also, Oracle does not always perform a full table scan on the driving table. Listing 7.8 indicates that the driving table is **STATS2**. Notice, as you read from the top down, that you encounter the **STATS2** table one line above the **STATS** table. The driving table, or inner table, should be the table that is the most selective. By selective, I mean the table that returns the fewest number of rows. Most of the time, Oracle makes the best choice of the driving table. However, when Oracle does not make the best choice of the inner table, more rows are returned, and these rows have to be joined to the next table in the join chain. To rigidly control the join chain, or the order the tables are joined, use the hint named **ORDERED**.

Listing 7.8 The driving table.

```
SQL> EXPLAIN PLAN FOR
  2  SELECT  STATS2.SNO, STATS.SEX
  3  FROM    STATS,      STATS2
  4  WHERE   STATS.SNO = STATS2.SNO;
Explained.

SQL> @explain
Query Plan                                                    COST
------------------------------------------------------------ ------
SELECT STATEMENT   CHOOSE                                   20,010
  NESTED LOOPS                                              20,010
    TABLE ACCESS FULL STATS2 ANALYZED                           10
    TABLE ACCESS BY ROWID STATS ANALYZED
          INDEX UNIQUE SCAN BTREE_UNIQUE_SNO ANALYZED
```

Suppose the query that joins the tables together is running too slowly and both of the join columns in the **WHERE** clause are indexed. You might try running an Explain Plan on the same query using the **ORDERED** hint. This hint looks at the order of the tables in the **FROM** clause from left to right. The order of the tables in the **FROM** clause defines the join chain. Also, the table to the far left is the driving table. Listing 7.9 is an example of a really, really bad hint. With the **STATS2** table as the driver in Listing 7.8, the estimated cost is 20,010, whereas the estimated cost using **STATS** as the driving table in Listing 7.9 is 35,244.

Listing 7.9 The **ORDERED** hint.

```
SQL> EXPLAIN PLAN FOR
  2          SELECT /*+ORDERED */ STATS2.SNO, STATS.SEX
  3          FROM   STATS,       STATS2
  4*         WHERE  STATS.SNO = STATS2.SNO;
Explained.

SQL> @explain
Query Plan                                                            COST
-------------------------------------------------------------- ------
SELECT STATEMENT   CHOOSE                                          35,244
  MERGE JOIN                                                       35,244
    TABLE ACCESS BY ROWID STATS ANALYZED                           35,083
          INDEX FULL SCAN BTREE_UNIQUE_SNO ANALYZED
    SORT JOIN
      TABLE ACCESS FULL STATS2 ANALYZED                                11

6 rows selected.
```

Sometimes you don't want to scan the entire table. To determine the cost of such a statement (using **ROWNUM**), run it through Explain Plan, as shown in Listing 7.10. The **OPTIONS** column contains **STOPKEY** and the **OPERATION** column contains **COUNT** as well as **SELECT STATEMENT** and **TABLE ACCESS**. **STOPKEY** indicates to stop at a particular value indicated by **ROWNUM**. For example, if you want to see four rows from a table, the **WHERE** clause is **WHERE ROWNUM** < 5. In this case, the query stops at the fifth row in the active set.

Listing 7.10 **ROWNUM** or **COUNT STOPKEY**.

```
SQL> EXPLAIN PLAN FOR
  2          SELECT    *
  3          FROM      TESTS
  4          WHERE     ROWNUM < 5500;
Explained.

SQL> @explain
Query Plan                                                     COST
---------------------------------------------------------- -----
SELECT STATEMENT   CHOOSE                                    571
  COUNT STOPKEY
    TABLE ACCESS FULL TESTS ANALYZED                         571
```

If a table has not been analyzed, no hints are given, and Oracle gets to choose the optimizer, then the rule-based optimizer gets the green light. However, as shown in Listing 7.11, the index is used and the query runs very slowly. Most of the table is retrieved. For each part number, the index is scanned for the key and the row is retrieved using the address of the index, which is the rowid. A lot of input/output occurs to read most of the index blocks and most of the data blocks.

Listing 7.11 Table not analyzed.

```
SQL> ANALYZE TABLE PARTS DELETE STATISTICS;
Table analyzed.

SQL>TRUNCATE TABLE PLAN_TABLE;
Table truncated.

SQL> EXPLAIN PLAN FOR
  2  SELECT      *
  3  FROM        PARTS
  4  WHERE       PNO > 99;
Explained.

SQL> @explain
Query Plan                                               COST
-------------------------------------------------------  -----
SELECT STATEMENT   CHOOSE
  TABLE ACCESS BY ROWID PARTS
    INDEX RANGE SCAN PARTS_PNO
```

Another big use of Explain Plan is to write several different SQL statements that return the same rows and then run Explain Plan on each of the statements, noting the estimated cost for each. Most of the time, the statement with the lowest cost will execute faster than statements with higher costs. Listings 7.12, 7.13, and 7.14 all return the same rows, but all three have different costs and elapsed times.

The three queries return the part numbers of all parts in the **PARTS** table that are not in the **TESTS** table. **MINUS** has a cost of 14,465 and requires nearly 56 seconds to execute. **MINUS** is one of Oracle's four set operators. The four set operators are **UNION**, **UNION ALL**, **INTERSECT**, and **MINUS**. **MINUS** identifies rows that are in one table and not in another based on all columns in the **SELECT** clause. Notice that full table scans are performed on **PARTS** and **TESTS**. In addition, both tables are sorted.

Listing 7.12 Using **MINUS**.

```
SQL>TRUNCATE TABLE PLAN_TABLE;
Table truncated.

SQL> EXPLAIN PLAN FOR
  2         SELECT PNO FROM PARTS
  3         MINUS
  4*        SELECT PNO FROM TESTS;
Explained.

SQL> @explain
Query Plan                                                  COST
------------------------------------------------------- -------
SELECT STATEMENT   CHOOSE                                  14465
  MINUS
    SORT UNIQUE
      TABLE ACCESS FULL PARTS ANALYZED                        26
    SORT UNIQUE
      TABLE ACCESS FULL TESTS ANALYZED                       571

6 rows selected.

SQL> SELECT PNO FROM PARTS
  2  MINUS
  3* SELECT PNO FROM TESTS;

    PNO
  -----
    222
   1944
   1950
   1972
   1976
   1978
   5500

7 rows selected.

Elapsed: 00:00:55.61
```

Another method for identifying values in one table that are not in another is to use **NOT EXISTS** in a correlated subquery. A correlated subquery references a column in the outer query in the inner query's **WHERE** clause. Also, for every row in the outer query table (the candidate table), the inner query executes. Listing 7.13 shows a correlated subquery. The inner query references the **PNO** column of the **PARTS** table (**PARTS.PNO**). This means that for every row in the **PARTS** table, the inner query fires against the **TESTS** table. Because there are 10,000 rows in the **PARTS** table, the inner query will fire 10,000 times. The cost is 26, and the query requires a little more than 27 seconds to execute. This is more than twice as fast as the **MINUS** in Listing 7.12. The **OPERATIONS** column indicates the use of a filter. A full table scan on the **PARTS** table, which contains 10,000 rows, is performed. Each of the 470,552 rows in the **TESTS** table is retrieved using an index.

Listing 7.13 Using **NOT EXISTS**.

```
SQL> TRUNCATE TABLE PLAN_TABLE;
Table truncated.

SQL> EXPLAIN PLAN FOR
             SELECT   PNO
             FROM     PARTS
             WHERE    NOT EXISTS
                      (SELECT 'MAUI'
                      FROM    TESTS
                      WHERE   PARTS.PNO = TESTS.PNO);
Explained.

SQL> @explain
Query Plan                                                          COST
------------------------------------------------------------------  ----
SELECT STATEMENT   CHOOSE                                             26
  FILTER
    TABLE ACCESS FULL PARTS ANALYZED                                  26
    INDEX RANGE SCAN TESTS_PNO_INDEX ANALYZED 10

SQL> SELECT PNO
     FROM   PARTS
     WHERE  NOT EXISTS
            (SELECT 'MAUI'
            FROM     TESTS
            WHERE    PARTS.PNO = TESTS.PNO);

   PNO
  ----
   222
  1944
  1950
```

```
  1972
  1976
  1978
  5500

7 rows selected.

Elapsed: 00:00:27.09
```

Another method for retrieving part numbers in the **PARTS** table that don't exist in the **TESTS** table is to use **NOT IN**. However, it's usually not a good idea to use **NOT IN**. On the surface, everything seems normal. The cost is a mere 26. Both tables are accessed using full table scans, the same as **MINUS**. However, when you execute a statement like this, you might have to wait a very, very long time. I cancelled the query using Ctrl+C after nearly 51 minutes. Listing 7.14 is a great example of the cost being very misleading.

Listing 7.14 Using **NOT IN**.

```
SQL> TRUNCATE TABLE PLAN_TABLE;
Table truncated.

SQL> EXPLAIN PLAN FOR
  2          SELECT   PNO
  3          FROM     PARTS
  4          WHERE    PNO NOT IN
  5                                  (SELECT PNO
  6*                                 FROM    TESTS);
Explained.

SQL> @explain
Query Plan                                                     COST
-------------------------------------------------------------  ----
SELECT STATEMENT   CHOOSE                                        26
  FILTER
    TABLE ACCESS FULL PARTS ANALYZED                             26
    TABLE ACCESS FULL TESTS ANALYZED                            571

SQL> SELECT PNO
  2  FROM   PARTS -- Pulled The Plug After 51 Minutes
  3  WHERE  PNO NOT IN
  4                    (SELECT   PNO
  5                     FROM     TESTS);
```

```
^CERROR:
ORA-01013: user requested cancel of current operation

no rows selected

Elapsed: 00:50:53.83
```

Table 7.1 provides comparisons on the queries in Listings 7.12, 7.13, and 7.14. Remember that the statement with the lowest cost does not *always* execute faster than a statement with a higher cost. Most of the time, though, a query with a lower cost will execute faster. Another assumption that is not always true is the number of steps in a plan indicate the speed of the query. In other words, two queries with 3 steps in one plan, and 12 steps in the other, might lead you to believe the query with 12 steps executes much slower than the query with 3 steps in its plan. Instead, the query with 12 steps may execute much faster than the query with 3 steps. A plan with many steps can sometimes execute quicker than a plan with fewer steps.

Another example, shown in Listing 7.15, illustrates the lowest cost possible for a SQL statement. Obviously, I'm talking about the pseudocolumn rowid. The first explained query uses the nonunique index on the **PNO** column of the **TESTS** table. **RANGE SCAN**, as opposed to **UNIQUE SCAN**, states that the index allows duplicates. Hence, Oracle scans the index. The cost is 24, and 10.72 seconds are required to retrieve the one row from the **TESTS** table, which contains 470,692 rows. Notice that the **ROWID** is included in the **SELECT** clause, so the **ROWID** can be used to retrieve the row from **TESTS**.

The next query, using the **ROWID** to retrieve the row, is explained. The best cost obtainable is 1, and that's what happens here. Also, note that it takes only 0.37 seconds to retrieve the row using its rowid. However, remember that rowids can change. Going from 10.72 seconds to 0.37 seconds using the **ROWID** is fantastic.

Table 7.1 Comparing costs and timings of three queries.

Query	Cost	Time	Access PARTS	Access TESTS
MINUS	14,465	55.6 Sec	Full table scan	Full table scan
NOT EXISTS	26	27.1 Sec	Full table scan	Index
NOT IN	26	50+ Min	Full table scan	Full table scan

Listing 7.15 The lowest cost possible.

```
SQL> TRUNCATE TABLE PLAN_TABLE;
Table truncated.

SQL> EXPLAIN PLAN FOR
  2          SELECT ROWID, PNO, TNO
  3          FROM   TESTS
  4          WHERE  PNO = 90 AND
  5*                TNO = 8100;
Explained.

SQL> @explain
Query Plan                                                         COST
------------------------------------------------------------------ -----
SELECT STATEMENT   CHOOSE                                             24
  TABLE ACCESS BY ROWID TESTS ANALYZED                                24
        INDEX RANGE SCAN TESTS_PNO_INDEX ANALYZED

SQL> SELECT ROWID, PNO, TNO
  2  FROM   TESTS
  3  WHERE  PNO = 90 AND
  4*        TNO = 8100;

ROWID                            PNO    TNO
----------------------------    ----  -----
00000CFE.0020.0003                90   8100

Elapsed: 00:00:10.72

SQL> EXPLAIN PLAN FOR
  2          SELECT PNO, TNO
  3          FROM   TESTS
  4*         WHERE  ROWID = '00000CFE.0020.0003';
Explained.

SQL> @explain
Query Plan                                                      COST
-------------------------------------------------------------  ------
SELECT STATEMENT   CHOOSE                                           1
  TABLE ACCESS BY ROWID TESTS ANALYZED                              1

SQL> SELECT PNO, TNO
  2  FROM   TESTS
```

```
 3* WHERE  ROWID = '00000CFE.0020.0003';

  PNO  TNO
  --- ----
   90 8100

Elapsed: 00:00:00.37
```

Listing 7.16 is an example of using bitmap indexes. The two columns **REGION_BIT_MAP** and **SEX** both have bitmap indexes. The **STATS** table has not been analyzed. Using the hint **ALL_ROWS**, Explain Plan reveals the following: First, **BITMAP AND** indicates that the bitmap indexes for both columns are merged in memory. Second, the merged bitmaps are converted to rowids. Finally, the rows from the **STATS** table are retrieved using the rowids. The cost of 5 is much too low since the table has not been analyzed. However, the hint **ALL_ROWS** is used, which causes Oracle to use the cost-based optimizer. Therefore, Oracle estimates or "guess-timates" on the fly and derives a very low number of 5. The cost is actually 2,032 after the table is analyzed.

Listing 7.16 Bitmap indexes.

```
SQL> EXPLAIN PLAN FOR
  2           SELECT --+ ALL_ROWS
  3                  SNO,    REGION_HASH
  4           FROM   STATS  /* 2,000 ROWS RETURNED  */
  5*          WHERE  REGION_BIT_MAP = 'W' AND  SEX = 'F';

SQL> @explain
Query Plan                                                   COST
---------------------------------------------------------- -----
SELECT STATEMENT   HINT: ALL_ROWS                                5
  TABLE ACCESS BY ROWID STATS                                    5
    BITMAP CONVERSION TO ROWIDS
      BITMAP AND
        BITMAP INDEX SINGLE VALUE
               BITMAP_REGION_BIT_MAP
        BITMAP INDEX SINGLE VALUE
               BITMAP_SEX
```

Summary

Explain Plan is an excellent tool to help you write more efficient SQL statements. However, many times, writing queries against the data dictionary to check on index status is faster and easier to perform. You'll have to create the table **PLAN_TABLE** and write your own query (or queries) against it. One of the biggest uses of Explain Plan is to submit several different queries and compare their costs. Most of the time, the lower cost query executes faster; however, this is not always the case. Another caveat is the number of steps in a plan. The plan with the fewest steps does not always execute faster than a plan with more steps. When explaining queries that join tables, identifying the driving table is important. The driving table is the first table you see when reading from the top down. Most of the time, Oracle makes the best selection of a driving table. However, you know your data better than Oracle. That's why the **ORDERED** hint exists. Finally, the cost is estimated, based upon MIC (Memory, I/O, CPU). The lowest cost possible is 1, using **ROWID**.

SQL Trace And TKPROF

CHAPTER 8

The purpose of SQL Trace and TKPROF is to pinpoint bottlenecks in long-running SQL statements by recording statistics to the nearest second for parses, executes, and fetches. I/O is also recorded for all three phases.

SQL Trace And TKPROF

What Is SQL Trace And TKPROF

SQL Trace is a utility (or tool) you can use to examine long-running queries to help pinpoint problem areas. You can activate SQL Trace either at the database level (not recommended) using **sql_trace=true** in the init.ora parameter file or at the session level using the **ALTER SESSION** command. Once this command is entered, Oracle starts keeping statistics for all SQL statements until you enter another **ALTER SESSION** command setting **sql_trace=false**. However, if the parameter **timed_statistics** is not set to **true**, all timings to the nearest second will be zero. Statistics are tracked for three phases of a cursor: parses, executes, and fetches. The statistics are stored in an ASCII file with a .trc extension. Once you stop SQL Trace, using the **ALTER SESSION** command, or exit the product, the .trc file is closed. This file is usually referred to as the "SQL Trace dump file." The trace file is stored in the path indicated by the parameter **user_dump_dest**. The most difficult part of this process is locating your trace dump file. I usually place a very important person's name as a column alias so a Unix **grep** command can quickly identify my own trace dump file.

The next step is to submit the unformatted trace file (trc.) into a report program called TKPROF, which stands for Trace Kernel Profile. This report program reformats the trace file into a formatted file, with a .prf extension. The output file from TKPROF is formatted according to the parameters entered on the operating system command line.

At this point, you read the formatted output file (.prf) from TKPROF and interpret the results. Perhaps you need to rewrite the query, because many queries can be solved using different techniques, or create additional indexes. These steps are illustrated in Figure 8.1.

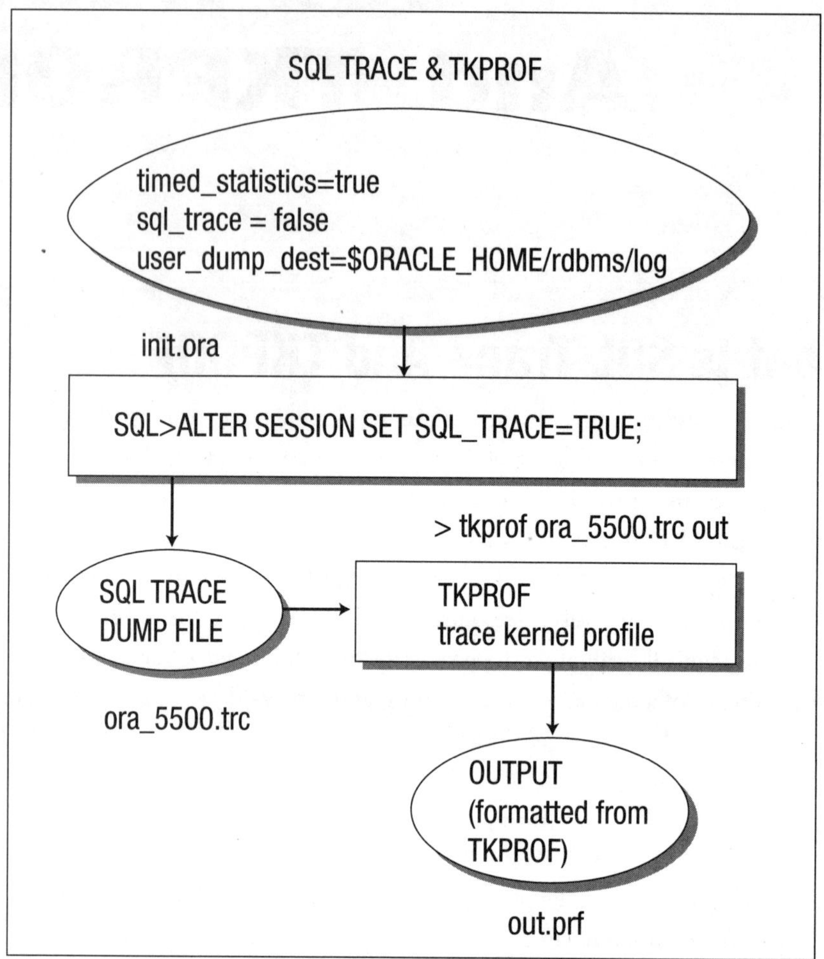

Figure 8.1
Using SQL Trace and TKPROF.

The Parameter File

Listing 8.1 contains the parameters and their current settings that are relevant to executing SQL Trace. The first parameter is **timed_statistics**. If this is not set to **true**, all of the timed statistics for parses, executes, and fetches will be zero. However, if you forget to change your init.ora file, you can enter the **ALTER SESSION** command setting **timed_statistics** equal to **true**.

The parameter **sql_trace** should very rarely, if ever, be set to **true**. If it is set to **true**, every Oracle session will create a trace dump file. On a busy system, you could fill up all of your disks in a short period of time. For this reason, the default value for **sql_trace** is **false**. However, if the Oracle DBA needs more detailed information about the Oracle database, then he or she might set **sql_trace** equal to **true** for a short period of time.

The parameter **user_dump_dest** contains the full path for where all trace dump files are stored. The question mark is a shorthand method of denoting the path for your Oracle home. On Unix platforms, the question mark is equivalent to **$ORACLE_HOME**.

The parameter **max_dump_file_size** indicates the maximum number of bytes for a trace dump file.

For earlier versions of Oracle7, there's a special parameter you set to **true** if you want to read your own trace dump files. The parameter's name is **_trace_files_public**. No, this is not a typographical error. Oracle has many special init.ora parameters starting with an underscore. When I worked at Oracle Corporation from 1988 through 1993, I saw a few very humorous emails referencing fictitious parameters. One parameter I particularly liked was _smoke_and_mirrors=always.

Listing 8.1 Parameter file.

```
SQL> SELECT SUBSTR(NAME,1,25) PARAM,
  2         SUBSTR(VALUE,1,25) CURRENT_SETTING
  3  FROM   V$PARAMETER
  4  WHERE  NAME IN('timed_statistics',
  5                 'user_dump_dest',
  6                 'sql_trace',
  7*                'max_dump_file_size');

PARAM                     CURRENT_SETTING
------------------------  ------------------------
timed_statistics          TRUE
sql_trace                 FALSE
user_dump_dest            ?/rdbms/log
max_dump_file_size        10240

SQL> ALTER SESSION SET TIMED_STATISTICS = TRUE;
Session altered.
```

Activating SQL Trace

To produce a trace dump file containing statistics for SQL statements, the **ALTER SESSION** command is used to set **SQL_TRACE** equal to **true.** This command can be issued from most Oracle products. This book uses the product SQL*Plus. You can also activate SQL Trace using the Oracle-supplied package named **dbms_session** and the procedure named **set_sql_trace.** You can even activate SQL Trace in another user's session using the package **dbms_system** and the procedure **set_sql_trace_in_session.** Listing 8.2 shows several commands to start tracing for a session.

Listing 8.2 Producing a trace dump file.

```
SQL> ALTER SESSION SET SQL_TRACE = TRUE;
Session altered.

(To see what procedures exist in the DBMS package
and the arguments and data types, write this query.)

SQL>  SELECT SUBSTR(TEXT,1,75) CODE
  2   FROM   DBA_SOURCE
  3   WHERE  NAME = UPPER('&DBMS') AND
  4          TEXT NOT LIKE '%--%' AND
  5*         TEXT LIKE '%procedure%';
Enter value for dbms: dbms_session

CODE
----------------------------------------------------------------------
  procedure set_role(role_cmd varchar2);
  procedure set_sql_trace(sql_trace boolean);
  procedure set_nls(param varchar2, value varchar2);
  procedure close_database_link(dblink varchar2);
  procedure set_label(lbl varchar2);
  procedure set_mls_label_format(fmt varchar2);
  procedure reset_package;
  procedure set_close_cached_open_cursors(close_cursors boolean);
  procedure free_unused_user_memory;

(If you know the package name and the procedure name,
but do not know how many arguments or data types to pass,
describe the package and the procedure.)

SQL> DESC DBMS_SESSION.SET_SQL_TRACE
```

```
PROCEDURE DBMS_SESSION.SET_SQL_TRACE
Argument Name                  Type                    In/Out Default?
------------------------------ ----------------------- ------ --------
 SQL_TRACE                     BOOLEAN                 IN


SQL> EXECUTE dbms_session.set_sql_trace(true)
PL/SQL procedure successfully completed.


(Now to activate SQL Trace in another user's session.)


SQL>  SELECT USERNAME,
  2          SID,
  3          SERIAL#
  4    FROM  V$SESSION;

USERNAME          SID SERIAL#
----------------- --- -------
                        1
                    2   1
                    3   1
                    4   1
                    5   1
INDY                6   3
OPS$PCASSIDY        8  13

7 rows selected.

SQL> EXECUTE dbms_system.set_sql_trace_in_session(6,3,true)
begin dbms_system.set_sql_trace_in_session(6,3,true); end;

*
ERROR at line 1:
ORA-06550: line 1, column 7:
PLS-00201: identifier 'DBMS_SYSTEM.
SET_SQL_TRACE_IN_SESSION' must be declared
ORA-06550: line 1, column 7:
PL/SQL: Statement ignored

SQL> CONNECT INTERNAL
Connected.
SQL> @$ORACLE_HOME/rdbms/admin/dbmsutil
SQL> EXIT
```

```
> sqlplus /
SQL> EXECUTE dbms_system.set_sql_trace_in_session(6,3,true)
begin dbms_system.set_sql_trace_in_session(6,3,true); end;

*
ERROR at line 1:
ORA-04068: existing state of packages has been discarded
ORA-04067: not executed, package body
        "OPS$PCASSIDY.DBMS_SYSTEM" does not exist
ORA-06508: PL/SQL: could not find program unit being called
ORA-06512: at line 1

SQL> EXECUTE sys.dbms_system.set_sql_trace_in_session(6,3,true)
PL/SQL procedure successfully completed.
```

Using SQL Trace

Listing 8.3 is a good example of looking at a long-running query. I submitted this query on Sunday evening at 8:49 P.M. The next afternoon at 12:18 P.M. (lunchtime) the query was still executing, so I cancelled it with a Ctrl+C. By looking at the output, you can see that this query had been running for nearly 15.5 hours. Note that Ctrl+C does not wipe out the SQL Trace session and output—it merely stops tracing.

To locate the correct trace dump file, change your directory to the path indicated by **user_dump_dest** in the parameter file. Then use an operating system command to search for your trace dump file. I use **ls** and **grep** to search for files containing the string "Sep, since this is the first day of September." Usually, I place a name such as Paige or Debra as a column alias and then search on that name.

Once you locate the appropriate trace dump file, you really don't want to look at it, because it's not formatted and does not make much sense. I used the Unix **more** command so you can see the contents and the format of the trace dump file.

Listing 8.3 The long-running query.

```
SQL> ALTER SESSION SET SQL_TRACE = TRUE;
Session altered.

SQL> SET TIMING ON
SQL> SET TIME ON
20:49:11 SQL> SELECT PNO
```

```
  2  FROM   PARTS
  3  WHERE  PNO NOT IN(SELECT PNO
  4*                   FROM   TESTS);

^C
ERROR:
ORA-01013: user requested cancel of current operation
6 rows selected.

Elapsed: 15:28:52.85

12:18:32 SQL> ALTER SESSION SET SQL_TRACE = FALSE;
Session altered.

12:18:48 SQL> EXIT

> cd $ORACLE_HOME/rdbms/log
/home3/oracle/7.3.2/rdbms/log

> ls -l *.trc | grep Sep
-rw-r--r--   1 ora73       10045 Sep  1 12:29 pete_ora_9817.trc

> more pete_ora_9817.trc
Dump file /home3/oracle/7.3.2/rdbms/log/pete_ora_9817.trc
Oracle7 Server Release 7.3.2.2.0 - Production Release
With the distributed, replication, parallel query
  and Spatial Data options
PL/SQL Release 2.3.2.2.0 - Production
ORACLE_HOME = /home3/oracle/7.3.2
System name:    SunOS
Node name:      dcidal
Release:        5.5.1
Version:        Generic
Machine:        sun4c
Instance name: pete
Redo thread mounted by this instance: 1
Oracle process number: 7
Unix process pid: 9817, image: oraclepete

Sun Aug 31 20:48:42 1997
*** SESSION ID:(6.3) 1997.08.31.20.48.42.000
APPNAME mod='SQL*Plus' mh=3375793674 act='' ah=403088694
=====================
PARSING IN CURSOR #1 len=35 dep=0 uid=8
ad='e02faa48'
```

```
ALTER SESSION SET SQL_TRACE = TRUE
END OF STMT
EXEC #1:c=3,e=16,p=2,cr=2,cu=0,mis=1,r=0,dep=0,og=4,tim=36374335
=====================
PARSING IN CURSOR #2 len=242 dep=0 uid=8
ad='e0329740'
select parameter, value     from v$nls_parameters
 ('NLS_SORT','NLS_CURRENCY','NLS_ISO_CURRENCY',
  'NLS_DATE_LANG
UAGE','NLS_NUMERIC_CHARACTERS',
      'NLS_LANGUAGE','NLS_TERRITORY'
))
END OF STMT
PARSE #2:c=1,e=1,p=0,cr=0,cu=0,mis=0,r=0,dep=0,og=4,tim=36374337
EXEC #2:c=1,e=1,p=0,cr=0,cu=0,mis=0,r=0,dep=0,og=4,tim=36374338
FETCH #2:c=0,e=0,p=0,cr=0,cu=0,mis=0,r=7,dep=0,og=4,tim=36374338
STAT #2 id=1 cnt=9
```

```
<<<<<<< A Lot Of The File Was Omitted >>>>>>>

PARSING IN CURSOR #1 len=85 dep=0 uid=8
ad='e02fa2f8'
SELECT PNO
FROM   PARTS
WHERE  PNO NOT IN(SELECT PNO
                  FROM   TESTS)
END OF STMT
PARSE #1:c=69,e=74,p=14,cr=58,cu=0,mis=1,r=0,dep=0,og=4,tim=36380585
EXEC #1:c=0,e=0,p=0,cr=0,cu=0,mis=0,r=0,dep=0,og=4,tim=36380586
Mon Sep  1 12:18:31 1997
FETCH #1:c=5308016,e=5573076,p=5547379,cr=5561968
tim=41953663
Mon Sep  1 12:29:00 1997
STAT #1 id=1 cnt=2427
STAT #1 id=2 cnt=2427
STAT #1 id=3 cnt=697561134
=====================
PARSING IN CURSOR #1 len=36 dep=0 uid=8
ad='e0267af0'
ALTER SESSION SET SQL_TRACE = FALSE
END OF STMT
PARSE #1:c=2,e=2,p=0,cr=0,cu=0,mis=1,r=0,dep=0,og=4,tim=42016533
EXEC #1:c=0,e=4,p=0,cr=0,cu=0,mis=0,r=0,dep=0,og=4,tim=42016537
```

Using TKPROF

The purpose of TKPROF is to output a formatted report using the correct trace dump file as input. Listing 8.4 illustrates how to view the syntax and sample commands using TKPROF. This example indicates that pete_ora_9817.trc is the name of the trace dump file used as input to TKPROF. The name of the formatted output file is long1.prf. Note that $HOME is a Unix technique for writing this file to the Unix user's home directory. A normal user does not have write privileges in the same directory where the trace dump files are stored. The string "**explain=/**" produces an Explain Plan at the end of the .prf formatted output file produced by TKPROF. This is a neat way to get "two for the price of one"—that is, SQL Trace and Explain Plan.

Listing 8.4 Using TKPROF.

```
> tkprof
  Usage: tkprof tracefile outputfile [explain= ] [table= ]
              [print= ] [insert= ] [sys= ] [sort= ]
  table=schema.tablename
  explain=user/password    Connect and issue EXPLAIN PLAIN.
  print=integer    List only the first 'integer' SQL statements.
  aggregate=yes|no
  insert=filename  List statements INSERT statements.
  sys=no  TKPROF does not list SQL statements run as user SYS.
  record=filename  Record nonrecursive statements
  sort=option      Set
  of sort options:
  prscnt  number of times parse was called
  prscpu  cpu time parsing
  prsela  elapsed time parsing
  prsdsk  number of disk reads during parse
  prsqry  number of buffers for consistent read during parse
  prscu   number of buffers for current read during parse
  prsmis  number of misses in library cache during parse
  execnt  number of execute was called
  execpu  cpu time spent executing
  exeela  elapsed time executing
  exedsk  number of disk reads during execute
  exeqry  number of buffers for consistent read during execute
  execu   number of buffers for current read during execute
  exerow  number of rows processed during execute
  exemis  number of library cache misses during execute
  fchcnt  number of times fetch was called
  fchcpu  cpu time spent fetching
```

```
  fchela  elapsed time fetching
  fchdsk  number of disk reads during fetch
  fchqry  number of buffers for consistent read during fetch
  fchcu   number of buffers for current read during fetch
  fchrow  number of rows fetched
  userid  userid of user that parsed the cursor

> tkprof pete_ora_9817.trc $HOME/long1.prf explain=/
TKPROF: Release 7.3.2.2.0 - Production on Mon Sep  1 13:02:18 1997
Copyright (c) Oracle Corporation 1979, 1994.  All rights reserved.
```

More TKPROF Examples

Listing 8.5 shows another method for using TKPROF. Using "**record=filename**" produces a SQL script file with all nonrecursive SQL statements wrapped with two **ALTER SESSION** statements—one to start SQL Trace and the other to end SQL Trace. Two other SQL statements are written to the file as well, and both are queries against **V$NLS_PARAMETERS**. At a later time, you can start the file and SQL Trace will be executed for you automatically.

Listing 8.5 More TKPROF examples: **record=**filename.

```
> tkprof pete_ora_9817.trc $HOME/long1.prf record=cornon

> ls cornon*
cornon.sql

> more cornon.sql
ALTER SESSION SET SQL_TRACE = TRUE ;
 <<<<<<< I Reformatted This File  >>>>>>>
 <<<<<<< So It Is More Readable   >>>>>>>
select parameter, value
from   v$nls_parameters
where (upper(parameter) in
 ('NLS_SORT','NLS_CURRENCY','NLS_ISO_CURRENCY','NLS_DATE_LANGUAGE',
   'NLS_NUMERIC_CHARACTERS', 'NLS_LANGUAGE','NLS_TERRITORY')) ;
select value
from   v$nls_parameters
where  (upper(parameter) = 'NLS_DATE_FORMAT') ;
SELECT PNO
FROM   PARTS
WHERE  PNO NOT IN(SELECT PNO
                  FROM   TESTS) ;
```

```
ALTER SESSION SET SQL_TRACE = FALSE ;

SQL> start cornon
```

The intent in Listing 8.6 is great: Produce a SQL script file that creates a table named **TKPROF_TABLE.** The file will also contain many **INSERT** statements that populate the table with data from TKPROF for the queries. You can use this information at a later time to compare the results. Unfortunately, there's a bug with this script. The table has 28 columns, but the **INSERT** statements reference only 27 columns. Data is missing for the column named *TICKS.* So, just drop the table, recreate the table with the *TICKS* column commented out, and re-un the script file named corinsert.ins.

Listing 8.6 More TKPROF examples: **insert=**filename.

```
> tkprof pete_ora_9817.trc $HOME/long1.prf insert=corinsert

> ls corins*
corinsert.ins

> more corinsert.ins
REM  Edit and/or remove the following  CREATE TABLE
REM  statement as your needs dictate.
CREATE TABLE  tkprof_table
(
 date_of_insert                       DATE
,cursor_num                           NUMBER
,depth                                NUMBER
,user_id                              NUMBER
,parse_cnt                            NUMBER
,parse_cpu                            NUMBER
,parse_elap                           NUMBER
,parse_disk                           NUMBER
,parse_query                          NUMBER
,parse_current                        NUMBER
,parse_miss                           NUMBER
,exe_count                            NUMBER
,exe_cpu                              NUMBER
,exe_elap                             NUMBER
,exe_disk                             NUMBER
,exe_query                            NUMBER
,exe_current                          NUMBER
,exe_miss                             NUMBER
```

```
,exe_rows                              NUMBER
,fetch_count                           NUMBER
,fetch_cpu                             NUMBER
,fetch_elap                            NUMBER
,fetch_disk                            NUMBER
,fetch_query                           NUMBER
,fetch_current                         NUMBER
,fetch_rows                            NUMBER
,ticks                                 NUMBER
,sql_statement                         LONG
);
INSERT INTO tkprof_table VALUES
(
  SYSDATE, 1, 0, 8, 0, 0, 0, 0, 0, 0, 0
, 1, 3, 16, 2, 2, 0, 1, 0
, 0, 0, 0, 0, 0, 0, 0
, 'ALTER SESSION SET SQL_TRACE = TRUE
');
INSERT INTO tkprof_table VALUES
(
  SYSDATE, 2, 0, 8, 1, 1, 1, 0, 0, 0, 0
, 1, 1, 1, 0, 0, 0, 0, 0
<<<<<<<  A Lot Of Inserts Removed >>>>>>>
<<<<<<<        >>>>>>>
<<<<<<<        >>>>>>>
INSERT INTO tkprof_table VALUES
(
  SYSDATE, 1, 0, 8, 1, 48, 52, 0, 0, 0, 1
, 1, 0, 0, 0, 0, 0, 0, 0
, 1, 5308016, 5573076, 5547379, 5561968, 7228, 6
, 'SELECT PNO
FROM   PARTS
WHERE  PNO NOT IN(SELECT PNO
                  FROM   TESTS)
');
INSERT INTO tkprof_table VALUES
(
  SYSDATE, 1, 0, 8, 1, 2, 2, 0, 0, 0, 1
, 1, 0, 4, 0, 0, 0, 0, 0
, 0, 0, 0, 0, 0, 0, 0
, 'ALTER SESSION SET SQL_TRACE = FALSE
');

SQL> START corinsert.ins
```

```
INSERT INTO tkprof_table VALUES
            *
ERROR at line 1:
ORA-00947: not enough values

SQL> DROP TABLE TKPROF_TABLE;
Table dropped.

SQL> edit corinsert.ins
REM  Edit and/or remove the following  CREATE TABLE
REM  statement as your needs dictate.
CREATE TABLE  tkprof_table
(
 date_of_insert                        DATE
,cursor_num                            NUMBER
,fetch_rows                            NUMBER
<<< Other columns removed to condense output. >>>
/* ,ticks                                 NUMBER   */
,sql_statement                         LONG
);

SQL> start corinsert.ins

SQL> SET LONG 20
SQL> SELECT FETCH_CPU FCPU,
  2         FETCH_DISK FDISK,
  3         SQL_STATEMENT
  4  FROM   TKPROF_TABLE;

     FCPU       FDISK       SQL_STATEMENT
------------ ------------ ----------------------------------
         0            0     ALTER SESSION SET SQ
         0            0     select parameter, va
         0            0     select value
         1            2     select obj#,type,cti
         3            3     select ts#,file#,blo
         6            0     select name,col#,seg
         3            4     select type,ts#,bloc
         1            0     select obj#,ts#,file
         1            2     select pos#,col# fro
         1            3     select owner#,name,n
   5308016      5547379     SELECT PNO FROM   PA

        0          0 ALTER SESSION SET SQ
```

The parameter "**sys=no**" in Listing 8.7 reduces the number of recursive SQL statements shown in the .prf output file produced by TKPROF.

Listing 8.7 More TKPROF examples: **sys=**no.

```
tkprof pete_ora_9817.trc $HOME/long1.prf sys=no
```

The parameter "**print=**" in Listing 8.8 limits the number of SQL statements you want to include in the .prf file. In this case, you want to see the first two nonrecursive SQL statements. (Perhaps you ran 50 slow-running SQL statements through SQL Trace, but only need to see the results for any two of them.)

Listing 8.8 More TKPROF examples: **print=**2.

```
tkprof pete_ora_9817.trc $HOME/long1.prf print=2
```

If you want to sort the SQL statements that were executed using SQL Trace, use the "**sort=**" parameter. In Listing 8.9, TKPROF sorts by CPU time spent for fetches. This is a descending sort.

Listing 8.9 More TKPROF examples: **sort=**fchcpu.

```
> tkprof pete_ora_9817.trc $HOME/long1.prf print=2 sort=fchcpu
```

Interpreting The TKPROF Output File

After you have submitted the very cryptic trace dump file (.trc) through TKPROF, you are ready to examine the output file (.prf). Listing 8.10 shows most of the output file from TKPROF, but not all of it. Oracle wrote nine recursive SQL statements to execute one SQL statement sent to SQL Trace. To save space, only the first recursive SQL statement is included. The other eight have been omitted. These eight recursive SQL statements were against the following Oracle tables: **V$NLS_PARAMETERS, OBJ$, TAB$, COL$, SEG$, IND$, ICOL$,** and **OBJ$.** Any table names that end with a dollar sign and are owned by **SYS** are the real Oracle tables. You can tell TKPROF not to include recursive SQL statements by using **SYS=NO** on the command line. If you are the curious type, you can write a query against **V$SQLAREA**, looking at the **SQL_TEXT** column. This column contains the SQL statements that currently reside in the shared SQL area of the shared pool. (See Listing 8.11 for more details.)

One really nice feature is that the columns are explained at the beginning of the output file. Also, notice that Oracle includes the command to produce the trace dump file—the **ALTER SESSION** command. You can include as many SQL statements as you want in SQL Trace and then sort the output by one or more of the many sort parameters listed when you enter **tkprof** by itself on the command line. (See Listing 8.4.)

Notice that very few statistics exist for the parse and execute phases of this SQL statement. Most of the statistics are in the fetch phase.

The "cpu" column for fetches indicates that 53,080.16 seconds were required to execute all the fetches. This equates to 14 hours, 44 minutes, and 40.2 seconds of CPU time during the fetch phase.

The "elapsed" column for fetches indicates that 55,730.76 seconds were required to perform all the fetches. This equates to 15 hours, 28 minutes, and 50.88 seconds.

The "disk" column for fetches required 5,547,379 physical reads of buffers from disk. The **PARTS** table has 10,000 rows and uses 169 blocks. The **TESTS** table has 469,712 rows and uses 3,759 blocks. This is an extremely large amount of I/O.

The "Explain Plan" portion of the report is produced using "**explain=scott/tiger**" on the command line for TKPROF (or in my case, "**explain=/**", because I have an **OPS$** account, OPS$PCASSIDY). Notice the phenomenally large number of rows read from the **TESTS** table (697,561,134). Again, the **TESTS** table contains 469,712 rows. If you divide 697,561,134 by 469,712, you get 1,485. This means that Oracle performed 1,485 full table scans of a 469,712-row table before the query was cancelled. Interestingly enough, six of the seven rows in the active set had been determined when the query was cancelled. Another two to three hours and the query probably would have completed.

Notice that both tables were accessed via full table scans. The bottom line is to rewrite this query. Almost 1,500 full table scans of a half-million-row table is absolutely absurd! Because there are indexes, you should try rewriting this query.

Just as the **ALTER SESSION** command to start SQL Trace is included in this file, so is the **ALTER SESSION** command to end this session of SQL Trace. You set **SQL_TRACE** equal to **false**. By the way, when you exit SQL*Plus, the SQL Trace session ends automatically.

The totals for all recursive and nonrecursive statements appear at the end of the .prf file.

Listing 8.10 Interpreting TKPROF output.

```
> cd
/home2/dci2/pcassidy/v7322

> ls long*
long1.prf

> more long1.prf
TKPROF: Release 7.3.2.2.0 - Production on Mon Sep  1 13:02:18 1997
Copyright (c) Oracle Corporation 1979, 1994.  All rights reserved.
Trace file: ././pete_ora_9817.trc
Sort options: default
********************************************************************
count    = number of times OCI procedure was executed
cpu      = cpu time in seconds executing
elapsed  = elapsed time in seconds executing
disk     = number of physical reads of buffers from disk
query    = number of buffers gotten for consistent read
current  = number of buffers gotten current mode (usually update)
rows     = number of rows processed by the fetch or execute call
********************************************************************
ALTER SESSION SET SQL_TRACE = TRUE

call      count      cpu   elapsed  disk    query   current  rows
Parse         0     0.00      0.00     0        0         0     0
Execute       1     0.03      0.16     2        2         0     0
Fetch         0     0.00      0.00     0        0         0     0
----------  --   ------  --------  ----  -------   -------  ----
total         1     0.03      0.16     2        2         0     0

Misses in library cache during parse: 0
Misses in library cache during execute: 1
Optimizer goal: CHOOSE
Parsing user id: 8  (OPS$PCASSIDY)
****************************************
select parameter, value
from
 v$nls_parameters     where (upper(parameter)
   in ('NLS_SORT','NLS_CURRENCY',
  'NLS_ISO_CURRENCY', 'NLS_DATE_LANGUAGE',
  'NLS_NUMERIC_CHARACTERS',
  'NLS_LANGUAGE','NLS_TERRITORY'))

call       count      cpu  elapsed   disk  query  current  rows
Parse          1     0.01     0.01      0      0        0     0
```

```
Execute       1      0.01      0.01       0        0         0     0
Fetch         1      0.00      0.00       0        0         0     7
---------- ----  ------- --------   -----   -----   -------  -----
total         3      0.02      0.02       0        0         0     7

Misses in library cache during parse: 0
Optimizer goal: CHOOSE
Parsing user id: 8  (OPS$PCASSIDY)
error during parse of EXPLAIN PLAN statement
ORA-01039: insufficient privileges on underlying objects of the view
parse error offset: 108

<<<<<<< 8 Recursive SQL Statements Removed Here >>>>>>>

SELECT PNO
FROM   PARTS
WHERE  PNO NOT IN(SELECT PNO
                  FROM   TESTS)

Call        count        cpu     elapsed      disk     query  current
--------    -----  ---------  ---------- -------   -------  -------
Parse           1       0.48        0.52         0         0        0
Execute         1       0.00        0.00         0         0        0
Fetch           1   53080.16    55730.76   5547379   5561968     7228
-------- ------   ---------   ---------   -------   -------  -------
total           3   53080.64    55731.28   5547379   5561968     7228

Misses in library cache during parse: 1
Optimizer goal: CHOOSE
Parsing user id: 8  (OPS$PCASSIDY)

Rows       Execution Plan
--------   ---------------------------------------------------
      0    SELECT STATEMENT   GOAL: CHOOSE
   2427     FILTER
   2427      TABLE ACCESS   GOAL: ANALYZED (FULL) OF 'PARTS'
697561134     TABLE ACCESS   GOAL: ANALYZED (FULL) OF 'TESTS'
********************************************************************
ALTER SESSION SET SQL_TRACE = FALSE

call   count   cpu  elapsed  disk  query  current  rows
------ -----  ----  -------  ----  -----  -------  ----
Parse      1  0.02     0.02     0      0        0     0
Execute    1  0.00     0.04     0      0        0     0
```

```
Fetch       0  0.00      0.00     0       0         0      0
------ -----  ----  -------  ----  -----  -------  ----
total       2  0.02      0.06     0       0         0      0

Misses in library cache during parse: 1
Optimizer goal: CHOOSE
Parsing user id: 8  (OPS$PCASSIDY)
*********************************************************************
OVERALL TOTALS FOR ALL NON-RECURSIVE STMTS
call     count        cpu   elapsed      disk     query current
------ ------  --------  -------- -------- -------- -------
Parse        4       0.52      0.56        0         0       0
Execute      5       0.04      0.21        2         2       0
Fetch        3   53080.16  55730.76  5547379  5561968    7228
------ ------  --------  --------  -------  -------  ------
total       12   53080.72  55731.53  5547381  5561970    7228

Misses in library cache during parse: 2
Misses in library cache during execute: 1

OVERALL TOTALS FOR ALL RECURSIVE STMNTS

call      count   cpu  elapsed  disk  query  current   rows
------   ------  ----  -------  ----  -----  -------  -----
Parse        12  0.06     0.10     0      0        0      0
Execute      16  0.00     0.00     0      0        0      0
Fetch        26  0.16     0.17    14     58        0     20
-------- -----  ----  -------  ----  -----  -------  -----
total        54  0.22     0.27    14     58        0     20
Misses in library cache during parse: 0

    5  user  SQL statements in session.
   12  internal SQL statements in session.
   17  SQL statements in session.
    1  statement EXPLAINed in this session.
*********************************************************************
Trace file: ./pete_ora_9817.trc
Trace file compatibility: 7.03.02
Sort options: default

       0  session in tracefile.
       5  user  SQL statements in trace file.
      12  internal SQL statements in trace file.
      17  SQL statements in trace file.
      12  unique SQL statements in trace file.
```

```
1  SQL statements EXPLAINed using schema:
    OPS$PCASSIDY.prof$plan_table
      Default table was used.
      Table was created.
      Table was dropped.
      183 lines in trace file.
```

Besides spotting recursive SQL statements in the TKPROF output file, you can also view them in the shared SQL area of the shared pool by using **V$SQLAREA** and the **SQL_TEXT** column. Listing 8.11 shows only the statements that are against the **SEG$** table. Using the recursive call in the .prf file, the matching query is highlighted.

Listing 8.11 Viewing recursive calls in the shared SQL area.

```
SQL> SELECT SUBSTR(SQL_TEXT,1,75) "Statement"
  2  FROM   V$SQLAREA
  3* WHERE  SQL_TEXT LIKE '%seg$%';

Statement
----------------------------------------------------------------
SELECT SUBSTR(SQL_TEXT,1,75) "Statement"
delete from seg$ where file#=:1 and block#=:2
insert into seg$ (file#,block#,type,ts#,blocks,extents
select file#, block# from seg$ where type = 3
select type,ts#,blocks,extents,minexts,maxexts,
update seg$ set type=:3,ts#=:4,blocks=:5,extents=:6,
6 rows selected.
```

Now, let's try rewriting the previous query that took more than 15 hours to execute and then run it through SQL Trace (because the lack of indexes is not the problem). You can always use the set operator **MINUS** if the data types are the same in order to locate column data in one table that's not in the other. You'll note in Listing 8.12 that the results are just short of extraordinary.

The total CPU time spent fetching was 48.01 seconds, compared to 14 hours, 44 minutes, and 40.2 seconds for the miserably long-running query.

The "elapsed" column for fetches indicates that 51.57 seconds were required, compared to 15 hours, 28 minutes, and 50.88 seconds.

The "disk" column for fetches indicates that 4,011 physical reads of buffers from disk were required, compared to 5,547,379 physical reads for the long-running query.

The **PARTS** table has 10,000 rows and uses 169 blocks, and the **TESTS** table has 469,712 rows and uses 3,759 blocks. This is an extremely small amount of I/O when compared to the long-running query.

Also note the very drastic reduction in the number of rows in the Explain Plan for the **TESTS** table. Using **MINUS** referenced all 470,552 rows twice. Notice that **SORT (UNIQUE)** is used to sort the part numbers in both tables. The long-running query performed nearly 1,500 full table scans on the **TESTS** table for a whopping total of 697,561,134 rows.

Listing 8.12 Rewriting the long-running query using **MINUS**.

```
SQL> SELECT PNO FROM PARTS
  2  MINUS
  3  SELECT PNO FROM TESTS;

   PNO
  ----
   222
  1944
  1950
  1972
  1976
  1978
  5500

7 rows selected.
Elapsed: 00:00:55.80

SQL> EXIT

> cd $ORACLE_HOME/rdbms/log
/home3/oracle/7.3.2/rdbms/log

> grep MINUS *.trc
pete_ora_11209.trc:MINUS

> tkprof pete_ora_11209.trc $HOME/fast1.prf explain=/

> cd
/home2/dci2/pcassidy/v7322
> more fast1.prf
>>>>>>>    A Lot Of Nonrecursive Data Stripped <<<<<<<
```

```
****************************************
SELECT PNO FROM PARTS
MINUS
SELECT PNO FROM TESTS

call     count    cpu  elapsed  disk  query  current  rows
------ ------   -----  ------- ----- ------ -------- -----
Parse        1   0.45     0.47     0      0        0     0
Execute      2   0.73     0.90     0      0        2     0
Fetch        1  48.01    51.57  4011   3928      419     7
------ ------   -----  ------- ----- ------  -------- ----
total        4  49.19    52.94  4011   3928      421     7

Misses in library cache during parse: 1
Optimizer goal: CHOOSE
Parsing user id: 8  (OPS$PCASSIDY)

Rows     Execution Plan
-------  ---------------------------------------------
      0  SELECT STATEMENT   GOAL: CHOOSE
  19993   MINUS
  10000    SORT (UNIQUE)
  10000     TABLE ACCESS   GOAL: ANALYZED (FULL) OF 'PARTS'
 470552    SORT (UNIQUE)
 470552     TABLE ACCESS   GOAL: ANALYZED (FULL) OF 'TESTS'

******************************************************************
```

Now, let's try rewriting this query once more and then run it through SQL Trace. This time we'll use **NOT EXISTS**. You'll note in Listing 8.13 that these results are also extraordinary.

The total CPU time spent for fetches was 21.79 seconds, compared to 14 hours, 44 minutes, and 40.2 seconds for the long-running query.

The "elapsed" column for fetches indicates that 26.15 seconds were required, compared to 15 hours, 28 minutes, and 50.88 seconds.

The "disk" column for fetches indicates that 2,161 physical reads of buffers from disk were required, compared to 5,547,379 physical reads for the long-running query. The **PARTS** table has 10,000 rows and uses 169 blocks, and the **TESTS** table has 469,712 rows and uses 3,759 blocks. This is an extremely small amount of I/O when compared to the long-running query.

NOT EXISTS used the index on the **TESTS** table to look up the 10,000 part numbers in the **PARTS** table. Ten thousand lookups using an index on the **PARTS** table is much more efficient than 1,500 full table scans of the **TESTS** table (for a whopping total number of 697,561,134 rows).

Listing 8.13 Rewriting the long-running query using **NOT EXISTS**.

```
SQL> SELECT PNO
  2  FROM   PARTS
  3  WHERE  NOT EXISTS(SELECT 'DEBRA'
  4                    FROM    TESTS
  5*                   WHERE   PARTS.PNO = TESTS.PNO);

SQL> EXIT

> cd $ORACLE_HOME/rdbms/log
/home3/oracle/7.3.2/rdbms/log

> grep DEBRA *.trc
pete_ora_11238.trc:WHERE  NOT EXISTS(SELECT 'DEBRA'

> tkprof pete_ora_11238.trc $HOME/corne.prf explain=/
> cd
> more corne.prf
*********************************************************************
SELECT PNO
FROM   PARTS
WHERE  NOT EXISTS(SELECT 'DEBRA'
                  FROM    TESTS
                  WHERE   PARTS.PNO = TESTS.PNO)

call     count    cpu  elapsed   disk  query  current   rows
------- -----  ------  -------  -----  -----  -------  -----
Parse       1    0.54     0.58     14     84        0      0
Execute     1    0.00     0.00      0      0        0      0
Fetch       1   21.79    26.15   2161  40170        2      7
------  -----  ------  -------  -----  -----  -------  -----
total       3   22.33    26.73   2175  40254        2      7

Misses in library cache during parse: 1
Optimizer goal: CHOOSE
Parsing user id: 8  (OPS$PCASSIDY)
```

```
Rows     Execution Plan
------   -------------------------------------------------
     0   SELECT STATEMENT   GOAL: CHOOSE
 10000    FILTER
 10000     TABLE ACCESS   GOAL: ANALYZED (FULL) OF 'PARTS'
 10000     INDEX   GOAL: ANALYZED (RANGE SCAN) OF 'TESTS_PNO_INDEX'
                (NON-UNIQUE)
```

Table 8.1 compares the results of the three queries that identify all part numbers in the **PARTS** table that are not in the **TESTS** table. Rewriting the long-running query using a correlated subquery with **NOT EXISTS** was the hero in this scenario. The real dog was the query using **NOT IN**.

Using Autotrace

Autotrace is a new environmental parameter available within SQL*Plus under Oracle7.3. When you set **autotrace** on, as in Listing 8.14, the query is executed, an unformatted Explain Plan is output to the screen, and client/server information is displayed. The client/server information at the end of the Autotrace output is very similar to the data produced by SQL Trace and TKPROF.

Listing 8.14 Using Autotrace.

```
SQL> SHOW AUTOTRACE
autotrace OFF

SQL> SET AUTOTRACE ON

SQL> SELECT PNO
     FROM   PARTS
     WHERE  NOT EXISTS(SELECT 'DEBRA'
                       FROM    TESTS
                       WHERE   PARTS.PNO = TESTS.PNO);

    PNO
  -----
    222
   1944
   1950
   1972
   1976
   1978
```

```
   5500
7 rows selected.

Elapsed: 00:00:40.83

Execution Plan
----------------------------------------------------------
 0      SELECT STATEMENT Optimizer=CHOOSE
 1      (Cost=26 Card=500 Bytes=13000)

 1    0   FILTER
 2    1      TABLE ACCESS (FULL) OF 'PARTS'
                (Cost=26 Card=500 Bytes=13000)

 3    1      INDEX (RANGE SCAN) OF 'TESTS_PNO_INDEX'
                  (NON-UNIQUE) (Cost=10 Card=820 Bytes=9840)

Statistics
----------------------------------------------------------
        740  recursive calls
          5  db block gets
      40254  consistent gets
       2175  physical reads
          0  redo size
        222  bytes sent via SQL*Net to client
        375  bytes received via SQL*Net from client
          3  SQL*Net roundtrips to/from client
0            sorts (memory)
1            sorts (disk)
2            rows processed

SQL Trace/TKPROF Output
call      count    cpu   elapsed   disk   query   current    rows
------    -----  ------  -------  ------  ------  -------  ------
Parse         1    0.54     0.58      14      84        0       0
Execute       1    0.00     0.00       0       0        0       0
Fetch         1   21.79    26.15    2161   40170        2       7
------    -----  ------  -------  ------  ------  -------  ------
total         3   22.33    26.73    2175   40254        2       7
```

Table 8.2 compares the output from Autotrace to the output of TKPROF.

Summary

Only use SQL Trace for troublesome, long-running SQL statements. Normally, you can check the existence of indexes writing queries on the data dictionary views **USER_INDEXES** or **USER_IND_COLUMNS**. If indexes exist and are properly used, execute the statement using Explain Plan. If Explain Plan does not reveal the problem, try SQL Trace/ TKPROF. You can also cause TKPROF to produce an Explain Plan output along with the normal report.

Table 8.1 Comparing SQL Trace/ TKPROF output from the three queries.

Method	Fetches CPU	Fetches Elapsed	Fetches Disk
NOT IN	53,080 Sec	55,730 Sec	5,547,379
MINUS	48 Sec	52 Sec	4,011
NOT EXISTS	21 Sec	26 Sec	2,161

Table 8.2 Autotrace compared to TKPROF.

Autotrace Parameter	TKPROF Parameter
consistent gets	query
physical reads	disk
SQL*Net roundtrips to/from client	count
rows processed	rows

Hints

HIGH PERFORMANCE

CHAPTER 9

The purpose of Oracle hints is to control which optimizer is used and how data is accessed. This chapter teaches you how to use hints.

Hints

Why Use Hints?

Occasionally, Oracle does not make the best decision in formulating a plan for executing a SQL statement. For instance, the wrong index is used, or the wrong table is selected as the driving or inner table. Or, perhaps, Oracle performs a full table scan when using an index would be faster. Another reason for using hints is upgrades. If you want to absolutely guarantee the method Oracle always uses on a statement, use a hint. Also, hints override the session and database levels of **OPTIMIZER_GOAL** and **OPTIMIZER_MODE**, respectively. Oracle Corporation is excellent about not discarding commands or syntax from previous versions. Finally, you know your data better than Oracle. So, by using a hint, the best method of accessing data can be forced. However, some of your hints may be ignored. You can combine hints for a SQL statement, as long as they are not conflicting hints such as FULL and INDEX.

Hint Syntax

The syntax for hints uses one of two methods, and both methods use a comment, followed by a plus sign "+", followed by the hint. You can use comments in SQL statements in two ways. One is to use the C language construct "**/* Comment */**". The other way to write a comment in a SQL statement is to use "--". Listing 9.1 shows two comments and the same hint with different formats. The two comments are equivalent, and the two hints are equivalent—just different formats. The Explain Plans show that Oracle takes these hints. The actual execution times (using the same hint in two different formats) are included to illustrate how to use the hints in an actual SQL statement. The **FULL** hint causes Oracle to perform a full table scan.

Listing 9.1 Two types of comments and hints.

```
SQL> SELECT PNO, TNO  /* One Way To Comment */
  2  FROM   TESTS     -- This Is Another Way
  3  WHERE  TNO = (SELECT MAX(TNO)
  4                FROM   TESTS T
  5                WHERE  TESTS.PNO = T.PNO)
  6         AND PNO < 11
  7* ORDER  BY PNO;

SQL> EXPLAIN PLAN FOR
  2  SELECT --+ FULL(TESTS)
  3  MAX(TNO)
  4  FROM   TESTS
  5* WHERE  PNO = 93;
Explained.

SQL> @explain
Query Plan                                      COST
---------------------------------------- -----
SELECT STATEMENT   CHOOSE                        571
  SORT AGGREGATE
    TABLE ACCESS FULL TESTS ANALYZED             571

SQL> SELECT --+ FULL(TESTS)
  2  MAX(TNO)
  3  FROM   TESTS
  4* WHERE  PNO = 93;

MAX(TNO)
--------
    8650

Elapsed: 00:00:39.58

SQL> EXPLAIN PLAN FOR
  2  SELECT /*+ FULL(TESTS) */   MAX(TNO)
  3  FROM   TESTS
  4* WHERE  PNO = 93;
Explained.

SQL> @explain
Query Plan                               COST
-------------------------------- -----
SELECT STATEMENT   CHOOSE                 571
  SORT AGGREGATE
```

```
    TABLE ACCESS FULL TESTS ANALYZED        571

SQL> SELECT /*+ FULL(TESTS) */   MAX(TNO)
  2  FROM    TESTS
  3* WHERE   PNO = 93;

MAX(TNO)
--------
    8650

Elapsed: 00:00:40.82
```

Why Hints Are Ignored

If the syntax for the hint is incorrect, the hint is ignored and no errors are generated. By incorrect syntax, I mean the wrong number of arguments is supplied to the hint. The first example in Listing 9.2 omits the table name as the only argument to be used with the **FULL** hint. Notice the absence of any error messages. However, the output from the Explain Plan indicates that the index is used instead of performing a full table scan. Because the incorrect number of arguments is supplied in the hint, Oracle just ignores the incorrect hint. To force Oracle to use the **FULL** hint, the hint should appear as **FULL(TESTS)**.

If table aliases are used, the table alias must be used in the hint. The second example in Listing 9.2 uses the table alias "T" in the **FROM** clause. For Oracle to use the hint, "T" or "t" must be used as the table name argument in the **FULL** hint instead of the actual table name **TESTS**. Once again, no error messages occur, but the hint is ignored. The hint should appear as **FULL(T)** to force Oracle to perform a full table scan on the table **TESTS**. The correct hint is shown in an Explain Plan for verification. The next example uses the table alias "t" (lowercase). However, the hint uses a capital "T." The table alias is *not* case sensitive. The Explain Plan indicates this is the case.

In addition, if the hint is completely out of context, it is ignored. For example, if you use the **HASH** hint in a query on a table that is not hashed, the hint is ignored because the table is not hashed. Obviously, if the hint is misspelled, then it is ignored. Listing 9.2 shows these two mistakes.

Oracle will also ignore conflicting hints. The conflicting hints **FULL** and **INDEX** are ignored. Oracle cannot possibly perform both a full table scan and use an index on the same query. It is like someone telling you to sit in the corner of a round room.

Finally, the rule-based optimizer supposedly ignores hints. However, it certainly does *not* ignore hints if statistics are available. Notice in both cases where the session **OPTIMIZER_GOAL** is set to **RULE** or the parameter **OPTIMIZER_MODE** is set to **RULE** that Oracle does *not* ignore the **FULL** hint. Next, the statistics are deleted from the **PARTS** table, and Oracle still uses the **FULL** hint even though the database parameter **OPTIMIZER_MODE** equals **RULE** and no table statistics exist. Hints take precedence over the database and session settings of **OPTIMIZER_MODE** and **OPTIMIZER_GOAL** respectively. Even when no statistics exist, Oracle uses the cost-based optimizer for hints **ALL_ROWS** or **FIRST_ROWS**. So, the next time someone tells you the rule-based optimizer does not take hints, you can tell him to take a hike!

Listing 9.2 When hints are ignored.

```
SQL> EXPLAIN PLAN FOR    -- Table Name Missing
  2  SELECT --+ FULL
  3  MAX(TNO)            -- Hint Ignored
  4  FROM   TESTS        -- Index Is Used
  5* WHERE  PNO = 93;
Explained.

SQL> @explain
Query Plan                                          COST
-------------------------------------------- ------
SELECT STATEMENT   CHOOSE                              4
  SORT AGGREGATE
    TABLE ACCESS BY ROWID TESTS ANALYZED               4
      INDEX RANGE SCAN TESTS_PNO_INDEX ANALYZED

SQL> EXPLAIN PLAN FOR  -- "T" Must Be Used
  2  SELECT /*+ FULL(TESTS) */  MAX(TNO)
  3  FROM   TESTS T
  4  WHERE  PNO = 93;
Explained.

SQL> @explain
Query Plan                                          COST
-------------------------------------------- ------
SELECT STATEMENT   CHOOSE                              4
  SORT AGGREGATE
    TABLE ACCESS BY ROWID TESTS ANALYZED               4
      INDEX RANGE SCAN TESTS_PNO_INDEX ANALYZED
```

```
SQL> EXPLAIN PLAN FOR  --Takes Hint Here Since "T" Is Used
  2  SELECT /*+ FULL(T) */  MAX(TNO)
  3  FROM   TESTS T
  4* WHERE  PNO = 93;
Explained.

SQL> @explain
Query Plan                                     COST
------------------------------------ -----
SELECT STATEMENT   CHOOSE                       571
  SORT AGGREGATE
    TABLE ACCESS FULL TESTS ANALYZED            571

SQL> EXPLAIN PLAN FOR     -- NOT CASE  SENSITIVE
  2  SELECT /*+ FULL(T) */  MAX(TNO)
  3  FROM   TESTS t
  4* WHERE  PNO = 93;
Explained.

SQL> @explain
Query Plan                                     COST
------------------------------------ -----
SELECT STATEMENT   CHOOSE                       571
  SORT AGGREGATE
    TABLE ACCESS FULL TESTS ANALYZED            571

SQL> EXPLAIN PLAN FOR
  2  SELECT --+ HASH(TESTS)
  3  MAX(TNO)      -- No Cluster Exists
  4  FROM  TESTS  -- Hint Ignored
  5* WHERE PNO = 93;
Explained.

SQL> @explain
Query Plan                                                COST
----------------------------------------------- -----
SELECT STATEMENT   CHOOSE                                    4
  SORT AGGREGATE
    TABLE ACCESS BY ROWID TESTS ANALYZED                     4
      INDEX RANGE SCAN TESTS_PNO_INDEX ANALYZED

SQL> SELECT INDEX_NAME   -- Name Of Index
  2  FROM   USER_INDEXES -- To Be Used In Hint
  3  WHERE  TABLE_NAME = 'TESTS';
```

```
INDEX_NAME
----------------------------
TESTS_PNO_INDEX

SQL> EXPLAIN PLAN FOR      -- Conflicting Hints
  2          SELECT
 /*+ FULL(TESTS) INDEX(TESTS TESTS_PNO_INDEX) */
  4          RESULTS
  5  FROM   TESTS
  6  WHERE  PNO = 222;
Explained.

SQL> @explain
Query Plan                                COST
---------------------------------- ------
SELECT STATEMENT   CHOOSE                     2
  TABLE ACCESS BY ROWID TESTS                 2
    INDEX RANGE SCAN TESTS_PNO_INDEX

SQL> ALTER SESSION SET OPTIMIZER_GOAL = RULE;
Session altered.

SQL> -- MYTH   EXPOSED !!!
SQL> -- Rule-based Optimizer Ignores Hints...NOT

SQL> EXPLAIN PLAN FOR
  2  SELECT --+ FULL(TESTS)
  3  PNO, TNO
  4  FROM   TESTS
  5* WHERE  PNO > 0;
Explained.

SQL> @explain
Query Plan                            COST
--------------------------------- ------
SELECT STATEMENT   RULE                 571
  TABLE ACCESS FULL TESTS ANALYZED    571

SQL> EXPLAIN PLAN FOR
  2  SELECT
  3  PNO, TNO  -- Return Table Of Nearly 1 Million Rows
  4  FROM   TESTS  -- Do NOT Want Oracle To Use An Index
  5* WHERE  PNO > 0;
Explained.
```

```
SQL> @explain
Query Plan                                         COST
------------------------------------------- ------
SELECT STATEMENT   RULE
  TABLE ACCESS BY ROWID TESTS ANALYZED
    INDEX RANGE SCAN TESTS_PNO_INDEX ANALYZED

SVRMGR> show parameter optimizer
NAME                               TYPE     VALUE
---------------------------------- ------   -----
optimizer_mode                     string   RULE
optimizer_percent_parallel         integer  0

SQL> EXPLAIN PLAN FOR
  2  SELECT --+ FULL(TESTS)
  3  PNO,  TNO
  4  FROM  TESTS
  5* WHERE PNO > 0;
Explained.

SQL> @explain
Query Plan                             COST
---------------------------------- -----
SELECT STATEMENT   RULE                 571
  TABLE ACCESS FULL TESTS ANALYZED     571

SQL> ANALYZE TABLE TESTS DELETE STATISTICS;
Table analyzed.

SQL> EXPLAIN PLAN FOR
  2  SELECT --+ FULL(TESTS)
  3  PNO,  TNO  -- With No Table Statistics
  4  FROM  TESTS
  5* WHERE PNO > 0;
Explained.

SQL> @explain
Query Plan                     COST
------------------------ ------
SELECT STATEMENT   RULE      571
  TABLE ACCESS FULL TESTS   571

SQL> ANALYZE INDEX TESTS_PNO_INDEX DELETE STATISTICS;
Index analyzed.

SQL> EXPLAIN PLAN FOR
```

```
  2  SELECT --+ FULL(TESTS)
  3  PNO,  TNO
  4  FROM  TESTS
  5* WHERE PNO > 0;
Explained.

SQL> @explain
Query Plan                        COST
------------------------ ------
SELECT STATEMENT    RULE      571
  TABLE ACCESS FULL TESTS     571
```

Optimizer Hints

Four hints pertain to the optimizer type. Remember Fric and Frac (with heavy emphasis on FRAC)? Once again you can use **FIRST_ROWS**, **RULE**, **ALL_ROWS**, or **CHOOSE** as one of the four hints. Figure 9.1 shows these four hints used to control which optimizer Oracle uses for a SQL statement.

Listing 9.3 shows the hint **ALL_ROWS**. **ALL_ROWS** invokes the cost-based optimizer and requests Oracle return *all* the rows in the quickest way possible. The cost-based optimizer uses bitmap indexes, but the rule-based optimizer does not. The hint **ALL_ROWS** invokes the cost-based optimizer, and Oracle uses both bitmap indexes. Notice the extremely low cost of 5. This number is derived "on the fly" because no statistics exist on the table for the optimizer to use—it performs a very

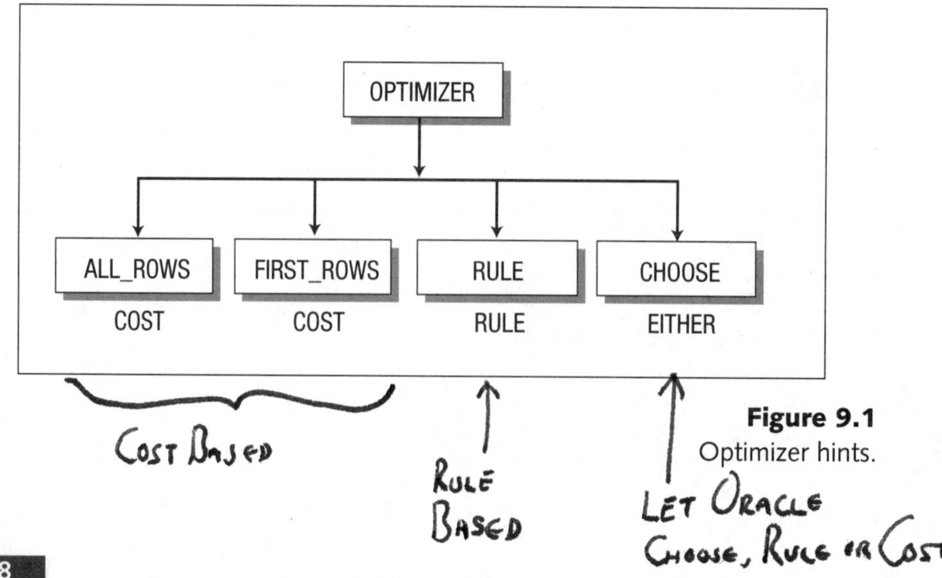

Figure 9.1
Optimizer hints.

quick estimate. The estimated cost of 5 is much too low. Another reason to use the hint **ALL_ROWS** is to override the parameter file setting of **OPTIMIZER_MODE**. If **OPTIMIZER_MODE** is set to **RULE** or **FIRST_ROWS** and you desire the fastest throughput, use the **ALL_ROWS** hint. Or, you might want to override the **OPTIMIZER_GOAL** setting for your session.

Listing 9.3 ALL_ROWS.

```
SQL> EXPLAIN PLAN FOR
  2  SELECT --+ ALL_ROWS
  3  SNO,    REGION_HASH
  4  FROM    STATS  /* 2,000 ROWS RETURNED */
  5* WHERE   REGION_BIT_MAP = 'W' AND SEX = 'F';

SQL> @explain
 Query Plan                                            COST
----------------------------------------------------- ------
SELECT STATEMENT   HINT: ALL_ROWS                          5
  TABLE ACCESS BY ROWID STATS                              5
    BITMAP CONVERSION TO ROWIDS
      BITMAP AND
        BITMAP INDEX SINGLE VALUE BITMAP_REGION_BIT_MAP
        BITMAP INDEX SINGLE VALUE BITMAP_SEX
```

Another method for forcing Oracle to use the cost-based optimizer is to use the **FIRST_ROWS** hint. **FIRST_ROWS** requests that Oracle retrieve the first row in the quickest way possible. Even though the **STATS** table has not been analyzed, the hint **FIRST_ROWS** causes the cost-based optimizer to be used. The cost-based optimizer computes the cost without any statistics available in the data dictionary. The cost of 5 is much too low in Listing 9.4. For a bitmap index to be used, the cost-based optimizer must be used. One way to cause the cost-based optimizer to be evoked for a SQL statement is to use the hint **FIRST_ROWS** or **ALL_ROWS**. Notice Oracle uses both bitmap indexes because the hint **FIRST_ROWS** is used. The plan for both **ALL_ROWS** and **FIRST_ROWS** is identical. Hints override the init.ora parameter **OPTIMIZER_MODE** and the **ALTER SESSION SET OPTIMIZER_GOAL** command.

Listing 9.4 FIRST_ROWS.

```
SQL> EXPLAIN PLAN FOR
  2  SELECT --+ FIRST_ROWS
```

```
  3  SNO,    REGION_HASH
  4  FROM    STATS     /* 2,000 ROWS */
  5* WHERE   REGION_BIT_MAP = 'W' AND SEX = 'F';

SQL> @explain
Query Plan                                                   COST
------------------------------------------------------------ -----
SELECT STATEMENT    HINT: FIRST_ROWS                             5
  TABLE ACCESS BY ROWID STATS                                    5
    BITMAP CONVERSION TO ROWIDS
      BITMAP AND
        BITMAP INDEX SINGLE VALUE BITMAP_REGION_BIT_MAP
        BITMAP INDEX SINGLE VALUE BITMAP_SEX
```

The optimizer of the future is the cost-based optimizer, not the rule-based optimizer. However, you know more about your data than Oracle does. If you have spent many hours tuning a particularly troublesome query and you want to ensure that Oracle always uses the same access method, you can use the **RULE** hint. Once again, as a reminder, the **RULE** hint overrides the current session-level setting for **OPTIMIZER_GOAL** as well as the current database setting of the parameter **OPTIMIZER_MODE**. Listing 9.5 shows you how to use the **RULE** hint. Notice there is no cost, which indicates the rule-based optimizer is evoked. Also, the string "**HINT: RULE**" indicates Oracle recognizes the hint.

Listing 9.5 RULE.

```
SQL> EXPLAIN PLAN FOR
  2  SELECT  --+ RULE
  3  TEMPERATURE, SEX
  4  FROM  STATS
  5  WHERE SNO > 800000;
Explained.

SQL> @explain
Query Plan                                             COST
------------------------------------------------------ -----
SELECT STATEMENT    HINT: RULE
  TABLE ACCESS BY ROWID STATS ANALYZED
    INDEX RANGE SCAN BTREE_UNIQUE_SNO ANALYZED
```

When you connect to an Oracle product, your default **OPTIMIZER_GOAL** is **CHOOSE**. The **CHOOSE** hint allows Oracle to make the choice of which optimizer to use for a SQL statement. If statistics are available for one of the tables in the statement, the cost-based optimizer is used. If no statistics are available for any of the tables in the SQL statement, the rule-based optimizer is used (unless a hint such as **ALL_ROWS** or **FIRST_ROWS** is used). If you alter your session to **RULE** before issuing the statement with the **CHOOSE** hint, the rule-based optimizer is used. If you alter your session to either **FIRST_ROWS** or **ALL_ROWS** before issuing the statement with the **CHOOSE** hint, the cost-based optimizer is used. Listing 9.6 shows how to use the **CHOOSE** hint. You'll notice that the **STATS** table is analyzed because the **NUM_ROWS** column is not null (1,000,018). Because statistics exist for the **STATS** table and the **CHOOSE** hint is used, Oracle uses the cost-based optimizer. Please be aware that this hint is not required in this situation because the **OPTIMIZER_MODE** setting has the default value of **CHOOSE** and the **OPTIMIZER_GOAL** also has the default value of **CHOOSE**. The next-to-last example in Listing 9.6 shows what happens when no statistics exist on a table and the **CHOOSE** hint is used. Because the **COST** column is null, the rule-based optimizer is used. Once more, the hint is not required. Because no statistics exist, the rule-based optimizer is used. You might wonder why you should ever use this hint. If the parameter **OPTIMIZER_MODE** or **OPTIMIZER_GOAL** is set to **ALL_ROWS** or **FIRST_ROWS**, Oracle will use the cost-based optimizer. If you want to override the database- or session-level settings, use the **CHOOSE** hint.

The last example in Listing 9.6 indicates that Oracle uses the cost-based optimizer even if no statistics exist on the **STATS** table because the **COST** column contains 237. But what if you only want analyzed tables to be queried using the cost-based optimizer? The answer is the **CHOOSE** hint.

Listing 9.6 CHOOSE.

```
SQL> SELECT NUM_ROWS     -- STATS Analyzed
  2  FROM   USER_TABLES -- Num_Rows Is Not Null
  3  WHERE  TABLE_NAME = 'STATS';

NUM_ROWS
--------
 1000018

SQL> EXPLAIN PLAN FOR
  2  SELECT /*+ CHOOSE */
  3  TEMPERATURE, SEX
```

```
  4  FROM    STATS
  5* WHERE   SNO > 999999;
Explained.

SQL> @explain
Query Plan                                           COST
---------------------------------------------- -----
SELECT STATEMENT   HINT: CHOOSE                         4
  TABLE ACCESS BY ROWID STATS ANALYZED                  4
    INDEX RANGE SCAN BTREE_UNIQUE_SNO ANALYZED

SQL> EXPLAIN PLAN FOR  -- Choose Hint Not Needed
  2  SELECT
  3  TEMPERATURE, SEX
  4  FROM    STATS
  5* WHERE   SNO > 999999;
Explained.

SQL> @explain
Query Plan                                           COST
---------------------------------------------- -----
SELECT STATEMENT   CHOOSE                               4
  TABLE ACCESS BY ROWID STATS ANALYZED                  4
    INDEX RANGE SCAN BTREE_UNIQUE_SNO ANALYZED

SQL> ANALYZE TABLE STATS DELETE STATISTICS;
Table analyzed.

SQL> EXPLAIN PLAN FOR
  2  SELECT /*+ CHOOSE */
  3  TEMPERATURE, SEX
  4  FROM    STATS
  5* WHERE   SNO > 999999;
Explained.

SQL> @explain
Query Plan                                 COST
------------------------------------ -----
SELECT STATEMENT   HINT: CHOOSE
  TABLE ACCESS BY ROWID STATS
    INDEX RANGE SCAN BTREE_UNIQUE_SNO

SQL> ALTER SESSION SET OPTIMIZER_GOAL = ALL_ROWS;
Session altered.
```

```
SQL> EXPLAIN PLAN FOR  -- Statistics Deleted
  2  SELECT            -- From The STATS Table
  3  TEMPERATURE, SEX
  4  FROM     STATS
  5* WHERE    SNO > 999999;
Explained.

SQL> @explain
Query Plan                                  COST
------------------------------------ -----
SELECT STATEMENT    ALL_ROWS                 237
  TABLE ACCESS BY ROWID STATS                237
    INDEX RANGE SCAN BTREE_UNIQUE_SNO

SQL> EXPLAIN PLAN FOR
  2  SELECT /*+ CHOOSE */
  3  TEMPERATURE, SEX
  4  FROM     STATS
  5* WHERE    SNO > 999999;
Explained.

SQL> @explain
Query Plan                                  COST
------------------------------------ ------
SELECT STATEMENT    HINT: CHOOSE
  TABLE ACCESS BY ROWID STATS
    INDEX RANGE SCAN BTREE_UNIQUE_SNO
```

Btree Indexes

Several hints control the use of btree indexes in Oracle. Refer to Figure 9.2 for the hints used with btree indexes.

Currently, four hints exist. Oracle recommends using the **INDEX_ASC** hint instead of the **INDEX** hint, because the optimizer could change in future releases of Oracle. Up to this point in time, Oracle8, scans btree indexes in ascending order. However, using the hint **INDEX_DESC** forces the index to be scanned from bottom to top.

Listing 9.7 shows the importance of btree index hints. In the one-million-row **STATS** table, the **REGION_BTREE** column has one value of "SE." A nonunique btree index exists on the column **REGION_BTREE**. However, when explained, Oracle

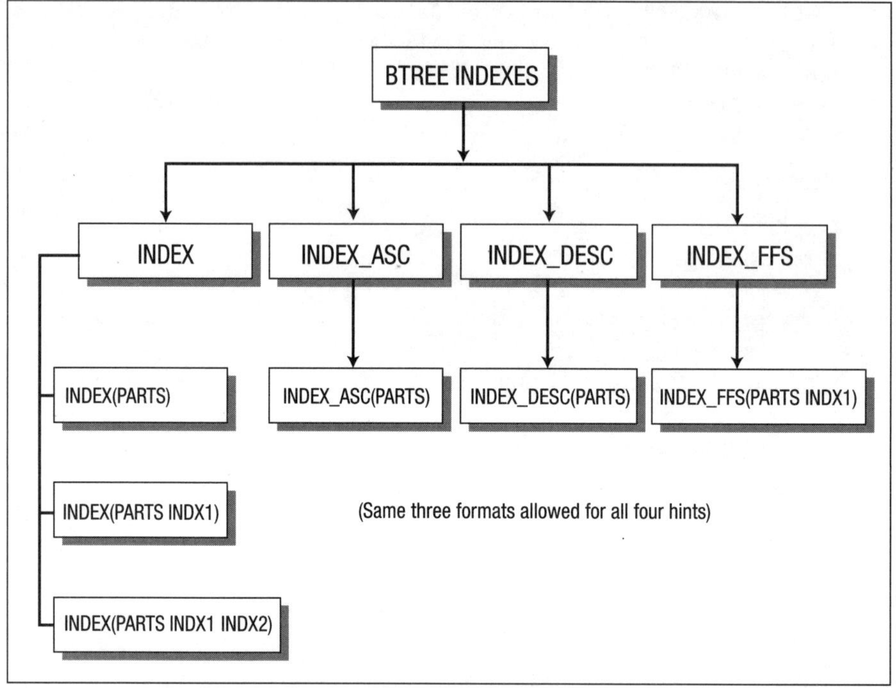

Figure 9.2
Btree index hints.

does not use the index but rather performs a full table scan. Oracle deduces that because there are eight distinct values and one million rows, there are 125,000 rows for each value. This full table scan would be eliminated if there were histograms on the **STATS** table. However, because no histograms exist, the **INDEX** hint is well in order. Notice the difference in the cost and elapsed times of the query with and without the **INDEX** hint. The cost of a full table scan is 3,958, and it requires 2 minutes and 12 seconds. The query using the **INDEX** hint has a higher cost of 4,898, but it only requires 1 second. This is another example of a query with a higher cost outperforming a query with a lower cost. Can you believe a time difference of 2 minutes and 11 seconds for a one-million-row table? What about a table with 175,000,000 rows?

Listing 9.7 INDEX.

```
SQL> SELECT REGION_BTREE, COUNT(*)
  2  FROM   STATS
```

```
  3  GROUP  BY REGION_BTREE;

REG  COUNT(*)
---  --------
E      125000
N      124999
NE     125000
NW       1000
S      125000
SE          1
SW     495000
W        4000

8 rows selected.

SQL> EXPLAIN PLAN FOR -- Full Table Scan For 1 Row
  2  SELECT  *         -- From 1,000,000 Rows
  3  FROM    STATS
  4  WHERE   REGION_BTREE = 'SE';
Explained.

SQL> @explain
Query Plan                             COST
---------------------------------- -----
SELECT STATEMENT   CHOOSE              3958
  TABLE ACCESS FULL STATS ANALYZED  3958

SQL> SELECT  SNO, SNAME, REGION_BTREE
  2  FROM    STATS
  3* WHERE   REGION_BTREE = 'SE';

    SNO SNAME                          REG
 ------ ----------------------------- ---
 375000 BETWEEN 300001 AND 600000     SE

Elapsed: 00:02:12.64

SQL> EXPLAIN PLAN FOR
  2  SELECT /*+ INDEX(STATS BTREE_REGION) */  *
  3  FROM    STATS
  4* WHERE   REGION_BTREE = 'SE';
Explained.

SQL> @explain
Query Plan                                      COST
----------------------------------------- -----
```

```
SELECT STATEMENT   CHOOSE                         4898
  TABLE ACCESS BY ROWID STATS ANALYZED            4898
    INDEX RANGE SCAN BTREE_REGION ANALYZED

SQL> SELECT /*+ INDEX(STATS BTREE_REGION) */  SNO
  2  FROM     STATS
  3* WHERE    REGION_BTREE = 'SE';

 SNO
--------
 375000

Elapsed: 00:00:01.10
```

Listing 9.8 illustrates the outcome of submitting more than one index name to the **INDEX** hint. An index is created on the **TNO** column of the **TESTS** table. Then, the table is reanalyzed because a new index exists. The cost of using the index on the part number column (**PNO**) is 4. The cost of using the index on the test number column (**TNO**) is 39. Therefore, the hint **--+INDEX(TESTS TESTS_TNO TESTS_PNO_INDEX)** causes Oracle to use the index with the lowest cost. In this case, the index on the part number column is used because its cost is 4 and the cost of the index on the test number column is 39. However, Oracle could use both indexes and combine the results under certain circumstances.

Listing 9.8 INDEX(TESTS INDX1 INDX2).

```
SQL> CREATE INDEX TESTS_TNO ON TESTS(TNO);
Index created.

Elapsed: 00:06:29.19

SQL> ANALYZE TABLE TESTS COMPUTE STATISTICS;
Table analyzed.

Elapsed: 00:03:04.01

SQL> EXPLAIN PLAN FOR -- Cost For TESTS_PNO_INDEX Is 4
  2  SELECT /*+ INDEX(TESTS TESTS_PNO_INDEX) */  *
  3  FROM   TESTS
  4  WHERE  PNO = 90;
Explained.
```

```
SQL> @explain
Query Plan                                    COST
--------------------------------------- -----
SELECT STATEMENT   CHOOSE                        4
  TABLE ACCESS BY ROWID TESTS ANALYZED           4
    INDEX RANGE SCAN TESTS_PNO_INDEX ANALYZED

SQL> EXPLAIN PLAN FOR  -- Cost For TESTS_TNO Is 39
  2  SELECT --+ INDEX(TESTS TESTS_TNO)
  3  *
  4  FROM   TESTS
  5  WHERE  TNO = 1;
Explained.

SQL> @explain
Query Plan                                    COST
--------------------------------------- -----
SELECT STATEMENT   CHOOSE                       39
  TABLE ACCESS BY ROWID TESTS ANALYZED          39
    INDEX RANGE SCAN TESTS_TNO ANALYZED

SQL> EXPLAIN PLAN FOR
  2  SELECT --+INDEX(TESTS TESTS_TNO TESTS_PNO_INDEX)
  3  *
  4  FROM       TESTS
  5  WHERE      TNO = 1 AND
  6             PNO = 90;
Explained.

SQL> @explain
Query Plan                                          COST
--------------------------------------------- -----
SELECT STATEMENT   CHOOSE                              4
  TABLE ACCESS BY ROWID TESTS ANALYZED                 4
    INDEX RANGE SCAN TESTS_PNO_INDEX ANALYZED
```

As you can see in Listing 9.9, Oracle uses the index with the lowest cost when no index names appear in the **INDEX** hint. Oracle uses the index on the part number column because it has a cost of 4. To retrieve one row from a 471,000-row table, 11.5 seconds are required.

Listing 9.9 INDEX(TESTS).

```
SQL> EXPLAIN PLAN FOR
  2  SELECT --+ INDEX(TESTS)
  3  *
  4  FROM       TESTS
  5  WHERE      TNO = 1 AND
  6*            PNO = 90;
Explained.

SQL> @explain
Query Plan                                          COST
------------------------------------------------ -----
SELECT STATEMENT   CHOOSE                              4
  TABLE ACCESS BY ROWID TESTS ANALYZED                 4
    INDEX RANGE SCAN TESTS_PNO_INDEX ANALYZED

SQL> SELECT
  2  --+ INDEX(TESTS)
  3  *
  4  FROM  TESTS
  5  WHERE TNO = 1 AND
  6*       PNO = 90;

    PNO    TNO R
 ------ ------ -
     90      1 F

Elapsed: 00:00:11.50
```

If you want Oracle to use both indexes and merge the index scans, use the **AND_EQUAL** hint. You probably won't use this hint that often, but it might be faster than just using one index. Listing 9.10 shows that using the **AND_EQUAL** hint is much faster for this query than using just one index. It requires 0.87 seconds! That's an improvement of 10.63 seconds for a table with less than one million rows. Just imagine the tremendous performance improvement for a table with 150,000,000 rows.

Listing 9.10 AND_EQUAL.

```
SQL> EXPLAIN PLAN FOR
  2  SELECT
  3  --+AND_EQUAL(TESTS TESTS_PNO_INDEX TESTS_TNO)
  4  *
  5  FROM  TESTS
```

```
  6  WHERE TNO = 1 AND
  7        PNO = 90;
Explained.

SQL> @explain
Query Plan                                          COST
--------------------------------------------- -----
SELECT STATEMENT   CHOOSE                              7
  TABLE ACCESS BY ROWID TESTS ANALYZED                 7
    AND_EQUAL
      INDEX RANGE SCAN TESTS_PNO_INDEX ANALYZED
      INDEX RANGE SCAN TESTS_TNO ANALYZED

SQL> SELECT
  2  --+AND_EQUAL(TESTS TESTS_PNO_INDEX TESTS_TNO)
  3  *
  4  FROM  TESTS
  5  WHERE TNO = 1 AND
  6*       PNO = 90;

   PNO    TNO R
------ ------ -
    90      1 F

Elapsed: 00:00:00.87
```

When using hints, be careful what you ask for. Hints allow a great deal of flexibility, but the incorrect hint can be outrageously costly. At least you have a large pool of hints to try with slow-running queries. You can also try rewriting the query. In Listing 9.11, Oracle uses the **USE_CONCAT** hint, but this hint causes three full table scans. The second example does not use the **USE_CONCAT** hint, but it accomplishes exactly the same result. When you see **CONCATENATION** in the output of Explain Plan, you know Oracle has transformed the query so that both indexes can be used. The last example shows that the hint plan is the same as the query without the hint.

Listing 9.11 USE_CONCAT.

```
SQL> EXPLAIN PLAN FOR
  2  SELECT /*+ USE_CONCAT(TESTS) */   *
  3  FROM   TESTS
  4  WHERE  PNO BETWEEN 1 AND 9000 OR
  5*        TNO BETWEEN 1 AND 7000;
Explained.
```

```
SQL> @explain
Query Plan                                  COST
------------------------------------------ -----
SELECT STATEMENT    CHOOSE                  1713
  CONCATENATION
    TABLE ACCESS FULL TESTS ANALYZED         571
    TABLE ACCESS FULL TESTS ANALYZED         571
    TABLE ACCESS FULL TESTS ANALYZED         571

SQL> EXPLAIN PLAN FOR
  2  SELECT *
  3  FROM    TESTS
  4  WHERE   PNO BETWEEN 1 AND 55 OR
  5*         TNO = 1;
Explained.

SQL> @explain
Query Plan                                               COST
------------------------------------------------------ ------
SELECT STATEMENT    CHOOSE                                 85
  CONCATENATION
    TABLE ACCESS BY ROWID TESTS ANALYZED                   46
      INDEX RANGE SCAN TESTS_TNO ANALYZED
    TABLE ACCESS BY ROWID TESTS ANALYZED                   46
      INDEX RANGE SCAN TESTS_PNO_INDEX ANALYZED

SQL> EXPLAIN PLAN FOR
  2  SELECT /*+ USE_CONCAT(TESTS) */  *
  3  FROM     TESTS
  4  WHERE    PNO BETWEEN 1 AND 55 OR
  5           TNO = 1;
Explained.

SQL> @explain
Query Plan                                      COST
---------------------------------------------- -----
SELECT STATEMENT    CHOOSE                        85
  CONCATENATION
    TABLE ACCESS BY ROWID TESTS ANALYZED          46
      INDEX RANGE SCAN TESTS_TNO ANALYZED
    TABLE ACCESS BY ROWID TESTS ANALYZED          46
      INDEX RANGE SCAN TESTS_PNO_INDEX
            ANALYZED
```

Oracle recommends the use of the hint **INDEX_ASC** instead of **INDEX**. Future releases of Oracle might not scan the btree indexes from top to bottom (in ascending order). By using the hint **INDEX_ASC**, you guarantee that the scan order of the index is in ascending order. Notice that the plan and cost are the same for the **INDEX_ASC** hint in Listing 9.12 and the **INDEX** hint in Listing 9.7.

Listing 9.12 INDEX_ASC.

```
SQL> EXPLAIN PLAN FOR
  2  SELECT /*+ INDEX_ASC(STATS BTREE_REGION) */  *
  3  FROM    STATS
  4* WHERE   REGION_BTREE = 'SE';
Explained.

SQL> @explain
Query Plan                                       COST
-------------------------------------------  -----
SELECT STATEMENT    CHOOSE                       4898
  TABLE ACCESS BY ROWID STATS ANALYZED           4898
    INDEX RANGE SCAN BTREE_REGION ANALYZED
```

Because Oracle scans indexes in ascending order, the hint **INDEX_DESC** is used to force Oracle to scan indexes in descending order. If you know the value searched for is near the end of the values in the index on a large table, this hint might speed up your query. Listing 9.13 indicates an eight-tenths of a second faster result using the **INDEX_DESC** hint on a one-million-row table when searching for the last entry in the index. This might not seem significant on the surface. But, if this were a 175,000,000-row table, the difference would be 2 minutes and 20 seconds. Notice that Oracle estimates the cost to be the same for both queries. Again, the lowest cost is 1 (and that is using the rowid). Therefore, a cost of 3 is excellent.

Listing 9.13 INDEX_DESC.

```
SQL> EXPLAIN PLAN FOR -- Last Entry Is 1,000,000
  2  SELECT --+ INDEX_DESC(STATS BTREE_UNIQUE_SNO)
  3  REGION_BTREE
  4  FROM   STATS
  5* WHERE  SNO = 1000000;
Explained.
```

```
SQL> @explain
Query Plan                                  COST
------------------------------------------ -----
SELECT STATEMENT   CHOOSE                      3
  TABLE ACCESS BY ROWID STATS ANALYZED         3
    INDEX RANGE SCAN DESCENDING
          BTREE_UNIQUE_SNO ANALYZED

SQL> SELECT --+ INDEX_DESC(STATS BTREE_UNIQUE_SNO)
  2  REGION_BTREE
  3  FROM   STATS
  4* WHERE  SNO = 1000000;

REG
---
NW

Elapsed: 00:00:00.13

SQL> EXPLAIN PLAN FOR   -- No Hint This Time
  2  SELECT REGION_BTREE
  3  FROM   STATS
  4* WHERE  SNO = 1000000;
Explained.

SQL> @explain
Query Plan                                  COST
------------------------------------------ -----
SELECT STATEMENT   CHOOSE                      3
  TABLE ACCESS BY ROWID STATS ANALYZED         3
    INDEX UNIQUE SCAN
          BTREE_UNIQUE_SNO ANALYZED

SQL> SELECT REGION_BTREE
  2  FROM   STATS
  3* WHERE  SNO = 1000000;

REG
---
NW

Elapsed: 00:00:00.93
```

Bitmap Indexes

Only one hint is related to bitmap indexes: **INDEX_COMBINE**. However, several "flavors" exist for this hint. Listing 9.14 indicates that both bitmap indexes are used. **BITMAP CONVERSION TO ROWIDS** indicates that the bits are converted to actual rowids. **BITMAP AND** indicates that the two bitmap indexes are merged into one, whereas **BITMAP INDEX SINGLE VALUE** merely indicates that Oracle uses the bitmap index.

Listing 9.14 INDEX_COMBINE.

```
SQL> EXPLAIN PLAN FOR     -- Table NOT Analyzed
  2  SELECT /*+ INDEX_COMBINE(STATS BITMAP_SEX) */
  3         SNO, REGION_HASH
  4  FROM   STATS         /* 2,000 ROWS */
  5* WHERE  REGION_BIT_MAP = 'W' AND SEX = 'F';
Explained.

SQL> @explain
Query Plan                                     COST
------------------------------------------- ------
SELECT STATEMENT   CHOOSE                         5
  TABLE ACCESS BY ROWID STATS                     5
    BITMAP CONVERSION TO ROWIDS
      BITMAP AND
        BITMAP INDEX SINGLE VALUE BITMAP_SEX
        BITMAP INDEX SINGLE VALUE
               BITMAP_REGION_BIT_MAP
```

Listing 9.15 does not use an index argument in the **INDEX_COMBINE(STATS)** hint. This permits Oracle to use the boolean combination of bitmap indexes with the lowest cost estimate. In this case, Oracle uses the union of both bitmap indexes, converts the bitmaps to rowids, and uses the rowids to retrieve the rows in the active set. Note that this command is entered after the **STATS** table has been analyzed.

Listing 9.15 INDEX_COMBINE(STATS).

```
SQL> EXPLAIN PLAN FOR
  2  SELECT --+ INDEX_COMBINE(STATS)
  3  *
  4  FROM        STATS
  5  WHERE       SEX = 'F' OR
  6              REGION_BIT_MAP = 'SE';
```

```
SQL> @explain
Query Plan                                          COST
-----------------------------------------  -------
SELECT STATEMENT   CHOOSE                          17,172
  TABLE ACCESS BY ROWID STATS ANALYZED             17,172
    BITMAP CONVERSION TO ROWIDS
      BITMAP OR
        BITMAP INDEX SINGLE VALUE
                     BITMAP_SEX
        BITMAP INDEX SINGLE VALUE
                     BITMAP_REGION_BIT_MAP
```

Join Orders

When you write a query that joins tables, Oracle creates a *join chain*. This chain is the order in which the tables are accessed and joined together. The most important table in this chain is the first table. The first table in this chain is called the *driving table* or the *inner table*. The two terms are synonymous. The driving table should be the most selective table in the chain. In other words, the first table in the chain should return the fewest number of rows. If this is not the case, the query will run slower—sometimes very much slower. Because you know your data better than Oracle, you can use the **ORDERED** hint to create the join chain. If you are joining three tables, you have six possible join chains. For example, if you are joining tables A, B, and C, you have the following possible join chains:

A, B, C

A, C, B

B, A, C

B, C, A

C, A, B

C, B, A

Listing 9.16 starts with a query that joins the **PARTS** and **TESTS** tables. Both tables do not have any indexes and have not been analyzed. As you can see, **TESTS** is the driving table, and Oracle performs a merge join. Notice that it takes only 1 minute and 43 seconds to execute. Obviously, the rule-based optimizer is used throughout Listing 9.16. With the rule-based optimizer, you can change the driving table by physically changing the order of the tables in the **FROM** clause (if Oracle ranks the tables equally). Because both tables are not analyzed and no indexes exist, Oracle uses the last table in the **FROM** clause as the driving table. This is the reason the first query uses **TESTS** as the driving table, and the second query uses **PARTS** as the driving table. You'll notice that the query that uses **PARTS** as the driving table is 25 seconds faster than the query that uses **TESTS** as the driving table. A dramatic performance gain can be accomplished by just changing the order of the tables in the **FROM** clause.

With the rule-based optimizer, the order of the tables in the **FROM** clause might be important when the ranking is the same for each table. If you want to force Oracle to join tables in a particular order, use the **ORDERED** hint. The next example uses this hint to force Oracle to use the **TESTS** table as the driving table. Notice the cost is 602. The mere presence of 602 in the **COST** column indicates that Oracle uses the cost-based optimizer when given the **ORDERED** hint. All of the listings in this chapter show this to be true.

The cost-based optimizer has gotten more intelligent with each release. The queries that use the **ORDERED** hint run significantly faster than the ones using the rule-based optimizer. The two queries without the **ORDERED** hint require 3 minutes and 50 seconds. The two queries without a hint require 1 minute 22 seconds. What a difference the cost-based optimizer makes!

Listing 9.16 ORDERED.

```
SQL> EXPLAIN PLAN FOR -- No Indexes, No Statistics
  2  SELECT  PNAME,       RESULTS
  3  FROM    PARTS,       TESTS--TESTS DRIVES
  4  WHERE   PARTS.PNO = TESTS.PNO AND
  5*         PARTS.PNO = 22;
Explained.

SQL> @explain
Query Plan                          COST
--------------------------- ------
SELECT STATEMENT   CHOOSE
  MERGE JOIN
    SORT JOIN
      TABLE ACCESS FULL TESTS
    SORT JOIN
      TABLE ACCESS FULL PARTS
```

```
SQL> SELECT PNAME,      RESULTS
  2  FROM   PARTS,      TESTS
  3  WHERE  PARTS.PNO = TESTS.PNO AND
  4*        PARTS.PNO = 22;

PNAME          R
-------------- -
................
Widget 22      F
Widget 22      P

485 rows selected.

Elapsed: 00:01:42.53

SQL> EXPLAIN PLAN FOR
  2  SELECT PNAME, RESULTS
  3  FROM   TESTS, PARTS--PARTS DRIVES
  4  WHERE  PARTS.PNO = TESTS.PNO AND
  5*        PARTS.PNO = 22;
Explained.

SQL> @explain
Query Plan                       COST
---------------------------- ------
SELECT STATEMENT   CHOOSE
  MERGE JOIN
    SORT JOIN
      TABLE ACCESS FULL PARTS
    SORT JOIN
      TABLE ACCESS FULL TESTS

SQL> SELECT PNAME,      RESULTS
  2  FROM   TESTS,      PARTS  -- PARTS Drives
  3  WHERE  PARTS.PNO = TESTS.PNO AND
  4*        PARTS.PNO = 22;

PNAME          R
-------------- -
................
Widget 22      F
Widget 22      P

485 rows selected.

Elapsed: 00:02:07.98
```

```
SQL> EXPLAIN PLAN FOR  -- TESTS Drives
  2  SELECT /*+ ORDERED */ PNAME, RESULTS
  3  FROM   TESTS, PARTS
  4  WHERE  PARTS.PNO = TESTS.PNO AND
  5*        PARTS.PNO = 22;
Explained.

SQL> @explain
Query Plan                          COST
--------------------------- -----
SELECT STATEMENT   CHOOSE        602
  MERGE JOIN                     602
    TABLE ACCESS FULL TESTS      571
    SORT JOIN
      TABLE ACCESS FULL PARTS     26

SQL> SELECT /*+ ORDERED */ PNAME, RESULTS
  2  FROM   TESTS, PARTS  -- TESTS Drives
  3  WHERE  PARTS.PNO = TESTS.PNO AND
  4*        PARTS.PNO = 22;

PNAME          R
-------------- -
................
Widget 22      F
Widget 22      P

485 rows selected.

Elapsed: 00:00:42.29

SQL> EXPLAIN PLAN FOR
  2  SELECT /*+ ORDERED */ PNAME, RESULTS
  3  FROM   PARTS, TESTS--PARTS DRIVES
  4  WHERE  PARTS.PNO = TESTS.PNO AND
  5*        PARTS.PNO = 22;
Explained.

SQL> @explain
Query Plan                          COST
--------------------------- ------
SELECT STATEMENT   CHOOSE        602
  MERGE JOIN                     602
    TABLE ACCESS FULL PARTS       26
    SORT JOIN
      TABLE ACCESS FULL TESTS    571
```

```
SQL> SELECT /*+ ORDERED */ PNAME, RESULTS
  2  FROM   PARTS, TESTS  -- PARTS Drives
  3  WHERE  PARTS.PNO = TESTS.PNO AND
  4*        PARTS.PNO = 22;

PNAME          R
-------------- -

...............
Widget 22      F
Widget 22      P

485 rows selected.

Elapsed: 00:00:40.07
```

The hint **STAR** forces Oracle to place the fact table at the end of the join chain, because it typically contains many millions of rows. **STAR** also causes this large table to be joined using a nested loop join. Listing 9.17 shows a lot of helpful information about **STAR** queries. Refer to Figure 9.3 for the tables used in the queries in Listing 9.17.

First of all, the setting of the parameter **hash_join_enabled** is **TRUE**. The Explain Plan output indicates that **INDY_CARS** is the driving table, the last table in the join

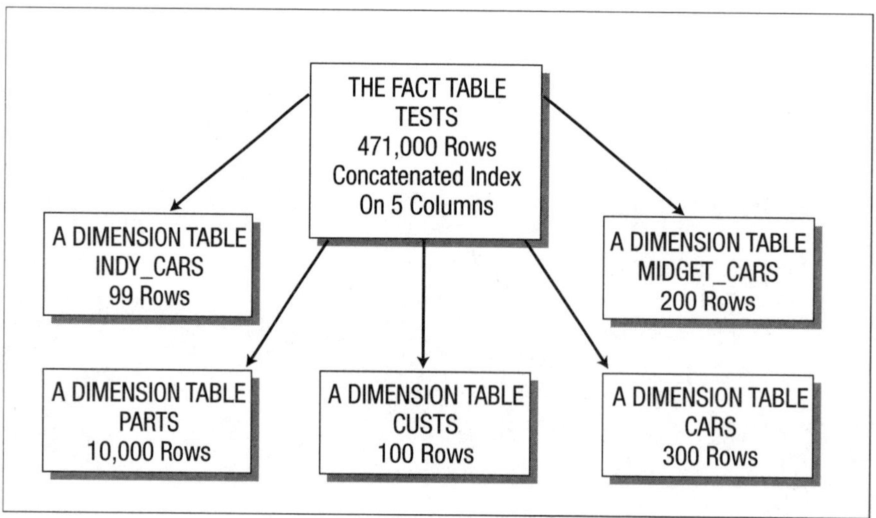

Figure 9.3
STAR configuration.

chain is the fact table **TESTS** (which is great), and the cost is 2.3E+07 (or 23,000,000). Also, many hash joins exist throughout the join chain.

The second example in Listing 9.17 shows the following when **hash_join_enabled** is **FALSE**: All tables are joined using sort-merge joins, the driving table is **TESTS** (which is the very last thing you ever want), the **MIDGET_CARS** table is the last table in the join chain (you want **TESTS** as the last table), and the cost is 2.1E+09 (or 2,100,000,000). The cost of 2,100,000,000 is 91 times as great as the cost of 23,000,000.

The third example accomplishes the same thing as the **STAR** hint. It uses three hints in one statement: **INDEX**, **ORDERED**, and **USE_NL(TESTS)**. The **INDEX** hint uses the concatenated index on the columns **PNO**, **CUSTID**, **CARID**, **INDYID**, and **MIDGETID** in the **TESTS** table. Oracle uses one nested loop join followed by four sort-merge joins. The driving table is **INDY_CARS**, and the last table in the join chain is **TESTS**. Finally, the cost is a huge 3.2E+17. Even though I majored in mathematics in college, I simply cannot comprehend the magnitude of this cost. Therefore, it seems you would *never* execute this query using these three hints. However, the appearance of **CARTESIAN** is a good indicator that the tables are being accessed very efficiently in the **STAR** query.

The last example in Listing 9.17 actually uses the hint **STAR**. As you can see, the plan is nearly identical to using the three hints in the previous example.

Listing 9.17 STAR.

```
SQL> SELECT SUBSTR(NAME,1,25) PARAM,
  2         SUBSTR(VALUE,1,25) CURRENT_SETTING
  3  FROM   V$PARAMETER
  4* WHERE  NAME LIKE '%' || LOWER('&Parameter') || '%';
Enter value for parameter: hash_join

PARAM                     CURRENT_SETTING
------------------------- -------------------------
hash_join_enabled         TRUE

SQL> EXPLAIN PLAN FOR
  2  SELECT RESULTS, PNAME,
  3         CUSTS.CNAME,
  4         NUM_DOORS,
  5         OWNER,
```

```
        NUM_FLIPS
FROM    TESTS,  -- Fact Table 471,000 Rows
        PARTS,  -- Dimension Table 10,000 Rows
        CUSTS,  -- Dimension Table    100 Rows
        CARS,   -- Dimension Table    300 Rows
        INDY_CARS,  -- Dimension Table 99 Rows
        MIDGET_CARS -- Dimension Table 200 Rows
WHERE   TESTS.PNO       = PARTS.PNO           AND
        TESTS.CUSTID    = CUSTS.CUSTID        AND
        TESTS.CARID     = CARS.CARID          AND
        TESTS.INDYID    = INDY_CARS.INDYID AND
        TESTS.MIDGETID = MIDGET_CARS.MIDGETID;
Explained.

SQL> @explain
Query Plan                                          COST
-------------------------------------------- -------
SELECT STATEMENT   CHOOSE                         2.3E+07
  HASH JOIN                                       2.3E+07
    TABLE ACCESS FULL INDY_CARS                         1
    HASH JOIN                                      991007
      TABLE ACCESS FULL CUSTS                           1
      HASH JOIN                                     39024
        TABLE ACCESS FULL MIDGET_CARS                   1
        HASH JOIN                                    3104
          TABLE ACCESS FULL CARS                        1
          HASH JOIN                                  1952
            TABLE ACCESS FULL PARTS ANALYZED           26
            TABLE ACCESS FULL TESTS ANALYZED          571

12 rows selected.

SQL> ALTER SESSION SET HASH_JOIN_ENABLED = FALSE;
Session altered.

SQL> TRUNCATE TABLE PLAN_TABLE;
Table truncated.

SQL> @cor9star
Explained.

SQL> @explain
Query Plan                                                    COST
------------------------------------------------------ -------
SELECT STATEMENT   CHOOSE                                   2.1E+09
```

```
 MERGE JOIN                                                  2.1E+09
   SORT JOIN
     MERGE JOIN                                              5.9E+07
       SORT JOIN
         MERGE JOIN                                          1697791
           SORT JOIN
             MERGE JOIN                                        49545
               SORT JOIN
                 MERGE JOIN                                     8254
                   SORT JOIN
                     TABLE ACCESS FULL TESTS ANALYZED            571
                   SORT JOIN
                     TABLE ACCESS FULL PARTS ANALYZED             26
               SORT JOIN
                 TABLE ACCESS FULL INDY_CARS                       1
           SORT JOIN
             TABLE ACCESS FULL CUSTS
       SORT JOIN
         TABLE ACCESS FULL CARS                                    1
   SORT JOIN
     TABLE ACCESS FULL MIDGET_CARS                                 1

22 rows selected.

SQL> get cor9star17
  1  BREAK ON NAME SKIP 1
  2  SELECT SUBSTR(INDEX_NAME,1,25) NAME,
  3  COLUMN_POSITION "POSITION",
  4  SUBSTR(COLUMN_NAME,1,25) COL_NAME
  5  FROM    USER_IND_COLUMNS
  6  WHERE   TABLE_NAME = 'TESTS'
  7  ORDER   BY NAME, "POSITION";
  8* CLEAR   BREAKS

SQL> @cor9star17
NAME           POSITION COL_NAME
-------------- -------- --------
STAR_ON_TESTS  1        PNO
               2        CUSTID
               3        CARID
               4        INDYID
               5        MIDGETID

TESTS_PNO      1        PNO

TESTS_TNO      1        TNO
```

```
SQL> ALTER SESSION SET HASH_JOIN_ENABLED = FALSE;
Session altered.

SQL> EXPLAIN PLAN FOR  -- A Baseball 3 Bagger!!
     SELECT --+ INDEX(TESTS STAR_ON_TESTS) ORDERED USE_NL(TESTS)
             RESULTS, PNAME,
             CUSTS.CNAME,
             NUM_DOORS,
             OWNER,
             NUM_FLIPS
     FROM    INDY_CARS,        --       99 Rows
             CUSTS,            --      100 Rows
             MIDGET_CARS,      --      200 Rows
             CARS,             --      300 Rows
             PARTS,            --   10,000 Rows
             TESTS             --  471,000 Rows
     WHERE   TESTS.PNO       = PARTS.PNO          AND
             TESTS.CUSTID    = CUSTS.CUSTID       AND
             TESTS.CARID     = CARS.CARID         AND
             TESTS.INDYID    = INDY_CARS.INDYID AND
             TESTS.MIDGETID = MIDGET_CARS.MIDGETID;
Explained.

SQL> @explain
Query Plan                                          COST
----------------------------------------- -------
SELECT STATEMENT   CHOOSE                        3.2E+17
  NESTED LOOPS                                   3.2E+17
    MERGE JOIN CARTESIAN                         4.2E+14
      MERGE JOIN CARTESIAN                       8.0E+09
        MERGE JOIN CARTESIAN                     4002001
          MERGE JOIN CARTESIAN                      2001
            TABLE ACCESS FULL INDY_CARS                1
            SORT JOIN
              TABLE ACCESS FULL CUSTS
          SORT JOIN
            TABLE ACCESS FULL MIDGET_CARS
        SORT JOIN
          TABLE ACCESS FULL CARS
      SORT JOIN
        TABLE ACCESS FULL PARTS ANALYZED
    TABLE ACCESS BY ROWID TESTS ANALYZED
      INDEX RANGE SCAN STAR_ON_TESTS

17 rows selected.
```

```
SQL> EXPLAIN PLAN FOR  -- Finally, The "Star" Of The Show
  2  SELECT --+ STAR
  3         RESULTS, PNAME,
  4         CUSTS.CNAME,  -- A Much Simpler Hint Than
  5         NUM_DOORS,    -- Using 3 Hints
  6         OWNER,
  7         NUM_FLIPS
  8  FROM   INDY_CARS,     --      99 Rows
  9         CUSTS,         --     100 Rows
 10         MIDGET_CARS,   --     200 Rows
 11         CARS,          --     300 Rows
 12         PARTS,         --  10,000 Rows
 13         TESTS          -- 471,000 Rows
 14  WHERE  TESTS.PNO      = PARTS.PNO        AND
 15         TESTS.CUSTID   = CUSTS.CUSTID     AND
 16         TESTS.CARID    = CARS.CARID       AND
 17         TESTS.INDYID   = INDY_CARS.INDYID AND
 18*        TESTS.MIDGETID = MIDGET_CARS.MIDGETID;
Explained.

SQL> start explain
Query Plan                                    COST
------------------------------------------ -------
SELECT STATEMENT   CHOOSE                  3.2E+17
  NESTED LOOPS                             3.2E+17
    MERGE JOIN CARTESIAN                   8.0E+13
      MERGE JOIN CARTESIAN                 4.0E+10
        MERGE JOIN CARTESIAN               2.0E+07
          MERGE JOIN CARTESIAN               10026
            TABLE ACCESS FULL PARTS ANALYZED    26
            SORT JOIN
              TABLE ACCESS FULL INDY_CARS        1
          SORT JOIN
            TABLE ACCESS FULL CUSTS
        SORT JOIN
          TABLE ACCESS FULL MIDGET_CARS
      SORT JOIN
        TABLE ACCESS FULL CARS
    TABLE ACCESS BY ROWID TESTS ANALYZED
      INDEX RANGE SCAN STAR_ON_TESTS

17 rows selected.
```

Joining Tables

Oracle uses several different methods to join tables. These methods are **MERGE JOIN**, **NESTED LOOPS**, HASH, and **CLUSTER**. Obviously, Oracle provides hints for all these methods. Listing 9.18 uses the hint **USE_MERGE**. When you use the **USE_MERGE** hint with the **ORDERED** hint, Oracle seems to recognize your hint.

Listing 9.18 USE_MERGE.

```
SQL> EXPLAIN PLAN FOR   -- TESTS Drives
  2  SELECT --+ USE_MERGE(TESTS)
  3  PNAME, RESULTS
  4  FROM     PARTS, TESTS
  5  WHERE    PARTS.PNO = TESTS.PNO AND
  6*          PARTS.PNO BETWEEN 30 AND 95;
Explained.

SQL> @explain
Query Plan                                          COST
------------------------------------------ --------
SELECT STATEMENT   CHOOSE                              67
  MERGE JOIN                                           67
    TABLE ACCESS BY ROWID TESTS ANALYZED               56
      INDEX RANGE SCAN TESTS_PNO ANALYZED
    SORT JOIN
      TABLE ACCESS BY ROWID PARTS ANALYZED              4
        INDEX RANGE SCAN PARTS_PNO ANALYZED

SQL> EXPLAIN PLAN FOR   -- TESTS Drives
  2  SELECT --+ USE_MERGE(PARTS)
  3  PNAME, RESULTS
  4  FROM     PARTS, TESTS
  5  WHERE    PARTS.PNO = TESTS.PNO AND
  6*          PARTS.PNO BETWEEN 30 AND 95;
Explained.

SQL> @explain
Query Plan                                          COST
------------------------------------------ --------
SELECT STATEMENT   CHOOSE                              67
  MERGE JOIN                                           67
    TABLE ACCESS BY ROWID TESTS ANALYZED               56
      INDEX RANGE SCAN TESTS_PNO ANALYZED
    SORT JOIN
```

```
    TABLE ACCESS BY ROWID PARTS ANALYZED            4
      INDEX RANGE SCAN PARTS_PNO ANALYZED

SQL> EXPLAIN PLAN FOR  -- Takes The Hint!!
  2  SELECT --+ORDERED USE_MERGE(PARTS)
  3  PNAME, RESULTS
  4  FROM     PARTS, TESTS
  5  WHERE    PARTS.PNO = TESTS.PNO AND
  6*          PARTS.PNO BETWEEN 30 AND 95;
Explained.

SQL> @explain
Query Plan                                       COST
---------------------------------------- -------
SELECT STATEMENT   CHOOSE                         145
  MERGE JOIN                                      145
    TABLE ACCESS BY ROWID PARTS ANALYZED            4
      INDEX RANGE SCAN PARTS_PNO ANALYZED
    SORT JOIN
      TABLE ACCESS BY ROWID TESTS ANALYZED         56
        INDEX RANGE SCAN TESTS_PNO ANALYZED
```

Listing 9.19 shows the hint **USE_NL** (used nested loop). Notice that Oracle ignores the hint and performs a sort **MERGE JOIN**. Even when the hint is used on each table, Oracle still ignores the hint. Another hint must be used.

Listing 9.19 USE_NL.

```
SQL> EXPLAIN PLAN FOR       -- PARTS Drives
  2  SELECT --+ USE_NL(PARTS)
  3  PNAME, RESULTS
  4  FROM     PARTS, TESTS  -- Ignores Hint
  5  WHERE    PARTS.PNO = TESTS.PNO AND
  6*          PARTS.PNO BETWEEN 30 AND 95;
Explained.

SQL> @explain
Query Plan                                       COST
---------------------------------------- --------
SELECT STATEMENT   CHOOSE                         145
  MERGE JOIN                                      145
    TABLE ACCESS BY ROWID PARTS ANALYZED            4
      INDEX RANGE SCAN PARTS_PNO ANALYZED
    SORT JOIN
```

```
      TABLE ACCESS BY ROWID TESTS ANALYZED        56
        INDEX RANGE SCAN TESTS_PNO ANALYZED

SQL> EXPLAIN PLAN FOR       -- TESTS Drives
  2  SELECT --+ USE_NL(TESTS)
  3  PNAME, RESULTS
  4  FROM     PARTS, TESTS  -- Ignores Hint Again
  5  WHERE    PARTS.PNO = TESTS.PNO AND
  6*          PARTS.PNO BETWEEN 30 AND 95;
Explained.

SQL> @explain
Query Plan                                      COST
----------------------------------------- -------
SELECT STATEMENT   CHOOSE                         67
  MERGE JOIN                                      67
    TABLE ACCESS BY ROWID TESTS ANALYZED          56
      INDEX RANGE SCAN TESTS_PNO ANALYZED
    SORT JOIN
      TABLE ACCESS BY ROWID PARTS ANALYZED         4
        INDEX RANGE SCAN PARTS_PNO ANALYZED
```

Because Oracle refuses to use the **USE_NL** hint in Listing 9.19, let's try combining the **ORDERED** hint with the **USE_NL** hint (see Listing 9.20). As you can see, Oracle uses the **PARTS** table as the driving table because of the **ORDERED** hint. Oracle also uses the **USE_NL** hint to cause a nested loop join on the **TESTS** table. Oracle uses an index to retrieve a row from **PARTS**; then, all matching rows are retrieved from the **TESTS** table using the index **TESTS.PNO**. The cost is 208. When **TESTS** is the driving table and the **USE_NL** hint is on the **PARTS** table, the cost is a whopping 3,210. This should not be surprising. After all, the index is used to retrieve each of the 471,000+ rows in the **TESTS** table. Next, the **PARTS** table is joined to **TESTS** using **NESTED LOOPS**. Oracle does not seem to respond to the **USE_NL** hint unless the **ORDERED** hint is used in the same query.

Listing 9.20 Combining hints.

```
SQL> EXPLAIN PLAN FOR--PARTS Drives
  2  SELECT   --+ORDERED USE_NL(TESTS)
  3  PNAME,   RESULTS
  4  FROM     PARTS, TESTS
  5  WHERE    PARTS.PNO = TESTS.PNO AND
  6*          PARTS.PNO BETWEEN 30 AND 95;
```

```
Explained.

SQL> @explain
Query Plan                                           COST
---------------------------------------------- --------
SELECT STATEMENT   CHOOSE                             208
  NESTED LOOPS                                        208
    TABLE ACCESS BY ROWID PARTS ANALYZED                4
      INDEX RANGE SCAN PARTS_PNO ANALYZED
    TABLE ACCESS BY ROWID TESTS ANALYZED
      INDEX RANGE SCAN TESTS_PNO ANALYZED

SQL> EXPLAIN PLAN FOR--TEST Drives
  2  SELECT --+ORDERED USE_NL(PARTS)
  3  PNAME, RESULTS
  4  FROM   TESTS, PARTS
  5  WHERE   PARTS.PNO = TESTS.PNO AND
  6*         PARTS.PNO BETWEEN 30 AND 95;
Explained.

SQL> @explain
Query Plan                                           COST
---------------------------------------------- -------
SELECT STATEMENT   CHOOSE                            3210
  NESTED LOOPS                                       3210
    TABLE ACCESS BY ROWID TESTS ANALYZED               56
      INDEX RANGE SCAN TESTS_PNO ANALYZED
    TABLE ACCESS BY ROWID PARTS ANALYZED
      INDEX UNIQUE SCAN PARTS_PNO ANALYZED
```

Another example of combining hints is illustrated in Listing 9.21. The hint **FULL** causes a full table scan, and the hint **FIRST_ROWS** causes Oracle to select the access method that returns the first row the quickest. The output from Explain Plan indicates that Oracle takes both hints.

Listing 9.21 Combining **FIRST_ROWS** and **FULL**.

```
SQL> EXPLAIN PLAN FOR
  2  SELECT  --+FIRST_ROWS FULL(TESTS)
  3  PNO,    RESULTS
  4  FROM    TESTS
  5* WHERE   PNO BETWEEN 50 AND 93;
Explained.
```

```
SQL> @explain
Query Plan                                   COST
--------------------------------- --------
SELECT STATEMENT   HINT: FIRST_ROWS        571
  TABLE ACCESS FULL TESTS ANALYZED         571
```

Another hint used in queries that join tables is the **USE_HASH** hint. This hint causes Oracle to join each table in the hint to other tables in the query using a hash join. The first example in Listing 9.22 causes Oracle to join the **PARTS** table to the **TESTS** table using a hash join. Notice that the **PARTS** table is the driving table in all the examples in Listing 9.22. The second example shows Oracle ignoring the hint. One reason why Oracle ignores the hint is the size of the **TESTS** table. A hash join hashes in memory the smaller of the tables to be joined. Because **PARTS** has 10,000 rows, no problem exists and Oracle takes the hint. But, **TESTS** has more than 471,000 rows, and it appears that this might be why Oracle ignores the hint. Sounds good doesn't it? However, the last example in Listing 9.22 shows something else. You cannot place the **USE_HASH** hint on the inner or driving table of the query. The third example shows that the syntax in the second example is correct. Remember, when a table alias is used in the **FROM** clause, the table alias must also be used in the hint; otherwise, Oracle will ignore the hint.

The last two statements in Listing 9.22 illustrate two additional methods—other than the hint USE_HASH—of permitting hash joins to occur without using hints. If the parameter **hash_join_enabled** is FALSE, use the **ALTER SESSION** command to override this setting to **TRUE**.

Listing 9.22 USE_HASH.

```
SQL> EXPLAIN PLAN FOR  -- Hint On Non-Driver OK
  2  SELECT /*+USE_HASH(TESTS) */ P.PNAME, TNO
  3  FROM   PARTS P,
  4         TESTS
  5  WHERE  P.PNO = TESTS.PNO AND
  6*        P.PNO = 90;
Explained.

SQL> @explain
Query Plan                                        COST
---------------------------------------- -------
SELECT STATEMENT   CHOOSE                            7
 HASH JOIN                                           7
```

```
    TABLE ACCESS BY ROWID PARTS ANALYZED              2
      INDEX UNIQUE SCAN PARTS_PNO ANALYZED
    TABLE ACCESS BY ROWID TESTS ANALYZED              4
      INDEX RANGE SCAN TESTS_PNO ANALYZED

SQL> EXPLAIN PLAN FOR  -- Hint On Driver, Ignores
  2  SELECT /*+USE_HASH(P) */ P.PNAME, TNO
  3  FROM   PARTS P,
  4         TESTS
  5  WHERE  P.PNO = TESTS.PNO AND
  6*        P.PNO = 90;
Explained.

SQL> @explain
Query Plan                                          COST
----------------------------------------- -------
SELECT STATEMENT   CHOOSE                              5
  NESTED LOOPS                                         5
    TABLE ACCESS BY ROWID PARTS ANALYZED               2
      INDEX UNIQUE SCAN PARTS_PNO ANALYZED
    TABLE ACCESS BY ROWID TESTS ANALYZED
      INDEX RANGE SCAN TESTS_PNO ANALYZED

SQL> EXPLAIN PLAN FOR  -- Hint On Driver, Ignores
  2  SELECT /*+USE_HASH(PARTS) */ PNAME, TNO
  3  FROM   PARTS,
  4         TESTS
  5  WHERE PARTS.PNO = TESTS.PNO AND
  6*        PARTS.PNO = 90;
SQL> @explain

Query Plan                                          COST
----------------------------------------- -------
SELECT STATEMENT   CHOOSE                              5
  NESTED LOOPS                                         5
    TABLE ACCESS BY ROWID PARTS ANALYZED               2
      INDEX UNIQUE SCAN PARTS_PNO ANALYZED
    TABLE ACCESS BY ROWID TESTS ANALYZED
      INDEX RANGE SCAN TESTS_PNO ANALYZED

SQL> EXPLAIN PLAN FOR  -- Hint On Non-Driver OK
  2  SELECT --+ORDERED USE_HASH(PARTS)
  3  PNAME, RESULTS
  4  FROM   TESTS,
  5         PARTS
```

```
  6  WHERE   PARTS.PNO = TESTS.PNO AND
  7*         PARTS.PNO = 90;
Explained.

SQL> @explain
Query Plan                                         COST
------------------------------------------ -------
SELECT STATEMENT   CHOOSE                            7
  HASH JOIN                                          7
    TABLE ACCESS BY ROWID TESTS ANALYZED             4
      INDEX RANGE SCAN TESTS_PNO ANALYZED
    TABLE ACCESS BY ROWID PARTS ANALYZED             2
      INDEX UNIQUE SCAN PARTS_PNO ANALYZED

SQL> SELECT SUBSTR(NAME,1,25) PARAM,
  2         SUBSTR(VALUE,1,25) CURRENT_SETTING
  3  FROM   V$PARAMETER
  4* WHERE  NAME LIKE '%' || LOWER('&Parameter') || '%';
Enter value for parameter: hash_join_enabled

PARAM                     CURRENT_SETTING
------------------------- -----------------------
hash_join_enabled         FALSE

SQL> ALTER SESSION SET  -- For Your Session Only
  2         HASH_JOIN_ENABLED = TRUE;
Session altered.
```

Clusters

If you ever write a query that joins a nonclustered table to a clustered table and you want Oracle to scan the cluster, use the hint **CLUSTER**. Listing 9.23 joins the nonclustered table **PARTS** to the clustered table **TESTS_IN_CLUSTER**.

Listing 9.23 CLUSTER.

```
SQL> SELECT CLUSTER_NAME,
  2         CLUSTER_TYPE,
  3         HASHKEYS
  4* FROM   USER_CLUSTERS;

CLUSTER_NAME     CLUSTER_TYPE HASHKEYS
---------------- ------------ --------
DEPT_AND_EMP     HASH                5
HUEY_DEWEY_LEWIE HASH            12097
```

```
PARTS_AND_TESTS   INDEX                0

SQL> SELECT TABLE_NAME
  2  FROM   USER_TABLES
  3  WHERE  TABLE_NAME LIKE 'PARTS%' OR
  4         TABLE_NAME LIKE 'TESTS%'
  5* ORDER  BY 1;

TABLE_NAME
--------------------
PARTS
PARTS_IN_CLUSTER
TESTS
TESTS_IN_CLUSTER

SQL> EXPLAIN PLAN FOR
  2   SELECT --+CLUSTER(TESTS_IN_CLUSTER)
  3          PARTS.PNAME,
  4          TESTS_IN_CLUSTER.TNO,
  5          TESTS_IN_CLUSTER.RESULTS
  6   FROM   PARTS,
  7          TESTS_IN_CLUSTER
  8* WHERE   PARTS.PNO = TESTS_IN_CLUSTER.PNO;
Explained.

SQL> @explain
Query Plan                                               COST
-------------------------------------------------- ------
SELECT STATEMENT   CHOOSE                                5602
  MERGE JOIN                                             5602
    TABLE ACCESS CLUSTER TESTS_IN_CLUSTER ANALYZED       5188
      INDEX FULL SCAN INDX_PARTS_AND_TESTS ANALYZED
    SORT JOIN
      TABLE ACCESS FULL PARTS ANALYZED                     26
```

Why make Oracle take time during parsing to determine the access method when you know the table is in a hash cluster? Try using the hint **HASH** if the table is in a hash cluster and measure the difference in performance. Listing 9.24 uses the **HASH** hint to retrieve all employees in department 10 from the hash-clustered table **EMP_IN_HASH**, which is in the hash cluster **DEPT_AND_EMP**.

Listing 9.24 HASH.

```
SQL> CREATE CLUSTER DEPT_AND_EMP
  2          (DEPTNO NUMBER(2,0))
```

```
  3         SIZE 30720 -- AVG_ROW_LEN(40) * 768
  4*        HASHKEYS 4;

SQL> CREATE TABLE EMP_IN_HASH
  2  (EMPNO     NUMBER(4),
  3   ENAME     VARCHAR2(10),
  4   JOB       VARCHAR2(9),
  5   MGR       NUMBER(4),
  6   HIREDATE  DATE,
  7   SAL       NUMBER(7,2),
  8   COMM      NUMBER(7,2),
  9   DEPTNO    NUMBER(2))
 10* CLUSTER DEPT_AND_EMP(DEPTNO);

SQL> SELECT CLUSTER_NAME,
  2         FUNCTION,
  3         HASHKEYS
  4  FROM   USER_CLUSTERS
  5* WHERE  CLUSTER_TYPE = 'HASH';

CLUSTER_NAME                   FUNCTION         HASHKEYS
------------------------------ --------------- ---------
DEPT_AND_EMP                   DEFAULT2                5
HUEY_DEWEY_LEWIE               HASH EXPRESSION     12097

SQL> SHOW LONG
long 80
SQL> SET LONG 19

SQL> SELECT SUBSTR(OWNER,1,12) "Owner",
  2         SUBSTR(CLUSTER_NAME,1,16) "Cluster Name",
  3         HASH_EXPRESSION "Hash Expression"
  4* FROM   USER_CLUSTER_HASH_EXPRESSIONS;

Owner        Cluster Name     Hash Expression
------------ ---------------- ------------------
OPS$PCASSIDY HUEY_DEWEY_LEWIE TRUNC(MOD(EMPNO,3))

SQL> SELECT COUNT(*)
  2  FROM   EMP_IN_HASH;

COUNT(*)
--------
    1792
```

```
SQL> SELECT DEPTNO,
  2         COUNT(*)
  3  FROM   EMP_IN_HASH
  4  GROUP  BY DEPTNO;

 DEPTNO COUNT(*)
------ ---------
     10       384
     20       640
     30       768

SQL> EXPLAIN PLAN FOR
  2  SELECT --+ HASH(EMP_IN_HASH)
  3              ENAME, DEPTNO
  4  FROM        EMP_IN_HASH
  5* WHERE       DEPTNO = 10;
Explained.

SQL> @explain
Query Plan                                        COST
---------------------------------------- -------
SELECT STATEMENT   CHOOSE                           10
  TABLE ACCESS HASH EMP_IN_HASH ANALYZED            10
```

Whenever you use **NOT IN** before a subquery, you can try using an antijoin if the query is running too slowly. One method to cause Oracle to use an antijoin whenever possible is to use the parameter **always_anti_join**. The possible settings for **always_anti_join** are MERGE and HASH. In Listing 9.25, **always_anti_join** is set to HASH. You can verify the current setting by writing a query using **V$PARAMETER**, or, if you have database administrator privileges, you can enter Server Manager and use the **SHOW PARAMETER** command.

The first Explain Plan in Listing 9.25 shows that Oracle performs full table scans using a filter. Oracle cannot use the antijoin approach because the **PNO** column in both tables, **PARTS** and **TESTS**, might contain nulls. To make Oracle use the hash antijoin, you must be a little creative in your statement. You must use **NOT NULL** in the outer and inner queries. This is why Oracle uses the hash antijoin in the second Explain Plan in Listing 9.25.

Because both tables allow nulls in the part number column, they are altered to disallow nulls. The next Explain Plan shows that Oracle uses the hash antijoin without having to use the extra code of **NOT NULL** in both queries. This is a direct result of the part number columns in both tables disallowing null values.

Listing 9.25 Antijoins using **always_anti_join**.

```
SQL> SELECT SUBSTR(NAME,1,25) PARAM,
  2         SUBSTR(VALUE,1,25) CURRENT_SETTING
  3  FROM   V$PARAMETER
  4* WHERE  NAME LIKE '%' || LOWER('&Parameter') || '%';
Enter value for parameter: anti

PARAM                     CURRENT_SETTING
------------------------- ------------------------
always_anti_join          HASH

SVRMGR> show parameter anti
NAME                TYPE   VALUE
------------------- ------ ----------
always_anti_join    string HASH

SQL> EXPLAIN PLAN FOR  -- Must Use NOT NULL
  2  SELECT PNO
  3  FROM   PARTS
  4  WHERE  PNO NOT IN(SELECT PNO
  5                    FROM   TESTS);
Explained.

SQL> @explain
Query Plan                                COST
----------------------------------------- -------
SELECT STATEMENT   CHOOSE                      26
  FILTER
    TABLE ACCESS FULL PARTS ANALYZED           26
    TABLE ACCESS FULL TESTS ANALYZED          571

SQL> EXPLAIN PLAN FOR
  2  SELECT PNO
  3  FROM   PARTS
  4  WHERE  PNO IS NOT NULL AND
  5         PNO NOT IN(SELECT PNO
  6                    FROM   TESTS
  7                    WHERE  PNO IS NOT NULL);
Explained.
```

```
SQL> @explain
Query Plan                                  COST
------------------------------------- -------
SELECT STATEMENT   CHOOSE                   2069
  HASH JOIN ANTI                            2069
    TABLE ACCESS FULL PARTS ANALYZED          26
    VIEW                                     571
      TABLE ACCESS FULL TESTS ANALYZED       571

SQL> ALTER TABLE PARTS MODIFY PNO NOT NULL;
Table altered.

SQL> ALTER TABLE TESTS MODIFY PNO NOT NULL;
Table altered.

SQL> EXPLAIN PLAN FOR -- PNO NUMBER NOT NULL
  2  SELECT PNO
  3  FROM   PARTS
  4  WHERE  PNO NOT IN(SELECT PNO
  5*                   FROM   TESTS);
Explained.

SQL> @explain
Query Plan                                          COST
------------------------------------------ --------
SELECT STATEMENT   CHOOSE                           2068
  HASH JOIN ANTI                                    2068
    INDEX FAST FULL SCAN PARTS_PNO ANALYZED           13
    VIEW                                             571
      TABLE ACCESS FULL TESTS ANALYZED               571
```

Another method of causing Oracle to perform antijoins is to use the hint HASH_AJ as shown in Listing 9.26. The current setting of the parameter **always_anti_join** is the default setting of **NESTED_LOOPS**. For Oracle to perform antijoins, you must now use either the **HASH_AJ** or **MERGE_AJ** hints.

Listing 9.26 HASH_AJ.

```
SQL> SELECT SUBSTR(NAME,1,25) PARAM,
  2         SUBSTR(VALUE,1,25) CURRENT_SETTING
  3  FROM   V$PARAMETER
  4* WHERE  NAME LIKE '%' || LOWER('&Parameter') || '%';
Enter value for parameter: anti
```

```
PARAM                        CURRENT_SETTING
------------------------ ------------------------
always_anti_join             NESTED_LOOPS

SQL> EXPLAIN PLAN FOR  -- Must Use Hint
  2  SELECT PNO        -- For Oracle To
  3  FROM   PARTS      -- Use Antijoin
  4  WHERE  PNO IS NOT NULL AND
  5         PNO NOT IN(SELECT PNO
  6                    FROM   TESTS
  7*                   WHERE  PNO IS NOT NULL);
Explained.

SQL> @explain
Query Plan                                  COST
------------------------------------ --------
SELECT STATEMENT   CHOOSE                     26
  FILTER
    TABLE ACCESS FULL PARTS ANALYZED          26
    INDEX RANGE SCAN TESTS_PNO ANALYZED        3

SQL> EXPLAIN PLAN FOR
  2  SELECT PNO
  3  FROM   PARTS
  4  WHERE  PNO IS NOT NULL AND
  5         PNO NOT IN(SELECT --+ HASH_AJ
  6                           PNO
  7                    FROM   TESTS
  8*                   WHERE  PNO IS NOT NULL);
Explained.

SQL> @explain
Query Plan                                 COST
------------------------------------ -------
SELECT STATEMENT   CHOOSE                  2069
  HASH JOIN ANTI                           2069
    TABLE ACCESS FULL PARTS ANALYZED         26
    VIEW                                    571
      TABLE ACCESS FULL TESTS ANALYZED      571
```

Listing 9.27 is an example of the hint **MERGE_AJ**. It's exactly like the hint **HASH_AJ** in Listing 9.26, except for one detail: The rows are merged. Notice that the hint for this query is really a poor hint; its cost is 20,783, compared to the **HASH_AJ** hint with a cost of 2,069.

Listing 9.27 MERGE_AJ.

```
SQL>  EXPLAIN PLAN FOR
  2   SELECT PNO
  3   FROM   PARTS
  4   WHERE  PNO IS NOT NULL AND
  5          PNO NOT IN(SELECT --+ MERGE_AJ
  6                            PNO
  7                     FROM   TESTS
  8*                    WHERE  PNO IS NOT NULL);
Explained.

SQL> @explain
Query Plan                                 COST
-------------------------------------- -------
SELECT STATEMENT   CHOOSE                20783
  MERGE JOIN ANTI                        20783
    INDEX FULL SCAN PARTS_PNO ANALYZED      85
    SORT UNIQUE
      VIEW                                 571
        TABLE ACCESS FULL TESTS ANALYZED   571
```

PARALLEL

If your platform has multiple CPUs, then Oracle has a deal for you! The deal is queries executing much faster than with one CPU. To take advantage of the parallel query feature, however, you really need six or more CPUs. If you have fewer than six CPUs, you'll experience linear performance gains instead of exponential gains. In other words, with one CPU, a query might require 20 minutes; with two CPUs 10 minutes, and so on. On a single-CPU system, you'll probably not experience significant performance advantages using the parallel query feature (unless CPU utilization is very, very low).

Parallel server processes are executed simultaneously by Oracle if the parallel query feature is activated in the parameter file. Parallel processes can be used on certain operations such as full table scans, sorts, certain create table commands, and create index commands. In Oracle8, it can be used for **INSERT**, **UPDATE**, and **DELETE** statements. You can also use this option while loading data simultaneously from several files using SQL*Loader.

You specify the degree of parallelism for a table when you create a table, alter a table, or use the hint **PARALLEL**. The degree of parallelism is the number of simultaneous processes allocated to perform certain operations like full table scans, sorts, creating indexes, and certain create table statements. You can override the degree of parallelism for a table by using the **PARALLEL** hint.

Listing 9.28 indicates that the default parallelism of a table is 1. The **TESTS** table's degree of parallelism is changed to 8, because you have eight CPUs. If you are using Oracle's Parallel Server Option, which has multiple instances using one set of database files, you can indicate the number of instances you want the server processes spread across. For instance, you could use **PARALLEL(DEGREE 8 2)** to tell Oracle to use four processes on each instance to perform the operation. The example in Listing 9.28 overrides the degree of parallelism of 8 with 6 for the query. Experimenting with the query shows that all eight server processes are not needed for this query, but six are. The last example in Listing 9.28 is another instance in which hints are combined. To force a full table scan using a degree of parallelism of 6, use the hint **PARALLEL(TESTS, 6) FULL(TESTS)**.

Listing 9.28 PARALLEL.

```
SQL> SELECT TABLE_NAME,
  2          DEGREE
  3  FROM    USER_TABLES
  4  WHERE   TABLE_NAME IN('PARTS', 'TESTS');

TABLE_NAME     DEGREE
---------- ----------
PARTS               1
TESTS               1

SQL> ALTER TABLE TESTS
  2         PARALLEL(DEGREE 8);
Table altered.

SQL> SELECT TABLE_NAME,
  2          DEGREE
  3  FROM    USER_TABLES
  4* WHERE   TABLE_NAME IN('PARTS', 'TESTS');

TABLE_NAME     DEGREE
---------- ----------
PARTS               1
TESTS               8
```

```
SQL> SELECT /*+ PARALLEL(TESTS, 6) */  *
  2  FROM        TESTS
  3  WHERE       PNO > 5;

SQL> SELECT --+ PARALLEL(TESTS, 6) FULL(TESTS)
  2   *
  3  FROM        TESTS
  4  WHERE       PNO > 5;
```

To execute a statement using one server process, use the **NOPARALLEL** hint. Or, you can use the **PARALLEL** hint with a degree of parallelism of 1. Listing 9.29 illustrates both situations. If the degree of parallelism for a table is 1, no hint is needed.

Listing 9.29 NOPARALLEL.

```
SQL> SELECT --+ NOPARALLEL(TESTS)
  3  *
  4  FROM        TESTS
  5  WHERE       PNO > 5500;

SQL> SELECT /*+ PARALLEL(TESTS, 1) */  *
  2  FROM        TESTS
  3  WHERE       PNO > 5500;
```

CACHE

If you have small tables that applications are constantly performing full table scans on and you want the table blocks to remain in memory as long as possible, consider using the **CACHE** hint. Normally, when Oracle performs a full table scan, the blocks read into the database buffer pool go to the least recently used end of Oracle's Least Recently Used (LRU) list. Using the **CACHE** hint moves the blocks to the most recently used end of the LRU list. This permits the blocks to remain in the database buffer pool for a longer period of time. Consequently, queries needing to read the blocks of the smaller tables are more likely to find them in memory. Because the blocks are in memory, no physical I/O is required, which equates to faster-running SQL statements and applications.

To specify a table's blocks be moved to the most recently used end of the LRU list after a full table scan is performed, use the **CACHE** entry when either creating or altering a table.

From Listing 9.30, you can see that the default setting for **CACHE** when creating tables is "no." To cache the **PARTS** table after a full table scan, you should alter the table. If you cringe when you hear the phrase "curiosity killed the cat," you can view the cached blocks by writing a query using the dynamic performance view **V$CACHE**. For this object to exist, the DBA must run a script named catparr.sql. For you to see this view, you must have DBA privileges. It's not necessary for you to see this view, but it is fun to see Oracle at work. Finally, you'll note that the rows in the **PARTS** table are indeed in file number 7. For the real DBAs of the world, to see the actual file name and path the blocks are in, you would write a query that joins the table to **V$DBFILE**.

Listing 9.30 CACHE.

```
SQL> SELECT TABLE_NAME,
  2         CACHE
  3  FROM   USER_TABLES
  4  WHERE  TABLE_NAME IN('PARTS', 'TESTS');

TABLE_NAME                     CACHE
------------------------------ -----
PARTS                              N
TESTS                              N

SQL> ALTER TABLE PARTS CACHE;
Table altered.

SQL> SELECT TABLE_NAME,
  2         CACHE
  3  FROM   USER_TABLES
  4* WHERE  TABLE_NAME IN('PARTS', 'TESTS');

TABLE_NAME                     CACHE
------------------------------ -----
PARTS                              Y
TESTS                              N

SQL> SELECT *    -- Full Table Scan Of PARTS
     FROM   PARTS;
.....................
10000 rows selected.

SQL> SELECT SUBSTR(NAME,1,12) "Name",
```

```
  2         KIND,
  3         STATUS,
  4         FILE#,
  5         BLOCK#   -- catparr.sql creates
  6  FROM   V$CACHE  -- dynamic view V$CACHE
  7* WHERE  NAME = 'PARTS';

Name         KIND         STAT  FILE# BLOCK#
------------ ------------ ---- ------ ------
PARTS        TABLE        XCUR      7  17932

SQL> SELECT PNO,    -- Just Having A Little Fun
  2         PNAME,
  3         SUBSTR(ROWID,15,4) "File Number"
  4  FROM   PARTS
  5  WHERE  ROWNUM < 2;

   PNO PNAME         File
------ ------------- ----
     1 Widget 1      0007

SQL> SELECT PNO,
  2         SUBSTR(PNAME,1,6) "PNAME",
  3         SUBSTR(NAME,1,34) "Full Pathname"
  4  FROM   PARTS,
  5         V$DBFILE
  6  WHERE  SUBSTR(PARTS.ROWID,15,4) = FILE# AND
  7*        ROWNUM < 2;

PNO PNAME    Full Pathname
--- -------- ----------------------------------
  1 Widget 1 /disk0/oradata/7.3.2/pete_temp.dbf
```

If you don't want a table's blocks placed in the most recently used end of the LRU list for a table whose definition is **CACHE**, use the hint **NOCACHE**. The **NOCACHE** hint places the table's blocks in the least recently used end of the LRU list. Listing 9.31 shows an example using the **NOCACHE** hint along with the **FULL** hint. The **FULL** hint is not needed because no **WHERE** clause exists and a full table scan is performed anyway. At first glance, it appears the hint fails. However, the **NOCACHE** hint does not remove the blocks from cache—it moves the blocks to the end of the least recently used end of the LRU list. If no server process performs a full table scan on **PARTS** and you wait awhile on a busy system, then the query using **V$CACHE** shows that the **PARTS** table's blocks are no longer in cache.

Listing 9.31 NOCACHE.

```
SQL> SELECT TABLE_NAME,
  2         CACHE
  3  FROM   USER_TABLES
  4* WHERE  TABLE_NAME IN('PARTS', 'TESTS');

TABLE_NAME                     CACHE
------------------------------ -----
PARTS                              Y
TESTS                              N

SQL> SELECT --+ NOCACHE(PARTS) FULL(PARTS)
  2             PNO, PNAME  -- Full Hint 4 Fun
  3* FROM       PARTS;

   PNO PNAME
------ --------------
...... ............
  9999 Widget 9999
 10000 Widget 10000

10000 rows selected.

SQL> SELECT SUBSTR(NAME,1,12) "Name",
  2         KIND,   -- At LRU End Of List
  3         STATUS, -- But Still In Cache
  4         FILE#,
  5         BLOCK#
  6  FROM   V$CACHE
  7* WHERE  NAME = 'PARTS';

Name         KIND         STAT  FILE# BLOCK#
------------ ------------ ---- ------ ------
PARTS        TABLE        XCUR      7  17932

SQL> SELECT SUBSTR(NAME,1,12) "Name",
  2         KIND,  -- After Waiting A While
  3         STATUS,
  4         FILE#,
  5         BLOCK#
  6  FROM   V$CACHE
  7* WHERE  NAME = 'PARTS';

no rows selected
```

Other Access Methods

The quickest method to retrieve rows from any Oracle table is to use the *rowid*. However, to use the **ROWID** in a query you must know the actual *rowid* of the row(s) you want to see. In Listing 9.32, the **ROWID** 00000CFE.0021.0003 retrieves part number 90 and test number 8,101.

Listing 9.32 ROWID.

```
SQL> SELECT PNO,
  2         TNO,
  3         ROWID  -- To Determine Rowid
  4  FROM   TESTS
  5* WHERE  TNO = 8101;

   PNO     TNO ROWID
 ------  ------ ------------------
    93    8101 00000568.003A.0003
    90    8101 00000CFE.0021.0003
    91    8101 00000D3E.006E.0003
    92    8101 00000D80.0076.0003

SQL> EXPLAIN PLAN FOR
  2  SELECT --+ ROWID(TESTS)
  3          *
  4  FROM       TESTS
  5  WHERE      TNO = 8101 AND
  6*            ROWID = '00000CFE.0021.0003';
Explained.

SQL> @explain
Query Plan                                  COST
--------------------------------------- -------
SELECT STATEMENT   CHOOSE                     1
  TABLE ACCESS BY ROWID TESTS ANALYZED        1
```

Miscellaneous

The hint **NO_MERGE**, shown in Listing 9.33, causes Oracle not to merge any views it might create in the course of a statement. This is not one of your "everyday variety" hints, and neither is the SQL statement that uses it.

Listing 9.33 NO_MERGE.

```
SQL> SET NUMWIDTH 5
SQL> COL JOB      NOPRINT
SQL> COL MGR      NOPRINT
SQL> COL COMM     NOPRINT
SQL> COL DEPTNO   NOPRINT

SQL> SELECT *     -- 14 Rows X 4 Rows = 56 Rows
  2  FROM   EMP, (SELECT *
  3*              FROM   DEPT);

EMPNO ENAME      HIREDATE    SAL LOC
----- ---------- -------- ------ ------
.......................................
 7876 ADAMS      12-JAN-83  1100 BOSTON
 7900 JAMES      03-DEC-81   950 BOSTON
 7902 FORD       03-DEC-81  3000 BOSTON
 7934 MILLER     23-JAN-82  1300 BOSTON

56 rows selected.

SQL> EXPLAIN PLAN FOR
  2  SELECT *
  3  FROM   EMP, (SELECT *
  4*              FROM   DEPT);
Explained.

SQL> @explain
Query Plan                  COST
-------------------------- ----
SELECT STATEMENT   CHOOSE
  NESTED LOOPS
    TABLE ACCESS FULL DEPT
    TABLE ACCESS FULL EMP

SQL> EXPLAIN PLAN FOR
  2  SELECT *
  3  FROM   EMP, (SELECT /*+ NO_MERGE */  *
  4*              FROM   DEPT);
Explained.

SQL> @explain
Query Plan                     COST
---------------------------- -----
SELECT STATEMENT   CHOOSE
```

```
NESTED LOOPS
  VIEW
    TABLE ACCESS FULL DEPT
  TABLE ACCESS FULL EMP
```

Summary

Oracle hints are very powerful weapons in the hands of developers and database administrators when used correctly. Hints override the database-level parameter **OPTIMIZER_MODE** and the session-level **OPTIMIZER_GOAL**. Hints are extremely flexible, and you can combine them. For a slow-running query, you can run it with a hint through Explain Plan and then note the cost. Most of the time, the query with the lowest cost outperforms the query with a higher cost. This way, you can tell immediately by looking at the plan output whether the hint might speed up the query.

HIGH PERFORMANCE

Joining Tables

CHAPTER 10

Many queries require data residing in several different tables. To process a query of this type, Oracle joins the tables together. This chapter teaches you the four methods of joins.

Joining Tables

The Join Chain

At parse time, the optimizer decides the order in which to join tables when the query contains more than one table in the **FROM** clause. The rows from the first table in the chain are joined to the rows in the second table in the chain. This process continues through the last table in the join chain. The first table in the join chain is the *inner table*, and the last table in the join chain is the *outer table*. Don't confuse the outer table with an outer join. The outer table is merely the last table in the chain. The order of the tables in the join chain is very important. Performance is greatly impacted by the order of the tables. Usually, the optimizer makes the best choice of table order in the join chain. However, you can rigidly control the join chain by using the **ORDERED** hint. The first table in the join chain is the key factor in writing fast queries that join tables. Oracle uses one of four methods to join tables together: sort merge, nested loop, hash, and index cluster. The sort merge join is typically the slowest.

The Driving Table

The first table in the join chain is called the *driving table*. This table should be the most selective table in the join chain. By selective, I mean the number of rows returned in the **WHERE** clause for the table should be the fewest. Many times, the driving table has the fewest number of rows, but this is not always the case. For example, a large table with a unique index used in the **WHERE** clause causes the optimizer to use this large table as the driving table. The driving table, or the *inner table*, is the first table referenced in the output of Explain Plan, reading the output from the top down.

How To Identify The Driving Table

The driving table is easily located in the Explain Plan output. Listing 10.1 shows that the driving table is **PARTS**, because it's the first table name to appear in the output, reading from the top of the output to the bottom (**INDEX UNIQUE SCAN** *PARTS*_PNO **ANALYZED**).

Listing 10.1 The driving table.

```
SQL> EXPLAIN PLAN FOR
  2  SELECT   PARTS.PNO, RESULTS
  3  FROM     TESTS, PARTS
  4  WHERE    PARTS.PNO      = TESTS.PNO
  5*          AND TESTS.PNO = 93;
Explained.

SQL> set echo off
SQL> @explain
Query Plan                                     COST
------------------------------------ -----
SELECT STATEMENT   CHOOSE                         4
  NESTED LOOPS                                    4
    INDEX UNIQUE SCAN PARTS_PNO ANALYZED 1
    TABLE ACCESS BY ROWID TESTS ANALYZED
      INDEX RANGE SCAN TESTS_PNO ANALYZED
```

The ORDERED Hint

One of the most powerful hints in Oracle is the **ORDERED** hint. This hint causes Oracle to create a join chain that matches the table order in the **FROM** clause. However, if your hint is not good, the cost becomes much higher, and the query will execute much slower than without the hint. However, the purpose of using Explain Plan is to allow you the luxury of trying hints and observing the cost. If your **ORDERED** hint results in a lower cost than without the hint, use the hint. Listing 10.2 uses the **ORDERED** hint. The driving table is **TESTS**, because it appears first in the **FROM** clause, and the outer table is **PARTS**, because it appears last in the **FROM** clause.

Listing 10.2 Using the **ORDERED** hint.

```
SQL> EXPLAIN PLAN FOR
  2  SELECT --+ORDERED
  3         PARTS.PNO, RESULTS
```

```
  4  FROM   TESTS, PARTS
  5  WHERE  PARTS.PNO      = TESTS.PNO
  6*        AND TESTS.PNO = 93;
Explained.

SQL> @explain

Query Plan                                    COST
----------------------------------  -----
SELECT STATEMENT   CHOOSE                        4
  NESTED LOOPS                                   4
    TABLE ACCESS BY ROWID TESTS ANALYZED 4
      INDEX RANGE SCAN TESTS_PNO ANALYZED
    INDEX UNIQUE SCAN PARTS_PNO ANALYZED
```

Types Of Joins

Figure 10.1 shows the four types of joins Oracle can choose. Typically, the slowest of the four is the sort merge join.

Sort Merge Join

Listing 10.3 shows a query that causes a sort merge join. No indexes exist on either table, and neither table is analyzed. Both tables are sorted before being merged. The driving table is completely irrelevant when a sort merge is performed. The first example shows that TESTS is the driving table, and it requires 2 minutes and 27.28

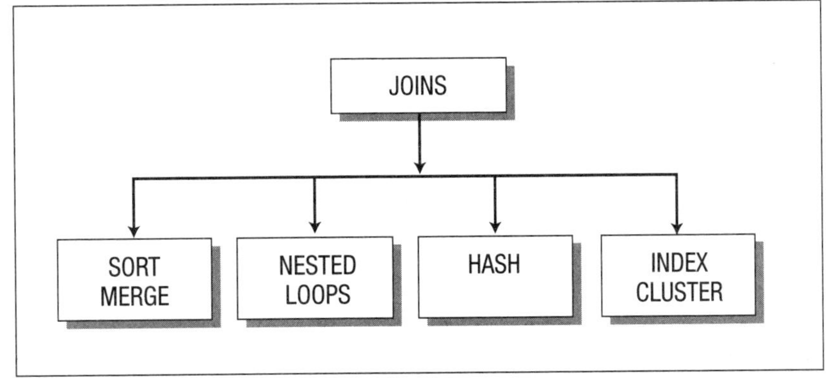

Figure 10.1
The four types of joins.

seconds to execute. In the second example, the order of the tables in the **FROM** clause is different than the order in the first example. Because no statistics exist for either table, Oracle uses the rule-based optimizer for both queries. Because no indexes exist on either of the **PNO** columns from these table, Oracle performs a sort merge join. Oracle examines the **FROM** clause and selects the last table to the reader's right as the driving table. When using the rule-based optimizer, rearranging the order of the tables in the **FROM** clause can change the order Oracle joins the tables in certain situations, where the ranking of several tables is the same. If the ranking is the same for a two-table join, for example, Oracle uses the table to the far right in the **FROM** clause as the driving table, even though it might not be the best choice. **PARTS** is the driving table in the second query, because it appears last in the **FROM** clause. The difference in the elapsed times is very small: The second query requires 2 minutes and 9.80 seconds to execute. You very rarely, if ever, want Oracle to perform full-table scans on all joined tables. The reason here is obvious—no indexes exist on the join columns of either table, which is really, really dumb.

Listing 10.3 A sort merge join.

```
SQL> SELECT SUBSTR(TABLE_NAME,1,15) "Table",
  2         SUBSTR(INDEX_NAME,1,20) "Index",
  3         DISTINCT_KEYS
  4  FROM   USER_INDEXES
  5  WHERE  TABLE_NAME = 'PARTS' OR
  6*        TABLE_NAME = 'TESTS';
no rows selected

SQL> SELECT SUBSTR(TABLE_NAME,1,15) "Table",
  2         NUM_ROWS
  3  FROM   USER_TABLES
  4  WHERE  TABLE_NAME = 'PARTS' OR
  5*        TABLE_NAME = 'TESTS';

Table            NUM_ROWS
-------------- ---------

PARTS
TESTS

SQL> EXPLAIN PLAN FOR
  2  SELECT PARTS.PNO, RESULTS
  3  FROM   PARTS, TESTS
```

```
  4  WHERE  PARTS.PNO = TESTS.PNO AND
  5         TESTS.PNO = 93;
Explained.

SQL>@explain
Query Plan                          COST
---------------------------- -----
SELECT STATEMENT   CHOOSE
  MERGE JOIN
    SORT JOIN
      TABLE ACCESS FULL TESTS
    SORT JOIN
      TABLE ACCESS FULL PARTS

SQL> SELECT PARTS.PNO, RESULTS
  2  FROM   PARTS, TESTS
  3  WHERE  PARTS.PNO = TESTS.PNO AND
  4         TESTS.PNO = 93;

    PNO R
 ------ -
     93 F
     93 P

8650 rows selected.

Elapsed: 00:02:27.28

SQL> EXPLAIN PLAN FOR
  2  SELECT  PARTS.PNO, RESULTS
  3  FROM    TESTS, PARTS
  4  WHERE   PARTS.PNO = TESTS.PNO AND
  5          TESTS.PNO = 93;
Explained.

SQL> @explain
Query Plan                          COST
---------------------------- ----
SELECT STATEMENT   CHOOSE
  MERGE JOIN
    SORT JOIN
      TABLE ACCESS FULL PARTS
    SORT JOIN
      TABLE ACCESS FULL TESTS
```

```
SQL> SELECT PARTS.PNO, RESULTS
  2  FROM   TESTS, PARTS
  3  WHERE  PARTS.PNO = TESTS.PNO
  4         AND TESTS.PNO = 93;
PNO  R
---  -
......
  93 F
  93 P

8650 rows selected.

Elapsed: 00:02:09.80
```

Now let's use the **FIRST_ROWS** hint to cause Oracle to use the cost-based optimizer, even though no statistics exist for either the **PARTS** or **TESTS** table. Notice in Listing 10.4 that the cost is 658 and **PARTS** is the driving table. Of greater interest is that Oracle uses a hash join to join the two tables. Also, note that the performance of this query is slower than the query in Listing 10.3. The query in Listing 10.3 requires 2 minutes and 9 seconds, whereas the query in Listing 10.4 requires 2 minutes and 16 seconds. In other words, the query that uses the hash join runs 7 seconds slower than the query that uses the sort merge join.

Listing 10.4 The **FIRST_ROWS** hint.

```
SQL> EXPLAIN PLAN FOR
  2  SELECT --+ FIRST_ROWS
  3         PARTS.PNO, RESULTS
  4  FROM   PARTS, TESTS
  5  WHERE  PARTS.PNO = TESTS.PNO AND
  6*        TESTS.PNO = 93;
Explained.

SQL> @explain
Query Plan                                 COST
---------------------------------------- -------
SELECT STATEMENT  HINT: FIRST_ROWS          658
  HASH JOIN                                 658
    TABLE ACCESS FULL PARTS                  26
    TABLE ACCESS FULL TESTS                 631

SQL> SELECT --+ FIRST_ROWS
```

```
  3         PARTS.PNO, RESULTS
  4  FROM   PARTS, TESTS
  5  WHERE  PARTS.PNO = TESTS.PNO AND
  6*        TESTS.PNO = 93;

 PNO R
---- --
.......
  93 F
  93 P

8650 rows selected.

Elapsed: 00:02:16.80
```

Listing 10.5 combines two hints, **FIRST_ROWS** and **ORDERED** to illustrate that the driving table makes no difference with respect to performance if no indexes exist on either column used in the **WHERE** clause. Note that the query requires 2 minutes and 13.48 seconds to execute. Remember, between each command in Chapters 1 through 14, the Oracle database is shut down and started up.

Listing 10.5 The **ORDERED** and **FIRST_ROWS** hints.

```
SQL> EXPLAIN PLAN FOR
  2  SELECT --+ FIRST_ROWS  ORDERED
  3         PARTS.PNO, RESULTS
  4  FROM   TESTS,  PARTS
  5  WHERE  PARTS.PNO = TESTS.PNO AND
  6         TESTS.PNO = 93;
Explained.

SQL> @explain
Query Plan                                COST
----------------------------------- ------
SELECT STATEMENT   HINT: FIRST_ROWS     658
  HASH JOIN                             658
    TABLE ACCESS FULL TESTS             631
    TABLE ACCESS FULL PARTS              26

SQL> SELECT --+ FIRST_ROWS  ORDERED
  2         PARTS.PNO, RESULTS
  3  FROM   TESTS,  PARTS
  4  WHERE  PARTS.PNO = TESTS.PNO AND
  5         TESTS.PNO = 93;
```

```
PNO R
--- -
.....
 93 F
 93 P

8650 rows selected.

Elapsed: 00:02:13.48
```

Another hint you can use is **ALL_ROWS**. The **ALL_ROWS** hint uses the cost-based optimizer and chooses the fastest access path and method to retrieve all of the rows in the active set. If you do not want to use a hint, you can use the **ALTER SESSION** command, as shown in Listing 10.6. Listing 10.6 shows the same cost (658) as the query in Listing 10.5. In addition, Oracle uses a hash join to retrieve rows from the two tables, using **PARTS** as the driving table. Moreover, the query requires 2 minutes and 20.02 seconds to execute; that is only seven seconds slower than the same query in Listing 10.5 that uses the hints **FIRST_ROWS** and **ORDERED**. However, the query in Listing 10.6 uses the **PARTS** table as the driving table, and the query in Listing 10.5 uses the **TESTS** table as the driving table. The best choice of a driving table belongs to **PARTS** with a cost of 26 compared to the cost of 631 for the **TESTS** table. So, the query in Listing 10.5 would execute faster if the **ORDERED** hint is omitted. The hint **FIRST_ROWS** normally outperforms the hint **ALL_ROWS**, since it is usually less work to bring back the first row the fastest way possible compared to returning all of the rows the quickest method possible.

Listing 10.6 The **ALL_ROWS** hint.

```
SQL> ALTER SESSION SET OPTIMIZER_GOAL = ALL_ROWS;
Session altered.

SQL> EXPLAIN PLAN FOR
  2  SELECT --+ ALL_ROWS
  3         PARTS.PNO, RESULTS
  4  FROM   PARTS, TESTS
  5  WHERE  PARTS.PNO = TESTS.PNO AND
  6*        TESTS.PNO = 93;
Explained.
```

```
SQL> @explain
Query Plan                              COST
-------------------------------- ------
SELECT STATEMENT   HINT: ALL_ROWS     658
  HASH JOIN                           658
    TABLE ACCESS FULL PARTS            26
    TABLE ACCESS FULL TESTS           631

SQL> SELECT --+ ALL_ROWS
  2          PARTS.PNO, RESULTS
  3   FROM   PARTS, TESTS
  4   WHERE  PARTS.PNO = TESTS.PNO AND
  5          TESTS.PNO = 93;

PNO R
--- -
.....
 93 F
 93 P

8650 rows selected.

Elapsed: 00:02:20.02
```

Another hint you can use when joining tables is **USE_NL**. In Listing 10.7, this hint causes a row from the **PARTS** table to join with matching rows from the **TESTS** table. Hints can be combined, and Listing 10.7 uses the **ORDERED** hint as well as **USE_NL**. Notice the cost of 12,646 here, compared to the cost of 658 in Listing 10.6. The hint **ALL_ROWS** has a much lower cost than the **ORDERED** and **USE_NL** hints in this listing. Remember, however, neither table is analyzed. The hint **ORDERED USE_NL(PARTS)** produces a catastrophic response time of 2 hours, 23 minutes, and 41.49 seconds.

Listing 10.7 The **ORDERED** and **USE_NL** hints.

```
SQL> EXPLAIN PLAN FOR
  2   SELECT --+ORDERED USE_NL(TESTS)
  3          PARTS.PNO, RESULTS
  4   FROM   PARTS, TESTS
  5   WHERE  PARTS.PNO = TESTS.PNO AND
  6          TESTS.PNO = 93;
Explained.
```

```
SQL> @explain
Query Plan                           COST
-------------------------- -----
SELECT STATEMENT    CHOOSE   12646
 NESTED LOOPS                12646
   TABLE ACCESS FULL PARTS      26
   TABLE ACCESS FULL TESTS

SQL> SELECT  --+ORDERED USE_NL(TESTS)
  2          PARTS.PNO, RESULTS
  3  FROM    PARTS, TESTS
  4  WHERE   PARTS.PNO = TESTS.PNO AND
  5          TESTS.PNO   = 93;
   PNO R
------ -
........
    93 P
    93 F
    93 P

8650 rows selected.

Elapsed: 00:02:03.03

SQL> EXPLAIN PLAN FOR
  2  SELECT --+ORDERED USE_NL(PARTS)
  3          PARTS.PNO, RESULTS
  4  FROM    TESTS, PARTS -- Really Slow
  5  WHERE   PARTS.PNO = TESTS.PNO AND
  6          TESTS.PNO = 93;
Explained.

SQL> @explain
Query Plan                           COST
-------------------------- ------
SELECT STATEMENT    CHOOSE      1151
 NESTED LOOPS                   1151
   TABLE ACCESS FULL TESTS       631
   TABLE ACCESS FULL PARTS

SQL> SELECT --+ORDERED USE_NL(PARTS)
  2          PARTS.PNO, RESULTS
  3  FROM    TESTS,  PARTS
  4  WHERE   PARTS.PNO = TESTS.PNO AND
  5          TESTS.PNO  =  93;
```

```
   PNO R
------ -
........
    93 P
    93 F
    93 P

8650 rows selected.

Elapsed: 02:23:41.49

SQL> EXPLAIN PLAN FOR
  2  SELECT  --+ORDERED USE_NL(PARTS) RULE
  3          PARTS.PNO, RESULTS
  4   FROM   TESTS, PARTS -- Parts Analyzed
  5   WHERE  PARTS.PNO + 0 = TESTS.PNO AND
  6              TESTS.PNO = 93;
Explained.

SQL> @explain
Query Plan                                  COST
------------------------------------ ------
SELECT STATEMENT   HINT: RULE               1151
  NESTED LOOPS                              1151
    TABLE ACCESS FULL TESTS                  631
    TABLE ACCESS FULL PARTS ANALYZED
```

Table 10.1 summarizes the results of the sort merge joins in Listings 10.3 through 10.7. Note that the hints **ALL_ROWS** and **FIRST_ROWS** cause Oracle to use the cost-based optimizer, even though no statistics are available. In addition, the use of the **USE_NL** hint suggests that you can be a hero or a zero, depending on which table you use in the hint.

Nested Loops Join

A nested loops join uses one row from the inner, or driving, table to join with all the matching rows from the outer table. Typically, this join is faster than a sort merge join.

One Unique Index And Neither Table Analyzed

Listing 10.8 shows a query that uses a nested loops join. One index exists on either of the two joined tables. In this case, the index is unique, and it's on the PNO

Table 10.1 Sort merge join results with no indexes and no statistics.

Listing	Type Of Join	Goal Or Hint	Driving Table	Type Of Access PARTS	Type Of Access TESTS	Cost	Elapsed Time
10.3	Sort merge	CHOOSE	TESTS	Full	Full	Null	2:27.28
10.3	Sort merge	CHOOSE	PARTS	Full	Full	Null	2:09.80
10.4	Hash	FIRST_ROWS	PARTS	Full	Full	658	2:16.80
10.5	Hash	FIRST_ROWS ORDERED	TESTS	Full	Full	658	2:13.48
10.6	Hash	ALL_ROWS	PARTS	Full	Full	658	2:20.02
10.7	Nested Loops	USE_NL (TESTS)	PARTS	Full	Full	12,646	2:03.03
10.7	Nested Loops	USE_NL (PARTS)	TESTS	Full	Full	1,151	2:23:41.49

column of the **PARTS** table. Furthermore, neither table is analyzed. A query using the data dictionary view **USER_TABLES**, with the column **NUM_ROWS** containing null values, shows that neither table contains statistics. The output from Explain Plan indicates that Oracle uses a **NESTED LOOPS** join to join the two tables, and the driving table is **TESTS**. Oracle retrieves a row from the driving table **TESTS**, and it retrieves the matching rows from the **PARTS** table using the unique index **PARTS_PNO**. The elapsed time is 2 minutes and 14.76 seconds to retrieve 8,650 rows.

Listing 10.8 A nested loops join with one index.

```
SQL> SET TIMING ON
SQL> CREATE UNIQUE INDEX
  2           PARTS_PNO
  3           ON PARTS(PNO);
Index created.

Elapsed: 00:00:10.95

SQL> SELECT SUBSTR(TABLE_NAME,1,15) "Table",
  2           NUM_ROWS
  3   FROM    USER_TABLES
  4   WHERE   TABLE_NAME = 'PARTS' OR
  5           TABLE_NAME = 'TESTS';
```

```
Table          NUM_ROWS
-------------- --------
PARTS
TESTS

SQL> EXPLAIN PLAN FOR
  2  SELECT  PARTS.PNO, RESULTS
  3  FROM    TESTS, PARTS
  4  WHERE   PARTS.PNO = TESTS.PNO AND
  5          TESTS.PNO = 93;
Explained.

SQL> @explain
Query Plan                      COST
------------------------- ------
SELECT STATEMENT   CHOOSE
  NESTED LOOPS
    TABLE ACCESS FULL TESTS
    INDEX UNIQUE SCAN PARTS_PNO

SQL> SELECT PARTS.PNO, RESULTS
  2  FROM   TESTS, PARTS
  3  WHERE  PARTS.PNO = TESTS.PNO AND
  4         TESTS.PNO = 93;

    PNO R
------- -
.........
     93 P
     93 F
     93 P

8650 rows selected.

Elapsed: 00:02:14.76
```

Listing 10.9 shows another query that uses a nested loops join. Only one index exists, and it's a unique index on the **PNO** column of the **PARTS** table. Neither table is analyzed, and the query uses the hint **FIRST_ROWS**. Because **FIRST_ROWS** causes Oracle to use the cost-based optimizer, the cost, without any actual statistics on either table, is 632. The driving table is **PARTS**, and each of the 10,000 rows from **PARTS** is retrieved using the unique index on the **PNO** column. Each row from **PARTS** is joined to the corresponding rows in **TESTS**.

Oracle performs a full-table scan on **TESTS**, which contains 470,552 rows. The query requires 2 minutes and 31.13 seconds to retrieve 8,650 rows.

Listing 10.9 A nested loops join using **FIRST_ROWS**.

```
SQL> EXPLAIN PLAN FOR
     SELECT --+ FIRST_ROWS
              PARTS.PNO, RESULTS
     FROM     PARTS, TESTS
     WHERE    PARTS.PNO = TESTS.PNO AND
              TESTS.PNO = 93;
Explained.

SQL> @explain
Query Plan                                   COST
-----------------------------------         -----
SELECT STATEMENT    HINT: FIRST_ROWS          632
  NESTED LOOPS                                632
    INDEX UNIQUE SCAN PARTS_PNO                 1
    TABLE ACCESS FULL TESTS

SQL> SELECT --+ FIRST_ROWS
              PARTS.PNO, RESULTS
     FROM     PARTS, TESTS
     WHERE    PARTS.PNO = TESTS.PNO AND
              TESTS.PNO = 93;

   PNO R
------ -
........

    93 P
    93 F
    93 P

8650 rows selected.

Elapsed: 00:02:31.13
```

Listing 10.10 shows another query that uses a nested loops join. A unique index exists on the **PNO** column of the **PARTS** table. Neither table is analyzed, and the query uses the hint **ALL_ROWS**. Because **ALL_ROWS** causes Oracle to use the cost-based optimizer, the cost, without any actual statistics on either table, is 632. The driving table is **PARTS**, and each of the 10,000 rows from **PARTS** is retrieved using the unique index on the **PNO** column. Each row from **PARTS** is joined to the corresponding rows in **TESTS**, with Oracle performing a full-table scan on **TESTS**, which contains 470,552 rows. The query requires 2 minutes and 18.17 seconds to retrieve 8,650 rows. The Explain Plan is the same for the hints **FIRST_ROWS** and **ALL_ROWS**, with a slight difference in elapsed times. The query using the **ALL_ROWS** hint in Listing 10.10 is 13 seconds faster than the **FIRST_ROWS** query in Listing 10.9.

Listing 10.10 A nested loops join using **ALL_ROWS**.

```
SQL> EXPLAIN PLAN FOR
  2  SELECT --+ ALL_ROWS
  3         PARTS.PNO, RESULTS
  4  FROM   PARTS, TESTS
  5  WHERE  PARTS.PNO = TESTS.PNO AND
  6         TESTS.PNO = 93;
Explained.

SQL> @explain
Query Plan                            COST
------------------------------ -----
SELECT STATEMENT   HINT: ALL_ROWS  632
  NESTED LOOPS                     632
    INDEX UNIQUE SCAN PARTS_PNO      1
    TABLE ACCESS FULL TESTS

SQL> SELECT --+ ALL_ROWS
  2         PARTS.PNO, RESULTS
  3  FROM   PARTS, TESTS
  4  WHERE  PARTS.PNO = TESTS.PNO AND
  5         TESTS.PNO = 93;

    PNO R
------- -
.........

     93 P
     93 F
     93 P

8650 rows selected.

Elapsed: 00:02:18.17
```

Table 10.2 Results of nested loops joins with a unique index on **PARTS.PNO** with no statistics.

Listing	Type Of Join	Goal Or Hint	Driving Table	Type Of Access PARTS	Type Of Access TESTS	Cost	Elapsed Time
10.8	Nested Loops	CHOOSE	TESTS	Index	Full	Null	2:14.76
10.9	Nested Loops	FIRST_ROWS	PARTS	Index	Full	632	2:31.13
10.10	Nested Loops	ALL_ROWS	PARTS	Index	Full	632	2:18.17

Table 10.2 summarizes the results of the queries that use nested loop joins on tables with one unique index and neither table analyzed.

PARTS Table Indexed And Analyzed

Listing 10.11 shows another query that uses a nested loops join. A unique index exists on the PNO column of the PARTS table. The PARTS table is analyzed, and Oracle uses the cost-based optimizer with a cost of 632 for this query. The driving table is PARTS, and each of the 10,000 rows from PARTS is retrieved using the unique index on the PNO column. Each row from PARTS is joined to the corresponding rows in TESTS, with Oracle performing a full-table scan on TESTS, which contains 470,552 rows. The query requires 2 minutes and 8.1 seconds to retrieve 8,650 rows.

Listing 10.11 The **PARTS** table, indexed and analyzed.

```
SQL> ANALYZE TABLE PARTS
  2          COMPUTE STATISTICS;
Table analyzed.

Elapsed: 00:00:13.47

SQL> SELECT SUBSTR(TABLE_NAME,1,15) "Table",
  2         NUM_ROWS
  3  FROM   USER_TABLES
  4  WHERE  TABLE_NAME = 'PARTS' OR
  5         TABLE_NAME = 'TESTS';
```

```
Table          NUM_ROWS
-------------- --------
PARTS             10000
TESTS

SQL> EXPLAIN PLAN FOR
  2  SELECT PARTS.PNO, RESULTS
  3  FROM   PARTS, TESTS
  4  WHERE  PARTS.PNO = TESTS.PNO AND
  5         TESTS.PNO = 93;
Explained.

SQL> @explain
Query Plan                               COST
------------------------------------ -----
SELECT STATEMENT   CHOOSE                 632
  NESTED LOOPS                            632
    INDEX UNIQUE SCAN PARTS_PNO ANALYZED 1
    TABLE ACCESS FULL TESTS

SQL> SELECT PARTS.PNO, RESULTS
  2  FROM   PARTS, TESTS
  3  WHERE  PARTS.PNO = TESTS.PNO AND
  4         TESTS.PNO = 93;

    PNO R
------- -
.........

     93 P
     93 F
     93 P

8650 rows selected.

Elapsed: 00:02:08.10
```

Listing 10.12 uses the hint **FIRST_ROWS**, which causes Oracle to perform a nested loops join. One unique index exists on the **PNO** column of the **PARTS** table, and the **PARTS** table is analyzed. The cost is 632 for this query, the driving table is **PARTS**, and each of the 10,000 rows from **PARTS** is retrieved using the unique index on the **PNO** column. Each row from **PARTS** joins to the corresponding rows in **TESTS** using a full-table scan on **TESTS**, which contains 470,552 rows. The query requires 2 minutes and 9.54 seconds to retrieve 8,650 rows.

Listing 10.12 A nested loops join using **FIRST_ROWS**.

```
SQL> EXPLAIN PLAN FOR
  2  SELECT --+ FIRST_ROWS
  3         PARTS.PNO, RESULTS
  4  FROM   PARTS, TESTS
  5  WHERE  PARTS.PNO = TESTS.PNO AND
  6         TESTS.PNO = 93;
Explained.

SQL> @explain
Query Plan                                    COST
---------------------------------------- -----
SELECT STATEMENT   HINT: FIRST_ROWS          632
  NESTED LOOPS                               632
    INDEX UNIQUE SCAN PARTS_PNO ANALYZED       1
    TABLE ACCESS FULL TESTS

SQL> SELECT --+ FIRST_ROWS
  2         PARTS.PNO, RESULTS
  3  FROM   PARTS, TESTS
  4  WHERE  PARTS.PNO = TESTS.PNO AND
  5         TESTS.PNO = 93;

    PNO R
------- -
.........

     93 P
     93 F
     93 P

8650 rows selected.

Elapsed: 00:02:09.54
```

Listing 10.13 uses the hint **ALL_ROWS**, which causes Oracle to perform a nested loops join. The cost is 632, and the driving table is **PARTS**. Oracle uses the unique index to retrieve each of the 10,000 rows from **PARTS**. A full-table scan retrieves the matching rows from the **TESTS** table. The query requires 2 minutes and 18.35 seconds to retrieve 8,650 rows.

Listing 10.13 A nested loops join using ALL_ROWS.

```
SQL> EXPLAIN PLAN FOR
     SELECT --+ ALL_ROWS
            PARTS.PNO, RESULTS
     FROM   PARTS, TESTS
     WHERE  PARTS.PNO = TESTS.PNO AND
            TESTS.PNO = 93;
Explained.

SQL> @explain
Query Plan                                     COST
---------------------------------------       -----
SELECT STATEMENT   HINT: ALL_ROWS               632
  NESTED LOOPS                                  632
    INDEX UNIQUE SCAN PARTS_PNO ANALYZED          1
    TABLE ACCESS FULL TESTS

SQL> SELECT --+ ALL_ROWS
            PARTS.PNO, RESULTS
     FROM   PARTS, TESTS
     WHERE  PARTS.PNO = TESTS.PNO AND
            TESTS.PNO = 93;

    PNO R
------- -
.........

     93 P
     93 F
     93 P

8650 rows selected.

Elapsed: 00:02:18.35
```

Listing 10.14 shows another example of a nested loops join—this time using the hint **RULE**. Oracle performs a full-table scan on **TESTS**, the driving table, and uses the unique index to retrieve matching rows in the **PARTS** table. When one column of the join clause is indexed and the other is not, Oracle uses the nonindexed table as the driving table. In Listing 10.14, the **PARTS.PNO** column is indexed, and **TESTS.PNO** is not. The query requires 2 minutes and 22.58 seconds to retrieve 8,650 rows.

Listing 10.14 A nested loops join using **RULE**.

```
SQL> EXPLAIN PLAN FOR
  2  SELECT --+ RULE
  3         PARTS.PNO, RESULTS
  4  FROM   PARTS, TESTS
  5  WHERE  PARTS.PNO = TESTS.PNO AND
  6         TESTS.PNO = 93;
Explained.

SQL> @explain
Query Plan                               COST
---------------------------------------- ----
SELECT STATEMENT   HINT: RULE
  NESTED LOOPS
    TABLE ACCESS FULL TESTS
    INDEX UNIQUE SCAN PARTS_PNO ANALYZED

SQL> SELECT --+ RULE
  2         PARTS. PNO, RESULTS
  3  FROM   PARTS, TESTS
  4  WHERE  PARTS.PNO = TESTS.PNO AND
  5         TESTS.PNO  = 93;
    PNO R
------- -
.........

     93 P
     93 F
     93 P

8650 rows selected.

Elapsed: 00:02:22.58
```

Table 10.3 summarizes the results of nested loops joins when a unique index exists on the **PNO** column of the **PARTS** table and statistics are available on the **PARTS** table.

Statistics On Both Tables And One Unique Index

Listing 10.15 starts by analyzing the **TESTS** table. Both tables are analyzed, and one unique index exists on the **PNO** column of the **PARTS** table. Oracle performs a nested loops join, uses the **PARTS** table as the driving table, and accesses each row with the unique index on the **PNO** column. A full-table scan retrieves matching

Table 10.3 Results of nested loops joins with a unique index and statistics on **PARTS**.

Listing	Type Of Join	Goal Or Hint	Driving Table	Type Of Access PARTS	Type Of Access TESTS	Cost	Elapsed Time
10.11	Nested Loops	CHOOSE	PARTS	Index	Full	632	2:08.10
10.12	Nested Loops	FIRST_ROWS	PARTS	Index	Full	632	2:09.54
10.13	Nested Loops	ALL_ROWS	PARTS	Index	Full	632	2:18.35
10.14	Nested Loops	RULE	TESTS	Index	Full	Null	2:22.58

rows in the TESTS table. The cost of this query is 632, and the query requires 2 minutes and 20.10 seconds to retrieve 8,650 rows.

Listing 10.15 Both tables analyzed.

```
SQL> ANALYZE TABLE TESTS
  2          COMPUTE STATISTICS;
Table analyzed.
Elapsed: 00:02:41.22

SQL>SELECT SUBSTR(TABLE_NAME,1,15) "Table",
  2        NUM_ROWS
  3   FROM  USER_TABLES
  4   WHERE TABLE_NAME = 'PARTS' OR
  5         TABLE_NAME = 'TESTS';

Table  NUM_ROWS
------ --------
PARTS     10000
TESTS    470552

SQL>SELECT SUBSTR(TABLE_NAME,1,15) "Table",
  2        SUBSTR(INDEX_NAME,1,20) "Index",
  3        DISTINCT_KEYS
  4   FROM  USER_INDEXES
  5   WHERE TABLE_NAME = 'PARTS' OR
  6*        TABLE_NAME = 'TESTS';
```

```
Table  Index      DISTINCT_KEYS
------ --------- -------------
PARTS  PARTS_PNO         10000

SQL> EXPLAIN PLAN FOR
  2  SELECT PARTS.PNO, RESULTS
  3  FROM   PARTS, TESTS
  4  WHERE  PARTS.PNO = TESTS.PNO AND
  5         TESTS.PNO = 93;
Explained.

SQL> @explain
Query Plan                                COST
---------------------------------------- ----
SELECT STATEMENT   CHOOSE                  632
  NESTED LOOPS                             632
    INDEX UNIQUE SCAN PARTS_PNO ANALYZED     1
    TABLE ACCESS FULL TESTS ANALYZED

SQL> SELECT PARTS.PNO, RESULTS
  2  FROM   PARTS, TESTS
  3  WHERE  PARTS.PNO = TESTS.PNO AND
  4         TESTS.PNO  =  93;

    PNO R
------- -
.........

     93 P
     93 F
     93 P

8650 rows selected.

Elapsed: 00:02:20.10
```

In Listing 10.16, the hint **FIRST_ROWS** causes Oracle to use a nested loops join. Also, **PARTS** is used as the driving table. Oracle uses the unique index to retrieve each row from **PARTS**, and it uses a full-table scan to retrieve matching records in **TESTS**. The cost of this query is 632, and the query requires 2 minutes and 20.84 seconds to retrieve 8,650 rows.

Listing 10.16 A nested loops join using **FIRST_ROWS**.

```
SQL> EXPLAIN PLAN FOR
```

```
  2  SELECT --+ FIRST_ROWS
  3         PARTS.PNO, RESULTS
  4  FROM   PARTS, TESTS
  5  WHERE  PARTS.PNO = TESTS.PNO AND
  6         TESTS.PNO = 93;
Explained.

SQL> @explain
Query Plan                                COST
----------------------------------------  ----
SELECT STATEMENT   HINT: FIRST_ROWS        632
  NESTED LOOPS                             632
    INDEX UNIQUE SCAN PARTS_PNO ANALYZED     1
    TABLE ACCESS FULL TESTS ANALYZED

SQL> SELECT --+ FIRST_ROWS
  2         PARTS.PNO, RESULTS
  3  FROM   PARTS, TESTS
  4  WHERE  PARTS.PNO = TESTS.PNO AND
  5         TESTS.PNO = 93;

    PNO R
------- -
.........

     93 P
     93 F
     93 P

8650 rows selected.

Elapsed: 00:02:20.84
```

In Listing 10.17, the hint **ALL_ROWS** causes Oracle to use a nested loops join. Also, the **PARTS** table is used as the driving table. Oracle uses the unique index to retrieve each row from **PARTS**, and it uses a full-table scan to retrieve matching records in **TESTS**. The cost of this query is 632, and the query requires 2 minutes and 9.68 seconds to retrieve 8,650 rows.

Listing 10.17 A nested loops join using **ALL_ROWS**.

```
SQL> EXPLAIN PLAN FOR
  2  SELECT --+ ALL_ROWS
  3         PARTS.PNO, RESULTS
  4  FROM   PARTS, TESTS
```

```
  5  WHERE  PARTS.PNO = TESTS.PNO AND
  6         TESTS.PNO = 93;
Explained.

SQL> @explain
Query Plan                                  COST
------------------------------------------- ----
SELECT STATEMENT   HINT: ALL_ROWS            632
  NESTED LOOPS                               632
    INDEX UNIQUE SCAN PARTS_PNO ANALYZED       1
    TABLE ACCESS FULL TESTS ANALYZED

SQL> SELECT --+ ALL_ROWS
  2         PARTS. PNO, RESULTS
  3  FROM   PARTS, TESTS
  4  WHERE  PARTS.PNO = TESTS.PNO AND
  5         TESTS.PNO = 93;

    PNO R
------- -
.........

     93 P
     93 F
     93 P

8650 rows selected.

Elapsed: 00:02:09.68
```

In Listing 10.18, the hint **RULE** causes Oracle to use a nested loops join. Also, **TESTS** is used as the driving table. Oracle uses a full-table scan to retrieve each row from **TESTS**, and it uses the unique index to retrieve matching rows from the **PARTS** table. Thequery requires 2 minutes and 10.25 seconds to retrieve 8,650 rows.

Listing 10.18 A nested loops join using **RULE**.

```
SQL> EXPLAIN PLAN FOR
  2  SELECT --+ RULE
  3         PARTS.PNO, RESULTS
  4  FROM   PARTS, TESTS
  5  WHERE  PARTS.PNO = TESTS.PNO AND
  6         TESTS.PNO = 93;
Explained.

SQL> @explain
```

```
Query Plan                                   COST
----------------------------------------     ----
SELECT STATEMENT   HINT: RULE
  NESTED LOOPS
    TABLE ACCESS FULL TESTS ANALYZED
    INDEX UNIQUE SCAN PARTS_PNO ANALYZED

SQL> SELECT --+ RULE
  2         PARTS.PNO, RESULTS
  3  FROM   PARTS, TESTS
  4  WHERE  PARTS.PNO = TESTS.PNO AND
  5         TESTS.PNO = 93;

    PNO R
------- -
.........

     93 P
     93 F
     93 P

8650 rows selected.

Elapsed: 00:02:10.25
```

Table 10.4 summarizes the results of nested loops joins with a unique index on the **PNO** column of the **PARTS** table; both tables are analyzed.

Table 10.4 Results of nested loops joins with a unique index and statistics on **PARTS/TESTS.**

Listing	Type Of Join	Goal Or Hint	Driving Table	Type Of Access PARTS	Type Of Access TESTS	Cost	Elapsed Time
10.15	Nested Loops	CHOOSE	PARTS	Index	Full	632	2:20.10
10.16	Nested Loops	FIRST_ROWS	PARTS	Index	Full	632	2:20.84
10.17	Nested Loops	ALL_ROWS	PARTS	Index	Full	632	2:09.68
10.18	Nested Loops	RULE	TESTS	Index	Full	Null	2:10.25

Statistics On Both Tables And Two Indexes

Now it's time to get real. Most joins have indexes on the foreign key columns, or at least they should in most situations. In Listing 10.19, a nonunique index is created on the **PNO** column of the **TESTS** table. Then, the **TESTS** table is reanalyzed because a new index exists. Notice the unbelievably low cost of 4; also, the response time of 1 minute and 35.22 seconds is the quickest of any query in this chapter so far. This is proof that foreign key columns should normally be indexed.

Oracle uses a nested loops join with **PARTS** as the driving table, and it uses the unique index to retrieve each row from **PARTS**. The optimizer also uses the index on the **PNO** column of **TESTS** to retrieve each matching row from the **TESTS** table.

Listing 10.19 Statistics and indexes on both tables.

```
SQL> CREATE INDEX TESTS_PNO
              ON TESTS(PNO);
Index created.
Elapsed: 00:04:53.91

SQL> ANALYZE TABLE TESTS
  2            COMPUTE STATISTICS;
Table analyzed.
Elapsed: 00:02:55.61

SQL> EXPLAIN PLAN FOR
  2  SELECT   PARTS.PNO, RESULTS
  3  FROM     TESTS, PARTS
  4  WHERE    PARTS.PNO = TESTS.PNO AND
  5           TESTS.PNO = 93;
Explained.

SQL> @explain
Query Plan                                  COST
------------------------------------------ ----
SELECT STATEMENT   CHOOSE                      4
  NESTED LOOPS                                 4
    INDEX UNIQUE SCAN PARTS_PNO ANALYZED       1
    TABLE ACCESS BY ROWID TESTS ANALYZED
      INDEX RANGE SCAN TESTS_PNO ANALYZED

SQL> SELECT PARTS.PNO, RESULTS
  2  FROM   TESTS, PARTS
  3  WHERE  PARTS.PNO = TESTS.PNO AND
```

```
  4          TESTS.PNO = 93;

    PNO R
------- -
.........

     93 P
     93 F
     93 P

8650 rows selected.

Elapsed: 00:01:35.22
```

Listing 10.20 shows that the selection of the driving table makes little difference in response time when the foreign key columns in the **WHERE** clause are indexed. The **ORDERED** hint forces Oracle to use **TESTS** as the driving table, because it appears first in the **FROM** clause. The optimizer uses a nested loops join, and it uses indexes on both tables to retrieve matching rows. Notice that the cost is 4 and the elapsed time is 1 minute and 37.49 seconds.

Listing 10.20 Nested loops using **ORDERED**.

```
SQL> EXPLAIN PLAN FOR
  2  SELECT --+ ORDERED
  3         PARTS.PNO, RESULTS
  4  FROM   TESTS, PARTS
  5  WHERE  PARTS.PNO = TESTS.PNO AND
  6         TESTS.PNO = 93;
Explained.

SQL> @explain
Query Plan                                  COST
---------------------------------------- ----
SELECT STATEMENT   CHOOSE                      4
  NESTED LOOPS                                 4
    TABLE ACCESS BY ROWID TESTS ANALYZED       4
      INDEX RANGE SCAN TESTS_PNO ANALYZED
    INDEX UNIQUE SCAN PARTS_PNO ANALYZED

SQL> SELECT --+ ORDERED
  2         PARTS.PNO, RESULTS
  3  FROM   TESTS, PARTS
  4  WHERE PARTS.PNO = TESTS.PNO AND
```

```
           TESTS.PNO  =  93;

    PNO R
------- -
.........

     93 P
     93 F
     93 P

8650 rows selected.

Elapsed: 00:01:37.49
```

In Listing 10.21, the **FIRST_ROWS** hint causes the same Explain Plan as the one in Listing 10.19. The only difference is in the elapsed times. The query in this listing is 14 seconds faster than the query in 10.19, which has no hints.

Listing 10.21 A nested loops join using **FIRST_ROWS**.

```
SQL> EXPLAIN PLAN FOR
     SELECT --+ FIRST_ROWS
            PARTS.PNO, RESULTS
     FROM   PARTS, TESTS
     WHERE  PARTS.PNO = TESTS.PNO AND
            TESTS.PNO = 93;
Explained.

SQL> @explain
Query Plan                                        COST
----------------------------------------------- ----
SELECT STATEMENT   HINT: FIRST_ROWS                  4
 NESTED LOOPS                                       4
   INDEX UNIQUE SCAN PARTS_PNO ANALYZED              1
   TABLE ACCESS BY ROWID TESTS ANALYZED
     INDEX RANGE SCAN TESTS_PNO ANALYZED

SQL> SELECT --+ FIRST_ROWS
            PARTS.PNO, RESULTS
     FROM   PARTS, TESTS
     WHERE  PARTS.PNO = TESTS.PNO AND
            TESTS.PNO  =  93;
    PNO R
------- -
.........
```

```
     93 P
     93 F
     93 P

8650 rows selected.

Elapsed: 00:01:21.75
```

In Listing 10.22, the **ALL_ROWS** hint causes the same Explain Plan as the ones in Listing 10.21 and 10.19. The only difference is in the elapsed times. The query in this listing is 13 seconds slower than the query in Listing 10.21, which uses the **FIRST_ROWS** hint, and is one second faster than the query in Listing 10.19, which uses both indexes.

Listing 10.22 A nested loops join using ALL_ROWS.

```
SQL> EXPLAIN PLAN FOR
  2  SELECT --+ ALL_ROWS
  3          PARTS.PNO, RESULTS
  4  FROM    PARTS, TESTS
  5  WHERE   PARTS.PNO = TESTS.PNO AND
  6          TESTS.PNO = 93;
Explained.

SQL> @explain
Query Plan                                  COST
----------------------------------------    ----
SELECT STATEMENT    HINT: ALL_ROWS             4
  NESTED LOOPS                                 4
    INDEX UNIQUE SCAN PARTS_PNO ANALYZED       1
    TABLE ACCESS BY ROWID TESTS ANALYZED
      INDEX RANGE SCAN TESTS_PNO ANALYZED

SQL> SELECT --+ ALL_ROWS
  2          PARTS.PNO, RESULTS
  3   FROM   PARTS, TESTS
  4   WHERE  PARTS.PNO = TESTS.PNO AND
  5          TESTS.PNO = 93;

    PNO R
------- -
.........

     93 P
```

```
     93 F
     93 P

8650 rows selected.

Elapsed: 00:01:34.22
```

In Listing 10.23, the **RULE** hint causes the optimizer to use **TESTS** as the driving table. Oracle performs a nested loops join. It retrieves each row from **TESTS** using the nonunique index and retrieves matching rows from **PARTS** using the unique index.

Listing 10.23 A nested loops join using **RULE**.

```
SQL> EXPLAIN PLAN FOR
  2  SELECT --+ RULE
  3         PARTS.PNO, RESULTS
  4  FROM   PARTS, TESTS
  5  WHERE  PARTS.PNO = TESTS.PNO AND
  6         TESTS.PNO = 93;
Explained.

SQL> @explain
Query Plan                                   COST
------------------------------------------ ------
SELECT STATEMENT   HINT: RULE
  NESTED LOOPS
    TABLE ACCESS BY ROWID TESTS ANALYZED
      INDEX RANGE SCAN TESTS_PNO ANALYZED
    INDEX UNIQUE SCAN PARTS_PNO ANALYZED

SQL> SELECT --+ RULE
  2         PARTS.PNO, RESULTS
  3  FROM   PARTS, TESTS
  4  WHERE  PARTS.PNO = TESTS.PNO AND
  5         TESTS.PNO  = 93;
    PNO R
------- -
.........

     93 P
     93 F
     93 P

8650 rows selected.

Elapsed: 00:01:37.43
```

Table 10.5 Results of nested loops joins with both tables indexed and analyzed.

Listing	Type Of Join	Goal Or Hint	Driving Table	Type Of Access PARTS	Type Of Access TESTS	Cost	Elapsed Time
10.19	Nested Loops	CHOOSE	PARTS	Index	Index	4	1:35.22
10.20	Nested Loops	ORDERED	TESTS	Index	Index	4	1:37.49
10.21	Nested Loops	FIRST_ROWS	PARTS	Index	Index	4	1:21.75
10.22	Nested Loops	ALL_ROWS	PARTS	Index	Index	4	1:34.22
10.23	Nested Loops	RULE	TESTS	Index	Index	Null	1:37.43

Table 10.5 summarizes the results of nested loops joins with both tables indexed and analyzed. Notice the tremendous speed of these queries. All the queries execute in less than 1 minute and 38 seconds (compared to 2+ minutes in previous queries).

No Statistics, But Indexes On Both Tables

Now let's delete the statistics from both tables, but keep the indexes, as shown in Listing 10.24. Then, the indexes on the join columns, **PARTS.PNO** and **TESTS.PNO**, need to be verified. Explain Plan shows that the optimizer performs a nested loops join. The rule-based optimizer uses **TESTS** as the driving table and retrieves each row using the nonunique index. Notice the elapsed time of 1 minute and 22.82 seconds.

Listing 10.24 No statistics, but two indexes.

```
SQL> ANALYZE TABLE PARTS
  2          DELETE STATISTICS;
Table analyzed.

SQL> ANALYZE TABLE TESTS
  2          DELETE STATISTICS;
Table analyzed.
```

```
SQL> SELECT  SUBSTR(TABLE_NAME,1,15) "Table",
  2          SUBSTR(INDEX_NAME,1,20) "Index",
  3          DISTINCT_KEYS
  4  FROM    USER_INDEXES
  5  WHERE   TABLE_NAME = 'PARTS' OR
  6          TABLE_NAME = 'TESTS';

Table           Index                DISTINCT_KEYS
-------------- -------------------- --------------
PARTS           PARTS_PNO
TESTS           TESTS_PNO

SQL> EXPLAIN PLAN FOR
  2  SELECT PARTS.PNO, RESULTS
  3  FROM   TESTS, PARTS
  4  WHERE  PARTS.PNO = TESTS.PNO AND
  5         TESTS.PNO = 93;
Explained.

SQL> @explain
Query Plan                          COST
------------------------------- ------
SELECT STATEMENT   CHOOSE
  NESTED LOOPS
    TABLE ACCESS BY ROWID TESTS
      INDEX RANGE SCAN TESTS_PNO
    INDEX UNIQUE SCAN PARTS_PNO

SQL> SELECT PARTS.PNO, RESULTS
  2  FROM   TESTS, PARTS
  3  WHERE  PARTS.PNO = TESTS.PNO AND
  4         TESTS.PNO = 93;

    PNO R
------- -
.........

     93 P
     93 F
     93 P

8650 rows selected.

Elapsed: 00:01:22.82
```

The query in Listing 10.25 uses the **FIRST_ROWS** hint, which invokes the cost-based optimizer, even though no statistics exist for either table. This forces the cost-based optimizer to derive a very unrealistic estimated cost of 3, which is much too low. Oracle retrieves rows from both tables using indexes.

Listing 10.25 A nested loops join using **FIRST_ROWS**.

```
SQL> EXPLAIN PLAN FOR
  2  SELECT --+ FIRST_ROWS
  3         PARTS.PNO, RESULTS
  4  FROM   PARTS, TESTS
  5  WHERE  PARTS.PNO = TESTS.PNO AND
  6         TESTS.PNO = 93;
Explained.

SQL> @explain
Query Plan                         COST
---------------------------------- ----
SELECT STATEMENT   HINT: FIRST_ROWS   3
  NESTED LOOPS                        3
    INDEX UNIQUE SCAN PARTS_PNO       1
    TABLE ACCESS BY ROWID TESTS
      INDEX RANGE SCAN TESTS_PNO

SQL> SELECT --+ FIRST_ROWS
  2         PARTS.PNO, RESULTS
  3  FROM   PARTS, TESTS
  4  WHERE  PARTS.PNO = TESTS.PNO  AND
  5         TESTS.PNO = 93;

    PNO R
------- -
.........

     93 P
     93 F
     93 P

8650 rows selected.

Elapsed: 00:01:29.34
```

The Explain Plans are identical in Listing 10.26 (**ALL_ROWS**) and Listing 10.25 (**FIRST_ROWS**). The query that uses the **FIRST_ROWS** hint is 8 seconds faster than the query that uses the **ALL_ROWS** hint.

Listing 10.26 A nested loops join using **ALL_ROWS**.

```
SQL> EXPLAIN PLAN FOR
  2  SELECT --+ ALL_ROWS
  3         PARTS.PNO, RESULTS
  4  FROM   PARTS, TESTS
  5  WHERE  PARTS.PNO = TESTS.PNO AND
  6         TESTS.PNO = 93;
Explained.

SQL> @explain
Query Plan                         COST
-------------------------------- ----
SELECT STATEMENT   HINT: ALL_ROWS   3
 NESTED LOOPS                       3
   INDEX UNIQUE SCAN PARTS_PNO      1
   TABLE ACCESS BY ROWID TESTS
     INDEX RANGE SCAN TESTS_PNO

SQL> SELECT --+ ALL_ROWS
  2         PARTS.PNO, RESULTS
  3  FROM   PARTS, TESTS
  4  WHERE  PARTS.PNO = TESTS.PNO AND
  5         TESTS.PNO = 93;
    PNO R
------- -
.........

     93 P
     93 F
     93 P

8650 rows selected.

Elapsed: 00:01:37.10
```

Table 10.6 summarizes the results of nested loops joins with both tables indexed, but neither one analyzed.

Table 10.6 Results of nested loops joins with both tables indexed but neither analyzed.

Listing	Type Of Join	Goal Or Hint	Driving Table	Type Of Access PARTS	Type Of Access TESTS	Cost	Elapsed Time
10.24	Nested Loops	CHOOSE	TESTS	Index	Index	Null	1:22.82
10.25	Nested Loops	FIRST_ROWS	PARTS	Index	Index	3	1:29.34
10.26	Nested Loops	ALL_ROWS	PARTS	Index	Index	3	1:37.10

Btree Index Cluster Join

The btree cluster **PARTS_AND_TESTS** contains two tables: **PARTS_IN_CLUSTER** and **TESTS_IN_CLUSTER**. The cluster key column for both tables is **PNO**. Listing 10.27 shows the current clusters and the tables in the cluster. Note that **PARTS_IN_CLUSTER** contains 10,000 rows, and **TESTS_IN_CLUSTER** contains 470,692 rows. The Explain Plan reveals that Oracle uses the cluster index **INDX_PARTS_AND_TESTS** to retrieve rows from **TESTS_IN_CLUSTER**. Note that the optimizer performs a nested loops join within the cluster. Hopefully, you'll notice the absolute absurd elapsed time of 26 minutes and 37.16 seconds.

Listing 10.27 A btree index cluster join.

```
SQL> SELECT CLUSTER_NAME,
  2         CLUSTER_TYPE
  3  FROM   USER_CLUSTERS;

CLUSTER_NAME                   CLUSTER_TYPE
------------------------------ ------------
DEPT_AND_EMP                   HASH
HUEY_DEWEY_LEWIE               HASH
PARTS_AND_TESTS                INDEX

SQL> SELECT TABLE_NAME,
  2         CLUSTER_NAME
  3  FROM   USER_TABLES
  4  WHERE  TABLE_NAME LIKE 'PARTS_IN%'
```

```
  5          OR
  6          TABLE_NAME LIKE 'TESTS_IN%';

TABLE_NAME        CLUSTER_NAME
----------------  ---------------
PARTS_IN_CLUSTER  PARTS_AND_TESTS
TESTS_IN_CLUSTER  PARTS_AND_TESTS

SQL> SELECT TABLE_NAME,
  2         INDEX_NAME
  3  FROM   USER_INDEXES
  4  WHERE  TABLE_NAME LIKE 'PARTS%' OR
  5         TABLE_NAME LIKE 'TESTS%';

TABLE_NAME        INDEX_NAME
----------------  --------------------
PARTS_AND_TESTS   INDX_PARTS_AND_TESTS
PARTS             PARTS_PNO
TESTS             TESTS_PNO

SQL> SELECT COUNT(*)
  2  FROM   PARTS_IN_CLUSTER;

COUNT(*)
--------
   10000

SQL> SELECT COUNT(*)
  2  FROM   TESTS_IN_CLUSTER;

COUNT(*)
--------
  470692

SQL> EXPLAIN PLAN FOR
  2  SELECT P.PNO, T.RESULTS
  3  FROM   PARTS_IN_CLUSTER P,
  4         TESTS_IN_CLUSTER T
  5  WHERE  P.PNO = T.PNO AND
  6         T.PNO = 93;
Explained.

SQL> @explain
```

```
Query Plan                                   COST
-------------------------------------------- ------
SELECT STATEMENT   CHOOSE
  NESTED LOOPS
    TABLE ACCESS CLUSTER TESTS_IN_CLUSTER
      INDEX UNIQUE SCAN INDX_PARTS_AND_TESTS
    TABLE ACCESS CLUSTER PARTS_IN_CLUSTER

SQL> SELECT P.PNO, T.RESULTS
  2  FROM   PARTS_IN_CLUSTER P,
  3         TESTS_IN_CLUSTER T
  4  WHERE  P.PNO = T.PNO AND
            T.PNO = 93;

    PNO R
------- -
.........

     93 P
     93 F
     93 P

8650 rows selected.

Elapsed: 00:26:37.16
```

Hash Join

Oracle also joins tables using the hash join method, as in Listing 10.28. Full-table scans are performed with each table divided into partitions. The number of partitions is determined by the amount of available memory. Oracle builds a hash table from one of the partitions that fits in memory. The larger partitions reference the hash table built from the smallest partition. Oracle can only perform hash joins on equality joins.

Listing 10.28 A hash join using **FIRST_ROWS**.

```
SQL> DROP INDEX PARTS_PNO;
Index dropped.

SQL> DROP INDEX TESTS_PNO;
Index dropped.
```

```
SQL> ANALYZE TABLE PARTS DELETE STATISTICS;
Table analyzed.

SQL> ANALYZE TABLE TESTS DELETE STATISTICS;
Table analyzed.

SQL> SELECT SUBSTR(NAME,1,25) PARAM,
  2         SUBSTR(VALUE,1,25) CURRENT_SETTING
  3  FROM   V$PARAMETER
  4  WHERE  NAME LIKE '%' || LOWER('&Parameter') || '%';

Enter value for parameter: hash_join

PARAM                     CURRENT_SETTING
------------------------- ------------------------
hash_join_enabled         TRUE

SQL> EXPLAIN PLAN FOR
  2  SELECT --+ FIRST_ROWS
  3         PARTS.PNO, RESULTS
  4  FROM   PARTS, TESTS
  5  WHERE  PARTS.PNO = TESTS.PNO AND
  6         TESTS.PNO = 93;
Explained.

SQL> @explain
Query Plan                            COST
------------------------------------ ----
SELECT STATEMENT   HINT: FIRST_ROWS   658
  HASH JOIN                           658
    TABLE ACCESS FULL PARTS            26
    TABLE ACCESS FULL TESTS           631

SQL> SELECT --+ FIRST_ROWS
  2         PARTS.PNO, RESULTS
  3  FROM  PARTS, TESTS
  4  WHERE  PARTS.PNO = TESTS.PNO AND
  5         TESTS.PNO = 93;

    PNO R
------- -
.........

     93 P
     93 F
     93 P
```

```
8650 rows selected.

Elapsed: 00:02:16.85
```

The **ALL_ROWS** hint in Listing 10.29 causes the optimizer to perform a hash join. Neither table has indexes or statistics. Even though no statistics are available for either table, the hint forces Oracle to use the cost-based optimizer. The cost of the hash join is 658. Oracle uses **PARTS** as the driving table, and it scans both tables using full-table scans. The elapsed time is 2 minutes and 14.23 seconds.

Listing 10.29 A hash join using **ALL_ROWS**.

```
SQL> EXPLAIN PLAN FOR
  2  SELECT --+ ALL_ROWS
  3         PARTS.PNO, RESULTS
  4  FROM   PARTS, TESTS
  5  WHERE  PARTS.PNO = TESTS.PNO AND
  6         TESTS.PNO = 93;
Explained.

SQL> @explain
Query Plan                           COST
-------------------------------- ----
SELECT STATEMENT   HINT: ALL_ROWS  658
  HASH JOIN                        658
    TABLE ACCESS FULL PARTS         26
    TABLE ACCESS FULL TESTS        631

SQL> SELECT --+ ALL_ROWS
  2         PARTS.PNO, RESULTS
  3  FROM   PARTS, TESTS
  4  WHERE  PARTS.PNO = TESTS.PNO AND
  5         TESTS.PNO  =  93;

   PNO R
------ -
........

    93 P
    93 F
    93 P

8650 rows selected.

Elapsed: 00:02:14.23
```

Now, both tables have indexes and statistics. Listing 10.30 uses the **USE_HASH** hint and forces a hash join with **PARTS** as the driving table. Both indexes retrieve the rows from their respective tables, and the cost of the query is 4. Total elapsed time to execute the query is 1 minute and 33.81 seconds.

Listing 10.30 The hint USE_HASH.

```
SQL> EXPLAIN PLAN FOR
  2  SELECT --+ USE_HASH(TESTS)
  3         PARTS.PNO, RESULTS
  4  FROM   PARTS, TESTS
  5  WHERE  PARTS.PNO = TESTS.PNO AND
  6         TESTS.PNO = 93;
Explained.

SQL> @explain
Query Plan                          COST
-------------------------------- ----
SELECT STATEMENT    CHOOSE             4
  HASH JOIN                            4
    INDEX UNIQUE SCAN PARTS_PNO        1
    TABLE ACCESS BY ROWID TESTS        2
      INDEX RANGE SCAN TESTS_PNO

SQL> SELECT --+ USE_HASH(TESTS)
  2         PARTS.PNO, RESULTS
  3  FROM   PARTS, TESTS
  4  WHERE  PARTS.PNO = TESTS.PNO AND
  5         TESTS.PNO = 93;

    PNO R
------- -
.........

     93 P
     93 F
     93 P

8650 rows selected.

Elapsed: 00:01:33.81
```

For Oracle to perform a hash join, the parameter **HASH_JOIN_ENABLED** must be set to **TRUE**. Listing 10.31 shows that you can't change the value of **HASH_**

JOIN_ENABLED using the ALTER SYSTEM command. However, you can change the value of HASH_JOIN_ENABLED using the ALTER SESSION command. Previously, the hints FIRST_ROWS and ALL_ROWS caused Oracle to perform a hash join when no indexes or statistics exist on the tables. However, in Listing 10.31, the optimizer performs sort merge joins because HASH_JOIN_ENABLED is set to FALSE. Finally, notice the power of hints in Oracle. Even though the value of HASH_JOIN_ENABLED is FALSE, the hint USE_HASH overrides this setting, and the optimizer performs a hash join.

Listing 10.31 HASH_JOIN_ENABLED = FALSE.

```
SQL> ALTER SYSTEM
  2        SET HASH_JOIN_ENABLED = FALSE;
ALTER SYSTEM
*
ERROR at line 1:
ORA-01092: ORACLE instance terminated. Disconnection forced

SQL> ALTER SESSION
  2        SET HASH_JOIN_ENABLED = FALSE;
Session altered.

SQL> EXPLAIN PLAN FOR
  2  SELECT --+ FIRST_ROWS
  3         PARTS.PNO, RESULTS
  4  FROM   PARTS, TESTS
  5  WHERE  PARTS.PNO = TESTS.PNO AND
  6         TESTS.PNO = 93;
Explained.

SQL> @explain
Query Plan                                  COST
------------------------------------------ ----
SELECT STATEMENT   HINT: FIRST_ROWS         662
  MERGE JOIN                                662
    TABLE ACCESS FULL PARTS                  26
    SORT JOIN
      TABLE ACCESS FULL TESTS               631

SQL> EXPLAIN PLAN FOR
  2  SELECT --+ ALL_ROWS
  3         PARTS.PNO, RESULTS
  4  FROM   PARTS, TESTS
```

```
    WHERE  PARTS.PNO = TESTS.PNO AND
           TESTS.PNO = 93;
Explained.

SQL> @explain
Query Plan                                 COST
--------------------------------- ----
SELECT STATEMENT    HINT: ALL_ROWS  662
  MERGE JOIN                        662
    TABLE ACCESS FULL PARTS          26
    SORT JOIN
      TABLE ACCESS FULL TESTS       631

SQL> EXPLAIN PLAN FOR
    SELECT --+ USE_HASH(TESTS)
           PARTS.PNO, RESULTS
    FROM   PARTS, TESTS
    WHERE  PARTS.PNO = TESTS.PNO AND
           TESTS.PNO = 93;
Explained.

SQL> @explain
Query Plan                          COST
--------------------------- ------
SELECT STATEMENT    CHOOSE       658
  HASH JOIN                      658
    TABLE ACCESS FULL PARTS       26
    TABLE ACCESS FULL TESTS      631
```

Table 10.7 summarizes hash joins. Listings 10.28 and 10.29 represent the results when neither table has indexes or statistics. Listing 10.30 represents the results when both tables are indexed and analyzed, and Listing 10.31 represents the results when the parameter **HASH_JOIN_ENABLED** is set to **FALSE**.

Summary

Oracle uses one of four methods to join tables. The nested loops method seems to be the fastest of the four, and sort merge the slowest. For Oracle to use the hash method of joining tables, the parameter **HASH_JOIN_ENABLED** must be set to **TRUE**. The optimizer joins tables using a cluster join when the tables are in a btree index cluster. Table 10.8 summarizes when Oracle uses one of the four join methods.

Table 10.7 Hash join results.

Listing	Type Of Join	Goal Or Hint	Driving Table	Type Of Access PARTS	Type Of Access TESTS	Cost	Elapsed Time
10.28	Hash	FIRST_ROWS	PARTS	Full	Full	658	2:16.85
10.29	Hash	ALL_ROWS	PARTS	Full	Full	658	2:14.23
10.30	Hash	USE_HASH (TESTS)	PARTS	Index	Index	4	1:33.81
10.31	Sort Merge	FIRST_ROWS	PARTS	Full	Full	662	
	Sort Merge	ALL_ROWS	PARTS	Full	Full	662	

Table 10.8 The four methods of joining tables.

Method	When Used
Sort merge	No indexes on either table and no cost hints
Nested loops	1. One index on either the primary or foreign key columns
	2. Both primary and foreign key columns indexed
	3. The hint USE_NL
Hash	1. No indexes on primary key or foreign key columns and No cost hints and **HASH_JOIN_ENABLED = TRUE**
	2. The hint HASH
Cluster	Tables are in a btree index cluster

HIGH PERFORMANCE

The Oracle Parallel Query Option

CHAPTER 11

The Oracle Parallel Query option is very powerful. This chapter teaches you how to use this option to speed up queries.

The Oracle Parallel Query Option

The Oracle Parallel Query option became available with Oracle7.1. This option permits several processes to simultaneously perform certain steps in a single SQL statement. Using several servers instead of one can improve performance for statements that are reading many blocks. This option does not require multiple CPUs, but to experience exponential gains in performance, you need between six and ten CPUs. This became evident at one of the customer sites I worked at, which had a machine with three CPUs and a table with 27 million rows. Using one server process requires 15 minutes for a particular query. Using a hint that requests two server processes requires 10 minutes, and a hint that requests three server processes requires 5 minutes, which is a linear progression in execution times. With eight CPUs, one might experience 15 minutes for one CPU, but only 2 seconds using eight CPUs. Figure 11.1 illustrates the results of these three queries using three different hints.

If your platform has one CPU, then this option probably won't do you much good, unless your CPU load is 30 percent or less. Moreover, this option requires the cost-based optimizer as well as statistics on the indexes and tables processed in parallel.

The Oracle Parallel Query option, or OPQ, performs parallel processing using two types of processes. One of the processes is the query coordinator, and the other is the query server process. The query coordinator is almost like the server process in non-parallel queries. It separates the various functions into parallel jobs and passes the jobs to the query servers. The query servers return the results to the query coordinator, and the query coordinator combines the results. The number of query servers given a single operation is the *degree of parallelism*. Figure 11.2 shows these two processes performing a query on the TESTS table.

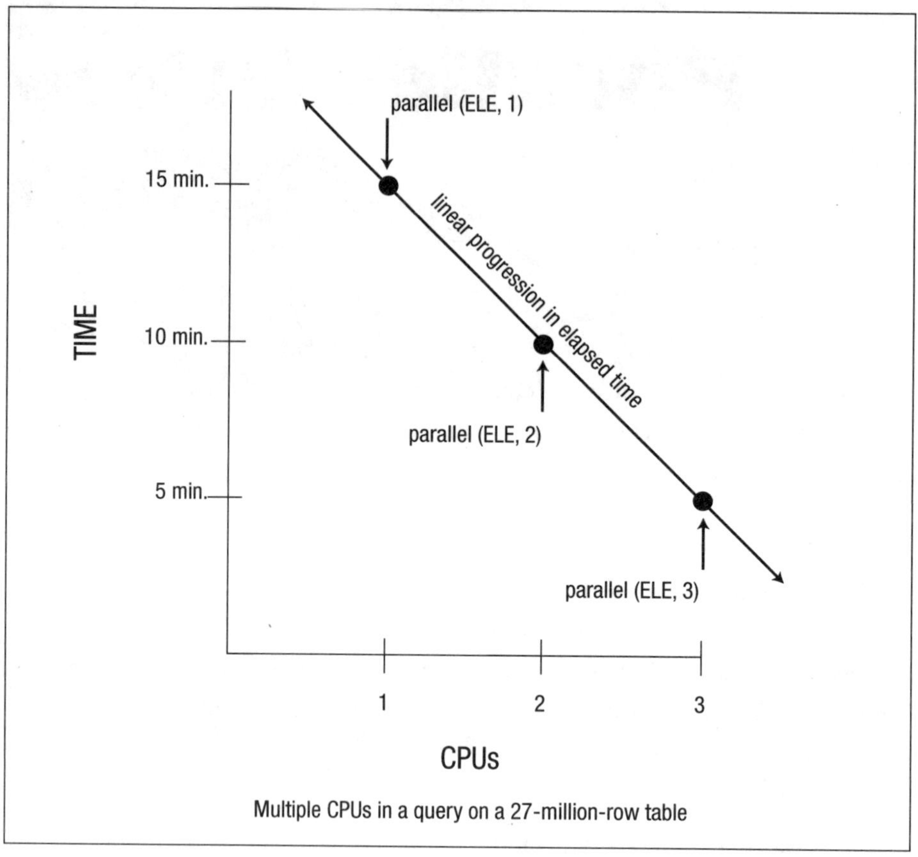

Figure 11.1
Multiple CPUs.

Init.ora Parameters

The parameter **parallel_min_servers** is the number of query server processes that Oracle creates after it starts up from the pool of query server processes. Oracle automatically increases this number up to the value of **parallel_max_servers.** If a query server process is idle for **parallel_server_idle_time**, Oracle kills the query server process. Listing 11.1 shows the parallel parameters and their current settings in our database.

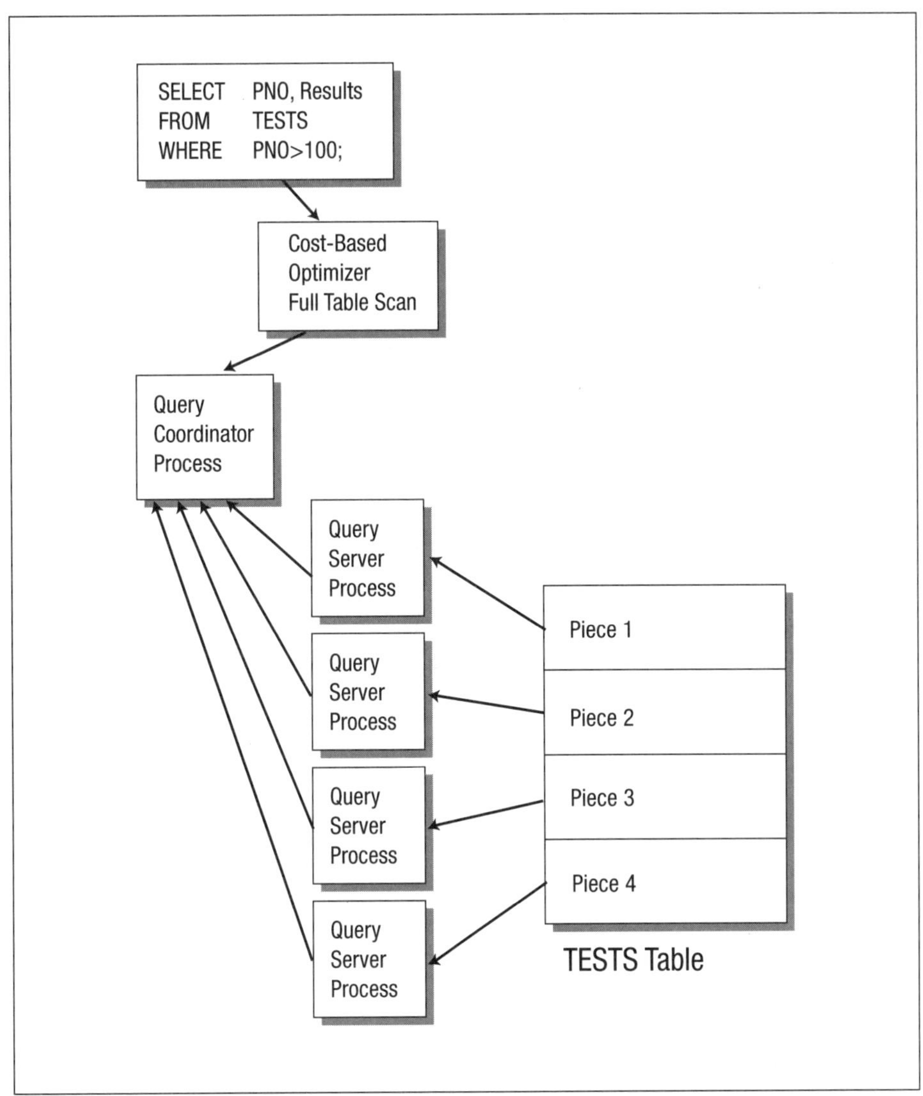

Figure 11.2
Parallel query processing.

Listing 11.1 Parallel parameters.

```
SQL> SELECT SUBSTR(NAME,1,30) PARAM,
  2         SUBSTR(VALUE,1,25) CURRENT_SETTING
  3  FROM   V$PARAMETER
  4  WHERE  NAME LIKE LOWER('%&Param%');
Enter value for param: par
```

```
PARAM                          CURRENT_SETTING
------------------------       ------------------------
recovery_parallelism           0
partition_view_enabled         FALSE
optimizer_percent_parallel     0
parallel_min_percent           0
parallel_default_max_instances 0
parallel_min_servers           0
parallel_max_servers           5
parallel_server_idle_time      5
```

Degree Of Parallelism

As mentioned earlier, the degree of parallelism is the number of server processes that simultaneously process certain steps in the plan of a SQL statement. To set the degree of parallelism, use the **CREATE TABLE** or **ALTER TABLE** commands. The degree of parallelism is also set using the parameter file or the **PARALLEL** hint. Listing 11.2 uses the **CREATE TABLE** command to set the degree of parallelism to 4 for the **TESTS** table. When Oracle performs a full table scan or a sort on **TESTS**, it uses four server processes instead of one. To override the degree of parallelism for a table, use the **PARALLEL** hint. Part of the **CREATE TABLE** command is a parallel option. If you have eight CPUs, you could create a table named **CARS** and specify Oracle use eight server processes for particular operations on the table using PARALLEL(DEGREE 8). Reader beware! Setting the degree of parallelism in the **CREATE TABLE** command causes Oracle to use many processes if the table is accessed by transactions that require full table scans, sorts, and so on. Remember, a SQL statement might have many steps. If several steps of a plan allow parallel processing, each step uses up to the default degree of parallelism. For instance, if the degree of parallelism is 8 for a table, two SQL statements execute using the table, and each SQL statement contains three steps that permit parallel operations, then Oracle will attempt to use 48 processes. Imagine using 48 processes for only two SQL statements. Before long on a busy system, you'll start receiving errors indicating that no more processes are allowed. On most Unix platforms, you'll receive semaphore errors. The solution is to use hints in SQL statements, and "mum's the word," except to developers and other database administrators. The same holds true for the **ALTER TABLE** command.

Listing 11.2 The **CREATE TABLE** command.

```
SQL> CREATE TABLE TESTS
  2          (PNO     NUMBER(7,0),
  3           TNO     NUMBER(4,0),
  4           RESULTS CHAR(1))
  5  PARALLEL(DEGREE 4   INSTANCES 1);
Table created.

SQL> SELECT NUM_ROWS,
  2         DEGREE,
  3         INSTANCES
  4  FROM   USER_TABLES
  5  WHERE  TABLE_NAME = 'TESTS';

NUM_ROWS  DEGREE     INSTANCES
--------  ------     ---------
               4             1

SQL> SET TIMING ON
SQL> ANALYZE TABLE TESTS
  2           COMPUTE STATISTICS;
Table analyzed.

Elapsed: 00:02:37.24

SQL> SELECT NUM_ROWS,
  2         DEGREE,
  3         INSTANCES
  4  FROM   USER_TABLES
  5  WHERE  TABLE_NAME = 'TESTS';

NUM_ROWS  DEGREE     INSTANCES
--------  ------     ---------
  470552       4             1
```

If the **PARALLEL** clause is not included in the **CREATE TABLE** command, use the **ALTER TABLE** command to define or set the degree of parallelism for the table, as shown in Listing 11.3.

Listing 11.3 The **ALTER TABLE** command.

```
SQL> ALTER TABLE TESTS
  2         PARALLEL(DEGREE 4   INSTANCES 1);
Table altered.
```

```
SQL> SELECT NUM_ROWS,
  2         DEGREE,
  3         INSTANCES
  4  FROM   USER_TABLES
  5* WHERE  TABLE_NAME = 'TESTS';
```

```
NUM_ROWS   DEGREE   INSTANCES
--------   ------   ---------
  470552        4           1
```

To override the default degree of parallelism on a table for a query, use the **PARALLEL** hint, as shown in Listing 11.4. The example in Listing 11.4 causes Oracle to use two server processes and one query coordinator process to perform a full table scan. Information relating to parallel query operations is stored in the columns **OBJECT_NODE** and **OTHER**. The explain.sql script now includes the **OBJECT_NODE** and **OTHER** columns and is saved to a file named **explain2.sql.** Notice Q52000 in the **OBJECT_NODE** column of the plan table. Also, note in the **OTHER** column of the plan table the hint Oracle writes to itself—**ROWID(A1)**. The Q52000 is the parallel server process and **ROWID(A1)** is a hint Oracle writes to itself to retrieve the rows the fastest way possible, by using **ROWID**. Oracle divides the work into ranges of rowids. As the query is running, enter the Unix command **ps** to view the parallel query processes. Note the processes **ora_p000_pete** and **ora_p001_pete.** Two steps in the execution plan of this SQL statement require multiple processes—a full table scan and a sort. The statement requires 44.9 seconds to execute.

Use **V$PQ_SYSSTAT** to observe the query server activity for the instance. Because **Servers Busy** is 0, obviously the servers are not busy. **Servers Highwater** is 2, and that's the number of query server processes used to execute the parallel query. If **Servers Started** is high (here it's only 2), increase the parameter **parallel_min_servers.**

Use **V$PQ_SLAVE** to indicate information about each active query server process and use **V$PQ_SESSTAT** to review query server activity for the last query and the totals for the current session. Use **V$PQ_TQSTAT** to identify the query coordinator and the slave processes. The query coordinator is the *consumer*, and the slave processes are *producers.* Oracle support uses **V$PQ_** dynamic performance views, and little documentation exists explaining its contents.

The hint **NOPARALLEL(TESTS)** causes Oracle to use one process. Note the execution time of 40.82 seconds. Using this one process is faster than the query that uses two processes (which takes 44.90 seconds). On a multiple-CPU platform, the parallel query that uses two processors runs faster than the query that uses one processor. You really need between six and eight CPUs to experience tremendous performance gains using the parallel query option.

Listing 11.4 Using the **PARALLEL** hint.

```
SQL> EXPLAIN PLAN FOR
  2  SELECT --+ PARALLEL(TESTS,2) FULL(TESTS)
  3         PNO, TNO, RESULTS
  4  FROM  TESTS
  5  WHERE PNO = 30
  6  ORDER BY PNO, TNO DESC, RESULTS;
Explained.

SQL> COL PLAN                       FORMAT A36
SQL> COL "Serv 1"                   FORMAT A7
SQL> COL "Operation Performed" FORMAT A25 WRAP
SQL> SET LONG 120
SQL> GET explain2
  1  SELECT  LPAD(' ', 2*(LEVEL-1)) ||
  2          OPERATION || ' ' ||
  3          OPTIONS || ' ' ||
  4  OBJECT_NAME || ' ' || OPTIMIZER || ' ' ||
  5  DECODE(ID,0,'COST=' || POSITION) "Plan",
  6  OBJECT_NODE "Serv 1", OTHER "Operation Performed"
  7  FROM    PLAN_TABLE
  8  START   WITH ID = 0
  9* CONNECT BY PRIOR ID = PARENT_ID

SQL> @explain2
Plan                                 Serv 1
------------------------------------ --------
SELECT STATEMENT   CHOOSE COST=635
  SORT ORDER BY
    TABLE ACCESS FULL TESTS ANALYZED :Q52000

Operation Performed
-------------------------
SELECT /*+ ROWID(A1) */ A
1."PNO",A1."TNO",A1."RESU
LTS" FROM "TESTS" A1 WHERE
ROWID BETWEEN :1 AND :2
AND A1."PNO"=30
```

```
SQL> SELECT --+ PARALLEL(TESTS,2) FULL(TESTS)
  2         PNO, TNO, RESULTS
  3  FROM   TESTS
  4  WHERE PNO = 30
  5  ORDER BY PNO, TNO DESC, RESULTS;

SVRMGR> !ps -aux | grep ora_p0
ora73 13470 27.6 ? 18:15:33  0:09 ora_p001_pete
ora73 13468 27.2 R 18:15:32  0:08 ora_p000_pete
ora73 13474  0.5 S 18:15:52  0:00 grep ora_p0

  PNO    TNO R
----- ------ -
   30      6 P
   30      5 F
   30      4 P
   30      3 F
   30      2 P
   30      1 F

901 rows selected.

Elapsed: 00:00:44.90

SQL> SELECT *   -- Are Servers Busy?
  2  FROM V$PQ_SYSSTAT;

STATISTIC                        VALUE
------------------------------  ------
Servers Busy                         0
Servers Idle                         0
Servers Highwater                    2
Server Sessions                      2
Servers Started                      2
Servers Shutdown                     2
Servers Cleaned Up                   0
Queries Initiated                    1
DFO Trees                            1
Local Msgs Sent                     39
Distr Msgs Sent                      0
Local Msgs Recv'd                   39
Distr Msgs Recv'd                    0
```

```
SQL> SELECT SLAVE_NAME, -- Active Query
  2         STATUS,     -- Server Processes
  3         SESSIONS SESS,
  4         MSGS_SENT_CUR MSGS_S_C,
  5         IDLE_TIME_TOTAL IDLE,
  6         BUSY_TIME_TOTAL BUSY,
  7         CPU_SECS_TOTAL CPU,
  8         MSGS_SENT_TOTAL MSGS_SENT MSGS_S
  9 FROM    V$PQ_SLAVE;

SLAV STAT SESS MSGS_S_C IDLE BUSY  CPU MSGS_S
---- ---- ---- -------- ---- ---- ---- ------
P000 IDLE    1        0    0    0   17     16
P001 IDLE    1        0    0    0   18     28

SQL> SELECT *  -- Most Recent Query
  2 FROM    V$PQ_SESSTAT;

STATISTIC            LAST_QUERY SESSION_TOTAL
-------------------- ---------- -------------
Queries Parallelized          1             2
DFO Trees                     1             2
Server Threads                2             0
Allocation Height             2             0
Allocation Width              0             0
Local Msgs Sent              39            78
Distr Msgs Sent               0             0
Local Msgs Recv'd            39            78
Distr Msgs Recv'd             0             0

SQL> SELECT *
  2 FROM    V$PQ_TQSTAT;

 DFO TQ_ID SERVER_TYP NUM_ROWS OPEN AVGL WAITS TIMEOUTS PROCESS
---- ----- ---------- -------- ---- ---- ----- -------- -------
   1     0 Producer        702    0    0     8        0 P001
   1     0 Producer        199    0    0     5        0 P000
   1     0 Consumer        901    0    0    32       12 QC
   2     0 Producer        199    0    0     5        0 P000
   2     0 Producer        702    0    0     8        0 P001
   2     0 Consumer        901    0    0    32       14 QC

SQL> EXPLAIN PLAN FOR
  2 SELECT --+ NOPARALLEL(TESTS) FULL(TESTS)
  3        PNO, TNO, RESULTS
```

```
  4  FROM   TESTS
  5  WHERE  PNO  =  30
  6  ORDER  BY 1,2 DESC,3;
SQL> @explain2
Plan                                   Serv 1
------------------------------------ ----------
SELECT STATEMENT   CHOOSE COST=635
  SORT ORDER BY
    TABLE ACCESS FULL TESTS ANALYZED

Operation Performed
------------------------


SQL> SELECT --+ NOPARALLEL(TESTS) FULL(TESTS)
  2         PNO, TNO, RESULTS
  3  FROM   TESTS
  4  WHERE  PNO = 30
  5  ORDER  BY 1,2 DESC,3;

 PNO  TNO R
---- ---- --
  30    6 P
  30    5 F
  30    4 P
  30    3 F
  30    2 P
  30    1 F

901 rows selected.

Elapsed: 00:00:40.82
```

Usage

As long as statements cause at least one full table scan, the following commands may process in parallel: **SELECT** statements, subqueries using **DELETE**, **UPDATE**, and **INSERT**, **CREATE TABLE**, **CREATE INDEX**, sorts, joins, merges, certain functions, and full table scans. SQL*Loader can also load data into Oracle tables in parallel using the direct path mode. This means several developers can add data to the same table at the same time to speed up the load. Listing 11.5 creates a table called **ALMOST_LIKE_TESTS**, and it asks Oracle to consider using eight query server processes. However, the parameter **parallel_max_servers** is 5, and Oracle uses all five processes and requires 4 minutes and 32.62 seconds to create the table in parallel.

Dropping the table **ALMOST_LIKE_TESTS** and re-creating it without the parallel processes requires 4 minutes and 33.95 seconds. With one CPU, to create a table with 470,552 rows without the use of the parallel option takes 1.33 seconds longer. What is simply amazing is the time it takes to create the table that uses **UNRECOVERABLE** (4 minutes and 35.58 seconds), which is supposed to be so much faster because no information is written to the redo log files. Well, **UNRECOVERABLE** is the slowest, so far, by 1.23 seconds (4:35.58-4:33.95). So, let's use both **UNRECOVERABLE** and **PARALLEL**. Once again—surprise!—using both **UNRECOVERABLE** and **PARALLEL** requires 4 minutes and 36.51 seconds.

Listing 11.5 CREATE TABLE X AS SELECT * FROM.

```
SQL> CREATE TABLE ALMOST_LIKE_TESTS
  2           PARALLEL (DEGREE 8)
  3  AS       SELECT *
  4           FROM   TESTS;
Table created.

Elapsed: 00:04:32.62

SVRMGR> !ps -aux | grep ora_p0
ora73 13625 21.8 ... R 19:37:08  0:09 ora_p003_pete
ora73 13623 20.5 ... R 19:37:07  0:08 ora_p002_pete
ora73 13619 14.1 ... S 19:37:06  0:05 ora_p000_pete
ora73 13621 13.6 ... S 19:37:07  0:05 ora_p001_pete
ora73 13627  0.5 ... S 19:37:08  0:00 ora_p004_pete
ora73 13631  0.4 ... S 19:37:37  0:00 grep ora_p0

SQL> DROP TABLE ALMOST_LIKE_TESTS;
Table dropped.

SQL> CREATE TABLE ALMOST_LIKE_TESTS
  2  AS       SELECT *
  3           FROM   TESTS;
Table created.

Elapsed: 00:04:33.95

SQL> CREATE TABLE ALMOST_LIKE_TESTS
  2  AS SELECT *
  3      FROM   TESTS
  4  UNRECOVERABLE;
Table created.

Elapsed: 00:04:35.58
```

```
SQL> DROP TABLE ALMOST_LIKE_TESTS;
Table dropped.

SQL> CREATE TABLE ALMOST_LIKE_TESTS
  2            PARALLEL (DEGREE 8)
  3  AS        SELECT *
  4            FROM   TESTS
  6  UNRECOVERABLE;
Table created.

Elapsed: 00:04:36.51
```

Creating an index requires a lot of overhead due to the sorting of the key of the index. The parallel creation of indexes is very fast. With one CPU and a small table, the results are very significant. In Listing 11.6, Oracle creates an index that uses five processes in 6 minutes and 17.73 seconds. Serially, to create a btree index on a column in a table of 470,552 rows requires 7 minutes and 2.68 seconds. The **CREATE TABLE** statement that uses the **PARALLEL** option sees a 45 second increase in speed. However, with just the use of **UNRECOVERABLE**, it requires 6 minutes and 10.71 seconds to create the index. This is 10 seconds faster than the statement that creates the index with **PARALLEL** and **UNRECOVERABLE**.

Listing 11.6 CREATE INDEX.

```
SQL> CREATE INDEX INDX_TESTS_TNO
  2            ON TESTS(TNO)
  3            PARALLEL(DEGREE 8)
  4            UNRECOVERABLE;
SVRMGR> !ps -aux | grep ora_p0
ora73 13815 32.0 R 20:12:10  0:14 ora_p003_pete
ora73 13813 16.3 R 20:12:09  0:08 ora_p002_pete
ora73 13811 10.2 S 20:12:09  0:04 ora_p001_pete
ora73 13809  8.3 S 20:12:08  0:04 ora_p000_pete
ora73 13821  0.5 S 20:12:48  0:00 grep ora_p0
ora73 13817  0.2 S 20:12:10  0:00 ora_p004_pete

Index created.

Elapsed: 00:06:17.73

SQL> DROP INDEX INDX_TESTS_TNO;
Index dropped.
```

```
SQL> CREATE INDEX INDX_TESTS_TNO
  2         ON TESTS(TNO);
Index created.

Elapsed: 00:07:02.68

SQL> DROP INDEX INDX_TESTS_TNO;
Index dropped.

SQL> CREATE INDEX INDX_TESTS_TNO
  2         ON TESTS(TNO)
  3  UNRECOVERABLE;
Index created.

Elapsed: 00:06:10.71
```

Another use of the Oracle Parallel Query option is to load data with multiple executions of the product SQL*Loader. Listing 11.7 shows the commands that execute SQL*Loader with different control files and data. Note that **parallel** is set to **true**, and Oracle uses a direct path instead of a conventional path. Four loads are performed on the same table at the same time.

Listing 11.7 SQL*Loader.

```
> sqlload / control=PAYMENT1.ctl direct=true parallel=true
> sqlload / control=PAYMENT2.ctl direct=true parallel=true
> sqlload / control=PAYMENT3.ctl direct=true parallel=true
> sqlload / control=PAYMENT4.ctl direct=true parallel=true
```

Full table scans also take advantage of the parallel option. In Listing 11.8, the degree of parallelism for the table **TESTS** is 4. Explain Plan indicates that the cost is 631 and that the parallel query option is used. Notice the hint Oracle writes to itself—**ROWID(A1)**. When the query is executed, Oracle uses four parallel query server processes named **ora_p000_pete**, **ora_p001_pete**, **ora_p002_pete**, and **ora_p003_pete**.

Listing 11.8 Full table scan.

```
SQL> SELECT DEGREE
  2  FROM   USER_TABLES
  3  WHERE  TABLE_NAME = 'TESTS';
```

```
   DEGREE
----------
        4

SQL> EXPLAIN PLAN FOR
  2  SELECT PNO,
  3         TNO,
  4         RESULTS
  5  FROM   TESTS;
Explained.

SQL> COL PLAN                       FORMAT A36
SQL> COL "SERV 1"                   FORMAT A10
SQL> COL "OPERATION PERFORMED" FORMAT A25 WRAP
SQL> @explain2
Plan                                  Serv 1
----------------------------------   --------
SELECT STATEMENT   CHOOSE COST=631
  TABLE ACCESS FULL TESTS ANALYZED  :Q66000

Operation Performed
-------------------------------
SELECT /*+ ROWID(A1) */ A1."PNO",
A1."TNO",
A1."RESULTS"
FROM "TESTS" A1
WHERE ROWID BETWEEN :1 AND :2

SVRMGR> !ps -aux | grep ora_p0
ora73 1296  0.9  4912 ? S 19:54:29  ora_p003_pete
ora73 1290  0.9  5868 ? S 19:54:28  ora_p000_pete
ora73 1294  0.7  4912 ? S 19:54:29  ora_p002_pete
ora73 1292  0.7  4908 ? S 19:54:28  ora_p001_pete
```

In Listing 11.9, note that Oracle uses parallel processing for both the full table scan and the sort. This is an interesting point. Because the degree of parallelism for the table TESTS is four, eight query processes could be used; however, Oracle only needs five.

Listing 11.9 Sorts.

```
SQL> EXPLAIN PLAN FOR
  2  SELECT PNO, TNO, RESULTS
  3  FROM   TESTS
  4  WHERE  PNO = 20
  5  ORDER  BY TNO DESC;
```

```
Explained.

SQL> @explain2
Plan                                    Serv 1
------------------------------------    ------
SELECT STATEMENT   CHOOSE COST=635
  SORT ORDER BY                         :Q68001

Operation Performed
------------------------
SELECT A1.C0 C0,A1.C1 C1,
A1.C2 C2,A1.C3 C3
FROM  :Q68000 A1
ORDER BY A1.C0 DESC

    TABLE ACCESS FULL TESTS ANALYZED :Q68000

Operation Performed
------------------------
SELECT /*+ ROWID(A1) */ A1."TNO" C0,
A1."PNO" C1,A1."TNO" C2,A1."RESULTS" C3
FROM

SQL> SELECT PNO, TNO, RESULTS
  2  FROM   TESTS
  3  WHERE  PNO = 20
  4  ORDER  BY TNO DESC;

SVRMGR> !ps -aux | grep ora_p0
ora73 1361  4.1  4992 ? S 20:23:16  0:16 ora_p001_pete
ora73 1359  4.0  5900 ? S 20:23:15  0:16 ora_p000_pete
ora73 1367  0.1  5356 ? S 20:23:17  0:00 ora_p004_pete
ora73 1363  0.1  4640 ? S 20:23:16  0:00 ora_p002_pete
ora73 1365  0.1  4048 ? S 20:23:17  0:00 ora_p003_pete
```

Summary

The OPQ option is great for multiple CPU systems with plenty of I/O bandwidth and unused memory. Regardless of the parallel operation, the query coordinator returns the results to a user, serially. For this reason, OPQ works best in statements that summarize or aggregate data. Use hints when using this option; also, do not use the **PARALLEL** clause when you create or alter the table (to prevent running out of processes).

HIGH PERFORMANCE

Application Tuning

CHAPTER 12

There's nothing like experience to teach you how to write the most efficient SQL statements in Oracle. In this chapter, I illustrate some of the tuning problems and solutions I've encountered over the past 10 years. In addition, I've included some experiences from my peers at Database Consultants, Inc. This chapter teaches you how to write more efficient SQL statements.

Application Tuning

Indexes

One fine Sunday afternoon, one of my best friends writes an anonymous PL/SQL block that attempts to update 550,000 rows in the one-million-row **STATS** table. His code loops 550 times, and each loop updates 1,000 rows at a time. The next afternoon at 4:30 P.M., another friend of mine notices the total frustration on my friend's face as he walks by his cubicle. He stops and asks, "What's going on?" He had to ask—after all, the guy's hat is on backwards, he needs a shave, shower, and a good night's rest. My overworked cohort says, "Oh, just trying to update 550,000 rows in this one-million-row table, and its been running since 11:00 P.M. last night." My friend is committing every 1,000 records; the job has run now for 17 and a half hours and only 421,000 records are updated. This job updates 400 rows per minute. My curious and helpful friend says, "I'm going to ask you a dumb question. Is your update using an index?" My tired comrade gives him a look that says "don't let the door hit you on your way out!"

He kills the job and creates a unique index on one column of the one-million-row table that he uses in the **WHERE** clause of the **UPDATE** statement. This takes approximately 9 minutes. He runs the same job, with loop counter changes, that he killed just minutes before, and it requires 18 minutes to update 129,000 rows in the one-million-row table. This means that 7,166 rows are updated per minute. Using a unique index is nearly 18 times faster than performing a full-table scan. The moral of this story is update statements can take full advantage of indexes as well as deletes and selects, and always verify which indexes exist on a table before executing a data manipulation statement that updates a table with many rows. By the way, my friend who forgot to check for indexes before updating has been working with the Oracle products for nine years. He simply assumed indexes existed on the columns referenced in the **WHERE** clause. Never assume; always verify by writing a query against either: **DBA_INDEXES, ALL_INDEXES, USER_INDEXES, DBA_IND_COLUMNS, ALL_IND_COLUMNS,** or **USER_IND_COLUMNS.** My friend's saga is described in Listing 12.1.

Listing 12.1 The **UPDATE** saga.

```
REM 17.5 HOURS AND KILLED THE JOB - NO INDEX ON SNO
SET TIMING ON
DECLARE     -- Updates 421,000 Rows In 17 + Hours
     strt   NUMBER    := 450001;
     ends   NUMBER    := 451000;
BEGIN
      FOR i IN 1..550 LOOP
          UPDATE STATS  SET ONE_THOUSAND_NUMBERS = i
                 WHERE  SNO BETWEEN  strt AND ends;
          strt := ends + 1;
          ends := (strt + 1000) - 1;
          COMMIT;
      END  LOOP;  -- Job Killed After 421,000 Rows Updated
END;
/

Control C to cancel operation.
Elapsed:  17:30:23.44

SQL> CREATE UNIQUE INDEX STATS_SNO
            ON STATS(SNO);
Index created.
Elapsed:  00:09:35.02

REM  This Time There Is A UNIQUE INDEX On The SNO Column
SET TIMING ON
DECLARE    -- Updates 129,000 Rows In 18 Minutes
     strt   NUMBER    := 871001;
     ends   NUMBER    := 872000;
BEGIN
  FOR i IN 422..550 LOOP
      UPDATE STATS
             SET ONE_THOUSAND_NUMBERS = i
      WHERE  SNO BETWEEN  strt AND ends;
      strt := ends + 1;
      ends := (strt + 1000) - 1;
      COMMIT;
  END  LOOP;
END;
```

```
/
Elapsed:  00:18:13.50
```

While teaching an Oracle course back in 1989 in Dallas, a student asks me, "Pete, aren't you going to say more about the **NOSORT** option?" So I point out that it's faster to create an index if the indexed column is loaded into the table in presorted, ascending order. The student is still not satisfied and asks if he can make a few remarks. I say okay, and this is what he shares with the class. He had been creating a unique index on the primary key column of a 176,000,000-row table, and after 19 days, the index still had not been created. So he called Oracle Support for help. Support asked him if he could reload the table in sorted order on the primary key column. He said yes. He killed the long-running **CREATE UNIQUE INDEX** command that had been going for 19 days and then reloaded the table. Then, he created the unique index using the **NOSORT** option, and it took between five and seven hours to complete.

I never forgot this student's experience. In Listing 12.2, the **NOSORT** option requires 6 minutes and 50.35 seconds to build an index on a date column for a one-million-row table. If you drop the index and re-create it without the **NOSORT** option, it requires 11 minutes and 28.64 seconds to build the same index. For a one-million-row table, this is a savings of 4 minutes and 38.29 seconds (11:28.64 minutes versus 6:50.35 minutes). For a table with 176,000,000 rows, around 13 hours and 36 minutes can be saved.

The last example in Listing 12.2 shows that Oracle stops the creation of an index and displays Oracle error 1409 when the data is not in ascending order in the table. However, it might be awhile before Oracle detects the error. In this example, 6 minutes and 39 seconds elapse before Oracle displays the error message.

Listing 12.2 NOSORT.

```
SQL> CREATE TABLE NO_SORT_DEMO
        (C1    DATE);

SQL> get cor12_4
DECLARE
    sdate DATE := '25-OCT-97';
BEGIN
  FOR I IN 1..1000000 LOOP
      INSERT INTO NO_SORT_DEMO
```

```
            VALUES(sdate);
            IF MOD(I,10000) = 0 THEN COMMIT;
            END  IF;
            sdate := sdate + 1;
        END   LOOP;
    END;
SQL> /

PL/SQL procedure successfully completed.

Elapsed: 02:41:59.70

SQL> CREATE INDEX INDX_C1
             ON NO_SORT_DEMO(C1)
     NOSORT;
Index created.

Elapsed: 00:06:50.35

SQL> DROP INDEX INDX_C1;
Index dropped.

SQL> CREATE INDEX INDX_C1
             ON NO_SORT_DEMO(C1);
Index created.

Elapsed: 00:11:28.64

SQL> CREATE UNIQUE INDEX
            BTREE_UNIQUE_SNO
            ON STATS(SNO)
     NOSORT;
       ON STATS(SNO)
          *
ERROR at line 3:
ORA-01409: NOSORT option may not be used;
rows are not in ascending order

Elapsed: 00:06:38.98
```

One day, a friend of mine, Steve Woods, of Lawton, Oklahoma, calls and asks me for some help on a very slow-running report. The table the report is based on is very dynamic, and it constantly grows in size. He says the first quarter report runs slow, the half-year report runs slower, the third quarter report runs really slow, and the year-end run is ridiculously slow, and he can't understand why. We look at the indexes on the underlying tables; several of the indexes are concatenated indexes. The first column of one of the concatenated indexes is in the **WHERE** clause. The rule-based optimizer uses the concatenated index to perform a full-table scan on the large table. The additional I/O is outrageous. I have him add a zero to the column, because it's numeric; the report runs much, much faster, because adding a zero to the indexed column causes Oracle not to use the index. Instead, it performs a full-table scan, which is what we wanted. If the column is of the data type **CHAR**, **VARCHAR2**, or **DATE**, you can concatenate a null to the column in the **WHERE** clause to cause Oracle to use a full-table scan on the table instead of using the index. Listing 12.3 shows how to suppress an index without using hints.

Listing 12.3 Lawton reports.

```
SQL> SELECT *
     FROM   STATS
     WHERE  SNO + 0 > 0;
```

I'm teaching a tuning class, and one of my students shows me a query that joins nine tables and has a **WHERE** clause that's nearly a page long. He asks me to take a look at it. I ask him what the problem is, and he tells me it just runs slow. I then ask him how long he has been working on this query. He states "several months." First of all, I suggest that all foreign key columns in the **WHERE** clause should have indexes. Second, I suggest that he experiment using the **ORDERED** hint with various permutations of the tables in the **FROM** clause and then run each through Explain Plan and note the cost. Usually, the plan with the lowest cost will execute the quickest. However, I tell him not to go overboard with the permutations. Because the query contains nine tables, the number of permutations is 9! (or 9*8*7*6*5*4*3*2*1, which equals 362,880). The most crucial position in the join chain is the first. Remember, the first table in the join chain should always be the table that returns the fewest number of rows or is the most selective. With a little work and knowledge of your tables, you can make a better selection of the driving table than Oracle can. Even though my student never contacted me later, I know he tuned that query to run much faster using the techniques I taught him in class. You can always try rewriting your query in Oracle like my former student did. Sometimes you are a hero, and other times you can be a zero. Another example of dramatic performance improvement illustrates the importance of rewriting a query.

A corporation has a parts table with approximately two million rows and a tests table with approximately nine million rows. A query requires nearly 72 hours to complete when joining the two tables. The query starts on Friday morning and ends sometime early the following Monday morning. A consultant observes each part has approximately the same number of tests for each of the two million parts, and asks if the corporation had tried clustering the two tables together. The answer is no, so the consultant creates a btree index cluster using the part number as the cluster key. The same query now executes in three to four hours. It's safe to say that this corporation is now sold on btree index clusters.

MINUS

A bank in America's "Windy City" has a correlated subquery that identifies any of the seven million or so checking account customers that do not have saving accounts. The bank has approximately two million saving accounts. The query works, but it requires more than 65 hours to complete. A consultant asks if anyone has tried rewriting the query, and the bank developer says no. So, the consultant rewrites the query using the set operator **MINUS**, and the query runs in several hours. Listing 12.4 illustrates this bank solution to the best of my memory.

Several months ago, I received an email from a former student of mine named Charles. This is what he said: "Pete, thanks for mentioning the power of **MINUS**. This week, by replacing a **NOT IN** with a **MINUS**, I reduced the elapsed time of a statement by 90 percent."

Another example is shown in Listing 12.4. The first query, which identifies all SNOs in the **STATS2** table that are not in the **STATS** table, uses the set operator **MINUS**. The second solution for the same problem uses a correlated subquery using **NOT EXISTS**. The **STATS2** table has 6,667 rows, and the **STATS** table has 1 million rows. The **STATS2** table has an index on the **SNO** column, and the **STATS** table does not. This is an absolute travesty of justice, as the elapsed times suggest. The cost for using **MINUS** is 49,522, and Oracle performs full-table scans on both tables. However, the cost is very misleading. The elapsed time for using **MINUS** is only 5 minutes and 1.27 seconds. The correlated subquery has a cost of only 11, performs a full-table scan on both tables, but runs forever! (I had to kill the job after 1 hour and 23 minutes, or this chapter would never be written. And, if **NOT IN** were used, we would probably retire before the query completes.)

To be more realistic, I create a nonunique index on the **SNO** column of the **STATS** table. Then, I analyze both the **STATS** and **STATS2** tables. The Explain Plan using **MINUS** has a very high cost (47,169) and performs a full-table scan on **STATS2**, but it performs an index fast full scan, which performs multiblock reads on the entire index and requires the cost-based optimizer, on the one-million-row table **STATS**. The **MINUS** query requires 4 minutes and 8.24 seconds to execute.

The query using **NOT EXISTS** has a cost of 11, performs a full-table scan on **STATS2**, and uses an index range scan on the **STATS** table. The real eye-opener here is the elapsed time, which is only 14.97 seconds. This is a tremendous improvement from the previous query using **MINUS**, which requires 4 minutes and 8.24 seconds. The **NOT EXISTS** query is 3 minutes and 54 seconds faster! In other words, the **NOT EXISTS** query runs 16.5 times faster than the query using **MINUS**. This is typically not the case—**MINUS** is normally faster.

The query using **NOT IN** has a cost of 11, performs a full-table scan of **STATS2**, and uses an index full scan to access rows from the **STATS** table. This query requires 33 minutes and 55.72 seconds to execute! Even though Oracle indicates that this query has the same cost as the **NOT EXISTS** query, the elapsed times are very, very different. The **NOT EXISTS** query, with a cost of 11, requires 14.97 seconds to execute. The **NOT IN** query, also with a cost of 11, requires 33 minutes and 55.72 seconds to execute. In situations like this, the cost must be taken with a grain of salt.

Listing 12.4 MINUS.

```
SQL> SELECT CUST_NAME FROM CHECKING
     MINUS
     SELECT CUST_NAME FROM SAVINGS;

SQL> DESC STATS2
 Name                          Null? Type
 ----------------------------- ----- ----------
 SNO                                 NUMBER(7)
 REGION                              VARCHAR2(3)

SQL> DESC STATS
 Name                          Null?    Type
 ----------------------------- -------- ----
 SNO                           NOT NULL NUMBER(7)
```

```
 SNAME                          VARCHAR2(30)
 REGION_BTREE                   VARCHAR2(3)
 REGION_BIT_MAP                 VARCHAR2(3)
 REGION_HASH                    NUMBER(1)
 SEX                            VARCHAR2(1)
 ONE_THOUSAND_NUMBERS           NUMBER(4)
 TEMPERATURE                    NUMBER(4,1)

SQL> SELECT SUBSTR(TABLE_NAME,1,10) "Table",
            SUBSTR(INDEX_NAME,1,17) "Index Name",
            SUBSTR(COLUMN_NAME,1,12) "Column Name",
            COLUMN_POSITION
     FROM   USER_IND_COLUMNS
     WHERE  TABLE_NAME IN('STATS','STATS2') AND
            COLUMN_NAME = 'SNO'
     ORDER  BY TABLE_NAME,
            INDEX_NAME,
            COLUMN_POSITION;

Table      Index Name        Column Name  COLUMN_POSITION
---------- ----------------- ------------ ---------------
STATS2     STATS2_SNO        SNO                        1
STATS2     STATS2_SNO_REGION SNO                        1

SQL> EXPLAIN PLAN FOR
     SELECT SNO FROM STATS2
     MINUS
     SELECT SNO FROM STATS;
Explained.

SQL> @explain
Query Plan                               COST
------------------------------------ -----
SELECT STATEMENT   CHOOSE               49522
  MINUS
    SORT UNIQUE
      TABLE ACCESS FULL STATS2             11
    SORT UNIQUE
      TABLE ACCESS FULL STATS ANALYZED   3958

SQL> SELECT SNO FROM STATS2   -- 6,667 Rows
     MINUS      -- Stats Has 1,000,000 Rows
     SELECT SNO FROM STATS;
```

```
    SNO
-------
5001944
5001950
5001976
5001978
5550000

Elapsed: 00:05:01.27

SQL> EXPLAIN PLAN FOR
  2  SELECT  SNO
  3  FROM    STATS2
  4  WHERE   NOT EXISTS
  5  (SELECT 'Debra,Paige,Bonnie,Toby'
  6  FROM    STATS
  7  WHERE   STATS2.SNO = STATS.SNO);
Explained.

SQL> @explain
Query Plan                              COST
------------------------------------ ----
SELECT STATEMENT   CHOOSE                 11
  FILTER
    TABLE ACCESS FULL STATS2              11
    TABLE ACCESS FULL STATS ANALYZED 3958

SQL> SELECT SNO
  2  FROM   STATS2
  3  WHERE  NOT EXISTS
  4  (SELECT 'Carole and Millie'
  5  FROM   STATS
  6  WHERE  STATS2.SNO=STATS.SNO);

^CERROR:
ORA-01013: user requested cancel of current operation

no rows selected

Elapsed: 01:23:21.20

SQL> CREATE INDEX STATS_SNO
  2  ON STATS(SNO);
```

```
Index created.

Elapsed: 00:11:22.00

SQL> ANALYZE TABLE STATS COMPUTE STATISTICS;
Table analyzed.

Elapsed: 00:14:33.43

SQL> ANALYZE TABLE STATS2 COMPUTE STATISTICS;
Table analyzed.

Elapsed: 00:00:05.58

SQL> EXPLAIN PLAN FOR
  2  SELECT SNO FROM STATS2
  3  MINUS
  4  SELECT SNO FROM STATS;
Explained.

SQL> @explain
Query Plan                                        COST
----------------------------------------------- ------
SELECT STATEMENT   CHOOSE                         47169
  MINUS
    SORT UNIQUE
      TABLE ACCESS FULL STATS2 ANALYZED              11
    SORT UNIQUE
      INDEX FAST FULL SCAN STATS_SNO ANALYZED 1459

SQL>  SELECT SNO FROM STATS2   -- Both Tables Indexed
  2   MINUS                    -- And Analyzed
  3   SELECT SNO FROM STATS;
      SNO
---------
  5001944
  5001950
  5001976
  5001978
  5550000

Elapsed: 00:04:08.24

SQL> EXPLAIN PLAN FOR
  2  SELECT  SNO
  3  FROM    STATS2
```

```
WHERE   NOT EXISTS
(SELECT 'Carole and Millie'
FROM    STATS
WHERE   STATS2.SNO = STATS.SNO);
Explained.

SQL> @explain
Query Plan                                   COST
-------------------------------------- -----
SELECT STATEMENT   CHOOSE                      11
  FILTER
    TABLE ACCESS FULL STATS2 ANALYZED          11
    INDEX RANGE SCAN STATS_SNO ANALYZED         3

SQL> SELECT  SNO
FROM    STATS2
WHERE   NOT EXISTS
(SELECT 'Debra,Paige,Bonnie,Toby'
FROM    STATS
WHERE   STATS2.SNO = STATS.SNO);

     SNO
--------
 5001978
 5001976
 5001950
 5001944
 5550000

Elapsed: 00:00:14.97

SQL> EXPLAIN PLAN FOR
SELECT SNO
FROM   STATS2
WHERE  SNO
       NOT IN(SELECT SNO
              FROM   STATS);
Explained.

SQL> @explain
Query Plan                                  COST
-------------------------------------- ----
SELECT STATEMENT   CHOOSE                     11
  FILTER
    TABLE ACCESS FULL STATS2 ANALYZED         11
```

```
    INDEX FULL SCAN STATS_SNO ANALYZED 9612

SQL> SELECT SNO
  2  FROM   STATS2
  3  WHERE  SNO
  4         NOT IN(SELECT SNO
  5                FROM   STATS);

    SNO
-------
5001978
5001976
5001950
5001944
5550000

Elapsed: 00:33:55.72
```

Rewriting Queries

Listing 12.5 shows the importance of rewriting queries that run too slowly. With little effort, the rewritten query can run much, much faster than the original. Here, the original statement requires more than five hours to run, and the rewritten statement using EXISTS requires only 35 minutes.

Listing 12.5 Rewriting queries.

```
SQL> DELETE FROM PLAYS  -- Killed After 5 Hours
            WHERE STREET IN(SELECT STREET FROM PLAYS
                                INTERSECT
                                SELECT STREET FROM PLAYS_TEMP);

SQL> DELETE FROM PLAYS  -- Executes In 35 Minutes
     WHERE EXISTS(SELECT 'ANN and BART'
                  FROM    PLAYS_TEMP
                  WHERE   PLAYS_TEMP.STREET =
                          PLAYS.STREET);
```

Frequency Of Commits

Listing 12.6 shows that the more frequently you commit, the slower the SQL script executes. The first example inserts one million rows and commits on every 10,000th row; it requires 2 hours, 41 minutes, and 59.7 seconds to insert one million rows into the table **NO_SORT_DEMO**. The second example in Listing 12.6 commits on every 1,000th row and requires 4 hours, 9 minutes, and 42.03 seconds to insert one million rows into **NO_SORT_DEMO**. This is a difference in time of 1 hour, 27 minutes, and 42.3 seconds. Remember, the less frequently you commit, the faster a script executes.

Listing 12.6 Commits.

```
SQL> get cor12_4
DECLARE
    sdate DATE := '25-OCT-97';
BEGIN
  FOR I IN 1..1000000 LOOP
      INSERT INTO NO_SORT_DEMO
      VALUES(sdate);
      IF MOD(I,10000) = 0 THEN COMMIT;
      END  IF;  -- Committing Every 10,000
      sdate := sdate + 1;
  END   LOOP;
END;
SQL> /

PL/SQL procedure successfully completed.

Elapsed: 02:41:59.70

SQL> TRUNCATE TABLE NO_SORT_DEMO;
Table truncated.

Elapsed: 00:00:05.31

SQL> DECLARE
    sdate DATE := '25-OCT-97';
BEGIN
  FOR I IN 1..1000000 LOOP
    INSERT INTO NO_SORT_DEMO
    VALUES(sdate);
    IF MOD(I,1000) = 0 THEN COMMIT;
    END  IF;  -- Committing Every 1,000
    sdate := sdate + 1;
  END   LOOP;
END;
```

```
SQL> /

PL/SQL procedure successfully completed.

Elapsed: 04:09:42.03
```

ESTIMATE Versus COMPUTE

You might have read a lot of "bad press" about estimating statistics on tables. The "experts" say not to do it—always use a full-blown **COMPUTE** instead. However, I have not found estimating statistics to be any problem whatsoever. I'm sure a couple instances exist where estimating might not be the best way to analyze a table. However, if 48 hours are required to compute statistics (as opposed to 30 minutes to estimate statistics) and the results are within 5 percent of each other, then what exactly is the problem? Listing 12.7 indicates the following. First of all, to compute the statistics on a one-million-row table requires 4 minutes and 44.32 seconds more than to estimate the statistics. Second, **ESTIMATE STATISTICS** is off by only .0215 percent on the **NUM_ROWS** column of the **USER_TABLES** data dictionary view and is off by only .0208 percent on the **DISTINCT_KEYS** column of **USER_INDEXES**. Third, **COMPUTE STATISTICS** shows a cost of 11, and **ESTIMATE STATISTICS** shows a cost of 3. Finally, the query based on estimated statistics executes 0.03 seconds slower than the query using computed statistics.

Listing 12.7 ESTIMATE STATISTICS.

```
SQL> ANALYZE TABLE NO_SORT_DEMO
  2          COMPUTE STATISTICS;
Table analyzed.

Elapsed: 00:04:58.61

SQL> SELECT NUM_ROWS
  2  FROM   USER_TABLES
  3  WHERE  TABLE_NAME = 'NO_SORT_DEMO';

NUM_ROWS
--------
 1000000

SQL> SELECT DISTINCT_KEYS
```

```
  2 FROM   USER_INDEXES
  3 WHERE  TABLE_NAME = 'NO_SORT_DEMO';

DISTINCT_KEYS
-------------
      1000000

SQL> EXPLAIN PLAN FOR
  2  SELECT *
  3  FROM   NO_SORT_DEMO
  4  WHERE  C1 < '25-DEC-99';
Explained.

SQL> @explain
Query Plan                                 COST
---------------------------------- ----
SELECT STATEMENT   CHOOSE                    11
  INDEX RANGE SCAN INDX_C1 ANALYZED   11

SQL> SELECT *
  2  FROM   NO_SORT_DEMO
  3  WHERE  C1 < '25-DEC-99';

C1
----------------
.........
22-DEC-99
23-DEC-99
24-DEC-99
791 rows selected.

Elapsed: 00:00:02.92

SQL> ANALYZE TABLE NO_SORT_DEMO
  2            DELETE STATISTICS;
Table analyzed.

SQL> ANALYZE TABLE NO_SORT_DEMO
  2            ESTIMATE STATISTICS;
Table analyzed.

Elapsed: 00:00:14.29

SQL> SELECT NUM_ROWS      -- Off By 215 Rows
  2  FROM   USER_TABLES   -- Or By .0215 %
  3  WHERE  TABLE_NAME = 'NO_SORT_DEMO';
```

```
NUM_ROWS
--------
 1000215

SQL> SELECT DISTINCT_KEYS  -- Off By 208
  2  FROM   USER_INDEXES   -- Or By .0208 %
  3  WHERE  TABLE_NAME = 'NO_SORT_DEMO';

DISTINCT_KEYS
-------------
      1000208

SQL> EXPLAIN PLAN FOR
  2  SELECT *
  3  FROM   NO_SORT_DEMO
  4  WHERE  C1 < '25-DEC-99';
Explained.

SQL> @explain
Query Plan                              COST
--------------------------------------- ----
SELECT STATEMENT   CHOOSE                  3
  INDEX RANGE SCAN INDX_C1 ANALYZED        3

SQL> SELECT *  -- 791 Rows
  2  FROM   NO_SORT_DEMO
  3  WHERE  C1 < '25-DEC-99';

C1
------------
.........
22-DEC-99
23-DEC-99
24-DEC-99
791 rows selected.

Elapsed: 00:00:02.95
```

One of my customers uses the parallel query option on a 27,329,308-row table, and it requires 33 seconds to estimate the statistics. I don't know the platform, but the customer is running Oracle7.3. Listing 12.8 shows the command to estimate the statistics on the 27,329,308-row table. The customer and I want to see how accurate **ESTIMATE** really is. When we execute a query on **DBA_TABLES**, Oracle returns

27,266,335 in the **NUM_ROWS** column. We are very impressed and excited that Oracle is so accurate when estimating statistics on a large table. The reason for all the excitement is due to **ESTIMATE STATISTICS** running so much faster than **COMPUTE STATISTICS**. The margin of error is less than a quarter of a percentage point.

Listing 12.8 Round two: COMPUTE versus ESTIMATE.

```
SQL> SET TIMING ON
SQL> ANALYZE TABLE T27MILLION
             ESTIMATE STATISTICS
             FOR COLUMNS VALUE SIZE 100;
Elapsed:  00:00:33.71

SQL> SELECT DEGREE,
            NUM_ROWS,
            CACHE
     FROM   DBA_TABLES
     WHERE  OWNER      = 'CLINT' AND
            TABLE_NAME = 'T27MILLION';

DEGREE   NUM_ROWS CACHE
------ ---------- -----
     3 27,266,335 N

SQL> SELECT 100 *
  2  ((27329308 - 27266335)/27329308) PCT_OFF
  3  FROM   DUAL;

PCT_OFF
-------
.230423
```

Removing Rows From A Table

To delete all rows from a table, use the **TRUNCATE TABLE** command if speed is important to you. In Listing 12.9, the **TRUNCATE TABLE** command requires 5.31 seconds to delete one million rows from the **NO_SORT_DEMO** table. The **DELETE** command, however, is another story. First of all, **DELETE** commands produce a tremendous amount of undo, or rollback segment, data. So much so, in this case, that rollback segment disk space runs out in rollback segment R01 after 2 hours and 18 minutes. As you can see, these two types of commands have a tremendous difference in elapsed times. However, you should be aware that the TRUNCATE command fires an implicit commit. If you accidentally enter the incorrect table name in the TRUNCATE command, all the rows from the incorrect table are deleted.

Listing 12.9 TRUNCATE versus DELETE.

```
SQL> TRUNCATE TABLE NO_SORT_DEMO;
Table truncated.

Elapsed: 00:00:05.31

SQL> DELETE FROM NO_SORT_DEMO;
DELETE FROM NO_SORT_DEMO
*
ERROR at line 1:
ORA-01562: failed to extend rollback
           segment number 2
ORA-01650: unable to extend rollback
           segment R01 by 512 in tablespace RBS

Elapsed: 02:18:39.12
```

Number Of Rows In A Table

You can determine the number of rows in a table in several ways. Listing 12.10 shows three methods. The first example analyzes the one-million-row table NO_SORT_DEMO, which requires 4 minutes and 58.61 seconds. Then a query is written against the data dictionary view USER_TABLES to observe the output of the column NUM_ROWS. The second example uses COUNT(*), which performs a full-table scan and requires only 1 minute and 56.94 seconds to execute (this is the fastest of all three methods used on the one-million-row table NO_SORT_DEMO). The last method uses the RULE hint to force Oracle to use the index on the C1 column, and it requires an outrageous time of 11 minutes and 26.05 seconds.

Listing 12.10 Number of rows in a table.

```
SQL> ANALYZE TABLE NO_SORT_DEMO
  2          COMPUTE STATISTICS;
Table analyzed.
```

```
Elapsed: 00:04:58.61

SQL> SELECT NUM_ROWS
  2  FROM   USER_TABLES
  3  WHERE  TABLE_NAME = 'NO_SORT_DEMO';

NUM_ROWS
--------
 1000000

SQL> SELECT COUNT(*)
  2  FROM   NO_SORT_DEMO;

COUNT(*)
--------
 1000000

Elapsed: 00:01:56.94

SQL> SELECT --+ RULE
  2  COUNT(*) - Force Use Of Index
  3  FROM   NO_SORT_DEMO
  4  WHERE  C1 > '01-JAN-97';

COUNT(*)
--------
 1000000

Elapsed: 00:11:26.05

SQL> EXPLAIN PLAN FOR
  2  SELECT --+ RULE
  3  COUNT(*)
  4  FROM   NO_SORT_DEMO
  5  WHERE  C1 > '01-JAN-97';
Explained.

SQL> @explain
Query Plan                           COST
------------------------------------ ----
SELECT STATEMENT   HINT: RULE
  SORT AGGREGATE
    INDEX RANGE SCAN INDX_C1 ANALYZED
```

ANY

Even though you can use **ANY** because it's part of the SQL language, you're much better off using the single group function **MAX**. Not only is this function, **MAX**, faster, but it's easier to write. Listing 12.11 compares **ANY** to **MAX**, and **MAX** is the winner. Four parts have test numbers 8101 that pass, 90 through 93. Both queries identify the number of tests for all part numbers less than any part number that passes test 8101. In our case, return the number of tests for all part numbers less than part number 93, which is 263,902 total tests for part numbers 1 through 92. Using **ANY** has a cost of 631, and it requires 3 minutes and 13.9 seconds to execute. Using **MAX(PNO)** also has a cost of 631 and uses two sort aggregates, but it only requires 1 minute and 48.96 seconds to execute. Once again, equal costs for different SQL statements does not mean the same elapsed times. Using **MAX(PNO)** is 1 minute and 25 seconds faster than using **ANY** for these two queries on the **TESTS** table, which has 470,552 rows.

Listing 12.11 ANY versus MAX.

```
SQL> SELECT COUNT(*)
     FROM   TESTS;

COUNT(*)
--------
  470552

SQL> SELECT PNO, TNO, RESULTS
     FROM   TESTS
     WHERE  TNO = 8101;

    PNO      TNO R
  -----  ------ -
     93     8101 P
     90     8101 P
     91     8101 P
     92     8101 P
SQL> EXPLAIN PLAN FOR
     SELECT   COUNT(TNO)
     FROM     TESTS
     WHERE    PNO < ANY (SELECT PNO
              FROM    TESTS
              WHERE   TNO = 8101 AND
              RESULTS     = 'P');
```

```
SQL> @explain
Query Plan                                          COST
----------------------------------------- ----
SELECT STATEMENT   CHOOSE                            631
  SORT AGGREGATE
    FILTER
      TABLE ACCESS FULL TESTS ANALYZED               631
      TABLE ACCESS BY ROWID TESTS ANALYZED             2
        INDEX RANGE SCAN INDX_TESTS_TNO

SQL> SELECT COUNT(TNO)
     FROM   TESTS
     WHERE  PNO < ANY (SELECT PNO
                       FROM   TESTS
                       WHERE  TNO = 8101 AND
                          RESULTS = 'P');

COUNT(TNO)
----------
    263902

Elapsed: 00:03:13.90

SQL> EXPLAIN PLAN FOR
     SELECT COUNT(TNO)
     FROM   TESTS
     WHERE  PNO < (SELECT MAX(PNO)
                   FROM   TESTS
                   WHERE  TNO = 8101 AND
                   RESULTS    = 'P');
Explained.

SQL> @explain
Query Plan                                          COST
----------------------------------------- ----
SELECT STATEMENT   CHOOSE                            631
  SORT AGGREGATE
    FILTER
      TABLE ACCESS FULL TESTS ANALYZED               631
      SORT AGGREGATE
        TABLE ACCESS BY ROWID TESTS ANALYZED           2
          INDEX RANGE SCAN INDX_TESTS_TNO

SQL> SELECT COUNT(TNO)
     FROM   TESTS
     WHERE  PNO < (SELECT MAX(PNO)
```

```
  4                         FROM   TESTS
  5                         WHERE  TNO = 8101 AND
  6     RESULTS                        = 'P');

COUNT(TNO)
----------
    263902

Elapsed: 00:01:48.96
```

ALL

As with **ANY**, you can use **ALL** because it's part of the SQL language, but you're much better off using the single group function **MAX**. This function is faster and easier to write. When using **MAX**, if the column value on the left side of the **WHERE** clause is more than the maximum value of all the values in the right side of the **WHERE** clause, then it follows that the value on the left is greater than all of the values on the right. Listing 12.12 compares **ALL** to **MAX**, and **MAX** wins. Both queries return the total number of tests for all part numbers greater than part number 93 that passes test number 8101. In our case, 198,000 tests exist on part numbers 94 through 10,000. Using **ALL** has a cost of 631, and it requires 3 minutes and 11.94 seconds to execute. Using **MAX(PNO)** also has a cost of 631 and uses two sort aggregates, but it only requires 1 minute and 45.47 seconds to execute. Using **MAX(PNO)** is 1 minute and 26 seconds faster than using **ALL** for these two queries.

Listing 12.12 ALL versus MAX.

```
SQL> EXPLAIN PLAN FOR
  2  SELECT COUNT(TNO)
  3  FROM   TESTS
  4  WHERE  PNO > ALL (SELECT PNO
  5                         FROM   TESTS
  6                         WHERE  TNO = 8101 AND
  7                            RESULTS = 'P');
Explained.

SQL> @explain
Query Plan                                     COST
-------------------------- ---------- ----
SELECT STATEMENT   CHOOSE                       631
```

```
  SORT AGGREGATE
    FILTER
      TABLE ACCESS FULL TESTS ANALYZED   631
      TABLE ACCESS BY ROWID TESTS ANALYZED 2
        INDEX RANGE SCAN INDX_TESTS_TNO

SQL> SELECT COUNT(TNO)
  2  FROM   TESTS
  3  WHERE  PNO > ALL (SELECT PNO
  4                    FROM   TESTS
  5                    WHERE  TNO = 8101 AND
  6                       RESULTS = 'P');

COUNT(TNO)
----------
    198000

Elapsed: 00:03:11.94

SQL> EXPLAIN PLAN FOR
  2  SELECT COUNT(TNO)
  3  FROM   TESTS
  4  WHERE  PNO >  (SELECT MAX(PNO)
  5                 FROM   TESTS
  6                 WHERE  TNO = 8101 AND
  7                    RESULTS = 'P');
Explained.

SQL> @explain
Query Plan                                    COST
------------------------------------------ ----
SELECT STATEMENT   CHOOSE                      631
  SORT AGGREGATE
    FILTER
      TABLE ACCESS FULL TESTS ANALYZED         631
      SORT AGGREGATE
        TABLE ACCESS BY ROWID TESTS ANALYZED     2
          INDEX RANGE SCAN INDX_TESTS_TNO

SQL> SELECT COUNT(TNO)
  2  FROM   TESTS
  3  WHERE  PNO >  (SELECT MAX(PNO)
  4                 FROM   TESTS
  5                 WHERE  TNO = 8101 AND
  6                    RESULTS = 'P');
```

```
COUNT(TNO)
----------
    198000

Elapsed: 00:01:45.47
```

Populate Numeric Primary Key Columns

To populate numeric primary key columns, you can use a table containing the last value in a primary key column for a particular table, or you can use a sequence. Listing 12.13 starts with the table approach. When a customer places an order, the sales agent presses the commit key when the order is complete. The **PRE-INSERT** block-level form's trigger fires and places the most current order number into the **order_number** item or field in the orders block of the form. The **FOR UPDATE** locks the row in the table **PK_VALUES**, if the row is not locked by another transaction. The last statement in the form's trigger increments the order number by 1 for the next transaction. Because this trigger Locks, Selects, and Updates (LSU), and Pistol Pete Maravich (who I played basketball with in 1958 at a basketball camp in North Carolina) went to Louisiana State University (LSU), I affectionately refer to this trigger as the Pistol Pete Trigger. This approach is outstanding, because no gaps are possible. However, on a busy system, you'll experience contention on the table containing the most current primary key values—in this case, the **PK_VALUES** table.

The other approach to populating numeric primary key columns is to use sequences. You use a sequence to populate a numeric column, particularly primary key columns by using the **CREATE SEQUENCE** command. The next available value can be in memory or on disk. If the next value is in memory, an instance crash or a sudden loss of power causes gaps because several values are in memory at once. For example, suppose the default is 20 values in memory for a sequence. If you lose power on your system, when power is restored, you'll be missing 20 order numbers. However, contention is minimal, even if the next available order number is on disk.

Listing 12.13 The Pistol Pete forms trigger versus a sequence.

```
SQL> CREATE TABLE PK_VALUES
           (NTABLE      VARCHAR2(30),
```

```
             LAST_VALUE NUMBER(9,0));
Table created.

SQL> INSERT INTO PK_VALUES
            VALUES('ORDERS', 5500);

SQL*Forms or Oracle Forms trigger.
Block level PRE-INSERT

SELECT last_value             -- "S" in LSU
INTO   :ORDERS.order_number
FROM   PK_VALUES
WHERE  ntable = 'ORDERS'      -- Possible Contention
FOR UPDATE;                   -- "L" in LSU

UPDATE pk_values              -- "U" in LSU
SET    last_value = last_value + 1
WHERE  ntable     = 'ORDERS';

SQL> CREATE SEQUENCE S_ORDERS
            START WITH 5500 -- Store On Disk
            NOCACHE;
Sequence created.

SQL*Forms or Oracle Forms trigger.
Block level PRE-INSERT

SELECT s_orders.nextval        -- Less Contention
INTO   :ORDERS.order_number   -- And Faster
FROM   DUAL;
```

Using Explain Plan

A friend of mine, Joe Cairns, has two tables. The first table's name is **PLAYS**, and it contains 10 million rows. The second table's name is **PLAYS_TEMP**, and it has 100,000 rows. Joe wants to delete 100,000 rows from **PLAYS** that match the 100,000 rows in **PLAYS_TEMP**. Listing 12.14 shows the long-running statement using **IN** and the fast-running statement using **EXISTS**. Joe says that the **DELETE** statement has been running for over five hours, and he asks me to take a look at it. First of all, I kill the statement using Ctrl+C. Then I run the statement through Explain Plan—the cost is 143,916. Then I rewrite the statement and run it through Explain Plan.

This time the cost is much lower—66,000. I then execute the revised statement, and it requires 35 minutes to run. By the way, the **SELECT** clause containing the string "ANN and BART" could be anything you want to use, because the string never displays anyway. For a slow-running query, try to rewrite it; then submit it to Explain Plan and observe the cost. If the cost is much lower, you might become a hero.

Listing 12.14 Rewrite and observe the cost.

```
SQL> DELETE FROM PLAYS  -- Killed After 5 Hours
     WHERE STREET IN(SELECT STREET FROM PLAYS
                     INTERSECT
                     SELECT STREET FROM PLAYS_TEMP);

SQL> DELETE FROM PLAYS
     WHERE EXISTS(SELECT 'ANN and BART'
                  FROM    PLAYS_TEMP
                  WHERE   PLAYS_TEMP.STREET =
                          PLAYS.STREET);
```

START WITH And CONNECT BY

Listing 12.15 starts by adding a column named **COMPONENT_OF** to the **PARTS** table, which is a foreign key column in **PARTS**. The primary key, the **PNO** column, is in the same table. This means **PARTS** is a recursive table, like the tables **EMP** and **PLAN_TABLE**, and you can use **START WITH** and **CONNECT BY**. The updates populate the **COMPONENT_OF** column to simulate a build of materials hierarchy, which provides part explosion reports. The table contains 10,000 rows, but it has no indexes or statistics. However, Oracle accesses the rows in the **PARTS** table using rowids. This query requires 2.81 seconds to return one row from a 10,000-row table.

Next, a unique index is created on the **PNO** column of the **PARTS** table and a nonunique index is created on the foreign key column **COMPONENT_OF**. Then, the table is analyzed to help the cost-based optimizer make the best decision when executing the SQL statements. Explain Plan shows a cost of 26, and the optimizer uses the unique index. The SQL statement requires 1.77 seconds to execute, with indexes on both columns in the **CONNECT BY** clause. This is a performance gain of 1.04 seconds for a 10,000-row table. If the table has 100,000,000 rows and the gain is linear, the improvement is 10,400 seconds, which is 173.333 minutes (or 2 hours, 53 minutes, and 20 seconds faster).

Listing 12.15 START WITH and CONNECT BY.

```
SQL> ALTER TABLE PARTS
  2        ADD COMPONENT_OF NUMBER(7);
Table altered.

SQL> UPDATE PARTS
  2  SET    COMPONENT_OF = 1
  3  WHERE  PNO BETWEEN 2 AND 1000;
999 rows updated.

SQL> UPDATE PARTS
  2  SET    COMPONENT_OF = 2
  3  WHERE  PNO BETWEEN 1001 AND 2000;
1000 rows updated.

SQL> UPDATE PARTS
  2  SET    COMPONENT_OF = 3
  3  WHERE  PNO BETWEEN 2001 AND 3000;
1000 rows updated.

SQL> UPDATE PARTS
  2  SET    COMPONENT_OF = 3000
  3  WHERE  PNO BETWEEN 3001 AND 4000;
1000 rows updated.

SQL> UPDATE PARTS
  2  SET    COMPONENT_OF = 4000
  3  WHERE  PNO BETWEEN 4001 AND 7000;
3000 rows updated.

SQL> UPDATE PARTS
  2  SET    COMPONENT_OF = 7000
  3  WHERE  PNO BETWEEN 7001 AND 10000;
3000 rows updated.

SQL> COMMIT;
Commit complete.

SQL> SELECT INDEX_NAME
  2  FROM   USER_INDEXES
  3  WHERE  TABLE_NAME = 'PARTS';

no rows selected
```

```
SQL> SELECT NUM_ROWS
  2  FROM   USER_TABLES
  3  WHERE  TABLE_NAME = 'PARTS';

NUM_ROWS
--------

SQL> SELECT COUNT(*)
  2  FROM   PARTS;

COUNT(*)
--------
   10000

Elapsed: 00:00:00.58

SQL> EXPLAIN PLAN FOR
  2  SELECT LPAD(' ', 3*LEVEL) || PNAME "Components"
  3  FROM   PARTS
  4  START  WITH PNO       = 9900
  5  CONNECT BY PRIOR PNO = COMPONENT_OF;
Explained.

SQL> @explain
Query Plan                         COST
------------------------------ ----
SELECT STATEMENT   CHOOSE
  CONNECT BY
    TABLE ACCESS FULL PARTS
    TABLE ACCESS BY ROWID PARTS
    TABLE ACCESS FULL PARTS

SQL> SELECT LPAD(' ', 3*LEVEL) ||
  2         PNAME "Components"
  3  FROM   PARTS
  4  START  WITH PNO      = 9900
  5  CONNECT BY PRIOR PNO = COMPONENT_OF;

Components
-----------------------------------------
Widget 9900

Elapsed: 00:00:02.81
```

```
SQL> CREATE UNIQUE INDEX
  2         INDX_PARTS_PNO
  3         ON PARTS(PNO);
Index created.
Elapsed: 00:00:11.80

SQL> CREATE INDEX
  2         INDX_PARTS_COM
  3         ON PARTS(COMPONENT_OF);
Index created.
Elapsed: 00:00:10.78

SQL> ANALYZE TABLE PARTS
  2           COMPUTE STATISTICS;
Table analyzed.

Elapsed: 00:00:10.79

SQL> EXPLAIN PLAN FOR
  2  SELECT  LPAD(' ', 3*LEVEL) || PNAME "Components"
  3  FROM    PARTS
  4  START   WITH PNO = 9900
  5  CONNECT BY PRIOR PNO = COMPONENT_OF;
Explained.

SQL> @explain
Query Plan                                COST
----------------------------------------- ----
SELECT STATEMENT   CHOOSE                   26
  CONNECT BY
    INDEX UNIQUE SCAN INDX_PARTS_PNO ANALYZED 1
    TABLE ACCESS BY ROWID PARTS ANALYZED
    TABLE ACCESS FULL PARTS ANALYZED        26

SQL> SELECT LPAD(' ', 3*LEVEL)
            || PNAME "Components"
     FROM   PARTS
     START  WITH PNO = 9900
     CONNECT BY PRIOR PNO = COMPONENT_OF;

Components
-----------------------------------------
Widget 9900

Elapsed: 00:00:01.77
```

```
SQL> DROP INDEX INDX_PARTS_PNO;
Index dropped.

SQL> DROP INDEX INDX_PARTS_COM;
Index dropped.

SQL> ANALYZE TABLE PARTS COMPUTE STATISTICS;
Table analyzed.

Elapsed: 00:00:09.52

SQL> EXPLAIN PLAN FOR
  2  SELECT LPAD(' ', 3*LEVEL)
  3         || PNAME "Components"
  4  FROM   PARTS
  5  START  WITH PNO = 9900
  6  CONNECT BY PRIOR PNO = COMPONENT_OF;
Explained.

SQL> @explain
Query Plan                                      COST
---------------------------------------------- ----
SELECT STATEMENT   CHOOSE                         26
  CONNECT BY
    TABLE ACCESS FULL PARTS ANALYZED              26
    TABLE ACCESS BY ROWID PARTS ANALYZED
    TABLE ACCESS FULL PARTS ANALYZED              26
```

UNION Or Multiple SELECTs

Listing 12.16 shows an index on the **TNO** column of the table **TESTS**, which contains 470,552 rows. Three separate queries on **TESTS** require 43.16 seconds, 42.99 seconds, and 42.63 seconds, respectively, for a total of 128.78 seconds (or 2 minutes and 8.78 seconds). The next query uses the **UNION** set operator and combines the three queries, but it runs slower without an index on the **PNO** column—2 minutes and 18.56 seconds. The **UNION** query is rewritten using **GROUP BY**. The **GROUP BY** query is much faster—it requires only 53.82 seconds to execute, which is 74.96 seconds faster than using the three separately written queries, and 84.74 seconds faster than the query that uses **UNION**.

Next, an index is created on the **PNO** column of the **TESTS** table. Now the three queries execute in 10.56 seconds, 10.77 seconds, and 11.98 seconds, respectively, which is a total of 33.31 seconds (compared to 2 minutes and 8.78 seconds without the index on the **PNO** column). The Explain Plan for the query that uses **UNION** to combine all three queries indicates a cost of 18, and the index on **PNO** is used for all three WHERE clauses. The query that uses **UNION** now requires only 29.96 seconds to execute, which is faster than the three separate queries by 3.35 seconds, and 4.57 seconds faster than the query that uses **GROUP BY**, even though **GROUP BY** has a lower cost (10).

Listing 12.16 **UNION** versus multiple **SELECT**s.

```
SQL> SELECT INDEX_NAME
  2  FROM   USER_INDEXES
  3  WHERE  TABLE_NAME = 'TESTS';

INDEX_NAME
------------------------------
INDX_TESTS_TNO

SQL> SELECT NUM_ROWS
  2  FROM   USER_TABLES
  3  WHERE  TABLE_NAME = 'TESTS';

NUM_ROWS
--------
  470552

SQL> SELECT MIN(TNO),
  2         MAX(TNO)
  3  FROM   TESTS
  4  WHERE  PNO = 80;

MIN(TNO) MAX(TNO)
-------- --------
       1     6401

Elapsed: 00:00:43.16

SQL> SELECT MIN(TNO),
  2         MAX(TNO)
  3  FROM   TESTS
  4  WHERE  PNO = 85 AND RESULTS = 'P';

MIN(TNO) MAX(TNO)
-------- --------
       2     7226

Elapsed: 00:00:42.99
```

```
SQL> SELECT MIN(TNO),
  2         MAX(TNO)
  3  FROM   TESTS
  4  WHERE  PNO = 90 AND RESULTS = 'P';

MIN(TNO) MAX(TNO)
-------- --------
       2     8101

Elapsed: 00:00:42.63

SQL> SELECT MIN(TNO), MAX(TNO)
  2  FROM   TESTS
  3  WHERE  PNO = 80
  4  UNION
  5  SELECT MIN(TNO), MAX(TNO)
  6  FROM   TESTS
  7  WHERE  PNO = 85 AND RESULTS = 'P'
  8  UNION
  9  SELECT MIN(TNO), MAX(TNO)
 10  FROM   TESTS
 11  WHERE  PNO = 90 AND RESULTS = 'P';

MIN(TNO) MAX(TNO)
-------- --------
       1     6401
       2     7226
       2     8101

Elapsed: 00:02:18.56

SQL> SELECT PNO, MIN(TNO), MAX(TNO)
  2  FROM   TESTS
  3  WHERE  (PNO = 80) OR
  4  (PNO = 85 AND RESULTS = 'P') OR
  5  (PNO = 90 AND RESULTS = 'P')
  6  GROUP  BY PNO;

    PNO MIN(TNO) MAX(TNO)
------- -------- --------
     80        1     6401
     85        2     7226
     90        2     8101

Elapsed: 00:00:53.82
```

```
SQL> CREATE INDEX INDX_TESTS_PNO
  2           ON TESTS(PNO);
Index created.

Elapsed: 00:06:20.82

SQL> SELECT MIN(TNO),
  2          MAX(TNO)
  3  FROM   TESTS  -- Index On PNO
  4  WHERE  PNO = 80;

MIN(TNO) MAX(TNO)
-------- --------
       1     6401

Elapsed: 00:00:10.56

SQL> SELECT MIN(TNO),
  2          MAX(TNO)
  3  FROM   TESTS
  4  WHERE  PNO = 85 AND RESULTS = 'P';

MIN(TNO) MAX(TNO)
-------- --------
       2     7226

Elapsed: 00:00:10.77

SQL> SELECT MIN(TNO),
  2          MAX(TNO)
  3  FROM   TESTS
  4  WHERE  PNO = 90 AND RESULTS = 'P';

MIN(TNO) MAX(TNO)
-------- --------
       2     8101

Elapsed: 00:00:11.98

SQL> EXPLAIN PLAN FOR
  2  SELECT MIN(TNO), MAX(TNO)
  3  FROM   TESTS
  4  WHERE  PNO = 80
  5  UNION
  6  SELECT MIN(TNO), MAX(TNO)
```

```
  7  FROM   TESTS
  8  WHERE  PNO = 85 AND RESULTS = 'P'
  9  UNION
 10  SELECT MIN(TNO), MAX(TNO)
 11  FROM   TESTS
 12  WHERE  PNO = 90 AND RESULTS = 'P';
Explained.

SQL> @explain
Query Plan                                    COST
------------------------------------------- ----
SELECT STATEMENT   CHOOSE                       18
  SORT UNIQUE
    UNION-ALL
      SORT AGGREGATE
        TABLE ACCESS BY ROWID TESTS ANALYZED     2
          INDEX RANGE SCAN INDX_TESTS_PNO
      SORT AGGREGATE
        TABLE ACCESS BY ROWID TESTS ANALYZED     2
          INDEX RANGE SCAN INDX_TESTS_PNO
      SORT AGGREGATE
        TABLE ACCESS BY ROWID TESTS ANALYZED     2
          INDEX RANGE SCAN INDX_TESTS_PNO

SQL> SELECT MIN(TNO), MAX(TNO)
  2  FROM   TESTS     -- Faster Than Separate
  3  WHERE  PNO = 80 -- With PNO Indexed
  4  UNION
  5  SELECT MIN(TNO), MAX(TNO)
  6  FROM   TESTS
  7  WHERE  PNO = 85 AND RESULTS = 'P'
  8  UNION
  9  SELECT MIN(TNO), MAX(TNO)
 10  FROM   TESTS
 11  WHERE  PNO = 90 AND RESULTS = 'P';

MIN(TNO) MAX(TNO)
-------- --------
       1     6401
       2     7226
       2     8101

Elapsed: 00:00:29.96
```

```
SQL> EXPLAIN PLAN FOR
  2  SELECT PNO, MIN(TNO), MAX(TNO)
  3  FROM   TESTS
  4  WHERE  (PNO = 80) OR
  5  (PNO = 85 AND RESULTS = 'P') OR
  6  (PNO = 90 AND RESULTS = 'P')
  7  GROUP  BY PNO;
Explained.

SQL> @explain
Query Plan                                          COST
-------------------------------------------------- ----
SELECT STATEMENT   CHOOSE                             10
  SORT GROUP BY
    CONCATENATION
      TABLE ACCESS BY ROWID TESTS ANALYZED             2
        INDEX RANGE SCAN INDX_TESTS_PNO
      TABLE ACCESS BY ROWID TESTS ANALYZED             2
        INDEX RANGE SCAN INDX_TESTS_PNO
      TABLE ACCESS BY ROWID TESTS ANALYZED             2
        INDEX RANGE SCAN INDX_TESTS_PNO

SQL> SELECT PNO, MIN(TNO), MAX(TNO)
  2  FROM  TESTS
  3  WHERE (PNO = 80) OR
  4   (PNO = 85 AND RESULTS = 'P') OR
  5   (PNO = 90 AND RESULTS = 'P')
  6  GROUP  BY PNO;

    PNO MIN(TNO) MAX(TNO)
------- -------- --------
     80        1     6401
     85        2     7226
     90        2     8101

Elapsed: 00:00:34.53
```

Summary

Be careful how you use indexes, because neither your experience level nor your IQ level can guarantee that you won't write slow-running statements that don't use indexes correctly. A perfect example is the **UPDATE** saga section of this chapter.

Remember, suppressing indexes is very powerful, and it works for both Oracle optimizers (cost-based and rule-based).

Set operators are our friends, so consider using them whenever possible. Most of the time, they're sweethearts in the tuning arena. Nevertheless, there are times when a correlated subquery that uses **NOT EXISTS** can really kick posteriors, which in this case is great, like David kicking Goliath. This leads to the beauty of Oracle. Many times you can become a hero just by rewriting a query. Also, watch the frequency of your commits. The more frequently you commit, the slower a batch program executes.

The argument of **ESTIMATE STATISTICS** versus **COMPUTE STATISTICS** will probably rage on forever, but I'm not convinced of the evils of estimating, mainly because of my observations on customer sites—some of which were shared in this chapter.

Be careful when you truncate a table. If you truncate the incorrect table, it could be "update the old resume" time. The **TRUNCATE** command fires an implicit commit, whether you want it to or not. Also, if you have any delete database triggers on the table you want to truncate, they will not fire. Looks like the fastest method for determining the number of rows in a table is to use the single group function **COUNT**(*). Moreover, when it comes to using **ANY** or **ALL**, use the single group function **MAX** instead, if possible. Also, when you're populating numeric primary key columns, consider using sequences, because contention is minimal, even if you store the next available value on disk.

One of the most important methods you can use is to rewrite your slow-running SQL statements through Explain Plan and then compare the costs. Normally, a query with a low cost runs faster than queries with higher costs. Also, if you use the **CONNECT BY** and **START WITH** clauses, you should probably index the columns in the **CONNECT BY** clause. Finally, if the appropriate columns in the **WHERE** clauses have indexes, then combining the multiple queries into one query is generally faster—either use the set operator **UNION** or use **GROUP BY**, depending on what you're attempting to accomplish.

Storage

CHAPTER 13

Nothing is worse than a badly fragmented Oracle database caused by improper storage parameters. This chapter teaches you to minimize fragmentation by using the proper settings for storage parameters such as PCTFREE *and* PCTUSED*.*

Storage

Row Chaining And PCTFREE

Only two types of chaining exist—the good type and the bad type. The good type exists because the data simply cannot and will not fit into one Oracle block. For instance, a **LONG** data type column can store up to 2 GB of data. Sorry, but there's no way in this world, or the world to come, to store 2 GB in a 2K, 4K, 8K, 16K, 32K, or 64K Oracle block. The other type of chaining, the bad type, can and should be eliminated. An example of the bad type of chaining is a block percent free setting that is much too low, causing blocks to chain. The percent free area of a block is reserved for updates of data that are wider than the data currently in the column. If there is not enough space for the updated data, Oracle chains the block to another block, and that means slower running queries on the table containing the low setting of percent free. An improper setting of **PCTFREE** can cause chaining.

The **PCTFREE** setting for a data block reserves space in a block for column expansion of data. The default setting of **PCTFREE** is 10 percent. A null column updated to a value uses the space marked as "percent free" for the actual update. Oracle does not push and slide rows around to make room for the update. On the other hand, a column with the value Sam that's updated to Ben does the update directly on top of the data value. In other words, Ben overwrites the previous value, Sam, and doesn't use the disk space marked as "percent free."

A heavily updated table that performs frequent column expansions requires a higher setting of **PCTFREE**. However, if **PCTFREE** is too large, fewer rows are inserted into each block, and the table requires many more blocks to store the data for the table. If **PCTFREE** is too small and frequent column expansions occur, the bad type of chaining occurs, and response time is much worse for queries on the chained table because data in the chained blocks is retrieved.

If rows chain from one Oracle block to another, you should correct this situation as quickly as possible. The major cause of chaining is an improper setting for **PCTFREE**. Column updates use the percent free space when the data is actually longer than what is currently in the column. For example, if Debra Kay marries Mark Smith, then Oracle places Smith in the percent free space of the data block. Oracle does not expand the column containing Kay so that it's large enough to hold Smith. Every column has a length indicator, followed by the data. If a column contains a null value, the length byte contains a zero, unless it's the last column of a table. Obviously, any column containing a null, when updated, uses the percent free space of the data block. If columns are frequently updated either from null values to non-null values, or, if the updated data is wider or longer than the data currently in the column, then the setting for **PCTFREE** should be higher than the default value of 10 percent for **PCTFREE**. If the value is not set higher, chaining occurs. Queries against a table containing chained rows will execute slower because Oracle reads the chained blocks as well as the regular data blocks.

Several methods exist to correct chaining. One method changes the setting of **PCTFREE**, exports the table, drops the table, and then imports the table. Another method creates a temporary table, copies the chained rows to the temporary table, and then deletes the chained rows from the original table. Finally, this method inserts the rows back into the original table from the temporary table.

The first method for detecting chained rows is shown in Listing 13.1. Figure 13.1 shows how to identify chained rows.

First, to determine the current setting of **PCTFREE**, write a query against **USER_TABLES**. Next, create the table **CHAINED_ROWS** using the Oracle-supplied SQL script file utlchain.sql; then analyze the **EMP** table, which inserts information into the table **CHAINED_ROWS** for every chained row in the **EMP** table. The next query indicates the number of chained rows. The last query joins the **EMP** table to the **CHAINED_ROWS** table to view the rows that are chained. Note that of the 224 rows in the **EMP** table, 128 are chained rows.

Listing 13.1 Chaining and **PCTFREE**.

```
SQL> SELECT PCT_FREE
  2  FROM   USER_TABLES
  3  WHERE  TABLE_NAME = 'EMP';
```

```
PCT_FREE
--------
       1

SQL> @$ORACLE_HOME/rdbms/admin/utlchain
SQL> create table CHAINED_ROWS (
  2    owner_name        varchar2(30),
  3    table_name        varchar2(30),
  4    cluster_name      varchar2(30),
  5    head_rowid        rowid,
  6    timestamp         date
  7  );
Table created.

SQL> ANALYZE TABLE EMP
  2          LIST CHAINED ROWS
  3          INTO CHAINED_ROWS;
Table analyzed.

SQL> SELECT COUNT(*)
  2  FROM   CHAINED_ROWS;

COUNT(*)
--------
     128

SQL> SELECT EMPNO, ENAME
  2  FROM   EMP E,
  3  CHAINED_ROWS C -- See 4 Chained Rows
  4  WHERE  E.ROWID = C.HEAD_ROWID AND
  5         ROWNUM < 5;

  EMPNO ENAME
------- ----------
   7369 SMITH
   7521 WARD
   7654 MARTIN
   7698 BLAKE

SQL> SELECT COUNT(*)
     FROM EMP;

COUNT(*)
--------
     224
```

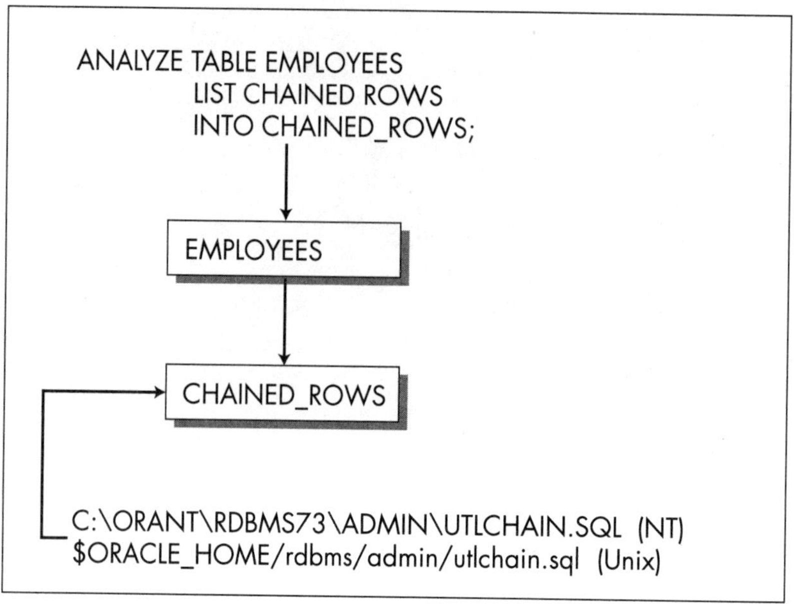

Figure 13.1
Identifying chained rows.

Listing 13.2 eliminates chaining by changing the **PCTFREE** setting to a higher value (if frequent updates occur and the updated data is wider than the current data). This table now requires more blocks, because more space is reserved for updates, but chaining is greatly reduced or eliminated. Next, the **CHAINED_ROWS** table is cleared out, and **EMPLOYEES** is exported using the **Exp** utility, dropped, and then imported using the **Imp** utility. The export utility, **Exp**, exports user objects, tables, or an entire Oracle database, and the import utility, **Imp**, does just the opposite. The table is then reanalyzed to verify that no chained rows exist. If you have an OPS$ Oracle user name, you don't need to enter a password to connect to Oracle products. In my case, my Oracle user name is OPS$PCASSIDY, and I connect to Oracle products using the forward slash (/) instead of an Oracle user name and password. Not many corporations use this feature—at least that's the case with the 150 I have worked with. Out of the 150, maybe four or five customers use this feature. This feature makes it easier for a user to log in; however, if a user is logged on his machine and then leaves the office, a security breach is possible because all Oracle users with OPS$ accounts realize **sqlplus /** will log them into SQL*Plus.

Listing 13.2 Correct chaining using **exp/imp**.

```
SQL> ALTER TABLE EMPLOYEES PCTFREE 20;
Table altered.

SQL> TRUNCATE TABLE CHAINED_ROWS;
Table truncated.

SQL> EXIT

> exp / tables=employees file=emp.dmp

> sqlplus /

SQL> DROP TABLE EMPLOYEES;
Table dropped.

SQL> EXIT

> imp / file=emp.dmp full=y

> sqlplus /

SQL> ANALYZE TABLE EMPLOYEES
  2           LIST CHAINED ROWS
  3           INTO CHAINED_ROWS;
Table analyzed.

SQL> SELECT COUNT(*)
     FROM CHAINED_ROWS;

COUNT(*)
--------
       0
```

Another method for eliminating row chaining is shown in Listing 13.3, which analyzes the table **EMPLOYEES**. Notice that 352 rows are chained. The table **HOLD_EMPS** is created to hold the chained rows. Next, the chained rows are deleted from the chained table and the **PCTFREE** setting is changed from 1 percent to 20 percent on the chained table **EMPLOYEES**, because many updates occur on this table. The chained rows are then inserted back into table **EMPLOYEES** from the table **HOLD_EMPS**. Note that all 448 rows are back in the **EMPLOYEES** table. Finally, all the existing rows from the table **CHAINED_ROWS** are truncated.

The **EMPLOYEES** table is then reanalyzed to verify that no rows are in the **CHAINED_ROWS** table. Because the number of rows in the **CHAINED_ROWS** table is zero, no chained rows exist in **EMPLOYEES** anymore, so the problem is fixed. This means queries on **EMPLOYEES** execute faster now.

Listing 13.3 Correct chaining using a temporary table.

```
SQL> ANALYZE TABLE EMPLOYEES
  2            LIST CHAINED ROWS
  3            INTO CHAINED_ROWS;
Table analyzed.

SQL> SELECT COUNT(*)
     FROM CHAINED_ROWS;

COUNT(*)
--------
     352

SQL> CREATE TABLE HOLD_EMPS
  2  AS SELECT *
  3  FROM   EMPLOYEES E,
  4         CHAINED_ROWS C
  5  WHERE E.ROWID = C.HEAD_ROWID;
Table created.

SQL> SELECT COUNT(*)
  2  FROM    HOLD_EMPS;

COUNT(*)
--------
     352

SQL> DELETE FROM EMPLOYEES
     WHERE  EMPLOYEES.ROWID
     IN(SELECT E.ROWID
        FROM   EMPLOYEES E,
               CHAINED_ROWS C
        WHERE E.ROWID = C.HEAD_ROWID);
352 rows deleted.
```

```
SQL> SELECT PCTFREE
     FROM   USER_TABLES
     WHERE  TABLE_NAME = 'EMPLOYEES';

PCT_FREE
--------
       1

SQL> ALTER TABLE EMPLOYEES
            PCTFREE 20;
Table altered.

SQL> INSERT INTO EMPLOYEES
  2  SELECT EMPNO,ENAME,JOB,MGR,
  3         HIREDATE,SAL,COMM,DEPTNO,
  4         C2,COMMENTS
  5  FROM   HOLD_EMPS;
352 rows created.

SQL> SELECT COUNT(*)
  2  FROM   EMPLOYEES;

COUNT(*)
--------
     448

SQL> COMMIT;
Commit complete.

SQL> TRUNCATE TABLE CHAINED_ROWS;
Table truncated.

SQL> ANALYZE TABLE EMPLOYEES
             LIST CHAINED ROWS
             INTO CHAINED_ROWS;
Table analyzed.

SQL> SELECT COUNT(*)
  2  FROM   CHAINED_ROWS;

COUNT(*)
--------
       0
```

Number Of Rows In A Table

You can determine the number of rows in a table in several ways. One way is to use the single group function COUNT(*). Listing 13.4 uses the COUNT(*) function.

Listing 13.4 Using COUNT(*).

```
SQL> SET TIMING ON
SQL> SELECT COUNT(*)
  2  FROM   STATS;

COUNT(*)
--------
 1000000

Elapsed: 00:00:46.77
```

You can also use the ANALYZE command to derive the number of rows in a table. In Listing 13.5, the STATS table is analyzed and a query is written to observe the contents of the NUM_ROWS column in USER_TABLES.

Listing 13.5 Number of rows using ANALYZE TABLE.

```
SQL> ANALYZE TABLE STATS
           COMPUTE STATISTICS;
Table analyzed.

Elapsed: 00:14:23.49

SQL> SELECT NUM_ROWS
  2  FROM   USER_TABLES
  3  WHERE  TABLE_NAME = 'STATS';

NUM_ROWS
--------
 1000000
```

Number Of Blocks In A Table

To determine the number of blocks in a table, you can use one of two methods. Listing 13.6 uses the group functions COUNT and DISTINCT on the combination of the block number and the file number. Oracle7 rowids permit the same block number in all database files. Therefore, you must concatenate the block number with the file number to retrieve unique blocks. **STATS** has 26,071 blocks that contain data.

Listing 13.6 Using **COUNT** and **DISTINCT**.

```
SQL> SELECT COUNT(DISTINCT SUBSTR(ROWID,1,8)
        || SUBSTR(ROWID,15,4)) BLKS_WITH_ROWS
     FROM   STATS;

BLKS_WITH_ROWS
--------------
         26071

Elapsed: 00:03:09.00
```

You can also use the **ANALYZE** command and a query on **USER_TABLES** to determine the total number of blocks in the table. Listing 13.7 shows how to analyze using **COMPUTE** and the query to retrieve the number of blocks in the **STATS** table. Note that the **ANALYZE TABLE** command indicates that 26,074 blocks exist; the **COUNT DISTINCT** query in Listing 13.6 shows 26,071 blocks. Using the functions **COUNT** and **DISTINCT** in the query returns the number of blocks actually containing data. Therefore, 26,071 blocks contain table data, two blocks are for overhead, and one block is empty.

Listing 13.7 Total number of blocks using **ANALYZE TABLE**.

```
SQL> ANALYZE TABLE STATS
                COMPUTE STATISTICS;
Table analyzed.

SQL> SELECT BLOCKS,
              EMPTY_BLOCKS
     FROM    USER_TABLES
     WHERE   TABLE_NAME = 'STATS';

BLOCKS EMPTY_BLOCKS
------ ------------
 26074            0
```

Average Row Length

To determine the average row length for a table, analyze the table, as in Listing 13.8 and then write a query, noting the value of the **AVG_ROW_LEN** column in the view **USER_TABLES**, **ALL_TABLES**, or **DBA_TABLES**. Or, if you ate a big breakfast, you can always write a query using the functions **AVG** and **VSIZE**. Each row in the table has 3 bytes of overhead, and every column has either 1 or 2 bytes of overhead, depending on the data type of the column and its size. For the **DEPT** table, all three columns have 1 byte of overhead. The number of bytes of overhead for each row is 3, and the column overhead for each row is 3. The average size of the data in all three columns is 14.25. Adding 3+3+14.25 gives you a sum of 20.25 bytes, which is only one-quarter of a byte different than the results of the **ANALYZE TABLE** command, which shows 20 bytes for the average row length.

Listing 13.8 Average row length using **ANALYZE TABLE**.

```
SQL> ANALYZE TABLE STATS
                COMPUTE STATISTICS;
Table analyzed.

SQL> SELECT AVG_ROW_LEN
  2  FROM   USER_TABLES
  3  WHERE  TABLE_NAME = 'STATS';

AVG_ROW_LEN
-----------
         47

SQL> ANALYZE TABLE DEPT
  2             COMPUTE STATISTICS;
Table analyzed.

SQL> SELECT AVG_ROW_LEN
  2  FROM   USER_TABLES
  3  WHERE  TABLE_NAME = 'DEPT';

AVG_ROW_LEN
-----------
         20

SQL> SELECT 3 ROW_OVERHEAD,
  2         3 *1 COL_OVERHEAD,
```

```
  3         AVG(VSIZE(DEPTNO))+AVG(VSIZE(DNAME))+
  4         AVG(VSIZE(LOC)) DATA_OVERHEAD
  5  FROM   DEPT;

ROW_OVERHEAD COL_OVERHEAD DATA_OVERHEAD
------------ ------------ -------------
           3            3         14.25
```

Extents

The goal for using Oracle objects is "larger and fewer extents." An extent is a contiguous set of Oracle blocks. More extents on a table means slower response time as the disk heads move from one spot on the disk to another to retrieve data. Listing 13.9 shows that the **BIG** table has 119 extents (out of a maximum of 121 for systems with a **DB_BLOCK_SIZE** of 2048 in the parameter file) and 90,000 rows. Clearly, the **BIG** table having 119 extents is not a good situation. Most Oracle experts agree that 10 is the largest number of extents a table or index should ever have. Therefore, the table **BIG** is exported. Note the huge amount of disk space in the size of the initial extent in the exported file—1,239,040 bytes. This occurs because the default for **COMPRESS** is "yes." Next, the table is dropped and then imported. Now 7 extents exist instead of 119. Note that the first extent is extent 0; therefore, extent 6 is really the seventh extent. This is a great reduction in the number of extents; queries against the **BIG** table will now execute faster. A full-table scan of the 90,000 rows in the **BIG** table requires 4 minutes and 19.49 seconds when there are 119 extents. When there are 7 extents, a full-table scan requires 3 minutes and 47.15 seconds. This is a savings of 32.34 seconds in response time for queries against the **BIG** table.

Listing 13.9 Extents.

```
SQL> SELECT MAX(EXTENT_ID)
  2  FROM   DBA_EXTENTS
  3  WHERE  SEGMENT_NAME = 'BIG';

MAX(EXTENT_ID)
--------------
           118

SQL> SELECT COUNT(*)
  2  FROM   BIG;
```

```
  COUNT(*)
----------
     90000

SQL> SELECT *
  2  FROM   BIG;

     BIGNO BNAME
---------- --------------------
     89992
     89993
     89994
     89995
     89996
     89997
     89998
     89999
     90000

90000 rows selected.

Elapsed: 00:04:19.49

SQL> SELECT INITIAL_EXTENT IX,
  2         NEXT_EXTENT NX,
  3         MIN_EXTENTS MINX,
  4         MAX_EXTENTS MAXX,
  5         PCT_INCREASE PCT
  6  FROM   USER_TABLES
  7  WHERE  TABLE_NAME = 'BIG';

        IX         NX       MINX       MAXX        PCT
---------- ---------- ---------- ---------- ----------
     10240      10240          7        121          0

SQL> EXIT

> exp / file=big.dmp log=bigc.dmp tables=big

> more big.dmp
CREATE TABLE "BIG"
("BIGNO" NUMBER(6, 0), "BNAME" VARCHAR2(20))
PCTFREE 10 PCTUSED 60 INITRANS 1 MAXTRANS 255
STORAGE(INITIAL     1239040
```

```
        NEXT         10240
        MINEXTENTS  7
        MAXEXTENTS  121
        PCTINCREASE 0
        FREELISTS   1
        FREELIST GROUPS 1) TABLESPACE "TEMP"

SQL> DROP TABLE BIG;
Table dropped.

SQL> EXIT

> imp / file=big.dmp full=y log=bigic.log

SQL> SELECT INITIAL_EXTENT IX,
  2         NEXT_EXTENT NX,
  3         MIN_EXTENTS MINX,
  4         MAX_EXTENTS MAXX,
  5         PCT_INCREASE PCT
  6  FROM   USER_TABLES
  7  WHERE  TABLE_NAME = 'BIG';

        IX         NX       MINX       MAXX        PCT
---------- ---------- ---------- ---------- ----------
   1239040      10240          7        121          0

SQL> SELECT COUNT(*)
  2  FROM   BIG;

  COUNT(*)
----------
     90000

SQL> SELECT MAX(EXTENT_ID)
  2  FROM   DBA_EXTENTS -- First Extent=0
  3  WHERE  SEGMENT_NAME = 'BIG';

MAX(EXTENT_ID)
--------------
             6

SQL> SELECT *
  2  FROM   BIG;
```

```
     BIGNO BNAME
---------- --------------------
     89992
     89993
     89994
     89995
     89996
     89997
     89998
     89999
     90000

90000 rows selected.

Elapsed: 00:03:47.15
```

Adding Disk Space To Tablespaces

Many times you'll run out of space in a tablespace. To correct this problem, you need to add a file to the tablespace, using the **ALTER TABLESPACE** command as shown in Listing 13.10, or resize one or more of the files in the tablespace using the **ALTER DATABASE** command. Both of these commands are very serious events in the life of your database. Only database administrators should ever enter these commands. The first command adds a 900MB file named pete_temp2.dbf to the tablespace TEMP. The **ALTER DATABASE DATAFILE** command assumes that the database file pete_temp2.dbf is 90MB, and it resizes this file to 120MB.

Listing 13.10 Enlarging tablespaces using **ALTER**.

```
SQL> ALTER TABLESPACE TEMP
     ADD DATAFILE '/disk0/oradata/7.3.2/pete_temp2.dbf'
     SIZE 900M;
Tablespace altered.

SQL> ALTER DATABASE DATAFILE
  2  '/disk0/oradata/7.3.2/pete_temp.dbf'
  3  RESIZE 120M;
Database altered.
```

If you don't like adding files to your database or resizing its existing files, you can use the **AUTOEXTEND** feature, shown in Listing 13.11. If no data files in your database are currently using the **AUTOEXTEND** feature, you receive error 942, indicating table **SYS.FILEXT$** does not exist. The table is created when a file is autoextended. You can see that the file pete_temp2.dbf is 41 MB. In Listing 13.11, the file is placed in **AUTOEXTEND** mode using the **ALTER DATABASE DATAFILE** command. This example allows Oracle to extend the file in increments of 10,000 bytes, up to a maximum file size of 44MB. Now the **SYS.FILEXT$** table exists, and you can identify all database files that are using the **AUTOEXTEND** feature.

Listing 13.11 Enlarging tablespaces using **AUTOEXTEND**.

```
SQL> !ls -l /disk0/oradata/7.3.2/pete_temp2.dbf
-rw-r-- 1 ora73 41945088 Nov 7 18:39
 /disk0/oradata/7.3.2/pete_temp2.dbf

SQL> SELECT V.NAME,
  2         F.MAXEXTEND,
  3         F.INC
  4  FROM   V$DBFILE V,
  5         SYS.FILEXT$ F
  6  WHERE  V.FILE# = F.FILE#;
        SYS.FILEXT$ F
            *
ERROR at line 5:
ORA-00942: table or view does not exist

SQL> ALTER DATABASE DATAFILE
  2  '/disk0/oradata/7.3.2/pete_temp2.dbf'
  3  AUTOEXTEND ON
  4  NEXT 10K
  5  MAXSIZE 44M;
Database altered.

SQL> SELECT V.NAME,
  2         F.MAXEXTEND,
  3         F.INC
  4  FROM   V$DBFILE V,
  5         SYS.FILEXT$ F
  6  WHERE  V.FILE# = F.FILE#;

NAME                                  MAXEXTEND INC
------------------------------------ --------- ---
/disk0/oradata/7.3.2/pete_temp2.dbf      22528   5
```

Preallocating Disk Space For Tables

If you want to manually preallocate an extent from a tablespace for a table, use the **ALTER TABLE** command, as shown in Listing 13.12. Here, a query is written that indicates the name of the tablespace the table is in and shows the database file(s) that are in the tablespace. In Listing 13.12, the **STATS** table is in the **STATS** tablespace, and the tablespace contains one database file named stats.dbf. Note that the file size of stats.dbf is 58MB and the amount of free space is 2,594 blocks. Next, an extent of 500K is preallocated for the **STATS** table. A query using **DBA_FREE_SPACE** reveals that 2,344 blocks are now free in the **STATS** tablespace. Subtracting 2,344 from 2,594 results in 250 Oracle blocks, which is 500K, because each Oracle block is 2,048 operating system bytes. The Unix **ls** command at the end of the listing shows that the operating system file is not changed by the **ALTER** command.

Listing 13.12 Preallocating extents for a table.

```
SQL> SELECT U.TABLESPACE_NAME,
  2  SUBSTR(F.FILE_NAME,1,35) "FILE NAME"
  3  FROM    USER_TABLES U,
  4          DBA_DATA_FILES F
  5  WHERE   U.TABLESPACE_NAME =
  6          F.TABLESPACE_NAME AND
  7          U.TABLE_NAME = 'STATS';

TABLESPACE_  FILE
NAME         NAME
-----------  -----------------------------------
STATS        /disk1/oradata/7.3.2/pete/stats.dbf

SQL> !ls -l /disk1/oradata/7.3.2/pete/stats.dbf
-rw-r-- 1 ora73 58722304 Nov 7 18:39
/disk1/oradata/7.3.2/pete/stats.dbf

SQL> COL TABLESPACE_NAME FORMAT A5
SQL> COL TABLESPACE_NAME HEADING TS

SQL> SELECT *
  2  FROM    DBA_FREE_SPACE
  3  WHERE   TABLESPACE_NAME = 'STATS';
```

```
TS     FILE_ID BLOCK_ID   BYTES  BLOCKS
----- ------- -------- ------- -------
STATS       4    26079 5312512    2594

SQL> ALTER TABLE STATS
  2  ALLOCATE EXTENT
  3  (SIZE 500K DATAFILE
  4  '/disk1/oradata/7.3.2/pete/stats.dbf');
Table altered.

SQL> SELECT *
  2  FROM   DBA_FREE_SPACE
  3  WHERE  TABLESPACE_NAME = 'STATS';

TS     FILE_ID BLOCK_ID   BYTES  BLOCKS
----- ------- -------- ------- -------
STATS       4    26329 4800512    2344

SQL> !ls -l /disk1/oradata/7.3.2/pete/stats.dbf
-rw-r-- 1 ora73 58722304 Nov 8 10:08
/disk1/oradata/7.3.2/pete/stats.dbf
```

Deallocating Empty Blocks From Tables

If a table has many empty blocks and you want to release them to the tablespace, use the **DEALLOCATE** clause of the **ALTER TABLE** command, as shown in Listing 13.13. To force empty blocks in the **STATS** table, 20,000 rows are deleted.

Listing 13.13 Releasing empty blocks in a table.

```
SQL> ANALYZE TABLE STATS
            COMPUTE STATISTICS;
Table analyzed.

SQL> SELECT BLOCKS,
  2         EMPTY_BLOCKS
  3  FROM   USER_TABLES
  4  WHERE  TABLE_NAME = 'STATS';
```

```
 BLOCKS EMPTY_BLOCKS
------- ------------
  26074            0

SQL> DELETE FROM STATS
  2  WHERE SNO
  3  BETWEEN 980001 AND 1000000;
20000 rows deleted.

SQL> SELECT *
  2  FROM   DBA_FREE_SPACE
  3  WHERE  TABLESPACE_NAME = 'STATS';

TS     FILE_ID BLOCK_ID   BYTES  BLOCKS
----- ------- -------- ------- -------
STATS        4    26329 4800512    2344
STATS        4    26079  512000     250

SQL> ALTER TABLE STATS
  2         DEALLOCATE UNUSED;
Table altered.
```

Coalescing Contiguous Extents

The goal for using tablespaces is "fewer and larger extents." However, as you create and drop tables, the extents for the tables return to the tablespace, and the tablespace becomes fragmented. Listing 13.14 begins with a query using **DBA_FREE_SPACE** and then indicates that the tablespace **STATS** has two extents free. A table named **FRAGMENTATION** is then created that requires six extents. The first extent requires 10 Oracle blocks, and the remaining five extents require 20 Oracle blocks. The output from **DBA_FREE_SPACE** now shows that 60 blocks are from one extent (250 – 60 = 190) and 50 blocks are from the other (2,344 – 2,294 = 50). The six extents allocated to the **FRAGMENTATION** table can be seen using **DBA_EXTENTS**. When the **FRAGMENTATION** table is dropped, six extents return to the **STATS** tablespace, which is fragmented temporarily. If the percent increase is not set to zero for the tablespace, the background process **smon** will automatically coalesce the tablespace. When coalescing occurs, neighboring contiguous extents are combined into one extent. However, the percent increase in this listing is zero for the **STATS** tablespace. The issue can be forced with the **ALTER**

TABLESPACE command, which makes the Oracle background process **smon** coalesce the **STATS** tablespace.

Listing 13.14 Coalescing.

```
SQL> SELECT *
  2  FROM   DBA_FREE_SPACE
  3  WHERE  TABLESPACE_NAME = 'STATS';

TS     FILE_ID BLOCK_ID   BYTES  BLOCKS
----- ------- -------- ------- -------
STATS        4    26329 4800512    2344
STATS        4    26079  512000     250

SQL> CREATE TABLE FRAGMENTATION
  2         (C1   NUMBER)
  3  STORAGE(INITIAL     20K
  4          NEXT        40K
  5          MINEXTENTS  6
  6          MAXEXTENTS  10
  7          PCTINCREASE 0)
  8  TABLESPACE STATS;
Table created.

SQL> SELECT *
  2  FROM   DBA_FREE_SPACE
  3  WHERE  TABLESPACE_NAME = 'STATS';

TS     FILE_ID BLOCK_ID   BYTES  BLOCKS
----- ------- -------- ------- -------
STATS        4    26139  389120     190
STATS        4    26379 4698112    2294

SQL> SELECT EXTENT_ID,
  2         BLOCK_ID,
  3         BLOCKS
  4  FROM   DBA_EXTENTS
  5  WHERE  SEGMENT_NAME = 'FRAGMENTATION'
  6  ORDER  BY 1,2;

EXTENT_ID BLOCK_ID  BLOCKS
--------- -------- -------
        0    26329      10
        1    26339      20
```

```
        2     26359       20
        3     26079       20
        4     26099       20
        5     26119       20

SQL> DROP TABLE FRAGMENTATION;
Table dropped.

SQL> SELECT *
  2  FROM   DBA_FREE_SPACE
  3  WHERE  TABLESPACE_NAME = 'STATS'
  4  ORDER  BY FILE_ID,
  5         BLOCK_ID;

TS    FILE_ID BLOCK_ID   BYTES  BLOCKS
----- ------- -------- ------- -------
STATS       4    26079   40960      20
STATS       4    26099   40960      20
STATS       4    26119   40960      20
STATS       4    26139  389120     190
STATS       4    26329   20480      10
STATS       4    26339   40960      20
STATS       4    26359   40960      20
STATS       4    26379 4698112    2294

SQL> SELECT PCT_INCREASE
  2  FROM   DBA_TABLESPACES
  3  WHERE  TABLESPACE_NAME = 'STATS';

PCT_INCREASE
------------
           0

SQL> ALTER TABLESPACE STATS
  2        COALESCE;
Tablespace altered.

SQL> SELECT *
  2  FROM   DBA_FREE_SPACE
  3  WHERE  TABLESPACE_NAME = 'STATS'
  4  ORDER  BY FILE_ID,
  5         BLOCK_ID;
```

```
TS     FILE_ID BLOCK_ID   BYTES BLOCKS
----- ------- -------- ------- ------
STATS       4    26079 5312512   2594
```

Striping

To manually stripe a table across disks in Oracle, you need to create a tablespace containing several disk files. Listing 13.15 stripes the table **INDY700** over five files. First, the tablespace **RACING** is created using five database files—each with a size of 100K and on different disk drives if possible. The table **INDY700** is created with a storage clause that uses **INITIAL** and **NEXT** extent sizes nearly as large as the file size of the five database files (95K); then, the number of minimum extents is set to 5, the number of files in the tablespace. This preallocates all five files to the **INDY700** table. Note that all five inserts place the rows in the same database file. Oracle does not insert the first row in the first file of the tablespace, the second row in the second file of the tablespace, and so on. Instead, one file fills and then the rows go into the next file in the tablespace until it is full, and so on.

Listing 13.15 Striping tables.

```
SQL> CREATE TABLESPACE RACING DATAFILE
  '/disk1/oradata/7.3.2/pete/r1.dbf' SIZE 100K,
  '/disk1/oradata/7.3.2/pete/r2.dbf' SIZE 100K,
  '/disk1/oradata/7.3.2/pete/r3.dbf' SIZE 100K,
  '/disk1/oradata/7.3.2/pete/r4.dbf' SIZE 100K,
  '/disk1/oradata/7.3.2/pete/r5.dbf' SIZE 100K;
Tablespace created.

SQL> CREATE TABLE INDY700
           (CARNO        VARCHAR2(4),
            COWNER       VARCHAR2(20),
            CHASSIS      VARCHAR2(3))
    STORAGE(INITIAL      95K
            NEXT         95K
            MINEXTENTS   5
            MAXEXTENTS   10
            PCTINCREASE  0)
    TABLESPACE RACING;
Table created.
```

```
SQL> INSERT INTO INDY700
  2  VALUES('99', 'BELINGER', 'OFY');
1 row created.

SQL> INSERT INTO INDY700
  2  VALUES('&CAR','&OWNER','&CHASSIS');
Enter value for car: 10
Enter value for owner: ZINK
Enter value for chassis: OFY
1 row created.

SQL> /
Enter value for car: 44
Enter value for owner: BROWN
Enter value for chassis: OFY
1 row created.

SQL> /
Enter value for car: 14
Enter value for owner: VUKY
Enter value for chassis: OFY
1 row created.

SQL> /
Enter value for car: 3
Enter value for owner: MEARS
Enter value for chassis: OFY
1 row created.

SQL> COMMIT;

SQL> SELECT ROWID, COWNER, CARNO
  2  FROM   INDY700;

ROWID              COWNER               CARNO
------------------ -------------------- -----
00000003.0000.000D BELINGER                99
00000003.0001.000D ZINK                    10
00000003.0002.000D BROWN                   44
00000003.0003.000D VUKY                    14
00000003.0004.000D MEARS                    3

SQL> SELECT SUBSTR(NAME,1,35) "File"
  2  FROM   V$DBFILE
  3  WHERE  FILE# = 13;
```

```
File
---------------------------------
/disk1/oradata/7.3.2/pete/r3.dbf
```

The High-Water Mark

The high-water mark for a table is significant when Oracle performs a full-table scan on the table. The high-water mark of a table indicates the maximum amount of space used by the table, much like the water mark left in a family bathtub after several children took a bath, except that high-water mark is normally a dirty ring around the tub. Regardless of the number of empty blocks, Oracle scans all the way to the high-water mark for a full-table scan. Use the Oracle-supplied package **DBMS_SPACE** and the procedure **UNUSED_SPACE**. Listing 13.16 shows a quick way to view the parameters and their modes, and data types in the procedure **UNUSED_SPACE** in the package **DBMS_SPACE** to determine the amount of unused space for a table. The procedure uses 10 parameters—three as input and seven as output. This means seven variables must be declared for the procedure to place the output values. (You can enter **VAR** to observe the variables currently defined in your session.) Next, the procedure in the package is executed and the output variables are prefaced with a colon (:) so that PL/SQL can return values into the variables. Using the output of this package and procedure as well as the data dictionary view **DBA_EXTENTS**, you can determine the high-water mark for a table. Because no unused blocks exist (**UBLKS=0**) and all blocks are used, the high-water mark is at the last block of the **STATS** table. The last used extent block ID from **DBMS_SPACE** is 18,442 (**LUXBID**), the same as the **BLOCK_ID** column from **DBA_EXTENTS**. Also, **LUBLK** is equal to the **BLOCKS** column of **DBA_EXTENTS** (7,635).

Listing 13.16 Using the package **DBMS_SPACE**.

```
SQL> DESC DBMS_SPACE.UNUSED_SPACE
PROCEDURE DBMS_SPACE.UNUSED_SPACE
 Argument Name                  Type     In/Out Default?
 ------------------------------ -------- ------ --------
 SEGMENT_OWNER                  VARCHAR2 IN
 SEGMENT_NAME                   VARCHAR2 IN
 SEGMENT_TYPE                   VARCHAR2 IN
 TOTAL_BLOCKS                   NUMBER   OUT
 TOTAL_BYTES                    NUMBER   OUT
```

```
 UNUSED_BLOCKS              NUMBER   OUT
 UNUSED_BYTES               NUMBER   OUT
 LAST_USED_EXTENT_FILE_ID   NUMBER   OUT
 LAST_USED_EXTENT_BLOCK_ID  NUMBER   OUT
 LAST_USED_BLOCK            NUMBER   OUT

SQL> VARIABLE TBLKS  NUMBER
SQL> VARIABLE TBYTES NUMBER
SQL> VARIABLE UBLKS  NUMBER
SQL> VARIABLE UBYTES NUMBER
SQL> VARIABLE LUXFID NUMBER
SQL> VARIABLE LUXBID NUMBER
SQL> VARIABLE LUBLK  NUMBER

SQL> VAR
variable   tblks
datatype   NUMBER

variable   tbytes
datatype   NUMBER

variable   ublks
datatype   NUMBER

variable   ubytes
datatype   NUMBER

variable   luxfid
datatype   NUMBER

variable   luxbid
datatype   NUMBER

variable   lublk
datatype   NUMBER

SQL> EXECUTE DBMS_SPACE.UNUSED_SPACE(    -
  2          'OPS$PCASSIDY',              -
  3          'STATS',                     -
  4          'TABLE',                     -
  5          :TBLKS,                      -
  6          :TBYTES,                     -
  7          :UBLKS,                      -
  8          :UBYTES,                     -
```

```
           :LUXFID,                  -
           :LUXBID,                  -
           :LUBLK)

SQL> @cor13_42

PL/SQL procedure successfully completed.

SQL> PRINT TBLKS

 TBLKS
------
 26075

SQL> PRINT UBLKS

 UBLKS
------
     0

SQL> PRINT LUXFID

LUXFID
------
     4

SQL> PRINT LUXBID

LUXBID
------
 18442

SQL> PRINT LUBLK

 LUBLK
------
  7635

SQL> SELECT EXTENT_ID,
            BLOCK_ID,
            BLOCKS
     FROM   DBA_EXTENTS
     WHERE  SEGMENT_NAME = 'STATS'
     ORDER  BY 1,2;
```

```
EXTENT_ID BLOCK_ID BLOCKS
--------- -------- ------
        0        2   9220
        1     9222   9220
        2    18442   7635
```

Separating Data From Indexes

For better throughput, you should always separate your indexes from the table data by placing the indexes in one tablespace and the data in another. Listing 13.17 shows you how to separate the data from the index using the **USING INDEX TABLESPACE** clause of the **CREATE TABLE** or **ALTER TABLE** statement with the primary key constraint. Oracle automatically creates a unique index on the **RACENO** column of the **IRL** table and does not allow nulls in the **RACENO** column. The name of the unique index is the same as the name of the primary key constraint—**PK_IRL_RACENO**. The **USING INDEX TABLESPACE INDEX_TS** clause tells Oracle to place the unique index in the tablespace **INDEX_TS** instead of the user default tablespace.

If you neglect to tell Oracle where to place the primary key unique index, the index is placed in the user default table space.

If you disable a primary key constraint, the index is dropped. When you enable the primary key constraint, use the **USING INDEX TABLESPACE** clause or else the unique index is created in the default tablespace of the user. Note that you can refer to the primary key constraint in the **ALTER TABLE** command as either **PRIMARY KEY** or the actual constraint name—in this case, **PK_IRL_RACENO**.

Listing 13.17 Separating data from indexes.

```
SQL> CREATE TABLE IRL
   (RACENO   NUMBER(4,0),
    RDATE    DATE,
    CITY     VARCHAR2(20),
       CONSTRAINT PK_IRL_RACENO
       PRIMARY KEY(RACENO)
       USING INDEX
       TABLESPACE INDEX_TS
       STORAGE(INITIAL   10K    -- Storage
               NEXT      10K    -- Clause
```

```
 11               MINEXTENTS  1    -- For
 12               MAXEXTENTS  4    -- Unique
 13               PCTINCREASE 0)) -- Index
 14  TABLESPACE STATS
 15  STORAGE(INITIAL   10K         -- Storage
 16          NEXT      10K         -- Clause
 17          MINEXTENTS  1         -- For
 18          MAXEXTENTS  4         -- Table
 19          PCTINCREASE 0);
Table created.

SQL> DESC IRL
Name   Null?    Type
------ -------- ----
RACENO NOT NULL NUMBER(4)
RDATE           DATE
CITY            VARCHAR2(20)

SQL> SELECT INDEX_NAME,
  2         UNIQUENESS,
  3         TABLESPACE_NAME
  4  FROM   USER_INDEXES
  5  WHERE  TABLE_NAME = 'IRL';

INDEX_NAME    UNIQUENES TABLESPACE_NAME
------------- --------- ---------------
PK_IRL_RACENO UNIQUE    INDEX_TS

SQL> DROP TABLE IRL;
Table dropped.

SQL> SELECT USERNAME,  -- Default Ts Is TEMP
  2         DEFAULT_TABLESPACE "DEF TS",
  3         TEMPORARY_TABLESPACE "TEMP TS"
  4  FROM   USER_USERS;

USERNAME     DEF TS TEMP TS
------------ ------ ------
OPS$PCASSIDY TEMP   TEMP

SQL> CREATE TABLE IRL          -- TEMP TS
  2     (RACENO   NUMBER(4,0),
  3      RDATE    DATE,
  4      CITY     VARCHAR2(20),
  5  CONSTRAINT PK_IRL_RACENO -- TEMP TS
```

```
PRIMARY KEY(RACENO));
Table created.

SQL> SELECT TABLESPACE_NAME
     FROM   USER_TABLES
     WHERE  TABLE_NAME = 'IRL';

TABLESPACE_NAME
--------------
TEMP

SQL> SELECT INDEX_NAME,
            UNIQUENESS,
            TABLESPACE_NAME
     FROM   USER_INDEXES
     WHERE  TABLE_NAME = 'IRL';

INDEX_NAME    UNIQUENES TABLESPACE_NAME
------------- --------- --------------
PK_IRL_RACENO UNIQUE    TEMP

SQL> DROP TABLE IRL;
Table dropped.

SQL> CREATE TABLE IRL
        (RACENO   NUMBER(4,0),
         RDATE    DATE,
         CITY     VARCHAR2(20),
     CONSTRAINT PK_IRL_RACENO
     PRIMARY KEY(RACENO)
     USING INDEX
     TABLESPACE INDEX_TS
     STORAGE(INITIAL   10K
             NEXT      10K
             MINEXTENTS  1
             MAXEXTENTS  4
             PCTINCREASE 0))
     TABLESPACE STATS
     STORAGE(INITIAL   10K
             NEXT      10K
             MINEXTENTS  1
             MAXEXTENTS  4
             PCTINCREASE 0);
Table created.
```

```
SQL> ALTER TABLE IRL
  2         DISABLE PRIMARY KEY;
Table altered.

SQL> SELECT INDEX_NAME, -- Index
  2         UNIQUENESS, -- Dropped
  3         TABLESPACE_NAME
  4  FROM   USER_INDEXES
  5  WHERE  TABLE_NAME = 'IRL';
no rows selected

SQL> ALTER TABLE IRL
  2         ENABLE PRIMARY KEY;
Table altered.

SQL> SELECT INDEX_NAME,
  2         UNIQUENESS,
  3         TABLESPACE_NAME
  4  FROM   USER_INDEXES
  5  WHERE  TABLE_NAME = 'IRL';

INDEX_NAME    UNIQUENES TABLESPACE_NAME
------------- --------- ---------------
PK_IRL_RACENO UNIQUE    TEMP

SQL> ALTER TABLE IRL  -- Drop Unique Index
  2     DISABLE CONSTRAINT PK_IRL_RACENO;
Table altered.

SQL> ALTER TABLE IRL
  2         ENABLE PRIMARY KEY
  3         USING INDEX
  4         TABLESPACE INDEX_TS
  5         STORAGE(INITIAL     10K
  6                 NEXT        10K
  7                 MINEXTENTS    2
  8                 MAXEXTENTS    4
  9                 PCTINCREASE   0);
Table altered.

SQL> SELECT INDEX_NAME,
  2         UNIQUENESS,
  3         TABLESPACE_NAME
  4  FROM   USER_INDEXES
  5  WHERE  TABLE_NAME = 'IRL';
```

```
INDEX_NAME     UNIQUENES TABLESPACE_NAME
-------------- --------- ---------------
PK_IRL_RACENO UNIQUE     INDEX_TS
```

To Cache Or Not To Cache

Normally, full-table scans don't cause blocks to appear in the MRU (most recently used) end of the LRU (least recently used) list, which the database writer maintains for blocks in the database buffer cache. However, if you create or alter the table using the **CACHE** option, the blocks of the table appear in the MRU end of the LRU list after a full-table scan. This means that other queries can perform logical reads on the block—because the block is probably already in memory—instead of performing physical reads from the disk, which are more expensive. Listing 13.18 assumes that many applications use the **INDY700** table. Also, the block should appear in memory after the first full-table scan so that other queries will find the block in the database buffer cache instead of on the disk.

Because the **CACHE** option is not on the **INDY700** table, the table should be altered and this option activated. A query using **V$DB_OBJECT_CACHE** reveals that the table is not in memory yet, because no full-table scans have taken place on **INDY700**. Next, a full-table scan is performed on **INDY700** and **V$DB_OBJECT_CACHE** is used again in the query. This time, Oracle finds the table in the database buffer pool.

Listing 13.18 Caching small tables.

```
SQL> ANALYZE TABLE INDY700
  2           COMPUTE STATISTICS;
Table analyzed.

SQL> SELECT NUM_ROWS,
  2           CACHE
  3  FROM    USER_TABLES
  4  WHERE   TABLE_NAME = 'INDY700';

NUM_ROWS CACHE
-------- ----
       4 N

SQL> ALTER TABLE INDY700 CACHE;
Table altered.
```

```
SQL> SELECT NUM_ROWS,
  2         CACHE
  3  FROM   USER_TABLES
  4  WHERE  TABLE_NAME = 'INDY700';

NUM_ROWS CACHE
-------- -----
       5     Y

SQL> COL KEPT FORMAT A4
SQL> SELECT SUBSTR(OWNER,1,12) "Owner",
  2         SUBSTR(NAME,1,12) "Name",
  3         TYPE,
  4         KEPT,
  5         NAMESPACE
  6  FROM   V$DB_OBJECT_CACHE
  7  WHERE  NAME = 'INDY700';

no rows selected

SQL> SELECT *  -- Full Table Scan
  2  FROM   INDY700;

CARN COWNER              CHASSIS
---- ------------------- -------
99   BELINGER            OFY
10   ZINK                OFY
44   BROWN               OFY
14   VUKY                OFY
3    MEARS               IRL

SQL> SELECT SUBSTR(OWNER,1,12) "Owner",
  2         SUBSTR(NAME,1,12) "Name",
  3         TYPE,
  4         KEPT,
  5         NAMESPACE
  6  FROM   V$DB_OBJECT_CACHE
  7  WHERE  NAME = 'INDY700';

Owner        Name    TYPE  KEPT NAMESPACE
------------ ------- ----  ---- ---------------
OPS$PCASSIDY INDY700 TABLE NO   TABLE/PROCEDURE
```

Summary

To prevent row chaining, you need to verify the accuracy of **PCTFREE** for your tables; also, you need to verify that the number of extents for your tables is 10 or less. When a tablespace runs out of disk space, don't slap another file on the tablespace like Oracle database administrators did in the past. Now, you can add more disk space to a tablespace by using the **ALTER DATABASE DATAFILE** command and resizing the database file. For extremely large tables, consider striping over several disks, and always separate your indexes from the table data by placing the indexes and the data in different tablespaces on different devices. Also, for small tables that are accessed frequently, consider caching them.

Oracle8 Programming

CHAPTER 14

This chapter contains many very practical SQL statements used by database administrators, developers, and end users. In addition, this chapter teaches you a lot of survival statements you can use to take full advantage of Oracle8.

Oracle8 Programming

Your Environment

You must know a lot about the Oracle8 environment. Listing 14.1 shows you how to identify release information about your database. Use the **CONNECT** command to connect to your Oracle8 database. Note that an error message appears if the service name is not correct. The **DEF** command shows what editor (if any) you are using, the release version (Oracle8.0.3.0.0), the options in effect (partitioning and objects), and the release number of PL/SQL (8.0.3.0.0). Another way to see the release versions and options is to use the **V$VERSION** dynamic performance view.

Listing 14.1 Determining which release you're running.

```
SQL> CONNECT SYSTEM/MANAGER@ORA802
ERROR: ORA-12154: TNS:could not resolve service name
SQL> CONNECT SYSTEM/MANAGER@ORA803
Connected.

SQL> DEF
DEFINE _EDITOR          = "vi" (CHAR)
DEFINE _O_VERSION       = "Oracle8 Enterprise
Edition Release 8.0.3.0.0 - Production
With the Partitioning and Objects options
PL/SQL Release 8.0.3.0.0 - Production" (CHAR)
DEFINE _O_RELEASE       = "800030000" (CHAR)
DEFINE _RC              = "0" (CHAR)

SQL> SELECT *
  2  FROM   V$VERSION;

BANNER
----------------------------------------
Oracle8 Enterprise Edition Release 8.0.3.0.0
```

```
- Production
PL/SQL Release 8.0.3.0.0 - Production
CORE Version 4.0.3.0.0 - Production
TNS for 32-bit Windows: Version 8.0.3.0.0
 - Production
NLSRTL Version 3.3.0.0.0 Production
```

If you work with more than one Oracle database, use **V$DATABASE** to view the current database, as shown in Listing 14.2. The name of the current database is ORACLE, and it has been around since 17-SEP-97.

Listing 14.2 Determining the database you're using.

```
SQL> DESC V$DATABASE
 Name                            Null?    Type
 ------------------------------- -------- -----------
 DBID                                     NUMBER
 NAME                                     VARCHAR2(9)
 CREATED                                  DATE
 RESETLOGS_CHANGE#                        NUMBER
 RESETLOGS_TIME                           DATE
 PRIOR_RESETLOGS_CHANGE#                  NUMBER
 PRIOR_RESETLOGS_TIME                     DATE
 LOG_MODE                                 VARCHAR2(12)
 CHECKPOINT_CHANGE#                       NUMBER
 ARCHIVE_CHANGE#                          NUMBER
 CONTROLFILE_TYPE                         VARCHAR2(7)
 CONTROLFILE_CREATED                      DATE
 CONTROLFILE_SEQUENCE#                    NUMBER
 CONTROLFILE_CHANGE#                      NUMBER
 CONTROLFILE_TIME                         DATE
 OPEN_RESETLOGS                           VARCHAR2(11)
 VERSION_TIME                             DATE

SQL> SELECT DBID,
  2         NAME,
  3         CREATED,
  4         LOG_MODE,
  5         CONTROLFILE_TYPE CTYPE,
  6         OPEN_RESETLOGS "RESET LOGS"
  7  FROM   V$DATABASE;

   DBID NAME   CREATED   LOG_MODE     CTYPE   RESET LOGS
------- ------ --------- ------------ ------- ----------
1.2E+09 ORACLE 17-SEP-97 NOARCHIVELOG CURRENT NOT ALLOWED
```

Listing 14.3 indicates that Oracle8 has many more data dictionary views than Oracle7. Oracle8 has 594 data dictionary views for this database, whereas Oracle7 might have anywhere from 154 to 278.

Listing 14.3 The number of data dictionary views for Oracle8.

```
SQL> SELECT COUNT(*)
  2  FROM   DICT;

COUNT(*)
--------
     594
```

You can use the public synonym **DICT** or the view name **DICTIONARY** to return all data dictionary names that contain a certain string in the **TABLE_NAME** column. Listing 14.4 prompts for a string, and "partition" returns six data dictionary views that have the string "partition" in their names. Eight views contain the name **OBJECTS**.

Listing 14.4 Data dictionary views by topic.

```
SQL> SELECT TABLE_NAME
  2  FROM   DICT
  3  WHERE  TABLE_NAME LIKE
  4    '%' || UPPER('&TN') || '%';

Enter value for tn: partition

TABLE_NAME
------------------------------

ALL_IND_PARTITIONS
ALL_TAB_PARTITIONS
DBA_IND_PARTITIONS
DBA_TAB_PARTITIONS
USER_IND_PARTITIONS
USER_TAB_PARTITIONS

SQL> SELECT TABLE_NAME
     FROM   DICT
     WHERE TABLE_NAME LIKE
      "%" || UPPER("&TN") || "%";

Enter value for tn: objects
```

```
TABLE_NAME
------------------------------
ALL_OBJECTS
ALL_REPGENOBJECTS
DBA_ANALYZE_OBJECTS
DBA_EXP_OBJECTS
DBA_OBJECTS
DBA_REPGENOBJECTS
USER_OBJECTS
USER_REPGENOBJECTS
```

To display all the data, redo, and control files in your database, use the query shown in Listing 14.5. Three dynamic performance views—**V$DATAFILE**, **V$LOGFILE**, and **V$CONTROLFILE**—provide the full path names for all three types of files in Oracle. You can use **V$DBFILE** as well as **V$DATAFILE** to view the full path names of all database files in your database. The database files do not include the control files or the redo log files.. The set operator **UNION** combines three queries into one query. The Oracle8 database in this listing has 10 files—one control file, two redo logs, and seven database files.

Listing 14.5 Database, redo, and control files.

```
SQL>SELECT SUBSTR(NAME, 1, 70)
FROM V$DATAFILE   -- NT Platform
UNION
SELECT SUBSTR(MEMBER, 1, 70)
FROM V$LOGFILE
UNION
SELECT SUBSTR(NAME, 1, 70)
FROM V$CONTROLFILE
ORDER  BY  1;

SUBSTR(NAME,1,70)
------------------------------
C:\ORANT\DATABASE\CTL1ORCL.ORA
C:\ORANT\DATABASE\EXT1ORCL.ORA
C:\ORANT\DATABASE\EXT2ORCL.ORA
C:\ORANT\DATABASE\EXT3ORCL.ORA
C:\ORANT\DATABASE\LOG1ORCL.ORA
C:\ORANT\DATABASE\LOG2ORCL.ORA
C:\ORANT\DATABASE\RBS1ORCL.ORA
```

```
C:\ORANT\DATABASE\SYS1ORCL.ORA
C:\ORANT\DATABASE\TMP1ORCL.ORA
C:\ORANT\DATABASE\USR1ORCL.ORA
```

Listing 14.6 shows the object type and the number of each object type that exists in the database. Note that you must have DBA privileges before you can see the views whose names start with "DBA" or "V$."

Listing 14.6 Displaying the count of each type of object.

```
SQL> SELECT OBJECT_TYPE,
  2         COUNT(*)
  3  FROM   DBA_OBJECTS
  4  GROUP  BY OBJECT_TYPE;

OBJECT_TYPE     COUNT(*)
--------------- --------
CLUSTER                9
DIRECTORY              1
INDEX                226
INDEX PARTITION        3
LIBRARY                5
PACKAGE              161
PACKAGE BODY         156
PROCEDURE              7
SEQUENCE              23
SYNONYM              820
TABLE                206
TABLE PARTITION        6
TRIGGER                3
TYPE                  63
TYPE BODY              2
UNDEFINED             16
VIEW                1019
```

To display the current settings for the parameters in the init.ora file, write a query using the **V$PARAMETER** dynamic performance table. Listing 14.7 shows the current settings for all parameters containing the string "object". As you can see, two parameters pertain to objects.

Listing 14.7 Displaying the current settings of init.ora.

```
SQL> get ora
  1  SELECT SUBSTR(NAME,1,30) PARAM,
  2  SUBSTR(VALUE,1,25) CURRENT_SETTING
  3  FROM   V$PARAMETER
     WHERE  NAME LIKE '%' ||
            LOWER('&Parameter') || '%';

Enter value for parameter: object

PARAM                          CURRENT_SETTING
----------------------------- ---------------
object_cache_optimal_size      102400
object_cache_max_size_percent 10
```

Oracle provides you with a set of packages named DBMS plus an extension name, such as **DBMS_OUTPUT**. Listing 14.8 shows 20 of the 87 package names in the database.

Listing 14.8 Displaying Oracle DBMS packages.

```
SQL> SELECT OBJECT_NAME   -- 87 Packages
  2  FROM   DBA_OBJECTS   -- Show 20 Here
  3  WHERE  OBJECT_NAME LIKE 'DBMS%'
  4         AND
  5         OBJECT_TYPE = 'PACKAGE'
  6         AND ROWNUM < 21
  7         ORDER BY 1;

OBJECT_NAME
-----------------------------
DBMSOBJG
DBMSOBJGWRAPPER
DBMS_ALERT
DBMS_APPLICATION_INFO
DBMS_AQ
DBMS_AQADM
DBMS_AQ_IMPORT_INTERNAL
DBMS_ASYNCRPC_PUSH
DBMS_BACKUP_RESTORE
DBMS_DDL
DBMS_DEBUG
DBMS_DEFER
DBMS_DEFERGEN
```

```
DBMS_DEFERGEN_AUDIT
DBMS_DEFERGEN_INTERNAL
DBMS_DEFERGEN_LOB
DBMS_DEFERGEN_PRIORITY
DBMS_DEFERGEN_RESOLUTION
DBMS_DEFERGEN_UTIL
DBMS_DEFERGEN_WRAP
```

Pseudocolumns

Oracle provides pseudocolumns to make your job easier. Pseudocolumns are not stored in any table, but can be referenced in all Oracle products. Some of the most common pseudocolumns are **SYSDATE**, **USER**, **UID**, **LEVEL**, **CURRVAL**, and **NEXTVAL**. Pseudocolumns are used in many SQL statements. For example, you can use the pseudocolumn **SYSDATE** to display the current date and time. Listing 14.9 shows **SYSDATE** in a **SELECT** statement using the **DUAL** table (because you only want to see the date once). The table named **DUAL** exists in every Oracle8 database and has since the first version of Oracle. It is a very special table, since it has only one column, named **DUMMY**, and contains only one row. Whenever you want to see something displayed once, use the **DUAL** table. I use it for calculations like summing three numbers. For example, the code **SELECT 12.25 + 2.75 + 30 FROM DUAL** returns a value of 45 one time. If this same query uses the **EMP** table, that contains 14 rows, you see 45 displayed 14 times, once for each row in Oracle's **EMP** table. The second example shows how to strip the time out of **SYSDATE** by using the function **TO_CHAR** with the mask HH:MI:SS (HH for hours, MI for minutes, and SS for seconds). The third example shows **SYSDATE** being used in an **INSERT** statement for a new employee named "THE PISTOL." "THE PISTOL" is not returned because the actual hour, minute, and second of the insert is stored in the **HIREDATE** column, and the **WHERE** clause does not match the time because time has transpired. Because the new employee "THE DEBBO" uses the string "12-NOV-97" for the date, Oracle finds a match—the default time for date strings is 12:00:00, and that's the contents of the **HIREDATE** column for each row of the **EMP** table. To strip off the time from a date data type column, use **LIKE** or **TRUNC**, and you'll see all the employees who were hired on 12-NOV-97. If you want to see the time to the left of the SQL prompt, just enter the command **SET TIME ON**.

Listing 14.9 Using **SYSDATE**.

```
SQL> SELECT SYSDATE
     FROM    DUAL;

SYSDATE
---------------
12-NOV-97

SQL> SELECT TO_CHAR(SYSDATE, 'HH:MI:SS') TIME
     FROM      DUAL;

TIME
-----------
02:15:44

SQL> INSERT INTO EMP
  2         (EMPNO,ENAME,HIREDATE) -- Actual Time
  3          VALUES(5555, 'THE PISTOL', SYSDATE);
1 row created.

SQL> INSERT INTO EMP
  2         (EMPNO,ENAME,HIREDATE) -- 12:00:00
  3          VALUES(7777, 'THE DEBBO', '12-NOV-97');
1 row created.

SQL> SELECT ENAME, HIREDATE
  2  FROM   EMP
  3  WHERE  HIREDATE = '12-NOV-97';

ENAME      HIREDATE
---------- ---------
THE DEBBO  12-NOV-97

SQL> -- WHAT HAPPENED TO "THE PISTOL" ?

SQL> SELECT ENAME,HIREDATE,
  2         TO_CHAR(HIREDATE,'HH:MI:SS') "Time"
  3  FROM   EMP
  4  WHERE  HIREDATE LIKE "12-NOV-97";

ENAME      HIREDATE  Time
---------- --------- --------
```

```
THE PISTOL 12-NOV-97 02:16:04
THE DEBBO  12-NOV-97 12:00:00

SQL> SELECT ENAME,HIREDATE,
  2  TO_CHAR (HIREDATE, 'HH:MI:SS') "Time"
  3  FROM   EMP
  4  WHERE TRUNC (HIREDATE) = '12-NOV-97';

ENAME      HIREDATE  Time
---------- --------- --------
THE PISTOL 12-NOV-97 02:16:04
THE DEBBO  12-NOV-97 12:00:00

SQL> SHOW TIME
time OFF
SQL> SET TIME ON
17:08:35 SQL> -- NOTICE WHAT HAPPENS
17:08:47 SQL> -- EVERY TIME I HIT ENTER
17:08:59 SQL> -- SEE HOW THE TIME CHANGES
17:09:08 SQL>
```

You can also use the pseudocolumn **SYSDATE** in date calculations. For example, if you add a positive number to a date, Oracle returns a date in the future. Forty-three days from now (November 12, 1997) is December 25, 1997. Also, if you subtract a number from a date, Oracle returns a date from the past. If you subtract a date column (such as **HIREDATE**) from **SYSDATE**, Oracle returns the number of days between the contents of the date column and today's date. Divide that total by 7 to derive the number of weeks. To display the number of months between the date column and **SYSDATE**, use the function **MONTHS_BETWEEN**, and for the number of years between the date column and **SYSDATE**, divide the result of the **MONTHS_BETWEEN** function by 12. The last example in Listing 14.10 displays the number of days Roonie has been alive. Use the function **TO_DATE** when using dates that are in a different format than the Oracle default date format, DD-MON-YY.

Listing 14.10 Using **SYSDATE** in date calculations.

```
SQL> SELECT SYSDATE + 43
  2  FROM   DUAL;
```

```
SYSDATE+4
-----------------
25-DEC-97

SQL>  SELECT ENAME,
      HIREDATE,
      TRUNC (SYSDATE - HIREDATE) "Days",
      TRUNC ((SYSDATE - HIREDATE)/7) "Weeks",
      TRUNC(MONTHS_BETWEEN(SYSDATE,HIREDATE)  "Mos",
      TRUNC ((MONTHS_BETWEEN (SYSDATE,
                 HIREDATE))/12) "Years"
      FROM   EMP          -- Only Want To See One Row
      WHERE  ENAME = "SMITH";

ENAME      HIREDATE    Days  Weeks   Mos   Years
---------- --------- ------ ------ ------ -------
SMITH      17-DEC-80   6174    882    202      16

SQL> COL "Roonie" FORMAT 99,999

SQL> SELECT   TRUNC(SYSDATE-TO_DATE('01/29/76',
                'MM/DD/YY')) "Roonie"
     FROM     DUAL;

 Roonie
-------
  7,958
```

If you're working with a recursive table (that is, a table with a foreign key column that references the primary key column) and both columns are in the same table, you can write self-joins using the recursive table, or you can write bill of materials or corporation hierarchy reports using the pseudocolumn **LEVEL** with the function **LPAD** to indent the output. A bill of materials report shows assemblies, subassemblies, and all parts that are part of an assembly. For example, a race car has several subassemblies like the chassis, the engine, and the body. Parts that belong to the engine subassembly are pistons, valves, cylinders, and gaskets. Listing 14.11 illustrates the following information: The "Sprint Car" row is LEVEL 1, because it's at the highest level of the tree. The "Engine" entry is LEVEL 3, because it's a component of "Chassis" at LEVEL 2, and "Chassis" is a component of "Sprint Car" at LEVEL 1. The **LPAD** function places spaces to the left of the part name. The number of spaces to the left of the part name depends on the result of LEVEL * 3. The

CONNECT BY and **START WITH** clauses cause Oracle to walk the tree. The **CONNECT BY** clause controls the direction of the walk (either up or down), and the **START WITH** clause tells Oracle where to begin walking. Oracle's **EMP** table is recursive because the **MGR** column is a foreign key that references the primary key column **EMPNO**. Another recursive table is **PLAN_TABLE**, which is used with the Explain Plan command. The primary key column in **PLAN_TABLE** is **ID**, and the foreign key column is **PARENT_ID**.

Listing 14.11 Using **LEVEL** with **LPAD**.

```
SQL> SELECT *
  2  FROM   PARTS;

   PNO PNAME            COMPONENT_OF
------ ---------------- ------------
     1 SPRINT CAR
     2 CHASSIS                     1
     3 AXLES                       2
     4 ENGINE                      2
     5 SKINS                       2
     6 DASH                        2
     7 OIL GAGE                    6
     8 TEMP GAGE                   6
     9 STEARING COLUMN             2
    10 STEARING WHEEL              9
    11 POP OFF DEVICE             10
    12 WHEELS                      3
    13 WING                       14
    14 ROLL CAGE                   2
    15 BRAKES                      3
    16 FUEL CELL                   2
    17 SHUT OFF SWITCH             6
    18 SEAT                       19
    19 FLOOR BOARD                 2
    20 FRONT WING                  2
    21 FUEL CAP                   16

SQL> COL "Bill Of Materials" FORMAT A30
  2  SELECT  LPAD(' ', 3*LEVEL)
  3         || PNAME "Bill Of Materials"
  4  FROM    PARTS
  5  CONNECT BY PRIOR PNO = COMPONENT_OF
  6  START   WITH PNAME   = 'SPRINT CAR'
```

```
SQL> @corbom

Bill Of Materials
------------------------------
   SPRINT CAR
      CHASSIS
         AXLES
            WHEELS
            BRAKES
         ENGINE
         SKINS
         DASH
            OIL GAGE
            TEMP GAGE
            SHUT OFF SWITCH
         STEARING COLUMN
            STEARING WHEEL
               POP OFF DEVICE
         ROLL CAGE
            WING
         FUEL CELL
            FUEL CAP
         FLOOR BOARD
            SEAT
         FRONT WING

SQL> COL Hierarchy FORMAT A18
SQL> SELECT  LPAD(' ',3*LEVEL) ||
  2                  ENAME Hierarchy
  3  FROM    EMP
  4  CONNECT BY PRIOR EMPNO = MGR
  5  START   WITH JOB        = 'PRESIDENT';

HIERARCHY
------------------
   KING
      JONES
         SCOTT
            ADAMS
         FORD
            SMITH
      BLAKE
         ALLEN
         WARD
```

```
        MARTIN
        TURNER
        JAMES
     CLARK
        MILLER
```

Another pseudocolumn is **ROWID**. Oracle8 rowids are very different than Oracle7 rowids. The Oracle8 rowid is extended, which means it includes the object number. On the other hand, a rowid in Oracle7 is restricted, which means it has no object number, but it does include the Oracle block number, the row number within the block, and the file number. Oracle8 provides a package named **DBMS_ROWID** to display Oracle8 rowids in Oracle7 format. As in previous versions of Oracle, the fastest way to retrieve a row is to use the rowid. However, you should note that rowids change when a table is exported, dropped, or imported. Listing 14.12 illustrates the use of **ROWID**.

Listing 14.12 Using ROWIDs.

```
SQL> SELECT ROWID,   -- Oracle8 Rowids
  2         PARTNO,  -- Are very, very
  3         PNAME,   -- Different from
  4         PCOST    -- Oracle7 Rowids
  5  FROM   AUTO_PARTS
  6  ORDER  BY PARTNO;

ROWID              PARTNO PNAME           PCOST
------------------ ------ ------------- ------
AAAAwCAAFAAAABiAAA      1 OFFY ENGINE    43000
AAAAwDAAGAAAAANAAA 300000 360 SPRINT     18000
AAAAwEAAHAAAAAXAAA 700000 OUTLAW ENGINE  22000

SQL> SELECT *
  2  FROM   AUTO_PARTS
  3  WHERE  ROWID = 'AAAAwEAAHAAAAAXAAA';

 PARTNO PNAME             PCOST
------- -------------- -------
 700000 OUTLAW ENGINE    22000

SQL> get cor8_r4
  1  SELECT PNAME,
  2         dbms_rowid.rowid_object(rowid) "Object#",
  3         dbms_rowid.rowid_block_number(rowid) BLK,
```

```
  4         dbms_rowid.rowid_row_number(rowid) RSN,
  5         dbms_rowid.rowid_relative_fno(rowid) RFILE#
  6* FROM   AUTO_PARTS
SQL> /

PNAME           Object#    BLK    RSN RFILE#
-------------- ------- ------ ------ ------
OFFY ENGINE       3074     98      0      5
360 SPRINT        3075     13      0      6
OUTLAW ENGINE     3076     23      0      7
```

Environmental Parameters

Oracle provides nearly 100 environmental parameters in SQL*Plus; we'll examine several of them in this section. Listing 14.13 shows a method of using the parameters **ACCEPT** and **PROMPT** to prompt the user for a department number and then assign that department number to a variable named **DNO**. Because **DNO** appears in the **WHERE** clause after the ampersand, the user is normally prompted to enter a value for **DNO**. However, in this case, **DNO** has a value because of the **ACCEPT** command, and the user is not prompted. If you use **ACCEPT** for a variable and include the same variable in a SQL statement, Oracle is smart enough not to prompt you again, since you already entered the value for the variable in the **ACCEPT** command. The whole point of **ACCEPT** is to customize what displays on the screen using **PROMPT** and to plug a value into the variable, without having to enter data when the SQL statement executes. The first example shows all the employees in Department 20. The second example in Listing 14.13 shows one method of placing a percent sign in the prompt—by using two percent signs, one after the other. The last example shows another method of displaying a percent sign in the prompt. A variable named **TEXT** is defined and a percent sign is placed at the end of the string that defines the value of **TEXT** (Please Enter Dept %). Then it's accepted into a variable called **X**, and the user is asked to input a value for **X** using the prompt **&TEXT** %. Because **TEXT** is already defined as "Please Enter Dept %", the user is not prompted twice, and the percent sign is displayed.

Listing 14.13 Using ACCEPT and PROMPT.

```
SQL> ACCEPT DNO PROMPT 'Please Enter Department Number: '
Please Enter Department Number: 20
```

```
SQL> SELECT *  -- Point here is operator not prompted
  2  FROM   EMP  -- When Oracle sees &DNO on next line
  3  WHERE  DEPTNO = &DNO;

EMPNO ENAME JOB       MGR HIREDATE   SAL COMM DEPTNO
----- ----- ------- ---- --------- ---- ---- ------
 7369 SMITH CLERK   7902 17-DEC-80  800           20
 7566 JONES MANAGER 7839 02-APR-81 2975           20
 7788 SCOTT ANALYST 7566 09-DEC-82 3000           20
 7876 ADAMS CLERK   7788 12-JAN-83 1100           20
 7902 FORD  ANALYST 7566 03-DEC-81 3000           20


SQL> ACCEPT X PROMPT 'Enter Dept %%'
Enter Dept %10
SQL> def x
DEFINE X               = "10" (CHAR)


SQL> DEFINE TEXT='Please Enter Dept %'
SQL> ACCEPT X PROMPT '&TEXT %'
Please Enter Dept %20
SQL> DEF X
DEFINE X               = "20" (CHAR)
SQL> DEF TEXT
DEFINE TEXT            = "Please Enter Dept %" (CHAR)
```

When you only want to prompt the user once and the variable is required several times in the same SQL statement, use double ampersands. In Listing 14.14, the first query identifies all employees who earn more than a particular employee, who have the same job as the employee, and who started work after the employee. If you use a single ampersand for all three occurrences, the user has to enter the name of the employee three times. In this listing, it appears that an employee named BIG BUCKS is paid too much, and employee BLAKE is underpaid. If you execute the query again, before "undefining" the variable **NAME**, you'll not be prompted to enter a value for **NAME**. You must enter **UNDEFINE NAME**.

The next example in Listing 14.14 prompts the user for a city and then displays the employees who work in that city. The user does not want the typical column name in the heading—in this case, **LOC**. Instead, the user wants the name of the city in the heading. Therefore, the variable preceded by double ampersands should be placed as a column alias in the **SELECT** clause, and the variable preceded by a single ampersand should be placed in the **WHERE** clause. The variable **CITY** in the **WHERE** clause will not prompt the user, because the user entered the city when prompted by the double ampersand variable **CITY** in the **SELECT** clause. By the way, if the "old" and "new" values bother you, set the environmental parameter **VERIFY** to **OFF**.

Listing 14.14 Using double ampersands.

```
SQL> get cb302
     SELECT *
     FROM   EMP
     WHERE SAL>(SELECT SAL
               FROM    EMP
               WHERE   ENAME='&&NAME')AND
          JOB=(SELECT  JOB
               FROM    EMP
               WHERE   ENAME = '&NAME') AND
     HIREDATE>(SELECT  HIREDATE
               FROM    EMP
               WHERE   ENAME='&NAME');

Enter value for name: BLAKE

EMPNO ENAME     JOB      MGR HIREDATE   SAL COMM DEPTNO
----- --------- ------- ---- --------- ---- ---- ------
8888  BIG BUCKS MANAGER      03-MAY-88 5500          30

SQL> /

EMPNO ENAME     JOB      MGR HIREDATE   SAL COMM DEPTNO
----- --------- ------- ---- --------- ---- ---- ------
8888  BIG BUCKS MANAGER      03-MAY-88 5500          30

SQL> UNDEFINE NAME
SQL> /

Enter value for name: BLAKE

EMPNO ENAME     JOB      MGR HIREDATE   SAL COMM DEPTNO
----- --------- ------- ---- --------- ---- ---- ------
8888  BIG BUCKS MANAGER      03-MAY-88 5500          30

SQL> UNDEFINE CITY
```

```
SQL> SELECT ENAME &&City
  2  FROM   EMP,  DEPT
  3  WHERE  EMP.DEPTNO = DEPT.DEPTNO
  4         AND LOC = '&City';

Enter value for city: DALLAS
old   1: SELECT ENAME &&City
new   1: SELECT ENAME DALLAS
old   4:        LOC        = '&City'
new   4:        LOC        = 'DALLAS'

DALLAS
------
SMITH
ADAMS
FORD
SCOTT
JONES

SQL> SET VERIFY OFF
SQL> UNDEFINE CITY
SQL> SELECT ENAME &&City
  2  FROM   EMP,  DEPT
  3  WHERE  EMP.DEPTNO = DEPT.DEPTNO
  4         AND LOC = "&City";

Enter value for city: DALLAS
DALLAS
------
SMITH
ADAMS
FORD
SCOTT
JONES

SQL> SELECT ENAME, LOC  -- To Verify Results
  2  FROM   EMP,   DEPT
  3  WHERE  EMP.DEPTNO = DEPT.DEPTNO AND
  4         LOC        = 'DALLAS';

ENAME      LOC
---------- ------------
SMITH      DALLAS
ADAMS      DALLAS
```

```
FORD       DALLAS
SCOTT      DALLAS
JONES      DALLAS
```

Functions

One of the many functions provided by Oracle is the modulo function named **MOD**. Listing 14.15 creates a table that contains all the employees whose employee number is a multiple of 3. Note that the employee number of FORD is 7902. If you sum up the digits in FORD's employee number, 7 + 9 + 0 + 2, the sum is 18, and 18 is a multiple of 3. Therefore, FORD's employee number, 7902, is evenly divisible by 3. The same is true for the other employees in the **MULTIPLE_OF_3** table.

Listing 14.15 Using **MOD**.

```
SQL> CREATE TABLE MULTIPLE_OF_3 AS
  2          SELECT *
  3.         FROM   EMP
  4          WHERE  MOD(EMPNO, 3) = 0;
Table created.

SQL> SELECT EMPNO, ENAME
  2  FROM  MULTIPLE_OF_3
  3  ORDER BY EMPNO;

  EMPNO ENAME
 ------ ----------
   7521 WARD
   7566 JONES
   7698 BLAKE
   7782 CLARK
   7788 SCOTT
   7839 KING
   7902 FORD
```

Another important function is **ROUND**. This function rounds up or down, depending on the value being rounded. The second argument can be either positive or negative. Listing 14.16 displays the output, varying the second argument of the function from -3 to +3. Positive values round to the right of the decimal, and negative values in the second argument round to the left of the decimal. Note that if you need to use **ROUND** when dealing with money, use 2 as the second argument to round to the nearest penny.

Listing 14.16 Using **ROUND**.

```
SQL> SELECT ROUND(347.864, -3) "-3",
            ROUND(347.864, -2) "-2",
            ROUND(347.864, -1) "-1",
            ROUND(347.864,  0) "0",
            ROUND(347.864,  1) "1",
            ROUND(347.864,  2) “2”, -- 1/100
            ROUND(347.864,  3) "3"
     FROM   DUAL;

     -3      -2      -1       0       1       2       3
------- ------ ------ ------ ------ ------ -------
      0     300     350     348  347.9 347.86 347.864
```

Thanks to one of my students in Tulsa for asking the following question: When we add new employees, regardless of their actual date started, we need to show in the employee table that their first day with the company is the first Monday of the following month. Can you do this in Oracle? The answer is yes, by using two functions: **LAST_DAY** and **NEXT_DAY**. The function **LAST_DAY** accepts a date argument and returns the date of the last day of the month. You no longer need to memorize that stupid poem about 30 days has September, and so on. Listing 14.17 shows that the employee actually started with the company on 27-AUG-95. The date returned from **LAST_DAY** is the first argument of **NEXT_DAY**. The function **NEXT_DAY** is then applied to the date at the end of the month, and it returns the date of the first Monday after the last day of the current month, which, in this case, is 04-SEP-95.

Listing 14.17 Using **LAST_DAY** and **NEXT_DAY**.

```
SQL> get cb71
  SELECT NEXT_DAY(LAST_DAY
      ('&Actual_Date'),'MONDAY') MON
  FROM   DUAL
SQL> /
Enter value for actual_date: 27-AUG-95
```

```
MON
---------
04-SEP-95

SQL> get cb73
  1  COL     "Last Day Of August Is"  FORMAT  A21
  2  SELECT LAST_DAY
  3 ('27-AUG-31') "Last Day Of August Is"
  4  FROM   DUAL
SQL> @cb73

Last Day Of August Is
---------------------
31-AUG-31

SQL> SELECT NEXT_DAY
  2  ('31-AUG-95', 'MONDAY') DOH
  3  FROM   DUAL;

DOH
---------
04-SEP-95
```

Most customers don't care too much for the standard date format (02-MAR-78); instead, they prefer the format 03/02/78. One method for using a preferred date format is to use the function **TO_CHAR**. Another means of changing the default format for all columns in your database of the date data type is to use the init.ora parameter **NLS_DATE_FORMAT**. You can override the **NLS_DATE_FORMAT** setting by using the **ALTER SYSTEM** command. Also, to control the date format for your session without using **TO_CHAR**, use the **ALTER SESSION** command. Listing 14.18 shows three of the four methods.

The purpose of the **COL** command is to shorten the width of the **DTE** column from 80 characters to 8. This prevents the output from wrapping. Without the "fm" in the argument mask of **TO_CHAR**, trailing spaces occur after the day of the week. If you change the date format for your session, all updates and inserts must use the same format as used in the **ALTER SESSION** command, or else you get Oracle error ORA-01843: not a valid month. If you enter the **ALTER SYSTEM** command to change the default date format, remember that you're changing the default format for the entire database, and this will impact all production jobs. If you're not an Oracle database administrator, you probably don't have the **ALTER SYSTEM** privilege—but if you do have this privilege, be careful. The **ALTER SYSTEM** command changes the setting for the entire database. If you change the date format to MM/DD/YY, all SQL statements abort if the date format is not MM/DD/YY. To display the current default date format for your database, write a query using **V$NLS_PARAMETERS**. If you're a developer or an end user, you'll not be able to view any of the V$ dynamic performance views unless your Oracle DBA grants you the necessary privileges. Finally, you should know that **TO_CHAR** can also be used to format numeric columns.

The quarterly report in this listing uses the functions **SUM**, **DECODE**, and **TO_CHAR**. The **TO_CHAR** function strips out the month in the format NOV (for November). The **DECODE** function works like a case statement or an **IF** statement. If the month is October, November, or December, then return the value in the **SAL** column to be summed to the **QTR4** bucket, else return a zero to be summed in the **QTR4** bucket.

Listing 14.18 Using **TO_CHAR** and **DECODE**.

```
SQL> get cb79
COL         DTE       FORMAT  A8
SELECT      ENAME,
TO_CHAR(HIREDATE, 'MM/DD/YY') DTE
FROM        EMP
WHERE       ROWNUM < 8
ORDER       BY HIREDATE DESC
SQL> @cb79

ENAME      DTE
---------- --------
CAROLE     12/11/68
DEBBO      04/02/81
PAIGE      02/22/81
BONNIE     02/20/81
TOBY       12/17/80
MILLIE     04/01/97
DON        04/02/81
ANN        02/20/81
BART       12/17/80

SQL> get cb80
SELECT TO_CHAR (HIREDATE,
'Day, "the" ddspth "of" Mon,
```

```
  3  "nineteen-hundred" yysp')
  4  FROM   EMP  -- Spaces after Friday
  5  WHERE  ROWNUM < 3;

TO_CHAR(HIREDATE,'DAY,"THE"
DDSPTH"OF"MON,"NINETEEN-
------------------------------------------------
Wednesday, the seventeenth of
Dec,nineteen-hundred eighty

Friday   , the twentieth of
Feb,nineteen-hundred eighty-one

SQL> SET HEADING OFF
SQL> SELECT TO_CHAR (HIREDATE,
  2  'fmDay, "the" ddspth "of"
  3   Mon,"nineteen-hundred" yysp')
  4   FROM  EMP -- FM Squeezes Data Together
  5   WHERE ROWNUM < 3;

Wednesday, the seventeenth of
Dec,nineteen-hundred eighty

Friday, the twentieth of
Feb,nineteen-hundred eighty-one

SQL> ALTER SESSION -- Just For My Session
  2        SET NLS_DATE_FORMAT = 'MM/DD/YY';
Session altered.

SQL> SELECT ENAME, HIREDATE
  2  FROM   EMP
  3  WHERE  ROWNUM < 2;

ENAME      HIREDATE
---------- --------
CAROLE     12/11/68

SQL> UPDATE EMP
  2  SET HIREDATE = '13-NOV-97'
  3  WHERE ENAME = 'KING';
UPDATE EMP
*
ERROR at line 1:
ORA-01843: not a valid month
```

```
SQL> ALTER SYSTEM SET
          NLS_DATE_FORMAT = "MM/DD/YY";
System altered.

SQL> DESC V$NLS_PARAMETERS
Name                           Null?        Type
------------------------------ ------------ ----
PARAMETER                      VARCHAR2(64)
VALUE                          VARCHAR2(64)

SQL> COL PARAMETER FORMAT A23
SQL> COL VALUE     FORMAT A12

SQL> SELECT *
  2  FROM   V$NLS_PARAMETERS
  3  ORDER  BY PARAMETER;

PARAMETER               VALUE
----------------------- ------------
NLS_CALENDAR            GREGORIAN
NLS_CHARACTERSET        WE8ISO8859P1
NLS_CURRENCY            $
NLS_DATE_FORMAT         MM/DD/YY
NLS_DATE_LANGUAGE       AMERICAN
NLS_ISO_CURRENCY        AMERICA
NLS_LANGUAGE            AMERICAN
NLS_NUMERIC_CHARACTERS  .,
NLS_SORT                BINARY
NLS_TERRITORY           AMERICA

SQL> SELECT ENAME,
  2  TO_CHAR(SAL,'$99,999.99') PRETTY_SAL
  3  FROM   EMP;

ENAME      PRETTY_SAL
---------- -----------
DEBRA        $4,800.00
PAIGE        $4,800.00
BONNIE         $555.00
TOBY           $222.00
CAROLE       $1,250.00
RUBY         $1,250.00
KERRY        $2,975.00
STAN         $2,850.00
MILLIE       $2,850.00
```

```
KEVIN         $2,850.00
BRIAN         $2,850.00
DON           $4,700.00
ANN           $2,975.00
BART          $2,975.00

SQL> get cb110
SET     FEEDBACK      OFF -- Quarterly Report Using DECODE
BREAK                 ON REPORT
COMPUTE SUM OF QTR1 ON  REPORT
COMPUTE SUM OF QTR2 ON  REPORT
COMPUTE SUM OF QTR3 ON  REPORT
COMPUTE SUM OF QTR4 ON  REPORT
COMPUTE SUM OF TOT_BY_YR ON REPORT
COL       QTR1    FORMAT   $999,990
COL       QTR2    FORMAT   $999,990
COL       QTR3    FORMAT   $999,990
COL       QTR4    FORMAT   $999,990
COL       TOT_BY_YR FORMAT $999,990
COL       "YEAR" FORMAT    A4
SELECT TO_CHAR(HIREDATE, 'YYYY') "YEAR",
SUM(DECODE(TO_CHAR(HIREDATE,'MON'),
'JAN',sal,'FEB',sal,'MAR',sal,0)) QTR1,
SUM(DECODE(TO_CHAR(HIREDATE,'MON'),
'APR',sal,'MAY',sal,'JUN',sal,0)) QTR2,
SUM(DECODE(TO_CHAR(HIREDATE,'MON'),
'JUL',sal,'AUG',sal,'SEP',sal,0)) QTR3,
SUM(DECODE(TO_CHAR(HIREDATE,'MON'),
'OCT',sal,'NOV',sal,'DEC',sal,0)) QTR4,
SUM(SAL) TOT_BY_YR
FROM      EMP
GROUP     BY TO_CHAR(HIREDATE, 'YYYY');
SET       FEEDBACK            ON
CLEAR     BREAKS
CLEAR     COMPUTES
CLEAR     COLUMNS

SQL> @cb110

YEAR      QTR1      QTR2      QTR3      QTR4  TOT_BY_YR
---- --------- --------- --------- --------- ---------
1980        $0        $0        $0      $800      $800
1981    $2,850    $8,275    $2,750    $8,950   $22,825
1982    $1,300        $0        $0    $3,000    $4,300
```

```
1983     $1,100         $0        $0        $0      $1,100
1995         $0         $0    $9,600        $0      $9,600
        --------   --------  --------  --------   ---------
sum      $5,250     $8,275   $12,350   $12,750     $38,625
```

Joins

Some queries require rows from the parent table that have no matching rows in the child table. When this situation exists, you must write an *outer join.* If you need a parts explosion report or a bill of materials (BOM), then you need to write a *self-join.* I might be the only one in the industry to say this, but I believe a hybrid of the self-join and the outer join exists—I call it a *self-outer join.* I cannot take credit for this amazing discovery, however. One of my students back in 1989 pointed it out to me and the rest of the class. Finally, there's the *horrible* join. Most people call this the *Cartesian product join.* (Believe it or not, there are times when you want to write a horrible join.) So, in summary, I propose that there are actually five types of joins: equi (or simple), outer, self, self-outer, and Cartesian. Now, let's examine these join types in more detail, starting with the outer join.

Outer Join

When you need to see rows from the parent table that have no matching rows in the child table, you must write an outer join. An outer join in Oracle requires the use of the symbols "(+)" in the **WHERE** clause. The "(+)" symbols go next to the column belonging to the table with a null row.

Listing 14.19 starts by identifying all part numbers in the **PARTS** table that have not been tested. In other words, the part numbers found in the **PARTS** table that do not exist in the **TESTS** table. The fastest method for determining these part numbers is to use the set operator **MINUS**. The output indicates that seven parts have no test results in the **TESTS** table. The next query attempts to display the part number, part name, and test results for parts 1944, 1976, and 1978. However, no matching rows in the **TESTS** table exist; consequently, no rows are returned.

If you want to see the part number and the part name for parts with no rows in the **TESTS** table, you must again write an outer join. In this case, you want null rows from the **TESTS** table to be joined with the part numbers in the **PARTS** table for part numbers 1944, 1976, and 1978. So, the symbols "(+)" should be placed in the

WHERE clause next to **TESTS.PNO**. The string **TESTS.PNO(+)** tells Oracle to join a null row from the **TESTS** table to any row from the **PARTS** table that does not have a matching part number in the **TESTS** table.

The Explain Plan output for the non-outer join shows three nested loop joins with each of the three using the appropriate index. Notice the extreme difference in response times between using an index and performing a full-table scan—it's nearly 3 minutes and 15 seconds faster to use an index than to use a full-table scan.

Also, note that the driving table for an outer join is always the non-outer join table. In this case, the **PARTS** table is the driving table. The outer join table is **TESTS** because of the **TESTS.PNO(+)** string in the **WHERE** clause.

Listing 14.19 Using an outer join.

```
SQL> SELECT PNO FROM PARTS
  2  MINUS
  3  SELECT PNO FROM TESTS;

     PNO
-------
     222
    1944
    1950
    1972
    1976
    1978
    5500

7 rows selected.

Elapsed: 00:01:14.64

SQL> EXPLAIN PLAN FOR  -- EQUI JOIN
  2  SELECT PARTS.PNO,
  3         PARTS.PNAME,
  4         TESTS.RESULTS
  5  FROM   PARTS,
  6         TESTS
  7  WHERE  PARTS.PNO = TESTS.PNO
  8         AND
  9         PARTS.PNO IN(1944,1976,1978);
Explained.
```

```
SQL>@explain
Query Plan                                        COST
---------------------------------------- -----
SELECT STATEMENT   CHOOSE                           15
  CONCATENATION
    NESTED LOOPS                                     5
      TABLE ACCESS BY ROWID PARTS ANALYZED           2
        INDEX UNIQUE SCAN PARTS_PNO ANALYZED
      TABLE ACCESS BY ROWID TESTS ANALYZED
        INDEX RANGE SCAN TESTS_PNO ANALYZED
    NESTED LOOPS                                     5
      TABLE ACCESS BY ROWID PARTS ANALYZED           2
        INDEX UNIQUE SCAN PARTS_PNO ANALYZED
      TABLE ACCESS BY ROWID TESTS ANALYZED
        INDEX RANGE SCAN TESTS_PNO ANALYZED
    NESTED LOOPS                                     5
      TABLE ACCESS BY ROWID PARTS ANALYZED           2
        INDEX UNIQUE SCAN PARTS_PNO ANALYZED
      TABLE ACCESS BY ROWID TESTS ANALYZED
        INDEX RANGE SCAN TESTS_PNO ANALYZED

SQL> SELECT PARTS.PNO,
            PARTS.PNAME,
            TESTS.RESULTS
     FROM   PARTS,
            TESTS
     WHERE  PARTS.PNO = TESTS.PNO
            AND
            PARTS.PNO IN(1944,1976,1978);

no rows selected

Elapsed: 00:00:01.25  (With indexes and statistics)
Elapsed: 00:03:15.58  (No indexes and statistics)

SQL> EXPLAIN PLAN FOR  -- OUTER JOIN
     SELECT PARTS.PNO,
            PARTS.PNAME,
            TESTS.RESULTS
     FROM   PARTS,      -- PARTS DRIVES
            TESTS
     WHERE  PARTS.PNO = TESTS.PNO(+)
            AND
            PARTS.PNO IN(1944,1976,1978);
Explained.
```

```
SQL>@explain
Query Plan                                    COST
---------------------------------------- -----
SELECT STATEMENT   CHOOSE                        15
  CONCATENATION
    NESTED LOOPS OUTER                            5
      TABLE ACCESS BY ROWID PARTS ANALYZED       2
        INDEX UNIQUE SCAN PARTS_PNO ANALYZED
      TABLE ACCESS BY ROWID TESTS ANALYZED
        INDEX RANGE SCAN TESTS_PNO ANALYZED
    NESTED LOOPS OUTER                            5
      TABLE ACCESS BY ROWID PARTS ANALYZED       2
        INDEX UNIQUE SCAN PARTS_PNO ANALYZED
      TABLE ACCESS BY ROWID TESTS ANALYZED
        INDEX RANGE SCAN TESTS_PNO ANALYZED
    NESTED LOOPS OUTER                            5
      TABLE ACCESS BY ROWID PARTS ANALYZED       2
        INDEX UNIQUE SCAN PARTS_PNO ANALYZED
      TABLE ACCESS BY ROWID TESTS ANALYZED
        INDEX RANGE SCAN TESTS_PNO ANALYZED

SQL> SELECT PARTS.PNO,
  2         PARTS.PNAME,
  3         TESTS.RESULTS
  4  FROM   PARTS,
  5         TESTS
  6  WHERE  PARTS.PNO = TESTS.PNO(+)
  7         AND
  8         PARTS.PNO IN(1944,1976,1978);

   PNO PNAME          R
------ -------------- -
  1944 Widget 1944
  1976 Widget 1976
  1978 Widget 1978

Elapsed: 00:00:01.11 (With indexes and statistics)
Elapsed: 00:02:22.07 (No indexes and no statistics)
```

Self-Join

When you have a recursive table like **EMP** or **PLAN_TABLE**, you'll sometimes need to write self-joins. A self-join is literally a table that joins to itself using the primary key and foreign key columns, which are in the same table. In Oracle's **EMP** table, the primary key column is **EMPNO**, and the foreign key column referencing the primary key column **EMPNO** is **MGR**. For **PLAN_TABLE**, the primary key column is **ID**, and the foreign key column referencing the primary key column **ID** is the **PARENT_ID** column. To produce a report that displays which part is a component of another component, visualize two tables that are identical—except in name. In Listing 14.20, you see **PARTS** and **C**, where **C** is a table alias for **PARTS** for the duration of the query. To join the two tables together, **COMPONENT_OF** is used in the **PARTS** table to hook up with the **PNO** column of the **C** table. Note that this query has one major problem—the top component, **SPRINT CAR**, is missing!

Listing 14.20 Using a self-join.

```
SQL> SELECT *
  2  FROM   PARTS;

    PNO PNAME              COMPONENT_OF
------- --------------- ------------
      1 SPRINT CAR
      2 CHASSIS                    1
      3 AXLES                      2
      4 ENGINE                     2
      5 SKINS                      2
      6 DASH                       2
      7 OIL GAGE                   6
      8 TEMP GAGE                  6
      9 STEARING COLUMN            2
     10 STEARING WHEEL             9
     11 POP OFF DEVICE            10
     12 WHEELS                     3
     13 WING                      14
     14 ROLL CAGE                  2
     15 BRAKES                     3
     16 FUEL CELL                  2
     17 SHUT OFF SWITCH            6
     18 SEAT                      19
     19 FLOOR BOARD                2
     20 FRONT WING                 2
     21 FUEL CAP                  16

21 rows selected.
```

```
SQL> SET     HEADING     OFF
     SELECT PARTS.PNAME ||
       ' is a component of ' ||
        C.PNAME
     FROM    PARTS,  PARTS C
     WHERE   PARTS.COMPONENT_OF = C.PNO
     /
     SET    HEADING     ON
SQL> @cb317b

CHASSIS is a component of SPRINT CAR
AXLES is a component of CHASSIS
ENGINE is a component of CHASSIS
DASH is a component of CHASSIS
FUEL CELL is a component of CHASSIS
FRONT WING is a component of CHASSIS
FLOOR BOARD is a component of CHASSIS
ROLL CAGE is a component of CHASSIS
SKINS is a component of CHASSIS
STEERING COLUMN is a component of CHASSIS
WHEELS is a component of AXLES
BRAKES is a component of AXLES
OIL GAUGE is a component of DASH
SHUT OFF SWITCH is a component of DASH
TEMP GAUGE is a component of DASH
STEERING WHEEL is a component of STEERING COLUMN
POP OFF DEVICE is a component of STEERING WHEEL
WING is a component of ROLL CAGE
FUEL CAP is a component of FUEL CELL
SEAT is a component of FLOOR BOARD
```

Self-Outer Join

In the previous example of the self-join, you saw that the top (or major) component, **SPRINT CAR**, was not displayed in the query. To force Oracle to display the part without a component, an outer join is used in Listing 14.21. Because a row in **PARTS** containing **SPRINT CAR** has to join with a null row in **C**, the outer join symbols "(+)" are placed on the "C" side by the sea shore (just kidding)...on the "C" side of the WHERE clause. Because this is a self-join and an outer join, why not just call it a *self-outer join?*

Listing 14.21 Using a self-outer join.

```
SQL> SET     HEADING     OFF
     SELECT PARTS.PNAME ||
     ' is a component of ' || C.PNAME
```

```
FROM   PARTS,  PARTS C
WHERE  PARTS.COMPONENT_OF = C.PNO(+)
/
SET    HEADING    ON
SQL> @cb318

CHASSIS is a component of SPRINT CAR
AXLES is a component of CHASSIS
ENGINE is a component of CHASSIS
DASH is a component of CHASSIS
FUEL CELL is a component of CHASSIS
FRONT WING is a component of CHASSIS
FLOOR BOARD is a component of CHASSIS
ROLL CAGE is a component of CHASSIS
SKINS is a component of CHASSIS
STEERING COLUMN is a component of CHASSIS
WHEELS is a component of AXLES
BRAKES is a component of AXLES
OIL GAUGE is a component of DASH
SHUT OFF SWITCH is a component of DASH
TEMP GAUGE is a component of DASH
STEERING WHEEL is a component of STEERING COLUMN
POP OFF DEVICE is a component of STEERING WHEEL
WING is a component of ROLL CAGE
FUEL CAP is a component of FUEL CELL
SEAT is a component of FLOOR BOARD
SPRINT CAR is a component of
```

If the user doesn't care for the output of "SPRINT CAR is a component of" and prefers to see "SPRINT CAR is a component of nothing," just add the **NVL** function to the **SELECT** clause. The null value function, **NVL**, requires two arguments. The first argument in this example (Listing 14.22) is **C.PNAME**, and the second argument is **"Nothing"**. If **C.PNAME** is a null, then Oracle returns the string in the second argument—"Nothing". If **C.PNAME** is not null, then data from the column is displayed. This produces the desired output. Queries using recursive tables such as **PARTS**, **EMP**, and **PLAN_TABLE** permit the use of **CONNECT BY** and **START WITH**, as well as self-joins and self-outer joins.

Listing 14.22 Using NVL in self-outer joins.

```
SQL> SET    HEADING    OFF
SELECT PARTS.PNAME ||
' is a component of '||
NVL(C.PNAME, "Nothing")
```

```
FROM   PARTS,  PARTS C
WHERE  PARTS.COMPONENT_OF = C.PNO(+)
/
SET    HEADING     ON
SQL> @cb318

CHASSIS is a component of SPRINT CAR
AXLES is a component of CHASSIS
ENGINE is a component of CHASSIS
DASH is a component of CHASSIS
FUEL CELL is a component of CHASSIS
FRONT WING is a component of CHASSIS
FLOOR BOARD is a component of CHASSIS
ROLL CAGE is a component of CHASSIS
SKINS is a component of CHASSIS
STEERING COLUMN is a component of CHASSIS
WHEELS is a component of AXLES
BRAKES is a component of AXLES
OIL GAUGE is a component of DASH
SHUT OFF SWITCH is a component of DASH
TEMP GAUGE is a component of DASH
STEERING WHEEL is a component of STEERING COLUMN
POP OFF DEVICE is a component of STEERING WHEEL
WING is a component of ROLL CAGE
FUEL CAP is a component of FUEL CELL
SEAT is a component of FLOOR BOARD
SPRINT CAR is a component of Nothing

SQL> COL "Bill Of Materials" FORMAT A30
    SELECT  LPAD(' ', 3*LEVEL) ||
            PNAME "Bill Of Materials"
    FROM    PARTS
    CONNECT BY PRIOR PNO = COMPONENT_OF
    START   WITH PNAME   = 'SPRINT CAR'
SQL> @cb319

Bill Of Materials
-----------------
   SPRINT CAR
      CHASSIS
         AXLES
            WHEELS
            BRAKES
         ENGINE
```

```
SKINS
DASH
   OIL GAUGE
   TEMP GAUGE
   SHUT OFF SWITCH
STEERING COLUMN
   STEERING WHEEL
      POP OFF DEVICE
ROLL CAGE
   WING
FUEL CELL
   FUEL CAP
FLOOR BOARD
   SEAT
FRONT WING
```

The **DEPT** and **HISTORY** tables contain departments 10, 20, 30, and 40. Debra is in department 44, and Paige is in department 77 in the **EMP** table. If you join the three tables together using a normal equi join, you won't see Debra or Paige. Because department numbers 44 and 77 don't exist in either of the two tables—department and history—each of the two tables need to have null rows joined to Debra's row and to Paige's row. Therefore, two outer join symbols need to be used—one for the **HISTORY** table, and one for the **DEPT** table. Listing 14.23 shows the query that displays employees with invalid department numbers. The first Explain Plan indicates that no statistics exist on any of the three tables, because the cost is null. It also indicates that Oracle performs a sort-merge join and uses the **EMP** table as the driving table. If you analyze any one of the three tables, Oracle will use the cost-based optimizer. Also, note that the cost is 5 and the optimizer uses hash-outer joins with **EMP** as the driving table.

There really is no official query type named a "horrible join," but there is a Cartesian product join where one row from a table is joined with every row of the other table. If you want to grant **SELECT** privileges on your **EMP** table to most users, but you don't want to use **PUBLIC**, use SQL to generate SQL. The trick is to *not* join the tables in the **WHERE** clause.

Listing 14.23 Three-table outer join and horrible join.

```
SQL> SELECT DISTINCT DEPTNO
  2  FROM   DEPT;
```

```
 DEPTNO
-------
     10
     20
     30
     40

SQL> SELECT *
  2  FROM   HISTORY;

 DEPTNO DUDE
 ------ ---------------
     10 ROY ROGERS
     20 HOPPY
     30 JOHN WAYNE
     40 RANDOLPH SCOTT

SQL> SELECT DISTINCT DEPTNO FROM EMP;

 DEPTNO
-------
     10
     20
     30
     44            DEBRA IS IN DEPT 44
     77            PAIGE IS IN DEPT 77

SQL> SELECT ENAME, -- Want To See Debra
  2         LOC,   -- And Paige
  3         DUDE
  4  FROM   EMP E,
  5         DEPT D,
  6         HISTORY H
  7  WHERE  E.DEPTNO = D.DEPTNO(+) AND
  8         D.DEPTNO = H.DEPTNO(+);

ENAME      LOC           DUDE
---------- -----------   ---------------
KERRY      NEW YORK      ROY ROGERS
KEVIN      NEW YORK      ROY ROGERS
STAN       NEW YORK      ROY ROGERS
PETE       DALLAS        HOPPY
CAROLE     DALLAS        HOPPY
ANN        DALLAS        HOPPY
BART       DALLAS        HOPPY
ALLEN      CHICAGO       JOHN WAYNE
```

```
BIG BUCKS  CHICAGO       JOHN WAYNE
BLAKE      CHICAGO       JOHN WAYNE
MARTIN     CHICAGO       JOHN WAYNE
JAMES      CHICAGO       JOHN WAYNE
DEBRA
PAIGE

SQL> EXPLAIN PLAN FOR
  2  SELECT ENAME,
  3         LOC,
  4         DUDE
  5   FROM  EMP E,
  6         DEPT D,
  7         HISTORY H
  8   WHERE E.DEPTNO = D.DEPTNO(+) AND
  9         D.DEPTNO = H.DEPTNO(+)
Explained.
SQL> SAVE cor3join

SQL> @explain8
Plan Tree
--------------------------------
SELECT STATEMENT   Cost =
  MERGE JOIN OUTER
    SORT JOIN
      MERGE JOIN OUTER
        SORT JOIN
          TABLE ACCESS FULL EMP
        SORT JOIN
          TABLE ACCESS FULL DEPT
    SORT JOIN
      TABLE ACCESS FULL HISTORY
SQL> TRUNCATE TABLE PLAN_TABLE;
SQL> ANALYZE TABLE EMP COMPUTE STATISTICS;
Table analyzed.
SQL> @cor3join

SQL> @explain8

Plan Tree
-----------------------------
SELECT STATEMENT   Cost = 5
  HASH JOIN OUTER
    HASH JOIN OUTER
      TABLE ACCESS FULL EMP
```

```
    TABLE ACCESS FULL DEPT
   TABLE ACCESS FULL HISTORY

SQL> select 'GRANT SELECT ON ' || table_name
  2      || ' TO ' || username || ';'
  3  from   user_tables,
  4         dba_users
  5  where username not in('SYS','SYSTEM')
            and table_name = 'EMP';

'GRANTSELECTON'||TABLE_NAME||'TO'||USERNAME||';'
------------------------------------------------
GRANT SELECT ON EMP TO DEBRA;
GRANT SELECT ON EMP TO PAIGE;
GRANT SELECT ON EMP TO CAROLE;
GRANT SELECT ON EMP TO STEVE;
GRANT SELECT ON EMP TO DEANNA;
GRANT SELECT ON EMP TO PHILLIP;
GRANT SELECT ON EMP TO LISA;
GRANT SELECT ON EMP TO JOSHUA;
GRANT SELECT ON EMP TO JAKE;
GRANT SELECT ON EMP TO KERRY;
GRANT SELECT ON EMP TO KEVIN;
GRANT SELECT ON EMP TO STAN;
GRANT SELECT ON EMP TO DON;
GRANT SELECT ON EMP TO ANN;
GRANT SELECT ON EMP TO BART;
GRANT SELECT ON EMP TO SCOTT;
```

Summary

Oracle has always been, and will always be, the very best database on the market. It runs on just about every platform known to man and does everything but make breakfast like the best hotel chain in the world. However, a certain level of complexity comes with the territory. This means that you end up writing a lot of queries on your own to examine the data dictionary.

Oracle also has many functions you can use. In my opinion, the most widely used functions are **DECODE**, **NVL**, and **TO_CHAR**. In addition, you can now write your own stored functions.

HIGH PERFORMANCE

Oracle8: New Features

CHAPTER 15

This chapter discusses the powerful new features offered in Oracle8. You'll learn how to use these features in this chapter.

Oracle8: New Features

New Features In Oracle8

Here are the new features that will be discussed in this chapter:

- Partitioned tables
- Enforcing constraints
- Using **INSTEAD OF** database triggers
- Index-organized tables
- Index partitions
- Parallel DML

Partitioned Tables

Oracle8 allows for the creation of partitions for tables. See Figure 15.1 for a diagram of this discussion.

The example in Listing 15.1 creates the **AUTO_PARTS** table in three partitions. Note that you must know what tablespaces exist before issuing the **CREATE TABLE** command. This example uses the tablespaces EXTRA1, EXTRA2, and EXTRA3. The next statement displays information about partitions using the data dictionary view **USER_TAB_PARTITIONS**. Because no rows are selected, no partitions exist in the database at the current time. The **CREATE TABLE** statement creates three partitions named AP250K, AP500K, and AP1MILLION. As rows are inserted into **AUTO_PARTS**, the value of the **PARTNO** column determines in which partition the row is placed. If a new part is added using part number 55, the row appears in partition AP250K, because 55 is less than 250,001. If a new part is added using part number 955,222, the row appears in partition AP1MILLION, because 955,222 is less than one million and more than 500,000.

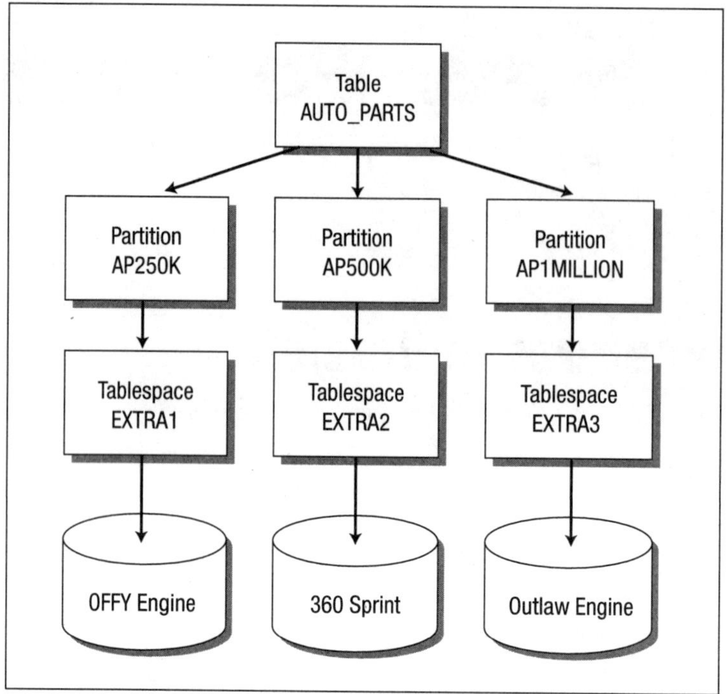

Figure 15.1
Partitions.

Partitions belong to tablespaces. Partition AP250K is in tablespace EXTRA1; partition AP500K is in tablespace EXTRA2; and partition AP1MILLION is in tablespace EXTRA3. Use the rowid to locate the file a row is in. Notice how much different Oracle8's rowids are than Oracle7's rowids. For example, Oracle8 rowids are unrestricted, whereas Oracle7 rowids are restricted. The Oracle8 rowid is extended, which means it includes the object number. The extended rowid has four components. The first component is the data object number, bytes 1–6 of the 18-byte character string. The second component is the relative file number, bytes 7–9. The third component is the block number, bytes 10–15, and the fourth component of the Oracle8 extended rowid is the slot number within the block, bytes 16–18. In contrast, rowids in Oracle7 format are restricted, with no object number, but they include the Oracle block number, the row number within the block, and the file number. Because of the advent of objects in Oracle8, the rowid has changed drastically. Thank goodness for the Oracle-supplied package **DBMS_ROWID**. To see the function names in the **DBMS_ROWID** package, write a query using **DBA_SOURCE**. To display the object number, use function **ROWID_OBJECT**. To display the block number, use function **ROWID_BLOCK_NUMBER**. To display the row number within the block, use the function **ROWID_ROW_NUMBER**. To display the file number, use function **ROWID_RELATIVE_FNO**. For example, the row containing "OFFY ENGINE" is object number 3074, block number 98, row number 0 in block number 98, and it appears in file number 5.

Use **V$DBFILE** to display the file that contains the row OFFY ENGINE. In this database, file c:\orant\database\ext1orcl.ora contains the OFFY ENGINE row.

Listing 15.1 Creating a table with partitions.

```
SQL> COL TABLESPACE_NAME FORMAT A15
SQL> COL STATUS          FORMAT A6

SQL> SELECT TABLESPACE_NAME,
  2         MIN_EXTLEN MINXLEN,
  3         STATUS,
  4         CONTENTS,
  5         LOGGING
  6  FROM   DBA_TABLESPACES;

TABLESPACE_NAME MINXLEN STATUS CONTENTS  LOGGING
--------------- ------- ------ --------- ---------
SYSTEM                0 ONLINE PERMANENT LOGGING
USER_DATA             0 ONLINE PERMANENT LOGGING
ROLLBACK_DATA         0 ONLINE PERMANENT LOGGING
TEMPORARY_DATA        0 ONLINE PERMANENT LOGGING
EXTRA1                0 ONLINE PERMANENT NOLOGGING
EXTRA2                0 ONLINE PERMANENT NOLOGGING
EXTRA3                0 ONLINE PERMANENT NOLOGGING

SQL> get cor14_4a
  1  SET    LONG      20
  2  SET    NUMWIDTH 6
  3  COL    PNAME     FORMAT A14
  4  COL    TS        FORMAT A6
  5  SELECT PARTITION_NAME PNAME,
  6         HIGH_VALUE,
  7         HIGH_VALUE_LENGTH HVL,
  8         PARTITION_POSITION POS,
```

```
  9          TABLESPACE_NAME TS,
 10          LOGGING,
 11          LAST_ANALYZED LAST,
 12          BUFFER_POOL BPOOL
 13  FROM    USER_TAB_PARTITIONS
 14  ORDER   BY POS
 15  /
 16* SET     LONG     80

SQL> @cor14_4a
no rows selected

SQL> get cor8_p1
  1  CREATE TABLE AUTO_PARTS
  2     (partno        NUMBER(7,0),
  3      pname         VARCHAR2(15),
  4      pcost         NUMBER(7,2))
  5  LOGGING
  6  PARTITION BY RANGE(partno)
  7      (PARTITION ap250k
  8        VALUES LESS THAN (250001)
  9        TABLESPACE EXTRA1,
 10       PARTITION ap500k
 11        VALUES LESS THAN (500000)
 12        TABLESPACE EXTRA2,
 13       PARTITION ap1million
 14        VALUES LESS THAN (1000000)
 15*       TABLESPACE EXTRA3)
SQL> /
Table created.

SQL> @cor14_4a

PNAME                HVL    POS TS     LOG LAST      BPOOL
------------- ------ ------ ------ --- --------- -------
AP250K                 6      1 EXTRA1 YES           DEFAULT
AP500K                 6      2 EXTRA2 YES           DEFAULT
AP1MILLION             7      3 EXTRA3 YES           DEFAULT

SQL> SELECT ROWID,  -- Oracle8 Rowids
  2         PARTNO, -- Are very, very
  3         PNAME,  -- Different from
  4         PCOST   -- Oracle7 Rowids
  5  FROM   AUTO_PARTS
  6  ORDER  BY PARTNO;
```

```
ROWID              PARTNO PNAME          PCOST
------------------ ------ ------------- ------
AAAAwCAAFAAAABiAAA      1 OFFY ENGINE    43000
AAAAwDAAGAAAAANAAA 300000 360 SPRINT     18000
AAAAwEAAHAAAAAXAAA 700000 OUTLAW ENGINE  22000

SQL> get cor8_r6
  1  SELECT SUBSTR(TEXT,1,70) CODE
  2  FROM   DBA_SOURCE
  3  WHERE  NAME = 'DBMS_ROWID'   AND
  4         TEXT NOT LIKE '%--%'  AND
  5*        TEXT LIKE '%function%'
SQL> /

CODE
----------------------------------------------
function rowid_create(rowid_type IN number,
function rowid_type(row_id IN rowid)
function rowid_object(row_id IN rowid)
function rowid_relative_fno(row_id IN rowid)
function rowid_block_number(row_id IN rowid)
function rowid_row_number(row_id IN rowid)
function rowid_to_absolute_fno(row_id IN rowid,
function rowid_to_extended(old_rowid IN rowid,
function rowid_to_restricted(old_rowid IN rowid,
function rowid_verify(rowid_in IN rowid,

SQL> get cor8_r4
  1 SELECT PNAME,
  2 dbms_rowid.rowid_object(rowid) "Object#",
  3 dbms_rowid.rowid_block_number(rowid) BLK,
  4 dbms_rowid.rowid_row_number(rowid) RSN,
  5 dbms_rowid.rowid_relative_fno(rowid) RFILE#
  6* FROM   AUTO_PARTS
SQL> /

PNAME           Object#    BLK    RSN RFILE#
-------------- ------- ------ ------ ------
OFFY ENGINE       3074     98      0      5
360 SPRINT        3075     13      0      6
OUTLAW ENGINE     3076     23      0      7

SQL> get cor8_r5
  1  SELECT *
```

```
  2  FROM   V$DBFILE
  3  WHERE  FILE# BETWEEN 5 AND 7
  4* ORDER  BY FILE#
SQL> /

 FILE# NAME
------ ----------------------------------
     5 C:\ORANT\DATABASE\EXT1ORCL.ORA
     6 C:\ORANT\DATABASE\EXT2ORCL.ORA
     7 C:\ORANT\DATABASE\EXT3ORCL.ORA
```

You can specify the partition name in the **FROM** clause of a **SELECT** statement if you know that the query retrieves rows from a single partition and you want to speed up the query a little. Listing 15.2 returns all rows in partition AP250K that have part numbers less than 249,555. The output from the table **PLAN_TABLE** indicates that the data returned is in partition number 1 because **NUMBER(1)** appears in the **PARTITION_START** and **PARTITION_STOP** columns. The second query returns all automobile parts whose part number is less than one million. This causes Oracle to use all three partitions, and the results of Explain Plan indicate this because **PARTITION_START** is partition number 1 and **PARTITION_STOP** is partition number 3. The **OPTIONS** column **CONCATENATE** indicates that the result sets from all three partitions are combined. The output is edited to fit the length constraints of this book.

Listing 15.2 **SELECTS** on partitioned tables.

```
SQL> SELECT *
  2  FROM AUTO_PARTS PARTITION (AP250K) A
  3  WHERE  A.PARTNO < 249555;

PARTNO PNAME             PCOST
------ -------------- ------
     1 OFFY ENGINE     43000

SQL> EXPLAIN PLAN FOR
  2  SELECT *
  3  FROM AUTO_PARTS PARTITION (AP250K) A
  4  WHERE  A.PARTNO < 249555;

SQL> SELECT ID,
  2  PARENT_ID PRNTID,
```

```
  3  SUBSTR(OPERATION,1,17) "Operation",
  4  SUBSTR(PARTITION_START,1,10) "PSTART",
  5  SUBSTR(PARTITION_STOP,1,10) "PSTOP",
  6  PARTITION_ID PID,
  7  SUBSTR(OPTIONS,1,7) "Options"
  8  FROM   PLAN_TABLE
  9  ORDER  BY ID, PARENT_ID;

    ID PRNTID Operation
------ ------ ----------------
     0        SELECT STATEMENT
     1      0 TABLE ACCESS

PSTART     PSTOP         PID Options
---------- ---------- ------ -------
NUMBER(1)  NUMBER(1)       1 FULL

SQL> EXPLAIN PLAN FOR
  2  SELECT *    -- Data From 3 Partitions
  3  FROM   AUTO_PARTS
  4  WHERE  partno < 1000000;
Explained.

    ID PRNTID Operation
------ ------ ----------
     0        SELECT STATEMENT
     1      0 PARTITION

PSTART     PSTOP        PID Options
---------  ---------- ----- -----------
NUMBER(1)  NUMBER(3)      1 CONCATENATED
NUMBER(1)  NUMBER(3)      1 FULL
```

If you use a partition name in the **FROM** clause, only rows satisfying the **WHERE** clause in the designated partition are returned. In Listing 15.3, the **WHERE** clause returns rows from partition AP250K because the partition AP250K appears in the **FROM** clause.

Listing 15.3 The **FROM** clause.

```
SQL> SELECT *
  2  FROM   AUTO_PARTS PARTITION (AP250K) A
  3  WHERE  A.PARTNO < 999999;
```

```
PARTNO PNAME              PCOST
------ ------------- -------
     1 OFFY ENGINE        43000

SQL> EXPLAIN PLAN FOR
  2  SELECT *
  3  FROM AUTO_PARTS PARTITION (AP250K) A
  4  WHERE  A.PARTNO < 999999;
Explained.

    ID PRNTID Operation
------ ------ ---------------
     0        SELECT STATEMENT
     1      0 PARTITION

PSTART     PSTOP        PID Options
---------- --------- ------ -------
NUMBER(1)  NUMBER(1)      1 FULL
```

Listing 15.4 shows how to create a view on a partition. This view is on the partition that includes all part numbers less than 250,000. The Explain Plan reveals that a full-table scan is performed on partition number 1 at a cost of 1.

Listing 15.4 Creating a view on a partition.

```
SQL> CREATE VIEW AP_250K AS
  2    SELECT *
  3    FROM AUTO_PARTS PARTITION (AP250K);
View created.

SQL> SELECT *
  2  FROM   AP_250K;

 PARTNO PNAME               PCOST
------- ---------------- -----
      1 OFFY ENGINE        43000

SQL> EXPLAIN PLAN FOR
  2  SELECT *
  3  FROM   AP_250K;
Explained.

SQL> @explain8
Plan Tree
```

```
------------------------------
SELECT STATEMENT   Cost = 1
  TABLE ACCESS FULL AUTO_PARTS

SQL> @explan8p

    ID  PRNTID Operation
------ ------- ----------------
     0         SELECT STATEMENT
     1       0 TABLE ACCESS

PSTART    PSTOP          PID Options
--------- --------- ------ -------
NUMBER(1) NUMBER(1)        1 FULL
```

If you want to relocate your most active partition to a tablespace that has files on its own disk, use the **MOVE PARTITION** clause in the **ALTER TABLE** command. Listing 15.5 starts by displaying the current tablespaces in the database and then displaying the partitions and their associated tablespaces. On this database, partition AP500K is the most active, and it should be moved to tablespace **EXTRA1**, because it's the least active tablespace in the database. Notice that the primary key index has a status of "UNUSABLE," which is a direct result of the **MOVE PARTITION** command. "UNUSED" is also caused by importing a partition or by using SQL*Loader or the **ALTER TABLE TRUNCATE PARTITION**, **ALTER TABLE DROP PARTITION**, and **ALTER TABLE SPLIT PARTITION** commands. To change the status of the index from **UNUSED** to **VALID**, you must either drop and rebuild the index, which you really don't want to do, or just rebuild the index using the **ALTER INDEX REBUILD** command. If the index is in a partition and you want to rebuild it, use the **ALTER INDEX REBUILD PARTITION** command, and the status of the index returns to **VALID**.

Listing 15.5 Moving a table partition.

```
SQL> SELECT TABLESPACE_NAME
  2  FROM   DBA_TABLESPACES;

TABLESPACE_NAME
------------------------------
SYSTEM
USER_DATA
ROLLBACK_DATA
```

```
TEMPORARY_DATA
EXTRA1
EXTRA2
EXTRA3
OBJECTS1

SQL> SELECT PARTITION_NAME,
  2         TABLESPACE_NAME
  3  FROM   USER_TAB_PARTITIONS;

PARTITION_NAME TABLESPACE_NAME
-------------- ---------------
AP500K         EXTRA2
AP250K         EXTRA1
AP1MILLION     EXTRA3

SQL> ALTER TABLE AUTO_PARTS
           MOVE PARTITION AP500K
           TABLESPACE EXTRA1
           NOLOGGING;
Table altered.

SQL> SELECT PARTITION_NAME,
  2         TABLESPACE_NAME
  3  FROM   USER_TAB_PARTITIONS;

PARTITION_NAME TABLESPACE_NAME
-------------- ---------------
AP500K         EXTRA1
AP250K         EXTRA1
AP1MILLION     EXTRA3

SQL> COL INDEX_NAME FORMAT A13
SQL> COL PARTITIONED FORMAT A11

SQL> SELECT INDEX_NAME,
  2         STATUS,
  3         PARTITIONED
  4  FROM   USER_INDEXES
  5  WHERE  TABLE_NAME = 'AUTO_PARTS';

INDEX_NAME    STATUS   PARTITIONED
------------- -------- -----------
PK_AUTO_PARTS UNUSABLE NO
```

```
SQL> ALTER INDEX
  2        PK_AUTO_PARTS
  3        REBUILD;
Index altered.

SQL> SELECT INDEX_NAME,
  2         STATUS,
  3         PARTITIONED
  4  FROM   USER_INDEXES
  5  WHERE  TABLE_NAME = 'AUTO_PARTS';

INDEX_NAME    STATUS PARTITIONED
------------ ------ -----------
PK_AUTO_PARTS VALID  NO
```

Listing 15.6 adds another table partition to the **AUTO_PARTS** table after a lot of agony. Currently, the **AUTO_PARTS** table is in three partitions: AP500K, AP250K, and AP1MILLION. Trying to add a partition to accommodate part numbers up to 8 digits in length fails, because the **PARTNO** column is a **NUMBER**(7) data type. Therefore, the table is altered and the part number is changed to data type **NUMBER(8,0)**. This fails as well, because neither the data type nor the length of a partitioned column can be changed. If you really need to work with 8-digit part numbers, you should re-create the table. For the purpose of this book, we can fudge and add a partition to handle part numbers between 500,001 and 700,000. As they say, "Nice play, Shakespeare." Well, at least you know the syntax for adding a partition. This is a nice lead-in to *splitting* partitions. If a partition is too large, you can split the partition into smaller ones. The last error states that the added partition must have an upper bound greater than the last upper bound. The last upper bound is one million, so the new partition must have an upper bound greater than one million; therefore, 700,001 produces an error message.

Listing 15.6 Adding a table partition.

```
SQL> get cor14_41
  1  COL    PARTITION_NAME  FORMAT A14
  2  COL    TABLESPACE_NAME FORMAT A15
  3  SET    LONG 15
  4  SELECT PARTITION_NAME,
  5         TABLESPACE_NAME,
  6         HIGH_VALUE
  7  FROM   USER_TAB_PARTITIONS
```

```
  8  WHERE  TABLE_NAME = UPPER('&TN')
  9  /
 10* SET    LONG 80
SQL> @cor14_41
Enter value for tn: auTO_PaRtS

PARTITION_NAME TABLESPACE_NAME HIGH_VALUE
-------------- --------------  -----------
AP500K         EXTRA1          500000
AP250K         EXTRA1          250001
AP1MILLION     EXTRA3          1000000

SQL> ALTER TABLE AUTO_PARTS
           ADD PARTITION AP1000500K
           VALUES LESS THAN (10005001)
           TABLESPACE EXTRA2
           NOLOGGING;

VALUES LESS THAN (10005001)
             *
ERROR at line 3:
ORA-01438: value larger than specified
           precision allows for this column

SQL> DESC AUTO_PARTS
Name   Null?    Type
------ -------- -----------
PARTNO NOT NULL NUMBER(7)
PNAME           VARCHAR2(15)
PCOST           NUMBER(7,2)

SQL> ALTER TABLE AUTO_PARTS
  2        MODIFY PARTNO NUMBER(8,0);
      MODIFY PARTNO NUMBER(8,0)
             *
ERROR at line 2:
ORA-14060: data type or length of a table
   partitioning column may not be changed

SQL> ALTER TABLE AUTO_PARTS
  2             ADD PARTITION AP700001K
  3             VALUES LESS THAN (700001)
  4             TABLESPACE EXTRA2
  5             NOLOGGING;
```

```
            ADD PARTITION AP700001K
                                *
ERROR at line 2:
ORA-14074: partition bound must
           collate higher than that of
           the last partition
```

Listing 15.7 splits the partition **AP1MILLION** into two partitions. However, the partition names don't quite match the noninclusive upper bounds. For instance, partition **AP1MILLION** has an upper bound of 750,000, and the partition **AP750001K** has an upper bound of one million. So, let's just rename the partitions instead of dropping and re-creating them. Each of the two partitions are temporarily renamed and then returned to the desired partition names **AP750001K**, with an upper bound of 750,000, and **AP1MILLION**, with an upper bound of one million.

Listing 15.7 Splitting and renaming partitions.

```
SQL> get cor8_par
  1  COL     PNAME FORMAT A10
  2  SET     LONG 10
  3  COL     TSNAME FORMAT A10
  4  SELECT  PARTITION_NAME PNAME,
  5          HIGH_VALUE,
  6          TABLESPACE_NAME TSNAME
  7  FROM    USER_TAB_PARTITIONS
  8* WHERE   TABLE_NAME = 'AUTO_PARTS'

SQL> @cor8_par

PNAME      HIGH_VALUE TSNAME
---------- ---------- ------
AP500K     500000     EXTRA1
AP250K     250001     EXTRA1
AP1MILLION 1000000    EXTRA3

SQL> ALTER TABLE AUTO_PARTS
         SPLIT PARTITION AP1MILLION
         AT (750001)
    INTO (PARTITION AP1MILLION TABLESPACE EXTRA3,
         PARTITION AP750001K  TABLESPACE EXTRA2);
Table altered.
```

```
SQL> @cor8_par

PNAME      HIGH_VALUE TSNAME
---------- ---------- ------
AP500K     500000     EXTRA1
AP250K     250001     EXTRA1
AP1MILLION 750001     EXTRA3
AP750001K  1000000    EXTRA2

SQL> ALTER TABLE AUTO_PARTS
  2  RENAME PARTITION AP1MILLION
  3             TO HOLD_PARTITION;
Table altered.

SQL> ALTER TABLE AUTO_PARTS
  2  RENAME PARTITION AP750001K
  3             TO HOLD_PARTITION2;
Table altered.

SQL> ALTER TABLE AUTO_PARTS
  2  RENAME PARTITION HOLD_PARTITION
  3             TO AP750001K;
Table altered.

SQL> ALTER TABLE AUTO_PARTS
  2  RENAME PARTITION HOLD_PARTITION2
  3             TO AP1MILLION;
Table altered.

SQL> @cor8_par

PNAME      HIGH_VALUE TSNAME
---------- ---------- ------
AP500K     500000     EXTRA1
AP250K     250001     EXTRA1
AP750001K  750001     EXTRA3
AP1MILLION 1000000    EXTRA2
```

Listing 15.8 shows how to drop a table partition. In this case, the partition named **AP1MILLION** is dropped.

Listing 15.8 Dropping a partition.

```
SQL> ALTER TABLE AUTO_PARTS
     DROP PARTITION AP1MILLION;
```

```
Table altered.

SQL> @cor8_par

PNAME      HIGH_VALUE TSNAME
---------- ---------- ------
AP500K     500000     EXTRA1
AP250K     250001     EXTRA1
AP750001K  750001     EXTRA3
```

Constraints

In Oracle8, you can create or alter a constraint using the **ENFORCE** option. The **ENFORCE** option of the **CREATE TABLE** and **ALTER TABLE** commands permits existing rows to violate the constraint, but new rows or changed rows must abide by the rules of the constraint. You can also set a constraint. For more detailed information, see *Oracle8 Server SQL Reference Release 8.0, Volume 2,* pages 4-611 and 4-612 for the **SET CONSTRAINT** command. Listing 15.9 shows how to add a primary key constraint to a table. The primary key constraint creates a unique index on the primary key column(s) and makes the column(s) not null. Be sure to use the **USING INDEX TABLESPACE** clause or else the unique index will be created in the default tablespace of the person altering the table. In this example, the unique index is created in the **USER_DATA** tablespace. Moreover, Oracle names the unique index the same name as the primary key constraint. If duplicate part numbers exist, the **ALTER TABLE** command fails, and the duplicates must be corrected before the primary key constraint can be created. To speed up large table loads, you can disable the primary key constraint, load your data, and then enable the constraint.

Listing 15.9 Adding primary key constraints.

```
SQL> ALTER TABLE AUTO_PARTS
  2        ADD CONSTRAINT PK_AUTO_PARTS
  3        PRIMARY KEY(PARTNO)
  4        USING INDEX
  5        TABLESPACE USER_DATA;
Table altered.

SQL> DESC AUTO_PARTS
 Name   Null?    Type
 ------ -------- -----------
 PARTNO NOT NULL NUMBER(7)
```

```
 PNAME          VARCHAR2(15)
 PCOST          NUMBER(7,2)

SQL> COL CONSTRAINT_NAME FORMAT A15
SQL> COL SEARCH_CONDITION FORMAT A16

SQL> SELECT CONSTRAINT_NAME,
            CONSTRAINT_TYPE,
            SEARCH_CONDITION
     FROM   USER_CONSTRAINTS
     WHERE  TABLE_NAME = UPPER('&Table');


Enter value for table: AUTO_PARTS

CONSTRAINT_NAME C SEARCH_CONDITION
--------------- - ------ ---------
PK_AUTO_PARTS   P

SQL> SELECT CONSTRAINT_NAME,
            CONSTRAINT_TYPE,
            STATUS,
            DEFERRABLE,
            DEFERRED,
            VALIDATED,
            GENERATED,
            BAD -- OUTPUT EDITED
     FROM   USER_CONSTRAINTS
     WHERE  TABLE_NAME = 'AUTO_PARTS';

CONSTRAINT_NAME C STATUS  DEFERRABLE
--------------- - ------ --------------
PK_AUTO_PARTS   P ENABLED NOT DEFERRABLE


DEFERRED  VALIDATED GENERATED BAD
--------- --------- --------- ---
IMMEDIATE VALIDATED USER NAME

SQL> COL INDEX_NAME    FORMAT A13
SQL> COL LOGGING       FORMAT A7
SQL> COL LAST_ANALYZED HEADING LAST
SQL> COL PARTITIONED   FORMAT A11
SQL> COL BUFFER_POOL   NOPRINT
```

```
SQL> SELECT INDEX_NAME,
  2         LOGGING,
  3         LAST_ANALYZED,
  4         PARTITIONED,
  5         GENERATED
  6  FROM   USER_INDEXES
  7  WHERE  TABLE_NAME = 'AUTO_PARTS';

INDEX_NAME    LOGGING LAST     PARTITIONED G
------------- ------- -------- ----------- -
PK_AUTO_PARTS YES     11/11/97 NO          N

SQL> SELECT INDEX_NAME,
  2         INDEX_TYPE,
  3         TABLE_TYPE,
  4         INCLUDE_COLUMN,
  5         TABLESPACE_NAME
  6  FROM   USER_INDEXES -- OUTPUT EDITED
  7  WHERE  TABLE_NAME = 'AUTO_PARTS';

INDEX_NAME    INDEX_TYPE TABLE_TYPE
------------- ---------- ----------
PK_AUTO_PARTS NORMAL     TABLE


INCLUDE_COLUMN TABLESPACE_NAME
-------------- ---------------
               USER_DATA

SQL> ALTER TABLE AUTO_PARTS -- NEXT, LOAD DATA
           DISABLE PRIMARY KEY;
Table altered.

SQL> ALTER TABLE AUTO_PARTS
  2        ENABLE PRIMARY KEY
  3        USING INDEX
  4        TABLESPACE USER_DATA;
Table altered.
```

Whenever constraints are enabled, they check the existing data in the table; therefore, they may require a lot of time to execute. However, in Listing 15.10, the **ENABLE NOVALIDATE CONSTRAINT** only checks new statements; it's much faster than the normal **ENABLE CONSTRAINT**, which checks all rows in the table. Placing a check constraint on the **PCOST** column ensures that the part cost is always less than

$50,000. When an attempt is made to update part number 1's cost to $69,000, Oracle error ORA-02290 results, as expected. To simulate a large table load, the check constraint is disabled and part number 1's cost is updated to $69,000. This update works because the check constraint is disabled. Next, the **ENABLE NOVALIDATE CONSTRAINT** clause is used in the **ALTER TABLE** command to enable the check constraint. Notice that it's successfully enabled, proving that the constraint does not validate preexisting data. Trying to update part number 1's cost to $55,000 violates the check constraint and the update rolls back. Notice that the **VALIDATED** column in **USER_CONSTRAINTS** contains a value of **NOT VALIDATED** for the check constraint in the data dictionary view **USER_CONSTRAINTS.** Finally, remember that if you try to enable the check constraint without using the **NOVALIDATE** option, your sins will follow you. Any violations of the check option cause an error.

Listing 15.10 Using **ENABLE NOVALIDATE CONSTRAINT**.

```
SQL> ALTER TABLE AUTO_PARTS
  2          ADD CONSTRAINT CK_AP
  3          CHECK(PCOST < 50000);
Table altered.

SQL> get cor14_24
  1  SET     LONG 15
  2  SELECT SUBSTR(CONSTRAINT_NAME,1,13) NAME,
  3         DEFERRABLE "DEF?",
  4         DEFERRED DEF,
  5         SUBSTR(VALIDATED,1,9) VAL,
  6         SUBSTR(GENERATED,1,9) GEN
  7  FROM   USER_CONSTRAINTS
  8  WHERE  TABLE_NAME = UPPER('&TN')
  9  /
 10* SET    LONG 80

SQL> @cor14_24
Enter value for tn: auto_PARTS

NAME          DEF?
------------ ---------------
PK_AUTO_PARTS NOT DEFERRABLE
CK_AP         NOT DEFERRABLE
```

```
DEF       VAL       GEN
--------- --------- ---------
IMMEDIATE VALIDATED USER NAME
IMMEDIATE VALIDATED USER NAME

SQL> UPDATE AUTO_PARTS
  2  SET    PCOST  = 69000
  3  WHERE  PARTNO = 1;

UPDATE AUTO_PARTS
*
ERROR at line 1:
ORA-02290: check constraint
           (SYSTEM.CK_AP) violated

SQL> ALTER TABLE AUTO_PARTS
  2        DISABLE CONSTRAINT CK_AP;
Table altered.

SQL> UPDATE AUTO_PARTS
  2  SET   PCOST  = 69000
  3  WHERE PARTNO = 1;
1 row updated.

SQL> ALTER TABLE AUTO_PARTS  -- DATA NOT VALIDATED
  2        ENABLE NOVALIDATE -- Very Fast!!
  3        CONSTRAINT CK_AP;
Table altered.

SQL> UPDATE AUTO_PARTS
  2  SET    PCOST  = 55000
  3  WHERE  PARTNO = 1;
UPDATE AUTO_PARTS
*
ERROR at line 1:
ORA-02290: check constraint
           (SYSTEM.CK_AP) violated

SQL> @cor14_24
Enter value for tn: auto_parts

NAME          DEF?
------------- --------------
PK_AUTO_PARTS NOT DEFERRABLE
CK_AP         NOT DEFERRABLE
```

```
DEF       VAL       GEN
--------- --------- ---------
IMMEDIATE VALIDATED USER NAME
IMMEDIATE NOT VALID USER NAME

SQL> ALTER TABLE AUTO_PARTS
  2         ENABLE CONSTRAINT CK_AP;
ALTER TABLE AUTO_PARTS
*
ERROR at line 1:
ORA-02293: cannot enable (SYSTEM.CK_AP)
Check constraint violated
```

Listing 15.11 uses the **ENFORCE** option, which allows existing rows to violate the constraint but prohibits new rows and new updates from violating the constraint.

Listing 15.11 Using **ENFORCE CONSTRAINT**.

```
SQL> ALTER TABLE AUTO_PARTS
  2         ENABLE CONSTRAINT CK_AP;
ALTER TABLE AUTO_PARTS
*
ERROR at line 1:
ORA-02293: cannot enable (SYSTEM.CK_AP)
Check constraint violated

SQL> ALTER TABLE AUTO_PARTS
  2         ENFORCE CONSTRAINT CK_AP;
Table altered.

SQL> UPDATE AUTO_PARTS
  2  SET PCOST = 55000
  3  WHERE PARTNO = 1;
UPDATE AUTO_PARTS
*
ERROR at line 1:
ORA-02290: check constraint
           (SYSTEM.CK_AP) violated
```

By using the **SET CONSTRAINT** command, you control when a deferrable constraint checks the data in a table. If you use the **IMMEDIATE** option, the constraint checks the data after each **INSERT**, **UPDATE**, or **DELETE** statement. If you use the **DEFERRED** option, the constraint checks the data when you commit your transaction. Listing 15.12 reveals that a problem seems to exist with this command in Oracle8.0.3 at the date of this writing. However, in the manual *Oracle8 Server Concepts Release 8.0, Volume 2* on page 20 of Chapter 23, the **ALTER SESSION** command is referenced, so let's try it. Also, in *Oracle8 Server SQL Reference Release 8.0, Volume 1* on page 68 of Chapter 4, **ALTER SESSION** is the command you need. Both Oracle manuals suggest the use of the **ALTER SESSION** command, and not the **SET CONSTRAINT** command as indicated on page 612 of Chapter 4 in *Oracle8 Server SQL Reference Volume 2*. None of the **SET CONSTRAINT** commands worked in Listing 15.12.

Listing 15.12 Using **ALTER SESSION SET CONSTRAINT**.

```
SQL> COMMIT;
Commit complete.

SQL> SET CONSTRAINT CK_AP DEFERRED;
unknown SET option "CONSTRAINT"

SQL> DEF _O_RELEASE
DEFINE _O_RELEASE  = "800030000" (CHAR)

SQL> SET HEADING OFF
SQL> SELECT TO_CHAR(SYSDATE,
  2  'fmDay, Month ddspth, yyyy HH:MI AM')
  3  FROM   DUAL;

Saturday, November fifteenth, 1997 1:51 PM

SQL> SET CONSTRAINT  CK_AP     IMMEDIATE;
SQL> SET CONSTRAINT  CK_AP     DEFERRED;
SQL> SET CONSTRAINTS ALL       IMMEDIATE;
SQL> SET CONSTRAINTS ALL       DEFERRED;
SQL> SET CONSTRAINTS CK_AP, C2 IMMEDIATE;
SQL> SET CONSTRAINTS CK_AP, C2 DEFERRED;

SQL> ALTER SESSION
  2         SET CONSTRAINT = DEFERRED;
Session altered.

SQL> ALTER SESSION
  2         SET CONSTRAINT = IMMEDIATE;
Session altered.
```

```
SQL> ALTER SESSION
  2       SET CONSTRAINT = DEFAULT;
Session altered.
```

You disable constraints for large table loads. Then, after you load the table with data, you enable the constraints. However, sometimes your constraints cannot be enabled because of violations. On very large tables, tracking down the violators can be time consuming. Before you can use the **EXCEPTIONS INTO EXCEPTIONS** clause, you must create the **EXCEPTIONS** table by executing a script named utlexcpt.sql. Normally, this file is located in $ORACLE_HOME/rdbms/admin on Unix platforms and C:\ORANT\RDBMS73\ADMIN on NT platforms.

In Listing 15.13, Maryellen's monthly salary is deliberately updated outside the boundaries of the check constraint by disabling the check constraint before the update. When an attempt is made to enable the constraint, error ORA-02296 results. Therefore, the same command is entered again, except this time the **EXCEPTIONS INTO EXCEPTIONS** clause is used. Don't be alarmed by the error message—the constraint cannot be enabled. Next, a query is written that counts the number of rows in the **EXCEPTIONS** table. In this example, one row is in violation of the check constraint. By joining the **EMP** and **EXCEPTIONS** tables together, you can determine which row is the violator. In this case, Maryellen's salary needs to be reduced below $5,500 a month, or the check constraint needs to be dropped and re-created with a higher monthly salary allowed. Remember that a constraint cannot be altered.

Listing 15.13 Finding constraint violators.

```
SQL> ALTER TABLE EMP
  2  ADD CONSTRAINT CK_EMP_SAL_RANGE
  3  CHECK(SAL BETWEEN 500 AND 5500);
Table altered.

SQL> @cons
Enter value for table: emp

CONSTRAINT_NAME TYPE SEARCH_CONDITION
--------------- ---- ------------------------
SYS_C006908        C EMPNO IS NOT NULL
PK_EMP_EMPNO       P
FK1_EMP_DEPTNO     R
CK_EMP_SAL_RANGE   C SAL BETWEEN 500 AND 5500
```

```
SQL> UPDATE EMP
  2         SET SAL = 7000
  3  WHERE ENAME    = 'MARYELLEN';
*
UPDATE EMP
ERROR at line 1:
ORA-02290: check constraint
(SYSTEM.CK_EMP_SAL_RANGE) violated

SQL> ALTER TABLE EMP
  2         DISABLE CONSTRAINT
  3         CK_EMP_SAL_RANGE;
Table altered.

SQL> UPDATE EMP
  2         SET SAL = 7000
  3  WHERE  ENAME   = 'MARYELLEN';
1 row updated.

SQL> ALTER TABLE EMP
  2         ENABLE CONSTRAINT
  3         CK_EMP_SAL_RANGE;

ALTER TABLE EMP ENABLE CONSTRAINT
*
ERROR at line 1:
ORA-02296: cannot enable constraint
(SYSTEM.CK_EMP_SAL_RANGE) - found
noncomplying values

SQL> @$ORACLE_HOME/rdbms/admin/utlexcpt
Table created.

SQL> ALTER TABLE EMP
  2         ENABLE CONSTRAINT
  3         CK_EMP_SAL_RANGE
  4         EXCEPTIONS INTO EXCEPTIONS;

ALTER TABLE EMP ENABLE CONSTRAINT
*
ERROR at line 1:
ORA-02296: cannot enable constraint
(SYSTEM.CK_EMP_SAL_RANGE) - found
noncomplying values
```

```
SQL> SELECT COUNT(*)
     FROM   EXCEPTIONS;

   COUNT
-------
       1

SQL> SELECT E.EMPNO,
            E.ENAME
     FROM   EMP E,
            EXCEPTIONS X
     WHERE  E.ROWID = X.ROW_ID;

  EMPNO  ENAME
-------  ----------
   7902  MARYELLEN
```

Working with the technique of using SQL to generate SQL, you can write a script similar to the one shown in Listing 15.14 to disable all constraints on a particular table. The script spools output to a file named disable.sql. The key is to sort by the constraint type, thus ensuring that the foreign key constraints are disabled before the primary key constraints; otherwise, error messages will result. The constraint type for a primary key constraint is P; for a foreign key constraint, the type is R (for referential integrity). Because R comes after P in the collating sequence (and we want it to be first), the constraint type is sorted in descending order. This is accomplished by entering **ORDER BY CONSTRAINT_TYPE DESC.** Notice that the foreign key constraints are disabled first and then the primary key constraints. Also, note the user-friendly constraint name—SYS_C007138. If you don't name your constraints, Oracle names them for you. Kind of a neat naming scheme, huh? By the way, with a little imagination, you can write another script that enables all the constraints on a table.

Listing 15.14 Using **DISABLE CONSTRAINT**.

```
SQL> get cb380
  SET ECHO     OFF
  SET HEADING  OFF
  SET FEEDBACK OFF
  SET PAGESIZE 60
  SPOOL disable.sql
  SELECT 'ALTER TABLE ' ||
```

```
            table_name ||
          ' DISABLE CONSTRAINT ' ||
            constraint_name || ';'
FROM   USER_CONSTRAINTS  -- FK's First
WHERE TABLE_NAME IN('DEPT','EMP')
ORDER   BY   CONSTRAINT_TYPE DESC;
SPOOL         OFF
SET ECHO      ON
SET HEADING   ON
SET FEEDBACK ON
START disable

ALTER TABLE EMP
DISABLE CONSTRAINT UN_EMP_ENAME;

ALTER TABLE EMP
DISABLE CONSTRAINT FK_EMP_DEPTNO;

ALTER TABLE EMP
DISABLE CONSTRAINT FK_EMP_MGR;

ALTER TABLE DEPT
DISABLE CONSTRAINT PK_DEPT_DEPTNO;

ALTER TABLE EMP
DISABLE CONSTRAINT PK_EMP_EMPNO;

ALTER TABLE EMP
DISABLE CONSTRAINT SYS_C007138;

ALTER TABLE EMP
DISABLE CONSTRAINT CK_EMP_SAL;
SQL> SET HEADING  ON
SQL> SET FEEDBACK ON
SQL> START disable

SQL> ALTER TABLE EMP
     DISABLE CONSTRAINT UN_EMP_ENAME;
Table altered.

SQL> ALTER TABLE EMP
     DISABLE CONSTRAINT FK_EMP_DEPTNO;
Table altered.
```

```
SQL> ALTER TABLE EMP
     DISABLE CONSTRAINT FK_EMP_MGR;
Table altered.

SQL> ALTER TABLE DEPT
     DISABLE CONSTRAINT PK_DEPT_DEPTNO;
Table altered.

SQL> ALTER TABLE EMP
     DISABLE CONSTRAINT PK_EMP_EMPNO;
Table altered.

SQL> ALTER TABLE EMP
     DISABLE CONSTRAINT SYS_C007138;
Table altered.

SQL> ALTER TABLE EMP
     DISABLE CONSTRAINT CK_EMP_SAL;
Table altered.
```

Remember, you cannot alter a constraint. To rename a constraint, you must first drop the constraint and then re-create it with the new name. If you don't name the constraint, as illustrated in Listing 15.15, Oracle names it SYS_C with six numbers at the end of the name. Here, Oracle has named the **NOT NULL** constraint on the **SAL** column SYS_C006921. Notice that more than one constraint can be placed on a column. The **SAL** column has two constraints—a **CHECK** constraint and a **NOT NULL** constraint. The constraint types are the same for the **CHECK** and **NOT NULL** constraints—that is, C. The constraint should be dropped and re-created with an appropriate name, such as **NN_EMP_SAL**.

Listing 15.15 Renaming SYS_C006921.

```
SQL> ALTER TABLE EMP
  2        MODIFY SAL NOT NULL;
Table altered.

SQL> DESC EMP
Name   Null?    Type
------ -------- -----------
SAL    NOT NULL NUMBER(7,2)

SQL> @cons
Enter value for table: emp
```

```
CONSTRAINT_NAME  TYPE SEARCH_CONDITION
---------------- ---- -----------------------
SYS_C006908      C    EMPNO IS NOT NULL
PK_EMP_EMPNO     P
FK1_EMP_DEPTNO   R
CK_EMP_SAL_RANGE C    SAL BETWEEN 500 AND 5500
SYS_C006921      C    SAL IS NOT NULL

SQL> ALTER TABLE EMP
          DROP CONSTRAINT SYS_C006921;
Table altered.

SQL> ALTER TABLE EMP
  2       MODIFY  SAL
  3       CONSTRAINT NN_EMP_SAL
  4       NOT NULL;
Table altered.

SQL> SELECT CONSTRAINT_NAME,
  2         CONSTRAINT_TYPE,
  3         SEARCH_CONDITION
  4         STATUS
  5  FROM   USER_CONSTRAINTS
  6  WHERE  TABLE_NAME = 'EMP'
  7         AND CONSTRAINT_TYPE = 'C';

CONSTRAINT_NAME  TYPE SEARCH_CONDITION
---------------- ---- -----------------------
SYS_C006908      C    EMPNO IS NOT NULL
CK_EMP_SAL_RANGE C    SAL BETWEEN 500 AND 5500
NN_EMP_SAL       C    SAL IS NOT NULL
```

To verify the format of a social security number, use the **TRANSLATE** function. This function requires three arguments. The first argument is the contents of the **SSN** column. The second argument is a list of characters to translate, and the third argument lists the characters into which the second argument's characters are translated. For instance, Listing 15.16 translates all numbers to 9 and dashes to D. Therefore, if the user enters 458-98-6754, this query translates the string into 999D99D9999. In this example, Dee Ana has her **SSN** column updated because her social security number is in an acceptable format. However, Phillip's social security number is not in the correct format, and the update fails.

Listing 15.16 Validate data format.

```
SQL> ALTER TABLE EMP
  2         ADD   SSN    VARCHAR2(11);
Table altered.

SQL> DESC EMP
Name      Null?    Type
-------- -------- ------------
EMPNO     NOT NULL NUMBER(4)
ENAME              VARCHAR2(10)
JOB                VARCHAR2(9)
MGR                NUMBER(4)
HIREDATE           DATE
SAL       NOT NULL NUMBER(7,2)
COMM               NUMBER(7,2)
DEPTNO             NUMBER(2)
SSN                VARCHAR2(11)

SQL>  ALTER TABLE EMP
  2   ADD   CONSTRAINT  CK_EMP_SSN
      CHECK(TRANSLATE(SSN,
             '0123456789-',
             '9999999999D') =
             '999D99D9999');
Table altered.

SQL> UPDATE EMP
  2  SET     SSN    = '123-45-6789'
  3  WHERE   ENAME = 'DEE ANA';
1 rows updated.

SQL> UPDATE EMP
  2  SET     SSN    = '12-345-6789'
  3  WHERE   ENAME = 'PHILLIP';
WHERE  ENAME = 'PHILLIP'
                     *
ERROR at line 3:
ORA-02290: check constraint(SYSTEM.CK_EMP_SSN)
```

Database Triggers

One of the biggest uses of database triggers is for auditing. Listing 15.17 shows a database trigger named ROY that audits all inserts, updates, and deletes applied to the **DEPT** table. After each row is inserted, updated, or deleted in the **DEPT** table, the trigger inserts one row into the **AUDIT_DEPT** table, because **ROY** is a row-level trigger (**FOR EACH ROW**). Four semicolons are missing so the trigger does not compile until corrected. To see more of the trigger code in **USER_TRIGGERS**, enter something like **SET LONG 500**.

Listing 15.17 Using triggers for auditing.

```
SQL> CREATE TABLE AUDIT_DEPT
      (WHO          VARCHAR2(30),
       WHEN         DATE,
       OLD_DEPTNO NUMBER(2,0),
       NEW_DEPTNO NUMBER(2,0),
       OLD_DNAME  VARCHAR2(14),
       NEW_DNAME  VARCHAR2(14),
       OLD_LOC    VARCHAR2(14),
       NEW_LOC    VARCHAR2(14));
Table created.

SQL> CREATE TRIGGER ROY
     AFTER INSERT OR
           UPDATE OR
           DELETE
     ON    DEPT
     FOR   EACH ROW
     BEGIN
          IF INSERTING THEN -- MISSING SEMICOLON
             INSERT INTO AUDIT_DEPT
             VALUES(USER,SYSDATE,NULL,:NEW.deptno,
                    NULL, :NEW.dname, NULL, :NEW.loc)
          ELSIF DELETING THEN -- MISSING SEMICOLON
             INSERT INTO AUDIT_DEPT
             VALUES(USER,SYSDATE,:OLD.deptno,NULL,
                    :OLD.dname,NULL,:OLD.loc,NULL)
          ELSIF UPDATING THEN -- MISSING SEMICOLON
             INSERT INTO AUDIT_DEPT
             VALUES(USER, SYSDATE,
                    :OLD.deptno, :NEW.deptno,
                    :OLD.dname,  :NEW.dname,
                    :OLD.loc,    :NEW.loc)
          END  IF -- MISSING SEMICOLON
     END;

SQL> SAVE cor14_21
```

```
SQL> /
Warning: Trigger created with
         compilation errors.

SQL> show errors
No errors.

SQL> COL TEXT FORMAT A40
SQL> COL TYPE FORMAT A10
SQL> COL NAME NOPRINT

SQL> SELECT *
  2  FROM   USER_ERRORS
  3  WHERE  NAME = 'ROY';

SQL> SELECT TEXT,
  2         SEQUENCE SEQ,
  3         LINE,
  4         POSITION POS
  5  FROM   USER_ERRORS
  6  WHERE  NAME = 'ROY';

TEXT                       SEQ LINE POS
-------------------------- --- ---- ---
PLS-00103: Encountered       1    6   7
 the symbol "ELSIF"
 when expecting one
 of the following:
 , ; return RETURNING_

SQL> @cor14_21
Trigger created.

SQL> UPDATE DEPT
  2  SET LOC = 'MAUI'
  3  WHERE DEPTNO IN(10,30);
2 rows updated.

SQL> SELECT WHO,
  2         OLD_LOC,
  3         NEW_LOC
  4  FROM   AUDIT_DEPT;
```

```
WHO    OLD_LOC        NEW_LOC
------ -------------- --------------
SYSTEM NEW YORK       MAUI
SYSTEM CHICAGO        MAUI

SQL> INSERT INTO DEPT
  2  VALUES(55,'IS','OAHU');
1 row created.

SQL> start cor14_30

WHO    OLD_LOC        NEW_LOC
------ -------------- --------------
SYSTEM NEW YORK       MAUI
SYSTEM CHICAGO        MAUI
SYSTEM                OAHU

SQL> DELETE FROM DEPT
  2  WHERE LOC = 'OAHU';
1 row deleted.

SQL> @ cor14_30

WHO    OLD_LOC        NEW_LOC
------ -------------- --------------
SYSTEM NEW YORK       MAUI
SYSTEM CHICAGO        MAUI
SYSTEM                OAHU
SYSTEM OAHU

SQL> SHOW LONG
long 80

SQL> SELECT TRIGGER_BODY
  2  FROM   USER_TRIGGERS
  3  WHERE  TRIGGER_NAME = 'ROY';

TRIGGER_BODY
-----------------------
BEGIN
      IF INSERTING THEN
         INSERT into audit_dept
         VALUES(us

SQL> SET LONG 500
```

Certain constructs don't permit DML through a view. DML is the acronym for data manipulation language, and includes the SQL statements **INSERT**, **UPDATE**, and **DELETE**. Some of the restrictive constructs are set operators, group functions, **GROUP BY**, **CONNECT BY** and **START WITH**, **DISTINCT**, and some joins. Listing 15.18 shows how to allow updates through the view **HEAD_COUNT**, using an **INSTEAD OF** trigger. If an employee is added to a certain department, the update fires the **INSTEAD OF** trigger for each row updated. When the **HC** column is updated by 1 for Department 10, the **INSTEAD OF** trigger fires and inserts a new employee in the **EMP** table in Department 10. A query using **HEAD_COUNT** verifies that the number of employees in Department 10 went from three to four.

Listing 15.18 Using INSTEAD OF triggers.

```
SQL> CREATE VIEW HEAD_COUNT AS
  2  SELECT DEPTNO, COUNT(*) HC
  3  FROM   EMP
  4  GROUP  BY DEPTNO;
View created.

SQL> SELECT *
  2  FROM   HEAD_COUNT;

 DEPTNO       HC
------- -------
     10       3
     20       5
     30       6
     44       1
     77       1

SQL> UPDATE HEAD_COUNT
  2  SET    HC = HC + 1
  3  WHERE  DEPTNO = 10;
UPDATE HEAD_COUNT
       *
ERROR at line 1:
ORA-01732: data manipulation
operation not legal on this view

SQL> CREATE TRIGGER UPDATE_HEAD_COUNT
  2  INSTEAD OF UPDATE ON HEAD_COUNT
  3  FOR EACH ROW
```

```
BEGIN
  IF :OLD.DEPTNO = 10 THEN
  INSERT INTO EMP(EMPNO,DEPTNO,ENAME)
    VALUES(10,10,'INSTEAD OF');
  ELSIF :OLD.DEPTNO = 20 THEN
  INSERT INTO EMP(EMPNO,DEPTNO,ENAME)
    VALUES(20,20,'INSTEAD OF');
  ELSIF :OLD.DEPTNO = 30 THEN
    INSERT INTO EMP(EMPNO,DEPTNO,ENAME)
    VALUES(30,30,'INSTEAD OF 30');
   END  IF;
END;
SQL> /
Trigger created.

SQL> SELECT *
     FROM   HEAD_COUNT;

 DEPTNO      HC
------- -------
     10       3
     20       5
     30       6
     44       1
     77       1

SQL> UPDATE HEAD_COUNT
     SET    HC = HC + 1
     WHERE  DEPTNO = 10;
1 row updated.

SQL> SELECT *
     FROM   HEAD_COUNT;

 DEPTNO      HC
------- -------
     10       4
     20       5
     30       6
     44       1
     77       1

SQL> SELECT EMPNO,
            ENAME,
            DEPTNO
```

```
FROM    EMP
WHERE   ENAME LIKE 'INS%';

EMPNO ENAME          DEPTNO
------- ---------- -------
     10 INSTEAD OF       10
```

Index-Organized Tables

Index-organized tables store the primary key and the data columns together in a btree index. Less space is required because the data is stored next to the primary key and no rowid is required. As a matter of fact, if you write a query using the pseudocolumn **ROWID**, you'll receive an error. Listing 15.19 creates an index-organized table named **AUTO_PARTS_INDEX_ORG**, because the **ORGANIZATION INDEX** clause is used. The **PCTTHRESHOLD** setting of 15 percent causes any rows exceeding 15 percent of the block size to be placed in the tablespace EXTRA2. The data dictionary view **USER_INDEXES** shows that the **INDEX_TYPE** column contains **IOT** (index-organized table). A PL/SQL script populates the table with 80,000 rows and analyzes the table. A query referencing **ROWID** will result in an error if **ROWID** is used by itself or if the Oracle-supplied package **DBMS_ROWID** is used. Analyzing this table requires 47.11 seconds, compared to 42.75 seconds for the normal table. The Explain Plan output shows a cost of 3. It also indicates that the index is used to retrieve all rows with a part number greater than 79,990 and that 0.66 seconds are required to actually retrieve the 10 rows. Notice that the rows return sorted on the primary key column **PARTNO**—79,991 through 80,000. Full-table scans return the rows in sorted order, as well, without the **ORDER BY** clause being used (note part numbers 1 through 4). Interestingly enough, the normal table with a separate btree index has a cost of 4 and requires only 0.17 seconds to retrieve 10 rows. (This is not what I expected.) Using **BETWEEN** requires 0.11 seconds to retrieve three rows from the 80,000-row, index-organized table, compared to 0.12 seconds for the normal table. Finally, a query returning one row requires 0.11 seconds on the index-organized table, but only 0.04 seconds on a normal table. Once again, this is not the expected outcome. Index-organized tables are supposed to be faster in equality- and range-type queries than normal btree indexes, but in these two cases, this is not the outcome. Perhaps much larger tables would indicate the expected results.

Note that you cannot create any indexes on the columns in an index-organized table—if you try, you'll receive Oracle error ORA-25182.

Listing 15.19 Index-organized tables.

```
SQL> get cor14_12
  1  CREATE TABLE AUTO_PARTS_INDEX_ORG
  2     (PARTNO        NUMBER(7),
  3      PNAME         VARCHAR2(15),
  4      PCOST         NUMBER(7,2),
  5      CONSTRAINT PK_AP_INDEX_ORG
  6                 PRIMARY KEY(PARTNO))
  7  ORGANIZATION INDEX TABLESPACE EXTRA1
  8  PCTTHRESHOLD 15
  9  INCLUDING PCOST
 10* OVERFLOW TABLESPACE EXTRA2
SQL> /
Table created.

SQL> SELECT INDEX_NAME,
  2         LOGGING,
  3         LAST_ANALYZED,
  4         PARTITIONED,
  5         GENERATED,
  6         BUFFER_POOL
  7  FROM   USER_INDEXES
  8  WHERE  TABLE_NAME = 'AUTO_PARTS_INDEX_ORG';

INDEX_NAME      LOG LAST_ANAL PAR G BUFFER_
--------------- --- --------- --- - -------
PK_AP_INDEX_ORG NO            NO  N DEFAULT

SQL> SELECT INDEX_NAME,
  2         INDEX_TYPE,
  3         TABLE_TYPE,
  4         INCLUDE_COLUMN IC,
  5         TABLESPACE_NAME TS
  6  FROM   USER_INDEXES
  7  WHERE  TABLE_NAME =
  8         'AUTO_PARTS_INDEX_ORG';

INDEX_NAME      INDEX_TYPE TABLE_TYPE IC TS
--------------- ---------- ---------- -- ------
PK_AP_INDEX_ORG IOT - TOP  TABLE       3 EXTRA1

SQL> SET TIMING ON
SQL> BEGIN
  2      FOR i IN 1..80000 LOOP
```

```
  3       INSERT INTO AUTO_PARTS_INDEX_ORG
  4       VALUES(i, 'Part # ' || i, i+.55);
  5       IF MOD(i,20000) = 0 THEN COMMIT;
  6       END  IF;
  7      END  LOOP;
  8* END;
SQL> /

Elapsed: 00:06:54.35

SQL> SELECT ROWID,
  2          PNAME
  3  FROM    AUTO_PARTS_INDEX_ORG
  4  WHERE   ROWNUM < 3;
FROM    AUTO_PARTS_INDEX_ORG
        *
ERROR at line 3:
ORA-02031: no ROWID for fixed tables
           or for index-organized tables

SQL> SELECT dbms_rowid.rowid_block_number
  2          (rowid) BLK,
  3          PNAME
  4  FROM    AUTO_PARTS_INDEX_ORG
  5  WHERE   ROWNUM < 3;
SELECT dbms_rowid.rowid_block_number(rowid) BLK,
       *
ERROR at line 1:
ORA-02031: no ROWID for fixed tables or
           for index-organized tables

SQL> SELECT COUNT(*)
  2  FROM AUTO_PARTS_INDEX_ORG;

COUNT(*)
--------
   80000

Elapsed: 00:00:22.46

SQL> ANALYZE TABLE
  2          AUTO_PARTS_INDEX_ORG
  3          COMPUTE STATISTICS;
Table analyzed.

Elapsed: 00:00:47.11
```

```
SQL> SELECT DISTINCT(IOT_TYPE)
  2  FROM   USER_TABLES;

IOT_TYPE
------------
IOT
IOT_OVERFLOW

SQL> EXPLAIN PLAN FOR
  2  SELECT *
  3  FROM AUTO_PARTS_INDEX_ORG
  4  WHERE PARTNO > 79990;
Explained.

SQL> get explain8
  1  SET ARRAYSIZE 1
  2  COL "Plan Tree" FORMAT A55
  3  SELECT lpad(' ',2*(level-1)) ||
  4  operation || ' ' || options
  5  || ' ' || object_name || ' ' ||
  6  decode(id,0,'Cost = ' ||
  7              position) "Plan Tree"
  8  FROM   PLAN_TABLE
  9  START  WITH id = 0
 10  CONNECT BY PRIOR id = parent_id
SQL> @explain8

Plan Tree
-----------------------------------
SELECT STATEMENT   Cost = 3
  INDEX RANGE SCAN PK_AP_INDEX_ORG

SQL> SELECT *
  2  FROM AUTO_PARTS_INDEX_ORG
  3  WHERE PARTNO > 79990;

 PARTNO PNAME           PCOST
------- ----------- -------
  79991 Part # 79991 79991.6
  79992 Part # 79992 79992.6
  79993 Part # 79993 79993.6
  79994 Part # 79994 79994.6
  79995 Part # 79995 79995.6
  79996 Part # 79996 79996.6
```

```
79997 Part # 79997 79997.6
79998 Part # 79998 79998.6
79999 Part # 79999 79999.6
80000 Part # 80000 80000.6

10 rows selected.

Elapsed: 00:00:00.66

SQL> SELECT *
  2  FROM   AUTO_PARTS_INDEX_ORG
  3  WHERE  ROWNUM < 5;

 PARTNO PNAME          PCOST
------- ------------ -----
      1 Part # 1        1.55
      2 Part # 2        2.55
      3 Part # 3        3.55
      4 Part # 4        4.55

SQL>  SELECT *
  2   FROM   AUTO_PARTS_INDEX_ORG
  3   WHERE  PARTNO BETWEEN 55000 AND 55002;

 PARTNO PNAME         PCOST
------- ----------- -------
  55000 Part # 55000 55000.6
  55001 Part # 55001 55001.6
  55002 Part # 55002 55002.6

Elapsed: 00:00:00.11

SQL> SELECT *
  2  FROM   AUTO_PARTS_INDEX_ORG
  3  WHERE  PARTNO = 55000;

 PARTNO PNAME         COST
------- ----------- -------
  55000 Part # 55000 55000.6

Elapsed: 00:00:00.11

SQL> CREATE INDEX NO_WAY_MAN
  2  ON AUTO_PARTS_INDEX_ORG(PNAME);
```

```
ON AUTO_PARTS_INDEX_ORG(PNAME)
         *
ERROR at line 2:
ORA-25182: feature not currently
available for index-organized tables
```

Normal tables, like those shown in Listing 15.20, have separate btree indexes for the primary key column(s) and therefore require more disk space. The **INDEX_TYPE** column displays **NORMAL**, which indicates a normal, separate btree index exists on the primary key (the part number column). To insert 80,000 rows into the normal table requires approximately 4 seconds more than to load the index-organized table. This is understandable, because the btree index is updated for each row inserted.

Listing 15.20 Non-index-organized tables.

```
SQL> CREATE TABLE AUTO_PARTS_NO_INDEX_ORG
  2     (PARTNO          NUMBER(7),
  3      PNAME           VARCHAR2(15),
  4      PCOST           NUMBER(7,2),
  5      CONSTRAINT PK_AP_NO_INDEX_ORG
  6                 PRIMARY KEY(PARTNO))
  7  TABLESPACE EXTRA3;
Table created.

SQL>  SELECT INDEX_NAME,
  2          LOGGING,
  3          LAST_ANALYZED,
  4          PARTITIONED,
  5          GENERATED,
  6          BUFFER_POOL
  7   FROM   USER_INDEXES
  8   WHERE  TABLE_NAME =
  9   'AUTO_PARTS_NO_INDEX_ORG';

INDEX_NAME         LOG LAST_ANAL PAR G BUFFER_
------------------ --- --------- --- - -------
PK_AP_NO_INDEX_ORG NO  14-NOV-97 NO  N DEFAULT

SQL> COL INDEX_NAME FORMAT A18
SQL> COL INDEX_TYPE FORMAT A10
SQL> COL TABLE_TYPE FORMAT A10
SQL> COL TS         FORMAT A6
```

```
SQL> SELECT INDEX_NAME,
            INDEX_TYPE,
            TABLE_TYPE,
            INCLUDE_COLUMN IC,
            TABLESPACE_NAME TS
     FROM   USER_INDEXES
     WHERE  TABLE_NAME =
     'AUTO_PARTS_NO_INDEX_ORG';

INDEX_NAME         INDEX_TYPE TABLE_TYPE     IC TS
------------------ ---------- ---------- ------ ------
PK_AP_NO_INDEX_ORG NORMAL     TABLE             EXTRA3

SQL> BEGIN
      FOR i IN 1..80000 LOOP
        INSERT INTO AUTO_PARTS_NO_INDEX_ORG
        VALUES(i, 'Part # ' || i, i+.55);
          IF MOD(i,20000) = 0 THEN COMMIT;
          END  IF;
      END  LOOP;
     END;
PL/SQL procedure successfully completed.

Elapsed: 00:06:58.81

SQL> SELECT ROWID,
            PNAME
     FROM   AUTO_PARTS_NO_INDEX_ORG
     WHERE  ROWNUM < 3;

ROWID              PNAME
------------------ -------------
AAAAwSAAHAAAAAcAAA Part # 1
AAAAwSAAHAAAAAcAAB Part # 2

SQL> SELECT COUNT(*)
     FROM AUTO_PARTS_NO_INDEX_ORG;

COUNT(*)
--------
   80000

Elapsed: 00:00:14.00

SQL> ANALYZE TABLE
         AUTO_PARTS_NO_INDEX_ORG
```

```
  3      COMPUTE STATISTICS;
Table analyzed.

Elapsed: 00:00:42.75

SQL> EXPLAIN PLAN FOR
  2  SELECT *
  3  FROM AUTO_PARTS_NO_INDEX_ORG
  4  WHERE PARTNO > 79990;
Explained.

SQL> @explain8

Plan Tree
----------------------------------------
SELECT STATEMENT   Cost = 4
  TABLE ACCESS BY INDEX ROWID
        AUTO_PARTS_NO_INDEX_ORG
    INDEX RANGE SCAN PK_AP_NO_INDEX_ORG

SQL> SELECT *
  2  FROM AUTO_PARTS_NO_INDEX_ORG
  3  WHERE PARTNO > 79990;

 PARTNO PNAME           PCOST
------- ------------ -------
  79991 Part # 79991 79991.6
  79992 Part # 79992 79992.6
  79993 Part # 79993 79993.6
  79994 Part # 79994 79994.6
  79995 Part # 79995 79995.6
  79996 Part # 79996 79996.6
  79997 Part # 79997 79997.6
  79998 Part # 79998 79998.6
  79999 Part # 79999 79999.6
  80000 Part # 80000 80000.6

10 rows selected.

Elapsed: 00:00:00.17

SQL>  SELECT *
  2   FROM AUTO_PARTS_NO_INDEX_ORG
  3   WHERE PARTNO BETWEEN 55000 AND 55002;
```

```
 PARTNO PNAME              PCOST
------- -------------- --------
  55000 Part # 55000    55000.6
  55001 Part # 55001    55001.6
  55002 Part # 55002    55002.6

Elapsed: 00:00:00.12

SQL> SELECT *
  2  FROM AUTO_PARTS_NO_INDEX_ORG
  3  WHERE PARTNO = 55000;

 PARTNO PNAME              PCOST
------- -------------- -------
  55000 Part # 55000    55000.6

Elapsed: 00:00:00.04
```

To create a global partitioned index, use either the **CREATE TABLE** command, as shown in Listing 15.21, or the **ALTER INDEX** command. The table named **RACES** now has an index with four partitions—IPART250K, IPART500K, IPART750K, and IPART1MILL.

Listing 15.21 Index partitions.

```
SQL> CREATE TABLE RACES
  2     (RACENO       NUMBER(8,0),
  3      DRIVERNO     NUMBER(6,0),
  4      DATE_OF_RACE DATE)
  5  TABLESPACE EXTRA1;
Table created.

SQL> get cor14_50
  1  CREATE INDEX PART_INDX
  2         ON RACES(DRIVERNO)
  3  GLOBAL PARTITION BY RANGE(DRIVERNO)
  4    (PARTITION IPART250K
  5      VALUES LESS THAN (250001)
  6      TABLESPACE INDEXES1 NOLOGGING,
  7     PARTITION IPART500K
  8      VALUES LESS THAN (500001)
  9      TABLESPACE EXTRA2 NOLOGGING,
 10     PARTITION IPART750K
 11      VALUES LESS THAN (750001)
```

```
12      TABLESPACE EXTRA1 NOLOGGING,
13     PARTITION IPART1MILL
14      VALUES LESS THAN (MAXVALUE)
15      TABLESPACE EXTRA3 NOLOGGING)
Index created.

SQL> COL DEFTS     FORMAT A9
SQL> COL ALIGNMENT FORMAT A9
SQL> COL LOCALITY  FORMAT A8

SQL> SELECT PARTITIONING_TYPE PTYPE,
  2         PARTITION_COUNT PCOUNT,
  3         LOCALITY,
  4         DEF_TABLESPACE_NAME DEFTS,
  5         ALIGNMENT
  6  FROM   USER_PART_INDEXES
  7  WHERE  INDEX_NAME = 'PART_INDX';

PTYPE PCOUNT LOCALITY DEFTS     ALIGNMENT
----- ------ -------- --------- ---------
RANGE      4 GLOBAL   USER_DATA PREFIXED

SQL> SELECT INDEX_NAME,
  2         INDEX_TYPE,
  3         TABLE_TYPE,
  4         STATUS,
  5         PARTITIONED
  6  FROM   USER_INDEXES
  7  WHERE  TABLE_NAME = 'RACES';

INDEX_NAME INDEX_TYPE TABLE_TYPE STATUS PAR
---------- ---------- ---------- ------ ---
PART_INDX  NORMAL     TABLE      N/A    YES
```

By using the **ALTER INDEX** command, as shown in Listing 15.22, you can flag an index partition as **UNUSABLE** if a problem exists with the tablespace the partition is in or if the partition itself is damaged.

Listing 15.22 Marking an index partition **UNUSABLE**.

```
SQL> get cor14_59
  1  COL    INAME     FORMAT A13
  2  COL    PNAME     FORMAT A10
  3  SET    LONG 10
  4  COL    TSNAME    FORMAT A10
```

```
  5  SELECT INDEX_NAME INAME,
  6         PARTITION_NAME PNAME,
  7         HIGH_VALUE,
  8         TABLESPACE_NAME TSNAME
  9* FROM   USER_IND_PARTITIONS
SQL> @cor14_59

INAME        PNAME      HIGH_VALUE TSNAME
------------ ---------- ---------- --------
PART_INDX    IPART250K  250001     INDEXES1
PART_INDX    IPART500K  500001     EXTRA2
PART_INDX    IPART750K  750001     EXTRA1
PART_INDX    IPART1MILL MAXVALUE   EXTRA3

SQL> ALTER INDEX PART_INDX
           MODIFY PARTITION IPART250K
           UNUSABLE;
Index altered.

SQL> SELECT INDEX_NAME INAME,
  2         PARTITION_NAME PNAME,
  3         STATUS,
  4         TABLESPACE_NAME TSNAME
  5  FROM   USER_IND_PARTITIONS;

INAME        PNAME      STATUS   TSNAME
------------ ---------- -------- ----------
PART_INDX    IPART250K  UNUSABLE INDEXES1
PART_INDX    IPART500K  USABLE   EXTRA2
PART_INDX    IPART750K  USABLE   EXTRA1
PART_INDX    IPART1MILL USABLE   EXTRA3
```

Listing 15.23 shows how to drop the index partition IPART500K. Note that you cannot drop the last partition in a global index. You should also be aware that index partitions can be split or merged.

Listing 15.23 Dropping an index partition.

```
SQL> ALTER INDEX PART_INDX
  2        DROP PARTITION
  3        IPART1MILL;
      IPART1MILL
      *
ERROR at line 3:
ORA-14078: you may not drop the
```

```
highest partition of a GLOBAL index

SQL> ALTER INDEX PART_INDX
  2  DROP PARTITION IPART500K;
Index altered.

SQL> SELECT INDEX_NAME INAME,
  2         PARTITION_NAME PNAME,
  3         STATUS,
  4         TABLESPACE_NAME TSNAME
  5  FROM   USER_IND_PARTITIONS;

INAME        PNAME      STATUS   TSNAME
------------ ---------- -------- ----------
PART_INDX    IPART250K  UNUSABLE INDEXES1
PART_INDX    IPART750K  USABLE   EXTRA1
PART_INDX    IPART1MILL USABLE   EXTRA3
```

Listing 15.24 shows you how to rebuild an index partition. (Unfortunately, it looks like this feature on this platform will need to be fixed in the next release.) The intent here is to rebuild index partition **IPART250K**, even though the status could be enabled to change back to **USABLE**. However, the command kicks you out of Oracle.

Listing 15.24 Rebuilding an index partition.

```
SQL> SELECT INDEX_NAME INAME,
  2         PARTITION_NAME PNAME,
  3         STATUS,
  4         TABLESPACE_NAME TSNAME
  5  FROM   USER_IND_PARTITIONS;

INAME       PNAME      STATUS   TSNAME
----------- ---------- -------- ----------
PART_INDX   IPART250K  UNUSABLE INDEXES1
PART_INDX   IPART750K  USABLE   EXTRA1
PART_INDX   IPART1MILL USABLE   EXTRA3

SQL> ALTER INDEX
  2       REBUILD PARTITION
  3       IPART250K;

ALTER INDEX
*
ERROR at line 1:
ORA-03113: end-of-file on communication channel
```

In Oracle8, the optimizer can be used to perform parallel inserts, updates, and deletes if **PARALLEL DML** is enabled. You enable **PARALLEL DML** using the **ALTER SESSION** command. Even then, there's no guarantee that the DML statement is processed in parallel, unless you submit a **PARALLEL** hint with the statement. Listing 15.25 illustrates how to enable **PARALLEL DML** for the session, followed by several examples that cause Oracle to process the statements in parallel.

Listing 15.25 Using **PARALLEL DML**.

```
SQL> ALTER SESSION
  2          ENABLE PARALLEL DML;
Session altered.

SQL> UPDATE /*+ PARALLEL(DRIVERS,2) */
  2  DRIVERS
  3  SET  DNO = DNO + 1;

SQL> CREATE TABLE DRIVERS_HISTORY
  2  AS SELECT *
  3  FROM   DRIVERS  -- Empty Table
  4  WHERE 1 = 2;
Table created.

SQL>INSERT /*+ PARALLEL(DRIVERS_HISTORY,2) */
  2 INTO DRIVERS_HISTORY
  3 SELECT --+ PARALLEL(DRIVERS,3)
  4 *
  5 FROM DRIVERS;
```

Summary

Oracle8 has some very powerful new features—particularly partitioned tables and indexes. Instead of creating a view on several **SELECT** statements using **UNION**s, like you did in Oracle7, you can now create partitions. In Oracle7, the partition scans all the very large tables in your view, regardless of the **WHERE** clause, whereas Oracle8 is smart enough to know what partitions to access to retrieve the data.

HIGH PERFORMANCE

Oracle8 Tuning And Oracle Objects

CHAPTER 16

This chapter examines some of the major changes made in Oracle8. For instance, the Oracle8 universal server includes some very exciting enhancements, such as objects. This chapter also teaches you the tuning changes that occur in Oracle8, as well as how to use objects. Also, every release of Oracle means changes to the optimizer. Fortunately, the changes are always for the better. This chapter covers those changes.

Oracle8 Tuning And Oracle Objects

Rowids

Oracle8 rowids are very different than Oracle7 rowids. The Oracle8 rowid is *extended*, which means it includes an object number. An extended rowid has four components. The first component is the data object number (bytes 1–6 of the 18-byte character string). The second component is the relative file number (bytes 7–9). The third component is the block number (bytes 10–15). Finally, the fourth component of an Oracle8 extended rowid is the slot number (bytes 16–18). On the other hand, a rowid in Oracle7 format is *restricted*, which means it has no object number. However, it does include an Oracle block number, a row number within the block, and a file number.

Listing 16.1 shows how very different the rowids are in these two versions of Oracle. For example, the OFFY ENGINE has the Oracle8 rowid AAAAwCAAFAAAABiAAA, and you can retrieve the row using this long string of characters. Also, Oracle8 provides you with a package named **DBMS_ROWID** that contains several functions to manipulate the rowid. The function **ROWID_OBJECT** returns the object number for the row; **ROWID_BLOCK_NUMBER** returns the Oracle block number the row is in; **ROWID_ROW_NUMBER** returns the row number within the Oracle block; and **ROWID_RELATIVE_FNO** returns the file number of the row. Note that several other functions appear at the end of Listing 16.1. To display the arguments, their data types, and the mode (whether IN, OUT, or IN/OUT), use the **DESCRIBE** command. Also, note that the function **ROWID_TYPE** contains a 1 for an Oracle8 rowid and a 0 for an Oracle7 rowid.

Listing 16.1 Using **ROWIDs**.

```
SQL> SELECT ROWID,  -- Oracle8 Rowids
  2         PARTNO, -- Are very, very
```

```
  3         PNAME,  -- Different than
  4         PCOST   -- Oracle7 Rowids
  5  FROM   AUTO_PARTS
  6  ORDER  BY PARTNO;

ROWID                PARTNO PNAME            PCOST
------------------ ------- ------------- ------
AAAAwCAAFAAAABiAAA       1 OFFY ENGINE    43000
AAAAwDAAGAAAAANAAA 300000 360 SPRINT     18000
AAAAwEAAHAAAAAXAAA 700000 OUTLAW ENGINE  22000

SQL> SELECT *
  2  FROM  AUTO_PARTS  -- Get The OFFY
  3  WHERE ROWID = 'AAAAwCAAFAAAABiAAA';

 PARTNO PNAME          PCOST
------- ------------- ------
      1 OFFY ENGINE    43000

SQL> get cor8_r4
  1 SELECT PNAME,
  2 dbms_rowid.rowid_object(rowid) "Object#",
  3 dbms_rowid.rowid_block_number(rowid) BLK,
  4 dbms_rowid.rowid_row_number(rowid) RSN,
  5 dbms_rowid.rowid_relative_fno(rowid) RFILE#
  6* FROM   AUTO_PARTS
SQL> /

PNAME            Object#    BLK    RSN RFILE#
-------------- ------- ------ ------ ------
OFFY ENGINE       3074     98      0      5
360 SPRINT        3075     13      0      6
OUTLAW ENGINE     3076     23      0      7

SQL> SELECT SUBSTR(TEXT,1,70) CODE
  2  FROM   DBA_SOURCE
  3  WHERE  NAME = 'DBMS_ROWID'  AND
  4         TEXT NOT LIKE '%--%'  AND
  5         TEXT LIKE '%function%';

CODE
-------------------------------------------
function rowid_create(rowid_type IN number,
function rowid_type(row_id IN rowid)
function rowid_object(row_id IN rowid)
```

```
function rowid_relative_fno(row_id IN rowid)
function rowid_block_number(row_id IN rowid)
function rowid_row_number(row_id IN rowid)
function rowid_to_absolute_fno(row_id IN rowid,
function rowid_to_extended(old_rowid IN rowid,
function rowid_to_restricted(old_rowid IN rowid,
function rowid_verify(rowid_in IN rowid,

SQL> DESCRIBE DBMS_ROWID.ROWID_CREATE
FUNCTION DBMS_ROWID.ROWID_CREATE RETURNS ROWID
 Argument Name Type   In/Out Default?
 ------------ ------ ------ --------
 ROWID_TYPE    NUMBER IN
 OBJECT_NUMBER NUMBER IN
 RELATIVE_FNO  NUMBER IN
 BLOCK_NUMBER  NUMBER IN
 ROW_NUMBER    NUMBER IN

SQL> DESC DBMS_ROWID.ROWID_TYPE
FUNCTION DBMS_ROWID.ROWID_TYPE RETURNS NUMBER
 Argument Name Type  In/Out Default?
 ------------ ----- ------ --------
 ROW_ID        ROWID IN

SQL> SELECT PNAME,
  2  DBMS_ROWID.ROWID_TYPE(ROWID) RTYPE
  3  FROM   AUTO_PARTS
  4  WHERE  PCOST < 65000;

PNAME          RTYPE
------------- ------
OFFY ENGINE        1
360 SPRINT         1
OUTLAW ENGINE      1

SQL> SELECT DBMS_ROWID.ROWID_TYPE
  2  ('00000ABC.0001.0004') RTYPE
  3  FROM DUAL;

 RTYPE
------
     0

SQL> DESC DBMS_ROWID.ROWID_TO_ABSOLUTE_FNO
FUNCTION DBMS_ROWID.ROWID_TO_ABSOLUTE_FNO RETURNS NUMBER
```

```
 Argument Name Type     In/Out Default?
 ------------- -------- ------ --------
 ROW_ID        ROWID    IN
 SCHEMA_NAME   VARCHAR2 IN
 OBJECT_NAME   VARCHAR2 IN

SQL> SELECT
  2  DBMS_ROWID.ROWID_TO_ABSOLUTE_FNO
  3  (ROWID,'SYSTEM','AUTO_PARTS') ABS_FNO
  4  FROM AUTO_PARTS;

ABS_FNO
-------
      5
      5
      7

SQL> DESC DBMS_ROWID.ROWID_TO_EXTENDED
FUNCTION DBMS_ROWID.ROWID_TO_EXTENDED RETURNS ROWID
 Argument Name   Type       In/Out Default?
 --------------- ---------- ------ --------
 OLD_ROWID       ROWID      IN
 SCHEMA_NAME     VARCHAR2   IN
 OBJECT_NAME     VARCHAR2   IN
 CONVERSION_TYPE NUMBER(38) IN

SQL> DESC DBMS_ROWID.ROWID_TO_RESTRICTED
FUNCTION DBMS_ROWID.ROWID_TO_RESTRICTED RETURNS ROWID
 Argument Name   Type       In/Out Default?
 --------------- ---------- ------ --------
 OLD_ROWID       ROWID      IN
 CONVERSION_TYPE NUMBER(38) IN

SQL> DESC DBMS_ROWID.ROWID_VERIFY
FUNCTION DBMS_ROWID.ROWID_VERIFY RETURNS NUMBER
 Argument Name   Type       In/Out Default?
 --------------- ---------- ------ --------
 ROWID_IN        ROWID      IN
 SCHEMA_NAME     VARCHAR2   IN
 OBJECT_NAME     VARCHAR2   IN
 CONVERSION_TYPE NUMBER(38) IN
```

Explain Plan

The only change made to the table **PLAN_TABLE** is the addition of three new columns that deal with partitions. The names of these new columns are **PARTITION_START**, **PARTITION_STOP**, and **PARTITION_ID**. Of course, this means your SQL statement using the table **PLAN_TABLE** will be different—that is, if you want to see any partition information. Listing 16.2 shows the new table **PLAN_TABLE** and an example of a statement using partition information. The output of the Explain Plan shows that the data is retrieved from the first partition—NUMBER(1).

Listing 16.2 The **PLAN_TABLE**.

```
SQL> get utlxplan
create table PLAN_TABLE (
    statement_id     varchar2(30),
    timestamp        date,
    remarks          varchar2(80),
    operation        varchar2(30),
    options          varchar2(30),
    object_node      varchar2(128),
    object_owner     varchar2(30),
    object_name      varchar2(30),
    object_instance  numeric,
    object_type      varchar2(30),
    optimizer        varchar2(255),
    search_columns   numeric,
    id               numeric,
    parent_id        numeric,
    position         numeric,
    cost             numeric,
    cardinality      numeric,
    bytes            numeric,
    other_tag        varchar2(255),
    partition_start  varchar2(255),
    partition_stop   varchar2(255),
    partition_id     numeric,
    other            long);

SQL> EXPLAIN PLAN FOR
SELECT *
```

```
FROM auto_parts PARTITION (AP250K) A
WHERE  A.PARTNO < 249555;

SQL> SELECT ID,
PARENT_ID PRNTID,
SUBSTR(OPERATION,1,17) "Operation",
SUBSTR(PARTITION_START,1,10) "PSTART",
SUBSTR(PARTITION_STOP,1,10) "PSTOP",
PARTITION_ID PID,
SUBSTR(OPTIONS,1,7) "Options"
FROM   PLAN_TABLE
ORDER  BY ID, PARENT_ID;

    ID PRNTID Operation
------ ------ ----------------
     0        SELECT STATEMENT
     1      0 TABLE ACCESS

PSTART     PSTOP         PID Options
---------- ---------- ------ ------
NUMBER(1)  NUMBER(1)       1 FULL
```

Objects

This is by far the most exciting part of this book. As far as I know, this is the only Oracle book in the world that compares traditional RDBMS queries to Oracle objects. In addition, Explain Plans and actual execution times are included. Listing 16.3 creates two standard RDBMS tables—**DEPTS_RDBMS**, with 1,000 rows, and **EMPLOYEES_RDBMS**, with 10,000 rows. Each of the 1,000 departments contains 10 employees. The **DEPTS_RDBMS** table has a unique index, **INDX_DEPTS_RDBMS**, on the **DEPTNO** column; the **EMPLOYEES_RDBMS** table has a nonunique index, **INDX_EMPLOYEES_RDBMS**, on the **EDEPTNO** column. Both tables are analyzed, and the output from Explain Plan indicates a cost of 4. Oracle joins the two tables using nested loops, and the driving table is **DEPTS_RDBMS**. Also, note that the optimizer uses both indexes to retrieve the 10 rows in the active set. Finally, by entering **SET TIMING ON** in the client/server environment, the elapsed time of this query is real: 550. (This equates to 0.55 seconds.) If you don't trust the second hand on your watch to time your queries, enter the command **SET TIMING ON** and observe the time displayed on the terminal after your statement executes. In the client/server environment, Oracle8 displays on your terminal real: 99999 where 99999 is in thousandths of a second. On a Unix machine, **SET TIMING ON** displays elapsed: 99:99:99.9 for hours, minutes, and seconds.

By running a PL/SQL script that loops one million times and observing the second hand on my wristwatch, I noted that 12 seconds elapsed. Comparing 12 seconds with the output of real, 12470, means that the output is in milliseconds. In other words, this script requires 12.470 seconds to execute.

Listing 16.3 A traditional RDBMS equi-join.

```
SQL> get cor16_rdepts
CREATE TABLE DEPTS_RDBMS
     (deptno     NUMBER(7,0),
      dname      VARCHAR2(20),
      city       VARCHAR2(20))
TABLESPACE OBJECTS1
SQL> /
Table created.

SQL> get cor16_r2
BEGIN
 FOR i IN 1..1000 LOOP
  INSERT INTO depts_rdbms
  VALUES(i,'MIS ' || i,'MAUI ' || i);
 END  LOOP;
END;
SQL> /
PL/SQL procedure successfully completed.
Elapsed: 00:00:03.55

SQL> CREATE TABLE EMPLOYEES_RDBMS
 (empno         NUMBER(6,0),    -- Create
  ename         VARCHAR2(20),   -- Fires
  salary        NUMBER(8,2),    -- Commit
  edeptno       NUMBER(7,0))
TABLESPACE     OBJECTS1;
Table created.

SQL> get cor16_o7
DECLARE
   startno   NUMBER  := 1;
   endno     NUMBER  := 10;
BEGIN
```

```
 5    FOR dno IN 1..1000 LOOP
 6     FOR eno IN startno..endno LOOP
 7      INSERT INTO employees_rdbms
 8      VALUES(eno,'Emp # ' || eno,
 9             200+dno, dno);
10     END  LOOP;
11     startno := endno;
12     startno := startno + 1;
13     endno   := startno;
14     endno   := endno + 9;
15    END  LOOP;
16  commit;
17* END;
/
SQL> /
PL/SQL procedure successfully completed.
 real: 54760

SQL> SELECT COUNT(*)
  2  FROM   EMPLOYEES_RDBMS;

 COUNT(*)
---------
    10000

 real: 5770

SQL> CREATE UNIQUE INDEX
  2  INDX_DEPTS_RDBMS
  3  ON DEPTS_RDBMS(DEPTNO);
Index created.
Elapsed: 00:00:02.39

SQL> ANALYZE TABLE DEPTS_RDBMS
  2           COMPUTE STATISTICS;
Table analyzed.
Elapsed: 00:00:02.57

SQL> CREATE INDEX -- FK INDEX
  2  INDX_EMPLOYEES_RDBMS
  3  ON EMPLOYEES_RDBMS(EDEPTNO);
Index created.
real: 5600
```

```
SQL> ANALYZE TABLE EMPLOYEES_RDBMS
  2          COMPUTE STATISTICS;
Table analyzed.
real: 2800

SQL> get cor16_o5
  1  EXPLAIN PLAN FOR
  2  SELECT e.ename,
  3         d.city
  4  FROM   employees_rdbms e,
  5         depts_rdbms d
  6  WHERE  d.deptno = e.edeptno
  7* AND    d.deptno = 550
SQL> /
Explained.

SQL> @explain
Query Plan                                COST
----------------------------------------- ----
SELECT STATEMENT   CHOOSE                    4
  NESTED LOOPS                               4
    TABLE ACCESS BY INDEX
          ROWID DEPTS_RDBMS ANALYZED         2
      INDEX UNIQUE SCAN
            INDX_DEPTS_RDBMS ANALYZED        1
    TABLE ACCESS BY INDEX
          ROWID EMPLOYEES_RDBMS ANALYZED     2
      INDEX RANGE SCAN
            INDX_EMPLOYEES_RDBMS ANALYZED    1

SQL> SELECT e.ename, e.salary,
  2         d.city
  3  FROM   employees_rdbms e,
  4         depts_rdbms d
  5  WHERE  d.deptno = e.edeptno
  6  AND    d.deptno = 550;

ENAME      SALARY CITY
---------- ------ --------
Emp # 5491    750 MAUI 550
Emp # 5492    750 MAUI 550
Emp # 5493    750 MAUI 550
Emp # 5494    750 MAUI 550
Emp # 5495    750 MAUI 550
```

```
Emp # 5496     750 MAUI 550
Emp # 5497     750 MAUI 550
Emp # 5498     750 MAUI 550
Emp # 5499     750 MAUI 550
Emp # 5500     750 MAUI 550

10 rows selected.

real: 550

SQL> SET TIMING ON
SQL> L
  1  BEGIN
  2    FOR i IN 1..1000000 LOOP
  3      NULL;     -- Real=Milliseconds
  4    END   LOOP; -- Watch Says 12 Secs
  5* END;      -- Oracle says real: 12470
SQL> /
PL/SQL procedure successfully completed.

real: 12470
```

Figure 16.1 is an overview of using pointers, or object identifiers, to retrieve rows from two tables without using the customary SQL join.

Listing 16.4 shows how to retrieve data from two tables without using the typical SQL join. First, an **OBJECT** data type named **DEPT_DATA** is created that contains three pieces of information. Note that as of this release, Oracle8.0.3.0, a bug exists—anytime you receive the message "Operation 77 succeeded," you've encountered the bug. This message simply means "Type created," and it's fixed in 8.0.3.1. When I worked for Oracle Corporation back in the late 1980s, a similar message displayed whenever Explain Plan was run. Instead of displaying, "Explained," Oracle displayed "Operation 50 succeeded." When I inquired about this matter, the kernel group informed me, after several emails, that "there are certain things one does not need to know about." On another occasion, I received the "Operation xx succeeded" message for every command I entered. In short, every command has an associated operation number. However, this problem is fixed in Oracle8.0.3.1.

Next, an object table named **DEPTS_OBJ** is created that has rows of the object type **DEPT_DATA**. A query using **USER_OBJECTS** indicates that the status is **VALID** for both the object type and the object table. Inserting rows into the object table

DEPTS_OBJ 1,000 Rows

DEPT_DATA Object TYPE		
DEPTNO	DNAME	CITY
number(7,0)	varchar2(20)	varchar2(20)
1 2 1000	IS IS IS	MAUI MAUI MAUI

EMPLOYEES_OBJ 10,000 Rows

ENO	ENAME	SALARY	DEPT_OID
number(6,0)	varchar2(20)	number(8,2)	POINTER ***REF (dept_data)***
1 2 10000	Emp# 1 Empl# 2 Empl# 10,000		Object Identifier Object Identifier Object Identifier

TO DISPLAY DATA FROM BOTH TABLES WITHOUT A SQL JOIN:

```
SQL>SELECT ename, salary
            DEREF(dept_oid)
      FROM  employees_obj
      WHERE eno between 8491 and 8500;
```

EXPLAIN PLAN COST = 35 and ELAPSED TIME OF real: 4780

Figure 16.1
Using pointers (or object identifiers).

DEPTS_OBJ requires the use of **DEPT_DATA**. Several rows are inserted into the object table **DEPTS_OBJ** and are selected to verify their existence.

Using **REF(x)** in the next **SELECT** statement returns the object identifier for department number 1. Every row, or instance, of an object table has an associated object identifier, or OID. Using **REF(x)** returned 86 characters, denoting the object identifier for department number 1. Note that the syntax requires the use of a table alias, which in this case is "x".

The next anonymous PL/SQL block populates **DEPTS_OBJ** with 1,000 departments, all on the island of Maui. Like they say, "Here today, gone to Maui." Then, the table **EMPLOYEES_OBJ** is created. It contains a pointer column named **DEPT_OID** that references each row in the table **DEPTS**. This column is populated with the object identifiers later in the next PL/SQL block. Ten employees are assigned to each of the 1,000 departments. **SELECT REF(d)** returns the object identifier for the particular department, and it places this OID into the **DEPT_OID** column of the table **EMPLOYEES_OBJ**. A query using **EMPLOYEES_OBJ** that returns only one row indicates that the **DEPT_OID** column contains an object identifier pointing to a row in the **DEPTS** table.

Because the contents of the **DEPT_OID** column are dereferenced, **DEREF (dept_oid)**, Oracle uses the OID in the **DEPT_OID** column to retrieve the matching row from the **DEPTS** table without the standard SQL join statement being written. Employee number 22 is in Information Systems (department number 3), which is in Maui. The output is not very pretty, so you might want to use the **COL** command to clean it up.

Listing 16.4 Look ma, no joins!

```
SQL> CREATE TYPE dept_data AS OBJECT(
       deptno     NUMBER(7,0),   -- User
       dname      VARCHAR2(20),  -- Defined
       city       VARCHAR2(20));
Operation 77 succeeded.  (Type created.)

SQL> DESC DEPT_DATA
 Name     Null?          Type
 ------   ------------   ----
 DEPTNO   NUMBER(7)
 DNAME    VARCHAR2(20)
 CITY     VARCHAR2(20)

SQL> CREATE TABLE DEPTS_OBJ OF dept_data;
Table created.

SQL> SELECT SUBSTR(OBJECT_NAME,1,15) ONAME,
            SUBSTR(SUBOBJECT_NAME,1,10) SUB,
```

```
          OBJECT_TYPE,
          STATUS
   FROM   USER_OBJECTS
   WHERE  OBJECT_NAME LIKE 'DEPT%';

ONAME     SUB  OBJECT_TYPE STATUS
--------- ---- ----------- ------
DEPT_DATA      TYPE        VALID
DEPTS_OBJ      TABLE       VALID

SQL> INSERT INTO depts_obj  -- Just A Try
   VALUES(dept_data(1,'MIS','MAUI'));
1 row created.

SQL> INSERT INTO depts_obj
   VALUES(dept_data(2,'AP','HANA'));
1 row created.

SQL> SELECT *
   FROM   DEPTS_OBJ;

 DEPTNO DNAME CITY
------- ----- ----
      1 MIS   MAUI
      2 AP    HANA

SQL> SELECT REF(x)          -- Returns 86
   FROM   depts_obj x -- Characters
   WHERE  deptno = 1;

REF(X)
------------------------------------
0000280209A7EB3895650511D1B65200A024
D7093AA7EB388A650511D1B65200A024D709
3A0200C1B40000

SQL> get cor16_15
   BEGIN
     FOR dno IN 1..1000 LOOP
       INSERT INTO depts_obj
       VALUES(dept_data(dno,'IS','MAUI'));
     END  LOOP;
   COMMIT;
   END;
SQL> /
```

```
PL/SQL procedure successfully completed.
 real: 14340

SQL> CREATE TABLE EMPLOYEES_OBJ
  (eno       NUMBER(6,0),
   ename     VARCHAR2(20),
   salary    NUMBER(8,2),
   dept_oid REF dept_data
             SCOPE IS depts_obj);
Table created.

SQL> DESC EMPLOYEES_OBJ
 Name     Null? Type
 -------- ----- -----------------
 ENO            NUMBER(6)
 ENAME          VARCHAR2(20)
 SALARY         NUMBER(8,2)
 DEPT_OID       REF OF DEPT_DATA

SQL> get cor16_16
 DECLARE
   startno  NUMBER := 1;
   endno    NUMBER := 10;
 BEGIN
  FOR i IN 1..1000 LOOP
   FOR j IN startno..endno LOOP
    INSERT INTO employees_obj
    SELECT j,'Emp# ' || j,222+j,
    REF(d)
    FROM depts_obj d
    WHERE d.deptno = i;
   END LOOP;
   startno := endno;
   startno := startno + 1;
   endno   := startno;
   endno   := endno + 9;
  END  LOOP;
 COMMIT;
 END;
SQL> @cor16_16

PL/SQL procedure successfully completed.
 real: 413580
```

```
SQL> SELECT *
  2  FROM    EMPLOYEES_OBJ
  3  WHERE   ROWNUM < 2;

  ENO ENAME   SALARY
----- ------ ------
    1 Emp# 1     223

DEPT_OID
------------------------------------
0000220208A7EB3895650511D1B65200A024
D7093AA7EB388A650511D1B65200A024D7093A

SQL> SELECT ename,
  2          salary,
  3          DEREF(dept_oid)
  4  FROM    employees_obj
  5  WHERE   eno = 22;

ENAME                         SALARY
----------------------- ---------
DEREF(DEPT_OID)(DEPTNO,DNAME,CITY)
-----------------------------------
Emp# 22                        244
DEPT_DATA(3, 'IS', 'MAUI')

SQL> COL "Dept Info" FORMAT A30
SQL> SELECT ename,
  2          salary,
  3          DEREF(dept_oid) "Dept Info"
  4  FROM    employees_obj
  5  WHERE   eno = 22;

ENAME    SALARY Dept Info(DEPTNO, DNAME, CITY)
------- ------ ------------------------------
Emp# 22     244 DEPT_DATA(3, 'IS', 'MAUI')
```

To speed up queries on the **EMPLOYEES_OBJ** table, an index is created on the pointer column containing OIDs and **DEPT_OID**. Another index is created on the **ENO** column in Listing 16.5. The table is analyzed to take full advantage of the cost-based optimizer. The Explain Plan output indicates that the cost-based optimizer shows a cost of 3 and uses both indexes to retrieve 10 employees from the

EMPLOYEES_OBJ table, which consists of 10,000 rows. The only different piece of information found in all the columns of the table **PLAN_TABLE** is the column **OTHER**. The string "ERROR: piece-wise fetching" is disturbing to say the least—this is not normal. I hoped that Oracle would provide new information in the table **PLAN_TABLE** regarding objects, but, unfortunately, no new information is provided by Explain Plan. The execution time is 4.78 seconds, which is 8.69 times slower than the traditional SQL join time of 0.55 seconds. The cost is 3 compared to the traditional SQL join cost of 4. Perhaps much larger tables might render a different outcome. To view the user-defined data types as well as the data found in each one, use **VALUE**.

Listing 16.5 Explain Plan using **DEREF**.

```
SQL> CREATE INDEX OID_INDEX
  2  ON EMPLOYEES_OBJ(DEPT_OID);
Index created.
 real: 6100

SQL> CREATE INDEX EMP_OBJ_ENO
  2  ON EMPLOYEES_OBJ(ENO);
Index created.
 real: 5160

SQL> ANALYZE TABLE EMPLOYEES_OBJ
  2            COMPUTE STATISTICS;
Table analyzed.
 real: 5330

SQL> EXPLAIN PLAN FOR
  2  SELECT ename,
  3         salary,
  4         DEREF(dept_oid)
  5  FROM   employees_obj
  6  WHERE  eno BETWEEN 8491 AND 8500;
Explained.

SQL> @explain
Query Plan                          COST
----------------------------- ----
SELECT STATEMENT   CHOOSE          3
 TABLE ACCESS BY INDEX
```

```
 ROWID EMPLOYEES_OBJ ANALYZED    3
   INDEX RANGE SCAN
   EMP_OBJ_ENO ANALYZED          2

SQL> SELECT OTHER FROM PLAN_TABLE;

OTHER
--------------------------
ERROR: piece-wise fetching

SQL>SELECT ename,
 2         salary,
 3         DEREF(dept_oid)
 4  FROM   employees_obj
 5  WHERE  eno BETWEEN 8491 AND 8500;

ENAME                             SALARY
-------------------- ---------------
DEREF(DEPT_OID)(DEPTNO, DNAME, CITY)
-----------------------------------
Emp# 8498                    8720
DEPT_DATA(850, 'IS', 'MAUI')

Emp# 8500                    8722
DEPT_DATA(850, 'IS', 'MAUI')

10 rows selected.

 real: 4780

SQL> SELECT VALUE(d)
  2  FROM   depts_obj d
  3  WHERE  deptno = 222;

VALUE(D)(DEPTNO, DNAME, CITY)
-----------------------------
DEPT_DATA(222, 'IS', 'MAUI')

SQL> COL OBJECT_NAME FORMAT A13
SQL> COL OBJECT_TYPE FORMAT A11
SQL> SELECT OBJECT_NAME,
  2          OBJECT_ID,
  3          OBJECT_TYPE,
  4          STATUS
```

```
FROM   USER_OBJECTS
WHERE OBJECT_NAME = 'DEPT_DATA'
OR    OBJECT_NAME = 'DEPTS_OBJ'
OR    OBJECT_NAME = 'EMPLOYEES_OBJ';

OBJECT_NAME    OBJECT_ID OBJECT_TYPE STATUS
------------- --------- ----------- ------
EMPLOYEES_OBJ       3816 TABLE       VALID
DEPTS_OBJ           3799 TABLE       VALID
DEPT_DATA           3468 TYPE        VALID
```

Table 16.1 shows the comparison between the traditional SQL join and the much newer objects approach. The facts suggest that using OIDs (object identifiers) on a table is much slower than a normal SQL join of two tables. This is in spite of the fact that using OIDs has a cost of 3, and both indexes and the traditional join have a cost of 4. The real execution time of using OIDs is 8.69 times longer than the more standard SQL join approach (4780 / 550 = 8.69).

Now let's compare the Oracle8 nested table feature to the typical two-table join. First of all, a nested table has repeating groups. Repeating groups can be implemented using **VARRAY**s of OIDs. A **VARRAY** is another method of implementing repeating groups like nested tables. In other words, the definition of first normal form is destroyed. By the way, my friend Don Burleson has recently published a great book titled *High Performance Oracle8 Tuning* published by The Coriolis Group, ISBN 1-57610-217-3, and he covers repeating groups rather extensively in the first chapter.

A nested table is very similar to the COBOL **OCCURS** clause—except with a nested table, data can appear many times in a particular column in a nested table. Figure 16.2 illustrates the structure of a nested table.

In the example shown in Listing 16.6, each department has exactly 10 employees. You're better off using an array of OIDs if you know you'll never have too many

Table 16.1 Comparing an object OID to the traditional SQL join.

Method	Cost	Elapsed	Real	Slowness
SQL join	4	0.55 sec	550	
OID	3	4.78 sec	4780	8.69

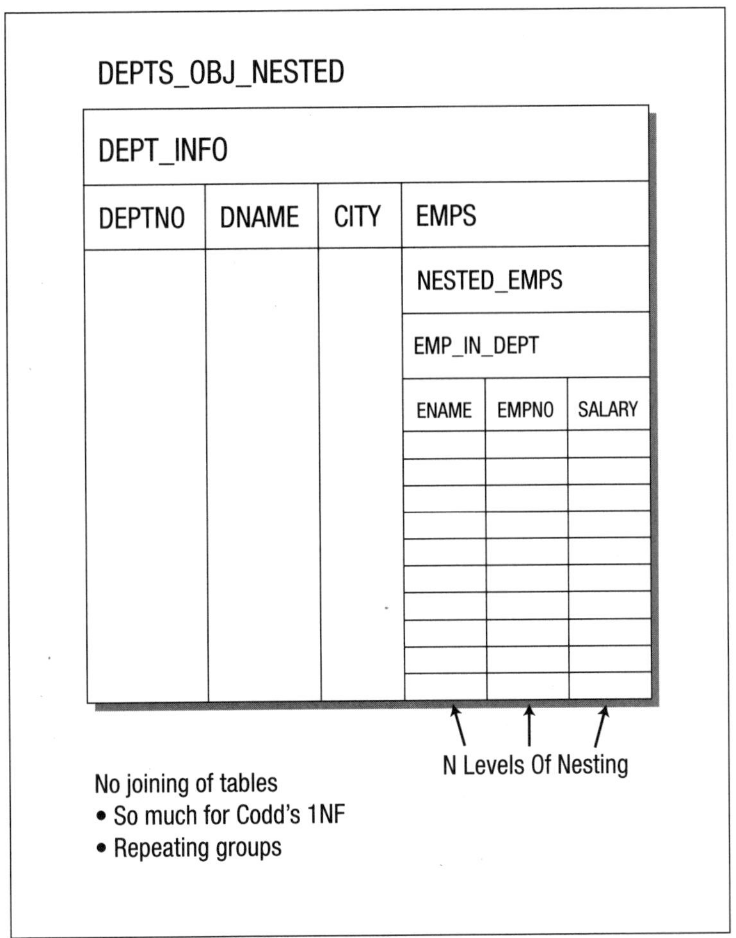

Figure 16.2
A nested table.

employees in a department. In this example, however, it's assumed that the departments will grow quickly. Once again, there's no need to join two tables because the department and employee information is all in one table—**DEPTS_OBJ_NESTED**.

First, a user-defined object data type named **EMP_IN_DEPT** is created to hold information about each employee in a department. Then, the nested table **NESTED_EMPS** is created to hold multiple employees for a particular department. **DEPT_INFO** is used to hold all the data for one department and one row in the table **DEPTS_OBJ_NESTED**. The object table **DEPTS_OBJ_NESTED** has a unique index on the object identifier (OIDINDEX), and **EMPS** is the name of the column that contains the multiple employees.

Several describes illustrate the structure of the objects. The **DESCRIBE** command is used to describe tables, views, synonyms, functions, and procedures in packaged procedures; user defined data types; and object tables. To describe the table **STATS**, you enter **DESC STATS** or **DESCRIBE STATS.** Displayed are the column names, data type of each column, the maximum width of the data in each column, and whether or not the column accepts null values. When you describe a function or procedure in a package, the number of arguments, the data type of each argument, and the mode of the argument—**IN**, **OUT**, or **IN OUT**—are displayed. Also, note the unique index **OID_DEPTS_NESTED.** This OID index resides on the column named **SYS_NC_OID$**. Loading data into objects is exciting when you have no packages, procedures, or functions written, so I tried inserting several rows before inserting the 1,000 departments, all with 10 employees. The nonunique index **DON_DEPTNO** on the **DEPTNO** column speeds up the queries.

Microsoft Word was used to drastically edit the query showing only one department. The format of the output data from objects is very undesirable. The output from Explain Plan shows a cost of 2. Also, the index **DON_DEPTNO** retrieves the instance (or row) representing department number 550, which requires 4.12 seconds. This query is 7.49 times slower than the query that joins the employee and department tables.

Listing 16.6 Nested tables.

```
SQL> CREATE TYPE emp_in_dept AS OBJECT
  2  (empno     NUMBER(6,0),
  3   ename     VARCHAR2(20),
  4   salary    NUMBER(8,2));
SQL> /
Type created.

SQL> CREATE TYPE nested_emps
  2  AS TABLE OF emp_in_dept;
SQL> /
Type created.

SQL> CREATE TYPE dept_info AS OBJECT
  2  (deptno    NUMBER(6,0),
```

```
  3  dname      VARCHAR2(20),
  4  city       VARCHAR2(20),
  5  emps       nested_emps);
  6  .
SQL> /
Type created.

SQL> CREATE TABLE DEPTS_OBJ_NESTED
  2  OF dept_info
  3  OIDINDEX oid_depts_nested
  4  TABLESPACE OBJECTS1
  5  NESTED TABLE EMPS
  6  STORE AS empsv8;
Table created.

SQL> CREATE INDEX DON_DEPTNO
     ON DEPTS_OBJ_NESTED(deptno);
Index created.

SQL> DESC DEPTS_OBJ_NESTED
 Name   Null? Type
 ------ ----- -----------
 DEPTNO       NUMBER(6)
 DNAME        VARCHAR2(20)
 CITY         VARCHAR2(20)
 EMPS         NESTED_EMPS

SQL> DESC NESTED_EMPS
 NESTED_EMPS TABLE OF EMP_IN_DEPT
 Name   Null? Type
 ------ ----- -----------
 EMPNO        NUMBER(6)
 ENAME        VARCHAR2(20)
 SALARY       NUMBER(8,2)

SQL> DESC EMP_IN_DEPT
 Name   Null? Type
 ------ ----- -----------
 EMPNO        NUMBER(6)
 ENAME        VARCHAR2(20)
 SALARY       NUMBER(8,2)

SQL> SELECT INDEX_NAME,
  2         COLUMN_NAME
```

```
  3  FROM   SYS.DBA_IND_COLUMNS
  4  WHERE  TABLE_NAME='DEPTS_OBJ_NESTED';

INDEX_NAME       COLUMN_NAME
---------------- ----------------
SYS_C001066      SYS_NC0000600007$
OID_DEPTS_NESTED SYS_NC_OID$

SQL> SELECT INDEX_NAME,
  2         UNIQUENESS
  3  FROM   SYS.DBA_INDEXES
  4  WHERE  TABLE_NAME
  5         ='DEPTS_OBJ_NESTED';

INDEX_NAME       UNIQUENES
---------------- ---------
SYS_C001066      UNIQUE
OID_DEPTS_NESTED UNIQUE

SQL> INSERT INTO DEPTS_OBJ_NESTED
  2  VALUES(1,'IS','Maui 1',
  3  nested_emps(
  4   emp_in_dept(1,'Emp# 1',222),
  5   emp_in_dept(2,'Emp# 2',223)));
1 row created.

SQL> SELECT *  -- Output Formatted
  2  FROM   DEPTS_OBJ_NESTED -MS Word
  3  WHERE  ROWNUM < 2;

   DEPTNO DNAME CITY
--------- ----- ------
        1  IS 1 Maui 1

EMPS(EMPNO, ENAME, SALARY)
-------------------------
NESTED_EMPS(
  EMP_IN_DEPT(1,  'Emp# 1', 223),
  EMP_IN_DEPT(2,  'Emp# 2', 224),
  EMP_IN_DEPT(3,  'Emp# 3', 225),
  EMP_IN_DEPT(4,  'Emp# 4', 226),
  EMP_IN_DEPT(5,  'Emp# 5', 227),
  EMP_IN_DEPT(6,  'Emp# 6', 228),
  EMP_IN_DEPT(7,  'Emp# 7', 229),
```

```
  EMP_IN_DEPT(8,  'Emp# 8', 230),
  EMP_IN_DEPT(9,  'Emp# 9', 231),
  EMP_IN_DEPT(10, 'Emp# 10', 232))

SQL> SELECT *  -- Unformatted
  2  FROM   DEPTS_OBJ_NESTED
  3  WHERE  ROWNUM < 2;

  -- DEPTNO DNAME     CITY
----------- -------- ------
EMPS(EMPNO, ENAME,  SALARY)
---------------------------
       1 IS 1                 Maui 1
NESTED_EMPS(EMP_IN_DEPT(1, 'Emp# 1', 223),
 EMP_IN_DEPT(2, 'Emp# 2', 224),
EMP_IN_DEPT(3, 'Emp# 3', 225),
EMP_IN_DEPT(4, 'Emp# 4', 226),
 EMP_IN_DEPT(5, 'Emp# 5', 227),
 EMP_IN_DEPT(6, 'Emp# 6', 228), EM
P_IN_DEPT(7, 'Emp# 7', 229),
EMP_IN_DEPT(8, 'Emp# 8', 230),
 EMP_IN_DEPT(9, 'Emp# 9', 231), EMP_IN_DE
PT(10, 'Emp# 10', 232))

SQL> ANALYZE TABLE
  2          depts_obj_nested
  3          COMPUTE STATISTICS;
Table analyzed.
 real: 1150

SQL> EXPLAIN PLAN FOR
  2  SELECT *
  3  FROM   depts_obj_nested
  4  WHERE  deptno = 550;
Explained.

SQL> @explain
Query Plan                           COST
-------------------------------- ----
SELECT STATEMENT   CHOOSE              2
  TABLE ACCESS BY INDEX                2
  ROWID DEPTS_OBJ_NESTED ANALYZED
    INDEX RANGE SCAN                   1
    DON_DEPTNO ANALYZED
```

```
SQL> SELECT *
  2  FROM    depts_obj_nested
  3  WHERE   deptno = 550;

  DEPTNO DNAME  CITY
-------- ------ --------
     550 IS 550 Maui 550

EMPS(EMPNO, ENAME, SALARY)
-----------------------------------
NESTED_EMPS(
  EMP_IN_DEPT(5491, 'Emp# 5491', 772),
  EMP_IN_DEPT(5492, 'Emp# 5492', 773),
  EMP_IN_DEPT(5493, 'Emp# 5493', 774),
  EMP_IN_DEPT(5494, 'Emp# 5494', 775),
  EMP_IN_DEPT(5495, 'Emp# 5495', 776),
  EMP_IN_DEPT(5496, 'Emp# 5496', 777),
  EMP_IN_DEPT(5497, 'Emp# 5497', 778),
  EMP_IN_DEPT(5498, 'Emp# 5498', 779),
  EMP_IN_DEPT(5499, 'Emp# 5499', 780),
  EMP_IN_DEPT(5500, 'Emp# 5500', 781))

 real: 4120
```

Once again, the Oracle8 option appears to execute slower than the traditional SQL join statement. Even with a slightly lower cost of 2 (compared to a cost of 4 for the SQL join), the nested table query requires 4.12 seconds to execute, which is nearly 7.5 times slower than the standard join of two tables. See Table 16.2 for comparison analysis between an Oracle8 nested table and a traditional SQL join.

Note that you can also use **VARRAYs** to store repeating groups of data, or you can even use **VARRAYs** to store an array of pointers (OIDs) to rows in other tables.

Table 16.2 Comparing a nested table to the traditional SQL join.

Method	Cost	Elapsed	Real	Slowness
SQL join	4	0.55 sec	550	
Nested	2	4.12 sec	4120	7.49

Reverse Key Indexes

If you're running Oracle8 using the OPS (Oracle Parallel Server) option on OLTP applications and one of your indexed columns is frequently updated, you can create an index that stores the bytes of the index in reverse key order to spread out your index entries across many blocks. However, Oracle does not change the rowids. If you have a reverse index on the employee name column and there's a strange name such as YDISSAC as an original entry in the employee table, the reverse key index would store this name as CASSIDY. Instead of storing the key CASSIDY in the index leaf block containing Cs, the reverse index entry YDISSAC is stored in the leaf block containing Ys. This process scatters employee names across many reverse index leaf blocks, and it allows multiple processes to retrieve index blocks much faster. Listing 16.7 illustrates the creation of a reverse key index named **REVERSE_INDX** on the **DNAME** column of the **IRL4VR** table. The query using **SYS.DBA_INDEXES** shows the **INDEX_TYPE** column value "NORMAL." I was hoping Oracle8 would indicate the type of index is **REVERSE**, but it does not. No big deal, but it would be nice to know when you have a **REVERSE** key index as opposed to a **NORMAL** btree index.

You need to watch out for a couple of things—one is the combination of the options **REVERSE** and **NOSORT**. You cannot combine these two options; if you try, you'll receive the error message "ORA-00900: invalid SQL statement." In *Oracle8 Server Concepts, Volume 1,* Chapter 7, page 25, the following appears:

"You cannot rebuild a normal index as a reverse key index; you must use the CREATE command instead."

Even Oracle makes a mistake every now and then, because a normal index can certainly be rebuilt as a reverse key index. For instance, I created a normal index named NORMAL_INDX on the **DNAME** column of the **IRL4VR** table and then very successfully rebuilt it as a reverse key index.

Listing 16.7 Using reverse key indexes.

```
SQL> CREATE TABLE  IRL4VR
  2  (DRIVER_NO     NUMBER(6,0),
  3   DNAME         VARCHAR2(20),
  4   INDY500_WINS NUMBER(2,0));
Table created.
```

```
SQL> SELECT *
  2  FROM   IRL4VR;

DRIVER_NO DNAME    INDY500_WINS
--------- -------- ------------
        1 VUKY SR.            3
        2 VUKY JR             0
        3 VUKY III            0
        4 LEE W               1
        5 AJ FOYT             4

SQL> CREATE INDEX REVERSE_INDX
  2         ON IRL4VR(DNAME)
  3         REVERSE;
Index created.

SQL> COL INDEX_NAME    FORMAT A12
SQL> COL INDEX_TYPE    FORMAT A10
SQL> COL LAST_ANALYZED HEADING LA
SQL> SELECT INDEX_NAME,
  2         INDEX_TYPE,
  3         UNIQUENESS,
  4         LAST_ANALYZED
  5  FROM   SYS.DBA_INDEXES
  6  WHERE  OWNER = 'PETE' AND
  7  TABLE_NAME = 'IRL4VR';
INDEX_NAME   INDEX_TYPE UNIQUENES LA
------------ ---------- --------- --------
REVERSE_INDX NORMAL     NONUNIQUE

SQL> DROP INDEX REVERSE_INDX;
Index dropped.

SQL> CREATE INDEX REVERSE_INDX
  2         ON IRL4VR(DNAME) -- Can't Use
  3         REVERSE          -- Both REVERSE
  4         NOSORT;          -- And  NOSORT
      NOSORT
         *
ERROR at line 4:
ORA-00900: invalid SQL statement

SQL> CREATE INDEX NORMAL_INDX
  2         ON IRL4VR(DNAME);
Index created.
```

```
SQL> ALTER INDEX NORMAL_INDX -- Doc Bug
  2       REBUILD REVERSE;
Index altered.
```

Parallel DML (PDML)

Oracle7.1 offers the parallel query option, which can dramatically speed up queries or SQL statements that contain **SELECT** statements. However, if you use **INSERT**, **UPDATE**, or **DELETE**, the statement does not take advantage of this Oracle7.1 option. However, in Oracle8, all DML (data manipulation) commands may use this option if your session has **PARALLEL DML** enabled by the **ALTER SESSION** command and the table has a degree of more than 1, or if you use the **PARALLEL** hint. Also, a DML statement that's part of a distributed transaction or a query using a remote table will not use the PDML feature. Listing 16.8 shows that the table **IRL4VR** has a degree of 8, which means that a degree of parallelism of 8 exists for certain SQL statements. This means Oracle attempts to use eight server processes when processing particular SQL statements.

However, before you can use this PDML feature, you must enable the session option **PARALLEL DML**. If you're really in a hurry and recovery is not an issue, you can use the **NOLOGGING** table feature. **NOLOGGING** is used for tables, indexes, partitions, and tablespaces, and it bypasses writing to the online redo log files, which makes the SQL statement execute much faster. A really neat feature of this option is the ability to use the **PARALLEL** hint in both the **INSERT** and **SELECT** commands, as illustrated in this listing. Moreover, the rows are appended to the end of the table without the use of the **APPEND** hint.

Listing 16.8 PDML inserts.

```
SQL> ALTER TABLE IRL4VR
  2       PARALLEL(DEGREE 8);
Table altered.

SQL> SELECT DEGREE
  2  FROM          SYS.DBA_TABLES
  3  WHERE         OWNER = 'PETE' AND
  4                TABLE_NAME = 'IRL4VR';
```

```
DEGREE
------
     8

SQL> ALTER SESSION
  2          ENABLE
  3          PARALLEL DML;
Session altered.

SQL> ALTER TABLE IRL4VR
  2          NOLOGGING;
Table altered.

SQL> SELECT LOGGING,
  2          DEGREE
  3   FROM   SYS.DBA_TABLES
  4   WHERE  OWNER = 'PETE' AND
  5          TABLE_NAME = 'IRL4VR';

LOGGING DEGREE
------- ------
NO           8

SQL> INSERT /*+ PARALLEL(IRL4VR,2) */
  2  INTO IRL4VR
  3  SELECT --+ PARALLEL(IRLHIST,6)
  4  *
  5  FROM IRLHIST;
500000 rows created.

SQL> COMMIT;
Commit complete.
```

The Oracle8 PDML feature also applies to **UPDATE** and **DELETE** statements, and Listing 16.9 shows an example. You want to use this feature when updating a lot of rows in a table. As a reminder, you must enable the PDML feature using the **ALTER SESSION** command to take advantage of parallel inserts, updates, and deletes. The **UPDATE** example requests three server processes, and the **DELETE** example requests two server processes. Oracle Corporation strongly recommends using a commit after executing PDML statements.

Listing 16.9 PDML updates and deletes.

```
SQL> ALTER SESSION
  2         ENABLE
  3         PARALLEL DML;
Session altered.

SQL> UPDATE /*+ PARALLEL(IRL4VR,3) */
  2  IRL4VR
  3  SET INTO INDY500_WINS =
  4      INDY500_WINS - 1;
550000 rows updated.

SQL> DELETE /*+ PARALLEL(IRL4VR,2) */
  2  FROM  IRL4VR
  3  WHERE INDY500_WINS < 2;
456000 rows deleted.

SQL> COMMIT;
Commit complete.
```

Other Parallel Hints

The APPEND hint in Listing 16.10 is used with the INSERT command to add data to a new block, not to the existing free space in a block. This hint works on both parallel and serial INSERT statements. The default of parallel inserts is APPEND. You can override APPEND by using the hint NOAPPEND.

Listing 16.10 Using the **APPEND** and **NOAPPEND** hints.

```
SQL> INSERT /*+ APPEND PARALLEL(IRL4VR, 6) */
  2  INTO IRL4VR
  3  SELECT *
  4  FROM   IRLHIST;
5 rows created.

SQL> COMMIT;
Commit complete.

SQL> INSERT /*+ NOAPPEND PARALLEL(IRL4VR, 6) */
  2  INTO IRL4VR
  3  SELECT *
  4  FROM   IRLHIST;
5 rows created.
```

```
SQL> COMMIT;
Commit complete.
```

The **PARALLEL_INDEX** hint in Listing 16.11 is used to make an index range scan on a partitioned index parallel. The partitioned index API on the **AUTO_PARTS** table is scanned using four concurrent servers.

Listing 16.11 Using the **PARALLEL_INDEX** hint.

```
SQL> SELECT /*+ PARALLEL_INDEX(AUTO_PARTS API,4) */
     FROM   AUTO_PARTS
     WHERE  PARTNO BETWEEN 5500 AND 200000;
```

Other Hints

Two more hints remain that are new in Oracle8—**STAR_TRANSFORMATION** and **DRIVING_SITE**. Listing 16.12 shows how to use **STAR_TRANSFORMATION**. First of all, the parameter **STAR_TRANSFORMATION_ENABLED** must be set to "true" before the optimizer will take a hint. If the star query is transformed, this hint forces the optimizer to use the plan with the lowest cost. Without this hint, the optimizer uses the best plan on the "untransformed" query. However, there's no guarantee that Oracle will transform the star query.

Listing 16.12 STAR_TRANSFORMATION.

```
SQL> SELECT --+ STAR_TRANSFORMATION
            RESULTS, PNAME,
            CUSTS.CNAME,
            NUM_DOORS,
            OWNER,
            NUM_FLIPS
     FROM   TESTS,   -- Fact Table 471,000 Rows
            PARTS,   -- Dimension Table 10,000 Rows
            CUSTS,   -- Dimension Table    100 Rows
            CARS,    -- Dimension Table    300 Rows
            INDY_CARS,  -- Dimension Table 99 Rows
            MIDGET_CARS -- Dimension Table 200 Rows
     WHERE  TESTS.PNO      = PARTS.PNO          AND
            TESTS.CUSTID   = CUSTS.CUSTID       AND
            TESTS.CARID    = CARS.CARID         AND
            TESTS.INDYID   = INDY_CARS.INDYID AND
            TESTS.MIDGETID = MIDGET_CARS.MIDGETID;
```

The **DRIVING_SITE** hint forces the optimizer to execute a query at the designated node where the table in your hint is located, using either one of the two optimizers—cost-based or rule-based. In Listing 16.13, the rows from **HAWAII_TABLE** are sent to the remote node on Maui, and the query is executed on Maui. The results are sent back from Maui to Oahu.

Listing 16.13 DRIVING_SITE.

```
SQL> SELECT --+ DRIVING_SITE(MAUI_TABLE)
     FROM   HAWAII_TABLE.
            MAUI_TABLE@HI
     WHERE  HAWAII_TABLE.ISLAND_NO =
            MAUI_TABLE.ISLAND_NO;
```

Summary

Oracle8 rowids are significantly different than Oracle7 rowids because of the inclusion of objects in Oracle8. Also, the package **DBMS_ROWID** is used to convert rowids in Oracle8 into a more readable format.

The Explain Plan table, **PLAN_TABLE**, has three new columns containing partition information. Also, with objects comes an entire suite of new verbs, such as **REF**, **DEREF**, and **VALUE**, as well as OIDs and user-defined data types. Apparently no new information is stored in the table **PLAN_TABLE**, because I queried every **VARCHAR2** column in this table and saw nothing pertaining to objects. Moreover, using the traditional SQL join seems to be faster than using OIDs (pointers) to reference data in other tables—that is, if the tables contain a small number of rows (10,000 or less).

Thanks to reverse key indexes, PDML features, and new parallel hints, statements execute much faster in Oracle8 than they did in Oracle7.

HIGH PERFORMANCE

Demonstration Tables

APPENDIX A

*This appendix lists the SQL statements that create the 1-million-row **STATS** table, the 100,000-row **BIG** table, the 10,000-row **PARTS** table, the 470,552-row **TESTS** table, and several other tables, as well as Oracle8 object types and tables.*

Demonstration Tables

Tables

The following SQL scripts create the tables referenced in this book.

STATS

STATS is a one-million-row table.

```
SQL> get p1.sql
 SET TIMING ON
 CREATE TABLE STATS
       (SNO                      NUMBER(7,0),
        SNAME                    VARCHAR2(30),
        REGION_BTREE             VARCHAR2(3),
        REGION_BIT_MAP           VARCHAR2(3),
        REGION_HASH              NUMBER(1,0),
        SEX                      VARCHAR2(1),
        ONE_THOUSAND_NUMBERS     NUMBER(4,0))
 TABLESPACE                      STATS
 STORAGE(INITIAL                 18M
         NEXT                    18M
         MINEXTENTS              3);
 DECLARE
       vsname          VARCHAR2(30);
       vsex            VARCHAR2(1);
       vregion_btree   VARCHAR2(3);
       vregion_hash    NUMBER(1,0);
       votn            NUMBER(4,0);
 BEGIN
  FOR i IN 1..1000000 LOOP
   IF i BETWEEN 1 AND 100000 THEN
     vsname := 'BETWEEN 1 AND 100000';
   ELSIF i BETWEEN 100001 AND 300000 THEN
     vsname := 'BETWEEN 100001 AND 300000';
```

```
    ELSIF i BETWEEN 300001 AND 600000 THEN
      vsname := 'BETWEEN 300001 AND 600000';
    ELSIF i BETWEEN 600001 AND 950000 THEN
      vsname := 'BETWEEN 600001 AND 950000';
    ELSE
      vsname := 'GREATER THAN 950000';
    END  IF;
    IF MOD(i,2) = 0 THEN
       vsex := 'M';
    ELSE
       vsex := 'F';
    END  IF;
 IF i BETWEEN 1 AND 124999 THEN
     vregion_btree := 'N';
     vregion_hash  := 8;
 ELSIF i BETWEEN 125000 AND 249999 THEN
     vregion_btree := 'NE';
     vregion_hash  := 1;
 ELSIF i BETWEEN 250000 AND 374999 THEN
     vregion_btree := 'E';
     vregion_hash  := 2;
 ELSIF i = 375000 THEN
     vregion_btree := 'SE';
     vregion_hash  := 3;
 ELSIF i BETWEEN 375001 AND 500000 THEN
     vregion_btree := 'S';
     vregion_hash  := 4;
 ELSIF i BETWEEN 500001 AND 995000 THEN
     vregion_btree := 'SW';
     vregion_hash  := 5;
 ELSIF i BETWEEN 995001 AND 999000 THEN
     vregion_btree := 'W';
     vregion_hash  := 6;
 ELSIF i BETWEEN 999001 AND 1000000 THEN
     vregion_btree := 'NW';
     vregion_hash  := 7;
 END  IF;
 INSERT INTO STATS
        VALUES(i,vsname,vregion_btree,
               vregion_btree,vregion_hash,
               vsex,votn);
 IF MOD(i,100) = 0 THEN COMMIT;
 END IF;
END  LOOP;
END;
```

STATS2

STATS2 is a table with 10,000 rows.

```
SQL> get stats2
CREATE TABLE STATS2
       (SNO      NUMBER(7),
        REGION   VARCHAR2(3))
```

```
SQL> get stats2b
BEGIN
 FOR i IN 1..10000 LOOP
  IF i BETWEEN 1 AND 1000 THEN
   INSERT INTO STATS2 VALUES(1000);
  ELSIF i BETWEEN 1001 AND 3000 THEN
   INSERT INTO STATS2 VALUES(3000);
  ELSIF i BETWEEN 3001 AND 6000 THEN
   INSERT INTO STATS2 VALUES(6000);
  ELSE
   INSERT INTO STATS2 VALUES(9999);
  END IF;
 END  LOOP;
END;
```

PARTS

PARTS contains about 10,000 rows.

```
SQL> get corbtc1
CREATE TABLE PARTS
       (PNO      NUMBER(7,0),
        PNAME    VARCHAR2(15),
        TIME_OF_INSERT DATE)
```

TESTS

TESTS is a 470,000-row table containing the test results of rows in the PARTS table.

```
SQL> get corbtc2
CREATE TABLE TESTS
       (PNO      NUMBER(7,0),
        TNO      NUMBER(4,0),
        RESULTS CHAR(1))
```

BIG

BIG is a table with 100,000 rows.

```
SQL> get cor13_big
CREATE TABLE        BIG
      (BIGNO        NUMBER(6),
       BNAME        VARCHAR2(20))
PCTFREE              0
PCTUSED             60
STORAGE(INITIAL     10K
        NEXT        10K
        MINEXTENTS  1
        MAXEXTENTS  121
        PCTINCREASE 0);
BEGIN
  FOR I IN 1..100000 LOOP
      IF I BETWEEN 1 AND 1999 THEN
         INSERT INTO BIG VALUES(I,'ONE THOUSAND');
      ELSIF I BETWEEN 2000 AND 5000 THEN
         INSERT INTO BIG VALUES(I,'BET 2K AND 5K');
      ELSE
         INSERT INTO BIG VALUES(I,NULL);
      END IF;
      IF MOD(I,15000) = 0 THEN COMMIT;
      END IF;
  END LOOP;
END;
```

Partitioned Table: AUTO_PARTS

AUTO_PARTS is an Oracle8 table with three partitions.

```
SQL> get cor8_p1
CREATE TABLE AUTO_PARTS
   (partno       NUMBER(7,0),
    pname        VARCHAR2(15),
    pcost        NUMBER(7,2))
LOGGING
PARTITION BY RANGE(partno)
    (PARTITION ap250k
        VALUES LESS THAN (250001)
        TABLESPACE EXTRA1,
     PARTITION ap500k
```

```
         VALUES LESS THAN (500000)
         TABLESPACE EXTRA2,
      PARTITION ap1million
         VALUES LESS THAN (1000000)
         TABLESPACE EXTRA3)
```

Index-Organized Table

AUTO_PARTS_INDEX_ORG is an Oracle8 index-organized table.

```
SQL> get cor14_12
CREATE TABLE AUTO_PARTS_INDEX_ORG
   (PARTNO          NUMBER(7),
    PNAME           VARCHAR2(15),
    PCOST           NUMBER(7,2),
    CONSTRAINT PK_AP_INDEX_ORG
               PRIMARY KEY(PARTNO))
ORGANIZATION INDEX TABLESPACE EXTRA1
PCTTHRESHOLD 15
INCLUDING PCOST
OVERFLOW TABLESPACE EXTRA2
```

Non-Index-Organized Table

AUTO_PARTS_NO_INDEX_ORG is a regular table.

```
SQL> CREATE TABLE AUTO_PARTS_NO_INDEX_ORG
   (PARTNO          NUMBER(7),
    PNAME           VARCHAR2(15),
    PCOST           NUMBER(7,2),
    CONSTRAINT PK_AP_NO_INDEX_ORG
               PRIMARY KEY(PARTNO))
               TABLESPACE EXTRA3;
```

AUDIT_DEPT

AUDIT_DEPT contains auditing information concerning the DEPT table and is populated by a database trigger on the DEPT table.

```
SQL> get cor14_20
CREATE TABLE AUDIT_DEPT
  (WHO        VARCHAR2(30),
   WHEN       DATE,
```

```
  4      OLD_DEPTNO NUMBER(2,0),
  5      NEW_DEPTNO NUMBER(2,0),
  6      OLD_DNAME  VARCHAR2(14),
  7      NEW_DNAME  VARCHAR2(14),
  8      OLD_LOC    VARCHAR2(14),
  9*     NEW_LOC    VARCHAR2(14))
```

Traditional DEPTS_RDBMS Table

DEPTS_RDBMS contains 1,000 rows and is joined to EMPLOYEES_RDBMS to compare to the Oracle8 technique of using OIDs instead of joining tables.

```
SQL> get cor16_rdepts
  1  CREATE TABLE DEPTS_RDBMS
  2      (deptno    NUMBER(7,0),
  3       dname     VARCHAR2(20),
  4       city      VARCHAR2(20))
  5* TABLESPACE OBJECTS1
SQL> /
Table created.

SQL> get cor16_r2
  1  BEGIN
  2   FOR i IN 1..1000 LOOP
  3    INSERT INTO DEPTS_RDBMS
  4    VALUES(i, 'MIS ' || i, 'MAUI ' || i);
  5   END  LOOP;
  6* END;
SQL> /
PL/SQL procedure successfully completed.
Elapsed: 00:00:03.55
```

Traditional EMPLOYEES_RDBMS Table

EMPLOYEES_RDBMS contains 10,000 rows of employees, with each department containing ten employees.

```
SQL> CREATE TABLE EMPLOYEES_RDBMS
  2   (empno      NUMBER(6,0),
  3    ename      VARCHAR2(20),
  4    salary     NUMBER(8,2),
  5    edeptno    NUMBER(7,0))
  6  TABLESPACE   OBJECTS1;
Table created.
```

```
SQL> get cor16_o7
DECLARE
  startno   NUMBER  := 1;
  endno     NUMBER  := 10;
BEGIN
  FOR dno IN 1..1000 LOOP
   FOR eno IN startno..endno LOOP
    INSERT INTO EMPLOYEES_RDBMS
    VALUES(eno,'Emp # ' || eno,
           200+dno, dno);
   END  LOOP;
   startno := endno;
   startno := startno + 1;
   endno   := startno;
   endno   := endno + 9;
  END  LOOP;
COMMIT;
END;
/
PL/SQL procedure successfully completed.
 real: 54760
```

OBJECTS

The following scripts create user-defined data types and object tables, and load the object tables. These object tables are compared to traditional joins. The table **DEPTS_OBJ** is an example of an Oracle8 object table.

Pointers Or OIDs (Object Identifiers)

An object table is comprised of user-defined data types and **dept_data** is an example.

```
SQL> CREATE TYPE dept_data AS OBJECT(
    deptno    NUMBER(7,0),
    dname     VARCHAR2(20),
    city      VARCHAR2(20));
Operation 77 succeeded.  (Type created.)

SQL> CREATE TABLE DEPTS_OBJ OF dept_data;
Table created.

SQL> get cor16_15
  BEGIN
```

```
    FOR dno IN 1..1000 LOOP
     INSERT INTO DEPTS_OBJ
     VALUES(dept_data(dno,'IS','MAUI'));
    END  LOOP;
COMMIT;
END;
SQL> /
PL/SQL procedure successfully completed.
 real: 14340

SQL> CREATE TABLE EMPLOYEES_OBJ
(eno      NUMBER(6,0),
 ename    VARCHAR2(20),
 salary   NUMBER(8,2),
 dept_oid REF dept_data
          SCOPE IS depts_obj);
Table created.

SQL> get cor16_16
DECLARE
  startno  NUMBER := 1;
  endno    NUMBER := 10;
BEGIN
 FOR i IN 1..1000 LOOP
  FOR j IN startno..endno LOOP
   INSERT INTO EMPLOYEES_OBJ
   SELECT j,'Emp# ' || j,222+j,
   REF(d)
   FROM DEPTS_OBJ d
   WHERE d.deptno = i;
  END LOOP;
  startno := endno;
  startno := startno + 1;
  endno   := startno;
  endno   := endno + 9;
 END  LOOP;
COMMIT;
END;
SQL> @cor16_16

PL/SQL procedure successfully completed.
 real: 413580
```

Repeating Groups Using A Nested Table

The following scripts create and load an Oracle8 nested table DEPTS_OBJ_NESTED.

```
SQL> CREATE TYPE emp_in_dept AS OBJECT
  2  (empno     NUMBER(6,0),
  3   ename     VARCHAR2(20),
  4   salary    NUMBER(8,2));
SQL> /
Type created.

SQL> CREATE TYPE nested_emps
  2  AS TABLE OF emp_in_dept;
SQL> /
Type created.

SQL> CREATE TYPE dept_info AS OBJECT
  2  (deptno     NUMBER(6,0),
  3   dname      VARCHAR2(20),
  4   city       VARCHAR2(20),
  5   emps       nested_emps);
  6  .
SQL> /
Type created.

SQL> CREATE TABLE DEPTS_OBJ_NESTED
  2  OF dept_info
  3  OIDINDEX oid_depts_nested
  4  TABLESPACE OBJECTS1
  5  NESTED TABLE EMPS
  6  STORE AS empsv8;
Table created.
```

HIGH PERFORMANCE

Useful SQL Scripts

HIGH PERFORMANCE

APPENDIX B

This appendix lists some important SQL statements that you'll frequently use. Oracle Corporation does not provide these scripts, with the exception of the scripts that begin with "utl".

Useful SQL Scripts

Explain Plan

```
SQL> get utlxplan - Oracle Does Provide
create table PLAN_TABLE (
   statement_id     varchar2(30),
   timestamp        date,
   remarks          varchar2(80),
   operation        varchar2(30),
   options          varchar2(30),
   object_node      varchar2(128),
   object_owner     varchar2(30),
   object_name      varchar2(30),
   object_instance  numeric,
   object_type      varchar2(30),
   optimizer        varchar2(255),
   search_columns   numeric,
   id               numeric,
   parent_id        numeric,
   position         numeric,
   cost             numeric,
   cardinality      numeric,
   bytes            numeric,
   other_tag        varchar2(255),
   partition_start  varchar2(255),
   partition_stop   varchar2(255),
   partition_id     numeric,
   other            long);
```

```
SQL> get explan8p
SELECT ID,
PARENT_ID PRNTID,
SUBSTR(OPERATION,1,17) "Operation",
SUBSTR(PARTITION_START,1,10) "PSTART",
```

```
  5  SUBSTR(PARTITION_STOP,1,10) "PSTOP",
  6  PARTITION_ID PID,
  7  SUBSTR(OPTIONS,1,9) "Options"
  8  FROM   PLAN_TABLE
  9* ORDER  BY ID, PARENT_ID

SQL> get explain8
  1  SET ARRAYSIZE 1
  2  COL "Plan Tree" FORMAT A55
  3  SELECT LPAD(' ',2*(LEVEL-1)) ||
  4  operation || ' ' || options
  5  || ' ' || object_name || ' ' ||
  6  DECODE(id,0,'Cost = ' || position) "Plan Tree"
  7  FROM   PLAN_TABLE
  8  START  WITH id = 0
  9* CONNECT BY PRIOR id = parent_id


SQL> get explain   ORACLE7
  1  SET ARRAYSIZE 1
  2  COL      "Query Plan" FORMAT A60
  3  SELECT  LPAD(' ', 2*(LEVEL-1)) ||
  4  operation || ' ' ||
  5  options || ' ' ||
  6  object_name || ' ' || OPTIMIZER "Query Plan",
  7  COST
  8  FROM    PLAN_TABLE
  9  START   WITH id = 0
 10* CONNECT BY PRIOR id = parent_id

HOW TO USE:
SQL> EXPLAIN PLAN FOR
  2  SELECT *
  3  FROM   STATS
  4  WHERE  SNO > 999999;
Explained.

SQL> @explain
Query Plan                               COST
-------------------------------------   ----
SELECT STATEMENT   CHOOSE                   4
  TABLE ACCESS BY ROWID STATS ANALYZED      4
    INDEX RANGE SCAN STATS_SNO ANALYZED
```

Data Dictionary

```
SQL> get dd
  SELECT TABLE_NAME
  FROM   DICT
  WHERE  TABLE_NAME LIKE '%'
  || UPPER('&TN') || '%';

HOW TO USE:
SQL> @dd
Enter value for tn: ROLE

TABLE_NAME
--------------
DBA_ROLES
DBA_ROLE_PRIVS
USER_ROLE_PRIVS
ROLE_ROLE_PRIVS
ROLE_SYS_PRIVS
ROLE_TAB_PRIVS
SESSION_ROLES
```

Constraints

```
SQL> get cor14_24
  SET    LONG 15
  SELECT SUBSTR(CONSTRAINT_NAME,1,13) NAME,
         DEFERRABLE "DEF?",
         DEFERRED DEF,
         SUBSTR(VALIDATED,1,9) VAL,
         SUBSTR(GENERATED,1,9) GEN
  FROM   USER_CONSTRAINTS
  WHERE  TABLE_NAME = UPPER('&TN')
  /
  SET    LONG 80

HOW TO USE:
SQL> @cor14_24
Enter value for tn: auto_PARTS

NAME          DEF?
------------ -------------
PK_AUTO_PARTS NOT DEFERRABLE
CK_AP         NOT DEFERRABLE
```

```
DEF       VAL       GEN
--------  --------- ---------
IMMEDIATE VALIDATED USER NAME
IMMEDIATE VALIDATED USER NAME
```

Init.ora Parameters

```
SQL> get ora
  1  SELECT SUBSTR(NAME,1,30) PARAM,
  2         SUBSTR(VALUE,1,25) CURRENT_SETTING
  3  FROM   V$PARAMETER
  4* WHERE  NAME LIKE '%' || LOWER('&Parameter') || '%'
```

```
HOW TO USE:
SQL> @ora
Enter value for parameter: timed_statistics

PARAM            CURRENT_SETTING
---------------- ---------------
timed_statistics TRUE
```

Tables

```
SQL> get tsf4tab
  1  SELECT U.TABLESPACE_NAME,
  2  SUBSTR(F.FILE_NAME,1,35) "FILE NAME"
  3  FROM   USER_TABLES U,
  4         DBA_DATA_FILES F
  5  WHERE  U.TABLESPACE_NAME =
  6         F.TABLESPACE_NAME AND
  7*        U.TABLE_NAME = UPPER('&TN')
```

```
HOW TO USE:
SQL> START tsf4tab
Enter value for tn: stats

TABLESPACE_ FILE_
NAME        NAME
----------  -----------------------------------
STATS       /disk1/oradata/7.3.2/pete/stats.dbf
```

```
SQL> get cons
  1  SET    LONG 30
```

```
SELECT SUBSTR(CONSTRAINT_NAME,1,15) "Name",
       CONSTRAINT_TYPE,
       SEARCH_CONDITION
FROM   USER_CONSTRAINTS
WHERE  TABLE_NAME = UPPER('&TN')
/
SET    LONG 80
```

```
HOW TO USE:
SQL> @cons
Enter value for tn: emp

Name           C SEARCH_CONDITION
-------------- - ------------------------------
PK_EMP_EMPNO   P
CK_EMP_SAL     C SAL BETWEEN 1000 AND 6000
FK_EMP_DEPTNO  R
```

Table Partitions

```
SQL> get cor14_41
COL    PARTITION_NAME  FORMAT A14
COL    TABLESPACE_NAME FORMAT A15
SET    LONG 15
SELECT PARTITION_NAME,
       TABLESPACE_NAME,
       HIGH_VALUE
FROM   USER_TAB_PARTITIONS
WHERE  TABLE_NAME = UPPER('&TN')
/
SET    LONG 80
```

```
HOW TO USE:
SQL> @cor14_41
Enter value for tn: auTO_PaRtS

PARTITION_NAME TABLESPACE_NAME HIGH_VALUE
-------------- --------------- ----------
AP500K         EXTRA1          500000
AP250K         EXTRA1          250001
AP1MILLION     EXTRA3          1000000
```

Table Blocks And Space Usage

```
SQL> get cor12_42
  1  ANALYZE TABLE PARTS
  2*          COMPUTE STATISTICS

SQL> get cor13_42
VARIABLE TBLKS              NUMBER
VARIABLE TBYTES             NUMBER
VARIABLE UBLKS              NUMBER
VARIABLE UBYTES             NUMBER
VARIABLE LUXFID             NUMBER
VARIABLE LUXBID             NUMBER
VARIABLE LUBLK              NUMBER

COL "Tot Blocks"            FORMAT 999,999
COL "Tot Bytes"             FORMAT 999,999
COL "Unused Blocks"         FORMAT 999,999
COL "Unused Bytes"          FORMAT 999,999
COL "Last Used Xtnt File#"  FORMAT 999,999
COL "Last Used Xtnt Blk#"   FORMAT 999,999
COL "Last Used Blk"         FORMAT 999,999

EXECUTE DBMS_SPACE.UNUSED_SPACE(    -
        'SYSTEM',                   -
        'DRIVERS',                  -
        'TABLE',                    -
        :TBLKS,                     -
        :TBYTES,                    -
        :UBLKS,                     -
        :UBYTES,                    -
        :LUXFID,                    -
        :LUXBID,                    -
        :LUBLK)                     -
;
SELECT  :TBLKS  "Tot Blocks",
        :TBYTES "Tot Bytes",
        :UBLKS  "Unused Blocks",
        :UBYTES "Unused Bytes"
FROM    DUAL;
SELECT
        :LUXFID "Last Used Xtnt File#",
        :LUXBID "Last Used Xtnt Blk#",
        :LUBLK  "Last Used Blk"
FROM    DUAL;
```

```
SQL> @cor13_42

PL/SQL procedure successfully completed.

  Tot Blocks    Tot Bytes Unused Blocks Unused Bytes
------------ ------------ ------------- ------------
       2,140    4,382,720           535    1,095,680

Last Used Xtnt File# Last Used Xtnt Blk# Last Used Blk
-------------------- ------------------- -------------
                   8               1,432           175
```

Table Size

```
SQL> get tabsize
SET      SERVEROUTPUT        ON
SET      VERIFY              OFF
DECLARE
 name_of_table VARCHAR2(30) := '&Table_Name';
 c1            NUMBER  := &Avg_Byte_Size1;
 c2            NUMBER  := &Avg_Byte_Size2;
 c3            NUMBER  := &Avg_Byte_Size3;
 c4            NUMBER  := &Avg_Byte_Size4;
 c5            NUMBER  := &Avg_Byte_Size5;
 c6            NUMBER  := &Avg_Byte_Size6;
 c7            NUMBER  := &Avg_Byte_Size7;
 no_columns    NUMBER  := &Number_Of_Columns_In_Table;
 no_col_250b   NUMBER  := &Number_Of_Columns_255b;
 no_col_250plus NUMBER := &Number_Of_Columns_255_Plus;
 row_size      NUMBER  := 0;
 blk_size      NUMBER  := &Block_Size;
 est_rows_per_blk NUMBER := 0;
 total_blk_header NUMBER := 0;
 initrans         NUMBER := &Init_Trans;
 space_available  NUMBER := 0;
 pct_free         NUMBER := &Pctfree;
 avg_rows_per_blk NUMBER := 0;
 total_table_blks NUMBER := 0;
 no_rows NUMBER := &Number_Of_Rows_In_Table;
 total_bytes      NUMBER := 0;
 total_meg        NUMBER := 0;
 total_gig        NUMBER := 0;
BEGIN
 row_size := (c1+c2+c3+c4+c5+c6+c7)+(3*no_col_250plus)
             +(1*no_col_250b) + 3;
```

```
    est_rows_per_blk := TRUNC(blk_size/row_size);
 total_blk_header := (57+(23*initrans))+(4+(2*est_rows_per_blk));
 space_available := (blk_size-total_blk_header) -
 ((blk_size-(57+(23*initrans))) * (pct_free/100));
   avg_rows_per_blk := space_available/row_size;
   total_table_blks := TRUNC(no_rows/avg_rows_per_blk);
dbms_output.put_line('You Need ' || TO_CHAR(total_table_blks,
     '999,999,999') || ' blocks for TABLE '
     || name_of_table);
total_bytes := TRUNC(total_table_blks * blk_size);
dbms_output.put_line('You Need ' || TO_CHAR(total_bytes,
     '999,999,999,999') || ' bytes for TABLE '
     || name_of_table);
 total_meg := TRUNC(total_bytes/1048576);
 IF total_meg >= 1000 THEN
    total_gig :=  ROUND(total_meg/1000);
    dbms_output.put_line('You Need ' || TO_CHAR(total_gig,
         '999,999,999,999') || 'GIG for TABLE '
         || name_of_table);
  ELSE
 dbms_output.put_line('You Need ' || TO_CHAR(total_meg
      '999,999,999,999') || 'MEG for TABLE '
      || name_of_table);
 END  IF;
END;
```

```
SQL>@tabsize

Enter value for table: CAROLE
Enter value for avg_byte_size1: 4
Enter value for avg_byte_size2: 4
Enter value for avg_byte_size3: 7
Enter value for avg_byte_size4: 2
Enter value for avg_byte_size5: 5
Enter value for avg_byte_size6: 4
Enter value for avg_byte_size7: 0
Enter value for number_of_columns_in_table: 6
Enter value for number_of_columns_255b: 6
Enter value for number_of_columns_255_plus: 0
Enter value for block_size: 4096
Enter value for init_trans: 1
Enter value for pctfree: 1
Enter value for number_of_rows_in_table: 3000000000
You Need 28,091,090 blocks for TABLE CAROLE
```

```
You Need 115,061,104,640 bytes for TABLE CAROLE
You Need 110 GIG for TABLE CAROLE

PL/SQL procedure successfully completed.
```

Index Partitions

```
SQL> COL DEFTS     FORMAT A9
SQL> COL ALIGNMENT FORMAT A9
SQL> COL LOCALITY  FORMAT A8

SQL> get cor14_51
SELECT PARTITIONING_TYPE PTYPE,
       PARTITION_COUNT PCOUNT,
       LOCALITY,
       DEF_TABLESPACE_NAME DEFTS,
       ALIGNMENT
FROM   USER_PART_INDEXES
WHERE  INDEX_NAME = 'PART_INDX'
SQL> /

PTYPE  PCOUNT LOCALI DEFTS     ALIGNMENT
------ ------ ------ --------- ---------
RANGE       4 GLOBAL USER_DATA PREFIXED

SQL> get cor14_59
COL    INAME      FORMAT A13
COL    PNAME      FORMAT A10
SET    LONG 10
COL    TSNAME     FORMAT A10
SELECT INDEX_NAME       INAME,
       PARTITION_NAME   PNAME,
       HIGH_VALUE,
       TABLESPACE_NAME TSNAME
FROM   USER_IND_PARTITIONS

SQL> @cor14_59

INAME         PNAME      HIGH_VALUE TSNAME
------------- ---------- ---------- ----------
PART_INDX     IPART250K  250001     INDEXES1
PART_INDX     IPART500K  500001     EXTRA2
PART_INDX     IPART750K  750001     EXTRA1
PART_INDX     IPART1MILL MAXVALUE   EXTRA3
```

Indexes

```
SQL> get indexes
SELECT SUBSTR(INDEX_NAME,1,20) NAME,
       UNIQUENESS,
       DISTINCT_KEYS DKEYS,
       STATUS
FROM   USER_INDEXES
WHERE  TABLE_NAME = UPPER('&TN')
```

HOW TO USE:

```
SQL> start indexes
Enter value for tn: tests

NAME           UNIQUENES DKEYS STATUS
-------------- --------- ----- ------
INDX_TESTS_PNO NONUNIQUE       VALID
INDX_TESTS_TNO NONUNIQUE       VALID
```

```
SQL> get con
BREAK  ON NAME SKIP 1
SELECT SUBSTR(INDEX_NAME,1,25) NAME,
       COLUMN_POSITION "POSITION",
       SUBSTR(COLUMN_NAME,1,25) COL_NAME
FROM   USER_IND_COLUMNS
WHERE  TABLE_NAME = UPPER('&TN')
ORDER  BY NAME, "POSITION"
/
CLEAR  BREAKS
```

HOW TO USE:

```
SQL> @con
Enter value for tn: emp

NAME         POSITION COL_NAME
------------ -------- --------
INDX_EMP_DCSH       1 DEPTNO
                    2 COMM
                    3 SAL
                    4 HIREDATE

INDX_EMP_JMH        1 JOB
                    2 MGR
                    3 HIREDATE

INDX_EMP_SAL        1 SAL
```

```
SQL> get cor14_53
  1  SELECT INDEX_NAME,
  2         INDEX_TYPE,
  3         TABLE_TYPE,
  4         STATUS,
  5         PARTITIONED
  6  FROM   USER_INDEXES
  7* WHERE  TABLE_NAME = 'RACES'
SQL> /

INDEX_NAME INDEX_TYPE TABLE_TYPE STATUS PAR
---------- ---------- ---------- ------ ---
PART_INDX  NORMAL     TABLE      N/A    YES
```

Pinning In The Shared SQL Area

Pinning is placing an object in the shared SQL area of the shared pool so the object will be found in memory and will not have to be reloaded. This improves performance.

```
SQL> DECLARE
     BEGIN
      FOR i IN(SELECT OWNER ||
       '.' || OBJECT_NAME NAME
       FROM   DBA_OBJECTS
       WHERE  object_type IN(
       'PACKAGE','PROCEDURE','FUNCTION')
       AND OWNER = 'OPS$PCASSIDY')
           LOOP
             dbms_shared_pool.keep(i.NAME);
      END  LOOP;
     END;
SQL> /

SQL> SELECT OBJECT_NAME
     FROM   USER_OBJECTS
     WHERE  OBJECT_TYPE
     IN('FUNCTION','PROCEDURE');

OBJECT_NAME
------------
ADD_NEW_DEPT
DAYS_OLD

SQL> EXECUTE DBMS_SHARED_POOL.KEEP('DAYS_OLD');
```

Index

A

C

D

E

J

L

M

T

U

V

Meet Advanced Demands with High Performance

The High Performance series explains the advanced tool features that introductory books just can't cover. The heavy-duty projects in each book force readers to think through the development process at an expert's level. These books strive for technical depth, presenting the underlying theory of the technology being discussed and backing it up with example code or demonstration projects.

Books in the High Performance series are edited by recognized industry experts Jeff Duntemann and Don Burleson. Co-founder and Editorial Director of The Coriolis Group, Jeff Duntemann is the author of seven books and innumerable articles on computer technology. Don Burleson has 15 years experience as an Oracle developer and is the author of numerous books and articles on database management.

High Performance Oracle8 Tuning
Donald Burleson
1-57610-217-3 • $49.99/$69.99 (US/CAN)
Available Now

High Performance Oracle Database Automation
Jonathan Ingram
1-57610-152-5 • $39.99/$55.99 (US/CAN)
Available Now

High Performance Oracle Data Warehousing
Donald Burleson
1-57610-154-1 • $39.99/$55.99 (US/CAN)
Available Now

High Performance Oracle8 SQL Programming & Tuning
Pete Cassidy
1-57610-213-0 • $39.99/$55.99 (US/CAN)
February 1998

High Performance Oracle8 Object-Oriented Design
David A. Anstey
1-57610-186-X • $39.99/$55.99 (US/CAN)
February 1998

High Performance Windows Graphics Programming
Stan Trujillo
1-57610-148-7 • $39.99/$55.99 (US/CAN)
Available Now

High Performance Windows NT 4 Optimization & Tuning
Arthur Knowles
1-57610-164-9 • $49.99/$69.99 (US/CAN)
Available Now

High Performance Visual Basic 5 Web Development
Scott Jarol
1-57610-063-4 • $39.99/$55.99 (US/CAN)
Available Now

High Performance Delphi 3 Programming
Don Taylor, Jim Mischel, John Penman and Terence Goggin
1-57610-179-7 • $49.99/$69.99 (US/CAN)
Available Now

High Performance ISAPI/NSAPI Web Programming
Tony Beveridge and Paul McGlashan
1-57610-151-7 • $39.99/$55.99 (US/CAN)
Available Now

High Performance Borland C++ Builder
Matt Telles
1-57610-197-5 8 $39.99/$55.99 (US/CAN)
Available Now

(800) 410-0192 • International Callers (602) 483-0192 • Fax (602) 483-0193 • www.coriolis.com

Prices and availability dates are subject to change without notice.
©1998 by Coriolis Group Books. All Rights Reserved. AT/GS 10/97